The Winn L. Rosch Hardware Bible

Winn L. Rosch

Brady Publishing

New York   London   Toronto   Sydney   Tokyo   Singapore

Brady Publishing

A Division of Prentice Hall Computer Publishing
15 Columbus Circle
New York, NY 10023

ISBN: 0-13-932260-4

Library of Congress Catalog No.: 92-18213

95 94 93 92   5 4 3 2

Printing Code: The rightmost double-digit number is the year of the book's printing; the rightmost single-digit number is the number of the book's printing. For example, 92-2 shows that the second printing of the book occurred in 1992.

Manufactured in the United States of America

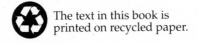 The text in this book is printed on recycled paper.

TO MY FATHER

Credits

Publisher
Michael Violano

Managing Editor
Kelly D. Dobbs

Editor
Burt Gabriel

Developmental Editor
Michael Sprague

Copy Editor
Jo Anna Arnott

Book Designer
Scott Cook

Cover Designer
HUB Graphics

Production Team
Christine Cook
Chuck Hutchinson
Roger Morgan
Juli Pavey
Michelle Self
Susan M. Shepard
Greg Simsic
John Sleeva
Marcella Thompson
Angie Trzepacz
Suzanne Tully

Illustrations on chapter openings were created by Bruce Sanders.

About the Author

Winn L. Rosch has written about personal computers since 1981 and has penned nearly 1,000 published articles about them—a mixture of reviews, how-to guides, and background pieces explaining new technologies. One of these was selected by The Computer Press Association as the best feature article of the year for 1987; another was runner up for the same award in 1990. He has written several other books about computers, the most recent of which are *The Winn L. Rosch PC Upgrade Bible* (Brady, 1991) and *The Micro Channel Architecture Handbook*, co-authored with Chet Heath (Brady, 1990). At present, he is a contributing editor to *PC Magazine, PC Week, PC Sources,* and *Computer Shopper.* His books and articles have been reprinted in several languages (French, Italian, German, Greek, and Portuguese).

Besides writing, Rosch is an attorney licensed to practice in Ohio and holds a Juris Doctor degree. He was appointed to, and currently serves on, the Ohio State Bar Association's Computer Law committee.

In other lifetimes, Rosch has worked as a photojournalist, electronic journalist, and broadcast engineer. For 10 years, he wrote regular columns about stereo and video equipment for The Cleveland Plain Dealer, Ohio's largest daily newspaper, and regularly contributed lifestyle features and photographs. In Cleveland, where he still lives, he has served as a chief engineer for several radio stations. He has also worked on electronic journalism projects for the NBC and CBS networks.

In his spare time, Rosch conducts experiments on spontaneous generation in his refrigerator and is researching a definitive study of Precambrian literature.

Limits of Liability and Disclaimer of Warranty

The author and publisher of this book have used their best efforts in preparing this book and the programs contained in it. These efforts include the development, research, and testing of the theories and programs to determine their effectiveness. The author and publisher make no warranty of any kind, expressed or implied, with regard to these programs or the documentation contained in this book. The author and publisher shall not be liable in any event for incidental or consequential damages in connection with, or arising out of, the furnishing, performance, or use of these programs.

Trademarks

Most computer and software brand names have trademarks or registered trademarks. The individual trademarks have not been listed here.

Acknowledgments

This book would not have been possible without the aid of the following people:

Bernie Wu, Archive Corporation; Rainer Schulz, CAE/SAR Systems; Bob Root and Sam Thompson, Carlyle Memory Products Group; Stephanie Campbell, Compaq Computer Corp.; John Simonds, Core International; Marty Alpert, Cumulus Corporation; Michael Dell and Ron Leonard, Dell Computer Corporation; Bob Goligoski, Grid System; Ken Plotkin, Hauppauge Computer Works; Jill Liscom and Mona Roberto, Hewlett-Packard, Inc.; Bobbie Crowell, Intel Corporation; Chet Heath, Jim Monahan, and Carey Ziter, IBM Corporation; John Klonick, Maxtor Corporation; Jennifer Roney, Miniscribe Corp.; Richard L. Sager, Mitsubishi Electric America; Kim Warnock, NCR Corporation; Dick Reiser, Priam Corporation; Catherine Hartsog, Quantum; Tim Mahoney and Debra Diamond, Rodime, Inc.; Dave Williams, Storage Dimensions, Inc.; Kathy Botz and Bob Flynn, Tecmar, Inc.; Philip Hage, 3M Company; and Burt Gabriel, Brady Publishing.

Publishers Acknowledgement

Portions of this second edition were contributed by Word Association, Inc. The publisher wishes to thank the members of Word Association for their hard work and dedication.

Contents

Introduction

Only a poor workman blames his tools when his job goes awry. But what kind of workman doesn't understand his tools, doesn't know how they work, and can't even tell a good tool from a bad one? Certainly, you would not trust such a workman on an important job—one critical to your business, one that may affect your income or budget, or one that may take control of your leisure pursuits. Yet far too many people profess ignorance about a tool vital to their businesses, their hobbies, or their households—the *personal computer.*

Indeed, the familiar PC is the most important business tool to emerge from electronic technology. It is vital to organizing, auditing, even controlling, most contemporary businesses. If fact, wherever work is to be done, you probably will find a PC at work. If you don't understand this modern tool, you will do worse than a bad job. Soon you may have no job at all.

Unlike a hammer or screwdriver, however, the personal computer is a tool that frightens those uninitiated into its obscure cabala. Tinkering with a personal computer is held in the same awe as open-heart surgery—except that cardiovascular surgeons are as apprehensive as the rest of us about tweaking around the insides of a computer. But computers are merely machines, made by people, meant to be used by people, and capable of being understood by people.

As with other tools, computers are only unapproachable by those inexperienced with them. An automobile mechanic may reel at the sight of a sewing machine. The seamstress or tailor may throw up his hands at the thought of tuning his car. The computer is no different. In fact, today's personal computer is purposely designed to be easy to take apart and put back together, easy to change and modify, and generally invincible except at the hands of the foolish or purposely destructive. As machines go, the personal computer is sturdy and trouble-free. Changing a card in a computer is safer and more certain of success than fixing a simple home appliance, such as a toaster, or changing the oil in your car.

The mystique surrounding the computer probably has its roots in several troubling aspects of the machine. First and foremost, the computer is a *thinking* machine—and that one word implies all sorts of preposterous nonsense. The thinking machine could be a devious machine, one hatching plots against you as it sits upon your desk, thinking of evil deeds that will cause you endless frustration. A thinking machine has a brain; therefore, opening it up and working inside is brain surgery, and the electronic patient is, just as the human, likely to suffer irreversible damage at the hands of an unskilled operator. A thinking machine must work the same unfathomable way as does the human mind—something so complicated that in thousands of years of attempts by geniuses, no one has yet satisfactorily explained.

But computers don't think—at least not in the same way as you do or Albert Einstein did. The computer has no emotions or motivations. The impulses traveling through it are no odd mixture of chemicals and electrical activity, of activation and repression. The computer deals in simple pulses of electricity, well understood and carefully controlled. The intimate workings of the computer are probably better understood than the seemingly simple flame that inhabits the internal combustion engine inside your car. Nothing mysterious lurks inside the thinking machine called the computer.

Computers are thought fearsome because they are based on electrical circuits. Electricity can be dangerous, as the ashes of anyone struck by lightning will attest. But inside the computer, the danger is low. At its worst, it measures 12 volts, which makes the inside of a computer as safe as playing with an electric train. Nothing that is readily accessible inside the computer will shock you, straighten your hair, or shorten your life. The personal computer is designed for tinkering, adding in accessories, and taking them out.

Computers are thought delicate because they are built from supposedly delicate electronic circuits, the same ones that their manufacturers warn about holding a cold water pipe before touching them, the same ones that cost $500 each. In fact, the one variety of electronic component that is really delicate requires extreme protection only when not installed where it belongs. Pulses of static electricity can damage circuits—while static pulses are a million times smaller than lightning bolts, the circuits inside semiconductor chips are a million times smaller and more delicate than you are—but circuitry in which the component is installed naturally keeps the static under control. Certainly a bolt of lightning or a good spark of static can still do harm, but the risk of either can be minimized simply. In most situations and workplaces, you should have little fear of damaging the circuits inside your computer.

Most people don't want to deal with the insides of their computers because the machines are complex and confusing. In truth, they are and they aren't. It all depends on how you look at them. Watching a movie on videotape is hardly a mental challenge, but understanding the whirring heads inside the machine and how the image is synchronized and how the hi-fi sound is recorded is something that will spin your brain for hours. Similarly, changing a board or adding a disk drive to a computer is simple. Designing the board and understanding the Boolean logic that controls the digital gates on it, however, take an engineering degree.

As operating systems get more complicated, computers are becoming easier to use. Grab a mouse and point it at an on-screen window, and you can be a skilled computer operator in minutes. That may be enough to content you. But you will be shortchanging yourself and your potential. Without knowing more about your system, you probably won't tap all the power of the PC. You won't be able to add to it and make it more powerful. You may not even know how to use everything that's there. You definitely won't know whether you've got the best computer for your purposes or some overpriced machine that can't do what simpler models excel at.

Although you don't need skill or an in-depth knowledge of computer or data-processing theory, you do need to know what you want to accomplish and what you can accomplish, the how and why of working with, expanding, even building a personal computer system.

The purpose of this book is to help you understand your present or future personal computer so that you can use rather than fear it. The text is designed to give you an overview of what makes up a computer system. The discussions will give you enough grounding in how the machine works so that you can understand what you are doing if you want to dig in and expand or upgrade your system. At the same time, the charts and tables will provide you with the reference materials you need to put that knowledge to work. As a whole, this book will help you understand your personal computer and give you the information you need to choose a computer and its peripherals. As you become more familiar with your system, this book will serve as a guide. It will even help you craft your own adapters and cables if you choose to get your hands dirty.

The computer is nothing to fear and need not be a mystery. It is a machine, and a straightforward one at that. A machine that you can master in the few hours it takes to read this book.

1

Background to an Industry Standard

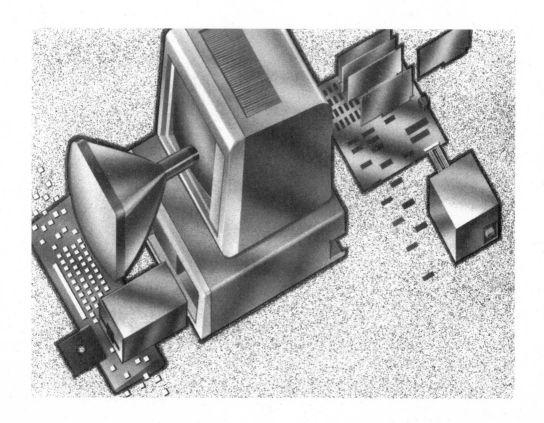

D efining a *personal computer* is one of those tasks that seems amazingly straightforward until you're charged to actually do it. When you take up the challenge, the term transforms itself into a strange cross-mating between amoeba and chamaeleon (biologists should shudder even at the thought of that one).

If the words were self-defining, a personal computer could be a machine meant to be used by one person instead of shared among a number of operators. But that definition includes such things as the expensive graphic workstation and the humble dedicated word processor. Another way to define the term might be by power. A personal computer would be one that lacks the computorial horsepower of a mainframe or minicomputer. Power alone no longer distinguishes machines. The quickest of today's personal computers easily outruns most minicomputers and even overlaps the low-end mainframe machines. You could try to define personal computer by price, but that definition, too, would be frustrated by reality. The price range is too wide to make any such limiting definition useful—you could buy a new personal computer priced anywhere from $200 to more than $20,000. Another way would be to define personal computer by reference to the machine that first put the term into public expression, the original IBM Personal Computer (PC). However, that machine is more than a decade old, an electronic antique with little relevance to today's world of personal computers.

The original PC can serve as a point of departure. Although the original PC has been long discontinued (the last one rolled off the production line in 1984), the PC still serves as an embodiment of the idea of the generalized personal computer. The IBM PC was the foundation of personal computer technology as it is now known. The IBM PC is the system that set the first standards—standards which helped other brands of personal computers earn success. Of course, these same standards have locked computer design into past technology and slowed progress. Today, although personal computers are 100 times faster than the original PC, they are just breaking out of the limitations imposed by that original design. Because the original PC and its offspring have proved so useful, the world has been slow to embrace new technologies that vary from those standards. Nearly 100 million reasons exist for this slow move away from the status quo—the machines still stuck, following that original admittedly flawed design.

Finally, the personal computer industry is putting the PC standard behind it and going off in new, more useful and powerful directions. New architectures and operating systems are giving you more computing power than may have been envisioned when the original IBM PC was introduced. Still, the latest computer hardware owes its heritage to the original PC. Consequently, one long look backward remains a good place to start any discussion of what a personal computer is and how it works.

Origins of the PC

This book would not exist, nor would the personal computer industry in its present form, were it not for a number of seemingly arbitrary, but at heart practical, decisions made at the IBM Corporation Entry Systems Division in Boca Raton, Florida, just as the decade of the 1980s was dawning. The culmination of that decision-making came on August 12, 1981, with the introduction of the IBM PC.

Far from idealists intent on starting a revolution, the PC was created as a machine for a limited number of people. Some sources inside IBM have stated that expectations were that about 100,000 Personal Computers would be sold, machines that would appeal primarily to hobbyists intent on exploring what computers could do. (But, of course, who probably would never do anything useful on the electronic curiosities. After all, useful computing work remained in the realm of the mainframe computer.) At the time, hobbyists were already exploring programming with other small computers. The IBM Personal Computer was seen as just another of these. Perhaps the machine would grab a toehold in the hobbyist market; perhaps the IBM Personal Computer served as a tool for exploring a new technological area (although IBM had already made a small computer, its model 5100, a suitcase-size portable machine, introduced in TK); or perhaps the project was just something some anxious engineers at IBM wanted to play with—with official sanction.

With such a market in mind, one design influence on the original Personal Computer can be understood. It was a machine of compromises designed to keep costs down, designed without any particular purpose in mind. In retrospect, that almost accidental element of the

Personal Computer design may have been IBM's masterstroke. That lack of purpose allowed the simple creation to grow into a variety of fields, to serve many masters, to be a true general-purpose computing instrument.

IBM was as surprised as the rest of the world when even in the initial months of its release, demand for the PC far outran supply, resulting in shortages and an unbelievable windfall to authorized IBM dealers who found that a little silicon could be worth its weight in gold.

Opportunist Design

If you want a full understanding of how a personal computer works, how it can be augmented, how it can be altered, you should start with examining all the issues that lead to the compromises in IBM's initial design. Exactly how this wildly successful collection of parts came together can only be conjectured about. The true motivations and design decisions underlying that first PC are forever the secret of IBM. The best guess that can be made is that the success of the PC stemmed from equal measures of serendipity and hard-nosed, bottom-line-oriented decision-making. IBM wanted to cash in on the success that small computers were having among hobbyists and, increasingly, small businesses. The desktop computer presented a tremendous opportunity—one that IBM did not want to miss—as it had with minicomputers. Most industry analysts attribute the astounding success of one-time number-two computer-maker Digital Equipment Corporation (DEC) in the 1970s and 80s to IBM's failure to move into the minicomputer field fast enough.

To create IBM's first true desktop machine, the company's engineers carefully pruned and grafted the ideas embodied in other small computers on the market with a scattering of minor changes and innovations to make their new product stand out. They put together a computer mostly made from off-the-shelf parts and components crafted by other manufacturers so that if the product misfired, losses would not be great, and IBM could go on to other, more important products in its bread-and-butter mainframe line. They borrowed design concepts from the machines that hobbyists were toying with, engineered around semiconductor parts widely available on the market that required no exotic proprietary design work, and exploited an operating system based on the most popular of those used in small business computers.

Computer Competitors

To understand why particular elements were chosen for the design of the PC, you need to remember what was going on in the small computer marketplace at the time. In 1980, the term "personal computer" was still evolving, much as was the hardware. The term didn't identify any particular type of machine because there was no prototypical small computer. The designs of machines varied widely, much more than the limited choices available today. Manufacturers had their own idea of what constituted the optimal design. Most of the available small computers could be divided into one of three major groups, however. Two of these groups were each dominated by a single manufacturer. The other was unified by a common operating system.

Apple Computer

The most important of the desktop computer competitors in terms of longevity and acceptance, the one that has survived the longest with the least alteration, was (and is) the original Apple II. (Its predecessor, Apple I, was more a design effort than a commercial product, something created in a garage by the common efforts of Steve Wozniak, a one-time Hewlett-Packard engineer and Steve Jobs, best regarded as a visionary salesman.) The design of the Apple II was innovative and clever; it introduced features and technologies that soon will become familiar in the discussion of the implementation of the IBM PC.

The original Apple II blazed a path as one of the first single-board computers that also featured a dedicated expansion bus into which accessories (and some necessities) could be attached. The Apple II was based on a single microprocessor and was a single-board computer because everything needed to make it work—at least in the most rudimentary way—was built onto a single (though large), glass-epoxy printed circuit board. Its expansion bus provided a way of connecting additional printed circuit boards almost directly to the microprocessor. Even the keyboard was combined into the housing for the electronics—a simple, practical, and cost-effective approach.

The central processing unit of the Apple II was its microprocessor brain, an integrated circuit that bore the designation 6502 (at the time, a respectable chip choice) that could perform eight-bit calculations at an operating speed of about one million cycles per second (megahertz).

Compared to the personal computers of today, the Apple II was rudimentary. The straightforward original design of the Apple II made no provision for lowercase letters, could put only 40 columns of text across the screen, and could be bought with as little as eight kilobytes of memory. For more permanent storage, the Apple II could route data from its electronic memory onto magnetic tape using a conventional audio cassette machine. Compared to what came before; however, the Apple II was groundbreaking. You could buy an Apple II, pull it from its box, plug it in, and have a working computer. Previous small computers universally required at least a moderate degree of technical knowledge, a great deal of patience to withstand the tedious process of assembling parts not necessarily meant to work together, and an overriding faith that they would, in fact, work.

Only later did Apple add features that have since become standard on all later personal computers: lowercase characters in 80 columns, bit-mapped graphics, and disk storage controlled by Apple DOS (Disk Operating System). Because the need for these added features was neither foreseen nor allowed for in the original design, they required some clever engineering (which was duly provided) to mix in. The result was a collection of workable but odd adaptations—for example, a memory structure in which alternate characters on-screen were separated into different blocks of memory. In retrospect, even on initial inspection, these weaknesses of the Apple II design were readily apparent and easily avoided in the designs of other manufacturers.

Tandy/Radio Shack

The second pre-PC small-computer design camp rallied under the Radio Shack flag. The familiar corner-store vendor of everything from batteries and toys to watches and telephones added small computers to its wide range of offerings by producing a number of machines based on different technologies, microprocessors, and operating systems.

The wide variety of the Radio Shack products was intended to appeal to the widest market. The leader at the time of the introduction of IBM's first machine was the TRS-80, a desktop computer that combined monitor, keyboard, and electronics into one box, all built around a Z80 microprocessor. Both cassette and floppy disk storage was available; the later using the TRS-DOS (widely known as Trash DOS to both its friends and detractors).

The punishment applied to the model designation is one of the reasons that this computer brand has officially disappeared from the market. After years of trashy jokes, Radio Shack's corporate parent Tandy Corporation elected to pull not only the TRS designation but also the Radio Shack label from its computer products and instead substituted its own name and less allusive model numbers.

Among the virtues of the TRS-80 were its capability to show 80-column text in upper- and lowercase characters. Among its biggest drawbacks were its styling, which was of the sort that appealed to those who found aesthetic ecstasy in the Cadillac tail-fins of a generation earlier. It was all rounded curves and metalized plastic, which might appeal to Buck Rogers more than a businessman.

CP/M

The third group of small computers huddled around the CP/M (Control Program for Microcomputers) operating system. CP/M linked the very popular and powerful 8080 and Z80 microprocessors with flexible disk drives. Its low cost and usefulness led to its wide use and its emergence as a standard.

CP/M-based computers typically enabled the use of 80-column text with lowercase characters in a text-oriented display that usually ran through a teletype interface, designed for computers constructed from separate terminals and central processing units that communicated through thin wires one bit at a time (serially).

The combination of microprocessor and operating system yielded enough power to handle many business chores, from word processing to bookkeeping. It was exactly what business needed; consequently, CP/M computers emerged as the business standard among desktop machines. In the early 80s more business-oriented software—which often consisted of more than a few dozen lines of BASIC code—was available for CP/M than any other computer operating environment.

The IBM Strategy

This environment provided IBM with the incentive for creating the PC. By then, the small computer market had grown to tens of thousands of machines per year, clearly too large to ignore—particularly since much of the growing base was among business users. Business, remember, is IBM's middle name.

Misstep Avoidance

Added to that incentive was IBM's generation-old minicomputer misstep. When IBM ignored the bottom rung of the ladder of computer power because the market was small and profits were minuscule, DEC gained a toehold in small computers and developed a loyal following. As DEC users graduated to higher power computers, DEC followed them by making what they needed, growing all the time, until the company had become IBM's chief rival.

Faced with the new flush of small computers, IBM decided to enter the market quickly but with minimum risk.

The Acquisition Angle

Perhaps the best way of accomplishing that end would be with the straightforward strategy of acquisition. IBM could simply buy a manufacturer of small computers and integrate the company and its products into the IBM corporate monolith—much as IBM later strode into the communications business by buying Rolm Corporation and gradually sucked the company into the Big Blue mainstream. The obvious choice would have been Apple. But Apple was not IBM's type of target. Apple had not yet aimed its products at business applications. Apple was still supplying hobbyists, not an IBM market.

Nor did Apple have much of a track record as a company and computer manufacturer. Of course, the same could be said about any company that had begun its life by building small computers. The industry itself was not that old, so the companies in the industry were understandably young. Nevertheless, Apple was a small start-up company with no track record and, according to normal business sense, a dubious future. Moreover, its sole product, the Apple II, just wasn't a very good design or one that fit the IBM business-oriented scheme of things.

Acquiring Radio Shack was never an alternative. Although Radio Shack, and its parent Tandy Corporation, had a proven track record of profits, computers had little to do with that. At the time, computers were a small part of the sales of the mass retailer. IBM would have to buy a restaurant to get a cup of coffee.

The other makers of small computers were even less attractive. IBM really didn't need to own someone's garage that was optimistically called a microcomputer factory.

The Roll-Your-Own Strategy

Developing its own machine was not quite so far-fetched. IBM had already made small computers in the guise of its transportable (by a stretch of the imagination and arm) Model 5100. Built without the benefit of such innovations as floppy disk drives, the 5100 primarily found use inside IBM but never did much as a commercial product.

Microprocessor Choice

There could be no doubt the IBM machine would be based on a microprocessor. The smart chips were what had originally made small computers practical and the industry possible. The question was which chip to use.

Apple's choice, the 6502, would have been considered dated even in 1981. An eight-bit chip, the 6502 processed and referenced data in memory just eight bits at a time and operated at a clock speed of about one megahertz. Its processing throughput paled in comparison to that achieved by the CP/M machines and their Z80 microprocessor.

Although the Z80 also is an eight-bit data engine, it is more efficient in handling code and can run faster than the 6502. Weighing more heavily in favor of the Z80 was the huge CP/M software library. IBM faced a marketing problem in designing a machine around the Z80 microprocessor, however. Such a product would hardly stand out from the pack of existing CP/M machines. An IBM CP/M computer would have no advantage over the hardware available from other manufacturers, no hooks for the IBM salesforce to use in marketing the machine.

The Intel 8088, on the other hand, was similar enough to the Z80 that software could be easily converted to run on it—at least that was the thought at the time. Moreover, the 8088 differed from the Z80 in two significant ways—it had wider internal registers and a greater memory addressing range.

Although the 8088 is truly an eight-bit processor in that information moves in and out of the chip eight bits at a time, its internal processing is sometimes performed 16 bits at a time because it has 16-bit registers. Although the Z80 could only address 65,536 bytes of memory (or 64K), the 8088 could handle 16 times as much: 1,048,576 bytes (1024K or 1M). At least potentially, the 8088 was a more formidable microprocessor. Even in the early 80s, more powerful chips were available, however. The bigger (and older) brother of the 8088, the 8086, for example, has the same 16-bit internal architecture, the same wide addressing range, but also used 16-bit connections with the outside world. The difference makes the 8086 potentially twice as fast as the 8088 even when operating at the same speed.

IBM had one good reason for foregoing the full 16-bit power of the 8086, however. In the early 80s, the price of microprocessor support chips (as well as memory) was much higher than today. For example, where a megabyte of memory costs in the neighborhood of $50 today, 16K of memory—one sixty-fourth as much—cost about that much when the first PC was introduced. Using a full 16-bit bus structure would add substantially to the cost of the computer that used it.

As a marketing move, going with a 16-bit architecture probably did not make sense to IBM's PC designers, particularly because the 16-bit internal nature of the 8088 would still enable IBM to advertise the erstwhile eight-bit PC as a 16-bit computer. Power was not a real issue. Although the 8086 brain would have resulted in a superior machine, the marketplace placed no demands on performance. After all, having a computer was vastly better than not having one, and in comparison the performance difference between 8-and 16-bit designs was insignificant. An 8-bit design would be easier—and faster—to implement, had no relative market disadvantage, and was less costly (a powerful advantage). The 8088 won out over the 8086.

Other chips were out of the running. The Motorola 6800, a full 16-bit chip, lost partly for the same reason as the full 16-bit 8086 and partly because it lacked easy CP/M translatability. The Texas Instruments family of microprocessors lost for the same reason. As a result, the 8088 was chosen—not quite an arbitrary or capricious decision, but one that lacked the foresight to see performance arising as a major issue in microcomputers.

Memory Issues

After a microprocessor is decided upon, the next choice is memory. Several aspects must be considered. The working memory of the computer system must be designed both physically (what sort of chips should be used, how should they be connected) and logically (what uses should the various memory locations be put to). In addition, mass storage—the holding zone for programs and data—must be decided upon.

The first part of the physical memory question—the hardware to use— was easily solved. At the time the PC was first designed, memory chips that held 16,384 bytes (16K) were the most plentiful and cost-effective. They also were the basis of most competing computers.

The least expensive and most popular of these stored their bytes in a one dimensional array, giving 16,384 places to store a single memory bit. (Other chips might store four bits at a location, half a byte or a nibble at a time.) A minimum of eight chips of these one-dimensional chips are required to hold bytes of information because of their one dimensional architecture.

To the basic and minimal eight, IBM added one more. In the mainframe business, data integrity is extremely important, so large computers use complex schemes for detecting and possibly correcting memory errors. IBM decided to include a form of memory-quality insurance in the PC, a system that would detect if a memory bit randomly should go bad. This approach, emphasizing data integrity, would distinguish IBM's personal computer efforts over the years.

The simplest possible detection scheme involves adding up all the bits in the byte and then adding in a special parity bit to ensure that the total is always even. If one bit changes, the total comes out odd, showing that an error must have occurred. The extra parity-check bit requires one additional RAM chip. Consequently, the PC was equipped with nine memory chips.

With a bit of prescience—the knowledge that most programs won't run with so little memory as 16K—IBM provided places for adding more memory. A total of 27 empty sockets enabled you to plug up to 64 kilobytes of memory into the original PC. With an eye to the future, IBM even made provisions for installing boards containing extra RAM, enabling the system to be expanded up to 512K, an amount that was more than any program could possibly require, or so IBM's engineers naively thought.

These engineers reserved the other half of the addressing range of the 8088 for special purposes. Some locations were used for video memory—storing the image that would appear on-screen in electronic form—others for the permanently recorded programs in ROM that are collectively called the Basic Input/Output System. Only a small fraction of this reserved memory area was actually put to use, but IBM made sure that the memory was there should it ever be needed. In fact, only about 20K of the potential of this reserved memory was initially used, 4K for video memory and 16K for the BIOS.

In mass storage, IBM almost indiscriminately exploited the same options other personal computer makers had used. Miniature (for the time) 5 1/4-inch floppy disks were a natural because of their use in other small computers and because of IBM's experience with their larger cousins, 8-inch drives, in other IBM products such as DisplayWriter.

Again, no one at the time foresaw a need for huge amounts of mass storage, so IBM elected to use only one side of the potentially two-sided disks, limiting capacity to 160 kilobytes but enabling the use of less-expensive drives. Although puny by today's standards, that capacity was substantially greater than the 80 to 130 kilobytes used in other small computers at the time.

IBM also hedged its mass storage bet by including a cassette port as part of the first PC. Instead of buying a $500 floppy disk drive, you could use your $20 portable tape recorder to remember programs and data, even exchange files with your friends. Even back then cassette tape was slow and inconvenient, in retrospect a particularly poor match for the PC. Should hobbyists actually be the major market for the somewhat undirected PC, the cassette port would undoubtedly find users.

The basic design of the original IBM PC reflects the new technology it embraced. The machine was built around a microprocessor and was essentially little more than an extension of the chip, enhanced with the necessities required to supply information to it and get results from it. The microprocessor-oriented design is termed a single-board microcomputer because all of its essential circuitry was located on one large printed circuit board. Like Apple (and many other computer makers) IBM provided expansion slots for adding accessories.

IBM might have made the PC a bus-oriented computer, one in which even the main brain is on an expansion board. Logic ruled against such a strategy, however. All the circuitry required would not have fit on a single expansion board. Therefore, IBM designed the PC with a large master circuit board holding the bulk of the system's circuits, the system board, which allowed for other expansion on it.

Language BASICs

To make a computer useful, it needs programs. That need can be accommodated in two ways—with ready-made programs called applications software (or simply applications) that only need be loaded into the computer to work, or using a programming language to enable the computer user to write his own software. At the time the PC was introduced, the number of applications for its was modest—principally only a handful instigated at IBM's behest. Moreover, most of the perceived market for the fledgling machine was seen in hobbyists who would want to dabble with programming themselves. In fact, they would be the reservoir that would supply the applications to be used by others. The PC provided a wonderful opportunity for this because the same inexpensive hardware that ran applications could be used for developing them. (Many earlier small computers required very expensive developmental systems, priced well out of the reach of the hobbyist, to create their software.)

The programming language that the PC got was BASIC, the Beginners' All-Purpose Symbolic Instruction Code, originally created as the name implies as an easy-to-learn language. Although many other languages were available, weighing in favor of IBM including BASIC in its PC was the acceptance of the language in the small-computer industry and among hobbyists, the small size of the language that made it usable on machines with limited memory, and IBM's own experience with BASIC in the 5100. Another programming language, APL (short for A Programming Language), also was used on the 5100—in many cases preferred by the users of the computer—but BASIC won.

Much to the consternation of compatible makers ever since, IBM stuffed a rudimentary form of BASIC into the ROM chips—unchangeable hardware—of the PC. Because mass storage was essentially optional in the first PCs, the machines would have been little more than vegetables without an internal programming language. BASIC gave even machines without mass storage a limited usefulness. It was always there waiting for you even if you had no disk drive, ready to run the programs you typed into your system at its prompt, able to save and load those programs from cassette tape if you were too cheap to buy a floppy disk drive.

In the beginning, some programmers took advantage of this BASIC and wrote applications that would use the language as it came with the machine. To achieve backward compatibility with the first generation of PCs—and to remain able to take advantage of this software— the BASIC language has been a standard part of every IBM personal computer since the beginning. It remains as an interesting anachronism, unnecessary as demonstrated by the vast array of clone computers, none of which include built-in BASIC. (Of course, these machines can load BASIC or any other programming language from disk to create and execute programs written using it.)

The Display System

Every computer needs a display system so that you can monitor its operation—see what you type or load from storage, follow the progress of calculations, and read and review the results.

In designing the display system for its original Personal Computer, IBM drew upon its experience won in the office with the making of millions of computer terminals. These essential characteristics were those that would appeal to your eye—it required sharp, easy-to-read characters and no annoying flicker. Moreover, for greater versatility in displaying information and maintaining those displays, IBM chose a particular technology for electronically organizing the data bound for the display. In its PC design, IBM broke away from the technology popular with mainframe computers and the typical implementations of machines—the so-called teletype video display by which the computer sends a string of characters to a terminal, each string broken into lines with carriage returns much the way a typewriter works (and exactly like the typewriter-gone-automaton called the teletype does; hence the name for the technology). Using a teletype interface, the computer sends out the lines without regard for where they will appear on-screen, and the circuitry in the display terminal does most of the worrying about where the text will appear on-screen. One line is posted beneath the previous one until the screen is filled, and then the terminal makes more room at the bottom by pushing the oldest line on the screen off the top, scrolling it into oblivion.

Another display technology had won favor with Apple Computer, however—one that was more versatile and better suited to systems with built-in display systems as opposed to computers with separate terminals. Called character-mapping, this technique divided the screen into a matrix of character positions and assigned each character position a memory location. The display system then matched the character designation in the map with the dot-pattern of the character stored elsewhere in a font library (which can be either RAM or ROM). Independently of the host microprocessor, the video system sends the appropriate dot information from the font library to the screen.

The advantage of this arrangement is that it is fast and efficient, from the microprocessor and memory point of view. It needs to deal with only efficient character codes. Only two kilobytes of data need to be moved or stored for a full 80-column-by-25-row screen of text. This arrangement also eliminates much of the cost of a terminal. Making it work only requires a display—essentially a picture tube and its control circuitry—instead of a complete terminal.

It gives the programmer an easy and absolute way of positioning characters on-screen. The program need only push the character code into the appropriate position in the matrix of display memory. With a teletype system, the programmer has no certain way of ensuring the absolute position of a character on-screen. The best that can be done is to use positioning codes that tell the terminal where to place the beginning character of each string. The program and programmer then must keep track of how many characters are sent to the terminal (to know when they move down to the next line) or send positioning codes every few characters. Either way, the programmer faces more work than simply selecting a matrix position.

In the IBM scheme of character mapping, an extra byte is added in the matrix for each character of the display to hold character attribute information—that is, an indicator as to whether the character should be displayed as dim, highlighted, underlined, or shown in reverse video. IBM also chose to put the character and attribute bytes for each on-screen cell adjacent to one another, using a total of four kilobytes of memory area. Although this arrangement seems obvious, it would have been just as effective to put the attributes in a second, separate map displaced from the first in memory. The advantages of each are esoteric—it is only important to know the exact arrangement used should you want to dabble in programming and take direct control of the PC display system.

The Keyboard

The display system is an excellent means for you to see what your computer is doing, but you need help at the other end, too, so that you can communicate with your PC and tell it what to do. Such is the job of the keyboard. Again, with the keyboard, different design variations are possible. Apple Computer demonstrated one technique with its Apple II by making the keyboard part of the computer, both physically and electrically. IBM also relied on its office experience to tether the keyboard to a cord so that it could be positioned to better suit the user. Although the separate keyboard design is more complex electrically—all the signals from the keyboard must be reduced to a form that can be sent through a narrow cable instead of being directly connected to the computer's circuitry, the flexibility of the separate keyboard design pays off in improving the workplace environment and even enabling the easy substitution and replacement of keyboards—in case of failure or just the need for something new under your fingers.

The keyboard and display system are only examples of the overall IBM philosphy in the original PC. IBM took the best ideas of the machines on the marketplace, refined them, and put them together in a single, clever computer. The bottom line was that the IBM PC was designed around many practical constraints at an almost totally unfocused market. It was almost as if IBM put the machine in stores to see who, if anyone, would buy it.

Much to the surprise of everyone, including IBM, people did buy it. Small businesses did. Huge corporations did. PCs sold so quickly that IBM couldn't make them fast enough.

The PC touched off a revolution. It spawned several succeeding and more powerful models. Its logical and practical design set the standard for a new industry. Dozens of manufacturers—from one-man-and-a-soldering-iron garage operations to multi-billion-dollar mega-corporations—created their own versions of the PC, each designed to be as compatible as possible with the IBM original.

These machines changed the way people worked and even the way they thought.

CHAPTER

The Motherboard

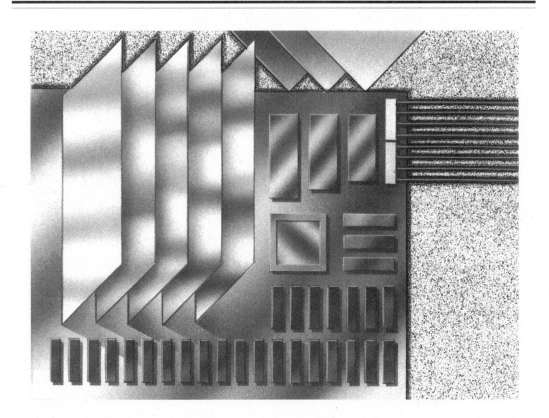

Traditionally the centerpiece of most personal computers, the motherboard is the physical and logical backbone of the entire system. The circuitry located on the motherboard defines the computer—its capabilities, limitations, and personality.

Nearly all PCs and compatible computers share one common feature: they are built with a single, large printed circuit board as their foundation. This one big board holds the most vital components that define the system—its microprocessor, support circuitry, and memory. Other additions to the system that enable it to increase in power or specialize to match a particular use plug into this central board. Without this one board, there would be no computer. This design is not inevitable; rather, its roots reach back to the original engineering choice made by IBM when it drafted its very first Personal Computer. IBM did not develop the idea of using a single, centralized board; they followed the emerging trends in the small-computer industry.

Small-Computer Designs

As the PC was being developed, two contrary philosophies dominated small-computer engineering. One united all the important components of the computer on a large board as in the PC, creating a *single-board computer*. The other design camp believed in diversity, putting the individual functional elements—microprocessor, memory, and input/output circuitry—on separate boards that plugged into connectors that linked them together through a circuit bus. Such machines are described as *bus-oriented computers*. Each of these designs has its strengths.

Bus-Oriented Computers

At the time the PC was developed, the bus-oriented design was the conservative approach. The bus gets its name because, like a Greyhound, all the signals of the bus travel together and make the same stops at the same connectors along the way. The most popular small business computers of that era were built around a bus standard termed *S-100*, the name indicating that the bus comprised 100 connections. Most larger computers used the bus-oriented design as well. The bus approach enabled each computer to be custom-configured for its particular purpose and business. Larger, more powerful processors, even multiple processors, could be added to the machine as needs dictated. The modular design enabled the system to expand as business needs expanded and allowed for easier service. Any individual board that failed could be quickly removed and replaced without circuit-level surgery.

Actually, the bus-oriented design originated as a matter of necessity because all the components required to make a computer would not fit on a circuit board of practical size. The overflowing circuitry had to be spread among multiple boards, and the bus was the easiest way to link them all together.

Single-Board Computers

The advent of *integrated circuits*, miniaturized assemblies that put multiple electronic circuit components into a single package often as small as a fingernail, and microprocessors greatly reduced the amount of circuit board required for building a computer. By the end of the 1970s, putting an entire digital computer on one circuit board first became practical. It was also desirable for a number of reasons. Primary among them was cost. Fewer boards means less fabrication expense and less materials cost. Not only can the board be made smaller, but the circuitry necessary to match each board to the bus can be eliminated. Moreover, single-board computers have an advantage in reliability. Connectors are the most failure-prone part of any computer system. The single-board design eliminates the bus connectors as a potential source for system failure.

On the downside, however, the single-board computer design is decidedly less flexible than the bus-oriented approach. The single-board has its capabilities forever fixed the moment it is soldered together at the factory. It can never become more powerful or transcend its original design. It cannot adapt to new technological developments.

Although the shortcomings of the single-board computer make it an undesirable (but not unused) approach for desktop computers, the design works well for many laptop and notebook computers. The compactness of the single-board approach is a perfect match for the space- and weight-conscious laptop design, and the lack of expansion is not a serious drawback. In fact, the laptop design attempts to shoehorn as many functions as possible into the small cases of the machines, leaving little (if any) room for expansion.

The PC Compromise

Rather than strictly following either the single-board or bus-oriented approach, IBM selected the middle ground and combined some of the best features of the single-board computer and the bus-oriented design. In the PC model, one large board hosts the essential circuitry that defines the computer, and slots are available for expansion and flexibility.

The history of the PC has been one of moving closer to the single-board computer design. As IBM has introduced new models, an increasing number of functions have been incorporated on the central circuit board. The original IBM PC did, in fact, lack only one feature to comprise a complete single-board computer—a display system. Mass storage was included in the form of a cassette port (equivalent to making the standard-equipment engine in an automobile a heavy-duty rubber band). With more recent models, however, IBM has moved the display system and advanced mass storage onto the main circuit board. At least three motivations underlie this migration. The basic requirements for a personal computer have risen so that the added features are now expected in every PC. Putting the basics required in a PC on the main circuit board lowers the overall cost of the system (for the same reason that a single-board computer is cheaper to make than the equivalent bus-oriented machine). In-creasing miniaturization has made possible cramming more functions on the main circuit board. The original PC had hardly a spare square inch for additional functions. Today, a computer ten times more powerful can fit a wide variety of standard features on a board half the size of the PC.

The trend today, however, is in the opposite direction. System designers now aim to make their PCs upgradeable by pulling essential features—such as the microprocessor—off the main board. This more modular design gives the manufacturer (and your dealer) more flexibility. New models can be introduced more quickly (the support circuitry need not be re-engineered), and inventories can be minimized. Instead of stocking several models, the manufacturer and dealer need only keep a single box on the shelf, shuffling the appropriate microprocessor into it as the demand arises. These modular systems also promise you upgradability, a concept desirable in the abstract (your PC need never become obsolete) but often impractical (upgrading is rarely a cost-effective strategy).

The flexibility of the bus-oriented design presupposes that you have a wide selection of plug-in boards available to you. After all, a slot that you can plug only one board into offers no advantage (other than the ability to discard the board) over having all the circuitry in one assembly. Consequently, the desirability of bus-oriented computers depends on the acceptance of the bus design as a standard. *Proprietary buses*—designs for which only a single manufacturer builds boards (often because the manufacturer refuses to reveal the technical workings of the bus to others)—fall short of the full flexibility of standardized buses. In effect, they offer little (if any) advantage over single-board designs.

Circuit Board Nomenclature

You're apt to hear a variety of names bandied about when those in the know—or those who think they are—discuss the large board around which their PCs are built. They speak of motherboards, system boards, planar boards, and backplanes as if they all were the same. Although the terms are used interchangeably in common parlance, the concepts underlying them are subtly different.

Mother and Daughterboards

Long before what was to become the 1991 Gulf War was proclaimed as the "Mother of All Battles" by Saddam Hussein, the biggest circuit assembly in any PC was colloquially known as the *motherboard*. In a way, this circuit assembly is the "mother of all boards," but not in the way Hussein intended to refer to the pre-eminence of the expected engagement. Rather, the term hints at the function of the board and its relationship to boards that plug into it, which are termed *daughterboards*. Drawing a direct analogy is fraught with strange images—you may imagine the smaller boards sucking from the larger one or the archaic concept of daughters clinging to their mother. Better to just think of the terms referring to the relative importance of the boards—mother is pre-eminent (mother knows best). No more sexism is implied in the terms than is implied by the Spanish assigning the female gender to a table radio. (After all, sex and language gender are entirely different concepts, and anyone doubting that must have missed one of the more important high school health classes.) Besides, the term daughterboard is more mellifluous than alternatives such as "sonboard" or the more generic "offspringboard." The motherboard-daughterboard relationship has nothing to do with size. Just as daughters can grow up to be taller than their mothers, daughterboards can be larger than the motherboards they plug into. In fact, the defining characteristic of the motherboard is not size or the circuitry it holds but the linkage it provides for expanding the system. Connectors rather than active circuitry are the essential elements of the motherboard. PCs can be (and have been) built with no components except expansion connectors and the electrical links between them on the motherboard.

System Board

IBM developed its own nomenclature for the system board that held the principal circuitry of its entire line of personal computers, from the original IBM PC through its successors, XT and AT. *System board* is an apt name because the board—or more correctly, the circuitry on the board—defines the entire computer system. And, yes, one reason for using the term was to create a gender-neutral term. IBM didn't want to take sides in the war between the sexes.

Expansion Boards

The gender-neutral term for daughterboard that matches the system board nomenclature is *expansion board*. The term seems apt in that these plug-in boards enable you to expand your system. But many PCs require you to plug in expansion boards just to get the thing to work— even an unexpanded PC requires some way of connecting a monitor. Nevertheless, expansion board is the accepted term, and the boards plug into connectors called *expansion slots* on the system board.

Planar Boards

Another gender-neutral term promoted by IBM for the motherboard, which first came into common parlance with the introduction of the Personal System/2 line of machines, was *planar board*. In conversation, IBM engineers often clip the term to the simple adjective, planar. Like most gender-neutral terms, planar board is less descriptive than the terms it is meant to replace. At face value, the term could not be more vague or all-embracing. All printed circuit boards are planar—flat— except, perhaps, for a few special-purpose flexible assemblies like those folded into cameras. Even system board is more precise because it at least describes the function of the circuit assembly.

Logic Boards

IBM has no monopoly on vague, gender-neutral terms. In the realm of the Apple Macintosh, the main circuit board inside a computer is often called a *logic board*. Of course, every circuit board inside a computer is based on digital logic, so the term could hardly be less specific.

Backplanes

Another name sometimes used to describe the motherboard in PCs is *backplane*. The term is a carry-over from bus-oriented computers. In early bus-oriented designs, all the expansion connectors in the machine would be linked together by a single circuit board. The expansion boards slid through the front panel of the computer and plugged into the expansion connectors in the motherboard at the rear. Because the board was necessarily planar and at the rear of the computer, the term backplane was perfectly descriptive. With later designs, the backplane found itself lining the bottom of the computer case.

Backplanes are described as *active* if, as in the PC design, they hold active logic circuitry. A *passive backplane* is nothing more than expansion connectors linked by wires or printed circuitry. The system boards of most personal computers could be described as active backplanes, although most engineers reserve the term backplane for bus-oriented computers in which the microprocessor plugs into the backplane rather than residing on it. The active circuitry on an active backplane under such a limited definition would comprise bus control logic that facilitates the communication between boards.

Motherboard Components

The motherboard of any computer that follows the IBM design scheme performs several major functions. At the most basic level, it is the physical foundation of the computer. It holds all the expansion boards in place, provides firm territory to attach connections to external circuit elements, and provides the base of support for the central electronics of the computer. Electrically, the circuitry etched upon it includes the brain of the computer and the most important elements required to nourish that brain. This circuitry determines the entire personality of the computer—how it functions, how it reacts to your every keystroke, and what it does.

No one part of the system board completely defines a computer's personality. Its essence is spread throughout the circuit traces and components.

The Microprocessor

The microprocessor does the actual thinking inside the computer. Which microprocessor of the dozens currently available is used determines not only the processing power of the computer but also what software language it understands (and thus what programs the computer can run).

Coprocessors

An adjunct to the microprocessor, the coprocessor enables a computer to carry out certain operations much faster. A coprocessor can make a computer run five to ten times faster in some operations.

Memory

Required by the microprocessor to carry out its calculations, the amount and architecture of the memory of a system determines how it can be programmed and, to some extent, the level of complexity of the problems upon which it can work.

BIOS

The *Basic Input/Output System* or *BIOS* of a computer is a set of permanently recorded program routines that give the system its fundamental operational characteristics. The BIOS determines what the computer can do without loading a program from disk and how the computer reacts to specific instructions that are part of those disk-based programs.

Expansion Slots

As portals that allow new signals to enter the computer and directly react with its circuitry, expansion slots allow new features and enhancements to be added to the system and enable the quick and easy alteration of certain computer prerequisites, such as video adapters.

Support Circuitry

A microprocessor, although the essence of a computer, is not a computer in itself (if it were, it would be called a computer). It requires a number of additional circuits to bring it to life: clocks, controllers, and signal converters. Each of these support circuits has its own way of reacting to programs, and thus helps determine how the computer works.

Printed-Circuit Technology

The "board" part of the motherboard name refers to the *printed-circuit board*. The term is sometimes confusingly shortened to PC board even when the board is part of some other, non-computer device. Today, printed-circuit boards are the standard from which nearly all electronic devices are made. The old alternative was point-to-point hand wiring. Actual physical wires connected circuit elements, each end soldered in place by hand (a workable, if not particularly cost-effective, technology in the days of tubes when even a simple circuit spanned a few inches of physical space). Today, point-to-point wiring is virtually inconceivable because a PC crams the equivalent of half a million tube circuits into a few square inches of space. Connecting them together with old-fashioned wiring would take a careful hand—and some very fine wire. The time required to cut, strip, and solder each wire in place would make building a single PC a lifetime endeavor.

Printed circuits allow all the wiring for an entire circuit assembly to be fabricated together in a quick process that can be entirely mechanized. The wires themselves are reduced to copper *traces*, a pattern of copper foil bonded to the *substrate* that makes up the support structure of the printed-circuit board. In computers, this substrate is usually green composite material called *glass-epoxy* because it has a woven fiberglass base filled and reinforced with an epoxy plastic. Less critical electronic devices (read "cheap") substitute a simple brownish substrate of phenolic plastic for the glass-epoxy.

The simplest circuit boards start life as a sheet of thin copper foil bonded to a substrate. The copper is coated with a compound called *photo-resist*, a light-sensitive material (hence the "photo" in the name). When exposed to light, the photo-resist becomes resistant to the effects of compounds, such as nitric acid, which strongly react with copper (hence the "resist" in the name). A negative image of the desired final circuit pattern is place over the photo-resist covered copper and exposed to a strong light source. The board is then immersed in an *etchant* that etches or eats away from the copper not protected by light-exposed photoresist. The result is a pattern of copper on the sustrate corresponding to the photographic original. The copper traces then can be used to connect the various electronic components that will make up the final circuit.

Two technologies are in wide use for attaching components to the printed-circuit board. The older technology is called *pin-in-hole*. Holes are drilled in the circuit board at the points components are to attach. The leads (wires coming out of the components) are inserted into and through the circuit board holes and soldered in place. The excess lead length is clipped off. In mass production, component leads are pre-trimmed, and all are soldered to the board at the same time using a technique called wave-soldering. The board passes just above the surface of a pool of molten solder across which a solitary wave rolls, just touching the board and soldering the leads to the traces. Both human workers and automatic insertion machines can handle pin-in-hole technology. Automatic machinery cuts labor costs and speeds production on long runs; assembly workers typically make prototypes and small production runs and often provide the sole means of assembly for tiny companies that can afford neither automatic machinery or to farm out their circuit-board work. *Surface-mount technology* promises greater miniaturization and lower costs than pin-in-hole. Instead of holes to secure them, surface-mount components are literally glued to circuit boards using solder paste, which temporarily holds them in place. After all the components are affixed to a circuit board, the entire board assembly runs through a temperature-controlled oven that melts the solder paste and firmly solders each component to the board.

System Board Makers

Because the motherboard defines each computer—its functions and capabilities—and because every computer is different, you could assume that every motherboard is different, too. Not exactly. Many different computers have the same motherboard designs inside. And oftentimes a single computer model might have any of several different motherboards, depending on when a particular computer came down the production line (and what motherboard the manufacturer got the best deal on).

OEMs

Although this variability of PCs and their motherboards may seem strange, it arises from a fact of marketing life long present in manufacturing. Brand names and manufacturers often have no closer association than the glue that holds on the nameplate. The brand name is owned by the company marketing a product at the wholesale or retail level. The company doing the marketing can handle the manufacturing itself, hire (contract or subcontract) another company to do the manufacturing for it, or simply buy parts or whole products made by someone else. Companies that supply the marketing organizations—and oftentimes the marketing organizations themselves—that follow this last strategy are known as *Original Equipment Manufacturers* or *OEMs*. The term, which has become almost meaningless through overuse and generalization, is now even accepted as a verb. An equipment maker OEMs to the marketing organization, and the marketing organization OEMs from the manufacturer.

OEM relationships often are as confusing as the terminology. Some manufacturing OEMs may market products under their own names, and marketing OEMs may build products other than those that they OEM. Sometimes the source of supply shifts. For example, Digital Equipment Corporation OEMed its first PCs from Tandy Corporation and then later began to manufacture some of its own products—without any outward indication of the different origins. One rationalization of this approach is that the marketing company—the brand name—stands behind the product that it sells. You depend on the warranty applied to the brand name (notwithstanding that the marketing company may merely send the product back to the original manufacturer for repair).

Integrators and VARs

The relationship between manufacturer and marketer can be tenuous. Some marketing organizations may invest as little time and effort as putting a nameplate on a finished product made by someone else. Others incorporate subassemblies into more powerful products, combine them with software, and submit them to thorough testing. Because they bring together components from different sources, integrating them, these latter companies are often termed *system integrators*. Because they take the original product and add more features or powers to it such as equipping a computer with a vertical software package (one designed for a particular industry), these organizations are sometimes called *value-added remarketers* (sometimes value-added retailers) or *VARs*.

The difference between the OEM and the company that entirely makes its own products is that you're likely to find the same system board inside many computers bearing the names of different OEMs. In many instances, you will find nothing to distinguish them but the case or the label. Such computers are essentially interchangeable, termed by economists as *commodities*. As with all commodities, the best of these look-alike-inside off-the-shelf computers is the one with the lowest price.

Physical Aspects of Motherboards

Although all motherboards aren't exactly interchangeable, some share physical characteristics that enable them to fit the same physical constraints. As a result, a computer maker that designs his products to accept a given-size of motherboard has his choice of products that screw in. Two major standards are followed for the physical size of motherboards. These standards follow the pattern set by IBM in its original designs for its personal computers.

Standard Dimensions

The motherboards of the original IBM Personal Computer measured about 8 1/2 x 11 inches and had 5 expansion slots spaced 1 inch apart in the left rear corner of the board (see fig. 2.1). Only the placement of the expansion slots emerged as a standard.

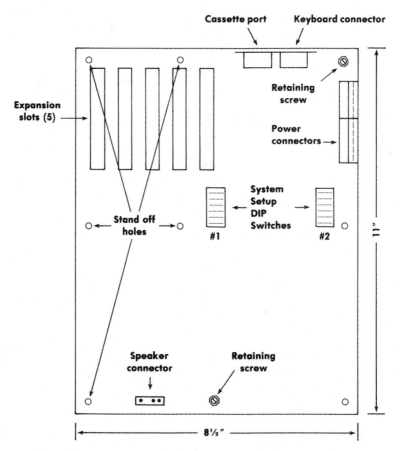

Figure 2.1. PC system board and screw placement.

Now accepted as a physical board standard by most motherboard makers is the original IBM XT design. The XT motherboard measured 8 1/2 x 12 inches (see fig. 2.2). Eight expansion slots, spaced at 0.8-inch intervals, were provided. More motherboards are made in this size than any other.

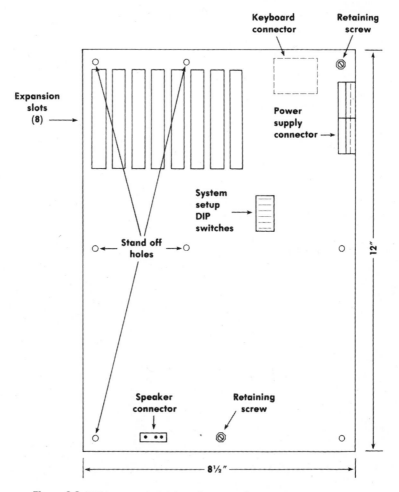

Figure 2.2. XT system board and screw placement.

If you have an original IBM Personal Computer and want to update it to a more modern motherboard, you are destined to be frustrated by more than the expansion slot spacing. Although the PC and XT system boards are nearly the same size, the patterns of their mounting holes do not match. The variations often amount only to a fraction of an inch, but they are enough to prevent the easy substitution of an XT-size motherboard for the original in a PC case.

The AT, in need of more space for more circuitry, extended all the way to 12 x 13 3/4 inches (see fig. 2.3). Motherboards requiring more space for circuitry—typically the first generation products of advanced designs—take advantage of the AT dimensions. As with the XT layout, the AT motherboard design allows for 8 expansion slots spaced at 0.8-inch increments.

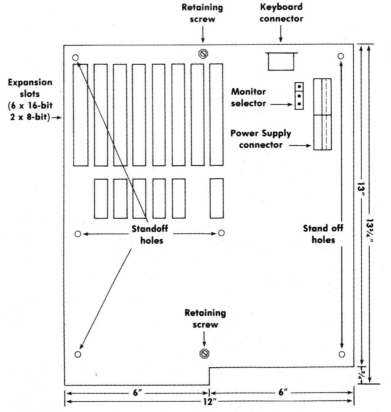

Figure 2.3. AT system board and screw placement.

No other motherboard supplanted the AT standard. The next IBM models—the PS/2 series—failed to set a new standard because few companies were willing to adopt Micro Channel Architecture for their expansion buses. Moreover, several different sizes of motherboards were used throughout the PS/2 line, sometimes even within the same model designation.

Major compatible manufacturers—Compaq, Epson, Leading Edge, Tandy, and so on—control the manufacture of both system board and case. They have the freedom to vary dimensions as may be required. For example, the original Compaq Portable motherboard was somewhat larger than that of the PC.

Small-footprint PCs, machines designed with smaller dimensions to cover less of your desktop, usually have motherboards that vary widely from the standard IBM sizes. Just as with laptop computers, small-footprint machines emphasize compact size over flexibility. They compromise expansion by reducing the number of expansion slots and drive bays to gain their more modest measurements. Shrinking the motherboard helps eke inches from the entire package. Besides losing expansion capabilities, the small-footprint design also ties the purchaser closer to the manufacturer. Because the motherboard is not a standard dimension, if it fails or if you want to upgrade it, you're stuck having to rely on the original manufacturer of the system. With standard-size motherboards, you have your choice of a variety of aftermarket motherboards to repair or upgrade your PC.

Mounting Hardware

A motherboard must somehow be mounted in its cabinet, and PC manufacturers have devised a number of ways to hold motherboards down. This simple-sounding job is more complex than you might think. The motherboard cannot simply be screwed down flat. The projecting cut ends of pin-in-hole components make the bottom uneven, and torquing the board into place is apt to stress it, even crack hidden circuit traces. Moreover, most PC cases are metal, and laying the motherboard flat against the bottom panel is apt to result in a severe short circuit. Consequently, the motherboard must not only be held secure, but it must be spaced a fraction of an inch (typically in the range 3/8 to 1/2) above the bottom of the case.

IBM solved this mounting problem ingeniously with the first PC. The motherboards in these machines—and those of the entire IBM line until the introduction of the PS/2—use a combination of screws and specialized spacers that make manufacture (and board replacement) fast and easy (see fig. 2.4). The design is amazingly frugal, using just two (sometimes three) screws. The balance of the mounting holes in the IBM's motherboards are devoted to nylon fasteners that insulate the boards from the metal chassis while holding them in place. These fasteners have two wings that pop through the hole in the motherboard and snap out to lock themselves in place. The bottom of these fasteners slides in a special channel in the bottom of the PC case. Mechanically, the two or three screws that hold the IBM motherboards in place and the nylon fasteners are designed to space the board vertically and fit special channels in the metal work of the case, enabling the boards to slide into place.

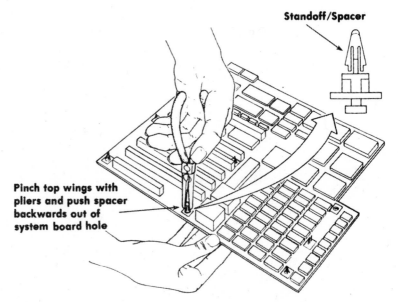

Figure 2.4. Close-up of the spacer used by IBM to mount the system board and the removal technique.

In the IBM design, removing the screws enables you to slide the motherboard to the left, freeing the nylon fasteners from their channel. Installing a motherboard requires only setting the board down so that the fasteners engage their mounting channel and then sliding the board to the right until the vacant screw holes line up with the mounting holes in the chassis. Because the number of screws is minimized, so is the labor required to assemble a PC—an important matter when you plan to make hundreds of thousands of machines.

In the PS/2 series, IBM simplified motherboard mounting by molding the required spacers into the plastic shell of the computers. Nevertheless, most machines still minimize the number of screws used for motherboard mounting.

Other personal computer makers developed their own means of mounting motherboards inside their machines.

These aftermarket manufacturers save the cost of welding the fastener-mounting channels in place by drilling a few holes in the bottom of the case and supplying you with a number of threaded metal or plastic spacers (usually nothing more than small nylon tubes) and screws. These spacers are meant to hold the system board the same height above the bottom of the chassis as would the IBM-style fasteners.

You could handle this kind of motherboard installation in one of two ways (see fig. 2.5). Either screw the spacers into the case, put the motherboard on top of them, and then screw the motherboard to the spacers, or you could screw the motherboard to the spacers and then try to get the spacers to fit the holes in the bottom of the case. Neither method is very satisfactory because you are faced with getting ten or so holes and screws to line up which, owing to the general lack of precision exercised by cut-rate manufacturers in making these cases, they never do. The best thing to do is compromise. Attach the spacers loosely to the motherboard and then try to get the screws at the bottom of the spacers to line up with the holes in the case. You should be able to wiggle them into the holes.

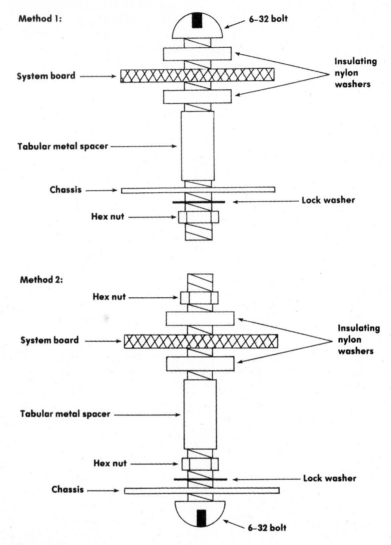

Figure 2.5. Do-it-yourself system board spacers.

Microprocessors

T he microprocessor is the heart and brain inside every personal computer. This tiny chip of silicon determines the speed and power of the entire computer by handling most, if not all, of the data processing in the machine.

All personal computers and a growing number of more powerful machines are based on a special type of electronic circuit called the *microprocessor*. Often termed "a computer on a chip," today's microprocessor is a masterpiece of high-tech black magic. It starts as a single slice of silicon that has been carefully grown as an extremely pure crystal, sawed thin with great precision, and is then subjected to high temperatures in ovens containing gaseous mixtures of impurities that defuse into the silicon and change its electrical properties. This alchemy turns sand to gold, creating an electronic brain as capable as that of your average arthropod.

As with insects and crustaceans, your PC can react, learn, and remember. Unlike higher organisms bordering on true consciousness, however, the microprocessor doesn't reason and is not self-aware. Clearly, although computers are often labeled as "thinking machines," what goes through their microprocessor minds is far from your thought processes and stream of consciousness. Or maybe not. Some theoreticians believe that your mind and a computer work fundamentally in the same way, although neither they nor anyone else knows exactly how the human mind actually works.

The operating principles of the microprocessor, on the other hand, are well understood. After all, microprocessor hardware was designed to carry out a specific function, and silicon semiconductor technology was harnessed to implement those functions. Nothing about what the microprocessor does is magic.

In fact, a microprocessor need not be made from silicon; scientists are toying with advanced semiconducting materials that promise higher speeds. A microprocessor also does not need to be based on electronics. A series of gears, cams, levers or pipes, valves, and pans could carry out all the logical functions exactly the same way as does one of today's most advanced microprocessors. Mechanical and hydraulic computers have, in fact, been built.

The advantage of electronics and the microprocessor is speed and size. Electrical signals travel at the speed of light; microprocessors carry out their instructions at rates up to several million per second. Without that speed, elaborate programs would never have been written. Executing one with a steam-driven computing engine might have taken lifetimes, not to mention warehouses full of equipment. The speed of the microprocessor and its small, portable size, make it into the miracle that it is.

The advantage of silicon is familiarity. An entire industry has arisen to work with silicon. The technology is mature; fabricating silicon circuits is routine, and the results are predictable. Familiarity also breeds economy. Billions of silicon chips are made each year. Although the processes involved are precise and exotic, the needed equipment and materials are readily available.

How Microprocessors Work

Reduced to its fundamental principles, the workings of a modern silicon-based microprocessor are not difficult to understand. They are the electronic equivalent of a knee-jerk. Every time you hit the microprocessor with an electronic hammer blow—the proper digital input—it reacts by doing a specific something, always the same thing for the same input, kicking out the same function. The complexity of the microprocessor and what it does arises from the wealth of inputs it can react to and the interaction between successive inputs. Although the microprocessor's function is precisely defined by its input, the output from that function varies with what the microprocessor had to work upon—and that depends on previous inputs. For example, the result of you carrying out a specific command—"Simon says lift your left leg"—will differ dramatically depending on whether the previous command was "Simon says sit down" or "Simon says lift your right leg."

Instruction Sets

The simple silicon circuits that microprocessors are made from don't understand English commands, however. They react to electronic signals. With today's microprocessors, each microprocessor command is coded as the presence or absence of an electrical signal at one of the pins of the microprocessor's package. These signals—each one representing a digital information bit that can be coded as a zero or a one—together make a bit pattern. Certain bit patterns are given specific meanings by the designers of a microprocessor and thus become a microprocessor instruction. For example, the bit pattern 0010110 is the instruction that tells Intel 8086-family microprocessors to subtract.

The entire repertoire of commands that a given microprocessor model understands and can react to is called that microprocessor's *instruction set* or its *command set*. Different microprocessor designs recognize different instruction sets.

Instruction sets can be incredibly rich and diverse. For example, a simple command to subtract is not enough by itself. The microprocessor also needs to know what to subtract from what, and it needs to know what to do with the result. The microprocessors used in PCs are told what numbers to subtract by variations of the subtract instruction, of which there are about seven, depending on what you count as a subtraction. Each different instruction tells the microprocessor to take numbers from different places and to find the difference in slightly different manners. Microprocessor *registers* handle some of these duties.

Registers

Before the microprocessor can work on numbers or any other data, it must first know what numbers to work on. The most straightforward method of giving the chip the variables it needs would seem to be supplying more coded signals at the same time the instruction is given. This simple method has its shortcomings, however. Somehow, the proper numbers must be routed to the right microprocessor inputs. Either the microprocessor and the computer circuitry would have to do the routing, or you would be stuck with manually loading the numbers into different inputs. The job is best left to the microprocessor (you wouldn't, for example, want to have to designate where to put each intermediate result in a lengthy calculation). All that signal routing would substantially complicate the external circuitry leading to the microprocessor.

Instead of working directly with two inputs simultaneously, today's microprocessors take one input at a time. The first input pattern is loaded into a special area called a *register*. A register functions both as memory and a workbench. It holds bit patterns until they can be worked upon or output. The register is also connected with the processing circuits of the microprocessor so that the changes ordered by the instructions actually appear in the register. Most microprocessors typically have several registers, some dedicated to specific functions (for example, remembering which step in a function the chip is currently carrying out) and some designed for general purposes.

Other microprocessor instructions tell the chip to put numbers in its registers to be worked on later and to move information from a register someplace else—for example to memory or an output port. Some microprocessor instructions require a series of steps to be carried out. For example, the subtraction instruction given previously tells the microprocessor to subtract an immediate number—one in memory— from another number in the microprocessor's *accumulator*, a particular register favored for calculations.

Everything that the microprocessor does consists of nothing more than a series of these one-step-at-a-time instructions. Simple subtraction or addition of two numbers may take dozens of steps, including the conversion of the numbers from decimal to the binary (ones and zeros) notation that the microprocessor understands. Computer programs are complex because they must reduce processes that people think of as one step in itself—adding numbers, typing a letter, moving a block of graphics—into a long and complex series of tiny, incremental steps.

Microcode

Instructions are the basic unit for commanding a microprocessor, telling it what to do. Internally, however, the circuitry of the microprocessor often has to go through several steps to carry out one instruction. The instruction tells the microprocessor to carry out a list of steps that make up one operation. The complete collection of these lists corresponding to each instruction is called the microprocessor's *microcode*.

Using microcode, microprocessor designers can easily give a chip a rich repertoire of instructions. One result of this is the seven different subtraction commands understood by PC microprocessors. The subtle variations between them make it easier to tell the microprocessor what to do. Fewer initial steps must be carried out for each operation.

Originally conceived by Maurice Wilkes at Cambridge University, the idea behind microcode was to enhance the instruction repertoire of early mainframe computers. Microcode allows simple but fast computers to take advantage of complex instructions. It adds a second layer to the microprocessor. In effect, the microcode is a secondary set of instructions that run invisibly inside the microprocessor on a *nanoprocessor*—essentially a microprocessor-within-a-microprocessor.

This microcode-and-nanoprocessor approach makes creating a complex microprocessor easier. The powerful data-processing circuitry of the chip can be designed independently of the instructions it must carry out. The manner in which the chip handles its complex instructions can be fine-tuned even after the architecture of the main circuits are laid into place. Bugs in the design can be fixed relatively quickly by altering the microcode—an easy operation compared to the alternative of developing a new design for the whole ship, a task that's not trivial when a million transistors are involved. The rich instruction set fostered by microcode also makes writing software for the microprocessor (and computers built from it) easier, reducing the number of instructions needed for each operation.

On the other hand, microcode imposes a penalty. The layering of nanoprocessor within the microprocessor introduces overhead. The nanoprocessor must go through several of its own microcode instructions to carry out every instruction you send to the microprocessor. More steps means more time taken for each instruction, slowing down processing. Nevertheless, the high speed at which microprocessor (and nanoprocessor) instructions can be carried out—possibly millions per second—makes this layered design not only feasible but also practical.

CISC and RISC

Microcode is not necessary for a microprocessor to operate, however. Instructions can be hard-wired into the design of a chip so that an instruction bit pattern directly causes the desired function. The result is that instructions can be executed at much higher speeds. On the downside, the complexity of a hard-wired microprocessor increases dramatically with every additional instruction. Practical designs are best made with small instruction sets.

John Cocke at IBM's Yorktown Research Laboratory analyzed the usage of instructions by computers and discovered that most of the work done by computers involves relatively few instructions. For example, given a computer with a set of 200 instructions, two-thirds of its processing involves using as few as 10 of the total instructions. Cocke went on to design a computer that was based on a few instructions that could be executed quickly. He is credited with inventing the *Reduced Instruction Set Computer* or RISC in 1974. In contrast, microcode-based systems with large instruction sets have come to be known as *Complex Instruction Set Computers* or CISC designs. In 1987, Cocke's work on RISC won him the Turing Award (named for computer pioneer Alan M. Turing, know best for his Turing Test definition of artificial intelligence), given by the Association for Computing Machinery as its highest honor for technical contributions to computing.

Cocke's research showed that most of the computing was done by basic instructions, not by the more powerful, complex, and specialized instructions. Further research at the University of California at Berkeley and Stanford University demonstrated that there were even instances where a sequence of simple instructions could perform a complex task faster than a single complex instruction could. The result of this research is often summarized as the 80/20 rule—that about 20 percent of a computer's instructions do about 80 percent of the work. The aim of the RISC design is to optimize a computer's performance for that 20 percent of the instructions, speeding up the execution as much as possible. The remaining 80 percent of the commands could be duplicated, when necessary, by combinations of the quick 20 percent. Analysis—and practical experience—has shown that the 20 percent could be made so much faster that the overhead required to emulate the remaining 80 percent was no handicap at all. Consequently, RISC designs have won great favor for new, high-speed microprocessor designs.

No sharp line demarcates the boundaries of complexity in chip design and the reduction in complexity possible with RISC designs. For example, an acknowledged RISC microprocessor, the M/2000 made by MIPS Computer Systems, has a very full repertoire of 115 instructions. Intel's 386, a CISC microprocessor, features about 144 instructions (depending on how you count). Although significant, the difference between the two is no watershed.

More important than the number of instructions that a computer or microprocessor understands in characterizing RISC and CISC is how those instructions are realized. Slimming down a computer's instruction set is just one way that engineers go about streamlining its processing. As the instructions are trimmed, all of the other ragged edges that interfere with its performance are trimmed off, and all that remains is honed and smoothed to offer the least possible resistance to the passage of data.

The most important distinguishing characteristics of the RISC philosophy is the elimination of microcode, an emphasis on speeding up the instructions most used by the computer, and a tighter bonding of machine and optimizing compiler (computer language) design. RISC designs exploit fast memory techniques like caching and pipelining. The RISC instructions themselves are more focused—each is designed to do only one thing. And the instructions are made more uniform so that all are the same size and handle operands similarly.

Clocked Logic

Microprocessors do not carry out their instructions as soon as the instruction code signals reach the microprocessor's pins that connect it to your computer's circuitry. If they did, they would quickly become confused. Electrical signals cannot change state instantly; they always go through a brief, though measurable, transition period. Moreover, all signals do not necessarily change at the same rate. Consequently, between commands to a microprocessor, there is always a period of confusion when the signals on the leads of the microprocessor are meaningless. To prevent the microprocessor from reacting to these invalid signals, the chip waits for an indication that it has a valid command to carry out. It waits until it gets a "Simon says" signal.

In today's PCs, this indication is provided by the system clock. The microprocessor checks the instructions given to it each time it receives a clock pulse—providing it is not already busy carrying out another instruction.

Most microprocessors cannot carry out one instruction every clock cycle, however. Following all the steps outlined in the microcode for an instruction can take more than 100 clock cycles. Moreover, all instructions are different. Some take a few cycles, others take dozens. The number of cycles required to carry out instructions varies with the microprocessor design. Some microprocessors are more efficient than others in carrying out their instructions. The trend today is to minimize the number of clock cycles needed to carry out a typical instruction. RISC designs are characterized by requiring the fewest clock cycles per instruction, typically fewer than 1.5 cycles per instruction on the average. Some CISC designs (such as the Intel 486, which operates at about 1.2 cycles per instruction) have achieved this efficiency level as well.

Programming Languages

A computer *program* is nothing more than a list of instructions. The computer goes through the instruction list of the program step-by-step, executing each one in turn. Each builds on the previous instructions to carry out a complex function. The program is essentially a recipe for a microprocessor or the step-by-step instructions in a how-to manual.

Microprocessors by themselves only react to patterns of electrical signals. Reduced to its purest form, the computer program is information, a set of ideas, that finds its final representation as the ever-changing pattern of signals applied to the pins of the microprocessor. That electrical pattern is difficult for most people to think about, so the ideas in the program are traditionally represented in a form more meaningful to humans. That representation of instructions is human-recognizable form is called a *programming language*.

Because the programming language is a coding scheme, it need not have a one-to-one correspondence between its symbols and the computer's instructions. Just as a microprocessor instruction can have several microcode steps, a single programming language symbol can indicate multiple microprocessor instructions.

Machine Language

The most basic of all coding systems for microprocessor instructions merely documents the bit pattern of each instruction in a form that humans can see and appreciate. This is an exact representation of the instructions that the computer machine understands, so it is termed *machine language.*

The bit pattern of electrical signals in machine language can be expressed directly as a series of ones and zeros such as the 0010110 subtraction instruction noted earlier. Note that this pattern directly corresponds to a binary (or base-two) number. As with any binary number, the machine language code of an instruction can be translated into other numerical systems as well. Most commonly, machine language instructions are expressed in *hexadecimal* form, that is in the base-16 number system. For example, the 0010110 subtraction instruction becomes 16 (hex).

Assembly Language

People can and sometimes do program in machine language. But the pure numbers assigned to each instruction require more than a little getting used to. After a while—weeks or months—of machine language programming, you begin to learn which numbers do what.

For humans, a better representation of machine language codes would involve mnemonics rather than strictly numerical codes. Descriptive word fragments can be assigned to each machine language code so that 16(hex) might translate into SUB (for subtraction). *Assembly language* takes this additional step, allowing programmers to write in more memorable symbols.

After a program is written in assembly language, it must be converted into the machine language code understood by the microprocessor. A special program, called an *assembler* does the necessary conversion. Most assemblers do even more to make the programmer's life more manageable. For example, they allow blocks of instructions to be linked together into a block called a *subroutine* which can later be called into action by using its name instead of repeating the same block of instructions again and again.

Most of assembly language involves directly operating the microprocessor using the mnemonic equivalents of its machine language instructions. Consequently, programmers must be able to think in the same step-by-step manner as the microprocessor. Every action that the microprocessor does must be handed in its lower terms. Assembly language is consequently known as a *low-level* language because programmers write at the most basic level.

Higher Level Languages

Just as an assembler can convert the mnemonics and subroutines of assembly language into machine language, a computer program can go one step further, translating more human-like instructions into multiple machine language instructions that would be needed to carry them out. In effect, each language instruction becomes a subroutine in itself.

The breaking of the one-to-one correspondence between language instruction and machine language code puts this kind of programming one level of abstraction farther from the microprocessor, a greater or higher abstraction. Such languages are called *higher level* languages. Instead of dealing with each movement of a byte of information, high-level languages allow the programmer deal with problems as decimal numbers, words, or graphic elements. The language program takes each of these higher level instructions and converts it into a lengthy series of digital-code microprocessor commands in machine language.

Higher level languages can be classified into two types: interpreted and compiled.

An *interpreted language* is translated from human to machine form each time it is run by a program called, appropriately enough, an *interpreter*. People who need immediate gratification like interpreted programs because they can be run immediately, without intervening steps. If the computer encounters a programming error, it can be fixed and immediately tested again. On the other hand, the computer must make its interpretation each time the program is run, performing the same act again and again. This repetition wastes the computer's time. More importantly, because the computer is doing two things at once, both executing the program and interpreting it at the same time, it runs more slowly. *BASIC*, an acronym for the Beginner's All-purpose Symbolic Instruction Code, is probably the most familiar interpreted programming language (but it is no longer the most commonly used language). Newer versions of BASIC also include compilers (see the discussion of compiled languages in the next section.)

Using an interpreted language typically involves two steps. First, you start the language interpreter program, which gives you a new environment complete with its own system of commands and prompts, then you execute the program. Although these two steps can be linked together so that there appears to be only one step—for instance, when you start BASIC with the name of a program to run on the DOS command line—the PC must still run the language interpreter before it can deal with a program.

Compiled languages cut the waste of interpreted languages. The programs written using them are translated from high-level symbols into machine language once. The resulting machine language is then stored and called into action each time you run the program. The act of converting the program from English into machine language is called *compiling* the program using a language program called a *compiler*. The original, English-like version of the program—the words and symbols actually written by the programmer—is called the *source code*.

Compiling a complex language program can be a lengthy operation, taking minutes, even hours. When the program is compiled, however, it runs quickly because the computer need only run the resulting machine language instructions instead of having to run a program interpreter at the same time. Most of the time, the compiled program runs directly from the DOS prompt—you just type the program name, and it loads and executes. Examples of compiled languages include C, COBOL, FORTRAN, and Pascal.

Because of the speed and efficiency of compiled languages, compilers have been written that take interpreted language source code and convert it into object code that can be run like any compiled program.

For example, a BASIC compiler will produce object code that will run from the DOS prompt without the need for running the BASIC interpreter.

No matter how high the level of the programming language, no matter what you see on your computer screen, no matter what you type to make your machine do its daily work, everything the microprocessor inside does is reduced to a pattern of digital pulses to which it reacts in knee-jerk fashion.

Microprocessor Construction

Getting an electrical device to respond in knee-jerk fashion rates as one of the greatest breakthroughs in technology. The first application was to extend the human reach beyond what could be immediately touched, beyond the span of the proverbial ten-foot pole. The simple telegraph is perhaps the best example. Closing a switch—pressing down on the telegraph key—sends a current down the wire that activates an electromagnet, causing the rattle at the other end that yields a message to a distant telegrapher. This grand invention is not just a Godsend to the deaf telegrapher but underlies all of modern computer technology—it puts one electrical circuit in control of another circuit that is a great or small distance away.

Logic Gates

From these simple beginnings, you can build a computer. Everything that a computer does involves one of two operations, decision-making and memory—in other words, reacting and remembering. The ability to control one signal with another signal enables you to carry out both operations with simple electrical circuits.

Start with that same remote mechanical design of the telegraph but couple it with a light switch—the arm of the telegraph pulls down the switch and flashes a light. Certainly, the electricity could be used to directly light the bulb, but there are other possibilities. For example, you could pair two telegraph arms together so that their joint effort would be required to throw the switch to turn on the light. Or you could link the two telegraphs so that a signal on either one would switch on the light. Or you could install the switch backwards so that when the telegraph is activated, the light would go *out*.

These three design examples actually provide the basis for building three different types of logic gate—the AND, OR and NOT gates, respectively—from which any digital computer could be built. These gates endow the electrical assembly with decision-making power. In the above examples, the decision is necessarily simple: when to switch on the light. But these same simple gates can be formed into elaborate combinations that make up a computer that can make complex logical decisions (using *Boolean logic*).

These same gates can be arranged to form memory. If the voltage controlled by a switch is fed back so that it, too, can energize and activate the switch, the gate will latch. That is, once you supply voltage to it, it will switch on and supply voltage to itself. Even when you discontinue providing the remote voltage, the switch will stay on, powered by its own output. In effect, it remembers after it has been turned on. (You can make this simple memory circuit forget—resume its original state—by putting a backward-connected remote-control switch in the feedback circuit so that it interrupts the latching voltage. This two-position memory system is called a *flip-flop* because it flips between two states.)

The essence of these designs is using one electrical current (or voltage) to control another. Technology has steadily refined the mechanisms for carrying out this action. The same principle underlying the telegraph-connected-to-a-switch example was soon refined into a single mechanism called a relay that's still used in modern electrical circuits.

The vacuum tube improved on the relay design by eliminating the mechanical part of the remote-action switch. Vacuum tubes harness the power of the attraction of unlike electrical charges and the repulsion of like charges, allowing a small charge to control the flow of electrons through the vacuum inside the tube. The advantage of the vacuum tube over the relay is speed. The relay operates at mechanical rates, perhaps a few thousand operations per second. The vacuum tube can switch millions of times per second. The first recognizable computers were built from tube-based logic gates—thousands of them.

Analog and Digital Circuits

Tubes also ushered in an entirely new technology. Using a small current to control a larger current (or a small voltage to control a larger voltage) is a process called *amplification*. The large current (or voltage) exactly mimics the controlling current (or voltage) but is stronger or amplified. In that every change in the large signal is exactly analogous to each one in the small signal, devices that amplify in this way are called *analog*. The intensity of the control signal can represent continuously variable information—for example, a sound level in stereo equipment. The electrical signal in this equipment thus is an analogy to the sound that it represents.

The limiting case of amplification occurs when the control signal causes the larger signal to go from its lowest value—zero—to its highest value. In other words, the large signal goes off and on—switching—under control of the smaller signal. The two states of the output signal (on and off) can be used as part of a binary code that represents information. For example, the switch could be used to produce a series of seven pulses to represent the numeral 7. In that information can be coded as groups of such numbers—digits—electrical devices that use this switching technology are described as *digital*. Note that this switching directly corresponds to the movement of the telegraph key and the switching of the relay. It allows the construction of logic gates, and from them, computers.

Semiconductors

The problems with tube-based electronics in computers are many. First is the space heater effect—tubes have to glow like light bulbs to work and they generate heat along the way, enough to melt rather than process data. Like light bulbs, tubes burn out. Large tube-based computers required daily shut-down and maintenance and several technicians on the payroll. And tube circuits are big. The house-sized monster computers of the 1950s-era science fiction would easily be outclassed in computing power by today's desktop machines. In the typical tube-based computer design, one logic gate required one tube. Consider that a PC may have hundreds of thousands of gates and you'll begin to see the size of the problem. Moreover, the bigger the computer, the longer it takes its thoughts to travel through its circuits, and the more slowly it thinks.

Making today's practical PCs took another true breakthrough in electronics, one that emerged in 1947 at Bell Laboratories: the transistor. A tiny fleck of germanium (later, silicon) formed into three layers, the transistor was endowed with the capability to let one electrical current applied to one layer alter the flow of another, larger current between the other two layers. Unlike the vacuum tube, the transistor needed no hot electrons because the current flowed entirely through a solid material—the germanium or silicon—hence, the common name for tubeless technology, *solid state*.

Germanium and silicon are special materials—actually, metals—called *semiconductors*. The term describes how these materials resist the flow of electrical currents more than do *conductors* (like the copper in wires) but not as much as *insulators* (like the plastic wrapped around the wires). By itself, being a poor but not awful electrical conductor is as remarkable as lukewarm water. But by infusing atoms of the impurities that wedge themselves into a crystal of a semiconductor's microscopic lattice structure dramatically alters the electrical characteristics of the material. The process of adding impurities is called *doping*. Some impurities add extra electrons—carriers of negative charges—to the crystal; others leave holes in the lattice where electrons would ordinarily be, and these holes act as positive carriers. Semiconductors are often described by the type of impurity that has been added to its structure, *N-type* for those with extra electrons (Negative charge carriers) and *P-type* for those with holes (Positive charge carriers). For example, ordinary three-layer transistors come in two configurations, NPN and PNP, depending on which type of semiconductor is in the middle.

Modern computer circuits mostly rely on another kind of transistor, one in which the current flow through a narrow channel of semiconductor material is controlled by a voltage applied to a gate (which surrounds the channel) made from metal-oxide. The most common variety of these transistors is made from N-type material and results in a technology called *NMOS*, an acronym for N-channel Metal Oxide Semiconductor. A related technology combines both N-channel and P-channel devices and is called *CMOS*—for Complementary Metal Oxide Semiconductor—because the N- and P-type materials are complements (opposites) of one another.

The typical microprocessor once was built from NMOS technology. While NMOS designs are distinguished by their design simplicity and small size (even on a microchip level), they have a severe shortcoming: they constantly sip electricity whenever their gates are turned on. In that about half of the tens or hundreds of thousands of gates in a microprocessor are switched on at any given time, NMOS chips can draw a lot of current. This current flow creates heat and wastes power, making NMOS unsuitable for miniaturized computers (which can be difficult to cool) and battery-operated equipment like laptop or notebook computers.

Some earlier and most contemporary microprocessors now use *CMOS* designs. CMOS is inherently more complex than NMOS because each gate requires more transistors—at least a pair per gate. But this complexity brings a benefit. When one transistor in a CMOS gate is turned on, its complementary partner is switched off, minimizing the current flow through the circuit. When a CMOS gate is idle, only maintaining its state, almost no power is required. During a state change, the current flow is large but brief. Consequently, the faster the CMOS gate changes state, the more current that flows through it and the more heat it generates. In other words, the faster a CMOS circuit operates, the hotter it becomes. This speed-induced temperature rise is one of the limits on the operating speed of many microprocessors.

CMOS technology can duplicate every logic function made with NMOS but with a substantial saving of electricity. On the other hand, manufacturing costs somewhat more because of the added circuit complexity.

Integrated Circuits

The transistor overcomes several of the problems of using tubes to make a computer. They are smaller than tubes and give off less heat because they need not glow to work. But every logic gate still requires one or more transistors (as well as several other electronic components) to build. Were you to allocate a mere square inch to every logic gate, the number of logic gates in a personal computer microprocessor would require a circuit board on the order of 16 feet square.

At the very end of the 1950s, Robert N. Noyce at Fairchild Instruments and Jack S. Kilby independently came up with the same brilliant idea—putting multiple semiconductor devices into a single package. Transistors are typically grown as crystals from thin-cut slices of silicon called wafers, typically thousands of transistors at a time on the same wafer. Instead of carving the wafer into separate transistors, the engineer linked them together (integrated) to create a complete electronic circuit all on one wafer. While Kilby linked the devices together with microwires, Noyce envisioned fabricating the interconnecting circuits between devices on the silicon itself. The resulting electronic device, for which Noyce applied for a patent on July 30, 1959, became known as the *integrated circuit* or IC. Such devices now are often called simply *chips* because of their construction from a single small piece of silicon, a chip off the old crystal. Integrated circuit technology has been adapted to both analog and digital circuitry. Their grandest development, however, is the microprocessor.

The IC has several advantages over circuits built from individual (or discrete) transistors, most resulting from miniaturization. Most importantly, integration reduces the amount of packaging—instead of one metal or plastic transistor case per logic gate, multiple gates (even millions of them) can be combined in one chip package.

Because the current inside the chip need not interact with external circuits, they can be made arbitrarily small, allowing the circuits to be made smaller, too. In fact, today the limit on the size of circuit elements inside an integrated circuit is mostly determined by fabrication technology—internal circuitry is as small as today's manufacturing equipment can make it affordably. The latest Intel microprocessors, which use integrated circuit technology, incorporate the equivalent of more than one million transistors using interconnections that measure about four-tenths of a micro (millionths of a meter) across. In the past, a hierarchy of names was given to ICs depending on the size of the circuit elements. Ordinary ICs were the coarsest. Large Scale Integration (*LSI*) put between 500 and 20,000 circuit elements together; Very Large Scale Integration (*VLSI*) puts more than 20,000 circuit elements on a single chip. The most recent products have become so complex (Intel's 486, for example has the equivalent of about 1.2 million transistors inside) that a new term has been coined for them, Ultra Large Scale Integration (*ULSI*).

Temperature Effects

The tight packing of circuits on chips makes heat a major issue. Heat is the enemy of the semiconductor because it can destroy the delicate crystal structure of the chip. If a chip gets too hot, it will be irrevocably destroyed.

Heat causes problems more subtle than simple destruction. Because the conductivity of semiconductor circuits also varies with temperature, the effective switching speed of transistors and logic gates also changes when chips get too hot or too cold. Although this temperature-induced speed change does not alter how fast a microprocessor can compute (the chip must stay locked to the system clock at all times), it can affect the relative timing between signals inside the microprocessor. Should the timing get too far off, a microprocessor might make a mistake, with the inevitable result of crashing your system. All chips have rated temperature ranges within which they are guaranteed to operate without such timing errors.

Because chips generate more heat as speed increases, they can produce heat faster than it can radiate away. Although it is unlikely the chip will get hot enough to damage itself without additional heat from an external source—your system will likely crash first—the crash is a penalty in itself. To avoid such problems, computer manufacturers often attach *heat sinks* to microprocessors and other semiconductor components to aid in their cooling.

A heat sink is simply a metal extrusion that increases the surface area from which heat can radiate from a microprocessor or other heat-generating circuit element. Most heat sinks have several fins, rows or pins, or some geometry that increases its surface area. Heat sinks are usually made from aluminum because that metal is one of the better thermal conductors, enabling the heat from the microprocessor to quickly spread across the heat sink.

Heat sinks provide *passive cooling* because they require no addition of energy—no power-using mechanism—to perform its cooling. Heat sinks work using *convection*; they transfer heat to the air which circulates past the heat sink. The air circulates because warmed air rises away from the heat sink with cooler air flowing in to replace it. In contrast, *active cooling* involves some kind of assist, either mechanical or electrical, in removing heat. The most common form of active cooling augments the passive effect of a heat sink with a fan, which blows a greater volume of air past the heat sink than would be possible with convection alone.

Inside the Microprocessor

The circuitry inside a microprocessor is divided into three functional parts: the *input/output unit* (or I/O Unit), the *control unit*, and the *arithmetic-logic unit* (or ALU). The last two are often jointly called the *central processing unit* (or CPU), although the same term often is used as a synonym for the entire microprocessor.

The *input/output unit* links the microprocessor to the rest of the circuitry of the computer, passing along program instructions and data to the registers of the control unit and arithmetic/logic unit. The I/O unit matches the signal levels and timing of the internal solid-state circuitry of the microprocessor to the other components inside the PC. For example, the internal circuits of a microprocessor are designed to be parsimonious with electricity so that they can operate faster and cooler. These delicate internal circuits cannot handle the higher currents needed to link to external components. Consequently, each signal leaving the microprocessor goes through a *signal buffer* in the I/O unit that boosts its current capacity.

The input/output unit can be as simple as a few buffers, or it can involve many complex functions. In the latest Intel microprocessors used to power some of the most powerful PCs, the I/O unit includes *cache memory* and *clock-doubling logic* to match the high operating speed of the microprocessor to slower external memory.

The *control unit* of a microprocessor is a clocked logic circuit that, as its name implies, controls the operation of the entire chip. Unlike more common integrated circuits, the entire function of which is fixed by hardware design, the control unit is more flexible. The control unit follows the instructions contained in an external program and commands the arithmetic/logic unit what to do. It receives instructions from the I/O unit, translates them into a form that can be understood by the arithmetic/logic unit, and keeps track of which step of the program is being executed.

The *arithmetic/logic unit* handles all the decision making—the mathematic computations and logic functions—that are performed by the microprocessor. It takes the instructions decoded by the control unit and either carries them out directly or executes the appropriate microcode to modify the data contained in its registers. The results are passed back out of the microprocessor through the I/O unit.

Distinguishing Microprocessors

All three parts of the microprocessor interact together. In all but the simplest microprocessor designs, the I/O unit is under control of the control unit, and the operation of the control unit may be determined by the results of calculations of the arithmetic/logic unit. The combination of the three parts determines the power and performance of the microprocessor.

Each part of the microprocessor also has its own effect on the processing speed of the system. The control unit operates the microprocessor's internal clock, which determines the rate at which the chip operates. The I/O unit determines the bus width of the microprocessor, which influences how quickly data and instructions can be moved in and out of the microprocessor. And the registers in the arithmetic/control unit determine how much data the microprocessor can operate on at one time.

Register Effects

Not only do microprocessors have differing numbers of registers, but the resisters may be of different sizes. Registers are measured by the number of bits that they can work with at one time. For instance, a 16-bit microprocessor should have one or more registers that each holds 16 bits of data at a time.

Adding more registers to a microprocessor does not make it inherently faster. The design of the microprocessors used in PCs allows performing only one operation at a time, involving at most two registers. However, a greater number of registers helps the software writer make more efficient programs. With more places to put data, information needs to be moved in and out of the microprocessor less often, potentially saving several program steps and clock cycles.

The width of the registers does, however, have a substantial impact on the performance of a microprocessor. The more bits assigned to each register, the more information that can be processed in every microprocessor operation. Consequently, a 16-bit register holds the potential of calculating twice as fast as an eight-bit register.

The performance advantage of using wider registers will depend on the software being run, however. For example, if a computer program tells the microprocessor to work on data 16 bits at a time, the full power of the 32-bit registers won't be tapped. For this reason, DOS, a 16-bit operating system written with 16-bit instructions, does not take full advantage of today's powerful 32-bit microprocessors. Nor do most programs written to run under DOS.

Bus Effects

The microprocessors used in IBM-compatible personal computers have two kinds of external connections to their input/output units: those that indicate the address of memory locations to or from which the microprocessor will send or receive data or instructions; and those that convey the meaning of the data or instructions. The former is called the *address bus* of the microprocessor; the latter, the *data bus*.

The number of bits in the data bus of a microprocessor directly influences how quickly it can move information. The more bits that a chip can use at a time, the faster it is. Microprocessors with 8-, 16-, and 32-bit data buses are all used in various IBM personal computers.

The number of bits available on the address bus influences how much memory a microprocessor can address. For instance, a microprocessor with 16 address lines can directly work with 2^{16} addresses. That's 65,536 (or 64K) different memory locations. The different microprocessors used in various PCs span a range of address bus widths from 20 to 32 bits.

Locating Your Microprocessor

Ordinarily, you should have no need to see or touch the microprocessor in your PC. As long as your computer works—and considering the reliability that most have demonstrated, that will be a long, long time—you really need have no concern over your microprocessor except to know that it is inside your computer doing its job. However, some modern system upgrades require that you plug a new microprocessor into your system or even replace the one that you have.

Before you can replace your microprocessor, you have to identify which chip it is. That's easy. As a general rule, all you have to look for is the largest integrated circuit chip on your computer's motherboard. Almost invariably it will be the microprocessor. That's only fitting because the microprocessor is also the most important chip in the computer.

If you find several large chips on your system board, odds are that one of them is the microprocessor. Others may be equally big because they have elaborate functions and need to make many connections with the system board, which means they need relatively large packages to accommodate their many leads. Almost universally, the microprocessor chip will be installed in a socket (which may or may not be visible) while most support chips will be soldered directly to the system board. Sometimes the microprocessor will be hidden under a heat sink, which you can identify by its heat-radiating fins. The appearance of each different microprocessor and its possible packages are discussed separately for each microprocessor model.

Microprocessor Family Tree

The history of microprocessor development has been mostly a matter of increasing these numbers. With each new generation of microprocessor, the number and size of its registers increases while data and address buses become wider. As a result, microprocessors and the personal computers made from them have become increasingly powerful.

The 4004 Family

The first true general-purpose microprocessor was first manufactured by Intel Corporation in 1971. As might be deduced from its manufacturer's designation, *4004*, this ground breaking chip had registers capable of handling four bits at a time through a four-bit bus. Puny by today's standards, these four bits—enough to code all numerals from zero to nine as well as other symbols—were just useful enough to make calculations. The 4004 could add, subtract, and multiply just as capably (but hardly as fast) as the much larger computers of the time.

In fact, that's how the 4004 originated. The chip was conceived by Ted Hoff of Intel Corporation in response to a 1969 request to Intel by a now-defunct Japanese calculator company, Busicom. The original proposal comprised some 12 chips to be used in different types of calculators. The small volumes of each design would have made development costs prohibited. Hoff, however, envisioned creating one general-purpose device that would satisfy the needs of all the calculators. It worked. The 4004 proved to be a success, ushering in the age of the low-cost calculators and giving designers a single solid-state programmable device for the first time.

Larger computers work not only with numbers but also with alphabetic symbols and text, something beyond the ken of the 4004. Making the microprocessor into a more general-purpose device required expanding the size of the chip's registers so that it could handle representations of all the letters of the alphabet and more. Although six bits could accommodate all upper- and lowercase letters as well as numbers—2^6 bits can code 64 symbols—it would leave little room to spare for punctuation marks and such niceties as control codes. In addition, the emergence of the eight-bit byte as the standard measure of digital data resulted in it being chosen as the register size of the next generation of microprocessor, Intel's *8008* introduced in 1972.

The 8008 was, however, at heart just an update of the 4004 with more bits in each register. It was an interesting and workable chip, and it found application in some initial stabs at building personal computers.

The 8080 Family

Intel continued development (as did other integrated circuit manufacturers) and, in 1974, created a rather more drastic revision, the *8080*. Unlike the 8008, it was planned from the start for byte-sized data. Intel bequeathed the 8080 with a richer command set, one that embraced all the commands of the 8008 but went further. This set a pattern for Intel microprocessors: every increase in power and range of command set enlarged on what had gone before rather than replacing it, ensuring backward compatibility (at least to some degree) of the software. The improvements made to the 8080 made the chip one of the first with the inherent capability to serve as the foundation of a small computer.

A few engineers had even better ideas for improving the 8080 and left Intel to develop these improvements on their own. After forming Zilog Corporation, they unveiled to the world the *Z80* microprocessor. In truth, the Z80 was an evolutionary development, an 8080 with more instructions, but it began a revolution by unlocking the power of the first widely accepted standard small-computer operating system, *CP/M*, an acronym for Control Program for Microcomputers.

An operating system is a special program that links programs, the microprocessor, and its related hardware such as storage devices. CP/M was developed by Digital Research and modeled on the operating systems used by larger computers but shrunk down to a size that would work on a microprocessor chip. Though hardly perfect, it worked well enough that it became the standard for many small computers used in business. Its familiarity helped the programmers of larger computers adapt to it and they threw their support behind it. Although CP/M was designed to run on the 8080, the Z80 chip offered more power, and it became the platform of choice to make the system work.

All the while Intel continued to improve on its eight-bit microprocessor designs. One effort was the *8085*, a further elaboration on the 8080 which was designed to use a single, five-volt power supply and to use fewer peripheral chips than its predecessor. Included in its design were vectored interrupts and a serial input/output port. Alas, it never won the favor of the small computer industry. Only a very few small computers, now almost entirely forgotten, were designed around the 8085.

The 8086 Family

In 1978, Intel pushed technology forward with its *8086*, a microprocessor that doubled the size of registers again to 16-bits and promised
ten times the performance of the 8080. The 8086 also improved on
the 8080 by doubling the size of the data bus to 16 bits to move information in and out twice as fast. It also had a substantially larger
address bus, 20 bits wide, that allowed the 8086 to directly control
over one million bytes, a megabyte, of memory.

As a direct descendent of the 8080 and cousin of the Z80, the 8086
shared much of the command set of the earlier chips. Just as the 8080
elaborated on the commands of the 8008, the 8086 embellished those
of the 8080. The registers of the 8086 were cleverly arranged so that
they could be manipulated either at their full 16-bit width or as two
separate eight-bit registers exactly like those of the 8080.

Segmented Memory

The memory of the 8086 was also arranged to be a superset of that of
the 8080. Instead of being one vast megabyte romping ground for
data, it was divided up into sixteen *segments* with 64 kilobytes each. In
effect, the memory of the 8086 was a group of 8080 memories linked
together. The 8086 looked at each segment individually and did not
permit a single large data structure to span across segments—at least
not easily.

In some ways, the 8086 was ahead of its time. Small computers were
based on eight-bit architectures, memory was expensive (that's why a
megabyte seemed like more than enough), and few other chips were
designed to handle 16 bits at a time. Using the 8086 forced engineers
to design full 16-bit devices which, at the time, were not entirely cost
effective.

The 8088 Downgrade

Consequently, a year after the introduction of the 8086, Intel introduced the *8088*. The 8088 was identical to the 8086 in every way—
16-bit registers, 20 address lines, the same command set—except for
one thing. Its data bus was reduced to eight bits, allowing the
8088 to exploit readily available eight-bit support hardware.

As a backward step in chip design, the 8088 might have been lost to history much like the 8085 had not IBM begun to covertly design its first personal computer around it. IBM's intent was evidently to cash in on the 8088 design. Its eight-bit data bus allowed the use of inexpensive, off-the-shelf support chips. Its 16-bit internal design gave the PC an important edge in advertising over the eight-bit small computers already available. And its 8080-based ancestry hinted that the wealth of the CP/M programs then available might easily be converted to the new hardware. In the long run, of course, these advantages have proven either temporary or illusionary. Sixteen-bit support chips have become available and cheap; the IBM name proved more valuable than the 16-bit registers of the 8088; and few CP/M programs were ever directly adapted to the PC.

In the end, what was important is that the lame 8088 microprocessor became the basis of a generation of small computers. The fast track to making compatible computers was paved with 8088s.

The 8086 is potentially twice as fast and almost completely compatible with the 8088. Consequently, manufacturers intent on selling performance engaged in the extra effort to design around the 8086. Even IBM chose the older yet more powerful 8086 to power its low-end PS/2s.

As compatible as they are, the 8088 and 8086 are not interchangeable. The need for eight additional data bits going into the chip requires eight more data lines or leads. The connections made to each of the two chips are thus different. The 8088 and 8086 are not identical pin-for-pin and are not plug-compatible. Computers must be designed for one chip or the other.

Low-Power Designs

The typical microprocessor requires a few watts of electricity to perform its function. When the electrical supply is drawn from a wall outlet, the amount of power is almost insignificant. A typical home has 10,000 watts or so at its disposal, and any individual outlet can supply about 2,000 watts. Batteries, however, aren't so munificent. An AA cell, for instance, might be expected to deliver 20 milliwatts—0.02 watts—or so. Switching to battery power to make a truly portable computer thus requires a drastic downward revision in the amount of power required for running the microprocessor.

The original 8086 and 8088 chips were designed using simpler but energy-wasteful NMOS technology. These chips were unsuitable for laptop and notebook computers, for which low power requirements are mandatory. To trim the electrical hunger of these NMOS designs, equivalent microprocessors based on CMOS technology were developed.

Versions of both the 8088 and 8086 are available in CMOS, distinguished by embedding a "C" in their designations, as in *80C88* and *80C86*. These low-power microprocessors are logically identical to their NMOS equivalents. They have the same command sets and run the same programs. However, they have different electrical requirements, so computers are designed to use either the CMOS or NMOS circuits. You can't directly substitute one for the other if you want to trim electrical requirements of your PC. (The only time such an exchange would be useful would be in a laptop computer, and these machines almost universally have CMOS microprocessors.)

Higher Integration

Just as the microprocessor incorporates thousands of discrete logic components on its tiny sliver of silicon, it is possible to build more functions into a single chip. Besides a microprocessor, a number of other special circuits are typically used in building a small computer, such as interrupt controllers, timing generators, and bus controllers. All of these functions can be designed to fit onto the same chip as the microprocessor circuitry.

Normally, all this extra circuitry would not be included because a microprocessor is a general-purpose device, not necessarily committed to becoming the basic of a desktop computer system. The additional circuitry might be wasted in something like an industrial process controller.

As the small-computer industry grew, however, the market for circuits optimized for that purpose reached the point that Intel felt safe in creating a more complete computer chip—an 8086—with most of its support circuitry on one substrate. Introduced in 1982 as the *80186*, this chip has served as the basis for a number of compatible computers and at least one turbo board. Intel also offers the *80188*, essentially an 8088 blessed with more on-chip support, much like the 80186.

Foreign Competition

Two chips directly interchangeable with the 8088 and 8086 are Nippon Electric Company's (NEC) *V20* and *V30*, respectively. The V20 can be used to replace an 8088; the V30 replaces the 8086. Although the NEC chips use the same command set as the Intel devices, they are not identical. Much of their microcode is different—more efficient because the NEC chips were designed with the benefit of hindsight. Replacing an 8088 with a V20 or an 8086 with a V30 can improve overall microprocessor throughput—and thus the speed of the computer around which it is based—from 10 to 30 percent.

Years of research and development go into the design of every integrated circuit. All of that work can be avoided in copying someone else's effort by *reverse engineering*, coming up with the design from the product itself instead of the product from the design. To prevent other companies from copying their chip designs, most makers of integrated circuits use all the legal protection available to them—patents, copyrights, and secrecy.

Sometimes, they will license other makers to use the *masks* they have designed to lay down the silicon circuitry of a chip to provide a *second source* for a product. This licensing or second sourcing earns the original designer a royalty and, often, greater acceptance of the chip because buyers of integrated circuits look askance at any product with a single source of supply. Second sources insulate against labor or manufacturing troubles and can sometimes reduce costs through competition. Intel licenses Advanced Micro Devices and IBM to produce many of its chips.

Identification and Packaging

The Intel 8088 and 8086—as well as the plug-compatible NEC V20 and V30—are packed in dual in-line pin (DIP) packages. That is, they are black, epoxy plastic rectangles about two inches long and half an inch wide. A row of connecting pins—a total of 40—line both of the long sides of the chip package like the legs of a shortchanged centipede. The number one pin of the two rows is the pin on the top left of the chip, on the same side as its orientation notch, when viewed from the top of the chip. Intel puts a dot-like indentation in the black epoxy just above pin one to help in its identification.

Intel identifies these chips with plain, silk-screen label, white on the black plastic case. A large lower-case "i" indicates Intel Corporation was the manufacturer. Advanced Micro Devices labels its chips with the initials AMD. On Intel chips, the top line of the chip label reveals its designation, often following the preface letter "P."

Speed Rating

These chips are available in two speed ratings, five and eight megahertz. Those labeled merely with their model designation (for instance, 8088) have the lower speed rating. Those with their model designations followed by a "-2" are rated at the higher speed. An 8088-2, for example, is rated to operate at up to eight megahertz.

On NEC microprocessors, the number following the chip designation represents the chip's speed rating in megahertz. In other words, a V20-8 is rated at eight megahertz.

The second line of the chip designation contains coded manufacturing information, including the week during which the chip was manufactured.

The 80286 Family

The introduction of IBM's Personal Computer AT in 1984 immediately focused attention on another of the Intel microprocessor family, the *80286*, which itself was introduced in 1982. Compared to its immediate forerunner, the 8086, the 80286 was endowed with several features that made it superior for personal computers. It used a full 16-bit data bus with 16-bit internal registers. It was also designed to run faster—initially at six Mhz, which quickly rose to eight and then to ten. Versions that operated at 12.5, 16, and even 20 Mhz also became available. Moreover, for its clock speed, it functions more efficiently, giving it even more of a performance advantage than its faster speed would imply. For example, although the first AT ran only 25 percent faster than the PC, it achieved throughput about five times greater.

Sixteen Megabytes

Most important of all in the long run, was the superior memory-handling ability of the 80286. Instead of the 20 address lines of the 8088/8086, the 80286 had 24. The four extra lines increase the maximum amount of memory the chip is able to address by 15 megabytes, up to a total of 16 megabytes.

Virtual Memory

The 80286 also allowed the use of *Virtual memory*. As the name implies, virtual memory is not made up of real, physical memory chips. Rather, it is information stored elsewhere, in a mass storage system, that can be transferred into physical memory when it needs to be worked on. The 80286 has a special provision for distinguishing each memory byte that is in real and virtual memory, although it requires additional circuitry to handle the actual swapping of bytes. The chip can track up to one gigabyte (1,024 megabytes or a billion bytes) of total memory—16 megabytes physical, 1,008 megabytes of virtual memory.

In theory, the upgraded memory-handling of the 80286 should have made the 1-megabyte addressing barrier faced by earlier Intel microprocessors a thing of the past. In reality and as a practical matter, the improvement was not realized.

The problem was partly a matter of compatibility, partly of tradition. By the time the 80286 was being readied for the market, the success of the IBM PC had already been ensured. A substantial software base had been built for the 8088 and 8086 microprocessors. Taking advantage of that software would speed the acceptance of the improved chip.

Real Mode

To maintain compatibility with the earlier chips, Intel's engineers endowed the 80286 with two operating modes: Real mode and protected mode. *Real mode* was designed to be nearly an exact duplicate of the way the 8086 was operated. The copying followed the 8086 so closely (as it had to do to ensure compatibility) that real mode brought along with it all the barriers of using the 8086, including the 1M limit on memory. The limit was necessarily imposed because the 80286 had to be able to recognize memory addresses just as an 8086 would.

Protected Mode

To take advantage of the improved memory handling of the 80286 architecture, Intel created *Protected mode*. Although not compatible with existing 8086 programs, protected mode allows all 16 megabytes of real and the gigabyte of virtual memory to be actively used by programs written specifically to take advantage of it.

As a faster 8086 with the capability to handle more memory, the 80286 proved immensely successful. However, protected mode did not win favor with programmers very quickly. Almost three years elapsed between the time of the introduction of the AT and the availability of an IBM-endorsed protected mode operating system, OS/2.

80286 Downside

Two reasons underlie the slow, begrudging support of the protected mode. For programmers working under the constraints of DOS, the problem was shifting between real mode and protected mode. Intel designed the process to be a one-way affair. After all, once you have tasted 16 megabytes, why would you want to go back to a measly one? Although the 80286 readily shifted gears from real to protected mode (the upshift was necessary because the chip starts functioning *only* in real mode), downshifting was not possible. Once in protected mode, the only way to regain real mode control was to reset the microprocessor, equivalent to rebooting the computer.

In addition, protected mode was only a partial fulfillment of the dreams of programmers. Although it did allow more memory to be used, it still operated with memory segments of 64 kilobytes. Instead of a free romping ground for their software, programmers got a bunch of little boxes that they had to shift their numbers between.

The 80386DX

Unlike the 80286, which was seemingly aimed at a brave new world beyond DOS, the next generation of Intel microprocessor opened its arms to DOS and the $16 billion software library built around it.

The 80386, introduced in 1985, combines the hard lessons won with the 80286 with the needs and dreams of programmers. It brought more speed, more power, and more versatility than every before available in an Intel microprocessor. It is able to handle nearly every chore of an 8088, 8086, and 80286, yet leaps beyond them in features and power.

The enlightenment embodied by the 80386 makes the 80286 look like a misfire—too late and too bad. Some former Intel employees have dismissed the shortcomings of the 80286 as a result of its design having been started earlier than even the 8086. The 80286 was the original idea of a chip to follow on the heels of the 8080, but may have proved too ambitions. The 8086 was born from a reappraisal of design objectives. Only later was the original idea marketed as the 80286.

In contrast, the 80386 (now designated 80386DX to differentiate it from the 80386SX downgrade was created in full awareness of the personal computer and the microprocessor market. Consequently, it had to accommodate all the features that were making other Intel processors sell. For example, its *instruction set* (the bit patterns it recognizes as commands to perform its various functions) is a superset of that of the 80286, so older software will run on the chip without a hitch. At the same time, the 80386 had to be designed to bring new features to the table so that it would be accepted in new designs, maybe even lure engineers away from the microprocessors made by other manufacturers who did not suffer from the handicap of segmented memory.

32-Bit Power

First and foremost, the 80386 was a leap ahead in raw power. It doubled the register size of previous microprocessors and data buses to 32 bits. Information could be moved into the chip and processed twice as fast as with 16-bit chips like the 80286.

Faster Clocks

The 80386 was designed from the beginning to be a fast chip, perhaps a product of the speed wars among AT-compatible computers. Using semiconductor technology called CHMOS, the first 80386 chips to be marketed started where the 80286 left off. Two ratings of 80386 were initially available, 12.5 and 16 Mhz, with the former pretty much ignored by speed-hungry computer designers. Shortly thereafter, a 20 Mhz version became available. In 1988 the limit became 25 Mhz, followed shortly by the 33 Mhz standard. Today, 80386 chips operating at 40 and 50 Mhz are offered by a few computer companies.

Temperature Limits

Note that some computer makers often operate chips (and not just 80386s) beyond the manufacturer's rating. This tactic works because there may be few differences between the designs of chips rated at different speeds. One major problem arises, however: Higher speed operation generates more heat because every logical thought involves a digital switching operation. Even with low-power CHMOS circuitry, each digital switch requires a burst of current that heats the chip. Faster operation means more current bursts in a given period, heating the chip even more.

Heat is the biggest enemy of semiconductor circuits. It can make them unreliable, and, if severe, it can destroy them. A small increase in clock speed can lead to a substantial, even surprising, increase in chip temperature. Running a microprocessor beyond its speed rating can make it unreliable or even ruin it forever. Heat sinks (finned metal plates mechanically in contact with the chip) help cool the chip by radiating the heat and may actually help improve reliability at higher speeds.

Improved Memory Architecture

Complementing the expansion of the data bus of the 80386 to 32-bits, the number of available address lines also was increased to 32. By itself, that expansion allows the 80386 to address directly up to four gigabytes of physical memory. In addition, the chip can handle up to 16 terabytes (that's a trillion bytes) of virtual memory. The chip has full facilities for managing all this memory built into its circuitry.

The big breakthrough in the 386 is the way in which this memory is organized. All of it can be addressed as one contiguous section, equivalent to the great open prairie for programs. Programs or data structures can be as large as the full memory capacity of the chip.

Dividing this memory into segments is possible, but optional. Segments are not, however, arbitrarily limited to 64 kilobytes in length. They can be virtually any size that's convenient for a program—or a programmer—to work with (as long as it is smaller than four gigabytes, a not insubstantial limit).

In addition, the 386 incorporates 16 bytes of *pre-fetch cache memory*. This special on-board memory area is used to store the next few instructions of the program that the chip is executing. Independently of the calculating portion of the chip, special circuitry loads software code into this memory before it is actually needed. This small cache helps the 80386 to run more smoothly, with less waiting as code is retrieved from system memory.

Multiple Modes

To maintain compatibility with previous Intel microprocessors—and thus with the library of DOS programs—the 386 was designed to be as compatible as possible with the 8086 and the 80286. As with these processors, the 80386 has a Real mode, complete with a one-megabyte addressing limit. The chip boots up in this mode and operates, for all intents and purposes, as if it were one of its older siblings.

From Real mode, the chip can be switched into Protected mode in which it functions like an 80286 except that it has more memory at its disposal, and it has more flexibility in manipulating this memory because of its variable segment size. In contrast with the 80286, the 80386 can switch modes with simple software commands and without being reset.

DOS Accommodations

A new mode called *Virtual 8086 mode* gives the 386 particular freedom in running DOS programs. In this mode, the chip simulates not just one 8086, but an almost unlimited number of them, all at the same time. This mode allows a single 80386 microprocessor to divide its memory up into many virtual machines, each one acting like it is an entirely separate computer equipped with an 8086 microprocessor.

Each of these virtual machines can run its own program, totally isolated from the rest of the virtual computers. That means that you can simultaneously run several DOS programs on one computer. Although this kind of multitasking was possible without the exotic architecture of the 80386, most such systems were either complex or shaky, and most of them required that software be specially written to proprietary standards to effect multitasking operation. The 386, on the other hand, makes multitasking control software almost trivial because all the hard work is done in hardware. Off-the-shelf DOS programs work without modification in most 386-based multitasking environments.

Original Sin

The 386 has suffered more severe teething pains than most microprocessors. Shortly after it was originally released, design errors were found that caused inaccuracies when the chip performed 32-bit mathematical operations. The problem was undiscovered in the first PC-compatible computers to use the chip because DOS uses only 16-bit operations. The random errors occurred only when software used the 32-bit mode of the 386.

The problem was quickly discovered and corrected, and 80386 chips manufactured after April, 1987, do not have the problem. According to Intel, all 386 chips manufactured after the correction was made are labeled with a *double sigma* symbol (see fig. 3.1). Some—but not all—earlier chips that were recalled before being delivered to users that potentially may show the problem have been stamped "For 16-bit Operations Only" by Intel. These chips will work with all 16-bit versions of DOS (which include versions through 5.0) and the initial releases of OS/2 (Versions 1.0 and 1.1), which do not use 32-bit mathematics.

Intel does not have a return policy for end-users except for products made by its PC Enhancement Operation, such as the Intel Inboard 386 (now discontinued) and the Snap In 386, a piggy-back 386 replacements for 286-based computers. Replacements for other products should come from the dealer where you obtained the product. If you find a potentially bad chip in your 386-based product manufactured by Intel, you should contact Intel Corporation PC Enhancement Operation in Hillsboro, Oregon for a replacement. The telephone numbers are 800-538-3373 in the United States or Canada, 503-629-7354 (Technical support) or 503-629-7000 (customer support) in other countries.

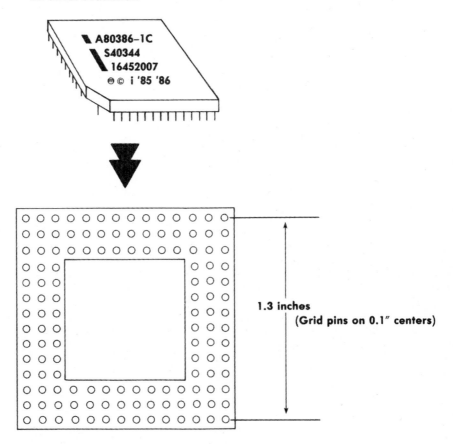

Figure 3.1. Pin-grid array socket (with PGA chip).

The 80386SX

Which of the virtues of the 80386 architecture is best depends on what you want to do with the chip. For many, speed is the thing. They want to roar through calculations lickety-split. A second saved on the recalculation of a spreadsheet or the drawing of a blueprint is an extra dollar earned. For these people, 32-bit power is the essence of the 80386 design.

But the other strengths of the 386 make it a more exciting chip to people who want to take advantage of its multiuser and multitasking power. The virtual 8086 mode is the best part of the 386 silicon to them, and the extensive memory-handling capabilities of the chip make it all the more valuable. Although the speed of the 80386 may be exciting, for these users it is unnecessary, particularly considering the modest performance increase the 32-bit chip brings to standard 16-bit software like DOS and OS/2.

Ultimate Compromise

For exactly this sort of person, Intel created the ultimate compromise, the 80386SX, a scaled-down 80386DX that loses power but not features. Just as the 8088 was derived from the 8086 to facilitate the use of cheaper eight-bit components, the 80386SX was created as a little sister to the 80386DX. Internally, the 386SX is nearly identical to the 386DX with full 32-bit registers and all of its operating modes, just as the 8088 is a 16-bit chip like the 8086 inside its epoxy case.

Only two differences of major import separate the 386DX from the 386SX. Instead of interfacing to a 32-bit memory bus, the 80386SX is designed for a 16-bit bus. Its 32-bit registers must be filled in two steps from a 16-bit I/O channel. And the 386SX is cheaper to manufacturer, although only moderately so in today's market. In fact, the price difference between the 80386DX and 80386SX chips is destined to become so small as to make the 386SX choice less and less popular, at least for cost considerations.

But the 386SX is no sluggard. Its initial version operated at a full 16 megahertz, twice as fast as Intel's first popular 80286 which operated at 8 Mhz. Despite its 16-bit I/O channel, the 386SX still races along faster than an 80286 with an equivalent speed rating because it can process instructions twice as fast after they're inside the chip (32-bits at a time instead of 16-bits at a time).

In addition, the 386SX understands the same 32-bit instructions as the 386DX. Just like the DX, the SX is backward compatible with the 16- and eight-bit instructions of previous Intel microprocessors.

A Brief History

Long before its introduction in June, 1988, the 386SX had been long rumored in the computer industry. Mostly it was known under its code name *P9*. Its final designation is likely an effort by Intel to cash in on the overwhelmingly favorable publicity garnered by the 386DX microprocessor.

The P9 was long rumored to be a plug-compatible upgrade for the 80286. In theory, you could pop out the old chip and pop in the 386 power of the P9. With the final 386SX design, however, that direct conversion is not possible.

Different Package

The 386SX is packaged entirely differently than the 80286, and the two chips will not fit in the same sockets. The main reason is that the 80286 multiplexed its bus connections (so that fewer physical wires are needed for a larger number of connections) while those of the 386SX are not multiplexed. As a result, the 386SX requires simpler interface circuitry than the 80286, facilitating its application in lower cost computers.

Future Play

Intel offered a piggy-back card, called the Snap In 386, that let you convert a 286-based PC to a 386. The Snap In 386 plugged directly into a 286 socket, offering a low-cost way of adding 386 features to existing computers.

On the other hand, the 386SX does demand a slight price premium over the 80286, and, when operating at its rated speed, it requires faster, more expensive memory. Computers based on the 80386SX generally are more expensive than their 80286 counterparts. However, the extreme popularity of the 386 architecture and the waning use of the 286 microprocessors are making the 386SX a better choice for any new acquisitions. In addition, as more and more software requires 386 features, the 386SX becomes even more desirable, and the 80286 becomes even more obsolete. Buy a computer equipped with a 386SX if you have an eye to the future; a 286 will only mire you in the past.

The 80386SL

The SL series of chip is designed for low-power, portable applications. The heart of the 386SL chip series is an 80386DX-compatible microprocessor. SL chips include power management circuitry, may operate at lower voltage than normal, and use less power inherently than conventional chips. Some models of the 386SL can operate on either 5 or 3 volts because of a dual, internal power plane. This chip can be used in conventional, 5V systems, or in low-power, portable or laptop designs. As this is written, Intel offers four 386SL chips:

➤ A 5v, 20/25 Mhz chip with cache

➤ A 5v, 16/20/25 Mhz cacheless chip

➤ A 3.3v 20 Mhz chip with cache

➤ A 3.3v 16/20 Mhz cacheless chip

The SL chip set includes additional features that give designers flexibility in creating custom systems. The SL CPU supports an optional flash memory disk, for example. Flash memory is Intel's term for non-volatile, read/write RAM. Flash memory is considerably slower than conventional RAM and requires special interfacing. With the SL chip, however, you can establish up to 16M of flash disk memory as a standard ISA data bus drive. The most obvious application for this memory disk is in portable or laptop machines. A floppy-based machine could include a 16M flash disk instead of a conventional magnetic hard drive to conserve power and size.

The SL chip includes a new, non-maskable interrupt called the system management interrupt (SMI) that is used to control what Intel calls the IdeaPort. A complementary resume instruction (RSM) is used in conjunction with the SMI interrupt to control transparently a variety of input/output pins. This facility could be used to enhance the SL chip's power-management features, for example, by sending shutdown signals to inactive peripheral devices. Designers can include SMI instructions within loadable device drivers or in system BIOS code so that they do not require operating system modification and, in fact, can operate transparent to the operating system.

Although the maximum clock speed for SL-series chips is 25 Mhz, the chip can be slowed down for certain operations to conserve power.

Remember that the faster a chip operates, the more power it consumes. On power-sensitive applications such as laptop and notebook computers, the clock divider feature can cut processor operating speed (divide by 2, 4, or 8) during operations that don't need speed, such as keyboard data entry. Then when calculations or I/O operations are underway, the processor can be returned to its maximum speed. This is part of the overall power management features that are part of the SL series chips.

Three battery warning inputs on the 386SL chip can be used to shutdown a system if the battery gets too low. These inputs also can be used to send warning beeps to a speaker to warn the user of an impending low battery condition or of system shutdown.

For more information on SL chip power management, see the discussion of the 80486SL later in this chapter.

The 80386SLC

The SLC series of chips is an interesting addition to current chip technology. IBM Corporation studied existing 80386 chips and the programs that ran on them and used this data to design a custom chip to be used in IBM PS/2 computers and other subsystems OEMed for third-party manufacturers. The 80386 SLC is pin-compatible with the Intel 80386 SX CPU. IBM designed the chip. Intel makes it for IBM. IBM sells it only within the computers and other subsystems they manufacturer as per an agreement between IBM and Intel.

The 386SLC currently is offered as standard with IBM's PS/2 model 56 SLC and Model 57 SLC. IBM also offers an upgrade option for customers with SX-based PS/2 machines. The 386SLC can provide up to 88 percent improvement in performance with some applications, according to IBM.

The SLC chip—or similar chips with other designations, since IBM is licensing the technology to other manufacturers—likely will begin showing up in a number of systems. And with good reason. The SLC design incorporates good features of several Intel chips and adds some enhancements that are uniquely IBM's.

Basically, the 386SLC chip is a 386 SX, Low power chip with Cache (That's where the SLC designation comes from). The SLC chip incorporates an 8K onboard cache (similar to the cache that is a standard part of 80486 chips), and it uses 5-volt, low-power technology that is part of Intel's SL series chips. In addition, the full, 80486SX instruction set is included in this chip.

A bus Snooping feature ensures that data in the chip's internal cache and external memory are consistent. The bus snooper works by monitoring the bus address lines that relate to the address range held in cache. If another device writes to any of these locations, the cache data is flagged as inconsistent with main memory. If data is requested from the location, the main memory data is used instead of the information being held in cache.

IBM also added another enhancement: by analyzing millions of instructions called by popular software applications, the company determined that certain instructions were used much more frequently than others. The SLC chip enhances or optimizes these instructions by reducing the number of clock cycles required to carry them out. That means the most-used instructions operate faster than they would in a standard 386SX or 486SX chip of comparable speed.

In fact, according to IBM, the onboard cache and optimized instruction set mean that a 386SLC chip operates about twice as fast as a conventional 386SX chip running at the same clock speed. And, the SLC technology is interesting in that a single chip is designed for 16, 20, and 25 Mhz operation. That means a low-end desktop or a laptop machine, for example, can be designed for the 386SLC and can operate at 16 Mhz, reducing the cost of peripheral components, and a full-featured desktop machine designed for 25 Mhz operation also can use the same chip.

Also, the SLC chip can operate in "asynchronous" mode, which means that the internal speed of the processor can be different from the external components (like Intel's DX2 chips, except the 386 SLC is not a clock doubler). This lets designers maximize internal processing speed while using lower cost peripheral components. This technique can improve overall computer performance without raising the cost significantly.

80386 Packaging

Because it has twice the number of data lines and 25 percent more address lines, the 386 naturally requires more connections than an 80286. Consequently, it is available packaged in a ceramic PGA-style housing with 132 pins projected from its bottom. These pins are arranged in three squares of increasing size, placed on a 14 x 14 grid with 0.100-inch spacing and the central pins removed. Pin one is closest to the cut-off corner of the case.

80386 Speed Ratings

As with the 80286, the speed ratings of the 386 chips are plainly marked after the model designation of the chip. The figure given there is the chip's maximum rated operating speed in megahertz. Hence, a chip marked 386-25 would be rated to operate at 25 megahertz.

Because of its unique input and output configuration, the 386SX uses its own package. Speed ratings are given on the chip in the same way as the 80286 and the 80386DX—as a number representing the rated speed in megahertz following the chip designation.

The 80486 Family

Introduced in 1989, the 80486 microprocessor was Intel's better 80386. The company classifies its most powerful chip as being in the 386 family, and indeed it is. The 486 will run all 386 software. In fact, from a software standpoint, the 486 is distinguished from the 386 by one flag, one exception, two page-table entry bits, six instructions, and nine control-register bits. Although that may sound like a lot, none of the programs designed for the 386 are likely to see the difference. The commands and controls of the 486 represent nothing more than a superset of the 386. That is, the 486 does everything the 386 does and a little more. Your programs operate as if the 486 is just a faster 386. For running DOS applications, the added features of the 486 remain unneeded and unused.

That small step is a notable difference from the giant leap between the 286 and the 386. Those two chips are qualitatively different from the software standpoint in that the 386 has an additional operating mode and advanced memory-management capabilities that are not built into the 286. The Virtual 8086 mode of the 386 is required to run multitasking applications such as Microsoft Windows in its enhanced mode and DESQview 386. The memory-management facilities of the 386 chip are key to extending the range of DOS beyond its traditional 640K byte addressing limit. Although the 486 retains these capabilities of the 386, it brings nothing more that will affect which programs you can run. Any of the software programs you lust after today will run on either a 386- or a 486-based PC.

From a hardware perspective, the 486 retains the principle features of the 386 that are important for the two chips to be compatible at the software level. Both chips have three operating modes (real, protected, virtual 8086), both have full 32-bit data and address buses allowing up to four gigabytes of memory to be directly addressed. Both support virtual memory that extends their addressing to 64 terabytes. Both have built-in memory-management units that can remap memory in 4K pages.

But the hardware of the 486 also differs substantially from the 386—or any previous Intel-architecture microprocessor—and all the changes spell speed. Most important of these are a streamlined hardware design, tighter silicon design rules (smaller details etched into the actual silicon that makes up the chip) an integral math coprocessor, and an internal memory cache.

The streamlined hardware design means that the 486 can think faster than a 386 microprocessor when the two are operating at the same clock speed. That is, a 33 Mhz 486 is faster than a 33 Mhz 386.

To some people, that seems contradictory because they confuse the processing of instructions with ticks of the clock. In most earlier microprocessors, carrying out a single instruction required multiple clock cycles, the exact number depending on the instruction itself. Some instructions required just one; others could take dozens. Because of its improved internal design, the 486 trims the number of clock cycles needed for most instructions. Many of the most common 486 instructions can be carried out in a single clock tick.

Size is the scourge of speed. Computer circuits are becoming so fast that the speed of light—actually the somewhat slower rate that it takes electrons and holes to travel through semiconductors—becomes a factor in limiting the performance of circuits. When signals have to travel long distances, they take a finite time in their traverses. Calculations can occur no quicker than the signals move. By integrating more functions onto a single slab of silicon, signals can be kept within near-microscopic confines instead of needing to travel extra inches to external support chips. In addition, the inevitable delays imposed by forcing signals through buffering and conditioning circuits are avoided by integration.

Inside the chip, size has a more important influence. The larger a logic circuit element is, the more power it can handle—and the more power it takes to make it work. Inside today's microprocessors, the primary limit on speed is heat dissipation. Run a chip too fast and its silicon will heat up until it boils its life away. Smaller circuits require less power, so they generate less heat and can operate faster. The 486 pioneered one-micron design rules, which means that the finest details etched into the chip measure one micron or one millionth of a meter across. The new 50 Mhz 486 has a 0.8 micro design, small enough to extend clock speeds to 100 Mhz.

Anyone having math-intensive applications such as statistical programs or graphics packages knows the value of a numeric coprocessor in accelerating system performance. The 486 incorporates all the necessary coprocessor circuitry—almost an exact duplicate of an 80387 chip—on the same slice of silicon. The new home for the coprocessor is more than a matter of convenience. Operating at the same clock speed as a 387 that's combined with a 386 microprocessor, the internal coprocessor of the 486 delivers about double the performance.

The difference is the proximity and direct connection between the processor and coprocessor circuitry. Commands and data for the 386 coprocessor need to travel from one chip to another across a printed circuit board, encountering all manner of delays along the way. The same instructions for a 486 math operation, on the other hand, simply step across a few microns right on the chip surface. It is like taking an express train instead of the local.

The faster a microprocessor operates, the more it suffers from the shortcomings of today's slow DRAM (Dynamic Random Access

Memory) chips. In some systems, microprocessors spend one-third or more of their time waiting for memory to catch up. The 486 helps minimize the effect of this memory slowdown by incorporating its own high-speed memory cache.

The 486 cache is organized as a four-way set-associative design that essentially splits up its 8K total size into four smaller, 2K caches, an arrangement that further enhances its performance, particularly on multi-threaded applications.

The internal cache uses write-through technology, which puts a higher premium on the integrity of the contents of both cache and system memory than it does on eking out the utmost in speed. When a 486 microprocessor wants to read from memory, it first checks the cache. When it writes, however, it updates both the cache and system memory at the same time, a process that holds the potential of adding delays in waiting for system memory to become ready.

Although the 8K cache is sufficient to match the 486 to commercially available memory chips, it doesn't offer the optimum match. Larger, external caches can further improve performance of the 486 chip, up to about 30 percent more, according to Intel. External caching techniques are discussed later.

The 486 microprocessor is available in a variety of speed ratings that top out at 66 Mhz but may be eventually extended to 100 Mhz or more. The faster the chip is operated, the faster it will perform in direct proportion to its clock speed. A 50 Mhz 486 will compute twice as fast as a 25 Mhz 486, for example, and the newest 66 Mhz chips offers a 30-percent speed improvement over the 50 Mhz chips. The newest chips—DX2/50 and DX2/66—are designed to plug directly into many existing 80486DX-33 socket for performance enhancement. Intel characterizes the two high-speed chip "upgrades" to 33 Mhz computers.

Whether you can upgrade any given 33 Mhz 386 system depends largely on the design of that system. The DX2/66, remember, is around 30-percent faster than even the 50 Mhz chips. Most 33 Mhz systems that were intended for upgrading were designed for the 50 Mhz chips. You can only upgrade directly to the 66 Mhz version if the rest of the computer circuitry is designed with enough margin to handle the extra fast speed. In addition, with the 66 Mhz chip, you almost certainly will need a heat sink, according to Intel designers. If your existing design does not include a heat sink, you likely will have to add one.

On the plus side, the 66 Mhz chips still communicate with the outside world at 33 Mhz, a fact that will help them operate with existing components, but other timing questions might cause problems, Intel said when the chip was announced.

When all the features of the 486 chip are put to work, the only competitors to the fastest 486-based computers are RISC workstations (But see the "future" discussion of the 586-family). The 486 can even hold its own with most of the RISC machines—if you count the speed of machines in millions of instructions per second (MIPS). The 486 scores 20 VAX MIPS at 33 Mhz and 41 MIPS at 50 Mhz, on par with all but the quickest RISC engines. You'll want to stick with the 486 if DOS is a big part of your life—no chip runs DOS better than a 486. Think RISC only if you have a particular application or advanced operating system in mind that only works with a specific RISC engine.

In addition to different speed ratings, the 486 chip comes in two models, the 486DX and the 486SX. The DX chip might be considered the 486 classic, the chip that was initially introduced and incorporates all the performance-enhancing features just discussed. The 486SX is the 486 Lite, a chip stripped of its internal numeric coprocessor. The difference is substantial, particularly when you pay for the chips.

The 80486SX

As initially conceived, the 486SX was the engine of choice for people who needed performance but didn't require a coprocessor. The pre-eminent example of such an application is a network server, where the paramount concern is response, but the data processing work is simple—mostly just moving data around. No number-crunching is necessary. Selecting the 486SX would deliver the high speed of the 486 family without the extra financial burden caused by adding the coprocessor section.

Using the 486SX as such an alternative presupposes that the chip is available with the same overall speed potential as the full-blown

486DX, which is not the case. The 486SX is available only in 20 and 25 MhZ versions from Intel. In effect, the 486SX is the low-end of the 486 line, and one that in the Intel scheme of things will replace the old 386 family.

That's the best view today. Consider the 486SX as a substitute for the 386DX microprocessor. The 486SX is available with similar speed ratings and is priced competitively with the 386DX. But the 486SX is faster than a 386DX running at the same clock speed because of its internal efficiencies. According to Intel, on some tests, the 486SX can double the performance of the 386DX when the two chips are running at the same clock speed.

From that standpoint, all else being equal—and that means primarily clock speed and price—a 486SX system is a better choice than a 386DX. But today the prices are rarely the same. You might buy a 386DX with twice the clock speed as a similar 486SX system for nearly the same price, for example, a 40 Mhz 386DX versus a 20 Mhz 486SX. The 386DX likely will delivery more for your money in this example. However, even this comparison depends on your applications. Some tests have shown that a 25 Mhz 486SX can outperform a 33 Mhz 386DX by as much as 40 percent under some conditions.

The lack of a coprocessor in the 486SX is not a life-long defect. Intel offers a coprocessor, the 487SX, to use with systems based on the 486SX to let you bring it to full power.

The 486SL

Intel's 80486SL is a low-power version of the 486SX chip designed for laptop and other portable or battery-powered applications. Early versions of the chip simply were designed to use less power, but later versions are designed to operate on 3.3 volts instead of the more standard 5 volts.

In addition, SL chips include built-in power management that Intel says can double battery life when compared to a standard SX chip. The power-management system delivers power when it is needed, but shuts things down when they are not needed. When you are entering data from the keyboard, for example, SL power management technology can turn off or place in stand by mode such peripherals as an internal modem or a hard drive. When you enter a save command, the hard drive powers up to save the data and then goes to sleep again until you need it.

If you don't use the keyboard or anything else for a period of time, power management can put the whole system into stand-by mode—or "suspend" mode as Intel calls it. In suspend mode, the computer draws very little power, which helps extend battery life. There's another benefit to the suspend mode: when you aren't using your laptop or portable computer you don't have to shut it off. DOS, Windows, and your current applications stay loaded, ready for use when you get back to them. Without power-management technology, you would have to turn off the machine to conserve power during extended periods of inactivity, but then you'd have to re-boot the system and re-load all of your software. Rebooting and loading software require considerable power to spin the hard drive and do POST (Power On Self Test) processes. With suspend, you simply put the computer to sleep and wake it up when you need it.

80486SLC2

Like the 386 SLC, the 486SLC2 is an IBM version of the 80486SX chip. (for more information on the SLC concept please refer to the section on the 386 SLC chip earlier in this chapter.) The differences between the 386SLC and the 486SLC2 include the following:

➤ The 486SLC2 uses 0.7 micro technology compared to the 386SLC's 1-micron design

➤ The 486SLC2 includes clock-doubling circuitry (like Intel's DX2 chips)

➤ The 486SLC2 uses a 3.3V, low-power supply

➤ The 486SLC2 doubles the 386SLC's onboard cache to 16K

IBM offers SLC technology with some of its mainline computer offerings and promises to provide even more enhancements with future designs. The future direction of the SLC includes improved performance through increased speed, a wider bus and larger cache, according to IBM. The company also is planning even lower voltage and lower power designs and is working on a better processor upgrade strategy that will include SLC technology.

Clock-Doubling 486s

Except for a few third-party upgrade boards (most generally difficult to install, costly and not always fully compatible with existing software), there has been no way to upgrade your computer for faster, better operation. Because later, faster chips weren't compatible with existing designs, you couldn't simply remove your existing CPU and plug in a newer one. With the release of Intel's 80486 family, however, that changed.

Most late-model 486-based motherboards use sockets compatible with Intel's DX2 high speed 486 chips. Two models of the DX2 are available as this is written, a 50 Mhz model and a 66 Mhz model. If your motherboard design includes a socket and circuitry designed to be upgraded to the DX2 chips, all you have to do is unplug the existing, 33 Mhz 486 chip and slip in one of the new DX2 models. You may also elect to purchase a computer that already uses a DX2/50 chip and upgrade it to 66 Mhz later. Then, if Intel decides to release a 100 Mhz DX2 chip (something being discussed but which Intel has not confirmed as this is written), you can upgrade again to an even faster chip.

Or, if your computer has an extra, 169-pin "overdrive" or "performance enhancement" socket, you can plug in a new "overdrive" chip. On 486SX-based systems, this is the same socket that was designed for the 487SX math coprocessor. The overdrive chip is essentially an enhanced 80486 microprocessor with the clock-doubling circuitry of the DX2 chips.

Actually, the overdrive socket is a way of adding a new, high-speed CPU without having to unplug the existing processor. When you insert an overdrive chip in the performance-enhancement socket, the existing CPU is disabled, and the new chip takes over at a higher speed. The overdrive ship includes math-coprocessor circuitry and also uses Intel's DX2 speed-doubling technology. This means that the overdrive chip operates at twice system clock speed internally but still communicates with the rest of the system at the existing system speed.

Two versions of the overdrive chip are available. One is designed to upgrade 16 Mhz or 20 Mhz systems, and there is another version for existing 25 Mhz systems. The 25 Mhz version includes a heat sink to help dissipate the additional heat generated by high-speed CPU operation. The overdrive concept is designed to provide end user upgrades. The existing CPU does not have to be removed, so even if it is soldered into the motherboard, a user can upgrade to higher speed and improved performance by simply inserting the new overdrive chip into the provided socket on the motherboard.

The DX2 and overdrive chips both speed up internal CPU processing, but they still communicate with the outside world at motherboard speeds. So if your existing 486 CPU is installed in a 25 Mhz system, the overdrive or DX2 chip may operate at 50 Mhz but still will exchange data with the rest of the system at 25 Mhz. A 66 Mhz, DX2 chip in a 33 Mhz system will communicate with the external computer at 33 Mhz. This technique should ensure maximum compatibility between the new, high-speed chips and the existing systems already installed in your computer.

Remember that although the upgrade process lets you speed up processing on your existing system, such an upgraded system won't run as fast as one designed from the ground up for 50 or 66 Mhz operation. The reason is obvious. When you plug a 50 Mhz chip into a 33 Mhz system, the computer's memory, BIOS, and controllers are still operating at the original system speed, and the CPU still is communicating with the rest of the system at the original speed.

A full-blown 50 or 66 Mhz system, on the other hand, includes memory and other components rated at the speed of the processor. How much these considerations affect final throughput speed of your system depends on your applications, primarily, but you should be aware that there will be differences. At the same time, however, a 50 Mhz chip in a 25 Mhz system should give you noticeable performance improvements, especially when your applications are compute-intensive as opposed to I/O intensive.

80486 Packaging

The 486 processor is housed in a 168-pin grid array package, similar to the 80386 chips. High speed chips—especially those operating at 25 Mhz and above—usually include heat sinks for enhanced cooling.

The 586 Family

As this book went to press, Intel was putting the finishing touches on chips to follow the 486 family. Although the company was not releasing any *official* information, high-end PCs with 240-pin expansion or overdrive sockets are being developed by some companies, and Intel was working on a chip designated the P5. The P5 chip was said to have 240 pins, so you should be able to upgrade existing 486 PCs that have the 240-pin sockets to the new 80586 CPU.

Intel delayed shipment of the 80586 from its first projections until early in 1993, primarily because the company wanted to ensure the availability of the chip in quantity before shipment started.

In addition, Intel acknowledged that discussion was underway within the company about a name change for the new series. Instead of calling it an 80586—the next logical nomenclature for a follow-on chip to the existing 80486 line—Intel was contemplating a name that contains some letters or all letters. This would help the firm protect its own name for the chip and prevent competitive companies from using the same name. It is a pretty good bet, however, that no matter what Intel calls their new chip, a good portion of the industry—including end users and developers—will call it a 586 anyway, at least for a reasonable time after it starts shipping.

Just what is an 80586? It is a 64-bit microprocessor, for one thing, and the internal cache is larger than that on 486 chips. The 586 chip was expected to include separate 8K instruction and data caches, for example, doubling the onboard cache now available with 80486 CPUs. The 586 is a large chip, about 16 mm on a side, and it contains the equivalent of 3 to 3.5 million transistors (switches), is capable of around 100 MIPS performance, and runs at about 66 Mhz.

The good news for current 486-based computer owners is that a scaled-down version of the 586 (586SX?) designed with a 64-bit internal architecture but with a 32-bit external bus compatible with the 486 may be part of the family. You could conceivably unplug your 486 CPU and stick in an adapter board or a smaller-than-normal 586 chip that would handle 586 software and still be compatible with existing 486 hardware. You may also be able to insert the down-scaled 586 in the performance-enhancement socket already available on some 486 computers.

Flash memory support chips are expected for the 586 line. Flash memory is a form of READ/WRITE, non-volatile memory that can replace the ROM (Read Only Memory) chips currently used to store a computer's BIOS (Basic Input Output System). Presently, significant hardware advances that occur after you purchase your computer can only be included in your machine by unplugging a set of ROM chips and replacing them with new chips. With flash memory, however, the BIOS could be upgraded with data from a floppy disk.

CHAPTER

Numeric
Coprocessors

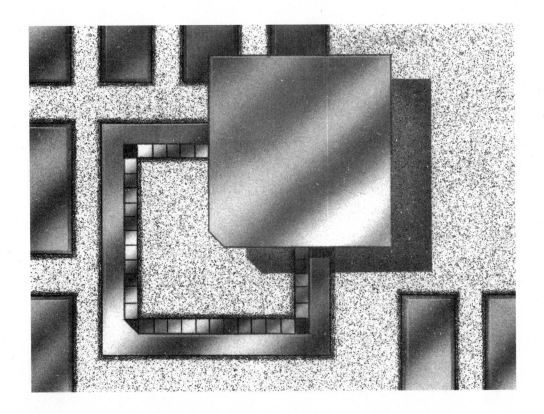

Most microprocessors are generalists designed to carry out a variety of logical operations. Adding a specialist chip called a *numeric coprocessor* can speed the complex mathematical operations carried out in a PC by factors approaching a hundredfold. Each of Intel's early microprocessors had its own, matching numeric coprocessor, but the latest generation of chips have integrated the coprocessor function into their silicon, making the stand-alone coprocessor obsolete.

Although the first microprocessors were designed for pocket calculators, neither they nor their immediate successors were designed to solve the most complex mathematical problems with the highest speed. By their very nature, these microprocessors were designed to handle a multitude of functions, of which complex math operations were of peripheral interest. After all, all mathematical operations can be created by judiciously manipulating simple addition—multiplication by repeating addition ad nauseum, subtraction by looking at things backward and inverting the addition, division by inverting the multiplication, and so on. Even the most complex math operations, such as determining trigonometric functions or square roots, can be carried out by variations on the addition theme. After all, you could build a mile-high building out of Legos if you have the mind to. Or, maybe not. The problem would be time; stacking a billion or so blocks would take more waking moments than the Fates deal us. Similarly, for the microprocessor, multiplying by a million using addition means a million or so steps. And even at microprocessor rates, carrying out each step can take substantial time—not enough that you'll go gray, but you may nevertheless feel like you are.

To accelerate numeric operations, most microprocessors incorporate more than simple addition operations in their command repertoires. But few include all possible math operations. There are just too many operations that are used too rarely to make the added design work and complex silicon work worthwhile. As a result, general-purpose microprocessors can be unbearably slow at complex mathematical operations.

The *coprocessor* is a special integrated circuit that works cooperatively with your microprocessor to speed up its operation. The most familiar of coprocessors are those designed to accelerate the same high-order math operations that were left out of the command set of the general purpose microprocessor. Other coprocessor are optimized to handle other specific functions—for example, making images on your display screen. Because the coprocessor is designed for a specific purpose, it can handle its particular functions many times faster than can the ordinary general-purpose microprocessor. In effect, the coprocessor relieves the microprocessor from needing to handle the hard stuff.

Although the concept sounds like a throughput miracle, the blessings brought by math coprocessors vary with your PC and the work you do. A given math coprocessor can dramatically accelerate calculations, but only certain calculations. Although the coprocessor chip can crunch numbers like a junk yard hydraulic ram, most of what you use your PC for, including number-intensive bookkeeping, may not benefit from a math coprocessor at all.

If that's not confusing enough, the math coprocessor marketplace is quickly becoming crowded and is dying at the same time. Once your choice of coprocessors was limited to exactly one chip that would work with your PC; today you have a choice of many from a range of vendors that at times (depending on lawsuit status) includes Cyrix Corporation, Integrated Information Technology, Intel Corporation, ULSI, and Weitek Corporation. All now offer, or have offered, chips that will plug into one of the coprocessor sockets that are standard in nearly all of today's PCs.

On the other hand, Intel Corporation developed a new strategy to get rid of its competition in the lucrative coprocessor market by making the future need for coprocessors unpredictable, even entirely eliminating the need for the chips. First, Intel made the coprocessor effectively obsolete (by introducing the 486), then brought it back (with the 486SX and its matching math coprocessor), and then destroyed it again (with its OverDrive upgrade chips).

For PCs that can use them, a modest investment in a coprocessor chip can bring immense performance improvements—or maybe not. The results you get depend on who you believe and the software that you run. For example, the benchmark tests written by the math coprocessor makers point to performance improvements of up to a hundredfold by plugging in a coprocessor. On most applications, however, the benefits of a math coprocessor are about as elusive as catching a glimpse of Comet Kahoutek. Most programs that you are apt to run won't gain any extra speed. Even the number-crunching that most business people use their PCs for (spreadsheet-based accounting) benefits little if at all from using a math coprocessor. Only computationally intense chores, such as statistics, engineering, and graphics, stand to gain much, and the margin of improvement a math coprocessor brings them hardly rises to the hundredfold claims of the chip manufacturers.

That's not to say that math coprocessors are overrated or worthless. If you have a job that can take advantage of one, there's no more cost-effective power boost you can give a coprocessor-starved PC. Today, the bottom line for coprocessors is that most people don't need them, but they don't hurt anything (except if you have to pay extra for the additional silicon) and are essentially unavoidable at the high end of the market. If you don't have a coprocessor in your PC today, you will eventually—either by adding one to what you have or when you inevitably move up to a more powerful system.

Fundamentals

The concept of a coprocessor is straightforward. A coprocessor is simply something that works in cooperation with your PC's microprocessor. The goal is performance won by greater efficiency through specialization and division of labor—the electronic equivalent of a miniature Industrial Revolution. To divide the labor, the coprocessor takes charge of some particular task normally relegated to the general-purpose microprocessor, relieving the main chip of some of its load. At the same time, the coprocessor is a specialist, designed to handle one particular task (and one task only) with the greatest possible efficiency. In sacrificing the need to be all things to all software, the specialist coprocessor can be trimmed down to the bare essentials required to perform its task most efficiently.

At heart, a coprocessor is a microprocessor; but, unlike a general-purpose microprocessor, a coprocessor is dedicated to its specific function, as a special-purpose device. Because its repertoire is somewhat limited, a coprocessor can concentrate on being the best in its field.

As microprocessors, coprocessors work just like all other microprocessors. They simply run programs that consist of a series of instructions. Unlike the main microprocessor in a PC, however, the coprocessor may not directly control the bulk of the machine. Instead, its lifeline is through the main microprocessor, which may send the coprocessor the program instructions it requires and then carry away the results.

In normal operation, the microprocessor handles all the functions of running the computer. However, when it encounters a task that's best handled by the coprocessor, it passes the data and instructions over and patiently awaits the answers.

Coprocessors do not share the same instruction set with the microprocessors that they complement. They have their own, special command sets. Consequently, programs must be specially written to take advantage of coprocessors. They must use the special coprocessor instructions if they want the coprocessor to do anything. Programs that are not written to use the coprocessor will not benefit by its availability.

The rule is worth repeating: by itself, a coprocessor will not improve the performance of your computer. You need to run software that has been specially written to include coprocessor instructions to take advantage of the speed and power of the coprocessor. Programs that do use the coprocessor can often run many times faster, a speed on the same order of magnitude as moving from a PC to an AT or PS/2.

The coprocessor won't automatically kick in when a tough problem crops up. Moreover, not only must an application be written to use a numeric coprocessor, but it also must match a particular coprocessor. If an application does not have coprocessor instructions that match those recognized by the coprocessor, the numeric coprocessor won't do anything.

The only way to be sure that the coprocessor will be active during the execution of a specific program is to check for an explicit statement from the program's publisher to that effect. There's no easy way to tell whether the coprocessor is working other than comparing performance with and without the chip installed.

Coprocessors have been designed for a variety of tasks, but the best known are those that are the subject of this chapter—the math coprocessor, which is also termed *numeric coprocessor*, or the floating-point unit (FPU). As the name implies, these chips specialize in manipulating numbers. In particular, they are designed to handle all the complex functions that gave you nightmares while you were day-dreaming in high school: long division, trigonometric functions, roots, and logarithms. These operations yield floating-point numbers, the type that math coprocessors are most adept at handling.

Floating-point describes a way of expressing values, not a mathematically defined type of number, such as integer, rational, or real number. The essence of a floating-point number is that its decimal point "floats" among a predefined number of significant digits rather than being fixed in place the way dollar values always have two decimal places.

Mathematically speaking, a floating-point number has three parts: a *sign*, which indicates whether the number is greater or less than zero; a *significant* (sometimes called a *mantissa*), which comprises all the digits that are mathematically meaningful; and an *exponent*, which determines the order of magnitude of the significant, essentially the location to which the decimal point floats.

Think of a floating-point number as being like those represented by scientific notation. But where scientists are apt to deal in base 10 (the exponents in scientific notation are powers of 10), math coprocessors think of floating-point numbers digitally in base#2—all 1s and 0s in powers of 2. In carrying out complex mathematical operations on floating-point numbers, the math coprocessor works much in the same way as a general-purpose microprocessor. Using digital logic, it processes patterns of bits containing information (the floating-point numbers) under the control of other bit patterns making up instructions. These operations are carried out in registers, special internal memory areas inside the coprocessor.

To make a computation, the math coprocessor first loads one of the numbers that it is to work on into one of its registers and then loads the second number into another register. Next, it reads the program instruction that tells the chip what particular operation it should carry out on the two numbers. The instruction starts another, miniature computer program running inside the coprocessor chip, and that program causes the circuitry of the coprocessor to actually calculate the desired answer. The entire set of programs inside the math coprocessor that respond to the various instructions that the chip understands are called its *microcode*.

After a result has been calculated, getting the answer out of the coprocessor requires the execution of another instruction. Alternately, the next instruction can make the coprocessor carry out another operation on the results of the first.

In that general-purpose microprocessors operate exactly the same way (load values, read instructions, and execute microcode), the math coprocessor can earn a speed advantage handling floating-point numbers only by carrying out commands faster. The basic commands understood by the general-purpose microprocessor are, in fact, handled with great efficiency. Instead of streamlining these common operations, most (but not all) numeric coprocessors concentrate on complex operations that would otherwise require a long series of steps. By combining all the steps into one operation that can be quickly computed, the coprocessor beats the general-purpose microprocessor at the numbers game. For example, a general-purpose microprocessor can compute an irrational root, but it might have to execute a loop of simple instructions hundreds of times to come up with the answer, performing hundreds of iterations of integer math. The coprocessor solves the same problem with a single instruction.

Certainly a microprocessor could be designed so that it could carry out all of the complex instructions handled by a math coprocessor. The Intel 486 microprocessor comes close to doing exactly that, appearing like that to your programs, although having a distinct internal structure comprising a general-purpose processor and special purpose floating-point unit. The coprocessor exists as a separate element for reasons tied to the history of the standardization of floating-point calculations and the technology of integrated circuits.

Addressing

To work properly with the main microprocessor in a PC, a coprocessor must share data. Somehow the microprocessor must be able to pass floating-point problems along to the coprocessor, and the coprocessor must be able to route the answers right back. Certainly, the potential range for communication method is wide—from Pony Express to telepathy—but practicality (not to mention functionality) leave but two main choices: linking to the main microprocessor through a direct connection of input and output ports through which they send and receive data and instructions, and exchanging data and instructions with the main microprocessor by passing bytes through memory.

The first type of coprocessor design is generally called *I/O mapped*; the second type, *memory mapped*. Because of fundamental differences in the way the two coprocessor designs operate, program code must be written to use one or the other technology. Most coprocessors work through one method or the other, although one coprocessor (the Cyrix EMC87) has two operating modes: one I/O mapped, one memory mapped.

I/O-Mapped Coprocessors

In the I/O-mapped design, both the microprocessor and the coprocessor are connected to the data lines that carry information—program instructions as well as the data that they work on—inside your PC. Normally, the main microprocessor carries out all of the instructions in most computer programs. Certain instructions are recognized by the math coprocessor as its own, however, and it can carry them out directly.

In a way, the I/O-mapped math coprocessor operates as a leech, a parasite that cannot live without the microprocessor it clings to. Only the microprocessor has circuitry to control your PC's address lines to find information. Consequently, proper operation of the coprocessor requires careful coordination of its work with that of the main microprocessor. The efforts of the two chips are coordinated through a direct hardware linkup (wires connecting the two chips) and are electrically controlled through input/output ports. These ports are internal to the two chips and, unlike the I/O ports used by your PC's peripherals, cannot be accessed directly by you.

Both the main microprocessor and the coprocessor have their own registers (in which all calculations take place) and internal control circuitry. As a result, the two chips can operate somewhat independently and simultaneously. That is, while your math coprocessor is wrestling with a particularly difficult problem, the microprocessor can do something else.

In theory, this design could add a degree of parallel processing to your PC. In reality, it often does not. Most programs send the math chip scurrying off in search of an answer and leave the microprocessor to wait until the results are found. Only a few programs take advantage of this parallel-processing capability.

Memory-Mapped Coprocessors

To communicate with your programs and the microprocessor, memory-mapped coprocessors use memory addresses as mailboxes. A small range of addresses (typically a 4K page) in far off paragraphs of your system's RAM (well above the 16 megabytes that most 386-based computers can use for physical RAM but within the four-gigabyte addressing range of the microprocessor) is cordoned off for such communications. The microprocessor pushes instructions for the coprocessor to one group of addresses and data to be worked on to other addresses. The coprocessor responds with its results in the same manner. No actual RAM chips are installed at these locations. Rather, the memory for holding the commands and data are part of the coprocessor's circuitry.

One obvious requirement of the memory-mapped design is that the coprocessor chip must have access to the address lines used by the microprocessor. In that I/O-mapped coprocessors have no need for this address information, address lines are not available at coprocessor sockets designed for I/O-mapped chips. Memory-mapped coprocessors thus require larger sockets with more pins to accommodate all the address lines to which they need access. The special sockets for memory-mapped coprocessors are termed EMC sockets because they use an Extended Math Coprocessor interface.

Because of the additional address-decoding logic they require, memory-mapped coprocessors are inherently more complex than I/O-mapped chips. They are more difficult to design and make and generally more expensive than equivalent (if there is such a thing) I/O-mapped chips.

In theory, a memory-mapped coprocessor can be faster than an I/O-mapped chip because the exchange of commands and data through memory is quicker than through the I/O route. Although I/O-mapped chips must move instructions and data in separate operations over several clock cycles, memory-mapped chips can acquire all the data and instruction they need in a single operation. Because address lines and data lines can be used simultaneously to move data and instructions between microprocessor and coprocessor, the memory-mapped coprocessor effectively has a 64-bit link with a 32-bit microprocessor (much as multiplexed data transfers give 32-bit Micro Channel machines a 64-bit data path).

In addition, after the information has been loaded into its memory range, the memory-mapped coprocessor is on its own. The I/O-mapped coprocessor requires more hand-holding. The main microprocessor first must read the instruction for the coprocessor and then poke the data into the proper port to get it to the coprocessor.

The big disadvantage of the memory-mapped coprocessor is that the interface has not been standardized. Each memory-mapped coprocessor has its own commands and uses its own distinct address range. In order to take advantage of the coprocessor, programs must know these secrets, so each memory-mapped math coprocessor requires its own version of a particular application. Few programs actually have such built-in support.

Intel Architecture

All coprocessors made by Intel Corporation and those from other manufacturers aimed to be compatible—that is, the chips designed to work with Intel's microprocessors from the 8088 up to the 486SX—share a number of common characteristics. All use the I/O-mapped design. More importantly, in conformance with the IEEE floating specification, all work with 80-bit registers, leaving the 8-, 16-, 32-, and 64-bit registers of Intel's microprocessors far behind.

Eighty bits seems somewhat arbitrary in a computer world that's based on powers of two and a steady doubling of register size from 8 to 16 to

32 to 64 bits. But 80-bit registers are exactly the right size to accommodate 64 bits of significant with 15 bits left over to hold an exponent value and an extra bit for the sign of the number held in the register.

The registers in Intel coprocessors (and the coprocessor circuits of the latest microprocessors) are not limited to this single data format, however. They can calculate on 32-, 64-, or 80-bit floating point numbers, 32- or 64-bit integers, and 18-digit binary coded decimal (BCD) numbers as well. (Binary Coded Decimal numbers simply use a specific 4-bit digital code to represent each of the decimal digits between 0 and 9.) Table 4.1 shows the formats of the different number types supported under the IEEE specification.

TABLE 4.1.
Coprocessor
Compatibility

Manufacturer	Model	Recommended Coprocessor
Amax Engineering	386 Business System	80287-6, -8, -10
American Logic Research	386/2	80287-10
American Logic Research	FlexCache 20386	80387-20
American Research	ARC 386i	80287-10
AT&T	6300	8087-2
AT&T	6300 Plus	80287 or 80287-6
AT&T	6386 Work Group System	80387-20
CAE/SAR	386	80287-10
CAE/SAR	CAE/SAR II	80387-25
Chicago Computer Conn.	CCC-386c	80287-6, -8, -10
Commodore	PC-10	8087 or 8087-3
Compaq	Deskpro 286 (8 MHz)	80287 or 80287-6
Compaq	Deskpro 286 (12 MHz)	80287-8
Compaq	Deskpro 386 (early)	80287-6 or -8
Compaq	Deskpro 386/16	80287-16
Compaq	Deskpro 386/20	80387-20
Compaq	Deskpro 86	8087-2
Compaq	Portable II	80287 or 80287-6
Compaq	Portable III	80287-8
Compaq	Portable 386	80287-20
Computer Classified	ST-386	80287-6, -8, -10
Computer Components	Heritage 386 (early)	80287-10
Computer Components	Heritage 386 (late)	80387-20
Computer Dynamics	Micro System 386	80387-16

continues

TABLE 4.1.
continued

Manufacturer	Model	Recommended Coprocessor
Core	ATomizer	80287-6
Corvus	386	80387-16
Dell	310	80387-20
Epson	Equity III	80287 or 80287-6
Everex	Step 386/20	80387-20
Herko Electronics	HEI Turbo 386 Tower	80287-10 or 80387-20
Hewlett-Packard	Vectra R5/20	80387-20
IDR	386 Workstation	80387-20
IBM	AT (6 or 8 MHz)	80287 or 80287-6
IBM	PC	8087 or 8087-3
IBM	PS/2 Model 30	8087-2
IBM	PS/2 Model 30 286	80287-10
IBM	PS/2 Model 50	80287-10
IBM	PS/2 Model 60	80287-10
IBM	PS/2 Model 70 (16 MHz)	80387-16
IBM	PS/2 Model 70 (20 MHz)	80387-20
IBM	PS/2 Model 70 (25 MHz)	80387-25
IBM	PS/2 Model 80 (16 MHz)	80387-16
IBM	PS/2 Model 80 (20 MHz)	80387-20
IBM	XT	8087 or 8087-3
IBM	XT Model 286	80287 or 80287-6
IBM	Portable PC	8087 or 8087-3
IBM	3270 AT	80287 or 80287-6
Intel	Inboard 386	80387-16
Intel	Inboard 386/PC	80387-16
Kaypro	386	80287-10 or 80387-16
Laser Digital	Pacer-386	80287-10
Micro 1	386 PC	80387-16
Mitsubishi	MP 386	80287-8 or 80387-16
NEC	APV-IV	80287 or 80287-6

Manufacturer	Model	Recommended Coprocessor
NCR	PC4	8087 or 8087-3
NCR	916	80287-10 or 80387-16
Northgate Computer Sys.	386/20 Northgate Power	80387-20
Osicom Technologies	Osicom 386	80287-10 or 80387-16
Pan United	Micro Lab 386	80287-8, -10 or 80387-20
PC Designs	GV 386	80287-6, -8, -10
PC Link	386/20	80387-20
PC's Limited	386/16	80387-16
Proteus Technology	286 Standard	80287-10
Proteus Technology	386A	80287-10
Sperry	PC/microIT	80287 or 80287-6
Tandon	PCA	80287 or 80287-6
Tandy	3000	80287 or 80287-6
Tandy	4000 (early)	80287-8
Tandy	4000 (late)	80387-16
Televideo	Tele/386	80287-10 or 80387-16
Toshiba	T5100	80387-20
VIPC	386 Colossus	80387-20
VIPC	System Micro 386	80287-8, -10 or 80387-20
Wang	380	80287-10
Whole Earth	386 Tower	80387-20
Wyse	pc286	80287-10
Wyse	pc386	80387-16 or 80287-6, -8, -10
Wyse	1400	8087 or 8087-3
Wyse	1500	8087 or 8087-3
Zenith	148	8087-2
Zenith	150	8087 or 8087-3
Zenith	158	8087-2
Zenith	160	8087 or 8087-3
Zenith	386	80287-6, -8, -10 or 80387-16
Zenith	Z200	80287 or 80287-6

Each Intel chip has eight of these 80-bit registers in which to perform their calculations. Instructions in your programs tell the math chip what format of numbers to work on and how. The only real difference is the form in which the math chip delivers its results to the microprocessor when it's done. All calculations are carried out using the full 80 bits of the chip's registers, unlike Intel microprocessors, which can independently manipulate its registers in byte-wide pieces.

The eight 80-bit registers in an Intel coprocessor also differ from those in a microprocessor in the way they are addressed. Commands for individual microprocessor registers are directly routed to the appropriate register as if sent by a switch board. Coprocessor registers are arranged in a stack—sort of an elevator system. Values are pushed onto the stack, and with each new number, the old one goes down a level. Stack machines are generally regarded as lean and mean computers. Their design is more austere and streamlined, which helps them run more quickly.

Numeric History

In the mid-1970s, there were no math coprocessors as they are known today. Nor were there any microprocessors. The only computers were mainframes and minicomputers, and all they did were floating-point operations. Oddly enough, however, all the different computers in the world came up with different answers when challenged by complex calculations. Not that they added two and two and deduced random numbers. Rather, when they calculated irrational numbers and rounded the values so that they could be stored and expressed in something less intractable than an infinite series of digits, the last few decimal places varied, depending on what make and model of computer did the thinking.

The core of the problem was, of course, that irrational numbers can only be approximated by the finite set of digits in our numerical system. Every computer and software designer PC had his own preferred means of dealing with the challenge of irrationality—rounding up or down at one or another decimal place in whatever numeric base was handiest—binary, octal, decimal, or whatever.

Of course, scientists weren't really thrilled to have the results of their calculations vary with the hardware on which they were computed. Before they became as irrational as their numbers, the Institute of Electrical and Electronic Engineers (the IEEE) formed an industry committee to develop standards for floating-point calculations. At the same time that scientists and engineers were trying to approach numbers more rationally, Intel was taking a more irrational approach to the design of its microprocessors. It already had created the successful 8080 and 8085 chips and was working on successors. As part of the development of its next generation of chips, the company decided to create a hardware implementation of the IEEE floating-point standard to handle the irrationalities. The new microprocessor would become the 8086, the immediate predecessor of the 8088 that served as the foundation of the IBM PC.

The decision had little to do with making PC programs run faster. At the time, only a few hobbyists were dabbling with desktop machines. But Intel foresaw advanced floating-point capabilities as being useful in robotic and numeric-control applications, considered one of the brightest markets for microprocessors back then.

From a marketing viewpoint, a microprocessor with elaborate floating-point capabilities seemed a good bet, but integrated circuit technology pushed the odds in the other direction. When the 8086 microprocessor was being developed in the years before its introduction in 1978, creating an integrated circuit was a much more exotic process than it is today. The technology was still primitive, and the size and number of components that could be grown and etched onto a wafer of silicon limited the complexity of possible (or at least affordable) integrated circuits. At the time, microprocessors were the most complex circuits ever designed.

The larger the chip, the more likely it was (and is) to contain some defect that would make it unusable. On the other hand, technology constrained how small the details of the chip design could be. If layouts were too small, they were more likely to suffer manufacturing defects, again making the chip unusable. For example, the smallest possible details in the 8086 microprocessor measured 5 to 10 microns across. (Today some chips are made with details 1/10 that width.)

Together, these two limits conspire to put an effective lid on the complexity of a given circuit at a given level of technical development. The 8086 pressed hard against those limits. Making the chip even more complex was out of the question even for the potentially lucrative market of digitally controlled electronic milling machines.

And probably unnecessary. Other chips made do without the need for dedicated floating-point units. There were no coprocessors for the 8080 and Z80 chips that were popular in the rudimentary desktop computers available at the time. Even the 4004, designed to be the heart of the hand-held calculator, lacked advanced floating-point capabilities. Most computer applications back then just didn't need a floating-point processor that followed the evolving IEEE standard.

8087

As a result of these very practical, if not rational, issues, Intel chose not to include advanced math functions in the silicon of the 8086 chip. Instead, the eminently useful and marketable math functions were relegated to a separate element, which eventually was produced as a commercial product in 1980—the 8087 math coprocessor.

The two-year lag between the introduction of the 8086 and its companion coprocessor arose from technical rather than marketing issues. The 8087 was just hard to design. According to Intel, when the 8087 was introduced, it was the most complex large-scale integrated circuit ever commercially manufactured.

Despite its complexity, the 8087 was not self-sufficient. It could function only in conjunction with an 8086 in a tightly bound symbiotic relationship. To simplify the too complex circuitry of the 8087, the chip's engineers took advantage of the interfacing and control circuitry built into the 8086. The main microprocessor reads and writes all program instructions from memory. When it encounters a numeric coprocessor instruction, it simply passes it along to the 8087. The 8086 also tells the 8087 what data its needs to act on, but the 8087 has its own bus connections to reach out and get what it needs. When the 8087 comes up with an answer, it passes the results back to the 8086. The microprocessor then can fit results back into the program.

The twin-chip approach to floating-point coprocessing has one big advantage—the 8087 can be paired with other microprocessors without the need to redesign the silicon. Intel wisely crafted the 8087 to complement the entire family of 8086-derived microprocessors. These include the 8088 used in PCs and XTs as well as the 80186 and 80188.

The 8087 fits into a 40-pin DIP socket that provides the chip with the same addressing and data-handling capabilities of the chips it was built to match. Although it can accept data from a 16-bit bus, it will also work without modification with the eight-bit bus of the 8088, automatically adapting itself as necessary. The 8087 ordinarily shares the same clock frequency with its microprocessor cohort and operates at the same speed.

Three versions of the 8087, differing by speed rating, have been made. The original chip, the plain 8087, was designed to operate at system clock speeds up to 5 Mhz; the 8087-2 operates at speeds up to 8 Mhz; and the 8087-1 operates at up to 10 Mhz.

Other than the rated speed, there is little difference between these chips. They understand the same commands and run the same software. The faster chips just produce results faster in a faster computer. Although a higher speed 8087 will work at a clock rate slower than its rating, there is no advantage to doing so. The speed of the system clock determines how fast the chip calculates. The rating of the chip determines only how fast a system the chip will work in.

All IBM PCs, XTs, 8086-based PS/2s, and nearly all compatible computers have sockets designed to accommodate the 8087. The IBM PC and XT line need nothing more exotic than the ordinary 8087. PS/2s and higher speed (so-called Turbo XT) compatibles generally require the 8087-2.

80287

In the original design of the 8087, Intel had the foresight to divide the chip's circuitry into two functional elements: a bus interface unit and the actual floating-point unit. The former links the chip to the rest of the system in which it is installed (the microprocessor in particular), and the latter performs the heavy-duty calculations. As a result, the math side of the 8087 could easily be adapted to match other micro-processor and environments by modifying only the bus interface. After all, that was the whole point of the IEEE floating-point standard. The form, function, and answers derived by the 8087 are defined by the standard, so they don't vary with the microprocessor or the computer built around it.

Intel took advantage of the split design of the 8087 to develop its next floating-point processor effort, the 80287. As introduced in 1985, the original 80287 took advantage of the floating-point section of the 8087 and coupled it with new interface logic to match the Intel's 80286 microprocessor chip. However, in the translation, some modifi-cations were made to the floating-point unit to reflect changes in the nascent IEEE standard.

As with the 8087, the bus control logic of the 80287 is designed to link to an 80826 and rely on the microprocessor host for system support. The 8087 itself won't work with the 80286 because of the wider address bus used by the newer microprocessor. In fact, the 80287 mates more tightly with the 80286 than its predecessor did with its microprocessor. The 80287 doesn't even have access to the address lines of the computer in which it is installed. All of its memory-related operations must be handled by the main 80286 microprocessor.

This addressless design enables the 80287 to deal with both the real and protected modes of the 80286 processor and enables the 80287 to address the full 16-megabyte range of that microprocessor. The 8087 operates only in real mode.

As with the 8087, the 80287 is packaged in a 40-pin DIP socket, but it obviously is not pin-for-pin compatible with the 8087. Moreover, the 80287 is designed to operate asynchronously; the 8087 normally is locked to the same clock that drives its host microprocessor. As a result, the 80287 does not necessarily operate at the same speed as its host microprocessor. The two chips—microprocessor and coprocessor—know how to adjust their operations, waiting as neces-sary, to match their data transfer cycles.

Ordinarily, the 80287 is connected with the same oscillator that runs the rest of an 80286-based PC. However, an internal divider slows down the clock frequency entering the 80287 to one-third its original speed before it reaches the floating-point circuitry. Hence, an 80287 operates at one-third the clock speed presented to it. In most 80286-based systems, the clock that runs the microprocessor is divided in half before being connected to the 80286. Typically, the original double-speed clock is connected to the 80287 so that the coprocessor effectively operates at two-thirds the microprocessor speed. For example, in an 8 Mhz IBM AT, the 80287 coprocessor runs at 5.33 Mhz.

Because the 80287 operates asynchronously, there's no need for its clock to be a multiple or submultiple of the microprocessor clock. In fact, some PCs give their 80287s their own dedicated clocks, enabling the engineers designing these systems to operate the coprocessors at whatever speed they want. By using a dedicated clock, they can boost the data throughput of their 80287s substantially (providing, of course, the chips can handle the racy speeds the engineers design).

The 80287 is also compatible with the 80386 microprocessor. However, the 80287 is not capable of operating at the same speeds as the 80386 and requires special interface designs to match it to the data bus used by the 80386. Moreover, because the 80287 is essentially a 16-bit chip, all communication between it and a host 80386 must be handled in 16-bit words, a potential (but not substantial) performance roadblock.

At various times, Intel has offered 80287 chips with four different speed ratings, all of which are not obsolete. All four have been replaced by two new coprocessors, the 287XL and 287XLT, which are based on a new floating-point unit design first implemented in the second generation of 387 coprocessors (explained in a later section in this chapter). Both of these chips are designed to operate at speeds up to 12.5 Mhz. The 287XL plugs into any socket designed to accommodate an ordinary 287 chip no matter the speed. The 287XLT is specifically designed for low-power applications and is not socket-compatible with other 287s. The 287XLT fits a PLCC (Plastic Leadless Chip Carrier) socket; the XL is compatible with the 40-pin DIP sockets used by earlier 80287 implementations.

The obsolete 80287 chips can be distinguished by their speed rating designations. The plain 80287 or 80287-3 operates at up to 5 Mhz; the 80287-6 runs at up to 6 Mhz; the 80287-8 runs at up to 8 Mhz; and the 80287-10 goes all the way to 10 Mhz. The four chips can be used interchangeably as long as the clock rate supplied to it is within the chip's operating range. There is no advantage to using a chip rated faster than the clock when a slower 80287 will work (and the prices for quicker chips tend toward the stratosphere).

Note that no Intel 80287 is rated to operate faster than the 12.5 Mhz 286XL and XLT. However, other companies offer higher speed clones of the 80287 capable of speeds up to 20 Mhz (providing the computer host can supply the necessary clock signal to its coprocessor socket). These chips are identified by their manufacturers' part numbers, which will contain the designation "287" and end with the speed rating "-20."

The Intel bus control logic design of the 80287 that makes the coprocessor rely on its microprocessor host for addressing information means that the 80287 is not limited by the 16-megabyte memory-handling capabilities of the 80286. The versatile design enables the 80287 to also operate with 386 microprocessors, and for two years the 80287 was the official Intel coprocessor for the 386.

The 80286 had shortcomings in the 386 environment. The 80286 was designed with a 16-bit interface; the 386 was capable of 32-bit operations. The 386 host had to translate wide data down to narrow size to slide it into the 80287. Moreover, the 80287 had been left behind by the still evolving IEEE floating-point standard. In fact, only after the 80287 was in production was the IEEE floating-point standard finally put into its final form, now known as ANSI/IEEE 754-1985. In some subtle ways, the 80287 and the finalized standard were at variance. Consequently, the 80287 is not the ideal math coprocessor, particularly for 386-based PCs. Nevertheless, a slow 80287 is faster on floating point operations than a 386 by itself, so even a lowly 80287 can be a worthy addition to a PC that will accommodate one.

387

When Intel began to design a coprocessor to match the 386, the old 8087 design was beginning to look long in the tooth. Not only had the venerable floating-point unit not kept up with the mutating IEEE proto-standard, it had not kept up with modern semiconductor design technology. Consequently, Intel decided to revamp the entire chip—bus-control logic and floating-point unit—when developing a matching coprocessor addition for the 386 microprocessor.

Intel put a design team to work on the 387 in Israel in parallel with its U.S.-based 386 design effort. The math coprocessor proved a bigger challenge than was anticipated, however, and the 387 lagged the introduction of the 386 by about two years. In the meantime, the venerable 80287 served as the arithmetic assistant to the 386.

When the new floating-point unit design was introduced, it not only implemented as the final IEEE standard but also proved faster than the old 8087/80287 floating-point unit by about a factor of five. After its introduction in 1987 as part of the 387 math coprocessor, the new floating-point unit became the foundation of all later Intel math coprocessors. It also serves as the foundation of the 387SX and the newest revisions of the 80287: the 287XL and 287XLT coprocessors. Much of its design is also carried over into the 486 microprocessor's floating-point section.

The 387 promises a similar degree of backward compatibility with the 80287 as the 80287 does with the 8087. The primary differences appear in error handling, mostly because of changes in the IEEE standard. These differences are easily managed by properly written software. On some problems, the 387 or 387SX may, in fact, deliver slightly different answers than would a 80287—not to the extent of adding two and two and getting 22 but deriving transcendental functions that may differ in the far right decimal place. Not that either microprocessor is wrong; the 387 and 387SX just conform better to the current IEEE standard.

Another change Intel made in updating the floating-point units of the 387 was endowing the chip with a greater range of transcendental functions, including sine, cosine, tangent, secant, and logarithmic functions. As a result, although the 387 and 387SX should be able to run all programs written for the 80287, the reverse is not necessarily true. Programs that take advantage of all the power of the 387 or 387SX may not run on the lesser chip. In general, however, code meant for the 8087 and 80287 will run on either the 387 or 387SX.

Although it can operate asynchronously, a 387 generally operates at the same speed as the 386 with which it is installed. Available versions have tracked the speed of the 386 as that microprocessor has become available in faster versions, all the way up to 33 Mhz.

The 387 even looks like a 386, only smaller. Its square 68-pin PGA (Pin Grid Array) case has the same slate-like appearance as the microprocessor. The speed rating of the chip is given in Mhz following the part number. Thus, a 387-20 is rated to operate at 20 Mhz.

The 387 design has not been static. When it became necessary to boost the 387 to 33 Mhz, further design improvements proved necessary. Intel switched from N-channel Metal Oxide Semiconductor (NMOS) technology to Complementary Metal Oxide Semiconductor (CMOS) and used new manufacturing processes that enabled details as fine as one micron to be etched in the chip's silicon. (Older 387s were limited to 1.5 micron details.) These improvements along with some tinkering in the floating-point unit itself yielded a performance improvement of about 20 percent. The same basic design is used for 50 Mhz chips.

On October 1, 1990, Intel upgraded its 16, 20, and 25 Mhz versions of the 387 chip to the same new technology used by the 33 Mhz and faster versions, giving each an extra 20 percent performance. The new chips are socket-compatible with the old and are essentially identical in appearance. The only way you can distinguish old technology 387s from new technology chips is by the numeric code under the part number. Old 387s always begin this line of 10 numbers with the letter "S." New technology chips lack the "S."

The 387SX, a math coprocessor complement for the 386SX microprocessor, was introduced in January, 1990, with this technology as well. Essentially, the 387SX is the same chip as the 387DX but was redesigned with a modified bus-interface unit to work with the 16-bit bus of the 386SX instead of a full 32-bit data bus. Intel offers versions of the 387SX to match all of its 386SX microprocessors, including speed ratings of 16, 20, and 25 Mhz.

487SX

The design of the original 486 microprocessor entirely eliminated the need for an external floating-point coprocessor. Intel simply put floating-point circuitry inside the main microprocessor (using the latest, fastest 387 design). Not only does the internal coprocessor design save a package (and eliminate the vagaries of one set of connections), but it also streamlines the communications between the main processor and coprocessor. With no external circuits to traverse, chip engineers can design an optimum transfer path operating at whatever width and speed yields the best match. Advances in chip design and fabrication technology made the more complex design possible with acceptable yields.

But not all computer chores require the power of a floating-point coprocessor. Although advancing technology enabled the incorporation of coprocessor circuitry along with the main microprocessor on the same slab of silicon, the combination was still more expensive to make than the general-purpose processor alone. Eliminating the coprocessor circuitry would enable the manufacture of a less expensive 486. In effect, the 486 without a coprocessor would be a fast 386—a chip with the benefit of the more efficient processing of the 486 but without the costly baggage of an unnecessary (for some applications) coprocessor. From this idea was born the 487SX coprocessor.

Conceptually, the 487SX is a second chance. If you bought a PC based on a 486SX and later discovered that you needed coprocessor power to get the most performance from your applications, the 487SX gave you the necessary math speed. The 486SX also enabled you to buy a less-expensive 486SX and later upgrade it to full 486DX power, spreading out the capital cost. Of course, Intel might have had more mundane reasons for introducing the 486SX—for example, it provided an outlet for 486DX chips with defective coprocessor units.

Whatever the reason for the existence of the 486SX-487SX pair, it labored under a handicap. One of the chief advantages of the 486DX was that it put microprocessor and coprocessor in a single package. The 486SX-487SX pairing split that design apart.

To sidestep that shortcoming, Intel developed a novel solution. The 487SX coprocessor is basically a 486DX in a slightly different package. The 487SX has an extra pin. Plugging in a 487SX automatically switches off the 486SX in a PC and substitutes the circuitry of the 487SX for all system operations. The extra pin on the 487SX handles this function. It also prevents your substituting a 486DX for a 487SX and vice versa. Although the 486SX chip is switched off when you install a 487SX, the 487SX design requires that you leave the 486SX in your PC. This expedient brings a benefit, for Intel, at least. You can't pry out your old 486SX and drop it into another PC, potentially eliminating another microprocessor sale for Intel.

All 487SX chips come in Pin Grid Array packages at speeds to match each of the 486SX microprocessors in the Intel line-up. Today, however, the 487SX has been rendered obsolete by Intel's OverDrive chips. For about the same price as the simple coprocessor function of the 487SX, an OverDrive chip brings clock-doubling and floating-point functions. The OverDrive is a better buy.

Strategically, the OverDrive line also gives the coprocessor competition a bigger challenge. No longer is cloning a coprocessor sufficient—the entire processor-coprocessor package must be duplicated. That's a big hurdle for the competitors to leap.

Considering the OverDrive and the poor publicity garnered by the "crippled" 486SX chip, the 487SX likely marks the end of Intel's dedicated coprocessor line. Certainly the company will manufacture coprocessors for older microprocessors as long as the market demands them (and keeps their manufacture profitable), but new floating-point units probably aren't in Intel's plans.

Compatible and Incompatible Coprocessors

The perfect product, according to apocryphal authorities, is one that costs a nickel to make, sells for a dollar, and is addictive. Coprocessors aren't quite addictive (although anything that improves the performance of your PC comes close), but otherwise fits the mold. Coprocessors, which at one time had list prices up to $1,000, cost but a few dollars to make. They represented one of the most lucrative areas of the semiconductor business. Understandably, most chip makers found crafting a successful coprocessor as alluring as a supposed sure thing would be to an inveterate gambler.

Although Intel licensed other chip makers to produce its microprocessor and coprocessor designs for the 80286 and 80287 families, the company has staunchly refused to license the 386 and 387. With the low cost of their production and high market prices, those chips proved immensely profitable for Intel—so profitable that a number of envious entrepreneurs invested in designing their own compatible products. Among these were Chips and Technology, Cyrix Corporation, Integrated Information Technology, and ULSI.

All of these coprocessors were designed through reverse engineering using "clean-room" techniques. That is, the designers don't pry into the exact layout of the original products but, instead, seek to duplicate the prototype by working back from its functions. Each of the resultant clones differs significantly from the Intel design. In fact, most compatible coprocessor manufacturers claim their products are superior to the original because of more efficient designs, aided by the big benefit of hindsight.

Although the clean-room technique sidesteps many copyright issues (the clone chips don't actually copy any part of the Intel design), they can run afoul of other legal protections instituted by Intel. For example, Intel Corporation holds many patents on chip fabrication, which it can choose to license or not. Withholding such a license can effectively block a company from making any chips, let alone clone coprocessors. Intel has asserted this protection to block some coprocessor manufacturers (successful, at least temporarily, against ULSI). It has also initiated suits against the other compatible coprocessor vendors, but has not prevented the sale of other clone chips. In true American tradition, the other vendors have responded with their own suits against Intel. As a result, clone coprocessors are shrouded with legal uncertainties.

Leave the complex legal maneuvering for the lawyers to worry about. If you buy a compatible coprocessor, you won't have to worry about the complexities of the law. No one will knock on your door and confiscate an unauthorized coprocessor. Rather, you should investigate all of your available options and take advantage of the one that suits you, your PC, and your budget best. Your choices are several.

Chips and Technologies SuperMathDX

Chipset maker Chips and Technologies broadened its product line first by releasing Intel-compatible microprocessors in 1991 and then releasing a line of 387-compatible coprocessors in 1992. The embodiment of the latter is the company's SuperMathDX line.

Although outwardly a 387, the SuperMathDX chips use an entirely different internal design. According to Chips and Technologies, the SuperMathDX chips can carry out some operations as much as six times faster than their Intel equivalents. Of course, this gain reflects only floating-point performance and gain on typical applications will be much smaller.

Socket-compatible with Intel's own 387-series of coprocessors, the SuperMathDX line uses the same 68-pin PGA package as the Intel chips. Compared to the Intel 387DX, however, the SuperMathDX line goes a bit further at the high end. Chips and Technologies coprocessors are available at speeds up to 40 Mhz.

Unique to the SuperMathDX series among today's coprocessors is on-chip power management circuitry, similar to that in laptop computer microprocessors, which reduces the power needs of the SuperMathDX chips. Typically, the chip needs about half a watt (100 milliamps at 5 volts) during operation. The SuperMathDX series conforms to the IEEE 754-1985 floating-point specification. According to Chips and Technologies, the entire series of chips is 100 percent compatible with Intel's 387 coprocessor line-up.

Cyrix 83D87

Cyrix Corporation was founded in 1988 to design and market advanced solid-state components. After the company was formed, the decision was made to develop Intel-compatible math coprocessors as its first product because of the ready market in an area that was without significant competition. The first of Cyrix's FasMath series of coprocessors were introduced in October, 1989, as the 83D87, a pin-compatible replacement for the Intel 387. A lower cost version for 386SX computers, the 83S87, was introduced in March, 1990.

The Cyrix products are designed to be completely compatible with the Intel 387 family of coprocessors. The Cyrix chips are engineered with an entirely different logic design based on the documented and undocumented functions of the Intel products. One of the most important differences is that the Cyrix chips rely more on hard-wired logic than microcode. Because of this design alternative, Cyrix chips often can achieve substantially greater speed than Intel's chips on floating-point operations.

Hard-wired logic is exactly what it sounds like. The bit patterns that make up commands directly trigger state changes in the solid-state circuitry of the chip. Each pattern (each logical instruction) must be specifically designed into the hardware of the coprocessor.

In microcode designs, instructions sent to the microprocessor cause the chip to run through several steps that make up the miniature internal program. The internal program tells the more general-purpose logic of the chip to carry out the function required of it.

The microcode design is the more structured approach. It gives the designer greater flexibility and can help get products to the market faster. The design also enables complex instruction sets to be handled by general-purpose circuits. But microcode can slow down the thinking process of the chip. Executing the microcode imposes another layer of overhead on every calculation.

On pure floating-point operations, the Cyrix chips can think nearly twice as fast as the official Intel 387 equivalents. The actual performance you get on commercial application software will show a more modest difference, however. Because of all the other operating overhead, you should expect to see only about a 10 percent difference between the Cyrix and Intel products.

Cyrix EMC87

Hoping to legitimize itself as more than merely the maker of clone chips, Cyrix has attempted to vault past the inherent limitations of I/O-mapped coprocessors by marketing its own memory-mapped design, the EMC87. Although based on the same processor architecture as the 387, with eight 80-bit registers and essentially the same command set, the EMC87 has completely revamped bus control logic. Cyrix claims a fivefold performance improvement over the Intel part. Again, however, most of the difference disappears when running actual applications because of other system overhead.

Unlike other memory-mapped coprocessors, however, Cyrix has built in complete Intel 387 compatibility in the EMC87. The Cyrix chip can operate either as I/O mapped or memory mapped, depending on the instructions given to it in your applications. With I/O mapped instructions, the Cyrix chip operates almost exactly like an Intel 387. With memory-mapped instructions, it rushes ahead in its native mode.

Of course, getting that memory-mapped speed requires software particularly written for the EMC87. Most existing applications have only Intel 387-style I/O-mapped instructions. Moreover, the EMC87 is incompatible with code written for other memory-mapped coprocessors, including the family of chips build by Weitek Corporation. Weitek and Cyrix memory-mapped chips use entirely different architectures for their floating-point units.

Because the EMC87 is memory mapped, it requires access to all the address lines used in 386 computers. Hence, it has a full complement of 121 pins and fits into the EMC socket normally reserved for a Weitek coprocessor.

Understanding the need for availability of software to create a demand for the chip, Cyrix offers a code converter that adapts assembly language code from I/O-mapped to memory-mapped instructions for the EMC87. This code-converter will work with any assembly language file, including those produced by higher level language compilers, such as Pascal or C. Although these free code converters may be interesting for software developers, they are of no value to you as an end user. They cannot convert commercial applications to make them compatible with the EMC87.

Until (and if) software publishers opt to take advantage of the EMC87, the chip will remain more a curiosity than an added enhancement. To help foster a user base, Cyrix priced the EMC87 identically with its 83D87. In that the two chips offer the same compatibility with Intel I/O-mapped instructions, the only reason to choose the 83D87 is the lack of socket accommodations in your PC for the larger EMC87.

IIT 3C87

At heart, Integrated Information Technology is a coprocessor company, producing both floating-point and video chips. Founded in 1988 by two engineers who left Intel to work for Weitek (one was actually a co-founder of Weitek), the company now offers chips compatible with Intel's 80287 and 387 using full CMOS designs based on 1.2 micron technology.

The IIT coprocessor design differs from the Intel original in that the IIT 3C87 has 32 80-bit registers instead of a mere eight. These registers are divided into four banks and are designed to facilitate 4 x 4 matrix math, which can accelerate drawing performance in graphics applications. Using just one of those four banks simulates an Intel-architecture coprocessor. Using all four requires special programs that use the IIT 4 x 4 matrix instruction.

IIT claims that the 3C87 can calculate 50 percent faster than an Intel 387 in its math functions. As with the Cyrix chips, however, actual program throughput is much more modest because of system overhead.

Unlike the Cyrix chips, the IIT coprocessor doesn't exactly duplicate the operation of the Intel 387. The exception handling of the Intel and IIT chips differs, much as it does between the 80287 and 387. Some chip makers have exploited that difference by writing special programs that show anomalous results when run on the IIT chips. With a bit of P. T. Barnum in their salesmanship, they claim that such results prove that the 3C87 is inaccurate. According to IIT, however, such odd answers only crop up when you purposely try to exacerbate the exception-handling differences by dividing by a near-zero number, such as 1,027. On normal application software, no anomalous results should appear.

IIT acknowledges that an early iteration of its 3C87 chip did have an internal bug that resulted in errors when using its arctangent operation when running AutoCAD under UNIX (and only with that application and operating system). This bug was corrected in June, 1990, and the company reports that no other problems have been reported in the 100,000 chips it has shipped.

ULSI MathCo 83C87

No longer a coprocessing contender—at least temporarily—the MathCo 83C87 from ULSI was removed from the market by legal action taken by Intel Corporation. Intel claimed that ULSI violated certain Intel chip patents in the manufacture of the 83C87, and the court agreed, enjoining ULSI from selling its chip products in early 1992.

ULSI stands for Ultra Large Scale Integration, which is the company's specialty—developing tiny products full of lots of circuitry. The

MathCo 83C87 was a reverse-engineered clone of the Intel 387. According to ULSI, the products of the MathCo 83C87 line were entirely socket-compatible with the various Intel chips that they mimic.

The ULSI products used CMOS technology and a streamlined design claimed to be more efficient than that of the Intel products. Each calculation performed by the MathCo 83C87 required fewer clock cycles than did the same operation on an Intel chip. For example, although an Intel chip requires 18 clock cycles to carry out a simple "add" instruction, the ULSI chip needed only three. Division, which takes an Intel chip about 80 cycles, was handled by the ULSI chips in 40. Of course these quicker calculations mean nothing if you cannot buy the chips, and the cloudy legal issues makes the future of the ULSI coprocessors doubtful.

Weitek 1167

Although other companies have concentrated on cloning Intel's own coprocessors, Weitek Corporation, in Sunnyvale, California, has gone its own direction, building memory-mapped coprocessors to its own standards. Founded by former Intel employees, Weitek has a better relationship with the world's favorite microprocessor maker than with the manufacturers of other clone chips. The company was formed in 1981 and, by 1985, was producing floating-point coprocessors for a variety of workstations, including those based on Motorola 68020 and Sun SPARC microprocessors. Around that time, Intel contracted with Weitek to develop a coprocessor for the 386 microprocessor. According to Weitek, the in-house Intel 387 program was behind schedule, and Weitek developed its product in parallel with the 387 team.

Unlike the 387, however, Weitek's effort was developed from multi-platform design. The initial Weitek product for the Intel environment split the one-package coprocessor into its constituent parts, using the same floating-point chips but different bus interface chips from coprocessors created for other microprocessor architectures. The first Weitek chip, the WTL1167, was consequently not a single chip but a multiple chip assembly on a small L-shaped printed circuit board. Three Weitek proprietary VLSI modules—the 1163, 1164, and 1165— were combined to create the coprocessor.

Although odd-looking and expensive, the WTL1167 has one great strength—it delivers even higher performance than the 387 on many numeric operations—in particular, CAD. Moreover, it works on all numeric operations, not just transcendental functions. According to Weitek Corporation, the WTL1167 could deliver from three to four times the performance of a 387 in machines designed to handle it. Again, such promises are meaningless because no one runs applications that exercise the coprocessor exclusively.

The Weitek WTL1167 and its successors accelerate your PC's floating-point performance purely through inherent processor efficiency, not by using an exotic command set. In fact, the Weitek chips lack both the rich command repertory and wider register width of the Intel chips. All Weitek coprocessors use 32-bit registers optimized to handle addition, subtraction, multiplication, division, negation, absolute value, comparison testing, data movement, and format conversion functions. Transcendental functions—the 387 specialty—are available through a subroutine library.

As with Intel coprocessors, the WTL1167 and other Weitek chips rely on special instructions passed to them by their host microprocessors, although those instructions are entirely different from those used by Intel's chips. The Weitek coprocessor instructions cause the host microprocessor to address certain areas of memory, well outside the range used by DOS or OS/2 programs. The addressing action itself, that is, the activation of certain patterns of these special address lines, tells the Weitek processor what operation to carry out.

The WTL1167 plugs into a special 121-pin socket with a pin out that is a superset of that used by the 387. Thus, either a 387 or WTL1167 often can be slipped into computers that use this socket.

A socket on the WTL1167 board itself provides a home for the expatriated 387, enabling you to put both chips in one system to reap the benefits of both. Even when you put both chips into your PC, however, the two coprocessors do not interact or work with one another. Instead, each one runs only the code designed specifically for it.

Weitek 3167

A three-chip design is inherently more expensive to build and less reliable than a single chip. Consequently, Weitek distilled the entire three-chip WTL1167 into a single chip, the Abacus 3167, which was introduced in April, 1988. With the exception of packaging, however, the 1167 and 3167 are essentially equivalent. They run the same applications and deliver the same performance.

Weitek 4167

In November, 1989, Weitek announced the 4167, a math coprocessor based on the 3167 but designed to enhance the Intel 486 microprocessor. According to Weitek, the 4167 can process floating-point math three to five times faster than a 486 alone, giving a 486-based PC the same math power as a RISC-based minicomputer.

The Abacus 4167 maintains full backward compatibility (Weitek calls it "full upward object-code-compatible") with the Abacus 3167 and runs all the same applications that execute on the 3167. However, the Abacus 4167 is not hardware compatible with the 3167. The 4167 offers 16 32-bit registers for adventurous programmers to play with, and requires a 142-pin socket.

The Case for and against Coprocessors

On the surface, coprocessors are a compelling concept. They show substantial performance improvements on floating-point mathematical operations, their precise design goal. If your work comprised nothing but floating-point operations, you could expect a coprocessor chip to work miracles. You would gain more speed by adding a coprocessor than from waiting for the next two or three generations of new microprocessors.

Unfortunately, no computer program—with the exception of benchmark tests and demonstrations developed by coprocessor makers—consists of nothing but floating-point operations. Even most number-intensive applications make scant use of floating-point operations.

Even on heavy-duty calculations, most applications devote only a fraction of their code to the actual math. They also need to devote time to processing display information, disk operations, and other housekeeping functions that are not aided by coprocessor operation. Consequently, only a fraction of the work done through any commercial application relies on the power of a coprocessor. Some programs have less overhead than others and thus accelerate more with the addition of a coprocessor. But all applications are sensitive to the tasks you call on them to carry out. For example, a spreadsheet used as a database will gain little from a coprocessor. Put the same program to work on financial projections, however, and the coprocessor will shift it into high gear. Consequently, the value of a coprocessor varies not only with the application that you run but with what you do with the application.

To gain any performance improvement from a coprocessor, you must have a need for transcendental functions. Typical accounting calculations don't have such requirements (unless, perhaps, you're planning for the hereafter). Engineering and scientific chores are those most likely to require transcendentals. Financial calculations that involve compound interest and the like will also take some advantage of a coprocessor.

Computer-Aided Design programs all benefit from the addition of a math coprocessor, but the advantage gained varies with the operation carried out. Loading images and screen regenerations can be handled in about half the time when a coprocessor is available. Hidden-line removal benefits only a little more than 10 percent.

No matter the application, normal data-entry performance won't change with the addition of a math coprocessor. Nor will the speed of standard DOS operations.

Whether you need a coprocessor becomes a personal choice. If you have an application that demands floating-point work, you would be foolish not to. Even with a "mere" 50-percent performance improvement on spreadsheet recalculations, there's no more cost-effective speed boost you can give to your PC. In the future, of course, a coprocessor will be unavoidable (it will be standard equipment packed inside the most powerful microprocessors).

5

Memory

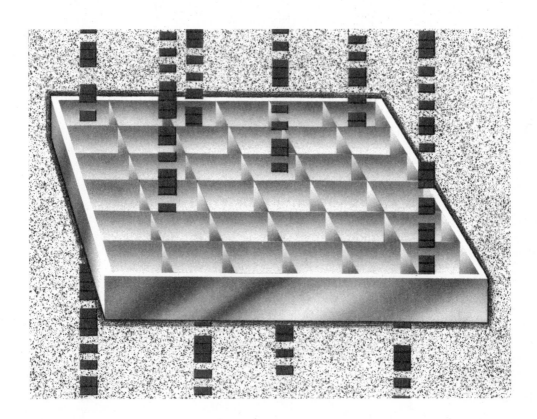

Memory is mandatory to make a microprocessor work. Memory is where all the bytes your PC's microprocessor needs to operate must be. Memory holds both the raw data that needs to be processed and the results of the processing. Memory can even be a channel of communication between the microprocessor and its peripherals. Memory comes in many types, described and delimited by function and technology. Each has its role in the proper function of your PC.

The difference between genius and mere intelligence is storage. The quick-witted react fast, but the true genius can call upon memories, experiences, and knowledge to find real answers. PCs are no different. A PC is nothing more than a switchboard without memory. Without memory, all of its reactions would have to be hard-wired in. The machine could not read through programs or retain data. It would be stuck in a persistent vegetative state, kept alive by electricity but able to react only autonomously.

A fast microprocessor is meaningless without a place instantly at hand to store programs and data for current and future use. Its internal registers can only hold a handful of bytes (and they can be slippery critters, as you know if you have tried to grab hold of one), hardly enough for a program that accomplishes anything truly useful. Memory puts hundreds, thousands, even millions of bytes at the microprocessor's disposal, enough to hold huge lists of program instructions or broad blocks of data. Without memory, a microprocessor is worthless even as a doorstop (most are too thin); with memory, a microprocessor is the herald of the information revolution.

That memory can take a variety of forms. A binary storage system, the kind used by today's PCs, can be built from marbles, marzipan, or metal-oxide semiconductors. Not all forms of memory work with equal efficacy (as you'll soon see), but the concept is the same with all of them—preserving bits of information in recognizable and usable form. Some forms of memory are just easier for an electronic microprocessor to recognize and manipulate.

The different forms of useful computer memory can be distinguished in a number of ways—for example, accessibility, function, technology, capacity, and speed.

Primary and Secondary Storage

Computer memory systems are often divided into two types: primary storage and secondary storage. Primary storage is that which is immediately accessible by the computer or microprocessor. Anything that is kept in primary storage is immediately accessible, ready to be used. This form of memory is called *on-line storage* because it is always connected to the computer, for instance, directly accessible through the address lines of a microprocessor. Because any specific part of this memory, any random byte, can be instantly found and retrieved, it is often termed *Random Access Memory* or *RAM*. No matter its name, primary storage is, in effect, the short-term memory of the computer. RAM is easy to get at but tends to be limited in capacity.

Long-term computer memory is termed *secondary storage*. Not only does this form of memory maintain information that must be kept for a long time, but also it holds the bulk of the information that the computer deals with. Secondary storage may be tens, hundreds, or thousands of times larger than primary storage. Because of its bulk, it is often termed *mass storage*. This data is held off-line and is not directly accessible by the computer. To be used, it must be transferred from secondary storage into primary storage.

Bits and Bytes

In digital computer systems, memory operates on a very simple concept. In principal, all that computer memory needs to do is preserve a single bit of information so that it can be recalled later. *Bit*, an abbreviation for *binary digit*, is the smallest possible piece of information. A bit doesn't hold much intelligence—it only indicates whether something is on or off, up or down, or something (one) or nothing (zero). However, when enough bits are taken collectively, they can code meaningful information. By storing as many single bits as needed in memory units, any amount of information can be retained.

People don't remember the same way as computers do. For us human beings, remembering a complex symbol can be as easy as storing a single bit. Although two choices may be enough for a machine, we prefer a multitude of selections. Our selection of symbols is as broad as the imagination. Fortunately for typewriter makers, however, we have reserved just a few characters as the symbol set for our language—26 uppercase letters, a matching number of lowercase letters, 10 numerals, and enough punctuation marks to keep grammar teachers preoccupied for entire careers. Representing these characters in binary form makes computers wonderfully useful. Add all those characters together and the lowest power of two that could code them all is 128 (or 27). Using an 8-bit code yields a capacity of 256 symbols, allowing all the odd diacritical marks of foreign languages and similar nonsense (at least to English speakers) to be represented by the same code. The usefulness of this 8-bit code has made eight bits the standard unit of computer storage—the ubiquitous byte.

Half a byte, a 4-bit storage unit, is called a *nibble* because, at least in the beginning of the personal computer revolution, engineers had senses of humor. Four bits can encode 16 symbols—enough for 10 numerals and six operators (addition, subtraction, multiplication, division, exponents, and square roots), making the unit useful for numbers-only devices, such as hand held calculators.

The generalized term for a package of bits is the *digital word*, which can comprise any number of bits that a computer might use as a group. The term *word* has developed a more specific meaning in the field of PCs, however. It refers to two bytes of data, 16 bits. A double word comprises two words, 32 bits.

To remember a single bit—whether alone or as part of a nibble, byte, word, or double word—computer memory needs only to preserve a single state, that is, whether something is true or false, positive or negative, a binary one or zero. Almost anything can suffice to remember a single state, whether a marble is in one pile or another, whether a dab of marzipan is eaten or molding on the shelf, whether an electrical charge is present or absent. The only need is that the memory unit has two possible states and that it will maintain itself in one of them once it is put there. Should a memory element change on its own, randomly, it would be useless because it does not preserve the information that it's supposed to keep. Although possibilities of what can be used for remembering a single state are nearly endless, how the bits are to be used makes some forms of memory more practical than others. The two states must be both readily changeable and readily recognizable by whatever mechanism is to use them. For example, a string tied around your finger will help you remember a bit state but would be inconvenient to store information for a machine. Whatever the machine, it would need a mechanical hand to tie the knot and some means of detecting its presence on your finger—a video camera, precision radar set, or even a gas chromatography system.

Random Access Memory

In digital computers, it is helpful to store a state electrically so that the machine doesn't need eyes or hands to check for the string, marble, or marzipan. Possible candidates for electrical state-saving systems include those that depend on whether an electrical charge is present or whether a current will flow. Both of these techniques are used in computer memories for primary storage systems.

The analog of electricity, magnetism, can also be readily manipulated by electrical circuits and computers. In fact, a form of magnetic memory called *core* was the chief form of primary storage for the first generation of mainframe computers. Some old-timers still call primary storage *core memory* because of this history. Today, however, magnetic storage is mostly reserved for mass storage because magnetism is one step removed from electricity. Storage devices have to convert electricity to magnetism to store bits and magnetic fields to electrical pulses to read them. The conversion process takes time, energy, and effort—all of which pay off for long-term storage (at which magnetism excels), but are unnecessary for the many uses inside the computer.

Primary storage has one important characteristic. Any of the basic units of storage can be instantly retrieved when it is needed. The microprocessor does not have to read through a huge string of data to find what it needs. Instead, it can zero in on any storage unit at random. Consequently, this kind of memory is termed *Random Access Memory*. More common is the acronym *RAM*.

Dynamic Memory

The most common memory inside today's personal computers brings RAM to life using minute electrical charges to remember memory states. Charges are stored in small capacitors. The archetypical capacitor comprises two metal plates separated by a small distance that's filled with an electrical insulator. A positive charge can be applied to one plate and, because opposite charges attract, it draws a negative charge to the other nearby plate. The insulator separating the plates prevents the charges from mingling and neutralizing each other.

The capacitor can function as memory because a computer can control whether the charge is applied to or removed from one of the capacitor plates. The charge on the plates can thus store a single state and a single bit of digital information.

In a perfect world, the charges on the two plates of a capacitor would forever hold themselves in place. One of the imperfections in the real world results in no insulator being perfect. There's always some possibility that a charge will sneak through any material. Although better insulators lower the likelihood, they cannot eliminate it entirely. Moreover, the circuitry that charges and discharges the capacitor also allows some of the charge to leak off.

This system seems to violate the primary principal of memory—it won't reliably retain information for very long. Fortunately, this capacitor-based system can remember long enough to be useful—a few milliseconds—before the disappearing charges make the memory unreliable. Those few milliseconds are long enough that practical circuits can be designed to periodically recharge the capacitor and refresh the memory. Because the changing nature of this form of memory and its need to be actively maintained by refreshing, it is termed *dynamic memory*. Integrated circuits that provide this kind of memory are termed *dynamic RAM* or *DRAM* chips.

In actual personal computer memories, special semiconductor circuits that act like capacitors are used instead of actual capacitors with metal plates. A large number of these circuits are combined to make a dynamic memory integrated circuit chip. As with true capacitors, however, dynamic memory of this type must be periodically refreshed.

Static Memory

Although dynamic memory tries to trap evanescent electricity and hold it in place, static memory allows the current flow to continue on its way, altering the path taken by the power, using one of two possible courses of travel to mark the state being remembered. Static memory operates as a switch that potentially allows or halts the flow of electricity.

A simple mechanical switch will, in fact, suffice as a form of static memory. The switch, alas, has the handicap that it must be manually toggled from one position to another by a human or robotic hand.

A switch that can be controlled by electricity is called a *relay*. Relay technology was one of the first used for computer memories. The typical relay circuit provides a latch. Applying a voltage to the relay energizes it, causing it to switch from not permitting electricity to flow to allowing it. Part of the electrical flow can be used to keep the relay energized, which would, in turn, maintain the electrical flow. Like a door latch, this kind of relay circuit stays locked until some force or signal causes it to change, opening the door or the circuit.

Transistors, which can behave as switches, can also be wired to act as latches. A large number of these transistor circuits miniaturized and combined make a static memory chip. *Static RAM* is often shortened to *SRAM* by computer professionals.

Read-Only Memory

Note that both the relay and the transistor latch must have a constant source of electricity to maintain their latched state. If the current supplying them falters, the latch will relax, and the circuit will forget. Similarly, if dynamic memory is not constantly refreshed, it also forgets. When the electricity is removed from either type of memory circuit, the information that it held simply evaporates, leaving nothing behind. Consequently, these electrically dependent memory systems are called *volatile*. A constant supply of electricity is necessary for them to maintain their integrity. Lose the electricity, and the memory loses its contents.

Not all memory must be endowed with the capability to be changed. Just as there are many memories that you would like to retain—your first love, the names of all the stars in the Zodiac, the answers to the chemistry exam—a computer is better off when it can remember some particularly important things without regard to the vagaries of the power line. Perhaps the most important of these more permanent rememberings is the program code that tells a microprocessor that it's actually part of a computer and how it should carry out its duties.

In the old-fashioned world of relays, you could permanently set memory in one position or another by careful application of a hammer. With enough assurance and impact, you could guarantee that the system would never forget. In the world of solid-state, the principal is the same, but the programming instrument is somewhat different. All that you need are switches that don't switch—or, more accurately, that switch once and jam. This permanent kind of memory is so valuable in computers that a whole family of devices called *Read-Only Memory* or *ROM* chips has developed. They are called read-only because the computer that they are installed in cannot store new code in them. Only what is already there can be read from the memory.

In contrast, the other kind of memory to which the microprocessor can write as well as read is logically termed *Read-Write Memory*. That term is, however, rarely used. Instead, read-write memory goes by the name RAM even though ROM also allows random access to its contents.

Mask ROM

If ROM chips cannot be written by the computer, the information inside must come from somewhere. In one kind of chip, the *mask ROM*, the information is built into the memory chip at the time it is fabricated. The mask is a master pattern that's used to draw the various circuit elements on the chip during fabrication. When the circuit elements of the chip are grown on the silicon substrate, the pattern includes the information that will be read in the final device. Nothing, other than a hammer blow or its equivalent in destruction, can alter what is contained in this sort of memory.

Mask ROMs are not common in personal computers because they require that their programming be carried out when the chips are manufactured; changes are not easy to make, and the quantities that must be made to make things affordable are daunting.

PROM

One alternative to a mask ROM is the *Programmable Read-Only Memory* chip or *PROM*. This style of circuit consists of an array of elements that work like fuses. Too much current flowing through a fuse causes the fuse element to overheat, melt, and interrupt the current flow, protecting equipment and wiring from overloads. Normally, the fuses in a PROM conduct electricity just like the fuses that protect your home electrical disaster. Like ordinary fuses, the fuses in a PROM can be blown to stop the electrical flow. All it takes is a strong enough electrical current, supplied by a special machine called a PROM programmer or PROM burner. PROM chips are manufactured and delivered with all of their fuses intact. The PROM is then customized for its given application using a PROM programmer to blow the fuses one by one, according to the needs of the software to be coded inside the chip. This process is usually termed *burning* the PROM.

As with most conflagrations, the effects of burning a PROM are permanent. The chip cannot be changed to update or revise the program inside. PROMs are definitely not something for people who can't make up their minds or for a fast changing industry.

EPROM

Happily, technology has brought an alternative to the PROM, the *Erasable Programmable Read-Only Memory* chip or *EPROM*. Sort of self-healing semiconductors, the data inside an EPROM can be erased, and the chip can be reused for other data or programs.

EPROM chips are easy to spot because they have a clear window in the center of the top of their packages. Invariably this window is covered with a label of some kind, and with good reason. The chip is erased by shining high-intensity ultraviolet light through the window. If stray light should leak through the window, the chip could be inadvertently erased. (Normal room light won't erase the chip because it contains very little ultraviolet. Bright sunshine does, however, and can erase EPROMs.) Because of their versatility, permanent memory, and easy reprogrammability, EPROMs are ubiquitous inside personal computers.

EEPROM

A related chip is call *Electrically Erasable Programmable Read-Only Memory* or *EEPROM* (usually pronounced "double-E PROM"). Instead of requiring a strong source of ultraviolet light, EEPROMs need only a higher than normal voltage (and current) to erase their contents. This electrical erasability brings an important benefit: EEPROMs can be erased and reprogrammed without popping them out of their sockets. EEPROM gives electrical devices, such as computers and their peripherals, a means of storing data without the need for a constant supply of electricity.

EEPROM has one chief shortcoming: it can be erased only a finite number of times. Although most EEPROM chips will withstand tens or hundreds of thousands of erase-and-reprogram cycles, that's not good enough for general storage in a PC that might be changed thousands of times each time you use your machine. This problem is exacerbated by the manner in which EEPROM chips are erased—unlike ordinary RAM chips in which you can alter any bit whenever you like, erasing an EEPROM means eliminating its entire contents and reprogramming every bit all over again. Change any one bit in an EEPROM, and the life of every bit of storage is shortened.

Flash RAM

A new twist to EEPROM is *Flash RAM*. Instead of requiring special, higher voltages to be erased, Flash RAM can be erased and reprogrammed using the normal voltages inside a PC. For system designers, that makes Flash RAM easy to use. Unfortunately, Flash RAM is handicapped by the same limitation as EEPROM—its life is finite (although longer than ordinary EEPROM) and (in most but not all cases) it must be erased and reprogrammed as a block.

The convenience of using Flash RAM has led many developers to create disk emulators from it. For most effective operation and longest life, however, these emulators require special operating systems (or modified versions of familiar operating systems) that minimize the number of erase-and-reprogramming cycles.

Memory Operation

No matter the type of memory—RAM or ROM, dynamic or static, erasable or flash—it all works the same. Essentially, memory is an elaborate set of pigeon holes like the post office workers use to sort local mail. A memory location, called an *address*, is assigned to each piece of information to be stored. Each address corresponds to one pigeon hole, unambiguously identifying the location of each unit of storage. The address is a label, not the storage location itself (which is actually a tiny electronic capacitor, latch, or fuse).

Because the address is most often in binary code, the number of bits available in the code determines how many such unambiguous addresses can be directly accessed in a memory system. An 8-bit address code permits 256 distinct memory location ($2^8 = 256$). A 16-bit address code can unambiguously define 16,256 locations ($2^{16} = 16,256$). The available address codes generally correspond to the number of address lines of the microprocessor in the computer, although, strictly speaking, they need not.

The amount of data stored at each memory location depends on the basic storage unit, which varies with the design of the computer system. Generally, each location contains the same number of bits that the computer processes at one time—so an 8-bit computer (like the original PC) stores a byte at each address, and a 32-bit machine keeps a full double word at each address.

The smallest individually addressable unit of today's 32-bit Intel microprocessors—the 386 and 486—is actually four double words, 16 bytes, a unit Intel calls a line of memory. Smaller memory units cannot be individually retrieved because the four least-significant address lines are absent from these microprocessors.

Most PCs that follow the IBM standard actually use more bits for each storage unit than these examples describe. IBM adds one extra bit called a *parity check bit* to every byte of storage. The parity check bit allows the computer to verify the integrity of the data stored in memory. When a byte is written into memory, the value stored in the parity check bit is set either to a logical one or zero in such a way that the total of all nine bits storing the byte is always odd. Every time memory is read, the PC totals up the nine bits of each byte, verifying that the total remains odd. Should the system detect an even total, it immediately knows that something has happened to cause one bit of the byte to change, making the stored data invalid.

Because IBM's engineers believe that having bad data is worse than losing information through a system crash—wrong data can result in erroneous paychecks, incorrect inventory reports, and bridges collapsing; a crash immediately notifies you that something is wrong—most PCs are designed to shut down when incorrect parity is discovered. If your system finds a wrong parity total in motherboard memory, it automatically displays the ominous message Parity Check 1 on your monitor screen and freezes its operations. A wrong total on expansion board memory elicits a Parity Check 2 error with the same fatal failing.

Parity checking can only locate an error of one bit in a byte. More elaborate error-detection schemes can detect larger errors. Better still, when properly implemented, these schemes can fix single-bit errors without crashing your system. Called *Error Correction Code* or *ECC*, this scheme in its most efficient form requires three extra bits per byte of storage. The additional bits allow your system not only to determine the occurrence of a memory error but to locate any single bit that changed so that the error can be reversed.

IBM uses ECC on its larger computers. The memories in PCs were small and reliable enough that the company's engineers did not feel the additional expense of ECC bits were justified. However, as total system capacities stretch beyond 16M, ECC may become a standard part of the memory systems of some PCs.

Memory chips do not connect directly to the microprocessor's address lines. Instead, special circuits that comprise the memory controller translate the binary data sent to the memory address register into the form necessary to identify the memory location requested and to retrieve the data there. The memory controller can be as simple as address decoding logic circuitry or an elaborate application-specific integrated circuit that combines several memory-enhancing functions.

To read memory, the microprocessor activates the address lines corresponding to the address code of the wanted memory unit during one clock cycle. This action acts as a request to the memory controller to find the needed data. During the next clock cycle, the memory controller puts the bits of code contained in the desired storage unit on the microprocessor's data bus. This operation takes two cycles because the memory controller can't be sure that the address code is valid until the end of a clock cycle. Likewise, the microprocessor cannot be sure that the data is valid until the end of the next clock cycle. Consequently, all memory operations take at least two clock cycles.

Writing to memory works similarly—the microprocessor first sends off the address to write to, the memory controller finds the proper pigeon hole, and then the microprocessor sends out the data to be written. Again, the minimum time required is two cycles of the microprocessor clock.

Reading or writing can take substantially longer than two cycles, however, because microprocessor technology has pushed into performance territory far beyond the capabilities of today's affordable DRAM chips. Slower system memory can make the system microprocessor and the rest of the PC stop while it catches up, extending the memory read/write time by one or more clock cycles.

Memory Speed

Memory speed deficiencies first appeared when IBM introduced the first AT computers with 80286 microprocessors. Ordinary memory chips could not keep pace with the speed of such a fast (by the standards of 1984) microprocessor. The 80286 could request bytes in such short order that memory was unable to respond. Consequently, wait states were added when the microprocessor requested information for memory.

A *wait state* is exactly what it sounds like; the microprocessor suspends whatever it's doing for one or more clock cycles to give the memory circuits a chance to catch up. The number of wait states required in a system depend on the speed of the microprocessor in relation to the speed of memory.

Microprocessor speeds are usually expressed as a frequency in Mhz, millions of cycles per second. Memory chips are rated by time in nanoseconds, billionths of a second. The two measurements are reciprocal. At a speed of 1 Mhz, one clock cycle is 1,000 nanoseconds long; 8 Mhz equals 125 nanoseconds; 16 Mhz, 62.5 nanoseconds; 20 Mhz, 50 nanoseconds; 25 Mhz, 40 nanoseconds; and so on.

Dynamic memory chips are speed-rated; the number usually is emblazoned on the chip following its model designation. The number reflects the access time of the chip given in nanoseconds with the rightmost zero left off to make the expression a little more compact. Hence, a chip that has -12 on it has an access time of 120 nanoseconds.

If this were the number of merit for chip speed, most of today's computers would have no problem. At 25 Mhz, for instance, one clock cycle is 40 nanoseconds, and the microprocessor requires at least two cycles between memory operations, a total of 80 nanoseconds. Chips rated at 70 nanoseconds are readily available and relatively inexpensive. In general, you'll do no harm installing quicker chips than a computer calls for, for instance putting 70 nanosecond chips into a system that calls for 80 nanosecond parts. The only detriment is that faster chips will likely cost you more—you'll be paying for speed that you don't need. Slower chips may not work or, more likely, work sporadically, leaving you vulnerable to parity check errors at unexpected times. The access time is not the only—or the most important—figure to describe a memory chip, however. More relevant is the cycle time, which does measure how quickly two back-to-back accesses can be made to the chip. The cycle time is generally about two to three times the access time of the chip. Hence, even an 70-nanosecond DRAM chip is not capable of reliably serving a 25 Mhz PC.

Static RAM chips have no need to be refreshed. Not only do their cycle times equal their access times, but they can operate faster. Static chips are readily available with ratings of 25 or 35 nanoseconds; the fastest common DRAM chips are rated at 60 or 70 nanoseconds. Unfortunately, because static chips are much more expensive than DRAM, static chips rarely are used for the primary storage of PCs.

To cope with the speed limitations of affordable DRAM memory chips, PC makers use a number of designs for their memory system. The most straightforward of these designs is simply to use the fastest possible chips, but even today's quickest DRAM chips lag far behind a 50 or 66 Mhz microprocessor. Another quick fix is to impose as many wait states as necessary—with not-so-quick results. A single wait state extends a normal memory cycle from two to three clock ticks—that's a big performance hit. With one wait state, a PC would operate at only two-thirds its potential speed. Two wait states cut performance in half.

Page-Mode RAM

A better way around the problem of speed mismatch is to look to technology. Special RAM chips that combine features of both dynamic and static memory can cut the effects of wait-states down to size. Two hybrid technologies have been used by PCs: page-mode RAM and static-column RAM.

Page-mode RAM chips allow part—but not all—of their storage to be read without wait states. These chips divide their total address range into smaller sections called pages. Each individual page can be accessed repeatedly without the imposition of wait states. Back-to-back accesses to different pages require wait states but no more than standard DRAM rated at the same speed.

Static-column RAM chips split their memory into rows and columns. Back-to-back accesses within a column can be made without wait states. Memory accesses crossing the boundaries between memory columns require the addition of wait states.

Technically, page-mode and static-column RAM are distinct chip technologies. In the static-column RAM arrangement, memory is logically laid out as a two-dimensional array, and sequential memory bits are organized in adjacent rows within a single column. Page-mode RAM chips break the total chip capacity into a number of pages, usually containing two kilobits. Despite this physical difference, in most practical applications, the two technologies yield exactly the same results: repeated accesses within a given range occur without wait states. In that most of the time programs require sequential bytes (the next instruction in a sequence or the adjacent character of data), this wait-state cutting technique is particularly effective. Wait state reductions of 60 percent or more are readily achieved.

The performance of static-column or page-mode memory systems depends on the page or column size that's used. The larger the page, the more likely the next bit of memory will be inside it and the better the chances of reading it without wait states. The performance improvement can be dramatic. Most programs execute within the limits of a 2K page most of the time, so overall system performance is boosted to near what it would be if system RAM was entirely static.

Banked Memory

Another clever technique, called *interleaved memory*, is like page-mode RAM in that it picks up speed on sequential memory accesses, but it does not suffer the limitation of small page sizes. Interleaved memory works by dividing the total RAM of a system into two or more banks. Sequential bits are held in alternate banks, so the microprocessor goes back and forth between banks when it reads sequential bytes. Although one bank is being read, the other is cycling so that the microprocessor does not have to wait. Of course, if the microprocessor must read logically noncontiguous bits, whether it encounters wait states is governed by the laws of probability.

In a typical interleaved memory system, system RAM will be divided into two banks, so the probability of encountering a wait state is about 50 percent. A four-way interleave can reduce wait-states by 75 percent.

Because interleaved memory does not require special memory chips, it is perhaps the most affordable method of speeding up system operation. Memory interleaving can also be combined with page-mode memory chips to further enhance system performance. Of course, you need an even number of memory banks to achieve a two-way interleave. With today's 32-bit microprocessors, the smallest single bank is typically 4 megabytes. Such systems often require 8 megabytes for a simple two-way interleave, 16 megabytes for four-way.

Memory Caching

With today's highest-performance microprocessors, the most popular memory-matching technique is *memory caching*. A memory cache interposes a block of fast memory (typically high-speed static RAM) between the microprocessor and the bulk of primary storage. A special circuit called a *cache controller* attempts to keep the cache filled with the data or instructions that the microprocessor is most likely to need next. If the information the microprocessor requests next is held within the static RAM of the cache, it can be retrieved without wait states. This fastest possible operation is called a *cache hit*. If the needed data is not in the cache memory, it is retrieved from ordinary RAM at ordinary RAM speed. The result is called a *cache miss*. Not all memory caches are created equal. Memory caches differ in size, logical arrangement, location, and operation.

A major factor that determines how successful the cache will be is how much information it contains. The larger the cache, the more data that will be in it, and the more likely any needed byte will be there when it's needed. Obviously, the best cache is one that's as large as and duplicates the entire system memory. Of course, a cache that big is also absurd. You could use the cache as primary memory and forget the rest. The smallest cache would be a byte, also an absurd situation because it guarantees the next read is not in the cache. Practical caches range from a 8K (as used internally by the 486 microprocessor) to 512K. Today, caches around 64K are the most favored.

The disadvantage of a larger cache is cost. More fast SRAM chips inevitably cost more, pushing up the overall cost of the system. Some manufacturers give you an option, scalable caches that allow you to start small and add more SRAM as you can afford it. If you expect to find the end of a rainbow sometime after buying your new 486, such a system deserves consideration.

The logical configuration of a cache involves how the memory in the cache is arranged and how it is addressed—that is, how the microprocessor determines whether needed information is available inside the cache. There are three major choices: direct-mapped, full associative, and set-associative.

The direct-mapped cache divides the fast SRAM of the cache into small units called lines (corresponding to the lines of storage used by Intel 32-bit microprocessors), each of which is identified by an index bit. Main memory is divided into blocks the size of the cache, and the lines in the cache correspond to the locations within such a memory block. Each line can be drawn from a different memory block, but only from the location corresponding to the location in the cache. Which block the line is drawn from is identified by a tag. For the cache controller (the electronics that ride herd on the cache) determining whether a given byte is stored in a direct-mapped cache is easy—just check the tag for a given index value.

The problem with the direct-mapped cache is that if a program regularly moves between addresses with the same indexes in different blocks of memory, the cache will need to be continually refreshed, which means cache misses. Although such operation is uncommon, it does slow down a direct-mapped cache.

The opposite design approach is the full-associative cache. In this design, each line of the cache can correspond to (or be associated with) any part of main memory. Lines of bytes from diverse locations throughout main memory can be piled cheek-by-jowl in the cache. The major shortcoming of the full-associative approach is that the cache controller must check the addresses of every line in the cache to determine whether a memory request from the microprocessor is a hit or miss.

A compromise between direct-mapped and full-associative caches is the set-associative cache, which essentially divides the total cache memory into several smaller direct-mapped areas. The cache is described as the number of "ways" it is divided into. Hence, a four-way set-associative cache resembles four smaller direct-mapped caches. This arrangement overcomes the problem of moving between blocks with the same indexes. Consequently, the set-associative cache has more performance potential than a direct-mapped cache. Unfortunately, the set-associative cache is also more complex, making the technology more expensive to implement. Moreover, the more "ways" there are to a cache, the longer the cache controller must search to determine whether needed information is in the cache. This ultimately slows down the cache, mitigating the advantage of splitting it into sets. Most

PC makers find a four-way set-associative cache to be the optimum compromise between performance and complexity.

Caches can be either internal or external to the microprocessor they serve. An internal cache is often also termed a *primary cache* and is built into the microprocessor's circuitry like the 8K cache of the 486 series of microprocessors. An external or secondary cache uses an external cache controller and memory chips. The primary cache holds more speed-up potential than a secondary cache because of its direct connection with the internal circuitry of the microprocessor. In 486 microprocessors, for example, the data path between the internal cache and the rest of the microprocessor is one line (16 bytes or 128 bits) wide. A transfer between the cache and microprocessor still requires two cycles, but in those two cycles all 16 bytes can be transferred. Because the 486 microprocessor has only 32 data lines, those same 128 bits normally would require four times longer (eight cycles) to transfer.

Some secondary caches are implemented with 128-bit buses and take advantage of a streamlined addressing mode of the 486 that allows four sequential data transfers without intervening address cycles. In other words, to move the cache data into the microprocessor takes five cycles (one address and four data transfers) instead of eight (four alternating address and data cycles). The internal cache still has a two-to-five performance advantage over this advanced addressing mode.

The shortcoming of the primary cache is capacity. The 8K internal cache of the 486 microprocessor occupies about one-third of the silicon used by the chip. Making it any larger would add prohibitively to the expense of making the microprocessor.

Sometimes, primary caches are divided functionally into instruction caches and data caches. The instruction cache stores only microprocessor instructions, and the data cache holds only data. This segregation can yield improvements in overall performance and is used effectively by some Motorola microprocessors. The Intel 486 uses a single, integrated cache for data and instructions.

Caches also differ in the way they treat writing to memory. Most caches make no attempt to speed up write operations. Instead, they push write commands through the cache immediately, writing to cache and main memory (with normal wait-state delays) at the same time. This write-through cache design is the safe approach because it guarantees that main memory and cache are constantly in agreement.

The quicker alternative is the write-back cache, which allows the microprocessor to write changes to cache memory, which the cache controller eventually writes back to main memory as time allows. The problem with the write-back cache is that there are times when main memory and the cache have different contents assigned to the same memory locations—for example when a hard disk is read and information is transferred into memory through a control system (the DMA system) that does not involve the microprocessor. The cache controller must constantly check the changes made in main memory and ensure that the contents of the cache properly track such alteration. This "snooping" capability makes the design of a controller more complex and, hence, expensive. For the utmost in performance, however, the write-back cache is the optimum design.

One preferred solution is to delegate all responsibilities for supervising the cache to dedicated circuits designed for that purpose. In the PC environment, a number of cache controller chips are available. Some chip sets also incorporate memory caching into their circuitry (see Chapter 8).

Video Memory

Memory access problems are particularly prone to appear in video systems. Memory is used in display systems as a frame buffer in which the on-screen image is stored in digital form with one unit of memory (be it a bit, byte, or several bytes) assigned to each element of the picture. The entire contents of the frame buffer is read from 44 to 75 times a second as the stored image is displayed on the monitor screen. All the while, your PC may be attempting to write new picture information into the buffer to appear on the screen.

With normal DRAM chips, these read and write operations cannot occur simultaneously. One has to wait for the other. The waiting negatively affects video performance, your system's speed, and your patience.

The wait can be avoided with special memory chips that have a novel design twist—two paths for accessing each storage location. With two access paths, this memory acts like a warehouse with two doors. Your processor can push bytes into the warehouse through one door while the video system pulls them out through another. Strictly speaking, this memory can take two forms. True dual-ported memory allows simultaneous reading and writing; video memory chips (often called VRAM for Video Random Access Memory) gives one access port full read and write random access while the other port only allows sequential reading (which corresponds to the needs of scanning of a video image).

Memory Location

One memory speed issue arises not from semiconductor technology but from system design. Where memory is located and how it is connected to the system microprocessor can have a dramatic effect on memory performance.

Memory is usually connected to the microprocessor's local bus. That means that the memory runs at the microprocessor's clock speed and connects through a bus as wide as the microprocessor's data bus. Many motherboards lack sufficient space for memory expansion and, consequently, relegate expansion memory to daughterboards. These daughterboards can link to the motherboard either with a proprietary connection that operates at full microprocessor speed and bus width or through a standard expansion bus, such as ISA, EISA, or Micro Channel.

The first kind of memory boards, which are often termed *proprietary memory boards*, generally impose no performance penalty on expansion memory. The latter boards can impose severe penalties in all systems more powerful than 8 Mhz AT compatibles. Higher speed machines (those with microprocessors operating in excess of 8 Mhz) suffer severely when memory is added through expansion slots. The slots typically operate at 8 Mhz or so, notwithstanding the higher speed of the microprocessor. Accessing this add-in memory thus requires the system to slow down to the 8 Mhz rate. A 66 Mhz machine would be effectively slowed to one-eighth speed when accessing expansion board memory.

The memory in classic AT bus slots imposes an additional slowdown on 386DX and 486 microprocessors because of the maximum 16-bit width of the bus. Because the memory bus would be only half the width of the microprocessor data bus, transferring data from memory to microprocessor automatically takes twice as long as it would with the full 32-bit connection used by motherboard and proprietary memory board RAM.

The simple rule is to keep memory out of normal expansion slots in any PC faster than an 8 Mhz AT if you want full performance. In some cases, however, sliding a few megabytes into an expansion slot makes good sense, such as when you have no other expansion, when a specialized application doesn't require the utmost in memory speed, or you already have a memory expansion board.

Some PCs have limited motherboard expansion capabilities and slotted memory may be the only kind that you can add. An all too common scenario is the system board that uses a proprietary memory expansion board, and you cannot acquire the needed proprietary board because the manufacturer is unreachable, out of business, or never bothered to make the boards in the first place.

If you just need a RAM disk to speed up program compiles or database sorts, expansion board memory may suffice. Although the RAM drive would not be as fast as one created using motherboard memory, it would nevertheless far out race any mechanical disk drive.

If you already have a populated memory expansion board, there's no reason not to put it to work if your PC will accept the board. As long as you configure the memory on the board to be addressed above the top of all system board memory, it will be the last to be used by your applications. Only when a program needs every last byte will it reach into slow-down territory. Certainly, performance will suffer at that point, but you'll be able to run software you wouldn't otherwise be able to.

Moreover, if you're using an environment like Windows that takes advantage of virtual memory techniques, the slow slotted memory will still outperform the virtual memory that is emulated by a mechanical disk drive. Although such slotted memory is not an ideal solution, it can be acceptable, affordable, and workable.

Logical Memory Organization

Although it may be made from the same kind of chips, not all memory in a PC works in the same way. Some programs are restricted to using only a fraction of the available capacity; some memory is off-limits to all programs.

Memory handling is, of course, determined by the microprocessor used to build a computer. Through the years, however, the Intel microprocessors used in PCs have dramatically improved their memory capabilities. In less than seven years, the microprocessor-mediated memory limitation was pushed upward by a factor of four thousand, far beyond the needs of any program written or even conceived (at least today).

But neither PCs nor applications have kept up with the memory capabilities of microprocessors. Part of the reason for this divergence has to do with some arbitrary design decisions made by IBM when creating the original PC. But the true underlying explanation is your own expectations. You expect that new PCs will be compatible with the old, run the same programs and use most of the same expansion hardware. To achieve that expected degree of compatibility, the defects and limitations of the original PC's memory system have been carried forward for ensuing generations to enjoy. A patchwork of improvements adds new capabilities without sacrificing (much of) this backward compatibility, but they further confuse the PC's past memories. The result is that PCs are stuck with a hierarchy of memory types, each with different capabilities and compatibilities—some useful to some applications, some useless to all but a few. Rather than improving with age, every advance adds more to the memory mix up.

Conventional Memory

Once upon a time, there was only one kind of memory to worry about, the kind of memory that your programs could use. There was only one operating system anyone was concerned about, DOS. Under DOS strictures, only 640K was available to your programs. For years, all programs abided by this 640K DOS memory limit. Since those early days, however, programs and operating systems have changed, as have your memory concerns. Although strictly speaking, DOS (starting with Version 5.0) is no longer confined to using just 640K of RAM, many familiar applications remain bound by the original DOS constraints.

The DOS memory limit cannot be credited to the crafters of the operating system, but rather was thrust on them by the design of the original PC. The PC's limit was, in turn, caused by a combination of pragmatic engineering and microprocessor limits.

To be used by a microprocessor, memory must be addressable. The 8088 microprocessor around which the PC was built imposed a memory addressing limit of one megabyte. As noted in Chapter 4, this one megabyte is termed *real mode memory*.

Out of this basic one-megabyte addressing range, IBM's engineers reserve certain sections for special system functions. In the initial design of the PC, just over half of its memory was reserved. The top half of the 8088 address range, 512K, was given over to providing an addressing range for the system's BIOS code and direct microprocessor access to the memory used by the video system. The first few kilobytes were reserved for specific hardware and operation system functions, to provide space for remembering information about the system and the location of certain sections of code that are executed when specific software interrupts are made.

The purposes assigned to each address range of memory can be charted to give a visual representation of memory usage. The result is a chart called a *memory map*. Figure 5.1 shows a memory map of the original IBM PC.

Even though 512K seemed generous in the days when 64K was the most memory other popular computers could use, the stinginess wastefulness of the original limit soon became apparent. Less than a year after the original PC was introduced, IBM engineers rethought their memory division and decided that an extra 128K could safely be reassigned to program access. That change left 384K at the upper end of the address range for use by video memory and BIOS routines.

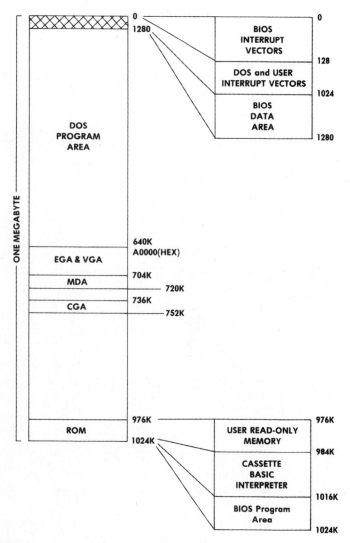

Figure 5.1. Memory map of the PC and XT.

This division persists, leaving us with the lower 640K addressing range assigned to the DOS Memory Area, also termed *conventional memory*. This range corresponds to the maximum contiguous memory area within the addressing range of the 8088 microprocessor and represents the extent of addresses that normal DOS programs can access. The design of DOS constrains programs to using memory that is logically contiguous. DOS permits programs to address any memory within an upper and lower bound (which it defines based on available memory and its assignment to utility functions). If there were a hole in DOS memory, for example, a range of addresses that did not correspond to memory chips, a program might inadvertently try to use the nonexistent range with deleterious results. The program (and your system) would crash. Until the advent of modern memory management hardware and software, this need for logical memory contiguity meant that DOS applications could only use 640K of RAM no matter how much memory was installed in your PC.

The upper limit to the DOS memory area is set by IBM's assignment of VGA memory, which begins immediately after the DOS 640K. The memory assigned to the original monochrome display system starts 64K higher. Some memory expansion boards and memory managers take advantage of the placement of monochrome display memory by giving DOS access to the 64K range used by VGA. With a propitious hardware/software combination, DOS and the applications that run under it can thus have access to a 704K range of RAM.

The lower limit to the DOS addressing range does not start at the first memory address because IBM has reserved some of this area for storing information needed by DOS and your programs. Included among the bytes at the bottom of the addressing range are interrupt vectors, pointers that tell the microprocessor the addresses used by each interrupt it needs to service. Also kept in these bottom bytes is the keyboard buffer, 16 bytes of storage that hold the code of the last 16 characters you pressed on the keyboard. This temporary storage allows the computer to accept your typing while it's temporarily busy on other tasks. The computer can then go back and process your characters when it's not as busy. The angry beeping your PC makes sometimes when you hold down one key for too long is the machine's way of complaining that the keyboard buffer is full and that it has no place to put the latest characters, which it will refuse to accept until it can free some buffer space. In addition, various system flags, indicators of internal system conditions that can be equated to the code of semaphore flags, are stored in this low memory range.

The hardware design of the PC restricts not just DOS but all operating systems to using only 640K of real mode memory. Consequently, the bottom 640K of memory is often described with the more general term *base memory*. Base memory is the standard foundation on which all IBM-compatible systems must be built.

Extended Memory

Memory beyond the megabyte addressable by the 8088 that can be accessed through the protected mode of the 80286 and 80386 microprocessors is generally termed *extended memory*. Up to 15M of extended memory can be added to a 286-based computer; nearly four gigabytes to a 386 or 486.

The usefulness of extended memory to DOS applications varies with the microprocessor installed in a PC. Only protected mode applications can use extended memory in 286 machines. But with 386 and later microprocessors, virtual 8086 mode allows software to split extended memory into one megabyte or smaller ranges that each act like base memory of an individual PC.

To be useful to DOS and its applications, using extended memory for virtual 8086 mode requires some kind of memory-management software. DOS versions before 5.0 required an add-on memory manager, such as Qualitas 386Max or Quarterdeck Office Systems Q-EMM. Current versions of Windows have built-in memory management. Extra memory management is irrelevant to OS/2 because it is a protected mode operating system designed to use extended memory.

Note, however, that no matter how much memory you have installed in your PC and no matter what memory-management scheme you use, your DOS applications will be limited to addressing no more than one megabyte and more typically only 640K. That's because the memory addressing limits of DOS applications are built into the applications themselves. Although you often can use extended memory to run several standard DOS applications under Windows or OS/2, each program is still internally constrained by the old DOS 640K addressing limit.

A few powerful DOS programs are exceptions to this rule. They can stretch into extended memory using DOS extenders, which are software toolkits comprising precoded memory-management routines that become embedded in the application itself. When a program is written using a DOS extender, it gets its own built-in memory manager. (You never see the DOS extender; you can only appreciate its results.)

DOS extenders work by loading a program through DOS in real mode and then switching program control to protected mode. The DOS extender provides all services normally given by DOS (because DOS can only operate in real mode). When an application in protected mode needs to step back for a function normally provided by DOS in real mode, the extender translates virtual protected-mode addresses into physical addresses, copies necessary data from extended memory into conventional memory, and switches back to real mode to carry out the function. When the real-mode function is completed, the extender reverses the process and switches back to protected mode.

Most applications that use DOS extenders typically have "386" in their names (for example, Paradox 386 or AutoCAD 386) because they are designed to run on 386 and later microprocessors. However, most of these programs are disappearing from the marketplace because the "386" name makes them seem obsolete in a world now dominated by 486 microprocessors. Moreover, programs specifically written to use OS/2 or Windows have access to extended memory without the need for a built-in DOS extender. (Of course, programs written for OS/2 or Windows are not DOS applications but OS/2 or Windows applications).

The larger expanses of extended memory add greater potential for program problems. With multiple megabytes out there for the taking, you can be tempted to run several extended DOS programs or operating systems that each have a built-in memory manager at the same time. Because DOS does not control how programs interact in extended memory, two programs in extended memory could potentially run into conflicts should each try to use the same block of RAM.

To prevent such conflicts, software writers have developed several methods for allocating extended memory among programs. The most primitive way is for a program that uses extended memory to reserve the blocks of extended memory it needs. Each extended memory program steals its own chunk of memory and that's that. The big problem is that programs only make this allocation when they load so that it cannot change with the program's needs. Should an application need multiple megabytes for only one little-used task, it would have to reserve all those megabytes when it starts, depriving all other programs of access to that memory.

Three standards have developed for extended memory managers to allow extended memory programs to work together: Extended Memory Specification, Virtual Control Program Interface, and DOS Protected Mode Interface.

Extended Memory Specification

Extended Memory Specification (XMS) was developed by AST Research, Intel Corporation, Lotus Development, and Microsoft Corporation to take advantage of several extended-memory capabilities. First appearing in 1987, XMS functions with all microprocessors that address extended memory (that is, 286 or better) and allows real-mode (DOS) applications to use that extended memory as well as a special block of real-mode memory normally out of DOS's reach. XMS is normally added to your system by loading an Extended Memory Manager driver in your PC's CONFIG.SYS file. The most familiar extended memory manager is HIMEM.SYS, which accompanies more recent versions of DOS and Windows.

Virtual Control Program Interface

Virtual Control Program Interface (VCPI) was developed by Phar Lap Software (the publisher of a popular DOS extender) and Quarterdeck Office Systems (creator of Q-EMM/386, an extended memory manager), and also first appeared in 1987. VCPI was developed specifically for the 386 microprocessor as a means of making virtual 8086-mode programs to cooperate and communicate using a software interrupt, specifically 67(Hex). Each VCPI application includes its own 386 control program. The first VCPI program loaded into your system takes the responsibility for linking control of that interrupt with each subsequent VCPI program loaded, so the first program acts as a memory manager for all the others.

DOS Protected Mode Interface

DOS Protected Mode Interface is the most recent extended memory management system that first appeared commercially along with (and built into) Windows 3.0. Version 1.0 of the standard was formally released in November, 1990, and applies to all microprocessors with extended memory capabilities. Although initially conceived by Microsoft as a proprietary standard that included all the functions of a DOS extender as well as a memory manager, the extent of the formal standard was scaled back to avoid conflicts with DOS extenders. Administration of the standard was given to an independent industry organization (the DMPI Committee).

Expanded Memory

In April, 1985, just months after the AT was introduced with its multiple megabytes of extended memory range, a major software publisher, Lotus Development Corporation, and a hardware maker, Intel Corporation, formulated their own method for overcoming the 640K limit of older DOS computers based on the 8088 microprocessor. A few months later, they were joined by Microsoft Corporation, and the development was termed the Lotus-Intel-Microsoft Expanded Memory Specification, LIM memory, EMS, or simply expanded memory. The initial version was numbered as EMS Version 3.0 to indicate its compatibility with then-current DOS 3.0. There was no EMS 1.0. When Microsoft joined, the spec was slightly revised and called Version 3.2.

The new memory system differed from either base memory or extended memory in not being within the normal address range of its host microprocessor. Instead, it relied on hardware circuitry to switch banks of memory within the normal address range of the 8088 microprocessor where the chip can read and write to it.

This technique, called *bank-switching*, was neither novel nor unusual, having been applied to CP/M computers based on the Z80 microprocessor to break through their inherent 64K addressing limit. Only the cooperative effort at standardization by oftentimes competing corporations was surprising.

The original EMS specification dealt with its expanded memory in banks of 16K. It mapped out a 64K range in the non-DOS memory area above the bytes used for display memory to switch these banks, up to four at a time, into the address range of the 8088. Up to eight megabytes of 16K banks of expanded memory could be installed in a system.

The Expanded Memory Specification included the definition of several function calls (pre-defined software routines) contained in special EMS software called the Expanded Memory Manager that were to be used by programs to manipulate the expanded memory. Because the memory areas beyond the DOS 640K range had been assigned various purposes by IBM, when the bank-switching area is assigned an arbitrary location, it could potentially conflict with the operation of other system expansion. Consequently, the specification allows several address locations for the bank-switching area within the range 784K to 960K.

Because programs had to be specially written to include the function calls provided by the EMS drivers, expanded memory does not allow ordinary software to stretch beyond the DOS limit. Moreover, the original Expanded Memory Specification put a burdensome limit on the uses of this additional memory—it could only be used for data storage. Program code could not execute in the EMS area. Adding EMS memory to your system also required special expansion boards with the required bank-switching hardware built into them. You couldn't just buy a handful of no-name memory boards and expect to put all their bytes to work.

The introduction of the AT and its potential of 16 megabytes of addressability overshadowed EMS until the hard reality of the inaccessibility of extended memory hit home. Only after three years did an extended memory operating system (OS/2 Version 1) become available, giving expanded memory a three-year head start in applications software development.

In fact, one of the most important uses of extended memory before the advent of truly useful extended memory programs, such as DOS 5.0, Windows 3.0, and OS/2 2.0, was emulating expanded memory. Special programs called *expanded memory managers* or *LIMulators* could make any kind of memory from base to extended to disk memory EMS compatible.

These software-only EMS products could be divided into two classes, those that took advantage of the paged virtual memory mapping capabilities built into the 80386 microprocessor (as well as 286 machines with the memory mapping hardware, such as Micro Channel PS/2s and AT-compatible machines built from the right chip sets) and those that copy 16K banks of memory from extended into base memory. The 386-style programs have a performance edge in that they can switch nearly instantly instead of requiring the host PC to go through the extra work of copying memory blocks. However, when you need EMS and the only way of getting it is with a copying-style LIMulator, the slower performance is but a small penalty.

Enhanced Expanded Memory Specification

Shortly after the introduction of EMS, a competing system was proposed by another cooperative association of otherwise competing computer products companies: AST Research, Quadram, and Ashton-Tate. Called the Enhanced Expanded Memory Specification or EEMS, it was an elaboration of the EMS idea (a superset of EMS) that allowed program execution and multitasking in the expanded memory area. The EEMS design enhancements included the capability to switch banks of up to 64K in size as well as using part of the DOS 640K area for switching banks. EEMS, too, required a special driver, special hardware, and software written to take advantage of its refinements, which were all different from those created for EMS.

EMS Version 4.0

In August, 1987, the two systems (EMS and EEMS) were brought together with the adoption of EMS Version 4.0. Because both EMS and EEMS are subsets of Version 4.0, software written for either system can run under it. Beyond the previous standards, often Version 4.0 supports up to 32M of bank-switched memory, all of which can support program execution and multitasking, and provided more than double the number of function calls to aid programmers in creating products to take advantage of it. Although EMS 4.0 is compatible with previous hardware designs, it requires new memory-management software to bring it to life. Although applications must be specially written to use its advanced function calls, those applications written for previous EMS or EEMS standards will operate within the limits of the specification for which they were originally designed.

According to its creators, the purpose of EMS 4.0 is to extend the life of 8088- and 8086-based computers. Although it can be useful as an alternative to a protected mode operating system to give programs access to greater memory, EMS 4.0 is not an operating system in itself. It merely affords facilities to software and operating system developers and requires an EMM program to be used effectively as a multitasking environment.

High DOS Memory

Memory-management software creates several other kinds of specialized memory in receptive computers. These include High DOS Memory or Upper Memory Blocks and the High Memory Area.

The reserved memory addresses beyond the nominal top of DOS memory and the upper limit of real mode memory (the area between physical addresses 640K and 1,024K) provide more space than is usually necessary for all the functions in a PC. Typically, tens or hundreds of thousands of memory addresses in this area are unused even in fully expanded PCs. Because these unused addresses appear in the real mode addressing range, they could be used by DOS. This entire range of 384K is called High DOS Memory.

By themselves, the vacant addresses in High DOS Memory are meaningless because no memory is assigned to them. However, PCs that support memory mapping (machines equipped with 386 or better microprocessors as well as 286 computers with the proper support circuitry) can remap extended memory into this address range. Although this remapped memory is not useful to DOS applications (because it is not contiguous), it can be used for executing self-contained chunks of code, such as driver software or terminate-and-stay-resident utilities.

Many memory-management programs (including DOS 5.0 and later) take advantage of the combination of these otherwise unused addresses and memory mapping to create what Microsoft calls Upper Memory Blocks. Special program loaders (such as DOS's LOADHIGH) driver and TSR software can be located in Upper Memory Blocks rather than the normal DOS 640K to leave more DOS memory for your applications. The trick to taking advantage of Upper Memory Blocks is finding the best fit between drivers and TSRs and the memory blocks. Each driver or program must fit entirely within the confines of a single contiguous memory block.

To make high DOS memory work in your PC, you must have suitable hardware (a 386, 486, or 286 with a chip set that supports memory mapping), a memory manager, and the special loader, and have physical memory available to remap. If your system has only 640K of memory, you can't remap anything into the high DOS range.

High Memory Area

Microprocessors with extended memory capabilities have an interesting quirk: they can address more than one megabyte of memory in real mode. When a program running on an 8088 or 8086 microprocessor tries to access memory addresses higher than one megabyte, the addresses "wrap" around and start back at zero. However, with an 286 or more recent microprocessor, if the twenty-first address line (which 8088s and their kin lack) is activated, the first segment's worth of accesses in excess of one megabyte will reach into extended memory. This address line (A20) can be activated during real mode using a program instruction. As a result, one segment of additional memory is accessible by 286 and better microprocessors in real mode.

This extra memory, a total of 64K minus 16 bytes, is called the High Memory Area. Because it is not contiguous with the DOS 640K, it cannot be used as extra memory by ordinary DOS applications. However, it can be used like Upper Memory Blocks for driver or TSR software. Unlike Upper Memory Blocks, however, only one driver or utility no matter its size (as long as it is less than 65,520 bytes) can be loaded into the High Memory Area. DOS 5.0 was rewritten to allow you to automatically move its kernel (about 40K or program code) into the High Memory Area, which it will do automatically in systems in which the High Memory Area is accessible. This relocation frees 40K of the normal DOS 640K for use by your DOS applications.

Shadow Memory

The latest 32-bit computers often provide for accessing memory through 8-, 16-, or 32-bit data buses. It's often most convenient to use a 16-bit data path for ROM BIOS memory (so only two expensive EPROM chips are needed instead of the four required by a 32-bit path). Many expansion cards that may have on-board BIOS extensions connect to their computer hosts through 8-bit data buses. As a result, these memory areas cannot be accessed nearly as fast as the host system's 32-bit RAM. This problem is compounded because BIOS routines, particularly those used by the display adapter, are among the most often used code in the computer.

To break through this speed barrier, many designers of 80386 computers use shadow memory. They copy the ROM routines into fast 32-bit RAM and use the page virtual memory mapping capabilities of the 80386 to switch the RAM into the address range used by the ROM. Execution of BIOS routines can then be speeded up by a factor of four or more (more because a greater wait states often are imposed when accessing slower ROM memory). Of course, the shadow memory is volatile and must be loaded with the BIOS routines every time the computer is booted.

Memory Packaging

An actual memory chip is a sliver of silicon smaller than a fingernail and so delicate that exposure to ordinary air will cause it to self-destruct. To make it easier to handle, memory chips (like all semiconductors) are hermetically sealed in a larger case that both protects the silicon and provides a convenient means of handling the chip and attaching it to circuit assemblies. This case is called the chip's packaging.

Almost universally, memory chips are individually packaged as integrated circuits that are commonly called *discrete chips*. Early PCs were designed to accept these discrete chips in their memory sockets, normally nine chips per memory bank. With the advent of 32-bit microprocessors, however, memory needs have become so large that discrete chips are inconvenient or impractical for memory. One bank typically would comprise 36 chips, and multiple banks would quickly consume more board space than is available in most PCs.

The modern alternative package is the *memory module*, which puts several discrete chips on a single small plug-in circuit board. Memory modules are more compact than discrete chips for two reasons. Chips are soldered to memory modules, eliminating space-wasting sockets and allowing the chips to be installed closer together (because no individual access is required). Moreover, because the discrete chips that are installed in the memory module never need to be individually manipulated except by machine, they can use more compact surface-mount packages. A single memory module just a few inches long can thus accommodate a full bank of memory.

If the instruction materials accompanying your computer did not specify the type of memory that it uses, you can tell just by taking a quick look. Discrete memory chips are nearly always located in a rectangular array on the system board, typically in multiple rows (usually four) of nine chips each, although some machines may use 18 chips rows or more than four rows. Some of the rows may be vacant sockets, allowing for memory expansion.

The give-away in identifying a computer that uses discrete memory chips is that all the chips in this chip array are identical—all usually will have the same identifying numbers on their cases. It is possible, however, for black sheep chips to appear because different chip manufacturers use different part numbers. Moreover, some computers may use different chip types in different rows of memory. Nevertheless, an array of multiple, similar chips is a good indicator of discrete memory.

You can tell if your computer is equipped with memory modules of some type by looking for several tiny circuit boards sticking up from your system board, usually at a right angle. A few computer designers spread out the memory modules, perhaps placing them between expansion slots. Usually, however, they're all located together in about a four-inch-square patch.

Discrete Chips

The evolution of the RAM chip has closely followed the development of the personal computer. The success of the small computer fueled demand for memory chips. At the same time, the capacity of memory chips increased and, except for a temporary rise in the late 1980s due to a worldwide shortage, their price has tumbled.

When the first PC was introduced, the standard RAM chip could store 16 kilobits of information, 16,384 bits or 2,048 bytes. These standard

RAM chips, the smallest capacity memory chips used by any PC-compatible computer, are now difficult to find (and consequently expensive) because they were quickly outmoded. Only a few tens of thousands of PCs used them, and the useful lives of most of those machines have ended.

By the time the XT was introduced hardly a year later, chips with a larger capacities (64 kilobit) proved to be more cost-effective. Although able to store four times more data, 64 kilobit chips cost less than four times the price of 16 kilobit chips. The PC system board was revised to accommodate the better memory buy, and the XT was designed to accept them. In a few years, 64 kilobit chips became so popular that their price fell below that of 16 kilobit chips.

By 1984, the best value in memory had become the next step larger, the 256 kilobit chip, and RAM chips of this size were chosen for the original AT. As the first 386-based PCs came on the market, the standard memory chip capacity had increased to one megabit. Today, four megabit chips are being marketed.

Most chip manufacturers aim at a factor of four to increase in the capacity of their products, so the next two generations of RAM chips will likely have 16 and 256 megabit capacities. The first 256 megabit chips are expected to become available by 1998. With the trend toward using more convenient memory modules, however, you're unlikely to deal with discrete chips of these capacities—or even four megabit chips.

Mixing discrete chips of different capacities in one PC can be chancy. Some PCs accept different capacities of chips but require that all chips installed in the system have the same capacity. For example, the machine might be able to use 64 kilobit, 256 kilobit, or 1 megabit chips, but won't accept a combination of different chip capacities. Other systems may accept mixtures of chip sizes, providing all the chips in a given bank have the same capacity. (You'll have to check your PC or motherboard manual to determine the rule your system follows.) The reasoning underlying this general rule is that if one chip in a bank had a smaller capacity from the others, then some address won't have sufficient bits to store a complete unit of storage. Errors would be inevitable. This rule is violated only in one case, when using four-bit chips, but this situation imposes even stricter requirements.

Discrete chip packages differ in ways besides capacity. They also can have different physical configurations—the plastic packages may be different shapes, and the pins that fit their sockets (or are soldered to circuit boards) vary in their arrangement. The most common memory chips remain those that use the Dual In-line Pin (or DIP) package, a small slab of plastic with two parallel rows of chips that emerge from either side of the package and then bend down at right angles to it. In general, the pins are spaced one-tenth inch apart, and the two parallel rows are separated from each other by four-tenths inch. The Single In-line Pin (or SIP) package turns the DIP on edge and drops all pins straight down from one edge with one-tenth inch spacing between the pins. The Zig-zag In-line Pin (or ZIP) package resembles the SIP but has two rows of pins one-tenth inch apart and alternating at one-tenth inch intervals. In effect, the pins in the two rows are offset from one another by half the spacing between the pins to create a zig-zag pattern. ZIP chips allow more connections for the same size chip as compared to SIPs.

Memory chips are also available in surface-mount packages, tiny (typically one-half inch) square blocks of epoxy that are designed to be soldered in place. These cannot be used for expanding system board memory because they won't fit into any standard socket.

Discrete chips also differ in how their capacity is accessed. The typical computer memory chip stores information in a series of addresses, typically about 256,000, one bit wide. The same capacity can be split four ways so that each address stores four bits. In that way, a 256-kilobit memory chip would store four bits at each of about 64,000 addresses. This style of chip, growing in popularity in display adapters and a few computer systems, is called a 4 x 64 kilobit chip, distinguishing it from the 1 x 256 kilobit conventional chip (although both can be legitimately called 256-kilobit chips). Similarly, 1 megabit parts are available either as 1 x 1,024 kilobit chips or as 4 x 256 kilobit chips.

The chief advantage of wider chips is that fewer are needed per memory bank, so when a system designer wants to skimp on the memory in a system, wider chips can be used. For example, you only need two 4-bit chips for byte-wide memory; you would need eight 1-bit chips for the same memory width. In PCs, 4-bit chips allow a building bank of memory from three chips (one additional chip is needed for parity checking), so the minimum 32-bit bank needed to power a 386 or 486 PC requires only 12 chips instead of 36, conserving motherboard space. This type of memory arrangement (with each byte comprised of one 1-bit chip and two 4-bit chips) is the only exception to the rule that you cannot mix chip capacities in a single memory bank.

When you order memory, you must be certain to get chips with the proper width. One-bit and 4-bit chips are not compatible even when they have the same total capacity.

The only certain way of identifying memory chips is through the manufacturer's designation stenciled onto the top of the chip case. However, most computers use a style of memory chip that's so ubiquitous to be nearly generic—bit-wide, dynamic RAM chips in DIP packages. Odds are that your computer, too, uses this kind of memory. If so, your only concern is the capacity of the individual chips, 64-kilobit, 256-kilobit, or 1 megabit. To confound you, every manufacturer uses its own nomenclature for this garden variety kind of memory chip. Table 5.1 lists the part numbers used by many major manufacturers for different chips.

TABLE 5.1.
Equivalency
Chart for Popular
DRAM Chips

1 MEGABIT DYNAMIC RAM CHIPS 1 bit wide organization, fast page mode:	
Fujitsu	MB81C1000P/PJ/PSZ
Hitachi	HM511000AP/AJP/AZP
Micron	MT4C1024PD/DJA/ZB
Mitsubishi	M5M41000AP/AJ/AL
NEC	uPD421000C/LA/V
Oki	MSM511000RS/JS/ZS
Siemens	HYB511000
TI	TMS4C1024N/DJ
Toshiba	TC411000BP/BJ/BZ/BFT
Vitelic	V53C100
1 bit wide organization, nibble mode:	
Fujitsu	MB81C1001P/PJ/PSZ
Hitachi	HM511001AP/AJP/AZP
Micron	MT4C1025PD/DJA/ZB
Mitsubishi	M5M41001AP/AJ/AL

continues

TABLE 5.1.
continued

1 bit wide organization, nibble mode:

NEC	uPD421001C/LA/V
Oki	MSM511001RS/JS/ZS
TI	TMS4C1025N/DJ
Toshiba	TC411001BP/BJ/BZ/BFT

1 bit wide organization, static column:

Fujitsu	MB81C1002P/PJ/PSZ
Hitachi	HM511002AP/AJP/AZP
Micron	MT4C1026PD/DJA/ZB
Mitsubishi	M5M41002AP/AJ/AL
NEC	uPD421020C/LA/V
Oki	MSM511002RS/JS/ZS
Siemens	HYB511002
TI	TMS4C1026N/DJ
Toshiba	TC411002BP/BJ/BZ/BFT
Vitelic	V53C102

4 bit wide organization, fast page mode:

Fujitsu	MB81C4256P/PJ/PSZ
Hitachi	HM514256AP/AJP/AZP
Micron	MT4C4256PD/DJA/ZB
Mitsubishi	M5M44256BP/BJ/BL/BVP/BRV
NEC	uPD424256C/LA/V
Oki	MSM514256RS/JS/ZS
TI	TMS44C256N/DJ
Toshiba	TC514256BP/BJ/BZ/BFT
Vitelic	V53C104

4 bit wide organization, static column:

Fujitsu	MB81C4258P/PJ/PSZ
Hitachi	HM514258AP/AJP/AZP
Micron	MT4C4258PD/DJA/ZB
Mitsubishi	M5M44258BP/BJ/BL/BVP/BRV
NEC	uPD424258C/LA/V
Oki	MSM514258RS/JS/ZS
Toshiba	TC514258BP/BJ/BZ/BFT
Vitelic	V53C106

4 bit wide organization, fast page write per bit:

Hitachi	HM514266AP/AJP/AZP
Mitsubishi	M5M44266BP/BJ/BL/BVP/BRV
NEC	uPD424266C/LA/V
Toshiba	TC514266BP/BJ/BZ/BFT
Vitelic	V53C105

4 MEGABIT DYNAMIC RAM CHIPS
1 bit wide organization, fast page mode:

Fujitsu	MB814100
Hitachi	HM514100AJ/AS/AZ
Micron	MT4C1004
Mitsubishi	M5M44100J/L
Mosaic	MDM14000
Motorola	MCM514100
NEC	MPD424100
Oki	MSM51400RS/JS/ZS
Panasonic	MN41C4000SJ/L
Samsung	KM41C4000
Siemens	HYB514100
TI	TMS44100
Vitelic	V53C400

1 bit wide organization, nibble mode:

Hitachi	HM514101AJ/AS/AZ
Mitsubishi	M5M44101J/L
NEC	MPD424101
Oki	MSM51401RS/JS/ZS
Samsung	KM41C4001

1 bit wide organization, static column:

Hitachi	HM514102AJ/AS/AZ
Mitsubishi	M5M44102J/L
NEC	MPD424102
Oki	MSM51402RS/JS/ZS
Panasonic	MN41C4002J/L
Samsung	KM41C40012

continues

TABLE 5.1.
continued

4 bit wide organization, fast page mode:

Fujitsu	MB81440
Hitachi	HM51440AJ/AS/AZ
Micron	MT4C4001
Mitsubishi	M5M44400J/L
Mosaic	MDM41000
Motorola	MCM514400
NEC	MPD424400
Oki	MSM514400RS/JS/ZS
Panasonic	MN41C41000SJ/L
Samsung	KM44C1000
Siemens	HYB514400
TI	TMS44400
Toshiba	TC514400AP/AJ/ASJ/AZ
Vitelic	V53C404

4 bit wide organization, static column:

Hitachi	HM514402AJ/AS/AZ
Mitsubishi	M5M44402J/L
NEC	MPD424402
Oki	MSM514402RS/JS/ZS
Toshiba	TC514402AP/AJ/ASJ/AZ

4 bit wide organization, static column:

Hitachi	HM514410AJ/AS/AZ
Mitsubishi	M5M44410J/L
NEC	MPD424410
Panasonic	MN41C41002SJ/L
Toshiba	TC514410AP/AJ/ASJ/AZ

SINGLE IN-LINE MEMORY MODULES (SIMMs)
256 KILOBYTE SIMMs

8-bit		9-bit	
Hitachi	HB561008	Fujitsu	MB85240
Micron	MT8C8256	Hitachi	HB561003
Mitsubishi	MH25608	Micron	MT8C9256
NEC	MC157	Mitsubishi	MH25609
Oki	MSC2328	NEC	MC41256A9

SINGLE IN-LINE MEMORY MODULES (SIMMs)
256 KILOBYTE SIMMs

8-bit		9-bit	
TI	TM4256GU8	NMB	MM256KOJ9
Toshiba	THM82500	Oki	MSC2331
		TI	TM42566U9
		Toshiba	THM92500

1 MEGABYTE SIMMs

8-bit width		9-bit width	
Fujitsu	MB85230	Fujitsu	MB85235
Hitachi	HB56A18	Hitachi	HB56A19
Micron	MT8C8024	Micron	MT8C9024
Mitsubishi	MH1M08AOJ	Mitsubishi	MH1M09AOJ
Motorola	MCM81000	Motorola	MCM91000
NEC	MC42100A8	NEC	MC421000A9
NMB	MM1M100J8	NMB	MM1M100J9
Oki	MSC2313	Oki	MSC2312
TI	TM024GAD8	TI	TM024EAD9
Toshiba	THM81000	Toshiba	THM91000

32-bit width		36-bit width	
Oki	MSC2327	Fujitsu	MB85236
Toshiba	THM322500	Hitachi	MB56D25636
		Micron	MT9D36256
		Mitsubishi	MH25636AJ
		Motorola	MCM36256
		NEC	MC424256A36
		Oki	MSC2320
		Toshiba	THM362500

2 MEGABYTE SIMMs
36-bit width

Hitachi	HB56D51236
Micron	MT8C36512
Mitsubishi	MH51236AJ
NEC	MC424512A36
Oki	MSC2321
Toshiba	THM365120

continues

TABLE 5.1.
continued

4 MEGABYTE SIMMs			
8-bit width		**9-bit width**	
Hitachi	HB56A48	Fujitsu	MB85285
Mitsubishi	MH4M08	Hitachi	HB56A49
Motorola	MCM84000	Hyundai	HYM594000
Oki	MSC2341	Mitsubishi	MH4M09AOJ
Toshiba	THM84000	Micron	MT9D49
		Motorola	MCM9L4000
		Oki	MSC2340
		TI	TMS4100EBD9
		Toshiba	THM94000
32-bit width		**36-bit width**	
Hitachi	HB56D132	Hitachi	HB56D136
Toshiba	THM321000	Mitsubishi	MH1M36
		Oki	MSC2350
		Toshiba	THM361020

The major exception to the generic memory rule are the few 80386-based machines which use more exotic chips (static-column or page-mode) to achieve greater performance than DRAM can deliver. If you're not certain of the memory technology that your computer uses, compare the legends on its memory chips to those listed in table 5.1. If you find a match, you're probably safe with expanding your system's memory with that chip or its equivalent.

As with coprocessors or any other chips you might install inside your computer, memory chips must be properly aligned in their sockets. That is, pin number 1 of the chip must fit into the corresponding pin 1 hole of the socket.

All chips have some means of identifying either pin 1 or the end of the chip at which pin 1 is located. Usually the pin 1 end of the chip is notched. Occasionally, a small circular depression (an indented dot) is located directly adjacent to pin 1. The end of the chip that is so marked is oriented to match the notch in the chip socket. Sometimes pin 1 of the socket is also identified with a silk-screened legend on the circuit board. Occasionally, all the pins in a socket will be denoted with numbers molded into the plastic of the socket itself.

An improperly oriented chip will likely fail immediately when you power up your computer. In fact, the backwards chip may short out and prevent your computer from booting at all. To avoid such disasters, double-check the orientation of every chip before you switch on your computer after adding any chips.

Sliding chips into sockets is not foolproof. The legs of ICs have a nasty tendency to go exactly where you don't want them. Sometimes, they fold outward and slide down outside the socket instead of making a connection. Sometimes they bend underneath the chip and don't make a connection. If a chip leg misses its place, you will encounter memory errors when you boot your computer, although the bent pin is unlikely to cause other damage to your system. Avoid such problems by carefully investigating each leg of every chip you install. Make certain that it fits properly into the hold provided in its socket.

If you discover a leg that is misplaced, simply pry the chip out of the socket, straighten the pin as best you can (don't flex the leg too much because they easily break off), and reinsert the chip.

You'll want to be careful when installing memory chips in your PC. Although it takes electricity to power a computer, the same force can be the worst enemy of your memory. A shuffle across a wool rug can charge you with up to 20,000 volts, just raring to zap a memory chip designed to operate on 5 volts. Although taking all the recommended precautions may be overkill (you don't have to ground yourself to a cold water pipe), there's no sense in taking chances. Grounding can be simply a matter of touching the case of your PC, even touching the plastic tube or foam your memory chips come in to your computer before you begin. The important thing is to make yourself, your computer, and the memory chips the same potential, which simply means linking them together before you actually touch the legs of the memory chip.

A few companies recommend that you leave the power cord plugged into your computer to ground it while your making the installation. You'll be safer to ignore that advice and unplug all cables from your computer before you begin. That way you can't accidentally try to install memory chips while the computer is running, an exercise guaranteed to be fatal to the memory chips.

Memory Modules

Memory modules are the large economy-size RAM to better suit the dietary needs of today's PCs. Besides the more convenient package that allows you to deftly install a number of chips in one operation, the memory module also better matches the way your PC uses memory. Unlike most chips, which are addressed at the bit level, memory modules usually operate in bytes. Where chip capacities are measured in kilobits and megabits, memory modules are measured in megabytes.

The construction of a memory module is straightforward, simply a second level of integration above the basic memory chip. Several chips are brought together on a small glass-epoxy circuit board with their leads brought together by circuit traces and terminated in an external connector suitable for plugging into a socket or soldering to another circuit board. This basic arrangement splits into two primary variations based on connector type.

Single In-line Memory Modules, more commonly known as SIMMs, use edge connectors. Like expansion boards, the connector is just a circuit board trace brought out to the edge of the module and, typically, plated with gold to prevent corrosion and to guarantee better contact. As with expansion boards, a SIMM is designed solely to plug into matching edge-connector sockets. The design allows the SIMM to be repeatedly added or removed without tools or damage.

Single In-line Pin Package modules, often shortened to SIPP, use pin connectors. Like SIP chip packages, the connections of a SIPP module are brought out as wire-like pins that hang down from the basic board in a single colinear row. The leads on a SIPP are designed for soldering in place, although sometimes they are installed in special sockets much like SIP chips. A SIPP socket often is nothing more than line of holes reinforced by contact cups in the circuit board to which the SIPP mates.

Functionally, SIMMs and SIPPs can carry the same memory chips, technologies, and capacities. However, their different mounting schemes make them mutually incompatible. When you want to add memory to your PC or replace a defective module, you'll have to specify whether it uses SIMMs or SIPPs.

Beyond packaging, you'll find a number of differences in memory modules. As with memory chips, these include access, capacity, and technology.

Although most memory modules have their storage arranged in bytes, they do not necessarily have an 8-bit bus width. Most PC memory modules are designed to the same standard as discrete chip memory systems (that means parity checking). Consequently, the most popular PC memory modules have 9-bit access (8 data bits and an extra bit for the parity check). Some computer systems (notably many Apple Macintoshs) and some specialized applications (such a printer and video memory) use 8-bit modules that lack parity checking. After all, a bad bit on your screen or printed on paper probably won't result in a billion-dollar business error.

As with discrete chips, the minimum memory you can add to a microprocessor will be a bank that matches the microprocessor's bus width. If you have a 32-bit microprocessor, such as a 386DX or 486, you'll need four 9-bit memory modules per bank. Memory expansion will also have to be made in four-module increments.

Some memory modules are designed for individual 32-bit addressing. That is, one module delivers full 32-bit bus width so that you can expand a system that uses such modules one module at a time. The most popular of these are the SIMMs used in many of IBM's PS/2s and are, consequently, termed IBM-style SIMMs. Because these SIMMs provide a 32-bit bus complete with four bits of parity checking, they are also termed 36-bit SIMMs. (They are also sometimes referred to as 72-pin SIMMs because their connectors have 72 connections.) The IBM SIMM design is versatile enough that the same 36-bit SIMMs can be used in 16-bit as well as 32-bit PS/2s.

Possibly memory module capacities are as wide as the imagination of the person soldering them together, though a number of standard sizes have arisen. The smallest commonly available modules store 256 kilobytes. The most popular capacities among 9-bit SIMMs are 1M and 4M. Larger sizes (8M and 16M) haven't caught on among 9-bit SIMMs because the smallest bank potentially made from them (32M) is bigger than most people currently want.

IBM-style 36-bit SIMMs are available in capacities including 1M, 2M, 4M, 8M, and 16M. Because only one such SIMM is required as standard system memory or as an expansion increment, the larger sizes are both useful and popular.

Memory modules follow the same mixing rules as chips: all the modules in a given bank of memory must have the same capacity. For example, in a 32-bit computer, the four modules that comprise one bank must have the same capacity. The seeming exception to this rule is machines that use IBM-style 36-bit SIMMs, which can generally be mixed without regard to capacity (although some memory boards may be more particular—check your manual). The important difference is that one IBM-style SIMM makes up an entire bank, so the rule really is not violated.

Because memory modules are made from discrete chips, they use the same underlying technologies. SIMMs made using static, dynamic, video, and page mode RAM technologies are available. As with discrete chips, different module technologies are not interchangeable, so you need to specify the correct type when ordering memory for your PC.

One way to identify memory modules is by part number. The manufacturer's part number given to a memory module is often stenciled on the side of the board opposite that carrying the individual memory chips. If it's not there (or anywhere else, as is often the case), you can identify the memory module from the nomenclature on its chip components. For instance, a module made from nine 256-kilobit chips rated at 80-nanoseconds is a 256 kilobyte, 80 nanosecond memory module.

For a better look when attempting to identify memory modules, you may want to pop the module from its socket. Just be careful because memory modules are made from discrete chips and consequently have the same sensitivity to static electricity. If you take the proper precautions, however, the removal process for SIPPs is easy—just pull each one out, applying even pressure to the two ends of the SIPP.

SIMMs are more difficult. Normally, SIMMs are latched into place by plastic fingers at either end of the slot in their connectors. Look closely and you'll see that the plastic of the socket has two latching fingers at each end. You must carefully pry these away from the SIMM. You can then lean the SIMM over a bit and pull it out. When you reinsert the SIMM, you must press it firmly in place until the fingers lock it down again and little round tabs appear in the latching holes in the SIMM near the fingers.

When installing SIMMs or SIPPs, remember that their orientation is important. In general, all SIMMs and SIPPs in a PC will face in the same direction. With SIMMs in modern, slanted sockets, that generally means the chips on the SIMM will be on the top of the SIMM once you lean it down into the socket. Most SIMM sockets have keying tabs on them to prevent your putting a SIMM in backwards. Should you try to insert a SIMM and discover that it refuses to fit, you probably have it in the wrong orientation or improperly seated.

Memory Errors

Memory chips (and memory modules) sadly seem to be the most likely solid-state part of your computer to fail. They can fail in one of two ways, with soft errors or hard errors.

Soft Errors

For memory chips, a soft error is a transient change. One bit in a chip may suddenly, randomly change state. Typically, one of the slightly radioactive atoms in the epoxy case of the chip will spontaneously decay and shoot out an alpha or beta particle into the chip. (There are a number of radioactive atoms in just about everything; they don't amount to very much but they are there.) If the particle hits a memory cell in the chip, the particle can cause the cell to change state, blasting the memory bit it contains.

This error can be detected thanks to the parity check bit assigned to each byte of memory. As soon as the error is detected, your machine shuts down with a parity error. However, the chip itself has suffered no damage from the particle blast, and as soon as you reboot your computer the error will be gone. Because such radioactive decay is rare and unpredictable, your machine is likely to resume processing and not have an error again for a long time.

There's nothing you can do to prevent soft errors, and there's nothing to do after they occur. The best you can hope for is to understand them.

Hard Errors

When some part of a memory chip actually fails, the result is a hard error. For instance, a jolt of static electricity can wipe out one or more memory cells. As a result, the initial symptom is that same as a soft error—a parity failure and your computer shuts down. The difference is that the hard error recurs. Your machine may not pass its memory test when you try to reboot it, or you may encounter repeated, random errors when a memory cell hovers between life and death.

Hard errors require attention. The chip in which the error originates should be replaced.

Finding a Bad Bank

Machines that follow the IBM standard facilitate finding memory errors by putting diagnostic messages on the screen during the Power On Self-Test procedure that your system goes through every time you turn it on. Sometimes, these diagnostic error codes will appear after a parity error. Unfortunately, the memory failure messages (and almost all other diagnostic messages provided by computers) are designed for service technicians rather than normal human beings. They are given in a numeric code that must be translated to zero in on the defective chip.

When PCs had dozens of memory chips in every bank, finding the one chip that went bad was a challenge. Trial-and-error chip swapping was out of the question unless you had time on your hands and a chip puller in them. You had to rely on diagnostics to locate the bad chip. Ultimately this meant consulting a look-up table or deciphering a complex formula to find the bad chip from the obscure numerical message reported by the diagnostic.

With modern SIMM-based PCs, however, the math of the chip-finding formula often takes longer than swapping a few modules. Most PCs have only four to eight memory modules, so the bad module can usually be located in a few minutes simply by swapping modules. If you want the most efficient means of locating a bad module, you can use a formula similar to the one for calculating the Tower of Hanoi puzzle. For example, you could shift a couple modules around and look for changes in the diagnostic error message, but the limited access in most PCs makes you remove the outermost modules to get to the inner ones. You ultimately end up pulling out most of the modules anyway. If you ever do encounter a hard error in one of your system's SIMMs, you'll probably find repair easier if you just exchange one module from inside your PC for a known good module (the replacement) and work your way through a memory bank.

CHAPTER

The Expansion Bus

Your PC's expansion bus enables your system to grow. The expansion bus provides a high-speed connection for internal peripherals that enhances the power of your PC. Standardized buses have spawned an entire industry dedicated to making interchangeable PC expansion boards. Where once a single standard sufficed, PC expansion has become specialized with expansion buses optimized for multi-user computers, high-performance video systems, and notebook machines.

The embodiment of your PC's bus is the expansion slot—a designated slice of airspace inside your system with an electrical connector at the bottom, a mounting bracket at the back end, and a promise of adding new powers and performance. The purpose of the expansion bus is straightforward: to enable you to plug things into the machine and, you hope, to enhance the machine's operation. The design of the expansion bus governs how your computer may grow; the bus standard is a primary determinant defining the compatibility of enhancement products. The design of the expansion bus also defines limits on system performance and ultimate system capabilities.

One of the greatest blessings for the small-computer industry was IBM's development of the expansion bus on the original PC. This development package gave the world a single standard where none existed before. Manufacturers of expansion boards have a set of dimensions and a layout of electrical signals to guide them in crafting their products. (The timing of those signals; however, was never explicitly defined by IBM.)

As expansion buses go, the chief asset of the PC bus was IBM's backing, which alone was the most compelling reason to use this bus. Compared to other expansion buses previously available, however, the PC bus was not remarkable. The IBM bus was a simple design devoid of technical innovation and in some ways was a backward step. For example, the *S-100* standard, which teetered near universal acceptance in CP/M computers only to be steamrollered by the IBM bandwagon, offered more flexibility and power. At least the S-100 standard accommodated 16 data lines; whereas the new IBM bus only accommo dated 8. S-100 provided connections for 100 expansion board signals (hence its name), versus only 68 for the PC bus.

In the end, simplicity and the lower costs associated with this simplicity became a PC bus virtue. Everything needed was available, and the bus was entirely workable. When the IBM PC became a runaway success, board makers had to adopt the PC bus to sell their products. The standard was born.

Bus Basics

Although the concept is simple, the expansion bus is not simple. The bus represents a complex system of design choices—some made by necessity; many picked pragmatically.

Most important of the necessities are the connections needed for moving data between the add-in circuits and the microprocessor and the rest of the computer. Among these connections are all the data and address lines from the microprocessor. In addition, special signals are required to synchronize the signals of the add-in circuitry with those of the host computer. Newer bus designs also include a means of delegating system control to add-in products and tricks for squeezing extra speed from data transfers.

Pragmatic concerns dictate how these connections are arranged, the connector used to link system to add-in, and the physical size of add-in products. Although some choices are constrained—for example, you need sufficient connections for the required circuits, and the choice of connectors should be made from commercially available products—the possibilities are almost limitless. Little wonder that so many bus designs have been created and used by various incompatible computer systems.

Data Handling

The most important function of an expansion bus is the transfer of data from the microprocessor to peripherals or between individual expansion boards. Ideally, the expansion bus should provide a data path that matches the data path of the microprocessor. When these data paths match, an entire digital word, or one of the double-words used by today's 32-bit chips, may ride across the bus in a single exchange. When the bus is narrower than the device that sends or receives the signals, the data must be repackaged for transmission; a double-word may need to be broken into two words or four bytes to fit a 16- or 8-bit bus. Circuitry to handle this packaging complicates both motherboards and expansion boards. A narrower bus slows the transfers, because moving a double-word might take two or four exchanges of data.

The fundamental factor in describing an expansion bus is the number of data lines the bus provides. More is always better, although adding more beyond the number of data connections on the host microprocessor adds undue complexity.

Addressing Limits

Having data is only half of what you need to make a successful transfer. You need to know where the information originates and where the information is to go. Imagine the delight of the dead letter office at the Post Office and the ever-increasing stack of stationery accumulating there if we all decided that appending addresses to envelopes was superfluous. Similarly, expansion boards must be able to address origins and destinations for data. The easiest method of doing this is to provide address lines on the expansion bus corresponding to those of the microprocessor.

As with microprocessor address lines, the address lines of the bus determine the maximum memory range addressable by the bus. Usually, a computer bus provides the full range of address lines used by a PC's host microprocessor. Some buses, however, shortchange on the number of address lines. When the addresses that are not included are those at the top of the range—for example, the most significant bits of each address—this strategy puts some addresses off limits to expansion boards. However, with 386- and 486-based PCs, deleting the two least significant address bits is common. Although this omission limits the precision with which memory can be identified, this omission works well with the 386 and 486, because the chips address memory in four-byte chunks only. The bus does not need to be more specific.

Arbitration and Bus-Mastering

In essence, the expansion bus of the original PC, as well as the later XT, was designed to be little more than an extension of the connections on the microprocessor. A bus connected directly to the microprocessor data and address lines is termed a *local bus*, because this bus is meant to service only the components in the close vicinity of the microprocessor. However, in the PC, a few electrical characteristics needed to be changed to enable system expansion and to isolate the microprocessor from more nefarious expansion board designs.

All connections to the chip are not assigned separate pins on the chip package. A few are combined, or multiplexed, to give the 8088 more legroom. These connections must be de-multiplexed before they can be used by the computer's other circuits. These de-multiplexed connections are then extended to the PC bus. In addition, the 8088 chip is not designed to supply sufficient power to run the numerous devices that might be plugged into an expansion slot. Consequently, the microprocessor connections are repowered; they are run through a digital amplifier called a *buffer* that boosts the current available for running accessories.

The PC bus design puts the microprocessor in direct contact and in direct control of everything on the expansion bus. Every byte transferred across the bus is moved by the microprocessor. For example, when the microprocessor wants to transfer a byte from one of the microprocessor registers to memory, one bus cycle is used to send out the address to which the data is to be sent. The memory system then prepares that address to receive the data. On the next bus cycle, the microprocessor puts the bit values of the data on the bus, and the memory subsystem collects the bits and stores them in DRAM chips. The speed of this simple bus-transfer operation is governed by the bus speed, which is directly linked to the microprocessor speed. Most bus operations are not so simple, however. The microprocessor must go through gyrations of machine language instructions for every byte transferred. With these more complex transfers, the speed of the microprocessor dominates all other factors in determining bus performance. This load is dropped on the microprocessor whether it is the source or target of the bus transfers and even when the chip need not be involved at all—for example, when bytes must move from hard disk to video memory to put a stored image on the monitor screen.

The microprocessor need not be burdened with controlling the expansion bus, however. Just as an executive delegates work to subordinates, a computer's microprocessor can delegate the control of the bus to special circuitry dedicated to the task, such as a *Direct Memory Access* or *DMA* controller. But even with a DMA chip controlling the actual movement of data, the microprocessor often must still set up and oversee the DMA transfers, tying up the chip throughout the bus transfer.

Another technology removes the microprocessor from the central position in controlling the bus and vests authority in special logic circuits, the *arbitrated expansion bus*. In the arbitrated bus design, the microprocessor abdicates the all-powerful position and takes its place as an equal to the expansion boards in the system. Although the microprocessor still controls the origination and receipt of bus transfers, the microprocessor need not be involved in transfers between other devices in the system.

A device that takes control of the expansion bus to mediate its own transfers is called a *bus master*. The device that receives the data from the master is termed the *bus slave* or *target*. The centralized circuitry in this design really does nothing more than determine which device takes control of the bus, a process called *bus arbitration*.

Synchronous and Asynchronous Operation

Because of the direct link between the microprocessor and expansion bus of the IBM PC, as well as the XT and Portable Personal Computer, the bus clock operates in lock-step with the microprocessor chip. That is, the clock that controls the PC bus operates at exactly the same speed as that which operates the microprocessor. In fact, it is exactly the same clock, controlled by the same vibrating quartz crystal.

Although this design was satisfactory for the PC, because of the modest speed potential of the 8088 microprocessor, the quick shift to faster microprocessors stretched the chip's clock speed beyond the capabilities of most expansion boards. The first increase in clock speed, from the 4.77 Mhz of the PC and XT to the 6 Mhz and then 8 Mhz of the AT, immediately made several expansion boards obsolete, because they could not reliably function in the faster systems. The introduction of even faster microprocessors made locking bus speed to the microprocessor clock untenable.

At 12 Mhz, many expansion boards became flaky, and at 16 Mhz, most expansion boards failed. The solution was to unlink microprocessor and bus speeds. Most faster PCs—and nearly all modern machines—do exactly that, run the microprocessor at one speed and the bus at another. To keep the two synchronized, the bus typically runs at a fraction of the microprocessor speed. For example, the expansion buses of most 33 Mhz PCs operate at 8.25 Mhz, one-quarter the microprocessor speed.

With correct designing, the bus need not be synchronized to the microprocessor. Such an *asynchronous expansion bus* gives the circuit designer more freedom in creating computers. Although an asynchronous bus increases the complexity of bus control logic, modern technology has shrunk all the required components onto a single ASIC making asynchronous buses both practical and affordable. All IBM Micro Channel computers, for example, operate with nominal bus speeds of 10 Mhz regardless of the system's microprocessor speed. Note, however, that an asynchronous bus can operate at virtually any speed. In fact, the speed of an asynchronous bus may be adjusted to match the maximum speed capabilities of each installed expansion board and then switch speeds depending on which boards are involved in the transfer.

Dual-Bus Computers

No law dictates that computers have just one expansion bus. In fact, a single bus imposes a great hardship. Because memory beyond that built into the computer's motherboard must be connected to the microprocessor's bus, the memory of a one-bus computer suffers the same speed restrictions as imposed on the expansion bus by slow boards. In other words, a 50 Mhz PC would slow to 8.25 Mhz every time memory is accessed, which means most of the time.

To get the most speed out of a machine, you want the microprocessor and memory to move as fast as possible. You cannot just jazz up the whole system, however, or you will outrun the cards you plug into the expansion bus. The answer is, of course, to separate memory and input/output functions.

Just as the microprocessor and the expansion bus need not run at the same speeds, no real need exists, other than design ease, to throttle memory down to I/O speed. You can split the expansion bus in two at the bus controller level, providing parallel data paths to memory and the input/output expansion bus. Memory can run at whatever ridiculous speed the chips you buy operate. The expansion bus can be kept to eight or so megahertz, making off-the-shelf expansion components run reliably.

In early 1987, Compaq Computer Corporation cleverly sidestepped this problem with the introduction of the first Deskpro 386, which operated at 16 Mhz. The first *dual-bus PC*, the Deskpro, was the first machine to provide a separate bus for memory, which operated at microprocessor speed, and a bus for input/output operations, which operated at the lower speeds tolerated by expansion. All modern PCs now use this dual-bus design or a more complex derivative drawn from this dual-bus design.

The Original PC/XT Bus

Perhaps this discussion makes the bus of a computer sound complex. In spite of the many connections, computer expansion buses are actually simple creatures. The classic PC bus is the best place to start examining how all the bus signals work together.

The 62 pins used by the PC/XT bus are as follows:

➤ Three electrical grounds

➤ Five pins supply the various voltages needed around the computer—two 5-volt direct current lines and one each for –5, 12, and –12 volts

➤ Twenty address lines

➤ Eight data lines

➤ Ten pins devoted to interrupts

➤ Several special-purpose connections to bring it all to life

Although the list of bus functions is complicated by a wealth of specialized terminology that makes it look as forbidding as the list of ingredients on a candy bar, everything is completely straightforward.

The *Oscillator* line supplies a signal, derived directly from the crystal oscillator, that runs all the clocks and timers inside the computer. Operating at 14.31818 Mhz, this oscillator is the single frequency standard of the entire computer.

The odd frequency on which PCs are based was actually derived from a very practical consideration. This frequency is exactly three times the speed at which the microprocessor operates and four times the frequency on which televisions and inexpensive computer monitors lock their color signals. This one oscillator serves multiple purposes through simple frequency dividers, running both the microprocessor and display system.

The *Clock* line on the bus is a signal derived from the Oscillator. This signal is electrically divided by four—to 4.77 Mhz—and supplied to the microprocessor and other system circuitry to time and synchronize all logical operations.

The *I/O Channel Check* line provides the microprocessor with an integrity check of the memory and of the devices connected to the PC bus. When the signal on this line is interrupted, the interruption indicates to the microprocessor that a parity check error has occurred. Grounding this line will effectively crash the system.

Supplying a pulse to the *Reset Driver* line of the PC bus instructs the whole system to reset or initialize itself. A signal is generated on this line whenever the system is turned on or power is interrupted.

The *Data Lines* carry digital information in parallel form throughout the computer. These same lines are used to move information to and from both memory and input/output devices. Eight data lines are used in the PC, identified with numbers from zero to seven. The zero line carries the least significant bit of each digital word of information.

The *Address Lines* are used for specifying locations in memory to and from which bytes of information are moved. The 20 total lines are identified with numbers 0 through 19, again with line 0 being the least significant.

Microprocessor Bus Control

To read or write memory, the microprocessor first sends the memory address to be used down the address lines and then pulses a special line called the *Address Latch Enable* to indicate to devices connected to the bus that a valid address has been sent. The devices should remember the address by *latching*—electronically locking their circuits to that address. Finally the microprocessor sends a signal down the *Memory Read Command* line to tell the memory controller to put the data at the indicated address on the data lines. Alternately, the microprocessor can send a signal down the *Memory Write Command* line, which indicates that the microprocessor has put a byte of information on the data lines and that the memory controller should store that information at the indicated addresses.

The same data lines are used for moving bytes to input/output devices through other special purpose lines on the bus. The *I/O Read Command* line tells a device to move information from an input port onto the data lines so that the microprocessor can read it into its registers. The *I/O Write Command* line instructs an input/output device to take the information on the data lines, put there by the microprocessor, and to move it to its output port.

Because the microprocessor can generate or demand data more rapidly than an input/output device or memory might be able to handle, the PC bus also includes a provision for making the microprocessor wait while the other part of the system catches up. By removing the "ready" signal from the *I/O Channel Ready* line, the memory controller or input/output device tells the microprocessor to pause for one or more clock cycles.

If the microprocessor does not find a ready signal on this line at the beginning of a clock cycle when it tries to use the bus, it waits until the start of the next clock cycle before trying again and continues to wait as long as the ready signal is not present. IBM specifications do not allow these delays to extend for longer than 10 clock cycles.

Direct Memory Access Bus Control

Information can be moved from one place in a PC to another much faster under DMA control than through the use of the microprocessor.

To make those moves, however, the DMA controller must take command of both the address and data lines. In addition, devices connected to the bus must be able to signal to the DMA controller to make those moves, and the controller needs to be able to signal back to the system when it's done. Several bus lines are used for these functions.

The *Address Enable* line is used to tell the DMA controller that the microprocessor has disconnected itself from the bus to let the DMA controller take command. After this signal is asserted, the DMA controller has charge of the address and data lines in addition to the memory and input/output read and write control lines.

At the end of a DMA memory move, a pulse is sent down the *Terminal Count* line. It's called Terminal Count, because the pulse represents the termination (end) of a count of the number of bytes moved in the DMA transfer. (The number of bytes to be moved must be declared before the transfer begins so that they can be appropriately counted.)

Devices indicate to the DMA controller that they want to make DMA transfers by sending signals down one of the three *DMA Request* lines. Each line is assigned a priority level corresponding to its numerical designation, with one having the highest priority, three the lowest.

To indicate that a request has been received by the DMA controller as well as to provide the rest of the system with an acknowledgment of the DMA request, four *DMA Acknowledge* lines are provided. Three are used to confirm the DMA requests across the bus, designated by numbers corresponding to the request acknowledged. The fourth, designated 0, acknowledges memory refreshing, which also deprives other devices access to the PC bus.

Finally, the PC bus provides for five *Interrupt Request* lines, which are used for hardware signals from various devices to the microprocessor to capture its attention and to temporarily divert it to a different process. The Interrupt Request lines are designated with numbers 2 through 7, in order of decreasing priority.

Interrupts 0 and 1 are not available on the bus but are used internally by the PC in its system board circuitry. The former is controlled by the system timer and generates a periodic interrupt at a rate of 18.2 per second. The latter is devoted to servicing the keyboard, generating an interrupt with each keypress. In addition, a special interrupt, called the *Non-Maskable Interrupt* or *NMI* because it cannot be masked or switched off in the normal operation of the system through software, is used to signal the microprocessor about parity errors.

Note that the NMI can be switched off through the *NMI Mask Registers*, which are available at I/O port 0A0(hex) in the PC and XT. (Similar functions are available in other IBM computers but at different ports.) By loading 00(hex) into this register, the NMI can be masked off and the computer will *not* shut down on parity errors. Loading 80(hex) to this register again turns on the NMI. Table 6.1 gives an example of how to do this using the DOS program DEBUG.

TABLE 6.1.
Turning NMI Off
Using DEBUG

To turn NMI off and prevent system halting with parity errors:	
DEBUG	; Load the DEBUG program
-rax	; Read the AX register
AX 0000	; System responds with current AX value
;0a	; Load the register with the port number, 0A(hex)
-o 00	; Output 00(hex) to the port in AX
-q	; Quit DEBUG to return to DOS
To turn NMI on and halt system upon detection of parity errors:	
DEBUG	; Load the DEBUG program
-rax	; Read the AX register
AX 0000	; System responds with current AX value
;0a	; Load the register with the port number, 0A(hex)
-o 80	; Output 80(hex) to the port in AX
-q	; Quit DEBUG to return to DOS

NOTE: *Port 0A(Hex) applies to PC-class machines. AT-class computers control NMI through port 070(Hex). Substitute this port number when using this routine on AT-style computers.*

XT Slot Eight

Normally, all the connectors on a bus have exactly the same signals available at the same positions. In the IBM environment, that congruency is normally the rule, but like all rules it has an exception. In IBM XT system units slot eight, the short slot nearest the power supply, differs electrically from all other 8-bit IBM PC-bus slots. One connection, which was noted as reserved in the original PC bus, is devoted to a *card selected* function.

Unlike other expansion slots, XT slot eight is electrically separated from the others. In ordinary operation, system board drivers pay no attention to slot eight. Only when the card selected line is activated does the system board respond and link up to the circuitry on the card. The card controls its isolation. This feature is designed to be taken advantage of by special purpose adapters (for instance, the multi-board emulation facility of the 3270 PC).

If you slide an expansion board that makes no special provision for slot eight into that slot, it won't work correctly. A few products will not function in slot eight, and their instructions (usually) warn you of that. Many vendors of short PC-bus expansion cards (the only ones that fit into slot eight) include a jumper or DIP switch on their boards to allow them to adapt to this special expansion slot. Before you use this slot, check the compatibility of the board you want to put there and modify its setup if necessary.

Table 6.2 shows the standard XT expansion bus pin-out.

TABLE 6.2.
Pin-Out of 8-Bit
PC Bus

Pin	Signal	Pin	Signal
B1	Ground	A1	Input/Output Channel Check
B2	Reset Driver	A2	Data 7
B3	+5 VDC	A3	Data 6
B4	Interrupt Request 2	A4	Data 5
B5	-5 VDC	A5	Data 4
B6	DMA Request 2	A6	Data 3
B7	-12 VDC	A7	Data 2
B8	Card Selected (XT Only)	A8	Data 1
B9	+12 VDC	A9	Data 0
B10	Ground	A10	Input/Output Channel Ready
B11	Memory Write	A11	Address Enable
B12	Memory Read	A12	Address 19
B13	Input/Output Write	A13	Address 18

continues

TABLE 6.2.
continued

Pin	Signal	Pin	Signal
B14	Input/Ouput Read	A14	Address 17
B15	DMA Acknowledge 3	A15	Address 16
B16	DMA Request 3	A16	Address 15
B17	DMA Acknowledge 1	A17	Address 14
B18	DMA Request 1	A18	Address 13
B19	DMA Acknowledge 0	A19	Address 12
B20	Clock	A20	Address 11
B21	Interrupt Request 7	A21	Address 10
B22	Interrupt Request 6	A22	Address 9
B23	Interrupt Request 5	A23	Address 8
B24	Interrupt Request 4	A24	Address 7
B25	Interrupt Request 3	A25	Address 6
B26	DMA Acknowledge 2	A26	Address 5
B27	Terminal Count	A27	Address 4
B28	Address Latch Enable	A28	Address 3
B29	+5 VDC	A29	Address 2
B30	Oscillator	A30	Address 1
B31	Ground	A31	Address 0

The 16-Bit AT Bus Extension

In the three years between the PC and the advent of the AT, the deficiencies of the original bus design had become apparent. Not only was the PC bus limited in its memory handling and the width of its data path to the capabilities of a microprocessor that was on the road to oblivion (the 8088), but many of the available system services were in too short supply for growth of the PC beyond a desktop platform for simple, single-minded jobs. For example, most systems ran out of hardware interrupts long before they ran out of expansion slots or clever ideas and expansion boards needing interrupts for control. At the same time, engineers were faced by the abundance of PC bus-based expansion products, many of those made by IBM, which would be rendered incompatible if the bus were radically changed. A complete redesign would require creating an entirely new line of expansion products for IBM and the compatibles industry, probably creating an outcry loud enough to weaken the IBM standard.

As a result of balancing these conflicting needs, the new AT bus was born a hybrid. It retains compatibility with most previous PC expansion products while adding functionality needed to push forward into full 16-bit technology. In addition, it contains a few new ideas (at least for PC-compatible computers) that hint at—and perhaps even foretell—the Micro Channel. Inherent in the AT bus, but almost entirely unused, are provisions for cohabitating microprocessors inside the system; these microprocessors are able to take control and share resources.

The big physical difference between the PC/XT bus and the AT bus was the addition of a second connector to carry more data and address lines—4 more address lines and 8 data—for a total of 16 data lines and 24 address lines, enough to handle 16 megabytes, the physical addressing limit of the 80286 chip. To make up for some of the shortcomings of the PC, which limited its expandability, the new AT bus also included several new interrupt and DMA control lines. In addition, IBM added a few novel connections. One in particular helps make expansion boards compatible across the 8- and 16-bit lines of the IBM Personal Computer. It signals to the host that the card in the socket uses the PC or AT bus.

Maintaining physical compatibility with the previous PC bus was accomplished with the simple but masterful stroke of adding the required new bus connections on a supplementary connector rather than redesigning the already entrenched 62-pin connector. Expansion cards that only required an 8-bit interface and needed no access to protected mode memory locations or the advanced system services of the AT could be designed to be compatible with the full line of 8- and 16-bit IBM-standard computers. Those needing the speed or power of the AT could get it through the supplemental connector. The design even allows cards to use either 8- or 16-bit expansion depending on the host in which they are installed.

The AT design also made it possible to sever the nearly direct connection between microprocessor and bus. As a result, a separate clock can be used for the microprocessor and the expansion bus (as well as the system timers). This change allowed expansion boards to operate at a lower speed than that of the microprocessor.

The AT design proved so satisfactory that a major standard-setting organization, the Institute of Electrical and Electronic Engineers (the IEEE) formed a committee that drew up a complete set of specifications for the bus, including bus timings. In other words, the IEEE certified the AT bus as a standard, which has since come to be known as *Industry Standard Architecture*. It also goes under several other names: ISA, classic bus, and AT bus. Table 6.3 shows the complete pin-out of the 16-bit AT bus.

TABLE 6.3.
Pin-Out of the
Standard 16-Bit
AT Expansion Bus

Pin	Signal	Pin	Signal
B1	Ground	A1	Input/Output Channel Check
B2	Reset Driver	A2	Data 7
B3	+5 VDC	A3	Data 6
B4	Interrupt Request 9	A4	Data 5
B5	-5 VDC	A5	Data 4
B6	DMA Request 2	A6	Data 3
B7	-12 VDC	A7	Data 2
B8	Zero Wait State	A8	Data 1
B9	+12 VDC	A9	Data 0
B10	Ground	A10	Input/Output Channel Ready
B11	Real Memory Write	A11	Address Enable
B12	Real Memory Read	A12	Address 19
B13	Input/Output Write	A13	Address 18
B14	Input/Ouput Read	A14	Address 17
B15	DMA Acknowledge 3	A15	Address 16
B16	DMA Request 3	A16	Address 15
B17	DMA Acknowledge 1	A17	Address 14
B18	DMA Request 1	A18	Address 13
B19	Refresh	A19	Address 12
B20	Clock	A20	Address 11
B21	Interrupt Request 7	A21	Address 10
B22	Interrupt Request 6	A22	Address 9
B23	Interrupt Request 5	A23	Address 8
B24	Interrupt Request 4	A24	Address 7
B25	Interrupt Request 3	A25	Address 6

Pin	Signal	Pin	Signal
B26	DMA Acknowledge 2	A26	Address 5
B27	Terminal Count	A27	Address 4
B28	Address Latch Enable	A28	Address 3
B29	+5 VDC	A29	Address 2
B30	Oscillator	A30	Address 1
B31	Ground	A31	Address 0
D1	Memory 16-Bit Chip Select	C1	System Bus High Enable
D2	I/O 16-Bit Chip Select	C2	Unlatched Address 23
D3	Interrupt Request 10	C3	Unlatched Address 22
D4	Interrupt Request 11	C4	Unlatched Address 21
D5	Interrupt Request 12	C5	Unlatched Address 20
D6	Interrupt Request 15	C6	Unlatched Address 19
D7	Interrupt Request 14	C7	Unlatched Address 18
D8	DMA Acknowledge 0	C8	Unlatched Address 17
D9	DMA Request 0	C9	Memory Read
D10	DMA Acknowledge 5	C10	Memory Write
D11	DMA Request 5	C11	Data 8
D12	DMA Acknowledge 6	C12	Data 9
D13	DMA Request 6	C13	Data 10
D14	DMA Acknowledge 7	C14	Data 11
D15	DMA Request 7	C15	Data 12
D16	+5 VDC	C16	Data 13
D17	Master	C17	Data 14
D18	Ground	C18	Data 15

16-Bit Data Bus Width

The obvious addition that's required when moving from 8 to 16 data bits is 8 additional data lines. These 8 new lines, designated Data 8 through 15, complete the sequence started with the first eight, increasing in significance with their designations.

Because both 8- and 16-bit devices may be present in one computer, some provisions must be made to indicate how many bits are actually to be used for each memory and input/output operation. IBM uses several signals to facilitate such matters. One of these is called *System*

Bus High Enable, and it must be active for 16-bit data transfers to take place. In addition, expansion cards indicate to the host system that the data transfer taking place is a 16-bit operation with the *Memory 16-bit Chip Select* and *I/O 16-bit Chip Select* signals depending on whether the transfer is from or to memory or an input/output device.

Besides slowing down memory access with the *I/O Channel Ready* signal, the AT bus also provides for a speedup signal. The *Zero Wait State* signal indicates that the current bus cycle can be completed without wait states.

24-Bit Addressing

To accommodate the full 16-megabyte physical address range of the 80286 microprocessor used in the AT, IBM expanded the number of memory address lines to 24. Rather than adding just four new lines, however, IBM elected to add eight.

The new address lines differ from the old in that they do not latch— that is, their value is not held by the system board throughout the memory cycle. Instead, they are asserted only until the Memory Read or Write command is given, at which point their value becomes undefined. The expansion board is charged with the responsibility for remembering the address for any longer period that it needs to. This technique can allow faster operation on the bus.

The *Memory Read* and *Memory Write* functions of the AT bus are shifted to the supplementary connector while the bus connections at the positions used by the Memory Read and Memory Write functions of the original (8-bit) PC bus are devoted only to operation on real mode memory.

Memory transfers within the one-megabyte real addressing range require that both the new and old Memory Read or Write lines be activated. When a Read or Write request is made to the area above the one-megabyte limit of real memory, however, only the supplementary connector Memory Read or Write lines are activated. Thus, an 8-bit card will never receive a command, or be able to issue one, that it cannot act upon.

Added System Services

To make up for the shortages of interrupts and DMA channels that often occur in PCs and XTs when multiple serial ports, hard disks, tape systems, and other peripherals are installed, IBM virtually doubled the number of each. Two sets of DMA controllers are available—one that yields four 8-bit channels, one with four 16-bit channels—one of which is reserved for use only on the system board. The operation and priorities assigned to DMA channels follow the pattern set with the PC. DMA channel 0 has the highest priority; DMA channel 7 has the lowest.

Also, the number of interrupts was nearly doubled in the AT, from 8 to a total of 15. Not all of these appear on the expansion bus, however. Five interrupts are reserved to the system board: interrupts 0, 1, 2, 8, and 13. In addition, the AT makes provisions for interrupt sharing so that one interrupt can be used for several functions.

Bus Sharing with Other Microprocessors

With the XT's slot eight, IBM made a token effort toward adding more power on the PC bus. With the AT, specific support is given to running more than one microprocessor on the bus.

The bus sharing works like a DMA cycle. The expansion card containing the visiting microprocessor first activates a DMA request and receives an acknowledgment back. After it has its acknowledgment, the visiting microprocessor activates the Master line on the bus, which gives the chip complete control of all address, data, and control lines of the bus. For a short period, it is the master in charge of the computer.

The short period is delimited by memory refreshing that requires host system access to RAM. If the visiting microprocessor tries to steal more than 15 microseconds at a time from the bus, the host may lose its memory and mind, because the chip gets total control, and the host cannot even refresh its own memory.

To prevent unwanted interruptions during memory refresh cycles, the AT bus also provides for a *Refresh* signal that serves as a warning as to what's going on.

Micro Channel Architecture

By 1987, the disparity between bus speed and microprocessor speed seemed ominous and limiting. With microprocessors forever gaining speed and the bus lock at the 8 Mhz rate, the expansion bus appeared to be the biggest bottleneck in every PC. A new standard was needed.

With the introduction of its PS/2 line of computers, IBM unveiled its solution—a stunning tour-de-force that represented a total break with the classic bus design that incorporated a multitude of the best ideas used in mainframe computers including bus-mastering with full prioritized arbitration. In addition, the new design provided an IBM-sanctioned 32-bit expansion bus to an industry without a 32-bit expansion standard.

The new bus premiered in the high end of the Personal System/2 line of personal computers. Its design was so radically different from the PC and AT buses that IBM coined a new name for it, *Micro Channel Architecture*, a registered trademark of IBM. (Although often abbreviated to MCA, these initials are also the trademark of another organization, a movie-and-media conglomerate once known as the Music Company of America.)

The Micro Channel may just be the most misunderstood innovation since the beginning of the personal computer. It's misunderstood because it was unexpected, unanticipated—and, in many instances, unwanted. Before the PS/2 introduction, what everyone wanted was a 32-bit expansion standard to rally around, one that would continue in the mold of the PC bus, an extension of the status quo. After all, everyone—both user and manufacturer—had a substantial investment in hardware built around the PC bus. Abandoning that standard could not help but be costly. If you had money tied up in a production line to manufacture PC-bus based computers or a thousand PC-bus expansion cards, moving to a new standard is definitely a bad thing.

If you look beyond mere monetary matters, however, it should be obvious that the PC bus had to go. The slow speed of the bus required, for backward compatibility, the biggest performance limit on 80386-based computers that use the PC bus. Even the Intel 25 Mhz slot is a bandaid of sorts. It does not alter some of the PC-bus design problems limiting its high-speed operation, such as the generation of interference.

Sever the link with the past, and system performance is unfettered. IBM, the creator of the PC bus, was perhaps the only organization in the world that could create a replacement for that standard, or, at least, a replacement that might be taken seriously.

Look at the Micro Channel and its history, however, and you will discover that performance may not be the major motivation behind its creation. According to IBM, work began on the Micro Channel as early as 1983—that's even before the AT with its extended PC bus went on sale. Little wonder, then, that there are hints of the Micro Channel in the AT.

The Micro Channel Standard

The Micro Channel came along at the same time IBM made the move to 32-bit processing, but it was not required for the upgrade. Rather, the Micro Channel merely marks a rethinking of the computer expansion slot and an improvement to match state-of-the-art technology. It endows the upper end of the PS/2 line—16-bit as well as 32-bit machines—with powerful new capabilities that fundamentally alter the way personal computers work, making them like more powerful mainframe computers.

Not all PS/2s use the Micro Channel, however. Micro Channel models start with the Model 50 and work their way up. The PS/2s with model designations less than 50 use a slightly modified PC bus, one whose primary difference from the original is that it has been physically flipped on its side. Electrically, it is the same old story.

The Micro Channel is a many splendored thing, nothing that you can put your finger on, hold in your hand, or even classify in one sentence. It's jargon that gives you a single handle to describe a wide collection of specifications and technologies. It's a set of redefined standards for linking various circuit elements and internal peripherals in the more powerful PS/2s.

In those specifications, the term Micro Channel Architecture defines the size and physical arrangement of the bus connectors used in the more powerful PS/2s, the electrical signals they carry, and the logical function that dictates how the entire system works.

Table 6.4 shows the pin-out of the 16-bit Micro Channel and variations for its 32-bit, video, and Matched Memory extensions.

TABLE 6.4.

The Micro Channel and Its Extensions

	Micro Channel Basic 8-Bit Section:		
Pin	Function	Pin	Function
A01	Card Setup	B01	Audio Ground
A02	Made 24	B02	Audio
A03	Ground	B03	Ground
A04	Address 11	B04	14.3 Mhz Oscillator
A05	Address 10	B05	Ground
A06	Address 09	B06	Address 23
A07	+5 VDC	B07	Address 22
A08	Address 08	B08	Address 21
A09	Address 07	B09	Ground
A10	Address 06	B10	Address 20
A11	+5 VDC	B11	Address 19
A12	Address 05	B12	Address 18
A13	Address 04	B13	Ground
A14	Address 03	B14	Address 17
A15	+5 VDC	B15	Address 16
A16	Address 02	B16	Address 15
A17	Address 01	B17	Ground
A18	Address 00	B18	Address 14
A19	+12 VDC	B19	Address 13
A20	Address Decode Latch	B20	Address 12
A21	Preempt	B21	Ground
A22	Burst	B22	Interrupt 09
A23	-12 VDC	B23	Interrupt 03
A24	Arbitration 00	B24	Interrupt 04
A25	Arbitration 01	B25	Ground
A26	Aribitration 02	B26	Interrupt 05
A27	-12 VDC	B27	Interrupt 06
A28	Arbitration 03	B28	Interrupt 07
A29	Arbitration Grant	B29	Ground
A30	Terminal Count	B30	Reserved
A31	+5 VDC	B31	Reserved
A32	Status Bit 0	B32	Channel Check

Micro Channel Basic 8-Bit Section:			
Pin	Function	Pin	Function
A33	Status Bit 1	B33	Ground
A34	Memory/Input Ouput	B34	Command
A35	+12 VDC	B35	Channel Ready Return
A36	Card Ready	B36	Card Selected Feedback
A37	Data line 00	B37	Ground
A38	Data line 02	B38	Data line 01
A39	+5 VDC	B39	Data line 03
A40	Data line 05	B40	Data line 04
A41	Date line 06	B41	Ground
A42	Data line 07	B42	Channel Reset
A43	Ground	B43	Reserved
A44	Data Size 16 Return	B44	Reserved
A45	Refresh	B45	Ground
A46	Key (No Contact)	B46	Key (No Contact)

Micro Channel 16-Bit Extension:			
Pin	Function	Pin	Function
A47	Key (No Contact)	B47	Key (No Contact)
A48	+5 VDC	B48	Data line 08
A49	Data line 10	B49	Data line 09
A50	Data line 11	B50	Ground
A51	Data line 13	B51	Data line 12
A52	+12 VDC	B52	Data line 14
A53	Reserved	B53	Data line 15
A54	Status Byte High Enable	B54	Ground
A55	Card Data Size 16	B55	Interrupt 10
A56	+5 VDC	B56	Interrupt 11
A57	Interrupt 14	B57	Interrupt 12
A58	Interrupt 15	B58	Ground

Micro Channel 32-Bit Extension:			
Pin	Function	Pin	Function
A59	Reserved	B59	Reserved
A60	Reserved	B60	Reserved
A61	Ground	B61	Reserved

continues

TABLE 6.4.
continued

Micro Channel 32-Bit Extension:			
Pin	Function	Pin	Function
A62	Reserved	B62	Reserved
A63	Reserved	B63	Ground
A64	Reserved	B64	Data line 16
A65	+12 VDC	B65	Data line 17
A66	Data line 19	B66	Data line 18
A67	Data line 20	B67	Ground
A68	Data line 21	B68	Data line 22
A69	+5 VDC	B69	Data line 23
A70	Data line 24	B70	Reserved
A71	Data line 25	B71	Ground
A72	Data line 26	B72	Data line 27
A73	+5 VDC	B73	Data line 28
A74	Data line 30	B74	Data line 29
A75	Data line 31	B75	Ground
A76	Reserved	B76	Byte Enable 0
A77	+12 VDC	B77	Byte Enable 1
A78	Byte Enable 3	B78	Byte Enable 2
A79	Data Size 32 Return	B79	Ground
A80	Card Data Size 32	B80	Translate 32
A81	+12 VDC	B81	Address 24
A82	Address 26	B82	Address 25
A83	Address 27	B83	Ground
A84	Address 28	B84	Address 29
A85	+5 VDC	B85	Address 30
A86	Reserved	B86	Address 31
A87	Reserved	B87	Ground
A88	Reserved	B88	Reserved
A89	Ground	B89	Reserved
Micro Channel Auxiliary Video Extension:			
Pin	Function	Pin	Function
AV10	Vertical Sync	BV10	ESYNC
AV09	Horizontal Sync	BV09	Ground
AV08	Blanking	BV08	Video data 5
AV07	Ground	BV07	Video data 4

Micro Channel Auxiliary Video Extension:			
Pin	Function	Pin	Function
AV06	Video data 6	BV06	Video data 3
AV05	ED Clock	BV05	Ground
AV04	Dot Clock	BV04	Video data 2
Micro Channel 32-Bit Extension:			
Pin	Function	Pin	Function
AV03	Ground	BV03	Video data 1
AV02	Video data 7	BV02	Video data 0
AV01	E Video	BV01	Ground
AV00	Key (No Contact)	BV00	Key (No Contact)
Micro Channel 32-Bit Matched Memory Extension:			
Pin	Function	Pin	Function
AM04	Reserved	BM04	Ground
AM03	Matched Mem Cyc Command	BM03	Reserved
AM02	Ground	BM02	Matched Mem Cyc Request
AM01	Matched Memory Cycle	BM01	Reserved

New Connectors

Some of the more obvious changes from the familiar PC bus seem so obvious as to be almost trivial. It uses physically different, smaller, connectors from those used by the aging PC bus. That alone makes the hardware intended for the PC bus incompatible with the Micro Channel.

The new connector choice seemed almost devious. In effect, IBM rendered all third-party peripherals obsolete in one bold stroke. The company honored itself with an instant head start against all other vendors in the design of enhancements for the more profitable top end of the PS/2 line.

If you didn't have a few million dollars tied up in PC expansion inventory and product designs, you might see a bright side to the adoption of miniaturization connectors. For one, they made it easier to engineer expansion boards based on *surface mount components*, miniaturized microchips that pack more functions into less space than ever before. Because the pin spacing on the new Micro Channel connectors—increments of 0.050 inch—corresponds to that of surface mount circuit components, the job of the layout artists (or drafting machine) is easier. On the negative side, they aren't amenable to garage-based engineering, because soldering them to circuit boards demands special equipment.

Miniaturization

IBM complemented the smaller connectors and smaller surface mount components by reducing the size of expansion boards, from the 4.75 x 13.5 of AT boards to 3.5 x 11.5 inches (see fig. 6.1). Surface mount components also help in this size reduction, because they require less power and thus produce less heat, allowing more miniaturization. For people who just use computers and don't have to worry about designing and building them, the smaller connectors, surface mount components, and smaller expansion cards is good news. Less desk space is overrun by rampaging computer equipment.

Unfortunately, much of the promise of miniaturization was slow to be fulfilled. Of all the Micro Channel computers that IBM introduced in the first year that the new bus was available, one, the Model 50, took advantage of the potentials of pygmy packaging. The other early Micro Channel computers, the Models 60 and 80, were actually larger than the original PC.

Smaller boards help manufacturers cut costs, after paying for developing the new designs. They require less of the glass-epoxy base materials from which the boards are built. That's only a small advantage, however, because the cost of components, development, and labor far outweigh the price of the glass-epoxy that makes up the board substrate.

Less Interference

On the interference front, the Micro Channel marks a quantum improvement over the PC-bus design. The radically altered arrangement of signals on the Micro Channel puts an electrical ground on every fourth pin. The many grounds and their proximity to the high frequency digital signals on the bus help reduce interference more than would be possible in PCs or ATs. That, in turn, makes achieving FCC certification less of a headache, giving designers one less thing to sit up nights worrying about.

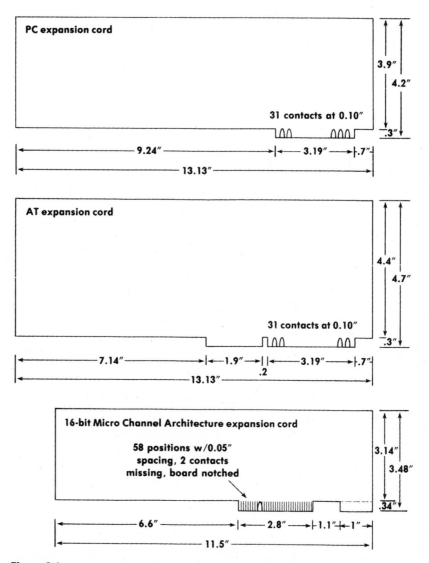

Figure 6.1. Comparison of expansion card dimensions.

More Speed

The better arrangement of signals in the Micro Channel also aids in increasing the maximum speed at which expansion boards can operate, because it increases the bandwidth of the bus. That means higher frequencies and data rates are possible. The first Micro Channels broke through the old IBM 8 Mhz barrier and pushed the limit up to 10. Even the 20 Mhz. Model 80-111 operates its expansion bus at 10 Mhz. The Micro Channel design does not impose 10 Mhz as an absolute speed limit, however. Undoubtedly, faster systems will be released.

Signal Enhancements

Rearranging signals and changing connectors were only a small part of the Micro Channel innovation. The new bus design adds extra data lines, more address lines, and several unexpected refinements such as channels for audio and video information.

More Data

The most expected and most awaited enhancement of the Micro Channel was its specification of 16 new data lines, stretching the width of the bus data path to 32 bits. The wider data path means that memory, input/output devices, and anything connected to the bus can be accessed twice as fast, all else being equal. The Micro Channel is the only IBM-endorsed standard for a 32-bit data bus.

More Addresses

The Micro Channel extended more than the data lines. It also goes beyond third-party AT-compatible 80386 designs by extending the address bus by 8 more bits, raising the total number of address lines from 24 to 32. That extension pushes the maximum addressable memory of the bus from 16 megabytes (same as the AT) to 4 gigabytes (billion bytes).

More Music

Other extensions made to both the 16- and 32-bit Micro Channel designs allow for integrating a single channel analog audio signal of medium fidelity—for instance, synthesized voice or music—with the IBM bus structure. Audio quality is designed to be nearly as good as FM radio, though potentially noisy, with a frequency range up to about 10 kilohertz. (Technically, the response is 50 Hz to 10 Khz +/– 3 dB.)

The *Audio* signal is the only analog signal on the Micro Channel. The Micro Channel specification allows an analog noise level of up to 50 millivolts, against a maximum analog signal of 2,500 millivolts, an inauspicious signal-to-noise ratio of about 32 dB.

Because this audio channel is incorporated as an extension to the bus, the Micro Channel allows expansion cards on the channel to exchange and independently process audio signals.

Video Extension

The video extension to the Micro Channel—a small auxiliary connector, usually on one slot only in each PS/2—allows expansion cards to access the Video Graphics Array circuitry that's built into the high-end PS/2s. You can plug a video coprocessor card into it that will enhance the performance of the VGA but will connect to your monitor through the video connector on the chassis. Moreover, the expansion card and VGA can exchange video information in analog form, which can be faster than moving bytes across the bus in digital form.

The video extension uses several important signals. Present here are horizontal and vertical synchronizing signals plus a special control line called ESYNC or Enable Sync. This line determines whether the synchronizing signals used in the video system originate on the planar board or from an adapter plugged into the Micro Channel. ESYNC is normally held to logical high. Bringing it low enables the system to use the synchronizing signals from the Micro Channel adapter.

Video data is transferred across the Micro Channel video extension in digital form using eight *Video Data Lines*. The data here is used to drive the VGA Digital-to-Analog converter on the system board.

Two clock signals and a special *blanking* signal are also provided. This last signal switches off the output VGA Digital-to-Analog converter to blank the screen. When this signal is high, the screen remains lit; a low darkens the screen.

Bus Arbitration

The Micro Channel's biggest break with traditional PC design is in its hardware-mediated bus arbitration scheme, a move that puts the high-end PS/2 on par with minicomputers. Although the PC bus was created solely for handling the needs of a single microprocessor working on one job at a time, Micro Channel PS/2s allow multiple microprocessors and ancillary devices to share the bus in an organized manner, permitting not only multitasking but also parallel processing.

The key words are hardware-mediated. The AT allowed bus sharing but required special software to control the system. All prioritizing had to be accomplished through programming, and little support was given to the programmer. Only the implementation of this hardware-mediation is new, however. The idea was borrowed from mainframe computers, an area in which IBM has some expertise.

The current PS/2 implementation of hardware bus arbitration allows up to eight microprocessors and eight other devices, such as DMA controllers, to share the single data bus of the Micro Channel without interfering with one another and without the need for elaborate software control systems. Engineers can add coprocessors, advanced communications, and high-resolution graphics subsystems to a PS/2 almost with impunity—and need not worry whether programmers will deliver the necessary code in time.

This hardware arbitration scheme could not be added to PCs or ATs without sacrificing backward compatibility, however. For the system to work correctly, all expansion cards—even those that do not exploit bus arbitration to take control—must implement its circuitry. Even if the bus were not modified, the expansion card would have to be. That alone would require an entire redesign of expansion card circuitry. But as long as the cards were being redesigned, adding the rest of the Micro Channel features were added.

New Configuration Procedure

Another indication of this conceptual shift is the Micro Channel's *Programmable Option Select* or *POS* feature, designed to make installation and expansion of system enhancements much easier and less confusing than in previous PCs. POS does away with all the DIP switches, jumpers, and headers that made configuring a system only a slightly less arcane ritual than an exorcism.

Using low-power, battery-backed CMOS memory, much like the AT uses for storing its disk drive types and memory endowment, each PS/2 can remember its own hardware configuration. That includes which board is supposed to be in each of its expansion slots and how that board should function in relation to the rest of the system.

Every different expansion board designed for the Micro Channel is assigned a unique identifying number that's coded into its firmware. When the system boots up, the PS/2 compares the installed options with its CMOS memory and files stored on its disk drive to detect changes to ensure the integrity of its setup. Also, the identifying numbers serve to link each Micro Channel board data file, holding information on using and installing the option. The setup files are automatically incorporated into the software setup procedure on the system *Reference Disk*, so you see one seamless installation procedure. In this way, one simple and familiar installation procedure takes care of any expansion board, no matter what its origins.

The PS/2 even eliminates the single switch located in every AT and nearly every compatible (including 80386-based models)—the one that selects the default monitor type. The VGA system renders it unnecessary, because signals in the monitor cable cause the VGA adapter to automatically adjust for either monochrome or color displays.

Level-Sensitive Interrupts

The Micro Channel also changes the number of the familiar signals carried over from the traditional PC-bus work. For instance, interrupts, which are edge-triggered on the PC bus, are level-sensitive on the Micro Channel. Systems based on the technology of the old PC sense interrupts only at the instant when the interrupt request changes state. In the Micro Channel design, the interrupt signal remains active during the interrupt.

While either edge-triggering or level-sensing works for interrupt signals, the latter design confers several benefits in computers in which interrupts are shared. The computer knows an interrupt is active just by examining a level-sensitive interrupt line. It must *remember* that an edge-triggered line has been set. As a result, level-sensing simplifies the design of the logic-sharing circuitry on expansion boards. It reduces the sensitivity of the interrupt controller to noise and transients. And it allows for a mixture of sharing and nonsharing hardware on the same interrupt level.

New Signals

In addition, some new signals have been defined on the Micro Channel bus, besides those used by the new hardware arbitration feature. For instance, *Card Selected Feedback* provides an indication from an expansion card to the host that the card is at the address it is supposed to be. Its primary use is during setup and diagnostics to help the system decipher what options are installed.

The *Channel Ready* line differs substantially from the I/O Channel Ready line of the PC bus. In the Micro Channel, it is used by devices connected to the bus to signal that they need more time to complete an operation, not to exceed 3.5 microseconds. Each connector has its own independent signal that is not bussed together with those from other connectors. All of the signals from every connector are combined logically, and if they all indicate that no additional time is needed, another special signal, *Channel Ready Return,* is created to make monitoring the condition of the bus easier.

Each connector in the Micro Channel also has its own *Card Setup* line that is used during setup and error-recovery procedures. Activating this signal allows the configuration data space on the expansion board in the connector to be read.

Rather than using separate lines for memory and input/output operations as does the PC bus, the Micro Channel uses a combination of three signals—*Memory/Input-Output, Status Bit One,* and *Status Bit Two* to define the type of bus cycle to be made.

Similar to the I/O Channel Check line of the PC bus, the *Channel Check* line of the Micro Channel is used to indicate serious error conditions, such as parity check errors.

The Micro Channel uses special signals to indicate the bus width of each card inserted into a connector. *Card Data Size 16* is generated by devices connected to the bus to tell expansion cards that 16 bits of information is available to them. The card signals back on Data Size 16 Return that it can handle 16-bit data. Similarly the signals Card Data Size 32 and Data Size 32 Return indicate and confirm 32-bit operations in 80386-equipped PS/2s, such as the Models 70 and 80.

Byte Enable Bits 0 through 3 are used to identify the type of data transfer carried across the bus. They permit Micro Channel components to move information 8-, 16-, 24-, or 32-bits at a time without ambiguity. This aids Micro Channel adapters in using any bus width that's an even multiple of a byte, so that 8-, 16-, and 32-bit expansion accessories can be mixed in the same computer.

Memory Address Enable 24, when not turned on, indicates that the microprocessor, or another device on the bus, is using the extended 32-bit addressing range of the 80386 microprocessor rather than the 24-bit range of the 80286.

Matched Memory Cycles

In addition to the wider 32-bit bus and the faster allowable clock speed of the Micro Channel, 32-bit versions of the system allow for a new data transfer mode. Called *Matched Memory*, this mode endows the Micro Channel with the potential of further quickening the pulse of data transfers between the planar board and expansion cards. The new signals take the form of another extension to the 32-bit bus that indicate to the 80386 that the data moving between devices can be synchronized at a higher rate. When memory or an 16- or 32-bit internal peripheral is capable of operating at this higher speed, it can use the Matched Memory provisions of the Micro Channel to speed each information transfer by 25 percent, from 250 nanoseconds per cycle to 187.

The Matched Memory extension to the Micro Channel adds eight possible connections, three of which are reserved for future use and two of which are grounds. The *Matched Memory Cycle* signal is activated by the host microprocessor to indicate that it can handle matched memory transfers. The *Matched Memory Cycle Request* line is driven active by a device on the bus to indicate that it wants transfers to be made in the faster Matched Memory mode, either as 16- or 32-bit data. A third signal, *Matched Memory Command* indicates that a Matched Memory cycle is active.

Burst Mode

In the original PC design, the flow of data across the expansion bus was never the smooth, consistent current implied by the term. Moving bytes was a function fraught with fits and stops, because data transfer operations were plagued by operating overhead. Moving each byte was a two-step operation—the address step to get ready and data-moving step to do the actual work. All those starts and stops dragged the flow of data, similar to the slow run of a local bus line with its stopping at every street corner to pick up and discharge passengers, making any journey seem to take forever. With this conventional design in computers, the processor becomes a point of congestion, because it is the only element capable of moving continuous blocks of data.

Micro Channel Architecture eliminates this bottleneck by allowing devices to move bursts or large blocks of data in its so-called *burst mode*. Rather than relying on the two-step microprocessor data-moving process, the Micro Channel allows transference of bursts of data blocks to and from input/output devices at rates of nearly 19 million characters or bytes per second (that's nearly 152 million bits per second) *without* the intervention of the microprocessor. To prevent congestion in the microprocessor, the Micro Channel also defines eight additional high-speed block-oriented paths between the input/output bus and memory.

Burst mode also requires some overhead, but much less than with PC- and AT-style block transfers. In burst mode, the system is first set up for moving the data by specifying the destination of the first byte to be transferred. Then the block of data is moved one byte right after another. Rather than a local or express bus trip, burst mode works like a chartered tour. It's a direct point-to-point operation that keeps together a group of sightseers.

Rather than using software signals to indicate that a transfer is taking place or has ended, the Micro Channel uses hardware—a special connection in the expansion bus. Operation of the burst mode is controlled by Micro Channel circuitry without the intervention of the microprocessor, so burst mode transfers can take place while the microprocessor is engaged in other activities (like processing data that has previously moved across the bus).

Streaming Data Mode

For most purposes and peripherals, the Micro Channel, as originally propounded, is fast enough even today. In fact, most expansion devices do just fine with an old ISA connection. However, what's fast one year quickly becomes slow as technology races ahead, and anticipating the need for faster bus transfers about two years after the introduction of the Micro Channel, IBM enhanced its performance with a special, faster data-transfer protocol, *streaming data mode*.

Designed to speed the movement of data between bus masters and slaves, streaming data mode is an optional Micro Channel implementation—that means that not all computers or peripherals need to be able to use it. Systems and devices designed to use it benefit from its up to eight-times-faster data transfers. Systems that cannot accommodate it won't encounter compatibility problems, however. They will just use their normal transfer methods should they be instructed to use the faster mode. In other words, under the Micro Channel specification, systems and peripherals will operate at the highest speed they can but won't suffer compatibility problems if they cannot handle the fastest transfers. In fact, no adjustments to the physical structure of the systems, mechanical or electrical definition of the connector interface, or redefinition of existing protocols was required to achieve the performance increase made possible by streaming data protocol.

The speed increase can be substantial. With no change in a system's timings or its signal definitions, streaming data mode can accelerate transfers by two to four times the initial or default data-transfer rate of the system in which it operates. In systems in which advanced streaming data support is engineered, greater gains are available. For example, Micro Channel Architecture allows a data multiplexing technique that yields an effective doubling of the data bus width—from 32 bits to 64 bits—for streaming data transfers. Altering system timing can double the transfer rate again. Ultimately, the existing streaming data protocol allows up to a sixteenfold increase in the speed of data transfers across the bus.

All of these advanced streaming data modes start out with a standard, or default, Micro Channel data transfer cycle. To move a word across the expansion bus, the Micro Channel (similar to most other computer buses) requires that an address be defined before a transfer can occur, even in its high-speed burst mode. Each transfer of a single word thus requires two cycles—one for setting up the address and one for actually moving the data.

Under the Micro Channel specification, the combined two operations require 200 nanoseconds (billionths of a second)—two cycles of the 10 Mhz Micro Channel bus clock. This speed allows five words to be transferred in each one-millionth of a second, 5 million words a second. Using 32-bit words, 4 bytes per word, that works out to a maximum effective data-transfer rate of about 20 megabytes of data per second.

That figure represents the potential throughput of the Micro Channel operating at its most basic level, its instantaneous data-transfer rate of its default data-transfer cycle. This is the highest rate at which the Micro Channel can move a byte at any given address to another address, the fastest possible rate at which a Micro Channel computer can *randomly* transfer data across its bus (absent some other enhancement, such as matched-memory mode). System overhead precludes real-world performance from ever achieving this rate under normal transfer modes. That's why burst mode, for example, is rated at only 19 million bytes per second.

The standard data-transfer methods on the Micro Channel have one strength. They allow random transfers—bytes can be selected from source locations at random and sent to a random set of destination locations, because an address is assigned to each byte for each transfer. However, the typical data transfer across an expansion bus is a series of random movements of bytes or words. Usually, an entire block of data is moved at a time, one word right after another. In such cases, the addresses that are indicated for each byte become redundant. If you know that you need to move 1,000 words as a group, when you know the first address, thereafter, you know where each word is supposed to go. The addresses given at the beginning of each of the transfers become redundant after the first transfer is completed. You know where every word, every byte, of each subsequent transfer is supposed to go. After you've located the first word, you need only maintain a running count to know where each subsequent word belongs.

It only makes sense to eliminate the requirement of sending out an address for one cycle before each word is transferred (at least, after the first word), much as the Micro Channel's burst mode does. Streaming data protocol eliminates every other cycle (the addressing cycle) of a transfer of a block of sequential data words. Eliminating one cycle cuts in half the time to transfer a word, from 200 nanoseconds to 100 nanoseconds, for each transfer after the first. Consequently, for transfers of blocks of data, streaming data mode effectively doubles the transfer rate to a theoretical peak of 40 megabytes per second. The longer the sequence of words to be transferred, the faster the overall rate and the closer it comes to the peak rate, because there's less setup overhead per data block that's streamed.

While streaming data mode and burst mode aim for the same results— an increase in the data transfer rate across the bus—they differ in mechanism used, speed achieved, and duration of the transfer. Burst mode is designed for handling smaller blocks of random data; whereas streaming data mode is capable of handling more extended sequential transfers. Although burst mode tops out at 20 megabytes per second data transfer rate, streaming data mode transfer rates up to eight times higher are already defined, and even higher rates may be possible. These improvements in streaming data mode arise from data multiplexing and reduced cycle times.

Data Multiplexing

IBM also added another optional feature to the Micro Channel as part of its so-called Micro Channel 2 announcement, *Data multiplexing*, which allows the ordinary 32-bit bus to support 64-bit transfers. The idea is to eliminate some of the redundancy of the bus when it's unnecessary. Note that the Micro Channel specification assigned 32 bus lines to carry data and another 32 lines to specify address information. Examine streaming data protocol and you'll see that those 32 address lines aren't doing anything during most of the streaming data transfer. In fact, the only time that they need to be active is for the single cycle at the beginning of the transfer of a data stream. For the balance of the transfer, those 32 address lines remain idle.

The key to the Micro Channel's speed is efficiency, putting all system resources to work. Those 32 idle address lines represent lost opportunity. By redefining them temporarily as additional data lines, the address lines can be used to double the width of the Micro Channel's data bus. That leads to an effective doubling of the data-transfer rate, up to 80 megabytes per second.

Using a single wire to carry more than one channel of information is a technique that's called *multiplexing*, so this mode is termed *multiplexed streaming data mode*.

All of the speeds given for effective bus throughput assume one condition: the Micro Channel uses a clock speed of 10 Mhz that results in a bus cycle time of 10 Mhz. Although this is the default speed of the Micro Channel, nothing constrains its speed to that rate. In fact, the Micro Channel specification allows a cycle time of one-half that rate, 50 nanoseconds. Operating with that reduced bus-cycle timing, the Micro Channel's streaming data mode produces an effective throughput approaching 160 megabytes per second.

Considering that the fastest hard disks now operate at an effective data-transfer rate of 15 megabits per second and the burst rate of the fastest network is 14 megabits per second, all of that speed might seem superfluous. However, when multiple bus masters need to make transfers at, or near the same time, every bit of bus bandwidth is needed.

Moreover, these extremely fast transfer rates make the Micro Channel fast enough that memory on the bus can serve the needs of the fastest of today's microprocessor memory caches. (A 32-bit microprocessor operating at 33 Mhz requires data at a 128 megabyte per second rate, well within the reach of the 160 megabyte per second Micro Channel.)

Bus Mastering Operation

As forbidding as bus mastering and arbitration under Micro Channel standard sounds, its operation is actually easy to conceptualize. It's just a system of several signals that serve as semaphores to notify each device sharing the bus when it is its turn to share the data bus. Sufficient controls are provided so that up to 16 different devices inside the host computer can share, with each superhighway in its initial explanations. Like the Interstate, the Micro Channel provides, according to IBM, multiple lanes going in every direction at the highest possible safe speed. Because it has more lanes, it can handle more traffic, speeding the flow of data around inside the system.

It's a good metaphor and could only be better were it to actually describe how the Micro Channel works. At best, however, it's misleading. The Micro Channel only provides two parallel paths for high-speed traffic running next to its (up to) 32 bits of data—one for its auxiliary audio signal and one for analog video information.

A more appropriate and descriptive highway analogy for the Micro Channel would be a Manhattan thoroughfare—one lined with traffic lights, kamikaze taxicabs, pedestrians, and a propensity for gridlock.

The Micro Channel works like the humble traffic cop, breaking up gridlock with a mixture of nerve, willpower, and guts. Just as the officer, armed with naught but his white gloves, keep hacks and hitchhikers out of harms way and keeps traffic flowing, the Micro Channel's hardware bus arbitration gives all the processors sharing the bus its own turn, assuring that none bogs down. Data processing flows along in as orderly and efficient a manner as possible. Like the policeman, the Micro Channel built highways to provide alternate data paths or eliminate waiting, it keeps everything orderly and under control, preventing collisions and accidents.

Micro Channel bus arbitration accomplishes this task by specifying the signal hierarchy each device must use to gain access to the data bus of the PS/2 in which it's running. The arbitration scheme also provides a means of resolving conflicting claims, when two or more devices demand their right to ride the bus. Hardware arbitration prevents the confusion of two devices trying to appropriate control of the Micro Channel at the same time.

New Lines

To implement this arbitration strategy, the Micro Channel adds several new lines to the old PC bus. Four of these, called *Arbitration Bus Priority Levels 0 through 3*, carry signals that code the level of priority assigned to each device that wants to take control of the Micro Channel, allowing for its 16 levels of priority.

In addition, two additional levels of priority are used by the devices on the system board of the PS/2 and do not appear on the Micro Channel. These special levels are used to assign the absolute top priority to memory refreshing (which preserves data integrity) and the nonmaskable interrupt (the familiar parity-check error signal).

Bus arbitration involves three additional signals. One, called *Pre-empt*, is used by expansion cards to indicate they require access to the Micro Channel. Another, *Arbitrate/Grant*, is sent out from the Micro Channel *Central Arbitration Control Point*, which manages use of the bus, to start a haggling process for bus access. A final signal, *Burst*, allows Micro Channel devices to retain control while they transfer multiple blocks of related data so that they don't have to go through arbitration until the entire transfer is complete. It's a "Do Not Disturb" sign for block data transfers.

Arbitration Process

The arbitration process begins when one or more devices want to take control of the Micro Channel and send that message to the Central Arbitration Point. After a pause appears on the data bus, the Arbitrator signals all devices connected to the Micro Channel that they should start bidding for control.

Each Micro Channel device that wants bus access then sends out its assigned priority level on the four Arbitration Bus Priority Level lines. Each Micro Channel expansion card checks these signals and ceases its efforts when it finds a higher priority level is being asserted. Conflicting claims of the same priority level should never appear, because the Micro Channel design does not allow two devices to be assigned the same priority.

These priority levels are assigned during the configuration process of each Micro Channel board and are stored on disk in the Adapter Description Files, disk files that are associated with each Micro Channel device during the Programmable Option Select process.

Hardware bus arbitration holds several advantages over the alternative technique, pure software control. With traditional PC architecture, however, such a software arbitration scheme would have to be governed by the host microprocessor, which necessarily handles all software instructions. This microprocessor-mediated process would involve substantial software overhead—the microprocessor monitoring every request from every device and deciding which should get control. When the microprocessor must break from its normal duties to oversee such housekeeping, system performance suffers. In addition, the microprocessor would always be tied up, because it would have to constantly monitor the bus. It could not be busy with its own chores while some other device peeked and poked through the system memory.

The Micro Channel breaks the connection between bus and microprocessor. No software is necessary, because all of the bus arbitration functions are built into the hardware of the expansion cards. It's a faster and, in the end, a cleaner system.

Bus Mastering Example

One application, perhaps unimportant today, that shows the advantage of Micro Channel hardware bus arbitration is the coprocessor card similar to the turbo boards used for enhancing the performance of older computers.

In a traditional PC-bus system, handling video (or any I/O) signals becomes a complex, software-intensive chore for a turbo board coprocessor. One of the more vexing complications is handling the display. Many programs write directly to the screen by pushing bytes of information into video memory. When these run on a coprocessor board, they write to its memory rather than the video RAM of the computer host, so nothing appears on the display. The coprocessor must simulate that video memory in its own address range, accept the data that's written there, and then transfer that information to the ordinary video memory of the host.

No matter how skillfully this operation double-writing and shift process is handled—and over the years turbo boards have improved immeasurably in their video handling—video updates always take substantially longer, because of the heavy overhead of dealing with two distinct memory systems.

On the Micro Channel, however, this operation is trivial. A co-processor board would merely map the normal video memory of its computer host into its own address range. When a program writes directly to video memory, the coprocessor board merely takes control of the Micro Channel and routes the display information exactly where it belongs. Overhead, is trivial and performance can be extraordinary.

Some coprocessors allow communication with their hosts using expensive dual-ported memory. The coprocessor writes to one port of the memory, and the host pulls the data out of the other. With the Micro Channel, data can be shared directly in any memory location, and ordinary RAM chips serve the purpose.

One of the most intriguing promises of the Micro Channel is parallel processing, breaking tough problems into small pieces to be simultaneously solved by multiple microprocessors. A single Model 80, for instance, might house eight 80386 microprocessors and deliver correspondingly fast performance—about on par with a VAX cluster (considering that a single 80386/80387 combination has nearly the same raw processing horsepower as a VAX 8600).

This parallel processing would, of course, require entirely new software. It's not a technology of today, but it is one that shows great promise in breaking the bottlenecks in mainframe processing. The Micro Channel makes those same potentials possible in a desktop computer.

Subsystem Control Block Architecture

By itself, bus mastering is a powerful and useless concept. Without a way for the computer to control the new feature through its software and operating system, the new hardware design cannot be exploited to its full potential. What's needed is a means to link the new hardware with the personal system's programs.

Subsystem Control Block Architecture serves that function. An architecture like Micro Channel Architecture, Subsystem Control Block Architecture is a software structure, a set of rules, and a philosophy. Its basic purpose is to define how operating systems can control one or more bus masters connected to the Micro Channel expansion bus. To do that, it provides a means for applications to take control over hardware resources. It specifies data structures (that is, the syntax of commands) and the method through which they are exchanged between parts of the computer system.

The responsibilities of Subsystem Control Block Architecture range from the mundane to the exotic. For example, part of the architecture provides error and status reporting protocols so all programs can depend on a standard interface to monitor the operation of the entire system. At the other end of the control continuum, it allows the dynamic assignment of system facilities among multiple masters.

One of the innovations introduced by Subsystem Command Block Architecture is *Command Chaining*, a powerful concept through which multiple bus masters can decide, according to prescribed algorithms, which of several potential control paths to follow. The path selection capability of Command Chaining allows for the Bus Master operations to be coordinated and predefined as "Macro" operations. Unlike a simple series of commands, however, the chain of command can be interactive, allowing the bus master subsystems the latitude to respond to changing conditions while operating.

In some ways, Subsystem Control Block Architecture is a way of avoiding the mass proliferation of system interrupts. It provides a means of control (independent of them) and helps avoid the overhead of interrupt operation. In fact, Subsystem Control Block Architecture owes its heritage to mainframe computer design (as does much of the Micro Channel), and it anticipates the further migration of mainframe operating system principles into the Personal Systems.

Subsystem Control Block Architecture provides the primary means for controlling complex hardware configurations that have multiple intelligent subsystems. The use of Subsystem Control Block Architecture extends the capabilities of the Micro Channel to support distributed multiprocessing—multiple microprocessors in a single system chassis serving a number of diverse users—in the future.

EISA

Technically, Micro Channel rated a masterstroke, essentially embodying the best of mainframe technology distilled down to PC size. But, in a fit of corporate hubris, IBM tied the use of MCA's proprietary technologies with hefty licensing fees at which the rest of the PC industry, accustomed to taking advantage of IBM-developed technology for free, balked. Moreover, IBM cursed Micro Channel with marketing so ineptly that it might have besmirched the reputation of Florence Nightingale, failing to satisfactorily explain why backward compatibility with PC and AT expansion boards was such an ill-considered concept. IBM's rationale was that the truly bad engineering behind the old bus and boards would hold back performance of new MCA systems. Advanced features such as level-sensitive interrupts would not tolerate old boards that used edge-triggered interrupts. Starting with a new standard opened the opportunity for doing things right, entirely re-engineering the bus for optimum high-speed operation and reliability. But most people believe the Micro Channel design was more a means for IBM to steal back the industry by obsoleting the products of other manufacturers.

The industry reaction to Micro Channel was the development of *Extended Industry Standard Architecture*, more commonly known as *EISA*. The basic design of EISA amounts to the features of Micro Channel implemented in technologies free from IBM's control—essentially, the greatest hits of expansion bus design. Although the exciting new bus standard certainly incorporates some original and clever thoughts, EISA really amounts to the greatest hits of computer buses, the best ideas drawn from other bus designs and the whole computer industry.

That description is not meant to be derogatory any more than it is accidental that EISA is so derivative. From its very beginnings, EISA was designed not as an original concept but as an enhancement to the familiar AT bus. The reality of EISA goes far beyond the mere specifying of how to add 16 new data lines to the classic AT bus. By borrowing the best ideas from other bus designs—features such as bus mastering, automated setup, and interrupt sharing—then mixing in its own new data-transfer modes, EISA has become a powerful and useful expansion design.

Of course, one contrary viewpoint would be to label EISA the computer equivalent of a camel—rather than a horse drawn by committee, a standard so executed. In fact, EISA was crafted by committee: the so-called "Gang of Nine" (AST Research, Compaq Computer Corp., Epson, Hewlett-Packard Company, NEC, Olivetti, Tandy, Wyse, and Zenith Data Systems), a group of erstwhile competitors that banded together to create their own standard in opposition to IBM's Micro Channel Architecture. The goal, announced September 13, 1988, was to design a 32-bit successor to Industry Standard Architecture—one that remained compatible to it rather than replacing it.

Backward Compatibility

Although committee-work often sounds synonymous to "kludge," this particular committee worked in the opposite direction. They recognized that ISA had become the classic kludge—an ill-defined standard at best—by the time the EISA group formed. At worst, the classic bus had grown into industry dominance lacking even bus-timing specifications, vital for determining how expansion cards interact. The EITHER had not formalized the all-important timing specifications for the AT bus until years after hundreds of manufacturers had gone in their separate directions. Because of the proliferations of boards, each following its own variation of the "standard," compatibility on the classic bus was chancy.

The future of the classic bus was even more disheartening. Its poor performance and limited data-handling fell far short of the needs of the fast 80286-based computers, must less those of the 386 and 486 machines. The task facing the EISA committee was to bring order from the chaos of the clouded.

To IBM, the original developer of the classic bus, the situation was so hopeless that the company's engineers decided that the only way out was to abandon the AT-bus standard altogether. The EISA committee thought otherwise. After all, computer users had billions invested in classic bus accessories, and the committee members had their fortunes tied to the old architecture as well. To try to preserve both investments, the committee created the EISA standard, brought together much of the rest of the personal computer industry, and ushered out a flurry of new products based upon it.

At its heart was full backward compatibility with the AT bus. Under EISA, all existing PC expansion boards are plug-compatible with newer, high-performance EISA computers, although the opposite is not true, and some exceptions do exist. To achieve this required some big compromises—for example, retaining the 8 Mhz bus speed limit. In addition, it demanded an entirely new kind of connector and unprecedented cooperation in a competitive industry.

Board Dimensions

The physical specifications between the old and new standards are remarkably similar. EISA expansion boards are the same size and shape as AT boards, with the standard setting the maximum (at 13.415 long and 4.5 inches high, from the top of the board to its bottom edge of the board) with smaller boards, such as so-called "short cards" still accepted. But EISA makes some specific changes aimed at ensuring future products are even more intercompatible than PC boards are today.

A seemingly minor change holds the potential for making a big difference. All measurements for EISA boards are specified from a common origin—that is, you measure all dimensions from a common starting point. For EISA, that point is the center of the expansion connector rather than an edge of the card. As a result, tolerances are smallest, and the fit of boards is best where it counts most, at the expansion connector. EISA boards should fit better than their predecessors.

Another EISA change may have greater implications for existing PC expansion boards. Although EISA accepts all physical configurations of current expansion boards, it prohibits in future products the addition of *skirts*, areas of board that dip down below the expansion connector to obtain slightly more space for component on the long bottom edge of the board. (EISA permits a "mini-skirt," however, one located between the expansion connector and card-retaining bracket.) The implication is clear, just as with current computers, not all slots in EISA machines allow the insertion of boards with skirts.

EISA Connector

The centerpiece of the EISA specification is its expansion connector, the design to ensure backward compatibility with PC-bus cards while allowing full 32-bit expandability of EISA peripherals. It adds 90 new connections (55 new signals) without increasing the size of the connector and accepts both EISA and classic-bus boards indiscriminately.

The clever, two-tier design of this connector actually represents a revision on the original EISA concept. The EISA connector originally announced in 1988 relied on what was, in effect, two parallel connectors—one providing the compatible link-up with existing expansion boards and another, offset from the expansion board, for 32-bit data transfers and addressing. The parallel-connector design was criticized for various deficiencies including its need for inordinately high insertion force (the effort required to plug a board into a slot). So much effort was believed to be required to squeeze a board into this connector that it nearly precluded the use of cost-saving automatic insertion machinery in the building of new computers.

Because the new EISA connector is physically the same size as a traditional expansion connector, it requires about the same insertion force—35 pounds—versus the 100-plus estimated for the proposed parallel connector. It should cause no problems for automatic insertion machinery.

The new connector achieves its combination of compatibility and full 32-bit expandability by branching out vertically rather than horizontally. In the new EISA connector, the contacts for enhanced functions are built into a second, lower level. Existing PC expansion boards can be inserted just about halfway into EISA slots to engage the PC bus contacts only. Five keys—plastic stops molded into the EISA connector—prevent older boards from being inserted further. EISA boards have cut-outs that fit into the keys and allow the boards to be fully inserted into the connector. This keying prevents old-bus cards from shorting out the EISA connections, which could potentially damage the EISA computer. After the card is fully inserted, both the upper and lower sets of contacts engage pads on the EISA board.

Because it needs deeper insertion, the edge connector on an EISA board is, consequently, a bit longer (about 0.2 inch) than that of a classic bus board.

Nothing stops EISA boards from fitting into ordinary 16-bit AT expansion slots, however. In fact, because of the odd arrangement of contacts on EISA boards, inadvertently inserting an EISA board into a old AT connector can potentially send signals into the wrong circuits—not enough fireworks to give Mr. Scott apoplexy, but sufficient to render the host system dysfunctional. Consequently, EISA boards should never be inserted into non-EISA computers although they physically fit the slots.

Power Limits

EISA also strives to maintain compatibility with the power demands of old-bus expansion boards. Under the EISA specification, a generous availability of power is assumed for each expansion slot, freeing peripheral designers from the need to use special low-power components. Over 45 watts at four different voltages are available to each EISA expansion slot.

Of course, such availability takes an optimistic view of the total reserves of the system power supply. Filling the eight slots envisioned in a complete EISA system with hungry expansion boards would require more than 325 watts of power. Even without considering the needs of mass storage devices and the system board itself, a fully expanded EISA computer would require a huge power supply. Then again, nothing about the EISA design implies expansion boards will require any more power than old-bus cards, so traditional power levels will probably be adequate.

32-Bit Expansion

The original impetus behind the search for a new bus standard was the inability of the 16-bit classic AT bus to deal with the 32-bit needs of the newer Inter microprocessors (specifically the 386DX and 486). The first step in wringing full performance from these chips is to move data around in the largest blocks they can manipulate in a single operation, specifically 32-bit double-words. Widening the *data path* to

32-bits in itself can double the speed of data transfers in an AT-style computer, all else being equal, which is definitely not the case of EISA. To gain this instant advantage over the classic bus, EISA expansion adds 16 new data lines.

Addressing Enhancement

The classic AT bus imposed another limit on higher powered microprocessors. Its 24 *address lines* enforce a maximum size of 16 megabytes on directly addressable memory (as opposed to bank-switched memory, like that available under the EMS standard). To accommodate the complete addressing capabilities of the 32-bit Inter microprocessors—4 gigabytes—EISA also broadens the address bus to a full 32-bits. The new address lines are labeled with the prefix LA in the pignut.

Note that EISA's endowment is more generous than a mere eight additional address lines. The standard also adds new lines for indicating some of the lower order address bits, to some extent duplicating the function of the classic bus but with an important change. The EISA lower order address lines (LA2 through LA16) are latching; they provide stable signals through the address cycle rather than just at its beginning. Note that the EISA address extensions (the upper eight bits) to the classic bus also latch.

Bus-Width Signaling

Sometimes, all 32-bits of the data bus are not needed in a data transfer. For example, a program may need to move only a byte from one memory location to another. EISA provides four new signals to indicate which bytes of the double-word of data on the bus are significant, the *Byte Enable* signals BE0 through BE4.

To maintain compatibility with as many classic bus expansion boards as possible, EISA is designed to accommodate devices that have either 8-, 16-, or 32-bit interfaces. This diversity requires some method of preventing a device dumping 32-bits of data to another device with only a 16-bit interface (half the data would be lost).

EISA provides two signals to indicate the data-transfer size a device can handle. To indicate that it has access to the full 32-bits of the EISA bus, a device sends the *EX32* signal. Similarly, the EX16 signal indicates that a device supports 16-bit transfers only. If neither signal is present, the system must assume that the particular device can handle only 8-bits of data at a time. (These signals supplement those on the classic bus that indicate 8- or 16-bit transfer width.)

Data-Width Translation

EISA doesn't stop with bus-width signaling. The standard also provides for the automatic translation of the width of bus signals, for instance breaking down the 32-bit signal of an EISA card into four sequential 8-bit signals digestable by classic bus expansion boards. A special integrated circuit, the EISA Bus Controller, moves data into the appropriate byte-lanes and translates the control signals on the bus accordingly.

New Transfer Modes

EISA goes well beyond just providing extra signals to add new data and addressing capacity to the classic bus. Other EISA enhancements also require new signals to be assigned to bus connections. These signals include support for burst-mode data transfers (MBURST and SLBURTS), new timing signals to help manage fast data transfers (START and CMD), even a signal to slow down the bus with wait states (EXRDY). EISA also adds slot-specific signals for managing bus arbitration (MREQx and MAKx), discussed later. Another slot-specific signal, one that redefines a signal assignment on the classic bus, is now called AENx. It enables each expansion board to respond independently, so each board can be addressed and controlled individually.

The nomenclature of these slot-specific signals alone limits EISA to its avowed maximum of 15 expansion slots per system (the "x" in the signal names is replaced by the hexadecimal designation of the slot), although the specification states that systems with more than eight slots are unlikely.

Under EISA standards, all the other signals on the classic bus retain their former definitions and functions to maintain backward compatibility with older expansion boards. The big challenge faced by the EISA engineers was to fit all these signals on a connector that would still allow the use of old expansion boards.

Compatibility is among the more formidable problems in squeezing more raw speed—more megahertz—from the AT bus. Simply increasing the clock speed, which synchronizes data transfers across the bus, is out of the question, because a speed increase can cause problems for existing expansion boards. Many classic bus boards won't operate at bus speeds much higher than the 8 Mhz used in the AT or the 10 Mhz used by some compatibles.

The Bus Clock

To help ensure compatibility, EISA does not increase the raw speed of the clock driving the expansion bus. The specification calls for a bus clock (BCLK) oscillating at a fixed rate between 6 and 8.33 Mhz, the latter figure is one-fourth the 33 Mhz clock speed of today's fastest microprocessors.

The bus speed is a submultiple of the system clock frequency, because the EISA is nominally a *synchronous bus*, it operates in lock-step with the host microprocessor, but not necessarily. Bus masters can assume control and alter some aspects of system timing to achieve higher data throughputs.

Such altered timings are necessary, because the bus speed limit is more severe than the megahertz would imply. The actual data-transfer rate of ISA is limited by its two-cycle per transfer limitation with the bus going through an elaborate hierarchy of commands for every transferred byte. Although EISA allows this data-transfer method, it also adds two faster schemes of its own: *compressed transfers* and *burst mode*. Compressed transfers are 50 percent faster since data can be moved every 1 1/2 bus cycles. Burst mode moves data every cycle, resulting in an effective transfer rate of 33 megabytes per second (8.33 Mhz bus speed and 32-bit data path).

Compressed Cycles

The key to EISA's compressed cycle operation is a special timing signal, CMD, which serves as a supplement to the bus clock. During compressed transfers, the CMD signal operates at twice the speed of the bus clock, and the data transfer is required to take place during its duration.

Burst Mode

In burst mode, the addresses for data transfer are asserted at the beginning (for writing data) or the end (for reading data) of every clock cycle. Actually, the data is put on the bus one-half or one-and-one-half cycles later, locked to CMD.

The EISA burst data mode has advantages as well as limitations. Unlike Micro Channel's streaming data mode in which only a starting address is specified, EISA burst mode can move noncontiguous data, because an address is given with each transfer. However, EISA allows only the least significant 10 address bits to change during a burst cycle, effectively limiting a burst data to addresses within a block of 1,024 doublewords in memory. In addition, EISA does not permit Reads and Writes to be mixed in a single burst, because of the differences in the timing of these signals.

Don't confuse the fast 33-megabyte-per-second maximum data-transfer rate with the even faster 33 Mhz operation of some once-regarded-as-fast PCs. Although both the EISA bus and the system memory of these computers are 32-bits wide, the maximum EISA bus clock speed remains 8.33 Mhz, effectively one-quarter the speed of system board memory. In other words, in EISA computers, slotted memory will still be slower than system board memory, just as in classic bus machines. High performance (which, for practical purposes, means all) EISA computers will still be built with proprietary memory expansion slots that operate at the full speed of the system (not the bus) clock.

DMA Issues

If any one part of the old AT needed improvement, it was its Direct Memory Access (DMA) system. While DMA controllers have the potential for speeding system operation, PCs and ATs failed to deliver on that promise. DMA transfers on these system can be painfully slow, so slow that DMA was abandoned for hard disk transfers in the AT.

On an AT, for example, DMA transfers ordinarily take place at the agonizing rate of one megabyte per second. Although a speed of two megabytes per second is theoretically possible using the three 16-bit DMA channels in the AT, DOS is limited to 8-bit transfers and, thus, the lower rate.

New DMA timings and techniques show some of the most creative aspects of the EISA design. Besides AT-compatible DMA transfers, EISA adds three new types, termed Types A, B, and C (the last also known as Burst DMA) all three can make 8-, 16-, or 32-bit transfers. In addition, multiple transfers can also be chained to send the same bytes to different locations. Under EISA standards, a maximum DMA data-transfer rate of 33 megabytes per second is available with 32-bit transfers in burst mode.

The default DMA timing is the slowest mode, AT-compatible 8-bit transfers. The EISA specification envisions the other modes being brought to life with software drivers. With the correct drivers, most classic bus expansion boards can take advantage of Type A transfers; a few can also take advantage of double-speed Type B transfers. EISA boards are required to use Type C or 32-bit transfers of any type.

Each type of DMA brings an improvement in data-transfer rate. For a given width of data path, Type A transfers are about 30 percent faster than AT-style DMA. Type B transfers double the AT speed. Type C transfers are more than four times faster than AT transfers.

Type A and B Transfers

For the most part, these speed increases are made just by specifying different data transfer protocols that involve fewer bus cycles in each DMA move. In the AT environment, each DMA move (8- or 16-bit) requires eight bus cycles, during most of which nothing is happening. Type A transfers merely trim two of the wasted bus cycles from each DMA move. Type B transfers are more extreme, cutting the number of cycles per DMA move to four. Because the newer expansion boards can operate at higher rates, many classic bus expansion cards can operate at these speeds.

Type C Transfers

Under the EISA specification, Type C DMA transfers compress all the necessary signal manipulations into a single bus cycle, with specific signal transitions occurring at the leading and trailing edges of the bus clock. Only EISA expansion cards are capable of this transfer method, and even they have their limitations. Only the 10 lowest-order bits of the address bus are allowed change within the confines of this tight timing, with the result that Burst Mode DMA transfers on EISA are limited to addresses within a single 1024-byte page.

DMA Addressing

In addition to creating high-speed transfer modes, the EISA specification also expands the reach of DMA. Because of addressing limitations, classic bus systems could provide DMA transfers only through the lowest 16 megabytes of memory addresses. EISA allows DMA transfers anywhere within a four-gigabyte range of physical memory.

The rate at which data can move during a DMA transfer depends on how many bits are moved at a time. All seven EISA DMA channels support up to 32-bits; the channels differ only in priority. The higher-numbered channels (5, 6, and 7) are serviced more often when an EISA system is heavily loaded.

Interrupt Control and Sharing

Speed and data connections aren't the only things in short supply in classic bus systems. System interrupts amount to a paltry few after even a modest number of expansion boards are plugged in. Nearly every device connected to the input/output channel—from hard disks to serial ports to video controllers—demands at least one interrupt for optimum performance.

Seven additional interrupts were added to the AT system design when the eight on the original PC proved too few. EISA could have done likewise and dosed new systems with new interrupt channels, but that strategy becomes overly complex and expensive as the number of interrupts increases.

The more moderate solution is to share interrupts between peripherals. With sharing, the 15 existing interrupts could potentially serve needs of an EISA system no matter how it might be expanded.

Maintaining classic bus compatibility and implementing interrupt sharing is a technological nightmare, however. The principle reason for this is the edge-triggered interrupts used by the AT bus. Level-sensitive interrupts are, of course, inherently less susceptible to noise and confusion. But using level-triggered interrupts in the PC environment is problematic. Getting level-sensitive interrupts to work with software that uses edge-triggered interrupts is one difficulty. Maintaining compatibility with existing edge-triggered boards is another, particularly considering that the two kinds of interrupts won't work together on a given interrupt control line. To maintain full backward compatibility, however, EISA must be able to mix the two types of interrupts without causing additional problems.

The EISA approach is to make each interrupt individually programmable between edge-triggered and level-sensitive operation. Old boards can use the edge-triggered interrupts they prefer, one board per interrupt. New EISA expansion boards can share the other interrupts that have been programmed to be level-sensitive.

The one remaining obstacle with this system is that level-sensitive interrupts require a different kind of hardware than does the edge-triggered variety. Because of this difference, plugging a board designed to use an edge-triggered interrupt effectively blocks the use of that interrupt by level-sensitive boards.

This difference in technology also holds the potential for damaging the hardware involved in the conflict. Thankfully, the EISA design minimizes this danger by specifying the inclusion of a current-limiting resistor in the interrupt lines of level-sensitive EISA boards. Nevertheless, EISA supports interrupt sharing only on EISA boards. Existing classic bus expansion cards cannot share interrupts with each other or EISA cards.

Bus Mastering

The most significant borrowing that EISA makes from Micro Channel is bus mastering. In EISA systems, both the operation and nomenclature differ from the IBM design—not just for the sake of originality but because IBM's designs are protected by patents and other intellectual property rights. In an EISA system, the arbitration control element is called the *Integrated System Peripheral* chip (and, strangely, not the EISA Bus Controller). The *ISP* acts just like the Micro Channel Central Arbitration Point and determines which system function gets control of the expansion bus.

Arbitration Priorities

Every arbitration system has rules. Mom, confronted with caring for a crowd of kids from the neighborhood may, for example, let the kid that screams the loudest go first in line just to get some peace and quiet. EISA has a much more pragmatic, more deterministic set of rules for priority. Control rotates through three classes of control: memory refreshing, DMA transfers, and a combination of the microprocessor and bus masters. In every control cycle, each one of these elements receives control in turn. If, however, several DMA channels request bus control, only one gets it per control cycle. In effect, control is like a menu in an old-fashioned Chinese restaurant—in each arbitration cycle, the system selects one from column A, memory refreshing; one from column B, DMA; and one from column C, the bus masters/ microprocessor.

Control rotates through the circle of those of the six EISA DMA channels needing it until all are served. Actually, this rotation is a pair of cycles, wheels within wheels. Three high-priority DMA channels (corresponding to the 16-bit channels in an AT system but allowed any transfer width under the EISA specification) going through one rotation and three lower priority channels in another rotation. One low-priority channel gets control for each complete cycle of three high-priority channels.

The microprocessor and bus masters form another wheel-within-wheel arrangement. Each time the microprocessor/bus master column is selected, either the microprocessor or a bus master gets control, whichever was not selected on the last cycle. In other words, the microprocessor is served half the time, the bus masters the other half. Another cycle selects which of the various bus masters gets served when the bus master selection pops up.

As a consequence of this arrangement, memory refreshing is assigned the highest priority in an EISA system. Every arbitration cycle includes memory refreshing. That's as it should be, because without memory refreshing, the system would crash. DMA transfers are next highest since one active DMA channel would get attention every cycle. The microprocessor has the next highest level of priority, getting control at least every other cycle. At best, any given bus master can only match the priority level of the microprocessor. If several are active, each gets control only after a delay of many arbitration cycles.

Arbitration Signals

Considering the complexity of this arbitration hierarchy, the hardware that brings it to life is actually simple. Only two slot-specific signals are necessary for each expansion board. The controlling logic is all contained inside the ISP chip, so the designers of expansion boards need not worry about complex decision-making circuitry.

When a bus master board wants to request bus access, it only needs to assert its Memory Request line (abbreviated MREQx, where x is the slot number, in EISA nomenclature). The ISP informs the bus master that it can take control of the bus by asserting the Memory Acknowledge (or MAKx) signal associated with the slot in which the bus master is located.

The EISA standard also allows a form of bus master to be built solely using the AT bus. Such cards use the DMA signals to control the bus, the DMA Request (DRQ) line to indicate a need to use the bus. Permission is sent back to the board on the associated DMA Acknowledge line (DAK).

Because these classic bus masters don't have access to all the EISA timing signals, they hold the potential for overstaying their welcome, getting so involved in a transfer as not to yield control to the one function that absolutely must have it—memory refresh. Consequently, the EISA design requires these boards to have built-in timing circuits to limit the duration of their bus access.

Automated Setup

At minimum, setting up all the technical wizardry that EISA's engineers have conjured into a system might seem to require a magic wand, what with addressing and interrupt considerations, not to mention four DMA types, the data-transfer modes, and the rest of the EISA variables. Even without the innovations, setting up an expansion board meant for the classic bus is generally an exercise in frustration that requires the careful matching of DIP switches and jumper settings with the needs of the board and the available interrupts and memory in the host system. Make one mistake—which is almost ensured owing to the deplorable state of most documentation—and the host system is likely not even able to boot, let alone diagnose the problem. Fortunately, EISA incorporates several strategies to alleviate these setup problems.

The EISA design automatically prevents conflicts in the assignment of some system resources. In addition, it incorporates a software-mediated setup procedure that finds, flags, and even corrects conflicts to the extent of automatically configuring the system. If that's not enough versatility, EISA also allows old-fashioned switch-and-jumper configuring of boards.

One inspired aspect of EISA automatically eliminates the conflict of input/output port assignments. In classic-bus computers, expansion boards were allowed to choose from any ports in the range 100(Hex) to 3FF(Hex) for their needs. You were left the job of assigning ports from a range within that selected by the board-maker. You also were left with the responsibility of detecting and resolving conflicting port assignments.

In contrast, the EISA design assigns a unique range of ports to each expansion slot. Boards are still confined to a limited range of three-digit hexadecimal addresses, but each expansion slot adds an extra digit to distinguish the ports used by its associated board from those in the other slots. This scheme makes it physically impossible for two boards to try to use the same I/O port addresses.

Each board also can be individually addressed to ferret out information stored in common locations. By selectively activating the AENx bus line for each slot, the host EISA system can query individual boards, isolate them, or just identify them.

Each make and model of EISA expansion board is assigned a unique *EISA Product Identifier*, which is stored on the board at input/output port addresses 0xC80(Hex) to 0xC83(Hex). The first two bytes store, in compressed form, a three-letter abbreviation identifying the board manufacturer (the characters "ISA" reserved to indicate generic classic-bus boards). The next byte encodes a two-digit product number, and the final byte encodes a two-digit revision number. The manufacturer's abbreviation is assigned by BCPR Services, the organization that distributes the EISA specification. Manufacturers create their own product and revision numbers. System boards are assigned identification numbers using a similar scheme.

Supplementing this slot- and card-identification arrangement is an *automated setup system*. Through a standardized setup program, you can allocate the resources of your EISA system resources or let the system automatically set itself.

This system brings together several diverse elements: Setup information is maintained in a hardware extension to the CMOS configuration memory used by AT-class computers. Additional battery-backed CMOS memory is assigned to remembering the essential parameters of the board installed in each expansion slot.

To load this information into memory, each EISA system manufacturer provides a setup program, either on disk or in ROM. This program integrates with each product that requires setup through configuration files, disk-based database records holding setup information in a standardized format set by the EISA specification. The setup program reads the disk-based data to customize itself for the setup needs of each specific product installed in the computer host.

The product identification numbers are used as a key. Stored in CMOS memory, they are used to look up configuration files each time the system is switched on. This system centralizes the nonvolatile memory needed for memorizing the setup of each board, eliminating the expense of incorporating such memory into each expansion product.

Even the interface of the setup program has been standardized across EISA machines so that if you can setup one, you know how to configure them all. If you don't, mastering the procedure is easy—you need only to pull down menus to choose the options you want.

Overall, EISA represents a well thought-out, tightly integrated system—though perhaps not particularly original. Although other extensions to the classic bus have been developed—notably the 32-bit expansion slots of Intel's OEM system boards—none won wide industry support. With the powerful Gang of Nine behind it, however, EISA automatically had that support. The weakness of EISA was that it initially—and for four years after its introduction—cost substantially more than ordinary ISA technology. The extra EISA circuitry added up to $1,000 to the price of a PC or motherboard at the retail level. Moreover, software support for EISA's advanced features was minimal even after the design was on the market for four years. For the general market, EISA (like Micro Channel) lost its window of opportunity—a better but older idea overtook the technology: local bus.

EISA can't be counted as a total failure, however. Many EISA systems have found applications in network servers—machines on which proud owners lavish any feature regardless of expense (or value). The bus design works well (though it falls short of the mark set by Micro Channel, at least technically), so there's no reason to avoid it. However, for most single-user systems with today's software, it offers no advantage to counter its added cost.

Local Bus

In a quest for ever greater performance from expansion boards, in 1991, many PC and peripheral manufacturers shifted their attention back a couple of generations to the familiar *local bus* concept. The underlying idea of their retro-thinking was that of the designers of the first IBM PC (and XT) expansion bus—to optimally match performance, connect peripherals directly to the microprocessor, and operate them at microprocessor speed with the same data path width.

With this seemingly backward technological step, engineers built systems that could flash quicker updates of monitor screens than ever possible. Little wonder. In theory, a local bus design can transfer data some 6 or 12 times faster than an EISA or ISA computer based on a 486 microprocessor running at 50 Mhz. The raw bus speed is about six times faster (50 versus 8.33 Mhz), and the bus is a full 32-bits wide.

Compared to the theories, however, the initial implementations of local bus came up short on two counts: real-world throughput and standardization.

The first local bus products to be introduced were dedicated solely to display systems, and they were able to deliver video performance that was only about 30 percent faster than connecting through the ordinary I/O bus. The modest improvement resulted from a number of factors. Part of the explanation is specific to video—the bus is not the only thing that holds back display performance. Generating a high-resolution image can absorb much of a microprocessor's power and time. In addition, with any local bus system, the microprocessor must also handle all of the bus transfer overhead.

Standardization is also a problem. For the first local bus systems, standards were not a problem, because they were never designed to be expansion buses. Rather, the local bus connection was a convenient and quick way to move motherboard video signals. Because no connector was involved in these local bus systems, there were no compatibility or standardization issues. But PC and peripheral makers saw the speed potentials of local bus and found that it would be an ideal solution for linking other devices requiring high data-transfer rates. They added connectors to motherboard local buses, and the issue of compatibility immediately arose.

In 1992, three designs rose in contention to become local bus industry standards—one based on a proposal by chipmaker *OPTi*, one hammered out by the Video Electronics Standards Association (VESA) called VESA Local Bus or *VL Bus*, and one developed at Intel Corporation, termed *Peripheral Component Interconnect* or PCI.

Contrary in Design

As noted earlier, one of the gravest limitations of the PC bus design was that it was a local bus. In fact, the concept of a local bus runs entirely contrary to the ideas embodied in the competing advanced expansion buses. While both Micro Channel and EISA move the host microprocessor from the center of bus control to the periphery to lighten overhead, a true local bus would cement it right back in the middle. Where EISA and Micro Channel give a dedicated bus controller responsibility for managing bus transfers, a true local bus demands the microprocessor take control of everything.

One result of this design is that getting better overall system performance requires increasingly powerful microprocessors. For a given processor power, EISA and Micro Channel can accomplish more (with appropriate software that takes advantage of bus mastering) when I/O demands become heavy. The overhead is shifted to the bus controller and the bus masters actually using the bus. Consequently, a 286 in some Micro Channel systems can run multithreaded applications with greater apparent speed than a faster chip in a system without an arbitrated bus.

You would expect an arbitrated-bus design to come from a company that aims at putting the least acceptable power in a computer package. Similarly, you would expect a company that specialized in making ever-more-powerful microprocessors to advocate local bus.

Of course, the world is not so simple. When reduced to matters of black and white, important issues lose their meaning. No local bus design standard is a pure local bus. For example, all require buffering to power the circuits needed to connect additional devices. Buffers are also required when you add slots to the bus to provide adequate power and to prevent problems in the slots from causing damage to the motherboard circuitry.

Actual local bus standards move even further away from being true local buses. The OPTi design, for example, is designed to operate asynchronously. The VL Bus and PCI both offer bus mastering and arbitration features.

In fact, the standard local buses are local buses in name only. Although that situation makes the nomenclature misleading, it's also the biggest strength of the renaissance of local bus. All three standards cleverly incorporate the speed of local bus while sidestepping its shortcomings (in varying degrees) as well as the drawbacks of the other advanced expansion buses. Moreover, all three converged toward a single standard, making local bus the best bet for high-speed PC expansion for next few years.

Speed Impediments

Without an undue number of headaches, engineers can design electronic circuits to operate at any reasonable speed—into the range of gigahertz. When it comes to expansion buses, however, they are teased by several quirks of technology. Some are purely electronic issues that cause high-speed buses to operate erratically and detrimentally interact with other electronic circuits by generating interference. In addition, engineers have to please people as well as the electrons in their circuits. Oftentimes, people are unwilling to accept their best design efforts—witness the warm reception of Micro Channel Architecture.

Electrical Limits

Expansion buses pose more engineering problems than other circuits, because they require balancing of several conflicting needs. The expansion bus must operate as fast as possible to achieve the highest possible transfer rate. And the expansion bus must provide a number of connectors for attaching peripherals, and these connectors must be spread apart to allow a reasonable thickness for each peripheral. In other words, the bus must stretch over several inches.

As speeds go up, so does the radiation potential of the signal; as circuit lengths increase, so does the radiation potential of the signal they carry. One way to minimize radiation is to keep speed low; another is to keep the bus short. Neither of these is entirely satisfactory if you want fast expansion that will accommodate several peripherals. With the correct layout of bus signals—for instance, the Micro Channel's interleaving of signals and grounds—the interaction between circuits can be kept to a minimum. However, maintaining backward compatibility with ISA boards and rearranging signals for higher speeds is a nearly unsolvable dilemma, as EISA demonstrates.

Compatibility Issues

The new local bus designs reflect a new understanding of compatibility issues that breaks through this former barrier. The EISA effort concentrated industry attention on backward compatibility at the expansion slot level. According to EISA, the best way to put your old expansion board to work was to shove them into any slot of a PC at random.

But taking advantage of your investment in old ISA boards doesn't require access to every slot. One reason for advancing to a new bus design is to gain the performance of new boards. You'll only want to retain the old boards that have no higher speed equivalents, because of some speed limit other than the bus such as an industry standard. For example, no modem is going to stress the capabilities of an expansion bus, because even the quickest modems with unusual modulation schemes and data compression can move data faster than about 38,400 bits per second. All you need is a number of slots large enough to accommodate your old boards—all slots don't have to be backwardly compatible.

That's exactly the approach taken by all the local bus standards. Rather than *slot-level* compatibility as demanded by the EISA consortium, they offer *system-level* compatibility. You can slide your old boards into one or more slots inside the system that are dedicated to backward compatibility. Other slots take advantage of local bus speed.

The design requires all local bus machines to have more than one expansion bus. In fact, all local bus PCs have three separate buses— the backwardly compatible conventional expansion bus (it can be either ISA, EISA, or Micro Channel), the high-speed local bus, and a separate bus dedicated to memory. Rather than replacing old bus designs, local bus supplements them, just giving an alternative for fast expansion. You get the best of both worlds and give up nothing.

Slot Limits

The status of local bus as a supplement is more than a matter of convenience. It's also a necessity if PCs are to have a reasonable degree of expansion. All the local bus standards limit the number of high-speed devices that can be connected to the bus to a total of three.

Note that the limit is measured in devices and not slots. Many local bus systems use a local bus connection for their motherboard-based display systems. These circuits count as one local bus device, so PCs with local bus video on the motherboard can offer at most two local bus expansion slots.

The three-device limit results from speed considerations. The larger the bus, the higher the capacitance between its circuits, because they have a longer distance over which to interact. Every connector added more capacitance. As speed increases, circuit capacitance increasingly degrades its signals. The only way to overcome the capacitive loses is to start with more signal. To keep local bus signals at reasonable levels and yet maintain high speeds, the standards enforce the three-device limit.

Local bus advocates are quick to point out that the three-device limit offers no practical disadvantage. Most PCs only need the high-performance edge offered by local bus technology for three devices— the video system, the mass storage system, and a network connection.

A high-speed SCSI host adapter allows the single local bus slot allocated to mass storage to link to multiple hard disks, disk arrays, and other devices. If you need more high-speed expansion than is afforded by a three-slot local bus system, you probably need more of a computer than an ordinary PC.

Design Incentive

Because local bus technology is old and the need for a new bus was perceived back in 1987, it might seem odd that the new local bus designs arose only four or five years later. The reason is at the root of the failure of the other advanced bus designs, only recently has a need arisen for high-speed bus transfers that can be translated into readily apparent performance gains. Micro Channel and EISA could speed up some transfers, but they did so on tasks that did not make a dramatic difference in the appearance of the overall operation of the machine. Nothing anyone did with an EISA or Micro Channel computer took much advantage of bus mastering, for example, and when it did, you couldn't see much change on your screen.

Local bus, on the other hand, makes a readily apparent visual difference. That appearance of improvement is its greatest marketing strength. With local bus, your PC seems to be operating faster. In fact, on tasks that are constrained by display speed—Computer-Aided Design and Windows applications, for example—local bus will make the overall operation of a PC faster.

Understandably, then, the organization making the biggest push for local bus standards is a committee of companies involved in PC video systems—VESA. Moreover, local bus started out not as an expansion bus but as a means to provide faster video in PCs.

Before the advent of the modern local bus designs, all PCs linked their video systems to the rest of the PC through the standard I/O bus. Even motherboards with built-in video circuitry electrically used the I/O bus as a link. This I/O bus connection became suspect only with the rise in acceptance of high-resolution video and graphical operating environments.

With early PCs, it was not a problem because most applications were *character-mapped*. A full screen of information was just an 80 x 25 array of characters stored in memory as two bytes per character (one byte in modified ASCII code, the other an attribute byte that specified color or emphasis). An entire screen of text data comprises only 4 kilobytes, which takes an insignificant time to transfer even across the original PC bus (the actual transfer time would be less than 1/500th second on a 4.77 Mhz bus one byte wide).

With graphics, the transfer needs increased dramatically. A screen of standard VGA 16-color graphics—today's least common denominator—consists of about 150K. Move up to a True Color (24-bit) image at 1024 x 768 resolution, and one screen of data increases to about 2.3M. If a system had no other overhead, that one screen would take one full second to transfer across the PC bus. In reality, such a transfer takes much, much longer when mediated by the system microprocessor which must also allocate its time for memory refreshing, subtle background processes (servicing the timer interrupt, for example), and calculating the image data bound for the screen.

Compaq first pushed video onto a 16-bit ISA connection with the introduction of its Deskpro 386 in 1987, doubling the potential transfer rate. Two other techniques have been used to improve video performance—coprocessor technology and bus-mastering. A coprocessor not only relieves the system microprocessor from most of the need for calculating screen images, it also removes the need to transfer blocks of data across the expansion bus except in the case of moving bit-images. Most displays are sent coded as instructions, which the coprocessor executes. Drawing instructions can trim the information transferred across the bus a thousandfold.

Bus mastering permits the video data to be transferred without tying up the system microprocessor, removing the overhead from the operation so that transfer speed approaches the theoretical rate. The first video system to use bus mastering was IBM's XGA, which also takes advantage of coprocessor technology.

These approaches have two weaknesses. Coprocessors don't accelerate the movement of bit-images, which are becoming increasingly common in desktop publishing and multimedia applications. Coprocessors and XGA also require that software specifically take advantage of their languages, so programs must be specially written for these display systems. The vast majority of applications cannot cash in on their speed.

Local bus breaks through the bus bottleneck by increasing the bus width of the video connection and kicking up the speed of transfers to near that of the microprocessor—typically from 33 to 66 Mhz. That gives local bus its theoretical four- to eightfold improvement in transfer rate due to its faster clock and another factor of two increase, thanks to its wider bus.

Local bus accelerates the aspect of video performance that coprocessors help least—the transfer of bit images. Consequently, local bus should not be seen as a replacement for video coprocessor technology but as a further enhancement to it. Similarly, bus mastering, although contrary to the true local bus philosophy, can further accelerate local bus performance. (In fact, bus mastering was included in the VL Bus design particularly to take advantage of XGA.) Local bus with coprocessing and bus mastering will give the greatest improvement in video speed you can get today.

Local Bus Standards

Existing local bus products are either proprietary or follow one of the three local bus standards. Newer products, however, will likely follow the accepted industry standard, VL Bus. Each design approach has its strengths and weaknesses, however, and you can benefit even from a proprietary system.

Proprietary Designs

The earliest of local bus products were systems with proprietary local bus designs, typically implemented as a dedicated video circuitry built into the motherboard. A few of these early, proprietary products put the video system on an expansion board and used a proprietary bus for the connection. They suffer the disadvantage of any proprietary design—your options are limited to what the manufacturer provides. Even when local bus slots are present, you're still limited, by proprietary bus designs, to the few expansion boards offered by the manufacturer of the PC.

If, however, you seek only better display performance, you can get exactly that from a proprietary local bus system. Moreover, your gratification will be immediate. Although you won't be able to take advantage of high-speed local bus expansion, you'll still get excellent display performance during the period before when local bus becomes common enough in the PC industry that pricing piracy ends.

OPTi Implementation

Chipset-maker OPTi developed its local bus as an adjunct to its DXBB PC/AT chipset (which consists of the company's 82C496 system/data controller, 82C206 integrated peripheral controller, and optionally 82C497 cache controller). As part of the data provided on this chipset, the company includes a suggested local bus connector design based on an EISA connector (access keys in the OPTi connector prevent standard EISA boards from plugging into an OPTi slot). The company has made no effort to ensure conformance with this design, and some manufacturers have opted for different connectors (for example, Hauppauge Computer Works uses a Micro Channel connector with OPTi-derived signals).

The OPTi chipset provides full control for the local bus connection but does not include arbitration or bus mastering. Consequently, building expansion boards based on the OPTi design incurs few added costs over building a standard ISA board. Motherboard design is also minimally different from ISA, because all the necessary signals come from the chipset.

The 82C497 cache controller permits the local bus to operate asynchronously from the microprocessor and other motherboard circuitry. This option allows PC designers to create PCs in which the microprocessor can be upgraded to a higher speed without altering the system board clock. In its documentation, OPTi indicates that its local bus should be operated at 33 Mhz, although some manufacturers have already designed peripherals based on the OPTi bus recommendation for 50 Mhz.

The OPTi design envisions the special local bus connector replacing that of an ordinary expansion slot. With this design, the one to three local bus slot positions would be constrained to using only local bus boards.

The OPTi connector provides little more than address and data lines. Interrupt, DMA, and other control functions are left to the host. Consequently there is no need for elaborate setup facilities.

VL Bus

The standard developed by the Video Electronics Standards Association, VESA Local Bus or *VL Bus* offers fully arbitrated high-speed expansion at up to 66 Mhz across a 32-bit bus. Because it is arbitrated, it requires control circuitry similar to that of Micro Channel or EISA but also offers their advantage as well: bus master transfers can be made across the VL Bus without the microprocessor's intervention.

The VL Bus definition allows for a variety of compatible configurations: 16- or 32-bit with two transfer modes—Type A and Type B—to allow for different host speeds. Type A transfers are typically used with microprocessors operating at 33 Mhz or slower; Type B, with microprocessors from 40 to 66 Mhz. The chief difference is the number of wait states imposed. Type A can generally complete write operations with zero wait states and reads with one. Type B transfers require three wait states.

Later expansion to 64-bit width (anticipating the 586 microprocessor) is anticipated. The board signals its maximum operating speed to its host during power-on self-test using its ID2, ID3, and ID4 signals coded. The local bus devices can determine what kind of microprocessor controls the host computer from the code of its ID0 and ID1. *Byte Enable* (BE0-BE3) bus signals are provided for negotiating the width of data transfers.

The standard connector for the VL Bus is a Micro Channel connector with 112 contacts with 0.050-inch spacing. The specification anticipates this connector fitting in either ISA, EISA, or Micro Channel slots in line with and one half-inch in front of the normal bus connector. Consequently, a VL Bus slot can be used either for a local bus board or normal expansion board. A VL Bus board may or may not make contact with the host computer's normal bus—that's left to the option of the board designer. Normally, the host computers normal I/O bus is used for interrupt control, although access to interrupt nine is provided by the VL Bus connector.

VL Bus avoids the handicap of overburdening the host microprocessor with transfer overhead by allowing bus-mastered transfers complete with a burst mode. All boards that take advantage of bus mastering must be able to operate as masters under the VL Bus specification. There are no VL Bus *slaves*. Operationally, during a bus master transfer, one board operates as a master, the other as a *target*.

The drawback to VL Bus is that it was not approved until June, 1992, and many local bus computers were designed and delivered before that auspicious date. Consequently, most first generation local bus computers do not follow the standard.

PCI

The Intel implementation of local bus remained undisclosed as this was written, but the company's design will likely be compatible with the VL Bus proposal and incorporate the same features, being more an enhancement to accommodate microprocessors more powerful than the 486. Included in PCI will be the capability for bus mastering and arbitration and other VL Bus features.

Note, too, that nothing precludes the use of the OPTi DXBB chipset with the VL Bus design. In other words, local bus standards are likely to converge on the VESA specification.

PC Card

Laptop and notebook computers are notorious for their lack of expansion options. The hardware is just too small to accommodate a standard expansion board, no matter the bus. Moreover, the power requirements of a typical desktop expansion board—in the vicinity of five watts—is about equal to what many notebook computers draw for all of their functions. However, an expansion standard is arising for small, portable computers—the *PC Card*.

The PC Card is an outgrowth of the memory cards that slide into laptop and notebook computers to expand their RAM capacity. But the PC Card specification is designed to accommodate a variety of devices besides memory—modems, hard disks, network adapters, or whatever you would slide into the expansion slot of a full-size PC.

The PC Card standard is governed by an international committee with over 220 members called the *Personal Computer Memory Card International Association* or *PCMCIA*, founded in 1989. It was formed after the advantage of using slide-in memory expansion cards (first introduced in today's form factor in 1985) became apparent and the diversity of designs became intolerable. The first generation PC Card, Release 1.0, was introduced in September, 1990.

Dimensions

The starting point for the PC Card was the 68-pin socket and form factor of the IC Card, first defined by the Japanese Electronic Industry Development Association. The initial version of the PC Card (now termed *Type I*) matched the IC Card in size and connector but added greater standardization. The card measured 2.126 x 3.37 inches and was 3.3 millimeters thick. To allow the use of thicker components, a new definition for *Type II* PC Cards was developed as Release 2.0 in September, 1991. Type II PC Cards are 5.0 millimeters thick but otherwise the same dimensions as Type I cards. The greater thickness allows the encapsulation of EEPROM chips in ceramic packages. Under development is a further standard, *Type III*, which allows PC Cards 10.5 millimeters thick. All three types of cards are 3.3 millimeters thick along their guide rails so thinner cards can fit newer, thicker slots.

Under Release 2.0, both Type I and Type II cards can be implemented in extended form. That is, they can be extended.

Electrical Connections

All PC Cards use the same 68-pin connector. They can connect with PCs that have either 8- or 16-bit data buses and allow addressing up to 64MB of memory on each card. Cards can operate at either 5 volts or 3.3 volts.

Beyond memory, the PC Card defines a standard input/output interface with control and interrupt signals similar to those of a full-size computer expansion bus. PCMCIA is also working on a 32-bit bus-mastering standard for future PC Cards.

Features

The PC Card standard accommodates the execution of ROM- or Flash RAM-based program code on the PC Card without first copying it to RAM, a feature called *Execute in Place*. A common BIOS interface is defined so that device drivers for PC Cards can be written to a common standard called *Socket Services*. The specification also defines a software head, termed a *tuple*, which can identify what kind of card is in a PC Card slot—its electrical characteristics and logical capabilities. Checking the tuple could reveal, for example, that a PC Card contains a hard disk that should not be formatted without a number of dire warnings.

The PC Card differs from older memory boards because it is designed for "hot" insertion. That is, installing a memory board in a notebook or laptop PC was normally done with the power switched off. The PC Card can be slid into place while the power is on, more like a game cartridge than an expansion board. Consequently, all hard disks become removable, and one slot can serve many functions within a single working session without rebooting the host PC. Besides peripherals, programs could be encoded in PC Card. These program cards could also hold their own nonvolatile memory to store your preferences and even templates and data.

The PC Card system is designed to take advantage of the standard File Allocation System used by floppy disks whether the card contains a true disk drive, RAM, ROM, or Flash memory. This expedient makes it relatively easy for software developers to create code that will work with any PC Card.

Note that nothing about the PC Card design is incompatible with the other standard buses, including ISA (on which it is based), EISA, or Micro Channel. In other words, PC Cards can be used to enhance full-size PCs as well as portable machines. One card can do it all—at least if desktop PCs ever grow PC Card slots.

7

The Basic Input/Output System

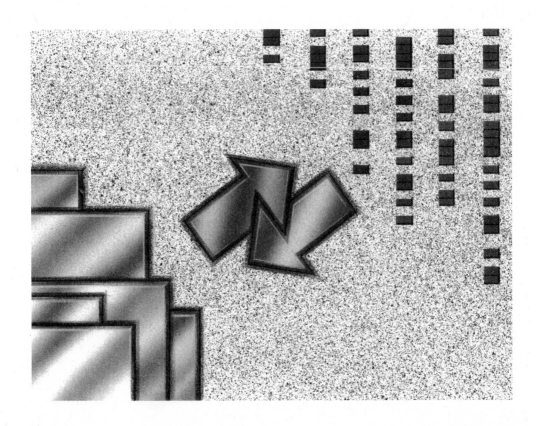

E very PC gets its personality from a set of built-in software routines called its Basic Input/Output System or BIOS. Although often less than 32 kilobytes of code, the BIOS controls many of the most important functions of the PC: how it interprets keystrokes, how it puts characters on the screen, and how it communicates through its ports. The BIOS also determines the compatibility of the computer and its flexibility in use. Although all BIOSs have the same function; all are not the same.

Just as the Minotaur, a man-beast half-breed, ruled the unfathomable Labyrinth, the inner mysteries and maze of your PC are governed by an odd mating of hardware and software called the *Basic Input/Output System* or BIOS. More than just a guard, however, the BIOS serves as a demigod that links the material hardware world of your PC and its circuits to the transcendent realm of software ideas and instructions. More than a link, the BIOS *is* both hardware and software. Like software, the BIOS is a set of instructions to the computer's microprocessor. Like hardware, however, these special instructions are not evanescent; rather, they are coded into the hard, worldly silicon of PROM chips. Due to the twilight state of programs like the BIOS, existing in the netherworld between hardware and software, such PROM-based programs are often termed *firmware*.

The BIOS of an IBM or compatible computer is special firmware, comprising routines that test the computer, give it its personality, help other programs mesh more smoothly with the electronics of the system, and (in IBM computers only), a programming language that enables you to use the machine without any other software (or even a disk drive).

The personality comes from the firmware code. This code determines how the computer will carry out the basic functions needed to make a working computer—how quickly they are carried out and how smoothly. In many PCs, this firmware also governs how the system board components interact, the chipset features that are used, even the amount of the microprocessor's time devoted to keeping memory working. The setup procedures in most new PCs are also held in the BIOS.

Every time your PC switches on, the BIOS immediately takes command. Its first duty is to run through a series of diagnostic routines—system checks—to ensure that every part of your PC's hardware is functioning correctly before you trust your time and data to it. One by one, the BIOS checks the circuits of your system board and memory, the keyboard, the disks, and each expansion board. If it finds a problem, it reports the problem with a code number on your monitor screen or as a coded series of beeps if an insufficient portion of your PC is working to display anything on the monitor.

After your PC is operating, the BIOS cannot rest. Its firmware includes several sets of routines that programs call to carry out everyday functions—typing characters on the screen or a printer, reading keystrokes, timing events. Programmers can create grand designs without concern for the tiny details, because this basic library is there.

BASIC is the least common denominator among programming languages, and the cassette BASIC in the IBM BIOS is the least common denominator among BASIC languages. Although it is easy to denigrate cassette BASIC, the language, if only minimally useful, is something. Rather than sticking a fat electronic tongue out at you when you try to boot up without a system disk with a message such as "Non-system disk or disk error," cassette BASIC gives you quick answers to math questions or runs simple programs. (You don't want to try complex programs without having a disk from which to load or save them.) Most people never need BASIC and may never want to see it, but it's there just in case.

The distinct parts of the BIOS work separately and distinctly although the code for each is contained inside the same silicon chip. The BIOS operates like a set of small *terminate-and-stay-resident programs* that are always in memory and at your beck and call. In this case, they are always in memory, because you cannot get them out. Such is the nature of nonvolatility.

BIOS Purpose

The design of any computer requires that many of the hardware elements of the machine be located at specific addresses within the range of the input/output ports of the computer. Other computer components may have registers of their own that are used in their control. Because of the number of separate components inside any computer, the potential number of possible variations is limitless. Software that attempts to control any of this hardware must correctly reach out to these registers. As long as all computers are crafted exactly the same, with the same ports used for exactly the same hardware with exactly the same registers, there should be no problem.

With the first PC, however, IBM reserved the right to alter the hardware at will. IBM made no guarantee that any of the ports or registers of the PC would be the same in any later computer. In the well-ordered world envisioned by IBM, programs would never need to directly address hardware. Instead, it would call up a software routine in the BIOS that has the addressing part of the instruction permanently set in its code. Later, computers with different hardware arrangements would use BIOS routines that worked like the old ones and were indistinguishable from them when used by application software. The addresses inside the routines would be changed, however, to match the updated hardware. The same software could thus work with a wide variety of hardware designs, giving the designer and manufacturer the flexibility to upgrade the entirety of system hardware should the need arise.

BIOS Shortcomings

The problem with BIOS routines is that no finite number (or at least no reasonable number) of routines could possibly cover all situations and software needs optimally. Consequently, using BIOS routines is sometimes advantageous, but oftentimes a bother. In particular, BIOS routines can make many computer functions slow, and performance problems are most evident in the video display. For example, all IBM BIOS routines are designed for putting information on the video display one character at a time. Text can be blasted onto the screen much faster by directly manipulating the hardware.

Using BIOS routines, software must first load particular registers with the character to display its attribute (color, underlining, or the like) and perhaps even its location on the screen. Then the program issues a software interrupt to give the BIOS control to do its job. The BIOS then runs through a dozen or more assembly language instructions to move the character onto the screen.

Taking direct control—avoiding the BIOS—means writing directly to the display memory on the video card. A program can write directly to the screen just by loading the appropriate address and moving the needed byte value to that address in one assembly language step. The dozens of steps saved in writing each character add up to real performance gains, the difference between watching changes slowly scroll down the screen and instant updates.

Another limitation imposed by handling all system operations through the BIOS is that the computer cannot do anything without the BIOS knowing. For example, when operated in standard modes, the BIOS routines function well and allows you to read, write, and format disks using the standard IBM disk formats. At the same time, however, these routines impose limits on what the drives can do. Controlled through the BIOS, drives perform similarly to products that have been blessed by IBM. But disk drives are more versatile than the BIOS gives them credit. They can read and write the disk formats used by other computer systems and others that can be used for copy-protecting disks. Thus, taking advantage of a disk drive's capabilities, beyond the powers officially sanctioned by IBM, means sidestepping the BIOS.

Direct Hardware Control

Bypassing the BIOS with programs that directly address the system hardware isn't difficult even when such a concept is forbidden by the IBM dream. In fact, so many software writers have taken their liberties with direct hardware control that many of the hardware features of personal computers are more standardized than the BIOS. Most prominent of these is the location of display memory. Writing directly to display memory has been so common that IBM has even thrown in the towel and stated that it will use its best efforts to preserve the status quo in the addresses used by display memory. Serial ports, too, have developed beyond BIOS control. Every program that uses a serial port at speeds higher than 9600 bits per second (19,200 on some machines) must sidestep the BIOS's serial communication routines.

Moreover, the PC hardware standard may just be a tighter standard than that set by the BIOS. Most compatibles do an exact job of mimicking all the hardware of a PC. The BIOS's that they use, however, are bound to be somewhat different, because of the demands of copyright laws. Hardware is actually more standardized (in many respects) than the BIOS firmware. Even IBM, in effect, admitted shortcomings of the BIOS-only restriction when they conceded that the hardware memory locations used by the video display will be supported for as long as possible.

Nevertheless, the BIOS offers other advantages to programmers. In many cases, using BIOS routines can simplify the writing of a program. Certain system operations are always available and can be easily accessed through software. These routines are reasonably well-documented and well-understood, removing many of the concerns and worries of the programmer.

BIOS Compatibility

The goal of the compatible computer manufacturer is to match the BIOS used by his machine with that inside the IBM AT. Even today's latest and most powerful machines must duplicate everything the old AT did. That minimum level of functionality is what all programs expect from a PC.

No matter how good it may be, the match cannot be perfect. The code used by IBM is protected by copyrights that forbid others from legally duplicating it. Instead, compatible makers are charged with writing their own BIOS routines without copying IBM's.

Because the copyright laws forbid the copying of someone else's work, compatible BIOSs are written "clean." That is, the programmers are kept from viewing the source code or having any knowledge of the routines it contains. Instead, they work from a list of instructions and functions that the BIOS carries out when given each specific instruction. In other words, they look at the BIOS they want to copy as a black box that takes an input and gives an output. The programmers then deduce the instructions that will give the desired results.

Working in this way is time-consuming and expensive. Few computer companies have the resources to do it all themselves. Consequently, the vast majority of compatible PC manufacturers buy the necessary BIOS firmware from specialist firms such as American Megatrends, Inc., Award Software, Phoenix Technologies, Ltd., or Mr. BIOS. This expedient gives them a BIOS known to work without worries about violating copyright protection.

Bought in bulk (to be installed in a full production run of PCs), the rights to use a compatible BIOS can be quite inexpensive—only a few dollars per copy. Buying an individual BIOS for a machine is more expensive, because you don't get the benefit of a manufacturer's mass-order bargaining power. Moreover, you must buy the PROM chip that holds the code while computer-makers often buy the code on disk or tape, making the copies they need (and have paid for) themselves. Consequently, buying a single copy of a BIOS can cost you $20 to $50 depending on what you buy and from whom.

Because each BIOS vendor must separately develop its own product, the exact code used by each BIOS version is different. As a result, BIOSs vary in their compatibility with the IBM XT standard.

One of the biggest differences between BIOSs has to do with entry points. The various code routines in each BIOS start and end at addresses assigned to the BIOS function in the PC memory map. The address at which each routine starts is called that routine's *entry point*. A few applications require that some entry points be at specific physical BIOS addresses. As with writing directly to system hardware, these address-specific programs seek to eke the utmost in performance from a PC. If the entry point of a BIOS differs from what the program expects, the probable results are a system crash.

IBM has maintained the same entry points with all of its BIOSs, and many compatible BIOSs use exactly the same addresses. A few do not. In general, the BIOSs with varying entry points have been written as programming modules that can be combined in various ways to suit the needs of a PC designer. What these modular BIOSs add in flexibility, they lose in compatibility.

Unlike programs that write directly to system hardware, however, programs that require specific BIOS entry points are rare. With the popularity of compatible computers and modular BIOSs, they will undoubtedly become rarer. Modern software is moving away from a compatibility dependency that goes down to the level of specific entry points.

One other compatibility issue with BIOSs is ensuring that a replacement BIOS is compatible with the computer in which you want to plug it. The job is not one to be taken lightly. All BIOSs are created to match specific hardware. That's part of their job—uniting different hardware designs so that they will work interchangeably with all software. Consequently, every BIOS is customized for the PC it will control. Computer motherboard manufacturers modify BIOSs to suit their purposes. A generic BIOS that works well in any PC does not exist. Should you want to change or upgrade your PC's BIOS for any reason, you'll need to get one that matches the exact model of computer you own.

BIOS Performance

The BIOS in a PC can affect the system's performance in two ways— the efficiency of the BIOS code and the control it affords over system resources. A better BIOS can thus give a PC a performance edge.

Because BIOS routines look like black boxes to programs with their specific contents essentially unknown (and uncared about), the assembly language instructions of each BIOS routine can vary considerably among different BIOSs. Some may have more instructions for a given function than others. Those with the fewest instructions to carry out a given function will be the most efficient. A program will need to execute fewer steps using fewer clock cycles every time it calls BIOS routines. As a result, the system runs faster.

Of course, this difference appears only when a program takes advantage of BIOS routines. Because most high-performance programs sidestep the BIOS to take direct hardware control, a better BIOS doesn't make much of an overall improvement on the quickest programs. For most people and software, the difference is nothing to worry about.

A more important performance difference depends on how a BIOS initiates its host computer. Some BIOSs do a better job in optimizing the relationship between the microprocessor's local bus and the input/output channel. With most modern chipsets, the relationship between the two is completely programmable. Moreover, most chipsets allow many performance-enhancing features, such as memory interleaving, to be switched on or off and others, such as cache operation, to be optimized. A simple BIOS can bring a PC to life without taking optimum advantage of these features, shortchanging on the performance potential built into the PC. A better BIOS automatically checks for the best operation of all available features. Through advanced setup procedures, it may also give you manual control of these vital system parameters so that you can second-guess its settings.

Unfortunately, you have no way of knowing how well a BIOS works just by looking at a PC. The only way to judge is to run your applications on the system and see what it does and how fast it does it. Although you can rarely narrow performance difference to BIOS effects (rarely will you find two PCs with the same system board but different BIOSs), at least you can determine whether a given system responds quickly enough to keep you happy.

PC BIOS Basics

The IBM BIOS made its debut with the first PC. From that point, it was probably the most copied set of software routines in the world. The PC BIOS laid out all the entry points used by subsequent IBM BIOS and thus most compatible BIOSs as well. It also defined the functions that could be, and must be, expected in any BIOS. And it established how the BIOS works. The AT BIOS that is now mandatory in every PC added a few enhancements without disturbing the underlying PC design. The IBM PC and AT BIOSs are thus the point of departure for understanding how a BIOS works.

BIOS Operation

The IBM BIOS is designed to work through a system of *software interrupts*. To activate a routine, a program issues the appropriate interrupt, a special instruction to the microprocessor. Table 7.1 lists the BIOS interrupts and their functions.

TABLE 7.1.
BIOS Interrupts
and Functions

Interrupt (Hex)	Function
00	Divide by zero
01	Single step
02	Nonmaskable interrupt
03	Breakpoint
04	Overflow
05	Print screen
06	Reserved
07	Reserved
08	System timer
09	Keyboard
0A	Reserved
0B	Reserved
0C	Reserved
0D	Reserved
0E	Floppy disk
0F	Reserved
10	Video
11	Equipment determination
12	Memory size determination
13	Floppy disk
14	Asynchronous communications
15	System services
16	Keyboard
17	Printer
19	Bootstrap loader
1A	System timer and real-time clock services
1B	Keyboard break
1C	User timer tick
1D	Video parameters
1E	Floppy disk parameters

Interrupt (Hex)	Function
1F	Video graphics characters
20 to 3F	Reserved for DOS
40	Floppy disk BIOS revector
41	Hard disk parameters
42	Reserved
43	Reserved
44	Reserved
45	Reserved
46	Hard disk parameters
47	Reserved
48	Reserved
49	Reserved
4A	User alarm
4B to 5F	Reserved
60 to 67	Reserved for user program interrupts
68 to 6F	Reserved
70	Real-time clock interrupt
71 to 74	Reserved
75	Redirect to nonmaskable interrupt
76 to 7F	Reserved
80 to 85	Reserved for BASIC
86 to F0	Used by BASIC interpreter when running BASIC
F1 to FF	Reserved for user program interrupts

The software interrupt causes the microprocessor to stop what it is doing and start a new routine. It does this by suspending the execution of the code that it is working on, saving its place, and searching a table held in memory that lists *interrupt vectors*. Each interrupt vector is a pointer that tells the microprocessor the location where the code associated with the interrupt is located. The microprocessor reads the value of the vector and starts executing the code located at the value stored in the vector.

The table of interrupt vectors begins at the very start of the microprocessor's memory, address 00000(Hex). Each vector comprises four bytes, and all vectors are stored in ascending order. The default values for each vector are loaded into RAM from the ROM containing the

BIOS when your computer boots up. Programs can alter these vectors to change the meaning of software interrupts. Typically, *terminate-and-stay-resident programs* (TSRs, pop-up programs such as SideKick and background programs such as Pro-Key) make such modifications for their own purposes.

Because there are less interrupts available than things one would want to do with the BIOS, different functions are available for many of the interrupts. These separate functions are identified by *parameter passing*. Information is handed over to the BIOS routine as a parameter, a value held in one or more of the registers at the time the software interrupt is issued. The BIOS routine may also achieve some result and pass it back to the program that called it.

Extendability

The IBM BIOS gains much of its versatility by being an *extendible BIOS*. That is, the full extent of the BIOS is not forever cast in the silicon of the single PROM chip holding the firmware. The IBM BIOS can accept additional code as its own into one integrated whole. Rather than replacing the BIOS PROM, this extendibility means that you can add additional PROM chips containing BIOS routines to your PC. The IBM BIOS will then incorporate the new routines.

All IBM BIOSs and compatible BIOSs are extendible, with one exception: those inside the very earliest PCs that allowed only 64 kilobytes of memory to be installed on their systems boards. Few of these machines are around any more, and most of them have been updated with replacement BIOSs.

The key to making the IBM BIOS extendible is an extra firmware routine that enables the BIOS to look for add-in code. During boot-up, the BIOS code reads through the address range that IBM set aside for firmware looking for code stored on add-in boards. If it finds a valid section of code, it adds those instructions to the BIOS repertory. For instance, new interrupt routines can be added or the function of existing routines can be changed.

The routine to extend the BIOS works as follows: During the Power On Self Test (POST), after interrupt vectors have been loaded into RAM, the resident IBM BIOS code instructs the computer to check its ROM memory for the occurrence of the special *preamble bytes* that mark the beginning of add-in BIOS routines. The BIOS searches for these preamble bytes in the absolute address range 0C8000(Hex) to 0F4000(Hex).

Should the BIOS find the special preamble bytes, it verifies that the subsequent section of code is a legitimate BIOS extension by performing a form of cyclical redundancy check on the specified number of 512 byte blocks. The values of each byte in the block are totaled using Module 0100(Hex) addition—the effect is the same as dividing the sum of all the bytes by 4096. A remainder of zero indicates that the extension BIOS contains valid code.

The preamble bytes take a specific form. Two bytes indicate the beginning of an extension code section: 055(Hex) followed by 0AA(Hex). Immediately following the two-byte preamble bytes is a third byte that quantifies the length of the additional BIOS. The number represents the amount of blocks 512 bytes-long needed to hold the extra code.

After a valid section of code is identified, system control (BIOS program execution) jumps to the fourth byte in the extension BIOS and performs any functions specified in machine language. Typically, these instructions tell the BIOS how to install the extra code. Finally, when the instructions in the extension BIOS are completed, control returns to the resident BIOS. The system then continues to search for additional blocks of extension BIOS. When it completes its search by reaching the absolute address 0F4000(Hex), it starts the process of booting your computer from disk.

The ROM chips containing this extra BIOS code need not be present on the system board. The memory locations used are also accessible on the expansion bus. This feature allows new ROM chips that add to the BIOS to become part of expansion boards that can be slid into the computer. The code required to control the expansion accessory thus loads automatically when the system boots.

Multiple sections of this add-on code will fit into any computer, limited only by the address range available. One complication is that no two sections of code can occupy the same memory area. Consequently, most expansion board makers for the PC series incorporate jumpers, or DIP switches, on their products to allow reassigning of the addresses used by their BIOS extensions to avoid conflicts, which is part of the justification for the complications required in setting up expansion boards.

Determining the Date

Nearly every BIOS identifies itself with a copyright message so that you can determine its manufacturer. (More specifically, the copyright message protects the writers of the BIOS from others copying their work.) In addition, most BIOSs include their latest revision date so that you can identify how recently its code was updated.

This BIOS date is not just interesting but is a useful diagnostic. As PCs have expanded their capabilities, BIOSs were revised to enable new operations. Sometimes older BIOSs won't work with new peripherals. The most important recent example occurred with early AMI BIOSs that did not work correctly with AT interface hard disk drives. After April, 1990, the problems were corrected; however many PCs remain equipped with the old code. Checking the BIOS date will tell you whether your system uses a BIOS predating the revision. AMI BIOSs dated 4-09-90 and later incorporate the fix.

Most BIOS chips have their date and revision number printed on labels affixed over their EPROM windows along with a copyright message. However, you can determine the BIOS date of your PC without opening your PC or even knowing what an EPROM chip looks like. You can examine the revision date embedded in the BIOS code using the DEBUG program supplied with DOS.

To check the BIOS date of your PC (or other computers—this procedure works on nearly all models), just run the DEBUG program.

At the hyphen prompt, type the following instruction:

```
D F000:FFF0
```

A mysterious-looking line of numbers and letters should appear on your screen. This line is divided into three parts horizontally. At left is the label of a memory location at which the display of 16 bytes begins—in this case, 0FFFF0(Hex). The central block of characters gives the individual contents of each of those 16 bytes of memory. The right block gives the ASCII representation of those values (if the value is a printable character). You should be able to read the date of the BIOS directly as it appears in the right column:

```
Run the Debug program that comes with most versions of DOS.
You'll need to have the program DEBUG.COM in the currently
logged disk and directory or accessible through the path
command. Then, type
```

```
  DEBUG
```

```
Once the Debug program loads, you'll see a hyphen prompt on
the screen. Type the following command in response to the
prompt:
```

```
  D F000:FFF0
```

```
Debug will respond with a display like that shown below; the
BIOS date appears in the right column:
```

```
F000:FFF0 EA AC 86 00 F0 20 30 39-2F 32 33 2F 38 37 FC 45
....09/23/87.E
```

```
To exit Debug, at the hyphen prompt type the Quit command,
simply the letter Q, as shown below:
```

```
  -Q
```

```
Debug will then return you to the DOS prompt.
```

System Identification Bytes

Part of the IBM ROM, but not strictly part of the BIOS, is IBM's *System Identification Bytes*. These two bytes of code can be read by programs so that the program knows the type of computer or system board on which it is attempting to run.

Originally, IBM assigned one byte to this purpose. Starting with the XT Model 286, however, IBM added a second byte to permit more specific identification. In IBM nomenclature, these bytes are the *Model Byte* and the *Submodel Byte*.

The Model Byte is located at absolute memory address 0FFFFE(hex), and the Submodel byte follows it. Table 7.2 lists the Model and Submodel Byte values for various IBM computers. Compatible computers generally use the byte value of the system to which they are the closest match.

TABLE 7.2.
IBM Model and
Submodel
Identification

System	Model Byte	Submodel Byte	Revision
PC	FF	none	none
XT	FE	none	none
Portable PC	FE	none	none
XT (1-10-86)	FB	00	01
XT (5-9-86)	FB	00	02
PCjr	FD	none	none
AT (original)	FC	none	none
AT (6-10-85)	FC	00	01
AT (11-15-85)	FC	01	00
XT Model 256	FC	02	00
PC Convertible	F9	00	00
PS/2 Model 30	FA	00	00
PS/2 Model 50	FC	04	00
PS/2 Model 60	FC	05	00
PS/2 Model 80	F8	00	00
PS/2 Model 80	F8	01	00

BIOS Data Area

After the BIOS code starts executing, it makes use of part of the host system's memory to store parameter values important to its operation. Included among the data stored are *equipment flags*, the base addresses of input/output adapters, keyboard characters, and operating modes. This *BIOS data area* comprises 256 bytes of memory, starting at absolute memory location 0000400(Hex). Table 7.3 lists the definition of some of the more important and interesting bytes in the BIOS data area.

TABLE 7.3.
Important BIOS
Data Area
Assignments

Address	Function
0400	Base address of first RS232 adapter (COM1)
0402	Base address of second RS232 adapter (COM2)
0404	Base address of third RS232 adapter (COM3) PS/2s only
0406	Base address of fourth RS232 adapter (COM4) PS/2s only
0408	Base address of first printer adapter (LPT1)
040A	Base address of second printer adapter (LPT2)
040C	Base address of third printer adapter (LPT3)

Address	Function
0410	Installed hardware flags
	Bit 0=IPL disk
	Bit 1=Numeric coprocessor
	Bit 2=Pointing device (except PC, XT, AT, and Convertible)
	Bit 4,5=Video mode
	01=40X25 color; 10=80X25 color; 11=80X25 mono
	Bit 6,7=Number of floppy disk drives
	Bits 9,10,11=Number of serial ports
	Bit 13=Internal model (Convertible only)
	Bits 14,15=Number of printer adapters
0412	Initialization flags
0413	Base memory size in kilobytes (0 to 640)
0417	Keyboard status flags
	Bit 0=Right Shift key pressed
	Bit 1=Left Shift key pressed
	Bit 2=Ctrl key pressed
	Bit 3=Alt key pressed
	Bit 4=Scroll Lock locked
	Bit 5=Num Lock locked
	Bit 6=Caps Lock locked
	Bit 7=Insert locked
0418	Additional keyboard status flags
	Bit 0=Left Ctrl key pressed
	Bit 1=Left Alt key pressed
	Bit 2=Sys Req key pressed
	Bit 3=Pause locked
	Bit 4=Scroll Lock key pressed
	Bit 5=Num Lock key pressed
	Bit 6=Caps Lock key pressed
	Bit 7=Insert key pressed
0419	Storage for alternate keypad entry

continues

271

TABLE 7.3.
continued

Address	Function
041A	Pointer to head of keyboard buffer
041C	Pointer to tail of keyboard buffer
041E to 042D	Keyboard buffer
043E	Diskette drive seek status
	Bit 0=Recalibrate drive 0
	Bit 1=Recalibrate drive 1
	Bit 2=Recalibrate drive 2
	Bit 3=Recalibrate drive 3
	Bit 7=Interrupt flag
043F	Diskette drive motor status
	Bit 0=Drive 0 motor on status
	Bit 1=Drive 1 motor on status
	Bit 2=Drive 2 motor on status
	Bit 3=Drive 3 motor on status
	Bits 4,5=Drive selected
	00=Drive 0; 01=Dive 1; 10=Drive 2; 11=Drive 3
	Bit 7 Write/Read operation flag
0440	Diskette drive motor count
0441	Last disk drive operation status flag
	00=No error
	01=Invalid disk drive parameter
	02=Address mark not found
	03=Write-protect error
	04=Requested sector not found
	06=Disk change line active
	08=DMA overrun on operation
	09=Attempted DMA access across a 64K boundary
	0C=Media type not found
	10=Cyclical Redundancy Check error on disk read
	20=General controller failure
	40=Seek operation failure
	80=Disk drive not ready

Address	Function
0449	Current video mode
044A	Number of columns displayed on monitor screen
044C	Length of regen buffer in bytes
044E	Starting address in regen buffer
0450 to 045F	Current cursor position for up to 8 pages
0460	Cursor mode setting
0462	Current page being displayed
0463	Base address for active video adapter board
0465	Current setting of the 3X8 register
0466	Current setting of the 3X9 register (video palette)
046C to 046F	Current timer count
0470	Flag indicating timer has rolled over since last read
0471	Flag indicating that Break key has been pressed
0472	Reset flag 1234=Bypass memory test 4321=Preserve memory on reset (Micro Channel PS/2s only) 5678=System suspended (Convertible only) 9ABC=Manufacturing test mode (Convertible only) ABCD=System POST loop mode (Convertible only)
0474	Hard disk status flag (results of last operation) 00=No error 01=Invalid function request 02=Address mark not found 03=Write protect found 04=Sector not found 05=Reset failure 07=Drive parameter activity failure 08=DMA overrun on an operation 09=Data boundary error 0A=Bad sector flag detected

continues

273

TABLE 7.3.
continued

Address	Function
	0B=Bad track detected
	0D=Invalid number of sectors on format
	0E=Control data address mark detected
	0F=DMA arbitration level out of range
	10=Uncorrectable ECC or CRC error
	11=ECC corrected data error
	20=General controller failure
	40=Seek operation failure
	80=Time out
	AA=Drive not ready
	BB=Undefined error occurred
	CC=Write fault on selected drive
	E0=Status error
	FF=Sense operation failed
0475	Number of hard disks installed
0476	Fixed disk drive controller port (XT only)
0478	Timeout counter for LPT1 printer response
0479	Timeout counter for LPT2 printer response
047A	Timeout counter for LPT3 printer response
047C	Timeout counter for COM1 serial device response
047D	Timeout counter for COM2 serial device response
047E	Timeout counter for COM3 serial device response
047F	Timeout counter for COM4 serial device response
0480	Base address of beginning of keyboard buffer
0482	Base address of end of keyboard buffer
0484	Rows displayed on monitor (less one)
0485	Character height (bits per character, EGA and thereafter)
0488	Feature bit switches
048B	Flag indicating last disk data rate selected
	Bits 6,7: 00=500K/sec; 01=300K; 10=250K/sec
048C	Status register flag
048D	Error register flag
048E	Hard disk interrupt flay

Address	Function
0490	Drive A media state flag
	Bits 1,2,3:
	000=360K disk/360K drive not established
	001=360K disk/1.2M drive not established
	010=1.2M disk/1.2M drive not established
	011=360K disk/360K drive established
	100=360K disk/1.2M drive established
	101=1.2M disk/1.2M drive established
	111=None of the above
	Bit 4=Media established
	Bit 5=Double-stepping required (360K disk in 1.2M drive)
	Bits 6,7: 00=500K/sec; 01=300K/sec; 10=250K/sec
0491	Drive B media state flag
	Same as above
0492	Drive A operation start state flag
0493	Drive B operation start state flag
0494	Drive A present cylinder flag
0495	Drive B present cylinder flag
0496	Keyboard mode state and type flags
	Bit 0=Last code was E1 hidden code
	Bit 1=Last code was E0 hidden code
	Bit 2=Right Ctrl key pressed
	Bit 3=Right Alt key pressed
	Bit 4=101/102-key (Advanced) keyboard installed
	Bit 5=Force Num Lock if read ID and KBX
	Bit 6=Last character was first ID character
	Bit 7=Read ID in progress
0497	Keyboard LED flags
	Bit 0=Scroll Lock on
	Bit 1=Num Lock on
	Bit 2=Caps Lock on
	Bit 3=Reserved (must be 0)

continues

TABLE 7.3.
continued

Address	Function
	Bit 4=Acknowledgment received
	Bit 5=Resend receive flag
	Bit 6=Mode indicator update
	Bit 7=Keyboard transmit error flag
04CE	Calendar (count of days since January 1, 1980)
0500	Print screen status flag
	00=Ready/okay
	01=Print screen in progress
	FF=Error

ROM BASIC

One section of code contained in the read-only memories of all IBM computers is not, strictly speaking, part of the IBM BIOS. Nor do compatible computer makers attempt to duplicate it, because it is protected not only by copyright law but also undocumented as to function and entry points. This section of code is actually a primitive programming language called *Cassette BASIC* or sometimes *ROM BASIC*.

The original purpose of the Cassette BASIC language was to enable the first IBM computer to do something—anything!—without the need for a disk drive. When you boot without a system disk in one of your drives, an IBM computer starts the Cassette BASIC language executing.

When the IBM PC was introduced, disks were by no means a standard. Many small computers worked well using only cassette recorders for mass storage. Cassette BASIC enabled the PC to boot up and load a program from tape (as well as run simple BASIC programs).

A more advanced version of the BASIC language was included with PC DOS. However, this BASIC code was designed to augment the Cassette BASIC already in an IBM computer's ROM. Because the code was already in the machine, there was no compelling need to duplicate it on the DOS disk. Loading BASIC or BASICA from disk simply adds new routines that augment Cassette BASIC.

Non-IBM computers do not have Cassette BASIC built into their ROMs. When a disk is not ready when you boot it, nothing happens. Worse, when you try to run the BASIC or BASICA language program included with PC DOS, they are likely to crash. The crash occurs because BASIC or BASICA cannot find the ROM code it needs to make itself into a complete language. It—and your machine—lose their minds.

The GWBASIC language sold directly by Microsoft and the BASIC interpreter languages that accompany many compatible computers do not need the ROM-based IBM Cassette BASIC to work; so those languages run on virtually any PC-compatible computer.

Supplementary BIOS Issues

Beyond the basic BIOS incorporated in every PC, some machines have added features that enhance or supplement traditional BIOS functions. The most dramatic of these improvements came with IBM's introduction of the PS/2 line of computers. Because of the innovations in the PS/2 design, IBM had to revise many aspects of its BIOS to handle added functions. An additional section of code was also added to help with multitasking software. The result was that BIOS firmware was more tightly integrated with the rest of the system. The BIOS was part of a complete system that included new system board hardware and special software for aiding in setup. The additions help the computer better adjust itself for the options and accessories that you install inside it.

Programmable Option Select

In the first few years of supporting PCs, IBM discovered that the vast majority of system problems arose from mis-set DIP switches on expansion boards or the interaction between mis-configured expansion boards. To eliminate these problems, IBM added a software-based configuration scheme called *Programmable Option Select* or *POS* to its Micro Channel computers.

POS eliminates the requirement for jumpers and DIP switches. All configuration is handled through software. Setup information is stored in CMOS memory and in special disk files. The PS/2 BIOS automatically loads the stored configuration information into each expansion board every time the system is booted. The BIOS also ensures the integrity of the setup information.

The POS process is keyed to adapter identification numbers, unique designations assigned to each model of Micro Channel adapter. These identification numbers are coded as four digits and stored as two bytes of data. Every Micro Channel expansion board must have such a number. Although IBM acts as a clearinghouse and attempts to prevent conflicts, some makers of Micro Channel accessories may invent their own numbers, creating the possibility of conflicts, or may copy the numbers used by IBM for similar adapters, perhaps to add legitimacy or an aura of compatibility to their products. Neither strategy is recommended, because there is no shortage of identifying numbers. The two-byte approach makes 65,536 numbers possible, so assigning a unique number to each expansion product will be possible for a long time.

The POS process begins by individually selecting each expansion slot and querying it for the presence of an adapter. If no adapter resides in the slot, there is no response. If an adapter is present, the POS procedure queries it for its adapter identification number. This number is compared to the value stored in CMOS memory assigned to that slot.

Adapter Description Files

If the two numbers match, the POS looks for an *Adapter Description File* on the boot disk. This special file contains setup information for configuring the associated adapter. If the file is found, its values are read, and the card is setup. Then the next slot is queried.

If the identifying number read from the card does not match the number stored in CMOS, or if the Adapter Description File is not found, an error results, and you must run the system configuration utility again.

IBM prescribes the exact contents and arrangement of the Adapter Description File, because its contents are used by the configuration utility on the PS/2 Reference Disk. All the prompts and option choices are listed in the file. These choices are read into and displayed by the configuration menu.

An Adapter Configuration File can be recognized by its filename extension ADF. The four numbers in the file name are the same as the identifying number assigned to the associated adapter.

Before a Micro Channel expansion board can be correctly configured, its associated ADF file must be transferred to the working copy of your Reference Disk. The configuration procedure provides an option for carrying out this copying process as the menu selection, Copy an option diskette.

Some Micro Channel options also include *diagnostic code modules* and *Power-On Self-Test Error Message Files*. These can be identified by their file names, which are also keyed to the identifying number of the option. Transfer these to the working copy of your Reference Disk, too.

The POS process has evolved with the PS/2 line of computers. Originally, the setup program controlling POS went through the list of installed peripherals once when it attempted an automatic setup. If it encountered a problem, it made no attempt to go back and reassign the resources given to a board that it had already configured. More recent versions of the POS configuration program cycle through all peripherals until all conflicts are resolved or until it runs out of options.

To update your configuration procedure, you usually only need to install a new peripheral. Because your PS/2 is running without conflicts as is, you need to worry about the configuration procedure only when you add a new peripheral. Most new Micro Channel boards come with code that updates their configuration routines, automatically giving you the benefits of the updated configuration procedure.

PS/2 Advanced BIOS

With the introduction of the Micro Channel PS/2, IBM revised its standard BIOS with the addition of new protected mode routines designed to facilitate the use of OS/2 and other advanced applications. Rather than integrating them into the existing BIOS, IBM chose to make the new routines a separate entity so that the PS/2 BIOS consists of two sections that take up nearly 128 kilobytes of read-only memory.

The first is called the *Compatibility BIOS* or *CBIOS*. It addresses the first megabyte of system memory only and is used by PC DOS. It is fully compatible with the previous IBM BIOS—hence its designation.

The second section of BIOS code is all new. It is called the *Advanced BIOS* or *ABIOS* and addresses all the memory within the 16-megabyte range of the 80286 microprocessor in its protected mode. The ABIOS is specifically designed to provide support for multitasking systems that include, of course, OS/2.

The ABIOS works substantially different from the operation of the CBIOS. Rather than using software interrupts and parameter passing for accessing hardware devices, it is based on a call system meant to integrate with programming language subroutines. To make use of an ABIOS routine, a program transfers control to a subroutine, which sends control back to the program after the routine is completed.

Unlike the CBIOS, the ABIOS is re-entrant. This feature enables it to issue a second call while waiting for the results of the first call. For example, a program can request that the ABIOS read a cluster of data from the system's disk drive. However, the disk might not be ready to transfer data. The ABIOS routine would let you know that the disk wasn't ready, but continues trying to read the disk. Because the ABIOS routine is re-entrant, the underlying program can issue a second call, such as to another disk drive. This re-entrant capability permits the ABIOS of Micro Channel PS/2s to operate in a true multitasking mode.

Few BIOS makers or PC vendors have chosen to clone IBM's ABIOS. Mostly because the OS/2 operating system had not won wide acceptance in its first years, few manufacturers worried about compatibility with it. Moreover, the important aspects of the ABIOS merely simplified the mode-switching of the 286 microprocessor. With 386 and more recent microprocessors capable of shifting between real and protected mode at will, the most important part of the ABIOS is irrelevant. Moreover, OS/2 has been recrafted for greater compatibility without ABIOS. Although the ABIOS adds benefits to PCs having or emulating it, don't consider its absence a grave shortcoming.

Support Circuitry

S upport circuits are the glue that holds a PC together, providing the signals that the microprocessor needs to operate as well as those signals that link the PC and its peripherals. Over the years of development, the form and nature of those support circuits have changed, but their function has remained consistent, part of the definition of an IBM-compatible PC.

Just as you can't build a house without nails, you can't put together a computer without support chips. A wealth of circuits is needed to hold together all the functions of a PC, to coordinate its operation, and to control the signals inside it. After all, you need more than a microprocessor to make a computer; otherwise a microprocessor would be a computer. Although some systems come close to being little more than microprocessors, today a personal computer still requires a number of support functions to make the microprocessor useful and to make the microprocessor work. Support chips provide a PC's microprocessor with the signals it needs to operate as well as generating the signals the rest of your PC requires to operate.

Those with a penchant for details will take glee in pointing out that it is possible to build a house without nails, what with space-age adhesives, drywall screws, and even peg-and-tenon construction. The correct response to such small-mindedness is to say, "Get real," and that's exactly the case with today's PCs. The real machines you can buy today have virtually eliminated the vast assortment of support chips found in ancient PCs. All the essential support can now be packaged in a single chip, sometimes inside the same package as the system microprocessor—no nails, no glue, just one prefabricated assembly.

Despite the physical lack of support chips in some of today's systems, the functions performed by these vital circuits remain. Only their form has changed to protect the profits. Even without nails, you need something to hold the studs, plates, and joists together (at least if you're building a conventional home).

Chip Sets

In early PCs, support circuits were constructed from a variety of discrete circuits (small, general-purpose integrated circuits, such as logic gates) and a few functional blocks that each had a specific function, although not one limited to a specific model or design of computer. These garden-variety circuits were combined to build all the necessary computer functions into the first PC.

As PCs became increasingly popular, enterprising semiconductor firms combined many of the related computer functions into a single package. Eliminating the discrete packages and all their interconnections helped make PCs more reliable. Moreover, because a multitude of circuits could be grown together at the same time, this integrated approach made the PC support circuitry less expensive. At first, only related functions were grouped together. As semiconductor firms became more experienced, and fabrication technology permitted smaller design rules and denser packaging, however, all the diverse support functions inside a PC were integrated into a few VLSI components individually termed *Application-Specific Integrated Circuits* or *ASICs*, collectively called a *chip set*.

The chip set changed the face of the PC industry. With discrete support circuitry, designing a PC motherboard was a true engineering challenge because it required a deep understanding of the electronic functions of all the elements of a PC. Using a chip set, a PC engineer need only be concerned with the signals going in and out of a few components. The chip set might be a magical black box for all the designer cares. In fact, in many cases, the only skill required to design a PC from a chip set is the ability to navigate from a road map. Most chip set manufacturers provide circuit designs for motherboards to aid in the evaluation of their products. Many motherboard manufacturers (all too many, perhaps) simply take the chip set maker's evaluation design and turn it into a commercial product.

Today, even chip sets are disappearing. A single chip is sufficient to hold all the support circuitry of an entire PC. Moreover, chip makers have already taken the final step—integration of the support circuitry with the microprocessor. Although a single-chip design has its benefits, particularly in space-critical applications such as notebook and hand-held PCs, it is not always the best approach. A multi-chip design allows hardware engineers more freedom to customize and optimize their products, which means a greater capability to tune in more speed. The semiconductor costs of one-chip and three-chip implementations are not significantly different, and the extra chips impose little penalty on desktop-size motherboards.

Timing Circuits

Although anarchy has much to recommend it should you believe in individual freedom or sell firearms, anarchy is an anathema to computer circuits. Today's data processing designs depend on organization and controlled cooperation. Timing is critical. The meaning of each pulse passing through a PC is dependent on time relationships. Signals must be passed between circuits at just the right moment for the entire system to work properly.

This time is critical in PCs because their circuits are designed using a technology known as *clocked logic*. All the logic elements in the computer operate synchronously. They carry out their designated operations one step at a time, and each circuit makes one step at the same time as all the rest of the circuits in the computer. This synchronous operation helps the machine keep track of every bit that it processes, ensuring that nothing slips between the cracks.

Clocks and Oscillators

The system clock is the conductor who beats the time that all the circuits follow, sending out special timing pulses at precisely controlled intervals. The clock, however, must get its cues from somewhere, either its own internal sense of timing or some kind of metronome.

An electronic circuit that accurately and continuously beats time is termed an *oscillator*. Most oscillators work on a simple feedback principle. Like the microphone that picks up its own sounds from speakers that are too near or turned up too high, the oscillator, too, listens to what it says. As with the acoustic feedback squeal the public address system complains with, the oscillator, too, generates it own howl. Because the feedback circuit is much shorter, however, the signal need not travel as far, and the frequency is higher, perhaps by several thousand times.

The oscillator takes its output as its input, amplifies the signal, and sends the signal to its output where it goes back to the input again in an endless, and out-of-control, loop. By taming the oscillator by adding impediments to the feedback loop and by adding special electronic components between the oscillator's output and its input, the feedback and its frequency can be brought under control.

In nearly all PCs, a carefully crafted crystal of quartz is used as this frequency-control element. Quartz is one of many piezoelectric compounds. Piezoelectric materials have an interesting property—if you bend one, it makes a tiny voltage. Or if you apply voltage to it in the right way, the piezoelectric material will bend.

Quartz crystals do exactly that. But beyond this simple stimulus-response relationship, quartz crystals offer another important property. By stringently controlling the size and shape of a quartz crystal, it can be made to resonate at a specific frequency. The frequency of this resonance is extremely stable and very reliable—so much so that it can help an electric watch keep time to within seconds a month. Although PCs don't need the absolute precision of a quartz watch to operate their logic circuits properly, the fundamental stability of the quartz oscillator guarantees that the PC will have a clock frequency within its design limits always available.

The very first IBM personal computer was designed around a single such oscillator built from a crystal that resonated at 14.31818 mega-hertz. The odd frequency was chosen for a particular reason: it's exactly four times the subcarrier frequency used in color television signals (3.58 Mhz), and the engineers who created the original PC thought compatibility with televisions would be an important design element of the PC. They were anticipating multimedia but looking for a cheap way of putting PC images on-screen. When the PC was released, no inexpensive color computer monitors were available (or necessary for almost non-existent color graphic software).

The actual oscillator in these early machines was made from a special integrated circuit, type 8284A, and the 14.31818 Mhz crystal. One output at the crystal's fundamental frequency was routed directly to the expansion bus. Another oscillator output was divided down by a discrete auxiliary chip to create the 1.19 Mhz frequency that was used as a time base for the PC's timer/counter circuit. The same chip also divided the fundamental crystal frequency by 3 to produce a frequency of 4.77 Mhz, the actual clock signal used by the microprocessor in the PC, determining the operating speed of the system microprocessor. This same clock signal also synchronized all the logic operations inside the PC and related 8-bit bus computers.

In that the 14.31818 crystal determines the speed at which a PC or related computer operates, you might think that you could speed up such a system and improve its overall performance simply by replacing the crystal with one that operates at a higher frequency. Although this strategy will actually increase the operating speed of a PC, it is not a good idea for several reasons.

One problem is easily solved. Although the standard 8088 micropro-cessor in the PC is rated at only 5 Mhz and may not operate properly at higher speeds, you can swap it for one that will handle a faster clock—an 8088-2 or NEC V-20, for example. But you'll have to up-grade other parts of the system to higher speed, too. A bigger obstacle is the one-oscillator design of the PC. Because all timings throughout the whole PC system are locked to that one oscillator, odd things will happen when you alter its frequency. The system clock won't keep very good time, perennially kept in a high-speed time warp. Software that depends on system timings may crash. Expansion boards might not work at the altered bus speed. Even your floppy disks may operate erratically with some software.

The goal in the oscillator/clock design of the PC seems to have been frugality rather than flexibility, versatility, or usability. In those early systems, one master frequency was cut, chopped, minced, and diced into whatever else was needed inside the computer. But as with trying to make a cut-rate system speed up, altering the frequency of any part of a computer with the PC oscillator design is likely to throw off all the other frequency-critical components. Consequently, when IBM rethought the basic concept of a personal computer and came up with its Advanced Technology approach, the oscillator was completely redesigned.

The more enlightened AT design broke the system clock free from the bondage of the timer and its oscillator. Instead of just one crystal and oscillator, the AT and every subsequent computer based upon its design (which means nearly all PCs) uses three. One is used to derive the system clock for synchronizing the bus, microprocessor, and related circuits. Another operates at 14.31818 Mhz and provides input to a timer/counter chip and a 14.31818 bus signal for compatibility with the PC. The third oscillator controls the CMOS time-of-day clock that runs on battery power even when the computer is switched off.

The oscillator of the original AT was much the same as that of the PC, to the extent of being based on the same 8284A timer chip and 14.31818 Mhz crystal. The oscillator's output was routed directly to the bus. Another output was divided down to 1.19 Mhz to feed the timer/counter circuit to maintain backward compatibility with the first PCs. In the original AT, a special circuit was dedicated to generating the system clock signal, a type 82284 System Clock Generator chip. The operating frequency of the microprocessor was governed by the crystal associated with this chip. The 82284 divides the crystal frequency in half to produce the clock that controls the speed of the microprocessor, bus, and associated circuitry. The original AT operated with a 6 Mhz clock derived from a 12 Mhz crystal; later ATs ran at 8 Mhz, derived from a 16 Mhz crystal.

• Replacing the crystal used by the 82284 oscillator will alter the speed of the microprocessor. This change likely will also affect the operating speed of the expansion bus. In the original AT design, the bus clock frequency was locked to the microprocessor clock. The bus and the microprocessor ran in lockstep. As designers pushed microprocessor speeds higher, however, bus devices could not keep up. Consequently, most modern PCs using the ISA expansion bus put a frequency divider between the microprocessor clock and the expansion bus.

Because the expansion bus clock is directly derived from the microprocessor clock, the two clocks are locked together, providing synchronous operation of the bus. However, the bus speed can be kept at a frequency low enough to be tolerated by most expansion boards. Most ISA systems strive to run the bus at the submultiple of the microprocessor clock that comes closest to the 8 Mhz that most expansion boards are designed to accommodate. The EISA bus design dictates a nominal 8 Mhz bus speed as well.

IBM took the oscillator designs of its PS/2 series in new directions but went to great lengths to maintain compatibility with previous systems. Even the first PS/2s merged much of the support circuitry on their motherboards into ASICs, with the system's oscillators and clocks among these newly integrated functions.

For example, the initial ISA PS/2s, the Models 25 and 30, put their timer, oscillator, and clock functions into two VLSI chips, which IBM called the System Support Gate Array and the I/O Support Gate Array. The former circuit generates the system clock, starting with the output of a 48 Mhz external oscillator. The System Support Gate Array divides this frequency by a factor of 6 to achieve the 8 Mhz that serves as the system clock. It also controls the refreshing of system memory, a function that in previous systems required the use of a channel of the system timer. In addition to these functions, the System Support Gate Array also controls which functions and devices (microprocessor, coprocessor, DMA controller, and so on) have command of the system bus.

The I/O Support Gate Array controls the serial and parallel ports, the floppy and hard disk controllers, the video system, and the real-time clock but does not contain the full circuitry for these functions. The I/O Support Gate Array also generates the 1.19 Mhz signal used by the system timer.

The direction of current PC clock and oscillator designs is exemplified by Chips and Technology's 82C836 (also called SCATsx), a one-chip VLSI device that incorporates most of the motherboard logic needed to construct an AT-style computer using an 386SX microprocessor. The 82C836 accepts a single, crystal-controlled oscillator signal (typically 32, 40, or 50 Mhz) and provides isolated output clock signals for the system microprocessor, the expansion bus, and the DMA system. The 82C836 also provides a 14.31818 Mhz I/O clock derived from a separate crystal or oscillator. The 82C836 will produce a microprocessor clock that's either exactly equal to or one-half, one-quarter, or one-eighth of the oscillator signal provided at its input. The bus clock can be set at either one-quarter, one-fifth, or one-sixth the input frequency. The DMA clock can be set at bus speed or one-half the bus speed. In short, using a chip set like the 82C836, the PC designer need only provide a single oscillator frequency, and all the necessary clock signals are automatically derived without further work or worry. Nevertheless, the designer is still allowed the flexibility of choosing among several bus and DMA speeds to match the particular system requirements.

Timers

The signals developed by the clocks and oscillators inside a PC are designed for internal consumption only. That is, they are used for housekeeping functions, locking together the operation of various circuit components. System timers serve more diverse functions. Unlike clocks and oscillators, which are fixed in frequency and purpose by hardware design, the PC's timers are programmable, so their output frequencies can be altered to suit the needs of special applications.

The timer signals in the original PC were generated from the system clock using a 8253 timer/counter integrated circuit chip. Actually three 16-bit timers in one, the 8253 derives several important signals from the system clock. One of its outputs controls the time-of-day clock inside the PC, another controls the memory refresh circuitry of the computer, and the third generates the tones made by the PC's speaker.

The 8253 timer/counter operates by counting the clock pulses it receives by reducing the value it holds in an internal register by one with each pulse it receives. In the PC series of computers, the signal that the 8253 timer/counter actually counts is a submultiple of the system clock, divided by four, to about 1.19 Mhz.

The 8253 can be set up (through I/O ports in the PC) to work in any of six different modes, two of which can be used only on the speaker channel. In the most straightforward mode, Mode 2, the 8253 operates as a frequency divider or rate generator. You load its register with a number, and it counts to that number. When the 8253 reaches that number, it outputs a pulse and starts all over again. Load the 8253 register with 2, and it will send out a pulse at half the frequency of the input. Load it with 1,000, and the output will be 1/1000th of the input. In this mode, the chip can generate an interrupt at any of a wide range of user-defined intervals. Because the highest value you can load into its 16-bit register is 216 or 65,536, the longest single interval it can count is about .055 second—that is, the 1.19 Mhz input signal divided by 65,536.

The six modes of the PC's 8253 timer/counter and their functions and programming are shown in table 8.1.

TABLE 8.1.
Operating Modes
of 8253 Timer/
Counter Chip

Mode	Operation
0—Interrupt on Terminal Count	Timer is loaded with a value and counts down from that value to zero, one counter per clock pulse.
1—Hardware Retriggerable One-Shot	A trigger pulse causes timer output to go low; when the counter reaches zero, the output goes high and stays high until reset. The process repeats every time triggered. Pulse length is set by writing a control word and initial count to chip before first cycle.
2—Rate Generator	Timer divides incoming frequency by the value of the initial count loaded into it.
3—Square Wave	Produces a series of square waves with a period (measured in clock pulses) equal to the value loaded into the timer.
4—Software Retriggerable Strobe	Timer counts down the number of clock cycles loaded into it; then pulses its output. Software starts the next cycle.
5—Hardware Retriggerable Strobe	Timer counts down the number of clock cycles loaded into it; then pulses its output. Hardware-generated pulse initiates the next cycle.

The time-of-day signal in the original PC used the 8253 timer/counter to count out its longest possible increment, generating pulses at a rate of 18.2 per second. The pulses cause the time-of-day interrupt, which the PC counts to keep track of the time. These interrupts can also be used by programs that need to regularly investigate what the computer is doing—for instance, checking the hour to see whether it's time to dial up a distant computer. Note that reprogramming this channel of a PC will have interesting effects on the time of day reported by the system, generally making the hours whiz by.

The speaker section of the 8253 works the same way, only it generates a waveform that is used to power the speaker and make sounds. Programs can modify any of its settings to change the sound of the speaker. Programs can also modify the channel that drives the memory controller, which will likely crash your computer. The timer/counter of the AT is similar to that of earlier IBM computers except that it is based on a chip. In the AT, it provides three outputs—one to generate the 18.2-per-second pulse that drives the time-of-day signal and interrupt; the second to provide a trigger for memory refresh cycles, fixed in the case of the AT to produce a signal with a period of 15 milliseconds; and a third to drive the speaker. Controls for these operate in the same way as those for the related PC functions and are found at the same I/O ports.

In its PS/2 series, IBM maintained the timer as a separate circuit, an 8253 (just as in IBM's previous PCs and XTs), and the timer is accessed and controlled through the same ports with the same commands. The newer IBM design differs, however, in the assignment of its three outputs. One still generates the 18.2-per-second pulses to serve as the system timer, and another controls the speaker. The other channel, used for DMA operations in PC and XTs, is used only for diagnostics in the Models 25 and 30. Its output is unconnected. Its former function is handled by the System Support Gate Array.In Micro Channel PS/2 models, the oscillator and timing functions are integrated into VLSI chips, but the function of the circuits remains compatible with the timers in previous computer models. However, some system timer functions were revised to help forestall disasters. As with Models 25 and 30, the system timer has been freed of its DMA duty, that chore being handled by a gate array. The timer channel and I/O port address, 041(Hex), nominally assigned to that function are undefined in Micro Channel PS/2s. A third timer channel is instead assigned a "watchdog" function, overseeing the Micro Channel expansion bus.

This timer channel monitors the 18.2-times-per-second time-of-day interrupt. The timer channel counts the number of these interrupts that do not arrive on schedule. Should the total number of missed interrupts reach a critical value, it reports an error to the system. If a program goes awry and interferes with proper operation of the system interrupts, the watchdog reports an error, allowing corrective action to be taken.

In a single-user, single-tasking system, the watchdog is of dubious value. When the interrupts go awry, both the executing program and the machine have effectively crashed. In a multitasking system, however, the watchdog gives the system a chance to save properly, executing applications from the effects of one that crashes.

The watchdog can be defeated or its timing values adjusted through the I/O ports that control the timer, as shown in table 8.2.

TABLE 8.2.

Registers and
Control of 8253
Timer

Register I/O Port Address	Function
040(Hex)	Timer 0 count
041(Hex)	Timer 1 count
042(Hex)	Timer 2 count
043(Hex)	8253 Control Register

Bit 0 - 0=Binary counter 16-bits
1=Binary-Coded Decimal (BCD) counter (four decades)

Bits 1 to 3—Mode select in binary form			
Bit 3	Bit 2	Bit 1	Mode
0	0	0	0
0	0	1	1
X	1	0	2
X	1	1	3
1	0	0	4
1	0	1	5

Bits 4 and 5—Read/Load		
Bit 5	Bit 4	Function
0	0	Counter latching operation
0	1	Read/load least significant byte only
1	0	Read/load most significant byte only
1	1	Read/load least significant byte first; then the most significant byte

Bits 6 and 7—Select counter		
Bit 7	Bit 6	Function
0	0	Select counter 0
0	1	Select counter 1
1	0	Select counter 2
1	1	Illegal instruction

Modern PCs based on commercial chip sets simply duplicate the functions of the AT's 8254-2 timer chip in their own silicon. The time-of-day and speaker timers in these machines are programmable exactly as they are in the AT. Many systems use a third timer channel in the traditional manner, to determine the intervals at which to refresh system memory. A few aim to prevent unintended disasters by relegating the memory refresh function to other circuits beyond the reach of your programs. As long as you don't plan to tinker with timers (that is, you don't do any hardware-level programming yourself), there's no reason to prefer one design over the other.

Real-Time Clock

Perhaps the most annoying characteristic of the first PCs was their bad habit of asking the time and date every time you switched them on. The inevitable response was to mash down twice on the Enter key to load in the defaults. Obediently the system would assume the day to be 1 January 1980 and the time midnight, and all your files would be time-stamped as if you had spent the wee hours of New Year's Day slaving away.

The AT and all more recent computers have avoided the problem by including a real-time clock among their support circuits. IBM set the pattern by using a specific clock circuit, an MC146818 chip. Based on low-power CMOS circuitry, the MC146818 is designed to run constantly whether your PC is switched on or off. A battery of some kind in your system supplies power when the PC is unplugged or otherwise turned off.

The MC146818 measures time by counting pulses of a crystal oscillator operating nominally at 32.768 kilohertz, so it can be as accurate as a quartz watch. (The MC146818 can be programmed to accept other oscillator frequencies as well.) Many compatible PCs tell time as imaginatively as a four-year-old child, however, because their manufacturers never think to adjust them properly. Most put a trimmer (an adjustable capacitor) in series with their quartz crystal, allowing the manufacturer—or anyone with a screwdriver—to alter the resonate frequency of the oscillator. Giving the trimmer a tweak can bring the real-time clock closer to reality—or further into the twilight zone. (You can find the trimmer by looking for the short cylinder with a slotted shaft in the center near the clock crystal. The trimmer is usually the only thing in a PC with a kilohertz rather than Mhz rating.)

The real-time clock has a built-in alarm function. The MC146818 can be programmed to generate an interrupt when the hour, minute, and second of the time set for the alarm arrives. The alarm is set by loading the appropriate time values into the registers of the MC146818.

Besides the real-time clock, the MC146818 also encapsulates the CMOS memory used for storing system configuration information. The original IBM design used the 64 bytes of storage inside the MC146818 for this purpose. Ten of those bytes store clock and alarm data, four store status information, and the remaining bytes are devoted to setup data, such as the number and type of disks installed, the amount of memory, and other system options. Table 8.3 lists the assignment of this memory in the original AT. Compatible PCs and Micro Channel machines added more CMOS memory for storing a wider variety of options.

Many chip sets emulate the MC146818 in their internal circuitry. In addition, special real-time clock modules (which also mimic the MC146818) with integral batteries are also available.

The CMOS memory of the MC146818 and the chip sets that emulate the MC146818 are not directly accessed by the host computer's microprocessor. They are reached through I/O ports. To read or write to CMOS memory, you must first indicate which address to access. To do this, you write an OUT instruction to I/O port 070(Hex) with the value of the CMOS address you want to access. To read that address, use an IN instruction to read the I/O port 071(Hex), and the value stored at the address will be returned to the microprocessor's AL register. To write to the address indicated by your first OUT command, use a second OUT instruction to I/O port 071(Hex) using the data to be written. These commands enable you—or, more likely, your programs—to read the real-time clock, set an alarm, or modify setup data. Because altering setup data can confuse your PC, be careful when tinkering with CMOS memory.

Interrupt Controllers

Intel microprocessors understand two kinds of interrupts: software and hardware. A *software interrupt* is simply a special instruction in a program that's controlling the microprocessor. Instead of adding, subtracting, or whatever, the software interrupt causes program execution to temporarily shift to another section of code in memory.

A *hardware interrupt* causes the same effect, but is controlled by special signals outside of the normal data stream. The only problem is that the microprocessors recognize far fewer interrupts than would be useful—only two interrupt signal lines are provided. One of these is a special case: the Non-Maskable Interrupt. The other line is shared by all system interrupts.

IBM's personal computer architecture nevertheless allows for several levels of interrupt, which are prioritized—a more important interrupt takes priority over one of lesser importance.

To organize the hardware interrupts of the PC-series of computers, IBM selected the 8259 Interrupt Controller. This chip handles eight interrupt signals, numbered 0 through 7, assigning each one a decreasing priority as the numeric designation increases. Table 8.3 lists the interrupt assignments of the PC, XT, Portable PC, and PCjr computers.

TABLE 8.3.
Interrupt
Assignments for
the PC, XT, and
Portable PC

Number	Function
NMI	Parity errors
0	System timer
1	Keyboard
2	EGA display PC network 3278/79 adapter
3	COM2

continues

TABLE 8.3.
continued

Number	Function
	PC network (alternate)
	3278/79 adapter (alternate)
	SDLC communications
	BSC communications
	Cluster adapter
4	COM1
	SDLC communications
	BSC communications
	Voice communications adapter (preferred)
5	Hard disk
6	Floppy disk
7	Printer
	Cluster adapter (alternate)

Eight hardware interrupts, of which only six were available on the expansion bus, quickly proved inadequate for complex systems, so IBM nearly doubled the number of hardware interrupts in the AT. The arrangement, assignment, and interplay of these interrupts were altered substantially from the PC design.

The near-doubling of interrupts was accomplished by adding a second interrupt controller chip (another 8259A) to the system architecture by cascading it to the first. The new chip is connected to another which, in turn, connects to the microprocessor. The chip closest to the microprocessor operates essentially as the single interrupt controller in a PC or XT. However, its interrupt 2 input is no longer connected to the PC bus. Instead, this chip receives the output of the second 8259A chip.

The interrupt channel on the bus that formerly led to the interrupt 2 input is now connected to interrupt 9 on the second chip. This interrupt signal must traverse two controllers before action is taken. Despite its new number, AT interrupt 9 functions just like PC interrupt 2, with the same priority activated by the same control line.

Although the 8259A controller still handles individual interrupts on a priority level corresponding to the inverse of the numerical designation of their inputs, the cascaded arrangement of the two controllers results in an unusual priority system. Top priority is given to interrupts

0 and 1 on the first chip. However, because the second chip is cascaded to interrupt 2 on the new chip, the new, higher-numbered interrupts that go through this connection get the next highest priority. In fact, interrupt 9 (which, remember, is actually the interrupt 0 input of the second 8259A controller) gets top priority of all interrupts available on the expansion bus. The rest of the interrupts connected to the second controller receive the next priority levels in ascending order up to interrupt 15. Finally, the remaining interrupts on the first chip follow in priority, from interrupt 3 up to interrupt 7. AT interrupt assignments are shown in table 8.4.

TABLE 8.4.
Interrupt Assignments for the AT and its Clones

Number	Function
NMI	Parity errors
0	System timer
1	Keyboard
2	Cascade input for second interrupt controller
3	COM2 PC network (alternate) SDLC communications BSC communications
4	COM1 SDLC communications BSC communications
5	LPT2
6	Disk controller Hard and floppy disk drive
7	LPT1 Data acquisition adapter General-purpose interface bus adapter Voice communications adapter (preferred)
8	Real-time clock interrupt
9	Software redirected to Interrupt OA(Hex) PC Network
10	Reserved
11	Reserved
12	Reserved
13	Coprocessor
14	Hard disk controller
15	Reserved

Just in case the 15 available interrupts (16 counting the special non-maskable interrupt) still don't stretch far enough, the AT bus makes provisions for interrupt sharing. IBM does not, however, implement interrupt sharing. That's left up to the designers of add-in components. Sharing involves designing device hardware to allow interrupt sharing and writing not only the code for the software routines that get carried out as a result of the interrupt, but also program code to sort through the shared possibilities, arbitrate conflicting interrupt calls, and put everything back together again at the end of the interrupt. Best done in assembly language, it's not stuff that timid programmers play with.

IBM's first ISA-bus PS/2 computers reverted back to the PC and XT design that supported a total of only eight interrupts. However, in these machines, IBM not only allows interrupt sharing but also takes advantage of it. Interrupt 1, assigned solely to the keyboard in PC-style computers, is shared among the keyboard, the pointing device (mouse), and the time-of-day clock in Models 25 and 30. Later classic bus PS/2s allowed the full AT interrupt selection.

The real PS/2 advance came with the Micro Channel machines and their level-sensitive interrupts. Although the level-sensitive interrupts work differently from and are incompatible with the edge-triggered interrupts used in previous IBM personal computers, the circuitry that controls them is familiar indeed. Micro Channel PS/2s use two 8259A interrupt controllers—exactly the same chips as other IBM personal computers—arranged exactly as are those in an ordinary AT. That is, the second 8259A is cascaded to the interrupt 2 channel of the first. Interrupt priorities are the same in both the AT and Micro Channel designs.

The 8259A chip is capable of either edge-triggered or level-sensitive operation. In Micro Channel computers, the chips are initialized in level-sensitive mode. Circuits external to the 8259A chips prevent their being set up in edge-triggered mode.

Chip sets used by modern PCs, including most EISA machines, incorporate the interrupt controller function. In general, the chip sets mimic the AT interrupt structure, cascading two levels of interrupts. Some, however, reorganize the interrupt structure to eliminate the two-tier approach.

In general, this change causes no problems. A few peripherals and programs depend on finding the exact AT interrupt structure and can demonstrate incompatibilities with these altered designs. The problems can often be avoided by reassigning interrupts so that the troublesome devices or software access interrupts strictly follow the AT standard. In other words, if a device has difficulty when using interrupt 2 or 9 in a PC, the problem often can be remedied by assigning it another interrupt.

Direct Memory Access

The best way to speed up system performance is to relieve the host microprocessor all of its housekeeping chores. One of the more time-consuming chores is moving blocks of memory around inside the computer—for instance, shifting bytes from a hard disk (where they are stored) through its controller into main memory (where the microprocessor can use it). The memory-moving chores can be handled by a special device called a Direct Memory Access or DMA controller.

This specialized chip needs to know only the base location from where bytes are to be moved, the address to where they should go, and the number of bytes to move. When it has received that information from the microprocessor, the DMA controller takes command and does all the dirty work itself. The DMA controller used in all IBM computers is completely programmable and is operated through a series of I/O registers.

DMA operations can be used to move data between I/O devices and memory. In theory, DMA operations could also expedite the transfer of data between memory locations, but this mode of operation is not supported by the basic IBM system design.

IBM first chose the 8237A-5 DMA controller for the PC and used the same chip in all later personal computers up to Micro Channel PS/2 models. The -5 in the designation is the speed rating of the chip, 5 Mhz, which closely matches the only clock in the PC and XT, 4.77 Mhz. Each transfer of a byte under DMA control requires five cycles of the system clock, a total of 1,050 nanoseconds.

The 8237A-5 affords these computers four separate DMA channels that can be used independently for memory moves. The PC design reserves one of these channels for refreshing system memory. The other three channels are available on the I/O bus. The PC and XT DMA can address only one megabyte, the maximum memory of those systems and the addressing limit of the eight-bit PC expansion bus.

In most IBM software, only one DMA channel is used at a time. Only on rare occasions, such as backing up a hard disk to floppy, are two channels needed. In such cases, it is convenient to pull data from the hard disk and immediately write it to the backup device. Many floppy disk-based backup systems do, in fact, use two DMA channels simultaneously for this purpose.

Normally, such operations should cause no problems. However, in 10 to 15 percent of the original PCs, such operations will not work properly because of defective 8237A chips. The chip errors don't normally show up (and didn't in the testing of the chips) because only one channel is typically used at a time.

The only sure cure for this problem is to replace the chip should its symptoms be noted. As this replacement is not easy—the ailing chip is soldered in place—and because the error is likely to occur only with a few backup programs, the procedure usually is not worthwhile. The better (and more affordable) strategy is to live with the bad chip, which won't otherwise misbehave, and avoid the software that causes the problem.

This problem does not occur with other computers because the design of the 8237A chip has been revised to eliminate it.

The AT and most more recent PCs based on the AT model use the same DMA chip as the PC and XT, the 8237A-5, but augment it with a second chip. As with the AT Interrupt Controller, one channel of one of the DMA controller chips is used to cascade the second chip. With four channels per chip and one used for cascading, the net yield to the system is seven DMA channels. Each of these channels can address the full 16-megabyte range of the 80286 microprocessor, the addressing limit of the AT expansion bus. Four of these DMA channels are eight bits wide and operate identically to those of the PC and XT. The other three channels on the second chip are a full 16 bits wide.

In the AT, each of the DMA controllers operates at one-half the microprocessor speed to stay within its speed rating. That is, in a 6 Mhz AT, the 8237A-5 operates at 3 Mhz. In an 8 Mhz AT, the 8237A-5 operates at 4 Mhz. Because each DMA cycle requires five clocks, each takes 1,666 nanoseconds in a 6 Mhz machine or 1,250 nanoseconds in an 8 Mhz machine. Note that even in an 8 Mhz AT in eight-bit mode, DMA transfers actually occur more slowly in the AT than in the PC. In 16-bit mode, however, AT DMA transfers are faster because the wider bus width permits more data to move through the controller. DMA transfers in AT systems are faster than those in PCs but still not that fast. In fact, IBM determined the speed to be inadequate for hard disk access. Consequently, AT-style systems avoid DMA control for hard disk access and, instead, use programmed I/O; that is, the microprocessor itself manages hard disk transfers. Of course, this eliminates problems of simultaneously using two DMA channels when backing up the hard disk.

The initial PS/2s lacking Micro Channel Architecture used an eight-bit DMA arrangement similar to that of the PC and XT. In these computers, however, the 8237A DMA chip operates at 4 Mhz. In addition, each DMA cycle requires six cycles of that clock rather than the five used in PC, XT, and AT systems. Each cycle of a DMA transfer thus requires about 1,500 nanoseconds. Newer classic bus PS/2s follow the AT model.

In IBM's Micro Channel Architecture, the DMA controller is incorporated into one of the very large-scale integration circuits on the system board. The design is functionally compatible with that of the AT and can mimic the operation of a pair of 8237A chips. However, the Micro Channel machines make an additional DMA channel available and offer an additional extended command set for control.

In a Micro Channel machine, DMA timing is essentially independent of the system clock. In general, each DMA cycle requires 600 nanoseconds from system board memory or 500 from an expansion board on the Micro Channel. Another few hundred nanoseconds of overhead are required to set up the entire transfer (which may consist of up to 64K cycles). Transfers can be either 8 or 16 bits at a time. Overall, Micro Channel DMA transfers are more than twice as fast as those of the AT, giving the newer computers a substantial performance advantage.

The initial Micro Channel design limited DMA addressing to 24 address lines, capping the reach of DMA to 16 megabytes of RAM. Starting with the PS/2 Models 90 and 95, Micro Channel DMA was given full 32-bit addressing.

Modern PCs integrate the DMA controller with the rest of the system support circuitry inside the chip set. They mimic a pair of cascaded 8237A DMA controllers. In general, the DMA systems of most classic bus systems are limited to addressing 16 megabytes by the bus itself. EISA machines allow full 32-bit addressing.

Other Support Functions

One additional support chip is necessary in every PC: a keyboard decoder. This special-purpose chip, an Intel 8042 in most PCs, an equivalent chip, or part of a chip set that emulates an 8042, links the keyboard to the motherboard. The primary function of the keyboard decoder is to translate the serial data that the keyboard sends out into the parallel form that can be used by your PC. As it receives each character from the keyboard, the keyboard decoder generates an interrupt to make your PC aware that you have typed a character. The keyboard decoder also verifies that the character was correctly received (by performing a parity check) and translates the scan code of each character. The keyboard decoder automatically requests the keyboard to retransmit characters that arrive with parity errors.

Each character in the serial data stream sent to the keyboard decoder comprises 11 bits—a start bit, eight bits of data, a parity bit, and a stop bit. The bits are synchronized to a clock signal originating inside the keyboard. In AT and more recent keyboards, the keyboard decoder can also send data to the keyboard to program its internal microprocessor. (Keyboards and scan codes are discussed more completely in Chapter 11, "Input Devices.")

Chip sets often include a variety of other functions to make the PC designer's life easier. These can include everything from controls for front panel indicator lights to floppy disk controllers. Exactly which functions are built into the chip set depends on the magnanimity of the chip set maker. Although adding more functions makes the chip set more complex and costly, a more feature-packed chip set can also give its maker a marketing advantage. Most modern chip set makers offer full-featured products that include floppy disk control circuitry, input/output ports (parallel, serial, mouse, keyboard, and game ports), and a connector for an embedded controller (IDE) hard disk. Some chip set manufacturers incorporate video (VGA) circuitry into their products as well.

If you're buying rather than designing a PC, you'll find no particular advantage in the extreme integration of today's single-chip PCs. Although a single-chip solution is, in theory, more reliable than a three-chip PC, the difference may be between whether the machine ultimately fails when your great-great grandchildren are playing with the system or when their children are reveling in the primitive glory of playing with an ancient PC. Probably the only important support circuit issue to ponder when purchasing a new PC is whether port, video, and floppy disk control circuitry on the motherboard can be defeated to eliminate I/O and interrupt conflicts with other expansion products. (IDE ports don't need defeatability because an unused IDE port acts as an expansion connector with nothing plugged in.) Other support chip issues represent only different paths to the same destination.

If a system doesn't have the right combination of support circuitry, it simply won't work like a PC. And if it has the right support circuitry, you'll have exactly what you should expect—a trouble-free PC that runs your favorite programs.

The
Power Supply

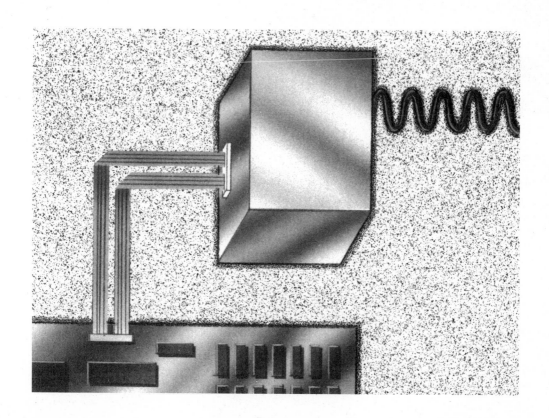

All practical computers made today operate electronically. Moving electrons (electricity) are the media of their thoughts. Electrical pulses course from one circuit to another, switched off or on in an instant by logic chips. Circuits combine the electrical pulses to make logical decisions and to send out other pulses to control peripherals. The computer's signals stay electrical until electrons colliding with phosphors in the monitor tube push out photons toward your eyes or generate the fields that snap your printer into action.

Of course, your computer needs a source for the electricity that runs it. The power does not arise spontaneously in its circuits but must be derived from an outside source. Conveniently, nearly every home in America is equipped with its own electrical supply that the computer can tap into. Such is the wonder of civilization.

But the delicate solid-state semiconductor circuits of today's computers cannot directly use the electricity supplied by your favorite utility company. Commercial power is an electrical brute, designed to have the strength and stamina to withstand the miles of travel between generator and your home. Your PC's circuits want a steady, carefully controlled trickle of power. Raw utility power would fry and melt computer circuits in a quick flash of miniature lightning.

For economic reasons, commercial electrical power is transmitted between you and the utility company as alternating current, the familiar AC found everywhere. AC is preferred by power companies because it is easy to generate and adapts readily between voltages (including to very high voltages that make long distance transmission efficient). It's called "alternating" because it reverses polarity, swapping positive for negative, dozens of times a second (arbitrarily, it is 60 Hz in America, 50 Hz in Europe).

The changing or oscillating nature of AC enables transformers to increase or decrease voltage (the measure of the driving force of electricity) because transformers only react to electrical changes. Electrical power travels better at higher voltages because waste (as heat generated by the electrical current flowing through the resistance of the long distance transmission wires) is inversely proportional to voltage. Transformers permit the high voltages used in transmitting commercial power, sometimes hundreds of thousands of volts, to be reduced to a safe level (nominally 117 volts) before it's led into your home.

As wonderful as AC is to power companies, it's an anathema to computer circuits. These circuits form their pulses by switching the flow of electricity tapped from a constant supply. Although computers can be designed that use AC, the constant voltage reversal would complicate designs so that juggling knives while blindfolded and riding a roller coaster would seem tame in comparison. Computers (and most electronic gear) use direct current or DC instead. Direct current is the kind of power that comes directly from a primary source, such as a battery. DC is a single voltage that stays at a constant level (at least constant as long as the battery has the reserves to produce it). Moreover, even the relatively low voltage that powers your lights and vacuum cleaner would be fatal to semiconductor circuits. Tiny distances separate the elements inside solid state circuits, and high voltages can flash across those distances like lightning, burning and destroying the silicon along the way.

The intermediary that translates AC from your electrical outlets into the DC that your computer's circuits need is called the *power supply*. As it operates, the power supply of your PC attempts to make the direct current that's supplied to your computer as pure as possible, as close to the ideal DC power as produced by batteries. The chief goal is regulation, maintaining the voltage as close as possible to the ideal that's desired by the circuits inside your PC.

Laptop and notebook computers have it easy. They work with low-voltage DC battery power, which is generated inside the battery cells in exactly the right form for computer circuits. However, even laptop and notebook computers required built-in voltage regulation because even pure battery power varies in voltage depending on the state of charge or discharge of the battery. In addition, laptop and notebook computers must also charge their batteries somehow, and their charges must make exactly the same electrical transformations as a desktop computer's power supply.

Power Supply Technologies

In electronic gear, two kinds of power supplies are commonly used: linear power supplies and switching power supplies. The former is old technology, dating from the days when the first radios were freed from their need for storage batteries in the 1920s. Switching power supplies rates as high technology, requiring the speed and efficiency of solid-state electronic circuitry to achieve the dominant position they hold today in the computer power market. These two power supply technologies are distinguished by the means used to achieve their voltage regulation.

Linear Power Supplies

The design first used for making regulated DC from utility-supplied AC was the linear power supply. At one time, the linear power supply was the only kind of power supply used for any electronic equipment. When another technology became available, they were slapped with the linear label because they used standard linear (analog) semiconductor circuits, although a linear power supply need not have any semiconductors in it.

In a linear power supply, the raw electricity from the power line is first sent through a transformer, which reduces its voltage to a value slightly higher than is required by the computer's circuits. Next, one or several rectifiers, usually semiconductor diodes, convert the now low-voltage AC to DC by permitting the flow of electricity in only one direction, blocking the reversals. Finally, this DC is sent through the linear voltage regulator, which adjusts the voltage created by the power supply to the level required by your computer's circuits.

Most linear voltage regulators work simply by absorbing the excess voltage made by the transformer, turning it into heat. A shunt regulator shorts out excess power to drive the voltage down. A series regulator puts an impediment, a resistance, in the flow of electricity, blocking excess voltage. In either case, the regulator requires an input voltage higher than the voltage it supplies to your computer's circuits. This excess power is converted to heat (that is, wasted). The linear power supply achieves its regulation simply by varying the waste.

Switching Power Supplies

The design alternative is the switching power supply. Although more complex, switching power supplies are more efficient and often less expensive than their linear kin. Although designs vary, the typical switching supply first converts the incoming 60 Hz utility power to a much higher frequency of pulses (in the range of 20,000 Hz, above the range of normal human hearing) by switching the utility power on and off using an electrical component called a *triac*.

At the same time that the switching regulator increases the frequency of the commercial power, it regulates the power using a digital technique called *pulse-width modulation*. That is, the duration of each power pulse is varied in response to the needs of the computer circuitry being supplied. The width of the pulses is controlled by the electronic switch; shorter pulses result in a lower output voltage. Finally, the switched pulses are reduced in voltage to the level required by the computer circuits by a transformer and turned into pure direct current by rectification and filtering.

Switching power supplies earn their efficiency and lower cost in two ways. Switching regulation is more efficient because less power is turned into heat. Instead of dissipating energy with a shunt or series regulator, the switching regulator switches all current flow off, albeit briefly. In addition, high frequencies require smaller, less expensive transformers and filtering circuits. For these two very practical reasons, nearly all of today's personal computers use switching power supplies.

PC Power Needs

Modern computer logic circuits operate by switching voltages with the two different logic states (true or false, one or zero) coded as two voltage levels, termed *high* and *low*. Every family of logic circuits has its own voltage standards. Most of today's PCs are built around the requirements of Transistor-Transistor Logic, which is most commonly referred to by its abbreviation TTL. In a TTL design, "high" refers to voltages above about 3.2 volts, and "low" means voltages lower than about 1.8. The middle ground is undefined logically, an electrical guard band that prevents ambiguity between the two meaningful states. Beside the signals, TTL logic circuits also require a constant supply voltage that they use to power their thinking; it provides the electrical forces which throws their switches. TTL circuits nominally operate from a 5-volt supply. The power supplies used by all full-size IBM personal computers and PS/2s are designed to produce this unvarying 5 volts in great abundance, commonly 20 or more amperes.

PCs often require other voltages as well. The motors of most disk drives (hard and floppy) typically require 12 volts to make them spin. Other specialized circuits in a PC sometimes require bipolar electrical supplies. A serial port, for example, signals logic states by varying voltages between positive and negative in relation to ground. Consequently, the –5 and –12 volts must be available inside every PC, at least if it hopes to use any possible expansion boards.

In laptop and notebook computers, most of which have no room for generic expansion boards, all of these voltages are often unnecessary. For example, many new hard disks designed for notebook computers use 5-volt motors, eliminating the need for the 12-volt supply.

In addition, the latest generation of notebook computer microprocessors and support circuits are designed to operate with a 3.3 volt supply. These lower voltage circuits cut power consumption because, all else being equal, the higher the voltage, the greater the current flow, and the larger the power usage. Dropping the circuit operating voltage from 5 to 3.3 volts cuts the consumption of computer power by about half (the power usage of a circuit is proportional to the square of the current consumed).

Voltages and Ratings

The power supplies that you're most likely to tangle with are those inside desktop PCs, and these must produce all four common voltages to satisfy the needs of all potential combinations of circuits. In practical desktop PC power supplies, each of these four voltages (+5, –5, +12, and –12) is delivered in different quantities (amperages) because of the demands associated with each. The typical PC has lots of logic circuitry, so it needs copious quantities of 5-volt power (20 to 25 amperes); it has two or three disk drives, so it needs quite a bit less 12-volt power (perhaps 4 or 5 amperes; and it has a few, almost trivial components requiring negative voltages—fractions of an ampere).

Most power supplies are rated and advertised by the sum of all the power they can make available, as measured in watts. The power rating of any power supply can be calculated by multiplying the current rating of each of the four voltages it supplies and summing the results. (Power in watts is equal to the product of voltage times current in amperes.) The power supplies in IBM computers range from 63.5 watts to 325; compatibles cover a similar range. Most modern full-size computers have power supplies of 200 to 220 watts.

Note that this power rating does not correspond to the wattage that the power supply draws from a wall outlet. All electronic circuits, and power supplies in particular, suffer from inefficiencies, linear designs more so than switching. Consequently, a power supply will require a wattage in excess of what it provides to your computer's circuits, at least when it is producing its full output. However, PC power supplies rarely operate at their rated output. As a result, efficient-switching power supplies typically draw less power than their nominal rating in normal use. For example, a PC with a 220-watt power supply with a typical dosage of memory (say 4 megabytes) and one hard disk drive will likely draw less than 100 watts while it is operating.

When selecting a power supply for your PC, the rating you require will depend on what boards and peripherals you want to fill your computer. A system board may require 15 to 25 watts; a floppy disk drive, 3 to 20 (depending on its vintage); a hard disk, 5 to 50; and a memory or multifunction expansion board, 5 to 10. If you sum the wattage requirements of the various items you need to plug into your PC, 200 watts, even 150 watts, should be more than adequate for any single-user system.

Supply Voltage

Most power supplies are designed to operate from a certain line voltage and frequency. In this country, utility power is supplied at a nominal 115 volts and 60 Hz. In other nations, the supply voltage and frequency may be different. In Europe, for instance, a 230 volt, 50 Hz standard prevails.

Most switching power supplies are willing to operate at either frequency, so that shouldn't be a worry when traveling. (Before you travel, however, check the ratings on your power supply to be sure.) Linear power supplies are more sensitive. Because their transformers have less reactance at lower frequencies, 60 Hz transformers draw more current than their designers intended when operated on 50 Hz power. Consequently, they are liable to overheat and fail, perhaps catastrophically. The switching power supplies in most PCs are also switchable. That is, they have a small switch on the rear panel which selects their operating voltage. Ensure that the switch is in the proper position for the power that is available before turning on your computer.

When traveling in a foreign land, always use this power supply switch to adjust for different voltages. Do not use inexpensive voltage converters. Often these devices are nothing more than rectifiers that clip half of the incoming waveform. Although that strategy may work for light bulbs, it can be disastrous to electronic circuitry. Using such a device can destroy your computer. It's not a recommended procedure.

IBM computers introduced since the XT Model 286 and a few compatibles have had auto-adjusting, autoranging, or universal power supplies that automatically adjust themselves to the prevailing voltage and frequency. If you have a computer with such a power supply, all you need to do is plug the computer in, and it should work properly. Note that some of these universal power supplies will accommodate any supply voltage in a wide range; others are limited to two narrow ranges, bracketing the two major voltage standards. In that you're unlikely to encounter a province with a 169.35-volt standard, these dual-range supplies are universal enough for world-wide use.

The Power-Good Signal

Beside the voltages and currents that the computer needs to operate, IBM power supplies also provide another signal called Power-Good. Its purpose is to tell the computer that all is well with the power supply and that the computer can operate normally. If the Power-Good signal is not present, the computer shuts down. The Power-Good signal prevents the computer from attempting to operate on odd-ball voltages (for instance, those caused by a brown-out) and damaging itself. A bad connection or failure of the power-good output of the power supply will also cause your PC to stop working just as effectively as a complete power supply failure.

Portable Computer Power

As with any PC, electricity is the lifeblood of laptop and notebook machines alike. But with these machines, emphasis shifts from power production to consumption. To achieve freedom from the need for plugging in, these totable PCs pack their own portable power, batteries. Although they are free from concerns about lightning strikes and utility bill shortfalls, they face a far less merciful taskmaster, gravity. The amount of power they have available is determined by their batteries, and weight constrains battery size to a reasonable value (the reasonableness of which varies inversely with the length of the airport concourse and the time spent traveling). Compared to the almost unlimited electrical supply available at your nearby wall outlet, the power that can be provided by a pound of batteries is minuscule, indeed, with total available energy measuring in the vicinity of five watt-hours.

The power supply in a laptop or notebook computer is consequently more concerned with minimizing waste rather than regulating. After all, battery power is close to ideal to begin with—smooth, unchanging DC at a low potential (voltage) that can be tailored to match computer circuitry with the proper battery selection. Regulation needs are minimal: a protection circuit to prevent too much voltage from sneaking in and destroying the computer, and a low-voltage detection circuit to warn you before the voltage output of the battery supply drops too low to reliably run the machine. Power-wasting shunt or series regulators are unnecessary because battery voltage is entirely predictable; it simply grows a bit weaker as the charge is drained away.

Rather than regulation, management is the principal power issue in a portable PC. Circuitry inside the system monitors which resources are being used and, more importantly, which are not. Anything not being used gets shut off—for example, the backlight on the display screen, the spin of the hard disk, even the microprocessor in some systems.

With but a few exceptions, all laptop and notebook computers also rely on a battery charger of some kind so that you can use rechargeable batteries for power. In essence and operation, the battery charger is little more than a repackaged power supply. Line voltage AC goes in, and low voltage DC (usually) comes out. The output voltage is close to that of the system's battery output, but always a bit higher. (A slightly higher voltage is required so that the batteries are charged to their full capacity.)

Most of the time, the battery charger/power supply is a self-contained unit external to the laptop. Although they typically contain more than just a transformer, most people call these external power supplies *transformers* or *power bricks*. The name was apt when all external battery chargers used linear designs with heavy transformers, giving the device the size and heft approaching that of an actual clay brick. Modern external power supplies use switching designs, however, and can be surprisingly compact and light.

Manufacturers favor the external power supply design because it moves unnecessary weight out of the machine itself and eliminates high voltages from anywhere inside the computer. The design also gives you something else to carry and leave behind as well as a connection that can fail at an inopportune time.

The brick typically only reduces line voltage to an acceptable level and rectifies it to DC. All the power-management functions are contained inside the PC.

No standard exists for the external battery chargers/power supplies of notebook and laptop computers. Every manufacturer, and often every model of PC from a given manufacturer, uses its own design. They differ as to output voltage, current, and polarity. You can substitute a generic replacement only if the replacement matches the voltage used by your PC and generates at least as much current. Polarity matching gives you two choices, right and wrong, and the wrong choice is apt to destroy many of the semiconductors inside the system. In other words, make certain of power polarity when plugging in a generic replacement power supply. (With most PCs, the issue of polarity reduces to a practical matter of whether the center or outer conductor of the almost-universal coaxial power plug is the positive terminal.) Also available are cigarette lighter adapters that allow you to plug many models of laptop and notebook computers into the standard cigarette lighter jack that's found in most automobiles. Again, you must match these to the exact make and model of PC you plan to use, being particularly critical of the polarity of the voltage.

Most external power supplies are designed to operate from a single voltage (a few are universal but don't count on it). That means you're restricted to plugging in and charging your portable PC to one hemisphere (or thereabouts) or the other. Moving from 117-volt to 230-volt electrical systems will require a second, expensive external charger. Experienced travelers often pack voltage converters to take care of electrical differences. Two kinds of converters are available: one that will work with laptop chargers, and one that will likely destroy the charger and the laptop computer as well.

Rectifying Power Converters

The simplest, smallest, lightest, and cheapest converters are nothing more than a diode (rectifier) that block half of the AC wave from getting through, effectively cutting the voltage in half. The result is an oddball half-wave electrical supply that's apt to wreak both havoc and disaster with critical electronic circuits, such as your PC and its power supply. Although these converters will work well with electric razors and hair dryers, never plug your PC into one.

Transformers

The other kind of converter is a simple transformer. Like all transformers, these converters are heavy (making them a joy to pack into an overnight bag). They are also relatively expensive. But they are safe for powering your PC because they deliver normal AC at their outputs. Of course, they require that you carry two power adapter bricks with your laptop computer, its power supply and the converter, that together will probably weigh more than the machine itself. In the long run, and the long concourse, you're better off buying a second battery charger/power supply for your PC.

Batteries

Think back to elementary school and you probably remember torturing half a lemon with strips of copper and zinc as another one of those world-relevant experiments, one meant to introduce you to the mysteries of electricity. Certainly, those memories will come in handy if you're stuck on a desert island with a radio, dead batteries, a case of lemons and strips of zinc and copper, but they probably seem as meaningless in connection with your PC as DOS 1.1. Think again. That juicy experiment should have served as an introduction to battery technology (and recalling the memories of it make a good introduction to this section).

Battery Technologies

The lemon demonstrated the one way that chemical energy can be put to work, directly producing electricity. The two strips of metal acted as electrodes. One gives off electrons through the chemical process of oxidation, and the other takes up electrons through chemical reduction; in other words, electrons move from one electrode, the *anode*, to another called the *cathode*. The acid in the lemon served as *electrolyte*, the medium through which the electrons were exchanged in the form of ions. Together the three elements made an electricity-generating device called a *Galvanic cell*, named after Eighteenth Century chemist Luigi Galvani. Several such cells connected comprise a battery.

Connect a wire from cathode to anode, and the electrons have a way to dash back and even up their concentration. That mad race is the flow of electricity. Add something in the middle, say a PC, and that electricity will perform work on its way back home.

All batteries work by the same principle. Two dissimilar materials (strictly speaking, they must differ in oxidation potential, commonly abbreviated as E0 value) serving as anode and cathode linked by a third material that serves as the electrolyte. The choice of materials is wide and allows for a diversity of battery technologies. It also influences the storage density (the amount of energy that can be stored in a given size or weight of battery) and nominal voltage output.

Batteries can be divided into two types, primary batteries in which the creation of electricity is irreversible. One or both of the electrodes is altered and cannot be brought back to its original state except by some complex process (like re-smelting the metal). Secondary or storage batteries are rechargeable; the chemical reaction is reversible by the application of electricity. The electrons can be coaxed back whence they came.

PC Battery Applications

The two battery types see widely different applications, even in PCs. Nearly every modern PC has a primary battery hidden somewhere inside it, letting out a tiny electrical trickle that keeps the time-of-day clock running while the PC is not. This same battery also maintains a few bytes or kilobytes of CMOS memory to store system configuration information. Storage batteries are used to power just about every laptop and notebook computer in existence. (A few systems use storage batteries for their clocks and configuration memory.)

The most common batteries in the world are primary cells based on zinc and carbon electrodes. In these zinc/carbon batteries (formally called a Leclanche dry cell but more familiar as the flashlight battery), zinc (the case of the battery) serves as the anode; a graphite rod in the center acts as cathode; and the electrolyte is complex mixture of chemicals (manganese dioxide, zinc chloride, and ammonium chloride). Alkaline batteries change the chemical mix to increase storage density and shelf life. Other materials are used for special-purpose batteries, but, with the exception of lithium, these have not found wide application in PCs.

The most common storage batteries in the world are the lead-acid batteries that are used to start automobiles. These have electrodes made from lead (anode) and lead oxide (cathode) soaked in a sulfuric acid electrolyte. Not only are these batteries heavy (they are filled with lead, after all), but they are filled with a corrosive liquid that can spill where it's not wanted, generally, anywhere. Some lead-acid batteries are sealed to avoid leakage.

Gelled-electrolyte lead-acid batteries (often called simple gel cells) reduce this problem. In these batteries, the electrolyte is converted to a colloidal form like gelatin, so it is less apt to leak out. Unlike most lead-acid batteries, however, gel cells are degraded by the application of continuous low-current charging after they have been completely charged. (Most lead-acid batteries are kept at full capacity by such "trickle" charging methods.) Consequently, gel cells require special chargers that automatically turn off after the cells have been fully charged.

In consumer electronic equipment, the most popular storage batteries are nickel-cadmium cells, a name that's often trimmed to *nicad*. These batteries use electrodes made from nickel and cadmium, as the name implies. Their most endearing characteristic is their capability to withstand in the range of 500 full charge and discharge cycles. They are also relatively lightweight, have a good energy storage density, and tolerate trickle charging. On the downside, cadmium is toxic.

Nickel-hydride batteries have all the good characteristics of nicads but lack the cadmium. Better still, they are able to store about 20 percent more power in a given cell. However, because they are relatively new on the market, they tend to be more expensive than nicads.

Clock Batteries

Nearly every PC since the AT was introduced in 1984 has had a time-of-day clock built into its system board circuitry. To keep proper track of the hours, days, and eons, this clock needs to run continuously even when the computer itself is switched off or unplugged. The source for the needed power is a small battery.

Different manufacturers have taken various approaches to supplying this power. IBM led the way by using lithium primary batteries in a plastic holder accessible at the rear of the system unit. With the first PS/2 computers, it moved the battery inside, but still relied on lithium technology. Some more recent machines use Dallas integrated clock modules (Dallas is the name of the manufacturer). These, too, have built-in lithium cells.

Lithium cells have several notable aspects. They offer a high energy density, packing a lot of power for their size. Moreover, they have a very long shelf life. Whereas conventional zinc/carbon dry cells lose potency after a year or so even when no power is being drawn from them, lithium cells keep most of their power for a decade. These qualities make lithium cells suited to providing clock power because today's solid-state clocks draw a minuscule amount of power—so small that, when battery and circuit are properly matched, battery life nearly equals shelf life.

The downside of lithium cells is that they are expensive and often difficult to find. Another shortcoming is that the metals used in them result in an output voltage of three volts per cell. A one-cell lithium battery produces too little voltage to operate standard digital circuits; a two-cell lithium battery produces too much.

Of course, engineers can always regulate away the excess voltage, and that's what's typically done. But poor regulator design will waste more power than is used, robbing the battery of its life. Some PCs suffer from this design problem and consequently give frightfully short battery life.

One advantage of the Dallas clock module is that its circuitry is matched with its built-in battery to optimize its life, which is about 10 years. The disadvantage of the module is that most are soldered to system boards, meaning that in 10 years you're guaranteed to need a visit to the repair shop to have the module replaced.

Many IBM-compatible computer makers avoid the expense and rarity of lithium batteries by adding battery holders for four (or so) type AA cells. In that zinc/carbon and alkaline cells produce 1.5 volts each, a four pack puts out the same 6 volts as a dual-cell lithium battery and can suffer the same problems in improperly designed PCs, only more so because the cells have shorter lives. A three-pack of AA cells produces 4.5 volts, which is adequate for most clock circuits and need not be hampered by regulation. Special alkaline PC battery modules are available that combine three ordinary cells into one package with the proper connector to match most system boards. The pin connectors used on system boards designed to accommodate such batteries follow a de facto standard.

Laptop and Notebook Power

Portable computers put contradictory requirements on their batteries—they must produce as much power for as long as possible, yet be as small and light as possible. Filling those needs simultaneously is impossible, so notebook and laptop computer batteries are always a compromise.

All three of the most popular storage batteries (lead-acid, nicad, and nickel-hydride) have been used in laptop computers. From your perspective as an end user, however, the technology doesn't matter as long as the result is a PC that you can carry without stretching your arms too long and can use without getting caught short too often. Odds are, however, you'll see nickel-hydride batteries increasing in popularity in laptop and notebook computers because of their greater storage density and less hazardous nature.

Rather than battery type, care is most important with computer batteries. If you take proper care of your PC's batteries, they will deliver power longer, both more time per charge and more time before replacement.

Early nicad batteries were infamous for their memory effect. That is, they remembered to what level they were discharged and after a while would only discharge to that level. The general recommendation was to fully discharge nicad batteries periodically to avoid this memory effect, perhaps as a monthly routine. Special utilities are available to perform this deep discharge (Traveling Software's Battery Watch includes one).

Deep discharge does not mean totally discharging the battery, however. Draining nearly any storage battery absolutely dry will damage it and shorten its life. If you discharge a nicad battery so that it produces less than about 1 volt (its usual output is 1.2 volts), it may suffer such damage. Laptop computers are designed to switch off before their batteries are drained too far, and deep discharge utilities don't push any farther, so you need not worry in using them. But don't try to deeply discharge your system's batteries by shorting them out; you risk damaging the battery and even starting a fire.

The makers of today's notebook and laptop computers claim that the nicad memory problem is no longer a worry. Batteries have been redesigned to avoid the problem. (Nickel-hydride batteries, being of even more recent design, should not suffer the problem either.) If you want to play it safe, however, you can still deeply discharge the batteries in your PC. But don't discharge the batteries solely to discharge them. Every battery cycle trims the life of the battery, and you'll be wasting a cycle. Only use the deep discharge utility when you've nearly discharged your system's battery and plan to recharge it again anyhow.

Most PC batteries and battery chargers are designed to allow you to leave them plugged in continuously without any detrimental effects on the battery. In fact, the best strategy is to leave your PC plugged in even after it is fully charged, detaching it from its charger only when you have to take the machine on the road. The trickle charge won't hurt it (in fact, the battery charging circuitry may switch off once the battery is charged) and you'll always be ready to roam.

Battery Safety

The maximum current that any battery can produce is limited by its internal resistance. Zinc/carbon batteries have a relatively high resistance and produce small currents, on the order of a few hundred milliamperes. Lead-acid, nickel-cadmium, and nickel-hydride batteries have very low internal resistances and can produce prodigious currents. If you short the terminals of one of these batteries, whatever produces the short (wires, a strip of metal, a coin in your pocket) will become hot because of resistive heating. For example, you can melt a wrench by placing it across the terminals of a fully charged automotive battery. Or you could start a fire with something inadvertently shorting the terminals of the spare nickel-cadmium battery for your laptop computer. Be careful and never allow anything to touch these battery terminals except the contacts of your laptop PC.

When a battery is charged, a process called *electrolysis* takes place inside. If you remember your high school science experiments, electrolysis is what you did to break ordinary water into hydrogen and oxygen using electricity. Hydrogen is an explosive gas; oxygen is an oxidizer. Both are produced when charging batteries. Normally, these gases are absorbed by the battery before they can do anything (such as explode), but too great a charging current (as results from applying too high a voltage) can cause them to build up. Trying to charge a primary battery will produce the same gas build-up. As a result, the battery can explode from too great an internal pressure or from combustion of the gases. Even if the battery does not catastrophically fail, its life will be greatly reduced. In other words, use only the charger provided with a laptop battery and never try to hurry things along.

Nearly all batteries contain harmful chemicals of some kind. Even zinc-carbon batteries contain manganese, which is regarded as hazardous. All batteries present some kind of environmental hazard, so be sure to properly dispose of them. Some manufacturers are beginning to provide a means of recycling batteries. Encourage them by taking advantage of their offers.

Desktop PC Power Supplies

Most PCs package their power supplies as a subassembly that's complete in itself and simply screws into the chassis and plugs into the system board and other devices that require its electricity. The power supply itself is ensconced in a metal box perforated with holes that let heat leak out while preventing your fingers from poking in.

In fact, the safety provided by the self-contained and fully-armored PC power supply is one of the prime advantages of the original IBM design. All the life-threatening voltages, in particularly, line voltage, are contained inside the box of the power supply. Only low, non-threatening voltages are accessible, that is, touchable, on your PC's system board and expansion boards. You can grab a board inside your PC even when the system is turned on and not worry about electrocution (although you might burn yourself on a particularly intemperate semiconductor or jab an ill-cut circuit lead through a finger).

But that's not to say grabbing a board out of a slot of an operating computer is safe for the computer's circuits. Pulling a board out is apt to bridge together some of the pin on its slot connector, if but for an instant. As a result, the board (and your PC's motherboard) may find unexpected voltages attacking, possibly destroying, its circuits. These surprises are most likely in EISA systems because of their novel expansion connectors. In other words, never plug in or remove an expansion board from a PC that has its power switched on. Although you may often be successful, the penalty for even one failure should be enough to deter your impatience.

In most PCs, the power supply serves a secondary function. The fan that cools the power supply circuits also provides the airflow that cools the rest of the system. This fan also supplies most of the noise that PCs generate while they're running. In general, the power supply fan operates as an exhaust fan; it blows outward. Air is sucked through the other openings in the power supply from the space inside your system. This gives dust in the air taken into your PC a chance to settle anywhere on your system board before getting blown out through the power supply.

Power Supply Selection

Two standards have emerged for the physical size of the PC power supply package, one that fits into the chassis of the original PC and XT, and another that fits the full-size AT chassis. AT-size power supplies are taller and wider than PC/XT models, measuring 5 7/8 inches high by 8 3/8 inches wide by 5 7/8 inches deep with a notch taken out of the inboard bottom corner to allow extra space inside the computer chassis for the system board. PC/XT-size power supplies measure about 4 3/4 x 8 3/8 x 5 1/2 inches.

Although it's obvious that the AT power supply won't fit into the smaller XT-size chassis, you may be surprised to discover that the smaller XT power supply also won't fit properly into an AT chassis. The placement of screws and other functional parts is different enough that the little box won't fit right in the big box.

Other system design variations may frustrate your power supply replacement efforts. The more effort that a PC maker uses in designing its own, identifiable system, the farther it varies from the accepted standards. Larger manufacturers, Compaq, Dell, IBM, NEC, Tandy, Zenith, and others, typically use a ground-up design philosophy that requires power supplies to be matched to a custom-designed case. That means they forego either of the two standard power supply packages for something that suits their purposes better. As a result, a power supply failure in one of these systems is a more expensive disaster than in systems from smaller manufacturers who use standard-size parts. A proprietary power supply may cost $400 or more; a standard power supply retails for $50 or less.

Beyond mere size, power supplies come in two classes: the generic and the glamorous. The generic power supplies make no claim except that they deliver the volts and amps you need. They likely originate in some part of the Far East that you can't pronounce or even imagine. These power supplies are the cheap ones with prices often below $50, and they work, at least for a while. In fact, many are likely to be the same units that nestle themselves in your favorite compatible computers.

The glamorous watt-makers promise some grand advantage over their generic siblings. More watts, less noise, more wind, whatever. The glamour demands a premium price and may earn a premium guarantee. Whether you need one depends on your sensibilities and motivations. Most PCs are adequately served by the low-end power supplies. If your PC operates without problems on a 100-degree day, you probably don't need better cooling, although a quieter fan will give anyone's ears a break. In other words, peace and quiet can overrule purely budgetary sense, but the decision is entirely personal.

Power Supply Mounting

Standard-size power supplies are also standard in their mounting. In all cases, the big chrome power supply box is held in place by four screws in the back panel of the computer. The front is secured by two fingers stamped from the computer chassis so that the power supply does not stress the rear panel of the PC.

After you remove the top of your computer's case and locate the power supply, you'll see that four of the screws in the rear panel roughly coincide with the four corners of the backside of the power supply. When you face the rear of the computer, the four screws will be on the left half of the rear panel, arranged roughly in a rectangle (see fig. 9.1). Remove these screws, and the power supply will be loose inside the chassis but not entirely free.

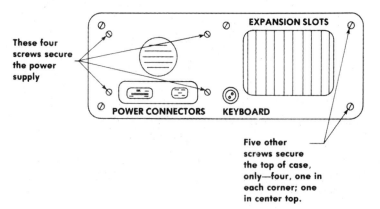

Figure 9.1. Power supply rear panel screws.

Before you attempt to lift the power supply out, remove the power supply connectors from each disk drive and the two connectors from the system board. Finally, slide the power supply box about one inch forward in the chassis till it bumps lightly against the rear of the disk drive bay or disk drives. The power supply should then lift out of the chassis without further ado.

Installing a new or replacement power supply is equally easy. The first step is to properly orient the supply so that the power switch protrudes through the notch cut in the top of the chassis. Then lower the power supply straight down into the chassis into the empty space left by the old power supply.

Before attempting to screw the new power supply into place, push it toward the front of the chassis and lightly into the drive bays. Then, while pressing it down, push it back toward the rear panel of the chassis. This front-then-back slide should slip the two steel fingers on the computer chassis through slots at the bottom of the power supply to hold it in place. You may also want to attach the power supply connectors before you screw the power supply down.

Finally, screw the power supply into place. Start all four screws but give them no more than two full turns before you have all four started. This will allow you to move the power supply slightly to line up all four holes. If you tighten one screw first, you may find that the rest of the holes in the power supply won't line up with those in the chassis. After all four screws have been started, drive them all home.

Power Connections

All IBM-standard PC, XT, and AT power supplies have two kinds of connectors dangling from them. Two of them go to the system board; the rest are designed to mate with tape and disk drives.

Mass Storage Power

The tape and disk drive connectors supply 5 and 12 volts to operate those devices. The connectors come in two sizes, which are polarized so that you cannot install them improperly. The original drive power connector was roughly rectangular in cross-section but had two of its corners chamfered so that it fit in its matching jack on the drive in only one orientation. The newer, miniaturized power connectors used by many 3.5-inch drives have a polarizing ridge that allows you to insert them only in the proper orientation. If either kind of drive connector doesn't seem to fit, don't force it! Instead, rotate it 180 degrees and try again. Likely it will slide into place. Figure 9.2 shows both styles of drive power connector and the voltages present on each of their pins.

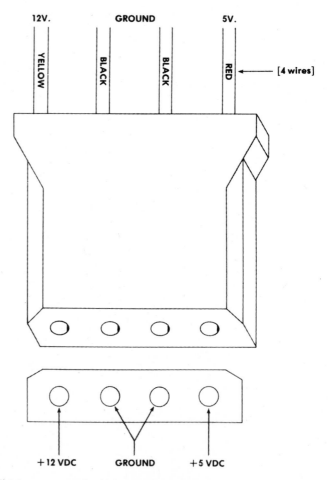

Figure 9.2. Mass storage device power connector.

PCs and some compatible computers are decisively frugal with their power connectors, supplying only two outlets. Powering more than two drives will require a Y-adapter that splits the power lines two ways. Although you can make such a cable if you have the right connectors, it's easier and often cheaper to buy one from a drive vendor ready-made. An even better idea is to replace the meager PC power supply with one that can supply more current because the factory standard supply really doesn't have the capacity for operating multiple mass storage devices other than their standard two-floppy endowment.

System Board Power

The two system board power connectors on standard power supplies are not identical. Each has its own repertoire of voltages. On most PC power supplies, these connectors are labeled P8 and P9. The lower number attaches to the mating connector on the PC system board, typically the one nearer the rear of the chassis.

Not all system boards match the two Burndy connectors standard on most power supplies. PS/2s often (but, again, not always) combine the two connectors into one. Other system board manufacturers some-times use slightly different Molex connectors. Unfortunately, Burndy and Molex connectors are not entirely compatible.

One difference between the two connector types is that the pins of a Burndy are rectangular. Molex system board connectors use smaller, square pins. Only with great effort can you mate dissimilar connectors. You'll want to check the style of pins required by your system board before you order a power supply. The only way to be sure about the style of connector is to disconnect one of them (with your PC switched off, of course) to examine the shape of its pins.

The Burndy connectors used by most power supplies are supposed to be keyed so that you cannot put one in the wrong place. Unfortu-nately, many replacement power supplies are shipped without the proper keying.

If you examine the power connectors meant to attach to the system board, you'll see that one side of the connector has one or more small tabs sticking out. If just one is longer than the rest, the connector is keyed. If all are the same length, the connector has not been keyed. You can key it by cutting off all but the one right tab using a pair of diagonal cutters. Figure 9.3 shows the proper keying of these connectors.

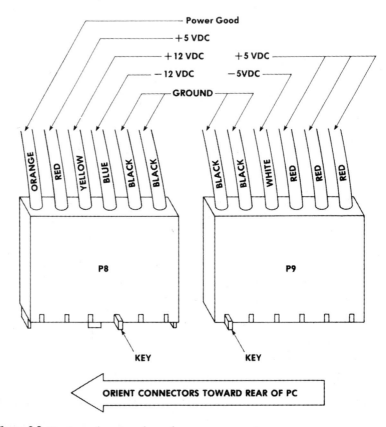

Figure 9.3. Keying of system board power connectors.

Another way of being sure that the system board connectors are in their proper positions is by the color codes of the wires. Proper installation puts black wires in the middle—that is, the black wires on the connectors adjoin one another.

Power Protection

Normal line voltage is often far from the 115-volt alternating current you pay for. It can be a rather inhospitable mixture of aberrations with spikes and surges mixed with noise, dips, and interruptions. None of these oddities is desirable, and some can be powerful enough to cause errors to your data or damage to your computer. Although you cannot avoid them, you can protect your PC against their ill effects.

Power Line Irregularities

Power line problems can be broadly classed into basic categories: overvoltage, undervoltage, and noise. Each of the problems has its own distinct causes and requires a particular kind of protection.

Overvoltage

The deadliest power line pollution is overvoltage, lightning-like high potential spikes that sneak into your PC and actually melt down its silicon circuitry. Often the damage is invisible, except for the very visible lack of image on your monitor. Other times, you can actually see charred remains inside your computer as a result of the over-voltage.

As its name implies, an overvoltage is gushing more voltage into your PC than the equipment is designed to handle. In general, and in the long run, your utility supplies power that's very close to the ideal, usually within about 10 percent of its rated value. If it always stayed within that range, the internal voltage regulation circuitry of your PC could take its fluctuations in stride.

Short duration overvoltages larger than that may occur too quickly for your utility's equipment to compensate, however. Moreover, many overvoltages are generated nearby, possibly within your home or office, and your utility has no control over them. Brief peaks as high as 25,000 volts have been measured on normal lines, usually due to nearby lightning strikes. Lightning doesn't have to hit a power line to induce a voltage spike that can damage your PC. When it does hit a wire, however, everything connected to that circuit is likely to take on the characteristics of a flash bulb.

Overvoltages are usually divided into two classes by duration. Short-lived overvoltages are called *spikes* or *transients* and last from a nano-second (billionth of a second) to a microsecond (one millionth of a second). Longer duration overvoltages usually are termed *surges* and can stretch into milliseconds.

Sometimes power companies do make errors and send too much voltage down the line, causing your lights to glow brighter and your PC to teeter closer to disaster. The occurrences are simply termed overvoltages.

Undervoltage

An undervoltage occurs when your equipment gets less voltage than its expects. An undervoltage can range from sags, which are dips of but a few volts, to complete outages or blackouts. Durations can vary from nearly instantaneous to hours (or days, if you haven't paid your light bill recently).

Very short dips, sags, and even blackouts are not a problem. As long as they are less than a few dozen milliseconds (about the blink of an eye), your computer should purr along as if nothing happened. The only exceptions are a few old computers that have power supplies with very sensitive Power-Good signals. A short blackout may switch off the Power-Good signal, shutting down your computer even though enough electricity is available.

Most PCs are designed to withstand prolonged voltage dips of about 20 percent without shutting down. Deeper dips or blackouts lasting for more than those few milliseconds will result in shut down. Your PC will be forced to cold start, booting up afresh. Any work you did not save before the undervoltage is lost.

Noise

Noise is a nagging problem in the power supplies of most electronic devices. It comprises all the spurious signals that wires pick up as they run through electromagnetic fields. In many cases, these signals can sneak through the filtering circuitry of the power supply and interfere with the signals inside the electrical device.

For instance, the power cord of a tape recorder might act like an antenna and pick up a strong radio signal. The broadcast could then sneak through the circuitry of the recorder and mix with the music that it's supposed to be playing. As a result, you might hear a CB radio maven croaking over your Mozart.

In computers, these spurious signals could confuse the digital thought coursing through the circuitry of the machine. As a practical matter, they don't. All better computers are designed to minimize the leakage of their signals from inside their case into the outside world to minimize interference from your computer affecting your radio and television. The same protection against signals getting out works extremely well against other signals getting in. Personal computers are thus well-protected against line noise. You probably won't need a noise filter to protect your computer.

Then again, noise filtering doesn't hurt. Most power-protection devices have noise filtering built into them because it's cheap, and it can be an extra selling point (particularly to people who believe they need it). Think of it as a bonus. You can take advantage of its added protection, but don't go out of your way to get it.

Overvoltage Protection

Spike and surge protectors are designed to prevent most short-duration, high-intensity overvoltages from reaching your PC. They absorb excess voltages before they can travel down the power line and into your computer's power supply.

Perhaps the most common overvoltage protection devices is the *varistor*, more formally known as the *metal oxide varistor* or *MOV*. Varistors work by conducting electricity only when the voltage across their leads exceeds a certain level. They can short out the excess voltage in spikes and surges before it can pop into your PC. The voltage at which the varistor starts clipping spikes is termed its *clamping voltage*.

The excess energy doesn't disappear but turns into heat, possibly destroying the varistor. It may give its life to protect your computer. Even bursts that don't completely destroy the varistor damage it slightly, and the damage is cumulative. In other words, the life of a varistor is finite, and it is shorted with every surge it shorts out. Eventually the varistor will fail, sometimes in its own lightning-like burst. Although it is unlikely this failure will electrically damage the circuits of your computer, it can cause a fire, which can damage not just your PC but your home, office, or self. Some manufacturers (for example, IBM) forego putting varistors in their power supplies to preclude the potential for fire, which they see as less desirable than a PC failure. A varistor can also fail more subtly; it will just stop sucking up surges. Unbeknownst to you, your PC can be left unprotected.

In any case, a good strategy is to replace varistors periodically to ensure that they are doing their job and to lessen the likelihood of their failure. How often to replace them depends on how dirty an electrical diet you feed them. Every few years is generally a sufficient replacement interval. Other devices are occasionally used to eliminate overvoltages. These include semi-conductors, ionized spark-gaps, and ferro-resonant transformers. Most of these devices function much like varistors but use different operating principles.

The most important characteristics of overvoltage protection devices are how fast they work and how much energy they can dissipate. Generally, a faster response time or clamping speed is better. Response times can be as short as picoseconds, trillionths of a second. The larger the energy-handling capacity of a protection device, the better. Energy-handling capacities are measured in watt-seconds or joules. Devices claiming the capability to handle millions of watts are not unusual.

Undervoltage Protection

Three devices help your computer deal with undervoltages. Voltage regulators keep varying voltages within the range that will run your PC but offer no protection against steep sags or blackouts. The standby power system and uninterruptible power system (or UPS) fight against blackouts.

Voltage regulators are the same devices that your utility uses to try to keep the voltage it supplies at a constant level. These giant regulators consist of large transformers with a number of taps or windings, which are outputs set at different voltage levels. Motors connected to the regulators move switches that select the taps that will supply the voltage most nearly approximating normal line voltage. These mechanical regulators are gargantuan devices. Even the smallest of them is probably big enough to handle an entire office. In addition, they are inherently slow on the electrical time scale, and they may allow voltage dips long enough for data to be lost.

Solid-state voltage regulators use semiconductors to compensate for line-voltage variations. They work much like the power supply inside your computer but can compensate over a wider range.

The saturable reactor regulator applies a DC control current to an extra control coil on the transformer, enough to "saturate" the transformer core. Once saturation is achieved, no additional power can pass through the transformer. Regulating the DC control current adjusts the output of the transformer. These devices are inherently inefficient because they must throw away power throughout their entire regulating range.

Ferro-resonant transformer regulators are "tuned" into saturation much in the same way as a radio is tuned, using a capacitor in conjunction with an extra winding. This tuning makes the transformer naturally resist any change in the voltage or frequency of its output. In effect, it becomes a big box of electrical inertia that not only regulates but also suppresses voltage spikes and reduces line noise.

The measure of quality of a voltage regulator is its regulation, which specifies how close to the desired voltage the regulator maintains its output. Regulation is usually expressed as the output variation for a given change of input. The input range of a regulator indicates how wide a variation in voltage variation that it can compensate for. This range should exceed whatever variations in voltage you expect to occur at your electrical outlets.

Blackout Protection

Both standby and uninterruptible power systems provide blackout protection in the same manner. They are built around powerful batteries that store substantial current. An inverter converts the direct current from the batteries into alternating current that can be used by your computer. A battery charger built into the system keeps the reserve power supply fully charged at all times.

Because they are so similar, the term *UPS* is often improperly used to describe both standby and uninterruptible power systems. They differ in one fundamental characteristic: the electricity provided by a standby power systems is briefly interrupted in the period during which the device switches from utility power to its own internal reserves. An uninterruptible power system, as its name indicates, avoids any interruption to the electricity supplied to the device it protects. If your PC is sensitive to very short interruptions in its supply of electricity, this difference is critical.

Standby Power Systems

As the name implies, the standby power system constantly stands by, waiting for the power to fail so that it can leap into action. Under normal conditions (that is, when utility power is available), its battery charger draws only a slight current to keep its source of emergency energy topped off. The AC power line that the standby supply feeds from is directly connected to its output, and thence to the computer. The batteries are out of the loop.

When the power fails, the standby supply switches into action, "switch" being the key word. The current-carrying wires inside the standby power supply that lead to the computer are physically switched from the utility line to the current coming from the battery-powered inverter.

The switching process requires a small but measurable amount of time. First, the failure of the electrical supply must be sensed. Even the fastest electronic voltage sensors take a finite time to detect a power failure. Even after a power failure is detected, there is another slight pause before the computer receives its fresh supply of electricity while the switching action itself takes place. Most standby power systems switch quickly enough that your computer never notices the lapse. A few particularly unfavorable combinations of standby power system and computer, however, may result in the computer shutting down during the switch.

Most standby power systems available today switch within one-half of one cycle of the AC current they are supplied; that's less than 10 milliseconds, quick enough to keep nearly all PCs running as though no interruption had occurred. Although the standby power system design does not protect against spikes and surges, most SPSs have other protection devices installed in their circuitry to ensure that your PC gets clean power.

Uninterruptible Power Systems

Traditionally, an uninterruptible power system supplied uninterrupted power because its output did not need to switch its output from line power to battery. Rather, its battery was constantly and continuously connected to the output of the system through its inverter. This kind of UPS was always supplying power from the batteries to your computer. Your computer was thus completely isolated from the vagaries of the AC electrical line. New UPS designs are more like standby systems but use clever engineering to bridge over even the briefest switching lulls. They, too, deliver a truly uninterrupted stream of power but can be manufactured for a fraction of the cost of the traditional design.

In an older UPS, the batteries are kept from discharging from the constant current drain of powering your computer by a large built-in charger. When the power fails, the charger stops charging, but the battery, without making the switch, keeps the electricity flowing to the connected computer. In effect, this kind of UPS is the computer's own generating station, only inches away from the machine it serves, keeping it safe from the polluting effects of lightning and load transients. Dips and surges can never reach the computer. Instead, it gets a genuinely smooth, constant electrical supply exactly like the one it was designed for.

Newer UPSs connect both the input power and the output of their inverters through a special transformer, which is then connected to your PC or other equipment to be protected. Although utility power is available, this kind of UPS supplies power through the transformer to your PC. When the utility power fails, the inverter kicks in, typically within half a cycle. The inductance of the transformer, however, acts as a storage system and supplies the missing half cycle of electricity during the switchover period.

The traditional style of UPS provided an extreme measure of surge and spike protection (as well as eliminating sags). Because no direct connection bridges the power line and the protected equipment, spikes and their kin had no pathway to sneak in. Although the transformer in the new style of UPS will absorb power-line irregularities, overall, it does not afford the same degree of protection. Consequently, these devices usually have other protection devices (like MOVs) built in.

Backup Power System Specifications

The most important specification to investigate before purchasing any backup power device is its capacity as measured in volt-amperes (VA) or watts. This number should always be greater than the rating of the equipment to which the backup device is to be connected.

In alternating current (AC) systems, watts don't necessarily equal the product of volts and amperes (as it should by the definition that applies in DC systems) because the voltage and current can be out of phase with one another. That is, when the voltage is at a maximum, the current in the circuit can be at an intermediary value. So the peak values of voltage and amperage may occur at different times.

Power requires both voltage and current simultaneously. Consequently, the product of voltage and current (amperage) in an AC circuit is often higher than the actual power in the circuit. The ratio between these two values is called the *power factor of the system*.

What all of this means to you is that volt-amperes and watts are not the same thing. Most backup power systems will be rated in VA because it is a higher figure thanks to the power factor. You must ensure that the total VA used by your computer equipment is less than the VA available from the backup power system. Alternately, you must ensure that the wattage used by your equipment is less than the wattage available from the backup power system. Don't indiscriminately mix the VA and watts in making comparisons.

To convert a VA rating to a watt rating, multiply the VA by the power factor of the backup power supply. To go the other way (watts to VA), divide the wattage rating of the backup power system by its power factor. (You can do the same thing with the equipment you want to plug into the power supply, but you may have a difficult time discovering the power factor of each piece of equipment. For PCs, a safe value to assume is 2/3.)

Standby and uninterruptible power systems are also rated as to how long they can supply battery power. This equates to the total energy (the product of power and time) that they store. Such time ratings vary with the VA the backup device must supply. Because of finite battery reserves, it can supply greater currents only for shorter periods. Most manufacturers rate their backup systems for given minutes of operation with a load of a particular size, rather than in more scientific fashion using units of energy. For example, a backup system may be rated to run a 250 volt-ampere load for 20 minutes.

If you want an idea of the maximum possible time a given backup supply can carry your system, check the ratings of the batteries it uses. Most batteries are rated in ampere-hours, which describes how much current they can deliver for how long. You can convert that rating to a genuine energy rating by multiplying it by the battery voltage. For example, a 12-volt, 6 amp-hour battery could, in theory, produce 72 watt-hours of electricity. That figure is theoretical rather than realistic because the circuitry that converts the battery from DC to AC wastes some of the power and because ratings apply to only new batteries. However, the numbers you derive will give you a limit. If you have only 72 watt-hours of battery, you can't expect the system to run your 250 VA PC for an hour. At most, you could expect 17 minutes. Realistically you might expect 12 to 15.

You probably won't need a lot of time from a backup power system, however. In most cases, five minutes or less of backup time should be sufficient because the point of a backup supply is not to keep a system running forever. Instead, the backup power system is designed to give you a chance to shut down your computer without losing your work. Shutting down shouldn't take more than a minute or two.

Different backup power systems also vary as to their output waveform. The perfect waveform is one that matches that from utility power, the sine wave. Sine waves are also the most difficult to generate, so most backup power systems actually generate square waves or modified square waves that approximate sine waves by adding square steps. Figure 9.4 shows the shapes of these different waveforms.

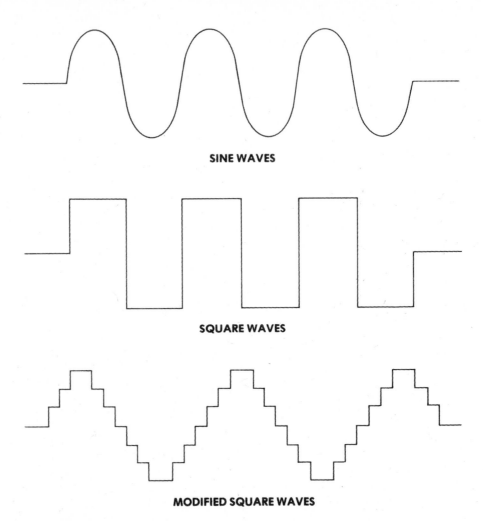

SINE WAVES

SQUARE WAVES

MODIFIED SQUARE WAVES

Figure 9.4. Power supply wave forms.

The least desirable is the ordinary square wave, which may cause the overheating of your PC's power supply. Because they power your computer from batteries only for a short time, the output waveform from standby power systems is less critical than that from a true uninterruptible power system.

Power Equipment Certification

When you switch on your desktop PC, you probably don't expect that the electricity inside will jolt out and send you corkscrewing, dropping you to the floor, your heart in fibrillation, your soul in limbo, and your coworkers gathered around in wonder about who will get your windowed office that they've all lusted after for years. Nor do you think of your workstation as a potential flame-thrower, a time-release modern Molotov cocktail that gives nightmares to fire marshals and Smokey the Bear. You have faith in the safety of your PC and the rest of your array of office equipment. But nothing about modern electronics makes equipment built from them inherently safe. Quite the contrary, all electrical devices have some shock potential. Voltages inside your PC's power supply are quite sufficient to electrocute you or to set your office aflame.

Worse, your shields against such prospective disasters may not be as impregnable as you think. For example, insurance kicks in only after the fact, little solace when you've been thrown onto your back, legs twitching. Government regulatory agencies react with enforced recalls and product bans even more slowly, only after a string of catastrophes hint that something not-so-subtle infects a certain product line. And anyone with memories of color televisions igniting apartments faster than you could say "instant on" knows that sometimes even companies with excellent reputations accidentally release potentially dangerous products.

Several testing and certification organizations do offer you the assurance that the equipment your trust your livelihood and life to is safe. Among these are the Canada Standards Association, Underwriters Laboratories Inc., and Verband Deutscher Elektrotechniker. The most familiar is Underwriters Laboratories (UL) because the organization has been active in the United States for about a century. The CSA is the Canadian equivalent; the VDE, German.

The trademarked stylized "UL" inside a circle means that independent safety engineers at Underwriters Laboratories have examined the design and a sample unit of the product and found it to meet their stringent safety standards. In addition, to assure you that the initial safety of your PC wasn't shortchanged later in production, other UL engineers occasionally spot check the manufacturer and random products off the assembly line.

Underwriters Laboratories

Underwriters Laboratories is not a government agency. Nor is it the child of some Sixties-vintage publicity-minded consumer-safety promoter. Rather, Underwriters Laboratories is an independent, non-profit organization that functions both as a safety engineering consultant and certification organization. It's a commercial business, one that earns its livelihood from manufacturers who pay for its services in detecting what's wrong with their products before they are put on the market.

Instead of governmental authority, the power of the UL arises from its standards and reputation—a particularly long reputation. The organization dates from almost as far back as commercial electrical power, well before the age of government regulations, consumer organizations, or even Upton Sinclair's exposés.

Founded in 1894 by William Henry Merrill, the UL was first known as the Underwriters' Electrical Bureau and primarily concerned itself with safety testing of the products of the fledgling electrical industry. At the time, the entire organization comprised three people, Merrill, Edward Teall, and W. S. Boyd, and was appropriately housed above a fire station in Chicago. Since then, the company has expanded both in employment (the roster now totals thousands), offices (four, one each in Northbrook, Illinois; Melville, New York; Research Triangle Park, North Carolina; and Santa Clara, California) and into other areas. It now sets standards and tests nearly any product about which there may be safety concerns, from PCs to space heaters and, appropriately, fire extinguishers. The organization was formally incorporated as Underwriters Laboratory Inc., in 1901.

Although they are theproduct of a private business, Underwriters Laboratories' standards can have legal significance. The standards developed by the UL can and have been incorporated into statutes and ordinances.

A particularly relevant example pertains in part to PCs. The National Electrical Code, which has been incorporated into the laws of numerous municipalities, specifies that as of July 1, 1991, any equipment intended to be electrically connected to a telecommunications network must be listed for that purpose. (National Electrical Code, Article 800-51, subparagraph i.) In communities enforcing the national code, your PC must be listed if you have a modem in it that you intend on connecting to a telephone line. A UL label on your PC would constitute the required listing.

Because Underwriters Laboratories is not an arm of the government, it cannot arbitrarily force a company to follow its standards. It relies instead on cooperation and contract. In order to use the UL logo, a company must enter into a contract with Underwriters Laboratories. In effect, it licenses the use of the trademarked symbol.

But Underwriters Laboratories does not just grant a license for the payment of a fee. To earn the right to use the logo, a company must agree to follow the appropriate UL standards. More importantly, the company must submit a sample of the equipment to Underwriters Laboratories so that it can be tested and certified to conform with the standard. The contract also imposes a continuing duty on the manufacturer to conform with the appropriate standard and gives the UL the right to check compliance. The UL can award its symbol to the products it chooses or withhold it and can enforce its conditions on the use of its symbol under federal law. The UL symbol can appear on any or all products in their class. The symbol indicates compliance with safety rather than performance standards, and it implies no relative measure of quality.

Computer Safety Standards

Computers, even electrical devices in general, are not the only or even primary concern of Underwriters Laboratories. The organization develops standards for and tests everything from building materials to fire alarm systems. Today, PCs must conform primarily with but one of hundreds of Underwriters Laboratory standards, designated as UL 1950.

The UL 1950 standard applies to all information technology equipment. First published on March 15, 1989, it becomes effective March 15, 1992, meaning equipment must meet the standard to be sold wearing the UL logo after that date. Computer equipment now being made is tested for conformance with the UL 1950 specifications.

In the 10 or 15 years before 1989, other standards have applied to data processing equipment: UL 478 for information-processing and business equipment and UL 114 for offices appliances and business equipment. UL 1950 replaces both.

The new standard was not arbitrarily created but represents an attempt to unite various standards in use around the world by the unaffiliated CSA, VDE, and others. Manufacturers can follow the guidance of one standard instead of several, perhaps conflicting, standards for equipment to be used in Europe, Canada, and the United States.

UL 1950 covers everything from ordinary desktop PCs and their peripherals (disk drives to printers) to mainframe computers to simple desktop calculators, even typewriters. Special standards with different requirements cover industrial computer devices that may have to work in severe environments, such as those with explosive fumes.

The inch-thick document covers nearly all aspects of equipment design and construction and outlines the testing procedure that Underwriters Laboratories applies. These range from insulation and wiring to mechanical strength and resistance to fire. Even relevant markings and identifications on the product are covered. If you're interested, the complete, copyrighted publication can be ordered directly from Underwriters Laboratories.

UL Recognition versus UL Listing

In granting its approval to electrical devices, Underwriters Laboratories uses three strictly defined terms: *listing*, *recognition*, and *classification*. Not interchangeable, the standards for each are different and even apply to different kinds of devices.

Recognition is an approval granted to electrical components, products that are not complete in themselves but are used in making a complete product. Light switches and computer power supplies are typical of equipment that earns UL recognition. Devices that are UL recognized are entitled to wear a special symbol, a slanted combination of the letter U and a backward R (for recognition).

Listing applies to complete products that you can buy—an entire appliance, monitor, or computer system unit. Listed products are allowed to wear the familiar UL trademark, the circle with the letters "UL" in it.

A UL listed product is often made from UL recognized components, but it doesn't have to be. Nor does the use of UL recognized components automatically confer a UL listing on the finished product. Rather, using UL recognized components helps the manufacturer more easily achieve a listing.

A UL listing means that a product is safe for use in the form in which it is delivered to you. A UL recognized product is safe when installed and used properly. The listing lifts the responsibility from you.

Although a UL recognized component might be safe in itself, there's always a possibility that it could be installed in a product in such a way to make it dangerous. For example, a heat-generating power supply could be shoehorned into a tight case that lacks adequate ventilation, leading to overheating and fire potential. Although the power supply was UL recognized, such a dangerous complete assembly could not be UL listed.

Any company that tells you that its PC is UL recognized is mistaken. It cannot be. The UL does not give recognition to complete computer systems. Manufacturers may rightly claim that a computer doesn't need to be listed because it is built from UL recognized components because a listing is voluntary and a computer legally need not be UL listed at all. The statement, while technically accurate, is misleading.

The operative words in such a statement are that the computer is not UL listed, so it gives you no assurance that the completed system complies with UL design and manufacturing standards. In other words, if you asked a PC maker whether its product is UL listed, and the response is that the system is made from UL recognized components, the answer is probably an evasion of the word "no."

UL *classification* generally applies only to commercial or industrial products that the UL tests for conformance with specific published standards or regulatory codes or have been evaluated with respect to certain hazards or to perform under specific conditions. A UL-classified device bears no specific symbol but instead may be marked with the UL's name and a statement indicating the extend of the classification of the product.

The Approval Process

Getting a product UL listed, recognized, or classified is a multi-step process. It all begins when the manufacturer voluntarily contacts Underwriters Laboratories. This first step can be a simple letter or phone call. The manufacturer then follows up by submitting a formal request for testing along with a product description, photos, instructions, brochures, and whatever else might be helpful in showing the UL exactly what the equipment is.

From the information provided, Underwriters Laboratories then determines what standards the product must meet and what tests will be necessary for assuring compliance with them. It then notifies the manufacturer of the testing requirements, including the number of samples required and the cost.

If the manufacturer agrees, it sends an application form, a deposit, and the requested samples to the UL, and the UL examines and tests the product.

Should the product pass scrutiny, Underwriters Laboratories issues a final report and sends the manufacturer notice of the listing of its product. Arrangements are made for follow-up procedures, including spot-checking of production. The manufacturer is then authorized to use the UL mark on its product and in brochures and advertisements for the product.

If the product fails UL testing, it notifies the manufacturer of the results and suggests changes necessary for passing the tests. The manufacturer can then make design corrections and resubmit the product.

Underwriters Laboratories approaches each product to be tested in a methodical way. In general, the testing procedure begins at the outside and works its way in.

The starting point for a PC is the power cord. UL engineers make sure that the power cord itself is suitable to the application, that it can carry enough current without overheating and that it is tough enough to withstand being trod upon.

From there, the UL safety engineers turn their attention to the case itself. Plastic cases are especially rigorously checked. They must be strong enough to withstand normal abuse, such as impacts and hot environments. After all, if the case breaks, you could injure yourself on the pieces or by accidentally touching the circuitry inside.

Flammability is another concern. Plastic cases must not contribute to the propagation of fires. Nor should it give off toxic fumes. These tests involve the classic trial-by-fire, in effect setting a torch to the PC being evaluated.

Even the ventilation holes in the case are checked. Here the engineer has several concerns. Ventilation slots must be large enough to allow air flow sufficient that the device doesn't become overheated. But the holes must also be yet small enough so that a user (or the child of a user) cannot poke a finger through and get a shock. They must also be located in such a way that something cannot fall inside and create a short circuit or fire.

Inside the case, the primary (utility) power is the principal concern. The UL engineers check the voltages present not only with everything operating normally, but also under fault conditions. Isolation between power and logic circuits is verified to make certain, for example, that when you grab the connector to unplug your printer, you're not surprised with a shockingly high voltage.

Equipment is also tested under operation to determine how hot is becomes under worst-case conditions. In the case of a PC, all of its expansion slots and drive bays would be filled so that the maximum load is put on the power supply and cooling systems. The PC (or other device) is then run until its temperature stabilizes, and the internal temperatures are measured. The primary concern is that excess heat won't cause degradation of components that could lead to fire or shock.

The amount of current the equipment actually draws is measured so that you know for sure what your electrical outlets will be called upon to supply. The UL also performs a leakage current test, so that you can be sure that when you lean against the case of a PC with your feet in a puddle, there's not enough current to give you a shock. In addition, a dielectric voltage test is performed to ensure that the insulation on the equipment is sufficient to protect you from electrical dangers.

The UL engineers even verify the printed ratings of the device, both those on the back of the equipment and those in the instruction manual, to be sure that they properly reflect the type of power the device may be plugged into and the amount of current it draws. They ensure that the information provided is adequate, at least about the electrical nature of the device, for you to properly use the equipment.

The UL doesn't stop with testing the single unit that the manufacturer first submits for evaluation. After all, a nefarious manufacturer might be tempted to build a super-rugged prototype, send it in for evaluation, then build the units it sells from the cheapest, flimsiest parts available. Consequently, to keep the UL mark on their equipment, manufacturers must agree to make follow-up tests on all of its products that come down the assembly line.

The follow-up tests the manufacturer must make on each unit it makes include a production-line dielectric voltage test and an earthing continuity test. For the former, a voltage is applied between the two electrical contacts of the unit's plug (the flat blades) and the ground connection (the round pin). Passing this test ensures that nothing in the manufacturing process damages any wiring in the unit that could cause a short circuit leading to shock potential from touching the units case. The earthing continuity test ensures that the ground pin on the power cord is actually connected to all user-accessible parts of the case. It assures that the case of every unit made is properly grounded.

Under terms of the contract with Underwriters Laboratories, the manufacturer opens its production facilities to random UL spot checks four times a year. Without notice, a UL engineer may knock on the door and ask to see the equipment being made and test units off the assembly line.

System Separator

A UL listing often sets apart the computers made by major manufacturers, the so-called first and second tiers of the industry, from the low-margin, low-cost makers that recently moved from garages into industrial parks. Computers from larger manufacturers, such as Compaq and IBM, all wear UL listings. Many mail-order systems do not.

One reason for this separation is that old-line manufacturers know that the major businesses that are their principal customers often require the assurance of UL listing on the products they buy. Another reason is that many smaller companies may not know what UL approval is all about or how to achieve it. And, perhaps the most compelling reason you don't see the UL label on bottom-of-the-barrel PCs, getting a UL listing can be expensive.

The computer maker must bear the entire cost of the UL approval process. Essentially, that means contracting with Underwriters Laboratories for the supply of safety engineering expertise.

Underwriters Laboratories charges for the time of its engineers who disassemble the computer to see how it is made and how its construction affects its safety. The manufacturer also must pay for the costs of testing the computer system. In addition to the time of the engineer, part of the cost of running the entire Underwriters Laboratories worldwide operation must be factored into the cost of achieving a listing, as well as the cost for follow-up inspections.

The exact charge by the UL for sending a product through the listing process varies with what the product is and, like any contract, it is subject to negotiation. According to UL publications, identical charge schedules apply to all investigations. Some products, however, may require more UL involvement and consulting work. One peripheral manufacturer reported that its average cost of submitting a product for UL evaluation ran between $3,000 and $5,000.

But that's just the starting point. Those charges assume a perfect product that's completely safe from an engineering standpoint. Underwriters Laboratories, after inspecting and testing the product, may make suggestions about improving the product's safety, suggestions the manufacturer must adhere to in order to gain a listing. Every one of those improvements will add to the development cost of the product.

Moreover, the manufacturer must submit the equipment to Underwriters Laboratories to be evaluated by testing that, at times, can verge on the destructive. For example, hand-held devices must undergo drop tests from one meter high onto a hardwood floor. After the test, the product must remain safe, but it need not remain operable. Other tests involve simulating faults, heating, and even applying flames to the equipment. Even if the evaluation sample comes back in a single piece after testing, it still may not be salable.

According to one company that manufacturers UL-listed peripherals, it writes off the cost of the evaluation sample as part of the UL approval process. For a small company making 586-based PCs, that's hardly a trivial expense.

All told, the cost of achieving a UL listing for a complete computer system starts at about $10,000 and could spiral upward if the original design were particularly inept from the standpoint of safety, according to companies contacted by *PC Magazine*. Some small-system vendors may have invested far less than that much capital in the entire design of their products. It may represent the complete profits from months of production in today's highly competitive low end of the PC market.

For many manufacturers, the cost of a UL listing is not a consideration. It's as much a necessity as a microprocessor in a PC. The UL labels broadens the market for the product. Although it doesn't insure against product liability lawsuits, a UL listing is evidence that the product design did meet recognized safety standards.

Whether to buy a product lacking a UL listing is a personal decision. Certainly, equipment lacking a UL listing can be just as safe as listed devices. But the UL logo gives you the assurance that the product wearing it has been independently tested for safety. It's one of the few forms of peace of mind you can buy.

10

Cases

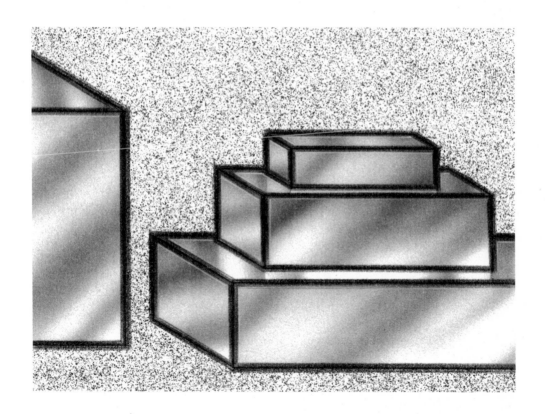

What holds your whole PC together is its case, but a case is more than a mere box. The case provides secure mountings for circuit boards and mass storage devices. It protects delicate circuitry from all the evils of the outside world, both mechanical and electrical, and it protects the world and you from what's inside the PC, both interference and dangerous voltages. Cases come in various sizes, shapes, and degrees of effectiveness to match your PC and the way you plan to use it.

The case is the physical embodiment of your PC. In fact, the case is the body of your PC. It's a housing, vessel, and shield that provides the delicate electronics of the computer a secure environment in which to work. The case protects against physical dangers, forces that might act against its circuit boards, bending, stressing, even breaking them with deleterious results to their operation. It also prevents electrical short circuits that might be caused by foreign objects that typically inhabit the office—paper clips, staples, letter openers, beer cans, and bridge-work. The case also guards against invisible dangers, principally strong electrical fields that could induce noise that would interfere with the data handling of your system, potentially inducing errors that would crash your system.

The protective shield of the case works both ways. It also keeps what's inside your PC inside your PC. Among the wonders of the workings of a computer, two in particular pose problems for the outside world. The electrical voltages inside the PC can be a shocking discovery if you accidentally encounter them. And the high-frequency electrical signals that course through the computer's circuits can radiate like radio broadcasts and interfere with the reception of other transmissions, which includes everything from television to aircraft navigational beacons.

Your PC's case also has a more mundane role. It gives you a place to put the things that you want to connect to your computer. Drive bays allow you to put mass storage devices within ready reach of your PC's logic circuits while affording the case's protection to your peripherals. In addition, your PC's case gives your expansion boards a secure mounting and gives them the same mechanical and electrical shelter as the rest of the system.

The case also can serve as the world's most expensive monitor stand, raising your screen to an appropriate viewing height, elevated above the clutter and confusion of your desktop.

Compounding the function of your computer's case is the need to be selective. Some of what's inside your PC has got to get out—heat, for instance. And some of what's outside needs to get in, such as signals from the keyboard and power from your electrical outlets. In addition, the computer case must form a solid foundation upon which your system can be built. It must give disk drives a firm base and hold electrical assemblies out of harm's way. Overall, the simple case may not be as simple as you think.

Mechanical Matters

The obvious function of the case is mechanical; you can see it and touch it as a distinct thing. And it steals part of your desktop, floor, or lap when you put it to work. It has a definite size, always too small when you want to add one more thing, but too large when you need to find a place to put it (and particularly when that place happens to be inside your carry-on luggage). The case also has a shape, which may be functional to allow you best access to all those computer accouterments, like the slot into which you shove your backup tapes. Shape and color also are part of your PC's style, which can set one system apart from the boring sameness of its computer kin.

In computers, form dictates function as much (if not more) than it does for any other type of office equipment. Computers have the shape they have so that they can hold what you want to put inside them, primarily all those expansion options that give your machine power and capability. The case has to be large enough to accommodate the expansion boards you want to plug in as well as provide adequate space for all the floppy and hard disks, optical disk drives, and tape drives your PC would not be complete without.

The sizes of both boards and drives are pre-ordained, set once long ago and forever invariant. The case must be designed around the needs of each. But creating a case is more than a matter of allocating box-like space for options. The case also has to provide a place for such mandatory system components as power supplies and loudspeakers. In addition, everything must be arranged to allow air to freely flow around everything to bring your PC's circuitry and peripherals a breath of cooling fresh air.

Not all computer manufacturers give that much thought to the cases into which they pack their products, however. Many (if not most) simply select a case from some other manufacturer that specializes in molding plastic and bending steel. Thanks to a mixture of the fore-thought of the case-maker and dumb luck, these amalgamations work out and everyone is happy—the case-maker who made the original sale, the computer-maker who gets a cheap box to slide his electrical works into, and you who get a deal on the system that you buy.

Nevertheless, you still have options when you select a PC or buy a case into which to put your own computer creation. To make the right decision and to be sure that your computer as a whole will suit your needs and continue to do so for a long life, you need to know your options and all of their ramifications.

PC/XT Cases

The place to begin a discussion of cases is with the first, the metal package that surrounded the original IBM PC and its younger cousin, the XT. These cases set the pattern for all machines to come, nearly all personal computers use some variation of the PC/XT layout. Although superficially identical, PC and XT cases are different, reflecting their difference in expansion slot spacing and number (1-inch spacing of five slots for the PC; 0.8-inch spacing and eight slots for the XT).

The fundamental design of these original cases was dictated by func-tion and fit. There was space at the front for two disk drives of the then-current miniature format (full-height 5.25-inch drives), a power supply tucked behind the drives, and a system board lining the rest of the case to the left. Its size was determined by the amount of circuitry required to build a computer. The height of the case was set by the needs of the full-height drives and the expansion board format.

The result is functional if not inspired. The computer's footprint (the amount of desk space required) measured 21 inches wide by 17 inches deep. Its height, to allow for expansion boards and 3/8-inch feet underneath, measured 5.5 inches.

Fabrication was designed to be easy and cheap, as suited a machine of unknown destiny. The bottom of the case formed the computer's chassis, the frame or foundation to which all the important mechanical components of the system are bolted. The top was simpler still, a flat piece of steel with the sides rolled down to a bottom lip. With this design, the chassis provided a full steel bottom, front, and back. The the lid and steel sides top, left, and right gave the PC steely protection and interference prevention on all sides. A molded plastic front panel added a decorative touch.

The chassis and lid mated at the rear panel, which quickly proved to be the weakest part of the design. Originally, IBM provided only three screws to hold the top to the bottom and to electrically connect the full-surround of shielding. Adding two screws, for a total of five, ensured better mechanical and electrical integrity.

The other weak aspect of the PC/XT case design was its provision for mounting disk drives. Full-height floppy disk drives slid into either of two bays formed from a steel tray. Drives were held in place on only one side because installation of a second drive made the space (and screw holes) between the two drives inaccessible. Consequently, drives were insecure in their mountings—so insecure that IBM had to add a screw through the bottom of the case to keep the hard disk of the XT in place. Moreover, the bay made no provision for half-height devices, an understandable situation considering that no half-height drives were readily available when the machines were introduced, but a major bother should you decide to upgrade one of these systems.

AT Cases

IBM improved their personal computer, and the AT eliminated these problems with a new case design that has remained the standard in the industry for nearly a decade. The foundation of the design was basically a continuation, a chassis with a matching lid, both fabricated from steel, and a decorative plastic front panel (and an easily removable plastic panel to fit over the rear of the machine). To accommodate the larger system board required by the AT's then-advanced design, the system unit was broadened by two inches (to 23 x 17 inches), and its height was increased by nearly an inch, allowing both taller expansion boards and accommodations for a stack of three half-height devices in the mass storage bays. A taller power supply with greater reserves was also fitted. To accommodate the large system board, however, the base of the power supply had to be cut away.

As with the PC, two side-by-side mass storage bays were installed, but IBM reserved the inboard (left) bay for hard disk drives that required no access to their front panels for media changes. Because the large system board required space for its circuits under the drive bay, this inboard bay had to end more than an inch above the bottom of the case, restricting it to a single full-height device; the outboard (right) bays provided space for three half-height drives.

Drive mounting was the real innovation of the AT case. Mass storage devices are secured on both sides by sturdy mounting rails that slide into channels on either side of the drive bay. The two-sided mounting prevents the drive in the bay from bouncing or rattling around during shipment as they would in one-sided PC mounting.

The new design makes drive removal and installation relatively easy, providing you have hands small enough or skin tough enough so that you don't bloody your knuckles reaching behind the drive to connect or disconnect its various cables. The mounting rails are secured by two brackets that screw into the front panel of the chassis. Most of the brackets are L-shaped, but one (which fits between the left and right bays) is U-shaped. With either style of bracket, the arm or arms of the bracket that project backward press against the drive mounting rail and hold it in its channel.

To pull out an AT drive, you only need to remove the two brackets holding its two mounting rails in place, and then slide the drive slightly forward. When you have adequate room behind the drive, you can unplug its cables (including the ground wire). With the drive free from its electrical tethers, you can finally pull it straight forward and out of the chassis.

Installing a drive is simply the reverse. Before sliding the drive into the bay, you first need to make sure that no cables are in the way of the drive. Then you can slide the drive about two-thirds of the way in so that you can connect its associated cables. After pushing the drive back as far as it will go, you can position one of the brackets over its associated screw hole, hold its arm against the end of the drive rail, and drive the screw home to hold the bracket in place. Affixing the second bracket in the same manner locks the drive securely in place.

The AT case also provided access control. A cylindrical key lock installed with an indicator panel on the left side of the front panel allowed you to lock the cover on the case (and electrically lock the keyboard).

IBM never developed the AT case beyond this arrangement, but various compatible computer makers refined the details. Most AT-compatible computers have added front panel access to all of the drive positions in the case. The internal bays of most machines also have been subdivided to accommodate either a pair of half-height drives or a single full-height device.

Miniaturization

A couple of inches might not seem like much, but the change between XT and AT cases represents a huge increase in apparent mass. While an XT resided on a desktop, an AT dominated it. But the larger size of the AT brought its own benefits, primarily the capability to use larger expansion boards that could pack more circuitry and features into an expansion slot.

Some compatible manufacturers hit upon the great compromise, an XT-size footprint in an AT-height case. The result was the mini-AT. A better description might be "tall-XT" cases because all their horizontal dimensions and accommodations (including system board size) match the XT standard; they equal the AT only in expansion slot area and drive-bay height. The advantage of this design is simply the smaller space it requires on your desk. The downside is the inevitable compromises, slicing off those inches eliminates some space in the expansion board area, so one or two slots may be pared off or truncated into short slots. Access inside is tighter, and the overall space savings is actually small.

The next step down in scale is the small-footprint PC, a case trimmed to smaller than the XT horizontal dimensions although typically AT height to accommodate those taller expansion boards. Again, the principal loss is in expansion, five or six slots instead of eight, and the partial loss of the internal drive bay. Some small footprint machines eliminate the internal bay entirely; others substitute quarters that accommodate nothing larger than a 3.5-inch hard disk, typically aligned on edge.

Today's smaller drives allow further reductions in bay and, thus, case size. The smallest of today's desktop machines typically hold two 3.5-inch removable-media drives side-by-side with another 3.5-inch hard disk bay hidden somewhere inside. These machines capitalize on the lower height as well as the more modest width of the miniature drives. To shave down the height of these tiny cases while conserving the capability of handling tall AT-size expansion boards, these machines move their options on edge. Instead of boards sliding into slots vertically, these tiny PCs align them horizontally. Typically, their system boards remain horizontal in the case and have a single AT-style expansion slot. A special expansion board rises vertically with additional AT-bus slot connectors on one side to allow you to slide in several ordinary expansion boards (typically three) parallel to the system board.

Besides the obvious space and expansion limitations of this miniaturized design, the horizontal expansion boards also have a shortcoming. The horizontal boards impede the normal convective air flow that would otherwise cool the components on the board. Moreover, the lower boards can serve as stoves, heating the boards installed atop them. As fewer expansion boards are installed in PCs (because of more functions being integrated on the system board) and large-scale integration trims the power consumption and heat generated by circuits, this problem decreases in magnitude. Nevertheless, if you have such a machine, you'll want to put the most component-laden of your expansion boards in the top slot so that the other boards can keep their cool.

IBM embraced the downsizing philosophy with the introduction of its initial PS/2 machines. By adopting smaller drives and abandoning the large size of older expansion boards, the company trimmed its desktop machines to a less domineering size. With Micro Channel expansion boards about one inch lower than XT boards, the height of desktop

Micro Channel PS/2s could be trimmed similarly. By cutting the number of slots to three (while maintaining the vertical orientation of expansion boards) IBM saved on the size of the system footprint without compromising convective cooling of the expansion cards.

More recent PS/2s have grown, however, as expansion needs have shifted. With the PS/2, IBM thought the old 5.25-inch form for drives could be safely abandoned. Then, of course, the CD ROM became mandatory for multimedia systems, and IBM was forced to enlarge its PS/2 cases (for example, the Models 57 and 90) to accommodate larger CD ROM and similar drives.

Laptop and Notebook Packaging

The ultimate in computer compression is the notebook PC, a machine shrunk as small as possible while still allowing your hands a grip on the keyboard (and your eyes a good look at the screen)—as thin as components will allow. Making machines this small means everything has got to give, you'll find compromises in nearly every system component.

The fewest of these compromises appear in mass storage. The need for tiny, flyweight drives for both notebook computers and machines of even smaller dimensions has been the principal driving force behind the miniaturization of floppy and hard disks. Drive manufacturers have been amazingly successful, reducing physical size and increasing capacity and improving performance and reliability.

The biggest compromises made for the sake of compact size appear in the user interfaces. Making a computer portable means making it a burden that a human being can bear, even one that will be willingly borne. And the portable must be something that can be packed rather than needing to be tethered with mooring ropes. Unfortunately some aspects of the user interface can't be compressed without losing usability; it's unlikely that human hands will be downsized to match the demand for smaller, lighter PCs, so the optimum size required for a keyboard won't shrink. But the temptation remains for the manufacturer to trim away what's viewed as excess, a bit around the edges from the function keys or eliminating some keys altogether in favor of key-combinations only contortionists can master.

Besides length and width, notebook computer makers have also trimmed the depth of their keyboards, reducing the height of keytops, not a noticeable change, as well as key travel. The latter can have a dramatic effect on typing feel and usability. Although the feel and travel of a keyboard is mostly user preference, odds favor greater dissatisfaction with the shrunken, truncated keyboards in miniaturized computers compared to full-size machines.

Displays, too, are a matter of compromise. Bulky picture-tube displays are out, replaced with flat screens whose size is limited by the dimensions of the rest of the notebook package. More importantly, compact systems are incompatible AT-bus expansion boards. The match is less than optimal. Full-size expansion boards are not built with the idea of conserving power, so a single board may draw as much power as the rest of a laptop computer with the result of cutting battery life commensurately. Consequently, most laptop PCs and nearly all notebook machines forswear conventional expansion boards. Instead they accommodate proprietary expansion products or rely on credit-card size expansion modules that follow the PCMCIA standard.

Access is one major worry with laptop cases. If you plan to expand the memory of your system, you'll want a laptop that lets you plug in memory modules or memory cards without totally disassembling the PC. The easiest machines to deal with have slots hidden behind access panels that allow you to slide in a memory card as easily as a floppy disk. Others may have access hatches that accommodate the addition of memory modules. The only shortcoming of either of these expansion methods is the amount of additional memory such machines support, generally 1 to 8 megabytes, enough for current applications, perhaps, but insufficient for the massive applications programmers stay up nights creating. Many notebook computers, especially the lower cost models wearing the house brands of mail-order companies, require that you remove the keyboard to access memory module sockets, a tricky job that demands more skill and patience than you might want to devote to such a task. A few computers even require unbolting the screen for accessing expansion sockets. If you plan on expanding a notebook or laptop system in the future, check both the permitted memory expansion capacity and the method for adding more RAM.

The key design feature of any laptop or notebook computer is portability. You'll want a machine that's packaged to be as compact and light as possible, commensurate with the ergonomic features that you will tolerate. Older laptops had built-in handles; newer machines have foregone that luxury. With PCs now weighing in under five pounds and sometimes measuring smaller than a stack of legal pads, that lack has become tolerable; you can either wrap your palm around the machine or tuck it into a carrying case.

At one time, the toughest laptop computers had cases crafted from metal, often tough but light magnesium, but nearly all machines today are encased in high-impact plastic. In general, they are tough enough for everyday abuse but won't tolerate a tumble from desktop to floor any more than would a clock, a camera, or other precision device. Inside you'll find foil or metal-enclosed subassemblies, but these are added to keep radiation within limits rather than minimize the effects of sudden deceleration after free-fall. In other words, laptop and notebook computers are made to be tough, but abuse can be as fatal to them as any other business tool.

Tower-Style Cases

At the other end of the packaging continuum from notebook and palm-size PCs are machines designed to be as large as logic allows, tower-style systems. Designed to stand upright on the floor, they are free from the need of minimizing the desk space they require. Instead, they concentrate on expandability, allowing as many expansion boards as standard system board designs permit and a wealth of drive bays.

The AT first brought legitimacy to installing personal computers on edge, using an afterthought mounting scheme, a cocoon to enclose a conventional AT machine on its end. The first mainstream PCs designed from the start for floor mounting were IBM's tower-style PS/2s, the venerable Models 60 and 80. Compatible computers used towers to take advantage of their more commodious drive accommodations. With some models having space for eight or more drives, freestanding tower-style PCs have become the choice for multi-gigabyte network servers.

Vertically mounting computer components causes no problems. Electronic circuits don't know which way is up. However, hard disks (particularly larger older models) may complain about installation on edge, particularly should they have been low-level formatted in horizontal orientation. The weight of a sturdy, old head mechanism can be enough to skew the head away from the center of disk tracks with the result that errors reading the disk can become appallingly frequent. The simple solution is to low-level format the disk in the same vertical orientation in which it will be used.

Another flaw in some tower-style cases is cooling. Most towers align expansion boards horizontally, stacking them one atop another much like small footprint PCs. Unless care is taken in providing cooling air flow, power-hungry boards low in the stack can cook those higher up. IBM anticipated such problems with its tower-style PS/2s by incorporating a plastic channel to direct air current across the expansion boards in those systems. Better tower-style PCs incorporate supplemental cooling fans.

Choose a PC with a tower-style case for its greater physical capacity for internal peripherals and its flexibility of installation wherever there are a few vacant feet of floor space. You'll also want to be critical about the provisions for physically mounting mass storage devices. Some towers provide only flimsy mounting means or require you to work through a Chinese puzzle of interlocking parts to install a drive. You'll want a system that provides a simple, secure mounting scheme for drives, typically something akin to the AT rail system.

Aberrations

Originality has never been the strong suit of the case designs for IBM-compatible computers. In general, that's good because compatible manufacturers have relied on tried and true designs. Along the way, however, some odd and impractical, if stylish, designs have emerged.

Mini-tower PCs fit the same oxymoronic classification as jumbo shrimp, taking a design created for maximum capacity and altering it for compact quarters. On the positive side, mini-towers minimize the materials that would go into making a PC case and they suffer no shortcomings beyond those of a true tower-style case. However, they require as much floor space as a full-height tower without the added capacity for mass storage devices. In other words, style overpowers function.

Flip-top cases seem like a good idea. They mimic the standard PC/XT configuration, but instead of using a lid that slides forward, they substitute a cover that lifts hatch-style. Although this design appears compelling—you can get easy access to what's inside your computer simply by lifting the lid as if your were opening the hood of your car—in the long run it may not be as desirable as you think. You still must pull whatever's atop the machine off to get inside. Worse yet, you may have to pull the plug on some of the peripherals that you have plugged into the expansion slots because the pivoting back end of the lid shears down on them. You either have to pull the plugs or you can access your expansion boards. The flip-top adds nothing but bother.

Device Mounting

Not only must devices fit into the chassis of a personal computer, they must attach securely in some way. Other components, too, require some means of attachment to the chassis so that your PC doesn't turn into a basketful of parts as soon as you touch it.

The most important of the components that somehow must fit and be affixed to the chassis is the power supply. For the most part, installing power supplies presents few problems. Most power supplies are standardized boxes that simply screw in place. Four screws suffice. (Power supply installation is covered in Chapter 9.)

Note, however, that all power supplies will not fit into all cases for both size and configuration reasons. Most power supplies follow the IBM style and put a big red on/off switch on an extension bracket to the right of the box. The cases of most systems, in particular those that explicitly follow the XT and AT standards, are notched at the right rear to allow access to these switches. A few cases, however, are designed to use power supplies with rear panel power switches. Usually the company that sells one variety of case offers power supplies that match (and vice versa). But if you're just replacing the case or the power supply, you'll have to be careful.

Don't forget that PC/XT and AT power supplies are different sizes and one will not fit in a case meant for the other. It's an obvious problem but one that can be eliminated if it's anticipated.

Mass storage devices present their own case-matching considerations. When you buy a complete computer system, you don't have to worry about interfaces, controllers, and the like. The manufacturer has done all the work and properly matched everything for optimum operation (you hope). Adding a new mass storage device to enhance your PC or replacing one that has failed provides you with several interesting challenges. Not only must the prospective product be matched electrically to your system, but also it must physically match your PC's case. After all, any device meant to be installed inside your system must, at minimum, physically fit in place.

Form Factors

Disk drives come in a variety of heights and widths. The basic unit of measurement of the size of a drive is the *form factor*. A form factor is simply the volume of a standard drive that handles a particular medium. Several form factors regularly find their ways into discussions of personal computers ranging in size from 8 inches to 1.3 inches, most of which allow for one or more device heights.

A full-size drive, one which defines the form factor and occupies all of its volume, is usually found in a first-generation machine. Its exact dimensions were chosen for whatever particular reason seemed fitting, perhaps allowing for the mood of the mechanical engineer on the day the blueprints were drafted. If the drive is a reasonable size and proves particularly successful, successful enough that other manufacturers eagerly want to cash in, others follow suit and copy the dimension of the product, making it a standard.

Device Heights

The second generation of any variety of hardware inevitably results in some sort of size reduction. Cost cutting, greater precision, experience in manufacturing, and the inevitable need to put more in less space gang up to shrink things down. The result of the downsizing process is a variety of fractional size devices, particularly in the 5.25-inch and

3.5-inch form factors. At 5.25 inches, devices are measured in sub-increments of the original full-height package. Devices that are two-thirds, one-half, one-third, or one-quarter height have all been manu-factured at one time or another. At the 3.5-inch form factor, sizes are more pragmatic, measured as the actual height in inches. The original 3.5-inch drives may be considered full-height and typically measure about 1.6 inches high. The next widely used size was an even inch in height. Sub-inch heights have been used for some devices, some as small as 0.6 inches.

However, before 3.5-inch drives had a chance to slim down to two dimensions, smaller form factors came into play—2.5, 1.8, and 1.3 inches. The 2.5-inch devices were designed primarily for notebook computers. Smaller drives fit palmtop computers, even on credit-card size expansion boards. Note that all of these applications for drives less than 3.5 inches are the sort in which the system (or at least its case or other packaging) is designed around the drive. In the foreseeable future, you're unlikely to tangle with one of these truly tiny products for use in a desktop PC.

The one important rule regarding small drives is that a device can always be adapted to fit a drive bay designed for a larger form factor. For example, kits to adapt 3.5-inch drives for 5.25-inch bays are readily available, often included with the drive itself. Going the other way is more difficult.

Device Installation

Internal installation of any mass storage device in a drive bay is actually quite simple. Most disk and tape drives are replete with multiple tapped holes on each side and bottom that will accept screws to hold the drive in place. Add the right screws and a few twists, and you can install a device in a couple of minutes. Anyone who knows the right end of a screwdriver to grab is qualified to install or remove a device from a drive bay.

But matters, and drive bays, are not quite so simple. You have to get access to the drive bay itself as well as the holes through which you must twist the screws. Some systems make playing hide-and-seek with the invisible man less of a challenge.

PC/XT-Style Drive Bays

The drive bays of the original PC, XT, and compatible computers patterned after them are based on a relatively straightforward (if ineffectual) mounting tray. The sides of the tray were bent upward and holes were provided to match the two tapped mounting holes on each side of the standard full-height 5 1/4-inch mass storage device. These screws are visible on the right side of drives in the right drive bay and the left side of drives in the left bay. Gaining access to the latter typically require a short screwdriver, a great deal of dexterity, and a tolerance for blood loss, or removing all or most of the expansion cards inside the computer.

The only challenge is lining up the holes tapped in the side of a device with the holes or slots in the sides of the drive bay. Slots impose an additional layer of merriment. You must align the font of the device with the front panel of the computer. You'll also need to use screws with large heads (binder head screws are best if you can acquire them from your hardware store) that won't slip through the slots.

As noted earlier, two screws on one side of a device provide less than adequate mounting security, particularly in inexpensive cases made from sheet-metal so thin you might expect it to be recycled soup cans. Slide a tape-cartridge drive into one of these bays, and you'll probably fold the entire bay half an inch over every time you shove in a tape. IBM added an extra screw for its XT hard disk drives for the sake of mechanical integrity, and you would be well advised to do the same. You'll need to mark the place on the bay that lines up with one of the screw holes in the bottom of the device you want to install and drill a matching hole in the bottom of the mounting tray. You'll then need to drill a matching hole in the bottom of the case, large enough for the entire screw (and screwdriver) to be pushed up to the bottom of the mounting tray.

Another difficulty you'll face is installing half-height devices in IBM's PC and XT device bays. You can install a single half-height drive in each slot simply by using these mounting holes and filling the empty space above the drive with blank half-height panel. Try to install two half-height drives in a single full-height bay, however, and you'll be screwing in the air. While most compatible computers provide two sets of drive-mounting holes or slots on each side of the mounting tray to allow installation of two half-height devices, one over the other, IBM gives you only one set of holes and trims off the upper sides of each bay so you can't simply drill your own.

The solution is to create a pair of half-height adapter plates. Basically just thin pieces of steel with a number of slots or holes in them, adapter plates allow you to assemble two half-height drives into a single unit that will install into a full-height drive bay. Figure 10.1 shows one form of adapter plate that is easily fabricated.

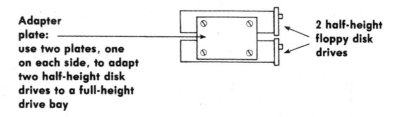

Adapter plate: use two plates, one on each side, to adapt two half-height disk drives to a full-height drive bay

2 half-height floppy disk drives

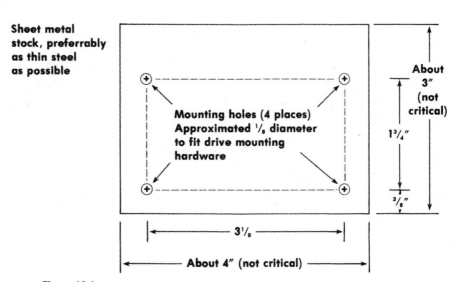

Sheet metal stock, preferably as thin steel as possible

Mounting holes (4 places) Approximated ⅛ diameter to fit drive mounting hardware

About 3" (not critical)

1¾"

⅜"

3⅛

About 4" (not critical)

Figure 10.1. Half-height drive adapter plate.

Installing drives with these adapters is more difficult than you may think. You can't just connect two drives with them and slide the whole assembly into the drive bay. The screw heads (and maybe the plates themselves) make the drive package too wide to slide through the front panel opening in the chassis.

The first step to a double-half-height installation is to connect the two drives on the side opposite that which attaches to the mounting tray. Once one plate is installed, you should be able to slide the drive stack into the computer as a single piece.

Once the two-drive stack is in its proper place but while you can still maneuver the drives in and out of the bay, install all the cables to both drives. Once everything is plugged in, slip the other mounting plate between the drives and the side of the drive bay. Secure this mounting plate and the drive by screwing through the two holes in the bay, through the mounting plate, and into the screw holes in the bottom drive. Finally, finish your work by screwing the top drive into place.

AT-Style Drive Bays

The improved drive mounting scheme developed for the AT imposes an additional step on device installation: mounting rails. These rails both solve and add problems to drive installation. On the positive side, they make a truly secure mounting system that will withstand even moderate earthquakes. On the negative side, the process of installing the rails allows you to make several missteps that you won't discover till too late, giving you the pleasure of screwing rails on and off your drive several times.

The first challenge in installing rails on a device is coming up with the rails themselves. Although IBM has been consistent in its rail design, using the same basic geometry for all AT-style cases as well as its tower-style ATs with mass storage sub-chassis, other manufacturers have not. You'll find many AT-compatible cases that simply duplicate the IBM mounting scheme in all of its dimensions. Others, particularly the larger manufacturers (such as Compaq), have opted for their own rail designs. Figure 10.2 shows the dimensions of the standard AT drive mounting rail and the similar rail used by Compaq.

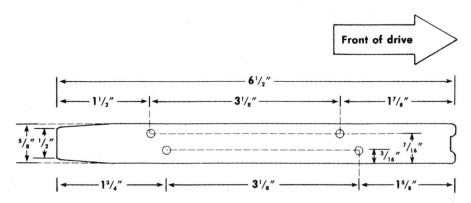

Left rail shown; right rail is mirror image

Use upper holes for full-height drive in internal bay
Use lower holes for half-height drive in half-height bays

B. Compaq drive mounting rail

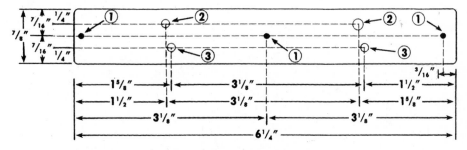

① = Hole for securing rail to computer
② = Hole for securing rail to disk drive
③ = Not used (make rail symmetrical so that it
        can be used on other side of drive

Figure 10.2. IBM AT and Compaq drive mounting rails.

True AT-style rails are easy to find. Many device vendors package AT-style rails with their products or pre-install AT-style rails before sending the device to you. The rails in compatible computers are so varied that finding the exact size you need means contacting the computer maker or an authorized dealer who stocks a complete array of parts.

Many makers of AT-style computers now alleviate this problem by filling all drive bays in their systems with rails, whether or not a drive is installed in each bay.

All sorts of AT-style rails are available. Official IBM rails are different for the right and left side of the drive and have only two installation holes. Aftermarket rails may have four or eight holes or slots and may be entirely symmetrical, even squared off at both ends. These rails are meant to be interchangeable between the right and left sides of the device you want to install. Although that's a laudable design consideration, the multiplicity of holes also imposes on you the challenge of finding which pair of the eight will put the device at the proper height in the bay and the proper distance from the front panel.

With true, asymmetrical IBM rails, proper orientation points the tapered end of the rail toward the rear of the drive. The screws to hold the rails in place then go into the lower pair of the two sets of mounting holes on the drive. With non-IBM AT-style rails, the general rule is to use the lower holes on the rail (when its tapered end is pointed toward the rear of the drive) to mate with the lower holes in the side of the device. Some odd rails may have holes in different positions, however. If you install rails on a new drive, make sure that the drive lines up in the proper vertical position before you secure its mounting brackets and try to reinstall the lid of the case.

After you have installed rails on a device, slide it into the bay in which you plan to use it. Push the device all the way back into the bay to ensure that the device fits at the proper height and depth to match with the computer's fascia panel. Once you're satisfied that the device fits properly, pull it part way out and make all the electrical connections to it. Then push the drive back to its final resting place. With AT-style cases, screw in the front panel brackets to hold the rails and device in place. With some compatibles, the bracket is part of the rail itself. These mate directly against the front panel of the computer.

PS/2 Bays

In the PS/2 series of computers, IBM refined its device-mounting schemes so that all devices could be installed or removed from their computer hosts without the use of tools. Devices conforming to the 3 1/2-inch form factor install on special plastic mounting sleds while 5 1/4-inch drives in most systems retain the AT rail system.

IBM-style drive sleds are one-piece plastic castings that screw into the bottom of 3 1/2-inch devices. The sled slides into guide rails, casts into the drive bay, and snaps into place using a plastic latch that is part of the sled. The IBM design holds the potential for making the sled an integral part of the device chassis, but such designs have not been accepted by drive makers. Figure 10.3 shows an IBM-style device sled.

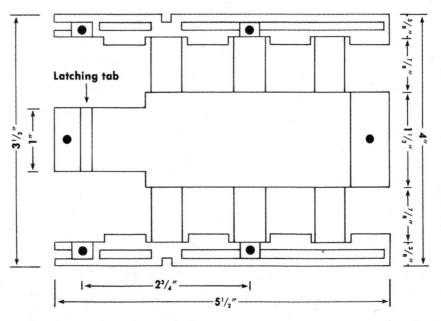

Figure 10.3. PS/2 3.5-inch hard disk mounting sled (dimensions approximate).

To access the drive bay to install or remove one of these sleds, you'll have to remove the front fascia panel from your PS/2. These are secured with by plastic snaps molded into the fascia. Just pry the front panel free at the seam running around it about half an inch behind its face. You should be able to pull it off using no tools other than your fingers.

A "floating" connector (one with some freedom of movement) at the rear of the bay automatically mates with an edge connector on the drive. Besides carrying the signals, this connector also supplies power to the drive, eliminating the need for a separate power connector.

When the drive is pushed fully into its bay, a latch at the bottom of the drive snaps down, locking the drive securely in place. To remove the drive, this latch must be released. To do so, simply lift up on the tab that's centered under the drive. Firmly pull the drive forward while lifting the tab to release the latch. After some initial effort, required to pull the drive from the connector at the back of the bay, the drive will pull easily and smoothly from the bay.

In the tower-style PS/2 systems that accept 5 1/4-inch devices, the AT-rail system is preserved but adapted to make the installation of drives free from the need for tools when rails are attached to each device (see fig. 10.4). Instead of the simple steel channels used in the AT, however, the PS/2 line uses a sturdy cage to hold drives. One or two drives fit into the cage, one of which can peek out the front panel of the computer, and are held down by screw pressure. Big blue daisy-like knobs of plastic turn the screws, designed to be spun without tools by firm pressure from the palm of your hand.

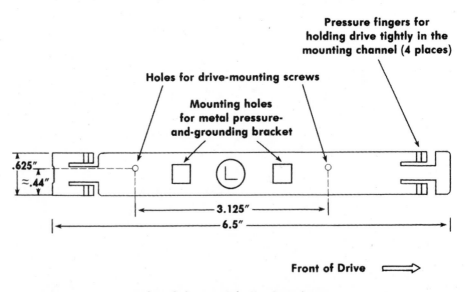

Figure 10.4. Internal hard disk rails for tower-style computers.

Drive installation in single-drive systems simply requires lowering the drive decked out in its mounting rails through the open center of the cage. The drive should be oriented so that the connectors at its rear will end up nearest the center of the chassis once the drive is positioned. Once you have lowered the drive into the cage, simply push it to the end of its travel and tighten down the blue daisies.

Two drive systems require a more complicated installation because one drive will block access for the other to the central open area of the chassis. The drive to be located at the rear of the chassis should be inserted first, as for a single drive installation. The second drive can then be slid into the cage through the opening in the front of the chassis. You'll want to snap out the front panel bezel to gain access. The front-mounted drive is tightened into place as for the rear unit.

Other Bays

Other compatible systems have gone in their own directions when it comes to device installation. Most, however, are variations of two designs: direct mounting and removable sub-bays.

Direct mounting is exactly as it sounds. As with the original PC, drives screw directly into bays in the computer host. The difference is that most compatible computers are more compatible with modern disk drive sizes. They accommodate the primary variations in disk form factors. The only trick is finding a way to access the screws meant to hold drives in place.

In some cases, access would be impossible. For example, a 3 1/2-inch drive bay may be squeezed in vertically next to a more conventional, larger bay with no provision for accessing the bottom of the bay. In these systems, the drive mounts to a subassembly, a sub-bay, that removes so that you can attach the drive directly to it, and then fits back in place secured by a more readily reached fastener. Another variation is the drive tray used by ALR tower-style PCs. Drives mount through their bottom screw-holes to trays, which then screw into the side of the tower. The cover-plate on the other side of the case is slotted to support the other side of each tray.

Cooling

Heat is the natural by-product of any electrical current flow. Some of the electricity in any circuit (except circuits made from superconductors) is turned into heat by the unavoidable electrical resistance of the circuit. Heat is also generated whenever an element of a computer circuit changes state. In fact, nearly all of the electricity consumed by a computer eventually turns into heat.

Inside the protective (and confining) case of the computer, that heat builds up, driving up the temperature. Heat is the worst enemy of semiconductor circuits; it can shorten their lives considerably or even cause their catastrophic failure. Some means of escape must be provided for the excess heat. In truth, the heat build-up in most PCs will not be immediately fatal to semiconductor circuits. For example, most microprocessors will shut down (or simply generate errors that will shut down your PC) before any permanent damage occurs to them or the rest of the components inside your PC. However, heat can cause circuits to age prematurely. It can trim the lives of circuit components. Keeping a system cool can thus prolong its life.

Passive Convection

The obvious way to make a PC run cooler is to punch holes in its case to let the heat out but keep the holes small enough so that other things, such as mice and milkshakes, can't get in. In due time, passive convection, less dense hot air rising with denser cool air flowing in to take its place, will let the excess thermal energy drift out of the case.

Active Cooling

Unfortunately, all IBM-standard computers (except for some laptops) produce heat faster than passive convection can rid it from the case. These machines need some form of active cooling, something that forces the heat away from the circuits. The means of choice is the fan.

Usually tucked inside the power supply, the computer's fan forces air to circulate both inside the power supply and the computer. It sucks cool air in to circulate and blows the heated air out.

The cooling systems of early PCs were particularly ill-conceived, however. The fans were designed mostly to cool off the heat-generating circuitry inside the power supply itself and only incidentally cool the inside of the computer. Moreover, the chance design of the system resulted in most of the cool air getting sucked in through the floppy disk drive slots. Along with the air, in came all the dust and grime that is floating around in the environment, polluting whatever media you have sitting in the drive.

The XT added more electric from the power supply but no better ventilation. And that brought its own problem. The airflow around expansion cards and the rest of the computer was insufficient (actually too ill-placed) to keep the temperature throughout the machine down to an acceptable level. As a correction to later models of the XT, IBM eliminated a series of ventilation holes at the bottom of the front of the chassis. The absence of these holes actually improves the air circulation through the system unit and keeps things cooler (see the "Ancient History" appendix).

Unfortunately, most computer manufacturers rely on cooling that has not advanced beyond the XT system. At most, these manufacturers will graft a heatsink onto the system microprocessor to provide a greater area to radiate heat. But most still rely on the fan in the power supply to do all the work of moving cooling air through the system.

Advanced Cooling

Some systems have more carefully thought-out cooling systems. IBM's tower-style PS/2s are exemplary, channeling the flow of cooling air to the places it is most needed. A few manufacturers add extra fans to supplement the air flow generated by the power supply fan.

In most systems, however, the cooling system can be improved. Booster fans that clamp on the rear panel of the computer and power supplies with beefed-up fans are available. These do, in fact, increase air circulation through the system unit, potentially lowering the internal temperature and prolonging the lives of components. Note that there is no reliable data on whether this additional cooling will increase the life of the components inside your PC. Unless you stuff every conceivable accessory into your machine, however, you're unlikely to need such a device except for the added measure of peace of mind it provides.

On the other hand, blocking the air path of the cooling system of any PC can be fatal, allowing too much heat to build up inside the chassis. Never locate a PC in cramped quarters that lacks air circulation (such as a desk drawer or a shelf on which it just fits). Never block the cooling slots or holes of a computer case.

Fan Failures

The fan inside a PC power supply is a necessity, not a luxury. If it fails to operate, your computer won't falter, at least not at first. But temperatures will build up inside. The machine, the power supply in particular, may even fail catastrophically from overheating.

The symptoms of fan failure are subtle but hard to miss. You'll be able to hear the difference in the noise your system makes. You may even be able to smell components warming past their safe operating temperature.

Should you detect either symptom, hold your hand near where the air usually emerges from your computer. (On PCs and ATs, that's near the big round opening that the fan peers through.) If you feel no breeze, you can be certain your fan is no longer doing its job.

A fan failure constitutes an emergency. If it happens to your system, immediately save your work and shut the machine off. Although you can safely use it for short periods, the better strategy is to replace the fan or power supply as soon as you possibly can.

Radio Frequency Emission

Beside heat, all electrical circuits radiate electromagnetic fields. Every flow of electrical energy sets up an electromagnetic field that radiates. Radio and television stations push kilowatts of energy through their antennae so that this energy (accompanied by programming in the form of modulation) will radiate over the countryside, eventually to be hauled in by a radio or television set for your enjoyment or disgruntlement.

Radio Frequency Interference

The electrical circuits inside all computers work the same way but on a smaller scale. They radiate electromagnetic energy whenever the computer is turned on, and when the thinking gets tense, so does the radiation.

A problem arises because the radiation from the computer circuitry occurs at a wide variety of frequencies, including the range occupied by your favorite radio and television stations, aviation navigation systems, and the eavesdropping equipment some initialed government agency has buried in your walls. Unchecked, these untamed radiations from within your computer will compete with broadcast signals not only for the ears of your radio but that of your neighbors. These radio-like signals emitted by the computer generate what is termed *radio frequency interference* or *RFI*, so called because it interferes with other signals in the radio spectrum.

FCC Regulation

Even if your PC doesn't exude 2 Live Crew or George Carlin reciting the seven words you can't say on the radio, the Federal Communications Commission is interested in what your PC is broadcasting. The government has set strict standards on the radio waves that your personal computer can emit, standards so severe that many computer makers fail to pay them heed. As a result, thousands of personal computers are sold illegally each year, possibly your next PC purchase.

You may not think of your PC as a radio transmitter, but it is. As with all electrical devices, a computer radiates electromagnetic fields. The frequencies at which your PC operates puts these fields in the range that a radio or television set might pick up. Of course these radio emissions are not intentional. They are an unwanted by product of a simple physical principal. Any moving electronic current, including the minuscule logic signals inside your PC, creates an electromagnetic field. If the current flow starts and stops or changes direction, it induces an electromagnetic field that causes radio waves that radiate into space. (Unchanging current flows produce steady-state or static fields.) The unintentional nature of these signals does not matter to the FCC. Almost anything that gets into the airwaves is within the jurisdiction of Commission. In fact, its oversight of signals starts at frequencies that you could hear if they were sound waves, 9,000 Hz, and keeps going almost to frequencies you could see as light waves, 300,000,000,000 Hz.

The Commission has created a body of rules and regulations that cover signals akin to those emitted by your computer, and it has Congressional authority to enforce its rules. It can, in fact, determine which computers can be sold and when, and which will haunt their designers as costly unmarketable products. Every personal computer and most computer peripherals sold in the United States must comply with these rules and regulations.

Nevertheless, few people (including the makers of many PCs and peripheral products) know what those rules govern, what they are meant to achieve, and why anyone should care. In ignorance or in defiance of the FCC's authority, many computer manufacturers offer PCs that for sale without regard to these rules. Selling such computers is illegal in the United States.

For the computer designer who is aware of and obedient to the FCC rules, complying with them is that last hoop to be leapt through, the final test before his life's work can nestle on your dealer's shelf. But the need for certification affects you, too. Because of this need for certification, your access to new technology is considerably slowed. Any computer product must be ready to be sold before it can be certified, and certification can take six to eight weeks. Automatically, the latest gear faces a month and a half or longer delay getting to market.

On the other hand, the good side of certification may seem slight. For example, FCC certification does not guarantee that a computer product is safe. Health and safety are not the concern of the FCC; a product that meets the FCC standards could, nevertheless, radiate harmful signals or contaminate your office with arcane poisons. The FCC rules also do not guarantee that a given computer product absolutely won't interfere with your radio or television reception. (That's why instructions for eliminating the interference caused by a computer is included in the manual of equipment that is properly certified.) All FCC certification shows is that a particular product won't exceed a given level of interference with broadcast services, such as television and radio transmissions (including cellular phones, emergency radio services, and the radio navigation equipment used by airplanes). Even though it doesn't seem like much, achieving that level of protection is something for which you and your neighbors should be thankful, even if it is often a big headache for computer manufacturers.

Interference

Interference was one of the most important reasons underlying the FCC's very existence. The Commission was created in 1934 primarily (but not exclusively) to sort out the mess made by early broadcasters who, in the 1920s, transmitted signals whenever, wherever, and however they wanted to, with the result that in some places the airwaves became a thick goulash from which no radio could successfully sort a program. The FCC was created to bring order to that chaos, and to do so it created strict rules to prevent interference between radio stations. As other services began to use the airwaves, the FCC set rules for them, too, always with the same purpose, to prevent signals from interfering with one another, not to limit what you could hear but to ensure that you could clearly hear what was there.

At first, the FCC was interested only in signals that were meant to be broadcast; however, the advent of modern computer equipment operating at high frequencies created a new source of radio interference. The clock frequencies of computers right now sit in the middle of communications frequencies and are edging up on the television and FM broadcast bands. (A few older computers operate at frequencies within the AM broadcast band, but IBM-standard PCs have never stooped so low.)

Potential radio and television interference doesn't seem like much of a cause for concern. Compared to the quality of network television programming, interference might be an improvement. But when the FCC took control and created the computer emission standards, the situation was more serious. At the time (the late 1970s) emissions from computer-like equipment were already proving to be a dangerous if not life-threatening problem. For example, according to the FCC, the police departments of several Western states reported their radios were receiving interference from coin-operated video games that were based on computer-style circuitry. At an East Coast airport, interference in aeronautical communications was traced to the computer-like electronic cash register at a drug store a mile away. Hobbyist-style computers and hand-held calculators were already on the market and were known to generate spurious radio signals. The Radio Shack TRS-80 was notorious for the television interference it generated. Even though the personal computer boom of the 1980's could not have been foreseen, the increased use of high-frequency digital logic circuitry promised that the situation could only become worse.

In a first attempt to regulate the emissions of personal computers, the FCC developed a special set of rules for them, enacted in October, 1979, as the infamous Subpart J of Part 15 that was emblazoned on the certification stickers on millions of PCs sold through 1989. In March of that year, Part 15 was rewritten with Subpart B to bring together computers and other equipment that generated similar interference. The new rules apply to all electronic equipment that inadvertently creates radio signals, equipment the FCC calls unintentional radiators, as opposed to devices that intentionally create radio signals for communications or related purposes. Of course, intentional radiators from television stations to garage door openers are also governed by the FCC rules.

Scope of Regulation

The new FCC rules specifically cover personal computers as well as other larger and smaller computer systems, from mainframes to pocket calculators. In addition, personal computer peripherals are also included. In fact, most peripherals must undergo the same certification process as computer systems. The rules explicitly define which peripherals require certification and which do not.

Peripherals, according to the FCC, include both internal and external devices used to enhance a personal computer. External devices connected to a PC require their own certification unless they are sold together with the computer, in which case the PC and peripheral must be certified together. Internal peripherals need not be certified only if they do not affect the speed or performance of the computer and do not connect with external cables. Serial communications boards or graphics boards would need to be certified because they have connectors for external devices. A turbo board upgrade board would require certification because it would increase the speed and radiation potential of the computer. A memory-only expansion board or a hard disk controller would not require certification.

Computer components that are ordinarily used only in making a computer at the factory are considered to be subassemblies and, as such, do not require certification. Once subassemblies are united to make a personal computer that will be sold to end users, the entire computer must be certified.

Cases, motherboards, and power supplies are specifically designated as subassemblies and need not, and cannot, be FCC certified. As things stand now, a computer motherboard does not require certification, but once that motherboard is installed in a case with a power supply sold as a personal computer, the entire assembly must be certified. Several organizations, including IBM, have lobbied to get motherboards separately certified, but as of this writing the efforts have not been successful.

The rules recognize that the testing apparatus required for compliance with verification is beyond the reach of the average computer hobbyist, and, implicitly, that the hobbyist may be beyond the reach of the FCC if just because the effects of his efforts are so minor. Consequently, the FCC rules allow a specific exception for the need for certification for home-made personal computers. For this exception to apply, the home-built PC must meet all three of the following criteria: one, it must not be marketed or offered for sale; two, it must not be made from a kit; and three, it must be made in quantities of five or fewer solely for personal use. Commercial computer kits, on the other hand, must be certified by the FCC.

Some kinds of commercial personal computer equipment are also specifically excluded from the need for certification under the FCC rules. Low-power devices are unlikely to radiate substantial interference, so equipment that uses less than six nanowatts (billionths of a watt) in its high-frequency circuits are specifically excluded. All current microprocessors use far more power than this. For example, a 50 Mhz 486 microprocessor uses about nine watts, about a billion times too much energy to sneak through the lower barrier of the requirements.

Equipment that operates at very low frequencies does not have to comply with the FCC rules that cover certification. A frequency of 9 Khz is the minimum cut-off for the FCC definition of digital device, so slower (more correctly, glacial) systems need not worry. The effective limit is actually much higher; devices operating at speeds lower than 1.705 Mhz that do not use AC power are also excluded.

Mice and joysticks are explicitly excluded from the need for certification because they contain no high-frequency circuits and use no high-frequency signals. However, a smart mouse with its own internal microprocessor would require certification.

FCC Classes

By now, most people are aware that the FCC divides digital devices into two classes, A and B, with entirely different standards as to allowable emissions and testing. The division is made on the basis of where the equipment is likely to be used. Class A digital devices are those that are suited only to business, commercial, and industrial applications. Class B applies to digital devices that are likely to be used in the home.

The FCC rules explicitly define all personal computers as Class B equipment. The rules also define the term *personal computer* so that just about anything that you might think of laying your hands on qualifies. What was classed as a *home* computer years ago, for example, the Commodore 64, is specifically included because the FCC included any computer that uses a television set as its display device in its personal computer definition. But the rules go even further. Computers with dedicated display systems, such as the PC that's probably sitting on your desk, meet the FCC definition as a personal computer if it has all three of the following characteristics:

1. It was marketed through a retail dealer or direct mail outlet.

2. Advertisements of the equipment are directed toward the general public rather than restricted to commercial users.

3. The computer operates on battery or 120-volt AC electrical power.

How a particular computer was actually sold does not matter. As long as a particular model has been offered for sale through a dealer or direct mail outlet, it meets the first requirement.

The definition of Class A equipment implicitly covers mainframe and minicomputers, most of which use industrial-strength 230-volt power. According to the rules, however, the most important distinguishing characteristic is that Class A devices are of such nature or cost that they would or could not be used at home by individuals. Here the FCC gives manufacturers an out; manufacturers or importers can apply to the FCC to have specific personal computers treated as Class A devices providing the computer is of such a nature (priced too high or delivering performance too high) that it is not suitable for residential or hobbyist use.

No hard and fast rule covers what is too powerful or too expensive to be a computer suitable for use in the home. One general (but not absolute) guideline used by the FCC is that a base retail price higher than $5,000 makes a computer more likely to be used in a business setting. Currently computers, based on 80486 or more powerful microprocessors may be powerful enough to likely earn the FCC's okay to be rated as Class A devices. As the power of PCs increases, prices plummet, and the expectations of home users skyrocket, this guideline will likely shift.

Note that a manufacturer cannot simply declare that a given computer is a Class A device. They must apply to the FCC for such a classification, and they had better be able to support their claims. The FCC confirms its classification with a letter notification.

All portable personal computers are considered to be Class B devices because their very portability makes them likely to be used in a residential setting. Although Class A portable computers are theoretically conceivable, for example, a machine dedicated to taking seismological measurements in oil prospecting, general-purpose portable PCs cannot qualify as Class A devices. In other words, any portable computer, from the smallest palmtop to an arm-stretching old lunchbox, offered to you for sale as a Class A device violates the FCC rules. Legally, such a computer cannot be sold in the U.S.

There's quite a substantial incentive for a manufacturer to want its products treated as Class A devices. Not only are the emission requirements more lax for Class A devices, a personal computer that's rated Class A does not require the long FCC certification process. Instead, a Class A device only needs to be verified by its maker to comply with the FCC rules. In other words, although Class B equipment must be certified by the FCC, a process which involves the FCC or a special lab actually testing the equipment, a Class A device is tested and verified to comply with the FCC rules by its manufacturer. The latter process is admittedly quicker. It also offers the potential for creative interpretation of the rules. For example, a manufacturer might succumb to marketing pressure and say that equipment is verified before it actually is. However, the FCC can double-check Class A verified equipment and prohibit its sale if it doesn't in fact meet the standard, and the FCC can punish those who fraudulently claim to have verified equipment.

Radiation Limits

The justification of the distinction between Class A and B devices may seem nebulous, and the different forms of testing procedures may seem insupportable. But there's good reason behind both.

The emission limits for a Class B device are not arbitrary or capricious. The limits represent a value believed by the FCC to be low enough that they will not cause interference to radio or television reception when there is more than one wall and 30 feet separating the computer and the television set or radio. That 30 feet and one wall is a reasonable description of the distance between one household and another (at least it's reasonable to the FCC). In other words, the standard is designed so that if Class B equipment causes interference at all, it will only be a bother in the home of the person owning the computer. The neighbors shouldn't have anything to worry about.

Class A equipment, on the other hand, may produce interference in equipment that's nearly 10 times farther away. The higher tolerance for interference is based on the assumption that most residential areas are substantially more than 30 feet from industrial or commercial buildings. This greater separation means that even with greater emissions, Class A devices should not bother the neighbors. However, in a residential neighborhood, a Class A device may cause interference to neighbors' radio and television reception.

Two kinds of emissions are covered by the limits in the FCC rules: conductive emissions, those that are conducted through the wires in the power cord; and radiation, the signals that are broadcast as radio signals from the computer into space. The maximum strength of the emissions varies with frequency.

The different testing arrangements, verification versus certification, for Class A and B equipment reflect some of the realities the FCC envisioned in the two types of computer equipment the rules are concerned with. Class B products are those mass-produced in the thousands or millions. Sending a sample to the FCC should be no hardship (except for the delay imposed in the certification process). Class A equipment may likely be unique, for example a custom-installed mainframe in an environmentally-controlled computer room. Sending a one-of-a-kind mainframe computer to the FCC testing lab would be impractical at best. Moreover, because more Class B than Class A devices are likely to be unleashed on the public, a higher degree of assurance against interference from the more popular equipment would seem warranted.

Under the FCC rules, commercial or industrial equipment can be sent to the FCC to be certified as Class B equipment, and Class B equipment can be used in business locations. The opposite is not true, however. Class A equipment should not be used in residential areas.

Enforcement

The law doesn't say that you cannot use a Class A device in your home, nor will the Radio Police break down your door if you do. The FCC rules implicitly allow you to get away with using a Class A device in your home, as long as no one notices. If, however, your computer causes interference to someone's radio or television reception, no matter whether your PC is a Class A or Class B device, you are responsible for eliminating the interference. If you don't, the FCC can order you to stop using your computer until you fix the interference problem. And if you don't obey the order, you may be fined or imprisoned. That threat alone should be sufficient to make you think twice about using a Class A device at home.

If that policy seems to incorporate more than a bit of Big Brother, you should be aware that the FCC also has the authority to demand to see your personal computer almost whenever they want. The FCC rules require that the owner of any Class A or B device (or any equipment subject to the FCC rules) make the equipment and any accompanying certification available for inspection upon request at any reasonable time (generally, that means 9 a.m. to 5 p.m. on workdays). You must also "promptly furnish" any FCC representative that calls upon you with such information as may be requested concerning the operation of your personal computer.

You needn't watch warily out your windows for big vans slowly driving down your street with dish antennae pointed in your general direction, however. Those vans are things of cheap spy novels and cheaper movies. In reality, the FCC uses ordinary-looking cars that may not even have an evident antenna. Moreover, the FCC doesn't arbitrarily go out looking for people holding Class A computers in their homes. The interference-locating equipment goes out in response to complaints, so odds are you'll hear from your neighbors before the FCC knocks.

The bigger concern of the FCC is that interference-causing equipment isn't sold in the first place so you don't get a chance to put wavy lines through all your neighbor's favorite TV shows. To that end, the FCC rules prohibit Class B equipment from being sold or offered for sale.

Class B personal computers that are not FCC certified cannot legally be advertised for sale, although ads announcing products with a disclaimer noting that the device is not certified (and thus, not available for sale) are permitted. If a company markets a computer that has neither been approved by the FCC as a Class A device nor certified as complying as a Class B device, the company may be ordered to stop selling the equipment and fined. If the company continues to flout the rules, company officials could be jailed. According to the FCC, most companies get into compliance right away.

Before a Class B device is certified, it can be displayed at shows and demonstrated with the appropriate disclaimer attached. The primary prohibition is against sales of non-certified equipment. For example, demonstrations units could be distributed, but "demo" models could not be sold to computer dealers for display.

Verification and Certification

The certification process requires that testing be done by the FCC or a special lab and that an example of the personal computer or peripheral be sent to the FCC Laboratory in Columbia, Maryland. The FCC will then test the device to determine whether its emissions are within the limits specified for Class B devices. If the unit qualifies, the FCC certifies the unit and issues a certification number, which may be an alphanumeric set of characters (manufacturers often select their own numbers).

Every model of a personal computer that differs as to case, power supply, or motherboard must be separately certified. If a manufacturer offers two case styles, desktop and floor-standing, and three system boards, 386SX, 386DX, and 486DX, each of the six configurations would need to be separately certified.

Computers from different vendors can share the same FCC number, providing they are identical units made by a single manufacturer differing only cosmetically, for example, in label or color. In the past, the FCC has required that it be notified about different trade names used on products that are certified, but this requirement was relaxed with the new (1989) rules. Computers with different packaging, processors, or power supplies cannot share an FCC certification number, even if they are made by the same manufacturer.

A personal computer need not be recertified if it differs from a certified model only in the addition of a certified peripheral. For example, a manufacturer could create a separate model by installing an extra FCC-certified serial board, and that new model would be covered by the certification of the old one.

A claim sometimes made by small computer makers, that a product is made only from FCC-certified subassemblies and thus does not require

FCC certification itself, is simply impossible. A PC cannot be built without a power supply, case, or motherboard, and these three subassemblies cannot be FCC certified. Any computer manufactured from subassemblies must be FCC certified as a completed unit.

All of these rules would seem to make FCC certification important only to computer manufacturers. After all, you are still liable for clearing up the interference generated by your PC no matter whether it's Class A or B. But FCC certification should be important to you.

Equipment Design

Achieving Class B certification takes a better design and better workmanship. Although a certification sticker is no guarantee that a particular product is well-made, that sticker does show that the PC or peripheral to which it is attached has met an important technical standard that uncertified equipment has not. Although you should not rely entirely on FCC certification when buying a PC, it does give you one more piece of evidence about the quality of your prospective purchase.

Manufacturers use a number of different strategies to minimize radiation. As speeds increase, manufacturers must be increasingly diligent.

The heavy steel case of the typical PC, XT, AT, or compatible computer does a reasonable job of limiting RFI. Plastic cases require special treatments to minimize radiation. The treatment of choice is a conductive paint, often rich with silver, which shields the computer much like the full metal jacket of other computers.

As PC operating frequencies increase, the spurious radiation becomes more pernicious. Any crack in the case may allow too much radio energy to leak out. If different parts of the chassis and the lid of the case are not electrically connected, RFI can leak out. In addition, any cable attached to the computer potentially can act as an antenna, sending out signals as effectively as a radio station.

A number of design elements help reduce RFI. Special metal fingers on the edge of the case and its lid ensure that the two pieces are in good electrical contact. Cables can be shielded. RFI absorbing ferrite beads can be wrapped around wires before they leave the chassis to suck up excess energy before it leaks out. Every one of these cures adds a bit to the cost of the computer, both for the materials and for their fabrication and installation. Moreover, it can take a substantial time to track down all the leaks and plug them.

Interference can also be minimized at the point of its origin. For example, IBM designed its PS/2s from the ground up to be inherently low in radio frequency emissions. Their system boards and the Micro Channel are designed in such a way that spurious radiation is at a minimum. The outer layers of the planar boards consist primarily of ground layers, which shield the high-frequency signals within the inner layers of the circuit board. Ground wires alternate with every few active conductors on the Micro Channel to partially shield the bus.

The bottom line is that a Class B device must be designed to be less likely to cause interference than a Class A computer. Not only does that mean you're less likely to get involved in an imbroglio with your neighbors about their television reception, it also means that a Class B computer may be built better with more attention to detail. In addition, lower emissions at radio frequencies generally go hand-in-hand with lower emissions at lower frequencies. That can be comforting should you worry about the health effects of low-frequency radiation.

11
Input Devices

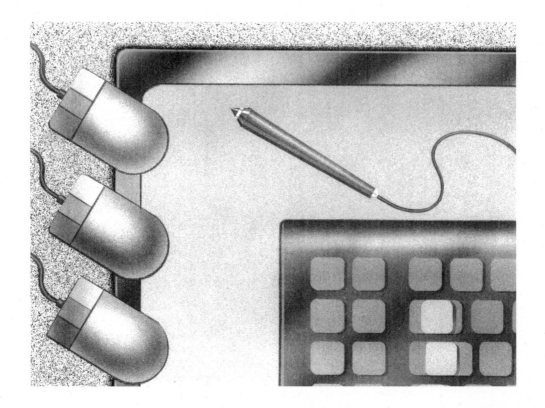

The input devices are the means by which you move information into your PC, the primary means by which you interact with your personal computer. The various available devices span an entire range of technologies, from the tactile to the vocal. Although they work in different ways, all accomplish the same task, allowing you to communicate with your computer.

The Keyboard

The primary input device for most computer systems is the keyboard, and until the time that voice recognition systems are perfected to the point they can recognize continuous speech, the dominance of the keyboard is not likely to change. As long as you're stuck with it, you might as well understand how it works.

IBM has offered nearly a dozen different keyboards with its variety of personal computers. Four really weren't mainstream products because two designs were meant only for the PCjr: one fit the short-lived Portable PC, one was designed particularly for the 3270 PC. The others marked a progression of adjustments in key layout and convenience features, including a smaller, more convenient alternative for crowded desks and versions for IBM's relaunched portable line.

The PC/XT Keyboard

Complaints began with the original PC/XT keyboard, introduced with the first PC (shown in fig. 11.1). Despite a vociferous outcry (primarily from the press) this design was kept as the IBM standard through the introduction of the AT, equipped as it was with a total of 83 keys. It put two vertical rows of function keys at the left of the main alphanumeric keypad, and forced cursor controls to share the same keypad with a calculator-style array of numbers for direct data entry. The Enter key was small and ambiguously identified with a bent arrow legend, and no indicators were provided for the three locking shift keys: Caps Lock, Num Lock, and Scroll Lock.

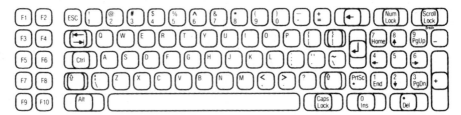

Figure 11.1. Layout of the original IBM PC and XT keyboards.

The complaints about the original design concerned mainly the layout of peripheral keys. The lefthand function keys did not correspond to the bottom-of-the-screen listings of function key assignments used by most programs. The lack of indicators led to a lot of mistypings of numbers for cursor movements and capital letters for lower case. Spreadsheets needed both a numeric keypad and cursor-control keys. Also, the Enter key was too small.

The AT Keyboard

After years of complaints in the press, IBM took heed and introduced a new keyboard layout with the AT. It had an additional key (Sys Rq, designed primarily for use with multiuser applications); enter was made bigger, Selectric-size; and indicators were provided for the locking Shift keys (see fig. 11.2.)

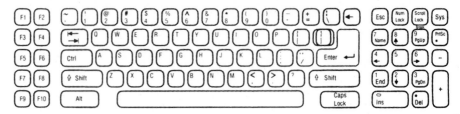

Figure 11.2. Original IBM AT keyboard layout.

In fact, the differences went much deeper. Unlike the PC keyboard, the AT keyboard was made programmable and was given its own set of commands, which could be relayed to it through the system unit. This fact alone made the AT keyboard incompatible with PC and XT system units. Although the connectors are the same, a PC/XT keyboard won't work when plugged into an AT, and an AT keyboard won't work when plugged into a PC or XT.

The IBM Advanced Keyboard

With the introduction of the upgraded AT, IBM also unleashed another new keyboard, termed the Advanced Keyboard by IBM but commonly also called the Enhanced Keyboard. Although electrically similar to the original AT product (to the extent that they can be plugged in interchangeably and it remains incompatible with PCs and XTs) the layout was altered again. The advance it made was a greater endowment of keys, to a total of 101 in the standard United States model. In international models, it gains one more (see fig. 11.3).

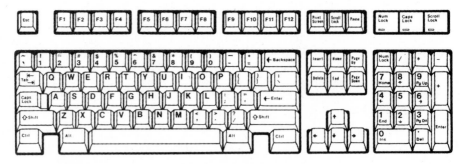

Figure 11.3. IBM advanced keyboard layout.

The key additions were several. A new, dedicated cursor-control pad was provided, separate from the combined numeric and cursor pad, and several other control keys were duplicated in another small pad. Two new function keys (F11 and F12) were added, and the whole dozen were moved to a top row, above and slightly separated from the alphanumeric area. Duplicate Ctrl and Alt keys were provided at either side of the space bar, and Caps Lock was moved to the former location of the Ctrl key.

One supposed blessing provided by the advanced design, the top row function keys, had been demanded by computer writers since the introduction of the PC. Finally, the function keys corresponded to the positions of on-screen key labels. The complainers soon learned that the left twin rows of function keys were much more convenient to use, particularly when needed in combination with Alt or Ctrl. What once could be done with one hand now required two.

Moreover, the relocated function keys proved to be more cumbersome to use. The smaller Enter key of the new design was more apt to be missed in fast typing. All in all, the keyboard was designed more for hunt-and-peck key bangers than proficient typists—probably the exact people who complained most loudly about the previous designs. In fact, probably the same people who complained that the letters are not arranged in alphabetic order.

PS/2 Keyboards

The PS/2 line universally uses the IBM Advanced Keyboard or a special reduced-size keyboard designed primarily for the tiny Model 25. The layout of the latter is shown in figure 11.4.

The only difference between the PS/2 and XT/AT Advanced Keyboards is the connector at the end of the removable cable. The PS/2 cable simply uses a miniature DIN connector in place of the standard DIN connector on PC/XT/AT keyboards. This cable is also removable so that you or IBM can substitute the proper cable to match the system you have.

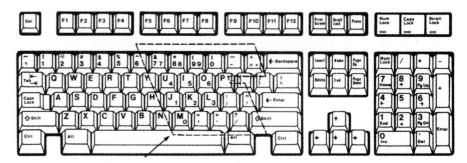

Figure 11.4. IBM Compact keyboard layout.

Compatible Keyboards

Compatible computer makers have striven to keep pace with IBM and have adapted their keyboards to the prevailing standard. Thus, they have followed suit in adopting the advanced design, its drawbacks notwithstanding. Some manufacturers have compounded the confusion created by IBM's troika of key layouts by adding their own subtle refinements, a complete elaboration of which would probably require a book of its own "Mystery of the Moving Keys." Anything out of the normal alphanumeric contingent is a candidate for roving anywhere around the keyboard.

One improvement made by many compatibles manufacturers is the inclusion of a compatibility switch, usually located on the bottom of the keyboard. The two positions of this switch allow you to select the electrical compatibility of the keyboard between the PC/XT and AT standards. One keyboard can thus be used with either type of system unit, providing you've put the switch in the correct position.

Several keyboards also include extra key caps to allow you to swap the position of the lefthand Ctrl and Caps Lock keys so that Ctrl falls in its more familiar position. The electrical relocation is handled either through another keyboard switch or through software that you must run on the host computer. Although these features cannot be added to an existing keyboard, they are worth looking for when buying a replacement.

Among non-standard keyboard designs introduced by third-party vendors are designs that offer a redundant set of function keys across the top of the board as well as in a pair of columns along the left side. Various designs have sought to isolate a set of cursor arrow keys from the numeric keypad.

Several manufacturers have introduced devices that incorporate a trackball or some altered form of a mouse to the keyboard itself. These keyboards include a special cable that incorporates both the keyboard wiring and a serial circuit for the mouse or trackball; the cables end with two plugs that must be attached to different ports on your computer. (On some machines which have keyboard ports on their front and serial ports on the back, this cabling arrangement can become a bit of a problem.)

Northgate is unusual among keyboard marketers in that it has designed some of its keyboards to work with the otherwise incompatible Tandy 1000 and AT&T 6300 models.

Some laptops offer ports that allow you to plug in a standard, full-sized keyboard when you are at your desk. A new breed of keyboards even get around the lack of such a port, connecting to laptops through the ubiquitous parallel port.

Keyboard Specifications

The standard spacing between keytops is 0.75 inches, measured from the center of each keytop to the next. Some tight laptops have tried to squeeze this down a bit. If you've got big hands, you're going to want a full-sized board.

Standard key travel—the distance a keytop must move to "make" a key—ranges from 3.5 to 4.5 millimeters for typical desktop models; laptops and notebooks and some standard boards have reduced key travel to the range of 2.5 to 3.8 mm. (0.14 to 0.18 inches.) Most keyboards require between 1.9 and 2.5 ounces of pressure to make contact.

Keyboard Technologies

No matter how their keys are arranged, all keyboards have the same function, detecting the keys pressed down by your fingers and relaying this information to your computer. Even though two keyboards may look identical, they may differ considerably in the manner in which they detect the motion of your fingers. The technology used for this process—how the keyboard works electrically—can affect the sturdiness and longevity of the keyboard.

Several technologies have been used for keyboards, ranging from the exotic (Hall-Effect switches, for example) to the mundane (switches that actually just switch). The two most common designs in PCs are the *capacitive* and *hard contact* keyboards.

Capacitive Keyboards

All the mainstream IBM keyboards—and those of the Portable PC and 3270 PC as well—are united by the sharing of a common mechanism: All operate using capacitive keyboard technology.

Capacitive keyboards are generally built around an etched circuit board. Two large areas of tin-and-nickel-plated copper form pads under each switch *station* (in keyboard terminology, each key is called a station). The pads of each pair are neither physically nor electrically connected to one another.

Pressing any key on the keyboard forces a circle of metalized plastic down, separating a pair of pads that lie just below the key plunger. Although the plastic backing of the circle prevents making a connection that would allow electricity to flow between the pads, the initial proximity of the pads results in a capacity change. Separating them causes a decrease in this capacitance change on the order of 20 to 24 picofarads decreasing to 2 to 6 picofarads. The reduction of capacitance causes a small but detectable current flow in the circuitry leading to the pads.

Some compatible capacitive keyboards do the opposite of the IBM design. Pressing the key pushes capacitive pads together and increases the capacitance. This backward process has the same effect, however. It alters the flow of current in a way that can be detected by the keyboard electronics.

A spring mechanism gives the IBM keyboard its tactile feel and delivers the infamous click of every keypress. The spring mechanism also returns the key to the top of its travel at the end of each keystroke. So called soft-touch keyboards often use foam as a spring mechanism and for cushioning the end of each keystroke.

Under control of a microprocessor (generally an 8048-series device in the most popular keyboards), all of the pads of the keyboard are scanned for current changes every few microseconds, and the minute current flow caused by a keystroke can be detected. Because there is a slight chance of random noise that could cause a current pulse similar to that generated by a keystroke, keyboards may require that the increased current flow be detected during two or more consecutive scans of the keyboard. (Although you might think scanning twice would slow things down, the entire check and verification operation occurs so quickly that some keyboards are capable of handling typing as fast as 300 characters per second—somewhat faster than the typical programmer or even the most rapid typist.)

After a keystroke has been detected, the microprocessor built into the keyboard then generates a scan code which indicates which key was struck. The scan code is then converted to serial data and relayed to the microprocessor in the computer's system unit.

Hard Contact Keyboards

The mechanism and electronics of the capacitive keyboard are relatively complicated and correspondingly expensive. A lower cost alternative is the hard contact design, such as was used in the two PCjr keyboard designs.

The PCjr was one of IBM's major errors in the PC marketplace, and the machine itself is all but consigned to the dust bin of history. However, there were a few unusual technologies employed in the machine worth examining. In the PCjr keyboard, each key operated as an individual switch. When you pressed down on a key, hard contact was made between the two poles of a switch. The connection conducted electricity which, detected through a matrix array, indicated which key was pressed.

The hard contact design required simpler circuitry to detect each keystroke, but still required a microprocessor to assign scan codes and serialize the data for transmission to the system unit.

The specific hard contact design of the PCjr keyboard was a marvel of simplicity. It was based on a molded rubber sheet which provided the spring action needed to return the keys to their rest positions as well as holding one of the contacts required for switching. This rubber was carefully tailored into domes which collapse under pressure in a controlled manner that gave a positive over-center action and feel to each key.

Many of the keyboards used by today's compatible computers are of a very similar hard contact design. Their advantage is low cost. Their primary disadvantage is that they may not last as long as capacitive keyboards. A common problem is that one key may deteriorate and suddenly get much stiffer, requiring greater pressure for activation than the rest. The solution to this problem is to get another keyboard.

Keytops

The most damning design aspect of the PCjr was probably its original keyboard which used small, tab-like keys termed chiclets (for the resemblance of the keys to the small, white, pillow-shaped, sugar-coated pieces of gum) by the derisive press. IBM's excuse for the radical design was that it allowed the use of templates with the keyboard, plastic or cardboard overlays which could be used to identify each key. Coincidentally, the smaller keys made the PCjr keyboard more difficult to type upon and eliminated any possibility that the low cost PCjr might replace the more expensive PC in business applications.

The updated PCjr keyboard, which was made available as a free upgrade, is electrically and mechanically identical to the original model. The only change was an increase in size of the keytops.

As with all other IBM designs, these keytops feature a concave cylindrical profile. A few non-IBM keyboards, primarily European products, have round, dish-shaped depressions in their keytops. The only difference is what feels best to you—and usually whatever is the most familiar feels best.

Cordless Keyboards

As a styling gimmick, IBM designed the PCjr keyboard to operate wirelessly. Two infrared-emitting LEDs on the rear edge of the keyboard sent out scan codes optically, which were then received by a photodetector embedded in the front panel of the PCjr system unit. When the keyboard was used in its wireless mode, it required four type-AA cells for power. For more reliable operation, IBM also offered a standard keyboard cable for the PCjr.

The PCjr keyboard cable used a telephone-style modular connector at the keyboard end and a Berg connector at the system-unit end. The Berg connector is difficult to obtain, thus making the manufacture of your own keyboard cable impractical. However, you can add extra length to it should your application (or desk arrangement) require simply by plugging in one or more standard telephone extension cables between the IBM cable and keyboard.

Key Layouts

QWERTY

Anyone new to typing will be amazed and perplexed at the seemingly nonsensical arrangement of letters on the keys of the typical computer keyboard. Even the name given to this esoteric layout has the ring of some kind of black magic or odd cabala—QWERTY. Simply a list of the first six characters of the top row of the nominal arrangement, the absurdity harks back to the keyboard of the first practical typewriter.

Actually, the first typewriter had its keys arranged alphabetically. But within a year of his invention, Christopher Sholes discovered what he viewed as a superior arrangement, the QWERTY system which is known and hated today.

Legend Debunked

A legend surrounds the QWERTY arrangements. According to the common myth, QWERTY came about because typists pounded on keys faster than the simple mechanisms of the first typewriters could handle the chore. The keys jammed. The odd QWERTY arrangement slowed down the typists and prevented the jams.

Sholes left no record of how he came upon the QWERTY arrangement, but it certainly was not to slow down speedy typists. High typing rates imply modern-day touch typing, 10 fingers flying across the keyboard. This style of typing did not arise until about 10 years after Sholes had settled on the QWERTY arrangement.

Other arguments about the QWERTY placement also lead to dead ends. For instance, breaking a strict alphabetic order to separate the keys and prevent the type bars (the levers which swing up to strike letters on paper) from jamming doesn't make sense because the arrangement of the typebars has no direct relationship to the arrangement of keys.

There is no doubt that the standard arrangement is not the only possible ordering of the alphabet—in fact, there are 26! (or 26 factorial, exactly 403,291,461,126,605,635,584,000,000) different possible arrangements of letters alone, not to mention the further complications of using rows of different lengths and non-alphabetic keys. But not only is QWERTY not the only possible layout, it's probably not the best.

Dvorak-Dealey Keyboard

The most familiar challenger to QWERTY, one that crawls in a distant second in popularity and use, is the Dvorak-Dealey letter arrangement, named for its developers, August Dvorak and William L. Dealey. The name is often shortened to Dvorak.

The Dvorak-Dealey design incorporates several ideas that should lead to faster typing. A basic goal is to foster the alternation of hands in typing—after you strike one letter with a key under a finger of your left hand, the next key you'll want to press will likely be under a right-hand finger. This hand alternation is a faster typing strategy. To make hand alternation more likely, the Dvorak-Dealey arrangement put all vowels in the home row under the lefthand's fingertips and the consonants used most often in the right hand's home row. Note that the Dvorak-Dealey arrangement was developed for speed and does nothing to make the keyboard more alphabetic or learning to use it easier (see fig. 11.5).

Figure 11.5. The Dvorak-Dealey key layout (as implemented in the PC-compatible Key Tronic KB 5150D).

The first publication of the Dvorak-Dealey keyboard was in the 1936 book *Typewriting Behavior*, authored by the developers of the new letter arrangement. To back up the philosophic and theoretical advantages attributed to the Dvorak-Dealey arrangement, tests were conducted in the '30s on mechanical typewriters, amounting to typing races between the QWERTY and Dvorak-Dealey key arrangements. Dvorak and Dealey ran the tests, and—not surprisingly—they came out the winner by factors as large as 30 percent.

Dvorak believed in both his keyboard and his test results and wrote papers promoting his ideas. Alas, the more he wrote, the greater his claims became. Articles like "There Is a Better Typewriter Keyboard" in the December, 1943, issue of *National Business Education Quarterly* has been called by some experts "full of factual errors." Tests run by the U.S. Navy and the General Accounting Office reported much more modest results for Dvorak.

Notwithstanding the exaggerated claims, the Dvorak layout does offer some potential advantages in typing speed, at least after you've become skilled in its use. The penalty for its increased typing throughput is increased difficulty in typing when confronted with a QWERTY keyboard.

The design of the PC makes converting to Dvorak relatively easy. While typewriters have to be redesigned for the new key arrangement, you can just plug a new keyboard into your PC. Commercial Dvorak keyboards are often available by special order.

In fact, if you don't mind your keytop legend bearing no likeness to the characters that actually appear on your screen (and in your files), you can simply reprogram your PC to think that it has a Dvorak keyboard by intercepting the signals sent by the keyboard to your computer and converting them on the fly.

Keyboard Use

Scan Codes

The internal microprocessor in all IBM keyboards identifies the keys that are pressed and converts the information so derived into scan codes, which are then sent serially to the host computer. Each press of a key generates two different scan codes—one when the key is pushed down and another when it pops back up. The two-code technique allows your computer system unit to tell when a key is pressed and held down—for example, when you hold down the Alt key while pressing a function key.

Each key generates a unique scan code. Even if the same legend appears on two keys, such as the duplicate number keys in the alpha-numeric and numeric-and-cursor keypads, the individual keys generate the same codes. The code for a given key is the same whether the Caps Lock or other Shift key is in effect. (Table 11.1 shows the scan codes sent by the keys of the different IBM keyboards.)

TABLE 11.1.
Scan Codes on
U.S. Keyboards

| Alphanumeric Key Area (all keyboards) | | |
Key	Make Code	Break Code
A	1E	9E
B	30	B0
C	2E	AE
D	20	A0
E	12	92
F	21	A1
G	22	A2
H	23	A3
I	17	97
J	24	A4
K	25	A5

Key	Make Code	Break Code
L	26	A6
M	32	B2
N	31	B1
O	18	98
P	19	99
Q	10	90
R	13	93
S	1F	9F
T	14	94
U	16	96
V	2F	AF
W	11	91
X	2D	AD
Y	15	95
Z	2C	AC
0 or)	0B	8B
1 or !	02	82
2 or @	03	83
3 or #	04	84
4 or $	05	85
5 or %	06	86
6 or ©	07	87
7 or &	08	88
8 or *	09	89
9 or (	0A	8A
• or ™	29	A9
- or _	0C	8C
= or +	0D	8D
[or §	1A	9A
] or †	1B	9B
¶ or ®	2B	AB
; or :	27	A7
' or "	28	A8
, or <	33	B3
/ or ?	35	B5
Left Shift	2A	AA
Left Ctrl	1D	9D

continues

TABLE 11.1.
continued

Key	Make Code	Break Code
Left Alt	38	B8
Right Shift	36	B6
Right Alt	E0 38	E0 B8
Right Ctrl	E0 1D	E0 9D
Caps Lock	3A	BA
Backspace	0E	8E
Tab	0F	8F
Space bar	39	B9
Enter	1C	9C

Numeric/Cursor Keypad Key	Make Code	Break Code
Scroll Lock	46	C6
Num Lock	45	C5
*	37	B7
–	4A	CA
+	4E	CE
Enter	E0 1C	E0 9C
1 or End	4F	CF
2	50	D0
3 or Pg Dn	51	D1
4	4B	CB
5	4C	CC
6	4D	CD
7 or Home	47	C7
8	48	C8
9 or PgUp	49	C9
0 or Ins	52	D2
Num Lock	E0 35	E0 B5

NOTE: *When the keyboard is in a shifted state, the make code of the Num Lock key changes to AA, and the break code changes to E0 B5 2A.*

Function Keys (F11 and F12 on Advanced and Compact keyboards only) Key	Make Code	Break Code
Esc	01	81
F1	3B	BB
F2	3C	BC

Key	Make Code	Break Code
F3	3D	BD
F4	3E	BE
F5	3F	BF
F6	40	C0

Key	Make Code	Break Code
F7	41	C1
F8	42	C2
F9	43	C3
F10	44	C4
F11	57	D7
F12	58	D8

Dedicated Cursor Area and Related Keys (Advanced and Compact Keyboards)		
Key	Make Code	Break Code
Up arrow	E0 48	E0 C8
Down arrow	E0 50	E0 D0
Left arrow	E0 4B	E0 CB
Right arrow	E0 4D	E0 CD
Insert	E0 52	E0 D2
Home	E0 47	E0 C7
Page Up	E0 49	E0 C9
Delete	E0 53	E0 D3
End	E0 4F	E0 CF

NOTE: *The keys send out different scan code when the keyboard is in a Shifted or Num Lock condition, effectively cancelling the effect of the locked Shift. That is, when the key is Shifted, its scan code is preceded by E0 AA, mimicking the effect of pressing Shift before the key and temporarily nullifying the Shift. The break code is followed by E0 2A, restoring the keyboard back to its Shifted condition. Similarly, when the keyboard is in Num Lock state, the make codes of these keys are preceded by E0 2A, and the break codes are followed by E0 AA.*

Page Down	E0 51	E0 D1
Scroll Lock	46	C6
Pause	E1 1D E1 9D C5	[None—Make only]
Print Screen	E0 2A E0 37	E0 B7 E0 AA

continues

TABLE 11.1.
continued

NOTE: *When the keyboard is in a Shifted state or the Ctrl key is held down when the Print Screen key is pressed, it sends out a make code of E0 37 and a break code of E0 B7. When the Alt key is held down, the make code of Print Screen becomes 54, and the break code becomes D4. The Pause key also acts differently in the shifted or Ctrl state, sending out the make code E0 46 E0 C6.*

| Embedded Cursor Keypad (Compact keyboard only) | | |
Key	Make Code	Break Code
; or : or *	37	B7
- or _	4A	CA
= or +	4E	CE
J or 1	4F	CF
K or 2	50	D0
L or 3	51	D1
U or 4	4B	CB
I or 5	4C	CC
O or 6	4D	CD
7 or &	47	C7
8 or *	48	C8
9 or (	49	C9
0 or)	52	D2

NOTE: *When Shift is active, the Scroll Lock key sends a scan code of 45 C5, which switches on the embedded numeric keypad on the Compact Keyboard. The scan keys of the following keys change to the indicated values during this state.*

Your computer receives these scan codes at a special I/O port. When a scan code is received by your computer, the keyboard controller chip notifies the microprocessor that a scan code is available to be read by issuing an interrupt. When that happens, your computer sorts through the scan codes and figures out which keys are pressed and in which combination. The program code for doing this is part of your system's BIOS. The computer remembers the condition of the locking Shift keys by changing special memory locations, called *status bytes* to reflect each change made in their condition.

Normally, you do not have to deal with scan codes. The computer makes the translation to numbers and letters automatically and invisibly. The converted information is used in generating the information that appears on your monitor screen, and it is also made available to the applications you run and even the programs you write. Sometimes, however, when you write your own programs, it is useful to detect every key change. You may, for example, want to cause something to happen when a certain key combination is pressed. Your program only needs to read the keyboard-input port and to compare what it finds there to a scan-code chart.

Keyboard Cabling

The scan codes are sent from the keyboard to your computer serially so only one wire conductor is needed to convey the *keyboard data* information. A second conductor is required to serve as a return path for the data signal, and, as a *ground*, it serves as common return for all the other circuits in the keyboard cable. To synchronize the logic in the keyboard with that in your computer, a separate wire is used for a keyboard clock signal. A fourth and final wire is used to supply the keyboard with the five-volt direct current power that it needs to operate. These four conductors are all that is necessary to link keyboard to computer.

Most PCs use standard five-pin DIN connectors for their keyboard connection. Pin 1 is assigned the keyboard clock; 2, keyboard data; 4, the ground; 5, the five volt electrical supply. One of the connections provided by the keyboard plug (pin 3) is assigned to carry a signal to reset the keyboard, but it is normally not used and need not be connected in normal keyboard cabling (see fig. 11.6).

Advanced keyboards generally use a modular (AMP) connector on the rear of the keyboard, allowing the cable itself to be easily replaced. The removable cable also allows one keyboard to serve both the old AT line and the new PS/2 line, which use different system-board input connectors. It has the following assignments: A, reserved; B, keyboard data; C, ground; D, keyboard clock; E, five volts; and F, reserved. When looking at the gold contacts of the connector, the contacts are labeled in reverse alphabetical order from left to right. Figure 11.7 shows the connector for the Advanced keyboards.

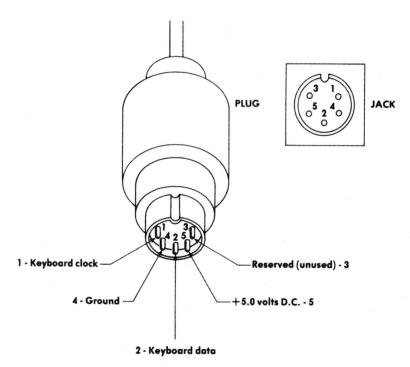

PLUG

JACK

1 - Keyboard clock

Reserved (unused) - 3

4 - Ground

+5.0 volts D.C. - 5

2 - Keyboard data

Figure 11.6. IBM PC, XT, AT keyboard connectors, 5-pin DIN connector.

PS/2s use different wire assignment in their six-pin miniature DIN connectors: Pin 1 is assigned keyboard data; pin 3, ground; pin 4, five volts; and pin 5, keyboard clock. Pins 2 and 6 are reserved, and the shield is attached as a chassis ground (see fig. 11.8).

Making a Keyboard Extension Cable

If you want to get away from your computer, you can lengthen the cable running between it and the keyboard that you've got to keep under your hands. Such keyboard extension cables are available in various lengths, already assembled, for prices that range from reasonable to outrageous.

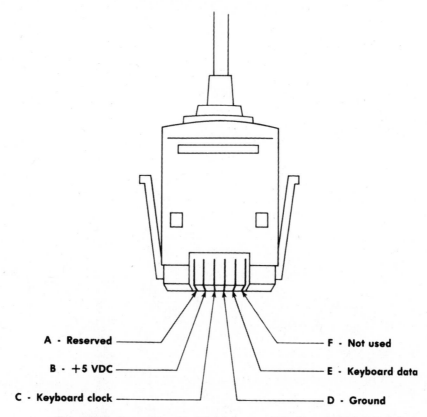

Figure 11.7. Connector for IBM Advanced Keyboards SDL (Modular) connector.

If you can't find a length that you want or refuse to pay five times what it would cost you to make your own extension cable, you can manufacture your own without much trouble. The 5-pin DIN connectors are available at Radio Shack. The part numbers are as follows: 5-pin plug (male), 274-003; 5-pin inline jack (female), 274-006; and 5-pin chassis mounting jack (female), 274-005. Each costs about $2.

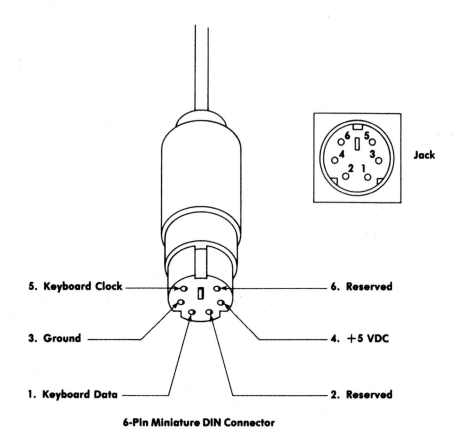

6-Pin Miniature DIN Connector

Figure 11.8. IBM PS/2 keyboard connector.

Although almost any wire will work, a shielded cable will reduce radio interference; one that uses stranded (as opposed to solid) conductors is recommended because stranded conductors withstand repeated flexure much better than solid wires.

You can cut the amount of soldering you must do in half and get exactly the right shielded, stranded cable by using Radio Shack's molded DIN patch cord (part number 42-2151) for your keyboard extension wiring. Although this cable has a male connector at each end, you can simply lop off one end of the cable and solder a female connector in its stead. These patch cords also work well as MIDI (Musical Instrument Digital Interface) cables.

Making extension cables for PS/2s is more difficult because miniature DIN plugs are more difficult to find. You may have to order them from a specialty electronics dealer.

Because IBM keyboards were not designed to be frugal with power—Advanced Keyboard, for instance, consumes 275 milliamps—the length of extension cable you can add is somewhat limited no matter the style of keyboard you're working with. The smaller gauge the cable (the higher the gauge number), the shorter the extension cable must be. Telephone cables have very little current capacity and their range is the most limited. Should the cable be too long, your keyboard will work erratically or not at all. If you want to make a really long cable, you'll have to experiment to prove its reliability.

Mice

For many people, the keyboard is the most formidable and forbidding aspect of a PC. It, as well as the uninformative and unforgiving user interface of DOS and OS/2 Version 1.0, are the major elements that alienate new PC users.

In an effort to make the computer more accessible, Douglas C. Engelbert of the Augmentation Research Center of the Stanford Research Laboratory developed a graphical/menu-driven on-screen user interface coupled to a special pointing device between 1957 and 1977. The pointing device allowed the user to indicate which menu selection he wanted by physically moving the device, which caused a corresponding on-screen movement of the cursor. One or more buttons atop the device allowed the user to indicate he wished to select a menu item.

The device was small enough to fit under the palm of a hand with the button under a fingertip. With a cord connecting the device to its computer host trailing like a tail, and the device's characteristic scurrying around the desktop to carry out its function, it quickly earned the name mouse. The whole process of moving the mouse and its on-screen representation is termed dragging the mouse.

The mouse idea was further developed by the Palo Alto Research Center of Xerox Corporation during the 1970s. Apple Computer, understanding the need to make computers easier to use to make them more accessible, incorporated the best of the Palo Alto ideas into its Macintosh, including the mouse, in 1983. IBM, more performance than ease-of-entry oriented, only made the mouse a built-in feature of its personal computers with the introduction of the Micro Channel PS/2 line, each machine of which incorporates a special *mouse port* in its planar board circuitry.

Clicking

In addition to the movement of the on-screen cursor, the mouse also has a function that enables it to select or identify elements of the screen. This process is called *clicking*. A "click" means a single, quick press of the left button, or a "double click," which means two quick presses of the left button. Generally you can adjust software parameters to determine just how quickly you must press the button for the action to be interpreted as a double click. If you leave too much time between clicks the application will assume you meant two single clicks.

In general, to drag an object—to move a screen icon from one place to another—you place the cursor or pointer on top of the object and hold down the left button while moving the mouse across the desktop. Except for a few newer products, or custom interfaces provided by the mouse vendor, most applications read only the left mouse button, even if the hardware has three or more buttons.

Mice can be distinguished by three chief differences—the number of buttons, the technology they use, and the manner in which they connect with their computer hosts.

Mouse Buttons

In purest form, the mouse has exactly one pushbutton. Movement of the mouse determines the position of the on-screen cursor, but a selection is made only when that button is pressed, preventing any menu selections that the mouse is inadvertently dragged across from being chosen.

One button is the least confusing arrangement and the minimum necessary to carry out mouse functions. Operating the computer is reduced to nothing more than whether you press the button or not. Carefully tailored menu selections will allow the single button to suffice in controlling all computer functions.

Two buttons allow more flexibility, however. For instance, one can be given a "Do" function and a second, "Undo" function. In a drawing program, one might "lower" the pen analog that traces lines across the screen while the other "lifts" the pen.

Of course, three buttons would be even better because the programmer would have more flexibility still. Or, possibly, four buttons would—but as the number of mouse buttons rises, the mouse becomes increasingly like a keyboard. It becomes a more formidable device with a more rigorous learning curve. A profusion of mouse buttons is counterproductive.

Three buttons is the practical limit because three positions are available for index, middle, and ring fingers while the thumb and pinkie grab the sides of the mouse. Most applications use two or fewer buttons, and the most popular mice are the two-button variety. There's nothing wrong with three-button mice—they can do everything two-button mice can and more—but most applications don't require the extra button.

The buttons you press as well as the movement of the mouse are relayed to your computer as a series of codes. (Figures 11.9 through 11.11 shows the codes used by many popular mice.)

The data arrives in the computer as a series of pulses that must be interpreted for correct movement. This is done by the interface or driver software that is loaded into memory with a DOS-level command, Microsoft Windows or as part of an application that supports the particular device you are using.

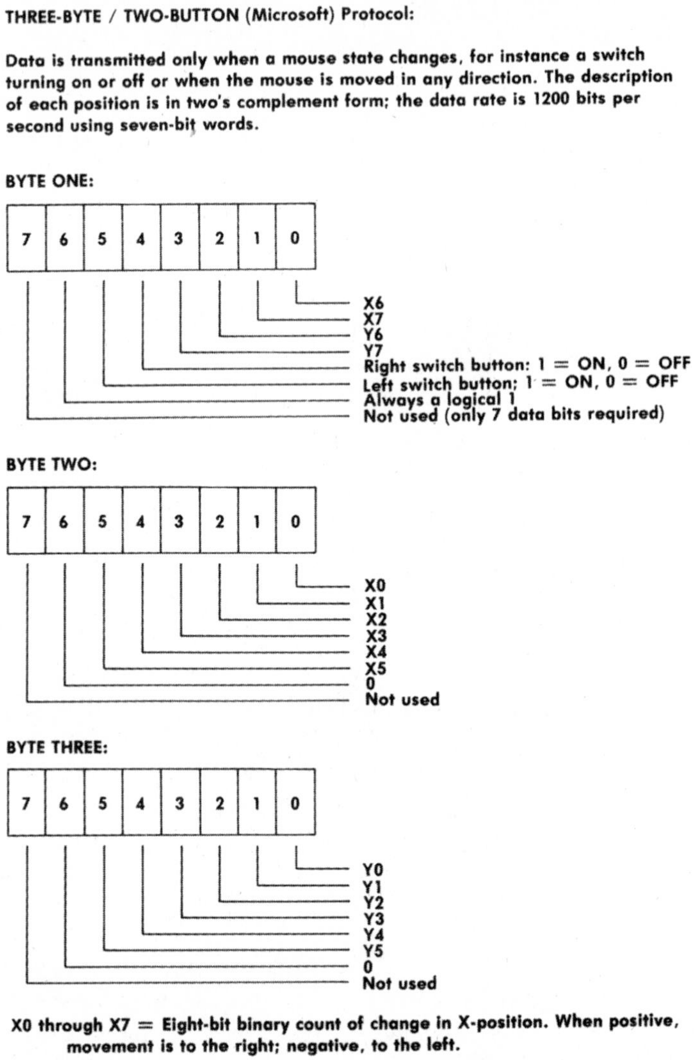

THREE-BYTE / TWO-BUTTON (Microsoft) Protocol:

Data is transmitted only when a mouse state changes, for instance a switch turning on or off or when the mouse is moved in any direction. The description of each position is in two's complement form; the data rate is 1200 bits per second using seven-bit words.

BYTE ONE:

```
7  6  5  4  3  2  1  0
                     └─── X6
                  └────── X7
               └───────── Y6
            └──────────── Y7
         └─────────────── Right switch button: 1 = ON, 0 = OFF
      └────────────────── Left switch button: 1 = ON, 0 = OFF
   └───────────────────── Always a logical 1
└──────────────────────── Not used (only 7 data bits required)
```

BYTE TWO:

```
7  6  5  4  3  2  1  0
                     └─── X0
                  └────── X1
               └───────── X2
            └──────────── X3
         └─────────────── X4
      └────────────────── X5
   └───────────────────── 0
└──────────────────────── Not used
```

BYTE THREE:

```
7  6  5  4  3  2  1  0
                     └─── Y0
                  └────── Y1
               └───────── Y2
            └──────────── Y3
         └─────────────── Y4
      └────────────────── Y5
   └───────────────────── 0
└──────────────────────── Not used
```

X0 through X7 = Eight-bit binary count of change in X-position. When positive, movement is to the right; negative, to the left.

Figure 11.9. Mouse control codes (courtesy of MSC Technologies, Inc.).

Y0 through Y7 = Eight-bit binary count of change in Y-position. When positive, movement is downward; negative indicates upward.

FIVE-BYTE / THREE-BUTTON (MSC Technologies) Protocol:

Five bytes are used as a data block. The beginning of the data block is indicated by a sync byte the first five bits of which are always 10000 (binary). The remaining three bits code the state of the three mouse pushbuttons. The next four bytes encode the change in the mouse's position since the last data block. The second and third bytes encode the change in the X- and Y-positions of the mouse since the last data block; the fourth and fifth byte encode the change in X- and Y-positions since the readings given in the second and third bytes. In effect, each data block encodes two changes of mouse position as two's complement, 8-bit binary numbers.

X7 and Y7 define the direction of mouse travel. When X7 is 0, it indicates motion to the right; Y7 at 0 indicates motion upward or in the direction of the mouse cord.

Codes are transmitted as eight-bit words at 1200 bits per second with no parity.

BYTE ONE:

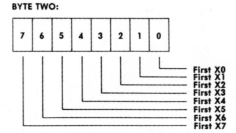

BYTE TWO:

Figure 11.10. Mouse control codes (courtesy of MSC Technologies, Inc.).

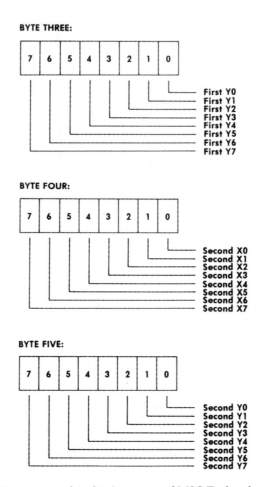

BYTE THREE:

| 7 | 6 | 5 | 4 | 3 | 2 | 1 | 0 |

First Y0
First Y1
First Y2
First Y3
First Y4
First Y5
First Y6
First Y7

BYTE FOUR:

| 7 | 6 | 5 | 4 | 3 | 2 | 1 | 0 |

Second X0
Second X1
Second X2
Second X3
Second X4
Second X5
Second X6
Second X7

BYTE FIVE:

| 7 | 6 | 5 | 4 | 3 | 2 | 1 | 0 |

Second Y0
Second Y1
Second Y2
Second Y3
Second Y4
Second Y5
Second Y6
Second Y7

Figure 11.11. Mouse control codes (courtesy of MSC Technologies, Inc.).

The Microsoft driver standard is the predominate definition; most alternate input devices, though they may offer their own standard as an "improved" alternate, are also Microsoft compliant. Microsoft provides software developers a mouse function library with 35 routines that can be accessed from many high-level languages. In addition, the Microsoft driver can be accessed directly by any language or application that can place calls to DOS interrupt 33H.

Among the functions supported by Microsoft-compliant mouse drivers are as follows:

Mouse Reset and Status

Show Cursor

Hide Cursor

Get Button Status and Mouse Position

Get Button Press Information

Read Mouse Motion Counters

Set Mouse Sensitivity

By the way, lefties: most mouse drivers will allow you to remap the buttons on the mouse to your preference.

Mechanical Mice

The first mouse was a mechanical design. It was based on a small ball that protruded through its bottom and rotated as the mouse was pushed along a surface. The ball rests loosely in a chamber bounded by sensing rollers.

As the mouse is moved along the desktop the ball touches the rollers (Microsoft calls theirs "shafts") which cause copper contacts, or brushes, to sweep across a segmented conductor. In function, the arrangement is similar to the brushes in an electric motor, except the rotating contacts inside a mouse are circuit board lands. The conducting strips are attached to a circular board in a spoke-like arrangement. The conducting wheel is called an "encoder." As the moving conductor steps across the segmented contacts, electrical impulses are generated and counted in the attached electronic circuitry.

The impulses can be either negative or positive, depending on the direction of rotation. The polarity of the pulses tells the electronics what direction the mouse is moving, and the speed of the pulses shows how fast the mouse is moving.

The two rollers inside the mouse ball cavity are opposed at 90-degrees to each other to measure horizontal and vertical movement. When both rollers are turning, the movement is oblique, and the electronics can interpret the relative speed and polarity of the pulses to compute the precise direction of movement.

One or more microswitches are used to accept the clicks that tell an application what is being selected. A switch closure is measured as a simple off or on condition. One quick closure is a single click; two closures in quick succession constitute a double click.

Although the ball is free to rotate in any direction, only four directions are detected, corresponding to two axes of a two-dimensional coordinate system. The movement in each of the four directions is quantified (in hundredths of an inch) and sent to the host as a discrete signal for each discrete increment of movement.

The mechanical mouse works on just about any surface. In general, the rotating ball has a coarse texture and is made from a rubbery compound that even gets a grip on smooth surfaces. In fact, you can even pick up a mechanical mouse and spin the ball with your finger (although you'll then have difficulty fingering the pushbuttons!)

On the other hand, the mechanical mouse requires that you move it across a surface of some kind, and all too many desks don't have enough free space to give the mouse a good run. (Of course, if all else fails, you can run a mechanical mouse across your pants leg or skirt, but you're likely to get some odd looks.) In addition, mechanical parts can break. A mechanical mouse tends to pick up dirt and lint that can impede its proper operation. You'll want to regularly clean your mechanical mouse even if you think your desktop is spotless.

Mechanical mice are made and sold by a number of companies, including IBM, Logitech, and Microsoft.

Optical Mice

The alternative technology to the mechanical mouse is the optical mouse. Instead of a rotating ball, the optical mouse uses a light beam to detect movement across a specially patterned *mouse pad*. No moving parts means that the optical mouse has less to get dirty or break.

The most popular optical mouse is made by MSC Corporation (at one time Mouse Systems Corporation, hence the name). The MSC mouse uses two pair of LEDs and photodetectors on its bottom, one pair oriented at right angles to the other. Its matching mouse pad is coated with an overlapped pattern of blue and yellow grids. Each pair of LEDs and photodetectors detects motion in either direction across one axis of the grid.

The light reflected from the pad bounces onto a small receptor inside the mouse, in some designs moving through a prism or lens onto a mirror which in turn reflects the light into a sensor. The reflective pad is segmented into a very fine grid of lines. As the mouse moves across these lines, the internal electronics reads the change in light, counting the pulses.

When the pulses are received and counted, the optical mouse functions like the mechanical and opto-mechanical designs. However, because there is no mechanical component as you move the optical mouse, it will feel decidedly different in your hand than the other designs. A felt-like covering on the bottom of the mouse makes it easy to slide across the plastic-coated mouse pad.

The big disadvantage of the optical mouse is that it does require you to use its special mouse pad. However, you have to put the pad somewhere, so you always have a place for your mouse to run. The pad itself can get dirty and can be damaged. The plastic coating can stick to your bare forearm on a humid day and lift off in sheets. In a normal, air-conditioned office environment, however, it should prove long-lasting and trouble-free.

Opto-Mechanical Mice

The opto-mechanical mouse is a hybrid design that falls between straight mechanical and straight optical. In this design the mechanical ball turns rollers as with the straight mechanical mouse, but instead of using mechanical electrical contacts, the opto-mechanical design rotates slotted or perforated wheels. An LED (light emitting diode) shines through the wheel and optical sensors count the resulting pulses.

The opto-mechanical mouse feels essentially the same in your hand as the straight mechanical design, and the function of the internal electronics is essentially the same. The difference is the way the electronic pulses are generated.

Serial Mice

In order to communicate its codes to your computer, the mouse must in some way be connected. Micro Channel PS/2s make the connection easy by providing a dedicated mouse port. PCs and many compatibles, however, have no such provision.

Most mice adapt to a port that is generally available, the standard serial port. Called serial mice, they simply plug in and deliver their movement codes to the serial port. Driver software for operating the mouse can give the mouse priority by generating an interrupt whenever a new mouse movement code appears at the port. The driver then passes along the mouse code to the software that is in control.

Advantages of serial mice include the fact that they readily plug into an existing port on most computers; this is also a disadvantage for some users who may already have modems, desktop networks, printers and other devices connected to serial outlets. Serial mice can easily be moved from one machine to another, as long as the appropriate driver software is installed on each computer.

Bus Mice

A serial connection works very well except for one problem: PCs that face a two-serial port limit may not have enough connections available to bring a mouse to life. The alternative is attaching the mouse to a dedicated mouse adapter that plugs into your computer's expansion bus. These so-called bus mice work identically with serial mice except they may use their own dedicated ports.

In most cases, these special mouse ports conform to the RS-232 standard and act just like serial ports except that they cannot be directly accessed by DOS because the operating system doesn't know what I/O addresses the port is assigned to. Otherwise, a bus mouse is just like any other mouse. It can use optical or mechanical technology and have any number of buttons.

If you have a spare serial port, you'll probably want a serial mouse because you pay extra for the bus mouse's adapter card. If you're short on serial ports, however, you'll likely want a bus mouse. The IBM PS/2 mouse is simply a bus mouse with the adapter built into the host computer.

Wireless Mice

Yet another variant of connection from the mouse to the computer is one that uses no connection at all: wireless mice. These devices are standard mechanical or optical units that send their codes to the computer using low-powered radio transmissions or infrared signals.

A wireless mouse is supposed to free the user from the relatively minor constraint of having a wire snake across the desk. It also would be of value in making a presentation from a lectern at a short distance from the computer.

Infrared technologies are cheaper to implement than radio systems, but they require an unobstructed path from the transmitter (the mouse) and the receiver (a box at the computer that plugs into a serial or bus port.) Infrared signals—like those used in television and VCR controllers—are good up to about 15 feet away from the receiver. The signals can be bounced off ceilings or walls if necessary.

Radio systems allow the receiver to be hidden, and there is no need for line-of-sight pathways for the signal.

Trackballs

Think of a trackball as an upside down mouse. Like the mouse, the ball rests loosely in a cavity where the moving ball causes sensors to move, tracking horizontal and vertical movement. The advantage of a trackball is that it can be incorporated into a keyboard platform, eliminating the need for extra desk space. Instead of moving the hardware across the desk, you use your hand to spin the ball. Your hand moves instead of the hardware.

One design of trackball gives you a large palm-sized ball to move, with small amounts of on-screen movement for large spins of the ball. An alternate design gives a small marble-like ball which yields greater cursor movement with fewer rotations.

Variations of trackballs are used in some designs of small clip-on mice intended to be used with laptop and notebook computers.

An important feature to look for in a trackball is a Drag/Lock button or function. This allows you to roll the ball without having to keep a finger on the trackball's button as you drag an element from one portion of the screen to another.

Joysticks

A joystick works essentially the same as a mouse, with separate sensors to monitor horizontal and vertical movement. Generally, instead of rollers, the joystick uses pressure-sensitive electronics or mechanical potentiometers which vary voltage by changing resistance in an electronic circuit.

Resolution

Resolution is the ability of an input device to interpret small distances. Newer mice designs generally support 400 points per inch (ppi) resolution, double that of earlier models. Some products even support resolutions of 700, 1,000 or more ppi, but beyond about 700 ppi, the device becomes almost too sensitive for the average user, particularly with VGA-quality or lower resolution screens.

Higher resolution with a mechanical or opto-mechanical mouse is based on more holes in the light wheel or more physical segments for the mechanical brush to pass over. Resolution with an optical mouse is determined by the spacing between the horizontal and vertical grid lines and the ability of the mouse electronics to read the grid.

In addition, some vendors change effective resolution—though not physical resolution—through software routines. By counting the actual pulses, then interpolating what would fall between the physical pulses, higher resolution performance can be simulated.

Resolution is more important in some applications than others. Using a mouse for word processing or a spreadsheet requires only the ability to move the cursor to a letter or a cell, both relatively coarse selections. If you are manipulating graphics, however, higher resolution could be important.

One difference you will notice quickly between a low resolution and a high resolution mouse, assuming everything else stays the same, is the speed of onscreen movement. The high resolution mouse seems much more sensitive, much quicker.

Many input devices let you vary the sensitivity—the relationship between the distance moved on the desktop and the distance moved on the screen. A higher sensitivity means that a smaller movement is required to move the pointer farther on the screen.

Similarly, acceleration usually can be varied through software settings. Acceleration is the relationship between the speed and distance of mouse movement and the speed and distance of cursor movement. As you move the physical mouse faster the onscreen pointer or cursor moves farther with each pulse received; cursor distance is reduced as the mouse slows down.

Light Pens

Sometimes, what you want to do with your computer is so obvious you could just point at the screen. If only you could move things around by pointing at them, you'd have instant, easy control.

A *light pen* lets you do exactly that. Shaped like a pen, but trailing a cord, the light pen lets your computer register positions on the screen when you point at them. The trick is inside the pen: At the tip is a photodetector that can detect changes in brightness; the picture tube in a computer monitor is lit by a scanning electron beam that lights tiny patches on the screen by scanning them back-and-forth and top-to-bottom. As each patch of the screen is struck by the beam, it briefly glows. The beam repeats its scan of the tube face so quickly—50 to 70 times a second—that although it appears continuously lit the sharp eye of the light pen knows that it is not.

The light pen registers the instant the patch on the screen lights up and then signals to your computer at that instant. Your computer can figure out exactly where the pen is because it knows where the scanning electron beam is all the time. From the light pen, then, the computer can tell where you are pointing on the screen.

You can use the light pen for anything that requires pointing. For example, with a painting program, you can draw on your monitor screen with a light pen as if it were filled with ink and the screen were paper. The light pen is used in graphic editing so that artists need only point to the screen or circle design elements they want to change or move.

All in all, the light pen is a wonderful idea but one that is inefficient, of low resolution limited to the sharpness that your monitor can display, and it makes your arm tired when you stretch it toward the screen all day long.

IBM provides an interface for a light pen on its graphics display adapters used with PCs, XTs, and ATs. The connector is simply a header on the card itself, requiring you to route a cable from inside the computer outside to the light pen. The light pen interface is not included on the IBM Monochrome Display Adapter because most light pens won't work with the IBM monochrome display. The lingering glow of the IBM green screens does not give the sharp on-off transition that the light pen needs to detect its position on the screen.

By itself, the light pen does little that's useful. It simply provides a signal at an input/output port, and it's up to your software to figure out what to do with the signal. To make a light pen useful, you'll need a special software driver or an application that is specifically written to use a light pen.

Touch Screens

Pointing is so natural (if impolite) that other technologies have been developed to exploit this human ability for data processing control. The most natural pointing device is, of course, the index finger and, in decreasing order of preference, the other four digits. Giving the computer some means of detecting what a finger is aiming at would turn the humble appendage into a true digital interface.

The *touch screen* is designed for exactly that purpose. This technology can detect the presence and location of a finger on or near the display screen of the computer. At least two methods of finger-detection have been employed. One form relies on actual contact with the surface of the screen to capacitively detect the presence of the finger. Another, used by Hewlett-Packard's Touch-Screen system, uses a special frame around the screen. This frame lines two perpendicular sides of the screen with LEDs emitting invisible light and on the two sides opposite with photodetectors. A finger approaching the screen breaks the constant light beam and allows the computer to determine its location.

Although a very natural interface, touch screen technology suffers its own logistical problems. As with light pens, reaching to the screen to perform normal daily work is a great way to build biceps and triceps, and otherwise tire yourself out. You're also apt to cover your screen with oily smudges, and if you share your computer with others less kempt than yourself, unknown contaminants and organisms.

The biggest problem with touch screen is the very practical matter of accuracy. Whereas light pens can zero in on any given pixel, the touch screen is much patchier in its pointing abilities. The screen is divided into a checkerboard pattern with resolution of about 16 x 16. While the touch screen can be used for making menu choices, it is hardly adequate for drawing or graphic editing on screen.

Touch screens have been effectively used to interface computers with a general public not versed in the intricacies of computing, enabling them to point at the function they wish to carry out. However, for a skilled computer user, the touch screen may be an exotic aberration.

Pen Computing

In theory, pen computers dispense with the cursor keys, mice, and keyboards and allow you to make your notes into information the computer can digest. The technology is just beginning to make its way out of the laboratories and onto the market; in some ways it is a solution in search of a problem.

Pen computers are based on an adapted operating system (DOS- or Windows-based) that recognizes pen movements that are called *gestures*. An important distinction can be drawn between programs that translate handwritten characters into computer-stored characters equivalent to keystrokes, and those systems that save an image of the handwriting as a vector-based graphic. The graphic programs treat the screen as an electronic piece of paper and the scratches you place upon it as "ink."

Although the character-recognition systems are supposed to be able to convert your writing to printed alphanumeric characters, the first implementations promised only about a 98-percent success rate per letter or number. That's not as good as it sounds; with five characters in an average word, we're talking about a true word-recognition rate of about 90 percent. Put another way, one out of 10 words will be misread.

On the plus side, designers say they expect the best uses of the pen computers will be in checklist applications such as inventory systems.

Hedging their bets, many pen computer makers offer systems that include keyboards or will work with an external one that can be plugged into a port.

Pen Operating Systems

The two major control programs for use with pen pointing devices are Microsoft's Windows for Pen Computing and GO Corp.'s PenPoint.

Windows for Pen Computing is a natural if you want to add pen pointing and handwriting recognition to an existing application running under Microsoft Windows. It will work with all of the huge number of printer drivers and other devices already designed for Windows. Files created with the pen operating system will work directly with standard Windows.

The Microsoft implementation includes a system to "train" the computer to recognize your handwriting.

PenPoint, which is preinstalled on a number of early pen-based systems, treats documents as if they were the pages of a notebook. Selecting a page will open the associated application under which it was created. The operating system is not compatible with DOS; files created under PenPoint must be converted before they can be run on another machine.

Alternative Input Devices

Manufacturers continue to search out other ways to give your computer a hand. The two biggest players in this market are Microsoft and IBM.

IBM's PS/2 Trackpoint is a small mouse/trackball for use in tight spaces. Microsoft's BallPoint Mouse clips onto the side of laptop keyboards for pointing purposes.

The ProHance Powermouse includes a full numeric keypad; Backspace and Escape keys; custom keys such as Menu, File, and Format; as well as 10 programmable keys with a template than can change functions with the applications.

Calcomp's Wiz is a combination mouse and graphics pad with multi-colored overlays for a range of applications. The mouse has six buttons and is capable of 1000 dot per inch (dpi) resolution). In addition, you can add an optional pen.

Key Tronic Corporation, a leading American keyboard maker, offers its "KeyMouse," a keyboard that includes a special grid-based switch for one of the character keys—usually the letter "J." When you turn on the mouse mode, this key becomes sensitive to directional pressure and moves a cursor around the screen like a mouse. Other implementations dedicate a special key to the mouse function.

Grid Systems Corporation is among the leaders in providing alternate input support for its portable and laptop machines. The GridPAD computer, for example, is packaged in a 9 x 12 inch box that's just over an inch thick. The top of the box is a drawing screen that uses an electronic pen for input. Users can write directly on the screen to fill out electronic facsimiles of business forms.

Another unusual Grid product is the Isopoint pointing device built into the keyboard below the spacebar on some models. The "Tootsie Roll" device is designed to roll and slide with the thumbs. It is a short cylinder that rests in a rectangular carrier parallel to the space bar. As you roll the cylinder up and back the cursor or pointer moves up and down on the screen; when you slide the cylinder to the right or left, the cursor moves accordingly. You press anywhere on the Isopoint to press the mouse button.

Interrupted Work

Every input/output device on a standard ISA bus computer requires an I/O address and an IRQ (interrupt request) setting so that the micro-processor knows where to look and what to do with the information. (Micro Channel and EISA boards are intelligent enough to handle these assignments by themselves.)

The I/O address, the device's location in memory, is expressed as a hexadecimal number. The IRQ is the wake-up call that a device sends to the processor.

Machines based on 286, 386 and 486 chips have 16 IRQs available; they are numbered from 0 to 15. Older 8088- and 8086-based ma-chines have just 8 IRQs, numbered from 0 to 7. If you use an 8-bit card in a 16-bit machine, you must assign that card to one of the first 8 IRQs.

I/O addresses are usually assigned to particular locations. Here are the standard assignments and defaults for some devices:

	I/O	IRQ
COM1	03F8H	IRQ4
COM2	02F8H	IRQ3
LPT1	0378H	IRQ7
LPT2	03BCH	IRQ5

Pay attention to the interrupts and memory assignments of the devices you plug into your computer's bus. You will have to reassign values if there are conflicts. Keep a list of all assignments you have made in a notebook near your computer; you can also use one of a number of utility and diagnostic programs that will generate a list of settings for devices already in your system.

12

The Display System

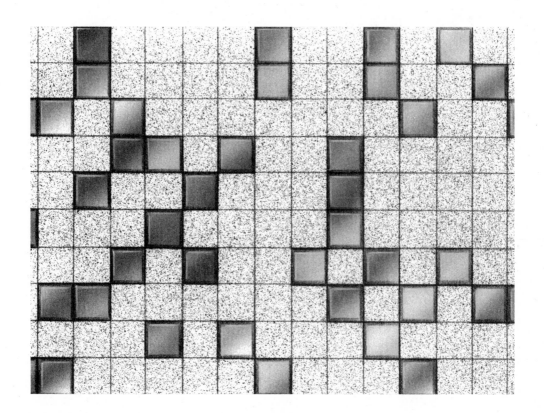

Your PC's display system allows you to see exactly what your PC is doing as it works. Because it gives you instant visual feedback, the display system makes your PC interactive. The display system also affects the speed of your PC and your pleasure (or pain) in using your machine. PCs use a number of different technologies in creating their displays, and the choice determines what you see, how sharply you see it, and how quickly.

Seeing is believing. If you couldn't see the results of your calculations or language manipulations, the personal computer would be worthless as a tool. You need some way of viewing the output of the computer system to know what it has done and why you're wasting your time feeding it data. Today's choice for seeing things that come from your computer is the video display, sort of like a television that substitutes a cable to your CPU for an antenna.

Display Fundamentals

Video was not always the primary output for thinking machines. Computers existed even before there was television, at least commercial television as we know it. These first data processors shared the same output, printed output, that was used by their predecessor, the mechanical adding machine. Before video, computers directly operated printers of some kind to show their results to an almost disbelieving world.

Teletype Output

The printer of choice was the Teletype machine, long used to convey words and numbers across continents. These early computers fed characters to the Teletype printer as if they had begun at some different keyboard one character at a time in a long series.

Video Terminals

Although the Teletype has reached a status somewhere between endangered species and museum piece, the method of data transmission and display that the Teletype used still does service to today's high-tech toys. Instead of hammering away at paper, however, these machines send their character strings to the electronic equivalent of the Teletype, the computer terminal. These terminals are often called *Video Data Terminals* (sometimes *Video Display Terminals*) or *VDTs* because they rely on video displays to make their presentations to you. They are terminal because they reside at the end of the communications line, in front of your eyes. A terminal at its most rudimentary is the classic dumb terminal, which merely displays each character exactly as it is received, on a phosphor-coated screen instead of paper. The refinements are few; instead of rattling off the edge of the paper, a too-long electronic line more likely will "wrap" down to the line below. The terminal never runs out of "paper"; it seemingly has a fresh supply of blank screen below that rolls upward as necessary to receive each additional line. Alas, the output it generates is even more tenuous than the flimsiest tissue and disappears at the top of the screen, perchance never to be seen again.

A smart terminal, on the other hand, has innate intelligence; that is, it has some of the data processing capabilities of a computer. A smart terminal recognizes special commands for formatting its display and may even be able to do some computer-like functions on its own. Often, however, the smartest of terminals is relegated to working like an ordinary dumb terminal.

A few other characteristics also distinguish the operation of a mechanical Teletype. The paper it prints on moves in only one direction. Neither the paper nor the output of the Teletype ever goes backward. Like a stock ticker, the Teletype merely churns out an unending string of text. The Teletype cannot type over something it did before, and it cannot jump ahead without patiently rolling its paper forward as if it had printed so many blank lines.

In the electronic form of the computer terminal, the Teletype method of text handling means that when one character changes on the screen, a whole new screen full of text must be generated and sent to the terminal. The system cannot back up to change the one character, so it must rush headlong forward, reworking the whole display along the way.

Mammoth primeval computers and rattling Teletypes might seem to have little in common with the quiet and well-behaved PC sitting on your desk. However, the simplest of programs still retain this most primitive way of communicating with your video screen. The programs generate characters and send them, one by one, to the video display. Instead of traveling across the globe, the text merely shuffles from one place in memory to another inside the machine. These programs, in effect, operate as if the video system of your computer was the screen of a terminal.

Many computers are limited to this form of video imagery, which, understandably, is often called a *Teletype display*. For IBM standard computers, from the first PC onward, Teletype displays are only a vestige of their ancestry that's used by rudimentary programs and sophisticated software on which the programmers have shirked responsibility for making things look better. Teletype-type output is, however, the highest level of support provided by the IBM system BIOS.

Actually, this BIOS support makes Teletype displays even slower. The IBM BIOS requires that each character must be individually manipulated by software. The standard system firmware only includes commands for taking each character from a program and squeezing it into the next video memory location. Each character thus requires the execution of series of program instructions, and even the chain of instructions takes time to execute.

Because of this software overhead, the actual speed of Teletype displays depends on the available microprocessor power. The faster the processor, the quicker the software runs, and the snappier the on-screen display.

Character Mapping

For years the most common means of displaying text on a PC screen was the *character-mapped* display. Using this technology, a special section of memory is reserved for storing the characters that will appear on the screen, and programs write text on the screen by pushing bytes into the proper places in that memory.

In the most common of the character-mapped display systems used by PCs, the screen is divided into a matrix, essentially a set of pigeon holes with each hole corresponding to one position on the screen that measures 80 characters wide and 25 high. To display a character on the screen, a program loads the corresponding code into the matrix cell. To put the image on the screen, the display system reads the entire matrix, translates into a serial data stream that scans across the monitor screen, and moves the data to the video output. From there, the signal is the monitor's problem.

Speed in making changes is one virtue of the character-mapped display system. Programs can push characters into any screen location in any order that they please, top, bottom, left, or right—even placing one letter atop another, overwriting the transitory existence of each. Screen updates occur quickly because only the character (or characters) needing to be changed have to be pushed into place. Once a character has been pushed into the display memory matrix, it stays there until changed by the program that put it there, or any other software that reaches into that area of memory.

For character mapping to work, your applications need to know the exact location of each screen memory address. For all applications to work on all PCs, the addresses used by each system must be the same, or there needs to be some means of determining what addresses are used. In the original PC, IBM reserved two blocks of addresses—one for color text and one for monochrome—in high DOS memory for holding characters for screen display, but it refused to make them an official IBM standard. However, software writers found that the only way to get acceptable speed from their software was to use this character-mapped mode. The industry's reliance on these addresses made them into unofficial standards with which even IBM refuses to tamper.

In the IBM scheme of things, your PC uses one set of screen memory addresses when it is operating in color mode and the other set when in monochrome. To determine which mode your system is currently using, the IBM BIOS provides a special flag, called the *video mode flag* (originally termed the *video equipment flag* by IBM) located at absolute memory location 0463(Hex). When this flag is set to 0D4(Hex), your system is running in color and the chain of addresses starting at B8000(Hex) is used for screen text memory. In monochrome, the flag is set to 0B4(Hex) to indicate the use of addresses starting at B0000(Hex). For compatibility reasons, all newer IBM video systems are also capable of operating through these same addresses even though they may store additional video information elsewhere.

Beyond this flag, the BIOS provides no character-mapped display support. That's good because there's no extra overhead burden for your programs in using character-mapped displays. In effect, your software simply writes directly to screen memory. Consequently, character-mapped mode is often called *direct writing*.

Character Boxes

In text modes, the display memory addresses hold codes that have nothing to do with the shapes appearing on the monitor screen except as a point of reference. The actual patterns of each character that appears on the screen are stored in a special ROM chip, called the *character ROM*, that's part of the video circuitry of the computer. The byte that defines the character is used by the video circuitry to look up the character pattern that matches it. The bit pattern from the character ROM is scanned and sent to the screen to produce the final image. Each on-screen character is made from an array of dots, much like the text output of a Teletype or dot-matrix printer. The several video standards used by IBM and other manufacturers build individual characters out of different size dot arrays. The framework in which the dots of an individual character are laid out, called the *character box*, is a matrix like a crossword puzzle. The character box is measured by the number of dots comprising its width and its height. For instance, a standard Video Graphics Array (VGA) text screen uses a 9 x 16 character box. Each character takes up a space on the screen measuring 9 dots wide and 16 dots high. Other display systems use character boxes of different sizes. The standard Monochrome Display Adapter character box measures 9 x 14; the standard Color Graphics Adapter character box, 8 x 8; the Enhanced Graphics Adapter character box, 8 x 14.

Individual characters do not necessarily take up the entire area that a character box affords. For instance, text characters on IBM monochrome displays keep one row of dots above and below that used by each character to provide visible separation between two adjacent lines of text on the screen.

Video Attributes

The character-mapped displays of the IBM standard do not store each letter adjacent to the next. Instead, each on-screen character position corresponds to every other byte of memory; the intervening bytes are assigned as attribute bytes. Even numbered bytes store character information; odd bytes store attributes.

The attribute byte determines the highlighting or color of the displayed character that's stored in the preceding memory byte. Monochrome and color attributes use different codes. Monochrome characters are allowed the following attributes: normal, highlighted (brighter on-screen characters), underlined, and reverse-video characters (dark on light instead of the normal light on dark). The different attributes can be combined. Note, however, that highlighted reverse-video characters make the character background brighter instead of highlighting the character shape itself. Monochrome display attributes are shown in figure 12.1.

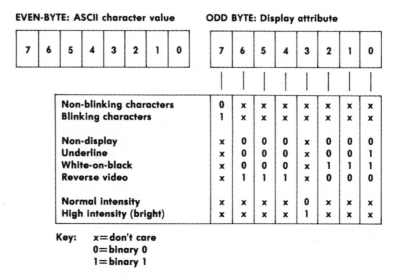

EVEN-BYTE: ASCII character value   **ODD BYTE: Display attribute**

	7	6	5	4	3	2	1	0
Non-blinking characters	0	x	x	x	x	x	x	x
Blinking characters	1	x	x	x	x	x	x	x
Non-display	x	0	0	0	x	0	0	0
Underline	x	0	0	0	x	0	0	1
White-on-black	x	0	0	0	x	1	1	1
Reverse video	x	1	1	1	x	0	0	0
Normal intensity	x	x	x	x	0	x	x	x
High intensity (bright)	x	x	x	x	1	x	x	x

Key: x=don't care
0=binary 0
1=binary 1

Figure 12.1. Monochrome text display attributes.

Color systems store two individual character hues in the attribute byte. The first half of the byte (the most significant bits of the digital code of the byte) codes the color of the character itself. The latter half of the attribute (the least significant bits) codes the background color. Color display attributes are shown in figure 12.2.

EVEN BYTE: ASCII character value   **ODD BYTE: Display attribute**

| 7 | 6 | 5 | 4 | 3 | 2 | 1 | 0 | | 7 | 6 | 5 | 4 | 3 | 2 | 1 | 0 |

FOREGROUND COLOR:

	7	6	5	4	3	2	1	0
Black	x	x	x	x	0	0	0	0
Blue	x	x	x	x	0	0	1	0
Green	x	x	x	x	0	0	1	0
Cyan	x	x	x	x	0	0	1	1
Red	x	x	x	x	0	1	0	0
Magenta	x	x	x	x	0	1	0	1
Brown	x	x	x	x	0	1	0	1
Light grey	x	x	x	x	0	1	1	1
Dark grey	x	x	x	x	1	0	0	0
Bright blue	x	x	x	x	1	0	0	1
Bright green	x	x	x	x	1	0	1	0
Bright cyan	x	x	x	x	1	0	1	1
Bright red	x	x	x	x	1	1	0	0
Bright magenta	x	x	x	x	1	1	0	1
Yellow	x	x	x	x	1	1	1	0
White	x	x	x	x	1	1	1	1

BACKGROUND COLOR:

	7	6	5	4	3	2	1	0
Black	x	0	0	0	x	x	x	x
Blue	x	0	0	1	x	x	x	x
Green	x	0	1	0	x	x	x	x
Cyan	x	0	1	1	x	x	x	x
Red	x	1	0	0	x	x	x	x
Magenta	x	1	0	1	x	x	x	x
Brown	x	1	1	0	x	x	x	x
White (light grey)	x	1	1	1	x	x	x	x
Non-blinking characters	0	x	x	x	x	x	x	x
Blinking characters	1	x	x	x	x	x	x	x

Key: x=don't care
0=binary 0
1=binary 1

Figure 12.2. Color text display attributes.

Because each character on the screen requires two bytes of storage, a full 80-character column by 25-character row of text (a total of 2,000 characters) requires 4,000 bytes of storage. In the basic IBM monochrome video system, 16K is allotted to storing character information. The basic (and basically obsolete) color system reserved 64K for this purpose.

Video Pages

The additional memory does not go to waste, however. It can be used to store more than one screen of text at a time, with each separate screen called a *video page*. Either basic video system is designed to quickly switch between these video pages so that on-screen images can be changed almost instantly. Switching quickly allows a limited degree of animation.

The basic IBM color system also has a special mode in which it displays text in 40 columns across the screen, an accommodation to people trying to use televisions instead of computer monitors as displays. Televisions are not as sharp as computer monitors. Fine, 80-column characters blur together on their screens. Half as many columns requires half as much storage, which in turn allows twice as many pages of video text.

Through the years, IBM has refined the quality of the display systems and increased the amount of memory devoted to video. In character-based displays, this additional memory has been put to work by offering new video modes that put more rows of text on the screen (up to 43) and by allowing an increased number of video pages. Third-party video systems may add their own text modes that permit up to 60 rows of text and 132 columns of characters on a single screen in text mode.

Block Graphics

Graphics are actually quite easy to display in any character-mapped text mode. Because one byte can encode 256 different characters, and the alphabet and other symbols total far short of that number, IBM assigned some special characters to some of the higher numbered bytes in its character set. Many of these extra characters are designed for drawing graphic images from blocks that entirely fill in the character matrix as well as many partially filled areas of different patterns.

Graphic images can be made by strategically locating these character blocks on the screen so that they form larger shapes. Other extra characters comprise a number of single and double lines as well as corners and intersections to draw borders around text areas. The characters are building blocks of the graphics images, and, consequently, this form of graphics is termed *block graphics*. Table 12.1 shows the block graphic characters used in IBM-standard computer systems.

To an IBM display system, block graphics are considered text and are handled exactly like ordinary text characters. All of the text attributes are available to every character of block graphics, including all of the available text colors, highlighting, and reverse-video characteristics.

Moreover, because block graphic displays are built in text mode, they can be pushed into video memory and onto the screen just as quickly as any other text, which is fast indeed. Block graphics are, in fact, the fastest graphics available on the PC.

On the other hand, block graphics offer the worst quality of the graphic display systems that PCs can use. The images made with block graphics are jagged and lumpy, in a word, blocky. Intricate shapes and fine details are impossible to create using large character blocks. Block graphic images are chunky, clunky, and otherwise aesthetically unappealing for most applications.

Then again, block graphics comprise the only graphics available on all IBM and compatible computer systems whether color or monochrome equipped. Block graphics are the minimum graphic standard and the least common graphic denominator among IBM display systems.

Bit-Mapped Graphics

One way to improve the poor quality of block graphics would be to make the blocks smaller. Smaller blocks would build an image with finer grain that could show more detail. The smaller the blocks, the better the image. However, physical aspects of the display system impose a distinct and unbreakable limit on how small each block can be: the size of the individual dots that make up the image on the video screen. The sharpest and highest quality image that could be shown by any display system would individually control every dot on the screen.

TABLE 12.1.
IBM Block Graphic Characters

ASCII	Character	ASCII	Character
169	⌐	170	¬
176	░	177	▒
178	▓	179	│
180	┤	181	╡
182	╢	183	╖
184	╕	185	╣
186	║	187	╗
188	╝	189	╜
190	╛	191	┐
192	└	193	┴
194	┬	195	├
196	─	197	┼
198	╞	199	╟
200	╚	201	╔
202	╩	203	╦
204	╠	205	═
206	╬	207	╧
208	╨	209	╤
210	╥	211	╙
212	╘	213	╒
214	╓	215	╫
216	╪	217	┘
218	┌	219	█
220	▄	221	▌
222	▐	223	▀

These dots are often called *pixels* (a contraction of the descriptive terms *picture element*), like atomic elements, the smallest building blocks which are known that reality can be readily constructed from. The terms *dot* and *pixel* are often used as synonyms, but their strict definitions are somewhat different. When a system operates at its limit, putting as many dots on the screen as it is physically capable of handling, the number of dots and the number of pixels are the same. Often, however, systems operate with somewhat less sharpness than they are capable of with the result that one pixel may be made from several on-screen dots.

The most straightforward way of handling the information to be displayed on such a screen is to assign some part of memory to each pixel, just as two bytes are given over to each character of a character-mapped display. In the IBM system, because the data controlling each pixel is stored as one or more memory bits, this kind of display system is often called *bit-mapped graphics*. Alternately, because each pixel or point on the video screen can be separately addressed through memory, this method of controlling the video display is often called *all points addressable graphics,* or *APA,* display.

In the bit-mapped graphics system, display memory stores an exact electronic representation of the on-screen image. This image is actually a time-slice of what you see. The software running on your PC is constantly sending new data into display memory to update the screen image. The memory temporarily stores or buffers the changes' frame until they are read out as a complete image frame dozens of times per second. Display memory thus serves as a frame buffer.

Bit-mapped graphics hold the potential for being much sharper than block graphics. More pixels mean more detail. The number of dots on a screen and the ultimate number of pixels are many times the number of characters that are displayed on that same screen—from 64 to 126 times greater.

However, bit-mapped graphics impose their own penalty: memory usage. Assigning a byte or two to each dot on the screen would take a prodigious amount of memory. Even the lowest quality graphics display that IBM offers would require 128K of memory to assign one byte to each dot. Although by today's standards 128K is not a lot of memory, it was at the time IBM introduced graphics for the PC. To keep the system affordable, IBM bequeathed only 16K of RAM to graphics information.

Fortunately, one byte per dot would be more lavish than necessary for simple displays. A single pixel cannot make a pattern, so there's no need to code for anything but whether the pixel is viewable, illuminated on the screen or invisibly dark. In simplest form, then, only one bit is needed to code each pixel and to indicate whether it glows. Each bit of memory would then be used to map what is revealed on the video display. As you might have guessed, 16K amounts to the minimum possible memory for controlling every dot on a screen that shows 640 dots horizontally and 200 vertically (the measurements of the minimum quality IBM video display). At today's standard 640 x 480 pixel resolution, 38,400 bytes would suffice for a full screen, easily accommodated in a 64K block of screen memory made using a bank of the smallest commonly available memory chips, those having 64 kilobits of storage.

Resolution

The number that quantifies the possible sharpness of a video image is called *resolution*. Resolution indicates how many individual pixels can be resolved across the screen. Because the quality of the electrical form of an image is independent of the screen that it is displayed on, physical measurements play no part in a resolution measurement. The number of pixels in an image does not vary with the size of the screen that it is displayed on. Hence, resolution is expressed without reference to units of linear measurement. Resolution is expressed as pixels or dots rather than dots per inch. For example, a standard VGA display has a resolution of 640 pixels horizontally by 480 pixels vertically in its native graphics mode. (A peculiarity of the VGA system makes its text and graphics resolutions different. VGA text has a resolution of 720 x 400 pixels.)

Graphics Attributes

What's lacking from this system is contrast and color. All bits are treated the same, and their associated pixels look about the same, either on or off. The result is a single-hued picture with no variation or shading, essentially the same sort of an image as a line drawing. Although that may be sufficient for some purposes (for instance, the display of a chart or graph that mimics the monochrome look of ink-on-paper), color and contrast can add impact.

The way to add color to bit-mapped images is much the same as adding color to character-based displays, adding attribute information. Additional memory is devoted to storing the attribute of each bit. The bit-mapped system works somewhat differently from the character-based mode, however. All of the memory devoted to a bit is used to describe it. Not a byte needs to be devoted to identifying a character or pattern for each picture element because each one is essentially a featureless dot.

A single bit per pixel results in what graphics folk call a two-color system much like the two-state digital system. All pixels are either on or off, white or black.

Color Planes

Adding a second dot per pixel doubles the number of possible displayable colors. (Shades, degrees of darkness or light, are considered different colors in the terminology of computer graphics.) Every additional bit assigned to each pixel likewise doubles the number of possible colors. Hence, with n bits, $2n$ colors are possible.

In computer graphics, the number of bits that are assigned to coding color information is sometimes described as the number of *color planes*. This term relates to the organization of display memory. The memory map of the graphic image can be visualized much like a Mercator projection of the world with latitude and longitude lines corresponding to the different positions of the bits that correspond to pixels in the image. Additional bits per each pixel add a third dimension, much like layers of maps stacked atop one another, a series of flat planes containing the color information.

Color planes are related to memory banks but are not exactly the same thing. For instance, to map more memory into the limited address space reserved for video under the IBM standard, some IBM video adapters use bank-switching techniques to move video memory bytes in and out of the address range of the host microprocessor. In some video modes, these banks correspond exactly to the color planes used by the video adapter. In other modes, several planes of video information may be stored in each bank by using bits in each byte of screen memory to indicate individual colors.

The more colors or color planes, the more storage is needed for encoding each pixel. Because the more colors used in an image, the better the apparent image quality and the more life-like its appearance, the temptation is to increase the bit-depth of each pixel as high as possible. Much to the dismay of purveyors of video memory, however, the human eye is limited in its ability to resolve individual colors. Color monitors are even more limited in the number of colors that they can display. Hence, once enough memory is assigned each pixel, further improvements will not improve appearances.

The practical limit on color is a bit-depth of 24, which allows a system to store and theoretically display any of 16,777,216 hues. Display systems with this bit-depth are termed *24-bit color* or *true color* systems.

True color is convenient in that one byte of storage is assigned to each pixel for each of the three additive colors (red, green, and blue). True color produces images of realistic quality, and imposes rather severe processing overhead on high-resolution systems.

Some people see true color as wasteful of memory and processor power in that most monitors cannot even approach displaying its color potential. Most monitors top out at about 262,144 colors, corresponding to the capabilities of an 18-bit display system. For general-purpose video displays, 215 or 32,768 hues are often sufficient. Accepted display standards correspond to each of these (as well as one intermediate) values.

The math for finding the amount of memory required to display a color graphics screen is straightforward. Simply multiply the number of pixels on the screen, that is, the resolution, by the bit-depth of each pixel, and then divide by 8 to translate bits into bytes. For example, a

VGA graphics screen comprises 307,200 pixels (that's simply 640 pixels times 480 pixels). With a bit-depth of 4 (allowing 16 colors on the screen), the minimum memory required is 1,228,800 bits. Divided by 8 bits per byte, that equates to 153,600 bytes of storage. The next-highest standard increment of memory is 256K, so you would need at least 256K of RAM to store a 16-color VGA image.

Direct Mapping

When the values stored in screen memory directly indicate what color will appear on the screen, as in the example in the previous paragraph, the colors are said to be *direct mapped*. Direct mapping allows any pixel to be any color, but most images are made from far fewer colors. After all, there are only 307,200 pixels on the VGA screen, so you can't possibly display them all at once. If you're judicious about your color pruning and the colors you display, you can make amazingly realistic images using a few bytes of storage by limiting the number of colors you put on the screen (which limits the storage you need). The problem is, of course, the optimum color selection for one image isn't the same as for another. A polar bear in a snowstorm is predominantly white; a black bear in a cave on a starless night would be predominantly black; and a still frame from a blockbuster movie would likely be mostly red.

The colors assigned to storage can be made to adapt to the image by using a color look-up table (CLUT). The CLUT serves as a spectral map. A limited amount of storage makes up the guideposts or pointers that indicate which particular color in a wide overall selection (called a *palette*) belongs to a particular pixel. The number of guideposts determines how many different colors can be on the screen at the same time. The number of colors in the palette is constrained by the size of the pointer. Each pixel on the screen needs only enough storage to indicate which pointer to use. For example, a VGA system using a single byte of storage for each pixel could access a color look-up table with 256 pointers allowing 256 different colors on the screen at a time. Each pointer has 18 bits of storage, allowing access to a palette of 262,144 different hues.

Color look-up tables conserve both memory and speed. The march of technology makes these issues increasingly irrelevant, however. As memory and microprocessor power becomes cheaper, CLUTs will become rarer, at least in new display standards. With progress currently stuck on VGA, however, CLUTs will be around for a long while.

Raster and Vector Graphics

The video display system that organizes the screen into a series of lines that's continually scanned dozens of times a second is termed a *raster display*. Although workable and the basis of all PC and PS/2 displays, as well as today's television and video systems, a raster display is not the only way to put a computer image on a monitor.

A completely different technique, *vector graphics*, does not regularly scan the screen at all. Instead, vector graphics precisely control the circuitry operating the horizontal and vertical deflection yokes. Vector graphics doesn't trace scan lines but, instead, draws figures the same way you would with a series of strokes of a paintbrush. To keep the screen lit, it constantly retraces the figures. This image-making technique is called vector graphics because the signals controlling the monitor drive the electron beam in the CRT as a series of vectors. Alternatively, this kind of display system is sometimes called a *stroker* because of the kinship to drawing brush strokes. Although not used on PCs, the term pops up occasionally in the descriptions of expensive computerized workstations.

Video Controllers

Images are loaded into screen memory by your PC's microprocessor or by dedicated video circuitry (which may itself include a full-fledged microprocessor). In simple display systems, your PC's microprocessor does all the work with either direct commands from your software to move bytes to specific memory locations, or through program calls to your PC's BIOS, which then handles the detail work (and commands the microprocessor to load values into particular screen memory locations). In more complex display systems, the microprocessor sends codes to the video processor, which either directly moves the data into screen memory, or generates the image and then moves it into memory. In any case, the final destination for screen-bound data is the screen memory of your PC.

Getting those bytes from memory to monitor is a much more complex matter. The image must be transformed from its comparatively static position in screen memory to a signal controlling a fast moving electron beam inside the picture tube of your monitor. The conversion is not as direct as you might think. The resemblance between the memory map and the on-screen image is only metaphoric. The bytes of video information are scattered among eight or more memory chips and must somehow be organized and find their way to the monitor. In addition, the monitor itself must be brought under the control of the computer.

These tasks are the job of the video controller, generally a special VLSI chip designed specifically for the task of turning memory bytes into video. IBM has used a number of video controllers, which compatible makers have duplicated in their designs.

The first IBM color and monochrome adapters relied on an off-the-shelf chip, the 6845, to handle its displays. More recently, IBM has switched to custom-designed and manufactured chips.

The primary job of the video controller in desktop PCs that use picture tubes is to serialize the data in display memory. The picture tubes are technically termed *cathode ray tubes,* or *CRTs,* because they have electron beams shot from a cathode (an electron emitter) to light the phosphors of the screen. The information that's so nicely laid out in two logical dimensions (horizontal and vertical) in the memory map must be converted to a long, serial train of pulses in the single dimension of time.

The principle underlying the conversion is elegant in its simplicity. Addresses in the memory map are just read off in sequential order, one row at a time. However, to make sure that the one-dimensional video information is not misinterpreted by your monitor, the video controller must mix with the stream of data a host of synchronizing and control signals.

When display systems not based on CRTs are used (for instance, the flat-panel liquid crystal displays, or LCDs, of most laptop computers), data for the display might not be serialized but nevertheless must be manipulated into a format that can be handled by the display. The flat-panel display is addressed in two dimensions, exactly like display memory, but the data often has to be channeled through a narrow electrical path. The video controller circuitry must convert the screen memory data into transferable form and reconstruct it once it gets to the display panel.

Retrace

CRT-based systems have particular signal requirements. To make the image you see, the electron beam in the CRT traces a nearly horizontal line across the face of the screen, and then, in an instant, flies back to the side of the screen from which it started but lower by the width of the line it already traced out. This quick zipping back is termed *horizontal retrace*, and, although quick, it cannot take place instantly because of the inertia inherent in electrical circuits. Consequently, the smooth flow of bytes must be interrupted briefly at the end of each displayed line or else the video information will be lost during the retrace process. The video controller must take each retrace into account as it serializes the image.

In addition, another variety of retrace must occur when the electron beam reaches the bottom of the screen: vertical retrace. The beam must travel as quickly as possible back up to its starting place, and the video controller must halt the flow of data while the beam is traveling.

Blanking

During retrace, if the electron beam from the gun in the tube was on, it would paint a bright line diagonally across the screen as the beam returns to its proper position. To prevent the appearance of this distracting line, the beam is switched off not only during retrace but also during a short interval on either side to give the beam time to stabilize. The interval in which the beam is off and cannot be turned on by any degree of programming is called *blanking* because the electron beam can draw nothing but a blank on the screen.

Most computer monitors don't fill their entire screens with data. They center (or try to) the image within darkened boarders to minimize the image distortions that sneak in near the edges of the screen. To produce these darkened, protected areas, the electron beam is held at the level that produces a black image for a short while before and after the data of each image line is displayed. These short intervals are termed the *front porch* and *back porch* of the signal. If you examined the signal, you would see that it dips down for blanking, and then pops up to an intermediate height (called *black level*) to create the porches between blanking and data. If you use your imagination, the black-level signals look like shelves, or porches.

Vertical Interval

The period during which the screen is blanked during the vertical retrace is called, appropriately, the *vertical interval*. The vertical interval's physical manifestation is the wide, black horizontal bar that's visible between image frames when your television screen or computer monitor picture rolls and requires adjustment of the vertical hold control.

Synchronizing Signals

The electron beam in the monitor is swept across the screen by a combination of magnetic fields. One field moves the beam horizontally, and another vertically. Circuitry in the monitor supplies a steadily increasing voltage to two sets of deflection coils to control the sweep of the beam. These coils are electromagnets, and the increasing voltage causes the field strength of the coils to increase and deflect the beam farther. At the end of the sweep of a line, the field that controls the horizontal sweep of the electron beam is abruptly switched off, returning the beam to the starting side of the screen. Likewise, when the beam reaches the bottom of the screen, the field in control of the vertical sweep switches off. The result is that the electron beam follows a tightly packed zig-zag path from the top of the screen to the bottom.

The primary difference between the two sweeps is that several hundred horizontal sweeps take place for each vertical one. The rate at which the horizontal sweeps take place is called the *horizontal frequency* of the display system. The rate at which the vertical sweeps take place is called the *vertical frequency* or *frame rate* of the system because one complete image frame is created every time the beam sweeps fully down the screen.

The electronics that generate the sweep frequencies used by a monitor are inside the monitor itself. However, the signals themselves must be synchronized with the data stream coming from the computer so that characters appear at their proper positions on the screen. If you lose sync, the ordinarily orderly screen display takes on the countenance of the tower of Pisa or the present day appearance of the Colossus at Rhodes.

To keep things organized, the video controller sends out special synchronizing signals. The video controller sends horizontal sync signals before each line is sent to the display, and it sends vertical sync signals before each frame.

Digital and Analog Display Systems

Two kinds of signals are used by different display systems to move video information from your PC to your monitor. The older IBM display standards, MDA, CGA, and EGA, all use digital signals, often termed *TTL* (for *transistor-transistor logic*, which are the family of electronic components used in their circuitry). The VGA and later standards use analog signals. The difference between the two is how they encode color information, and the number of colors each system can encode.

Digital signals are like the thoughts of your PC, each signal has one of two states. Information is conveyed by the pattern of several signals. Digital monitor signals use a parallel code that's been specifically tailored to monitors. Under the CGA standard, the digital video code comprises four signals, three (one for each of the additive primary colors) that determine whether a specific electron gun assigned to those colors is on or off. The fourth signal increases the intensity of all four signals simultaneously. This digital signal code is often called *RGBI* for the names of the four signals: red, green, blue, and intensity.

RGBI signals can encode 16 colors because a 4-bit system has 16 possible values. The EGA system uses a 6-bit code, a signal for the three colors and an intensity signal assigned to each. The resulting 6-bit code allows the transmission of 64 different colors. The MDA system uses only a single video signal, but it can have three states corresponding to black, moderate-intensity, and high-intensity images.

Analog signals can assume practically any value, and so can encode a virtually unlimited number of colors, as many as the phosphors in the monitor is capable of displaying. The signals are called *analog* because their electrical strength equates to (is analogous to) the brightness of the electron beam inside the CRT and the image on the tube face. Because analog signals are more versatile, nearly all newer video standards, VGA and up, now use them.

Digital-to-Analog Converters

Internally, your PC uses nothing but digital signals in its digital circuits. To translate those digital codes into the analog signals used by today's monitors, display adapters use special integrated circuits called *digital-to-analog converters*. Often abbreviated as DAC, the same chips also masquerade under the name RAMDAC, which is short for *random access memory digital-to-analog converter*.

DACs are classified by the number of digital bits in the digital code they translate. For example, an 8-bit DAC converts the levels encoded in 8-bit digital patterns into 256 analog levels. In color systems, each primary color or channel requires a separate DAC, a total of three. Add the number of bits of each DAC, and you'll get the number of bit-planes of color that a system can display. This number is its palette. The number of simultaneous on-screen colors is limited by the amount of display memory. With adequate storage, three 8-bit DACs yield a 24-bit True Color system.

In most display systems, all DACs are created equal. All DACs are rated in the same number of bits. The VGA system, for example, has three 6-bit DACs to create an 18-bit system with a palette potential of 262,144 hues. Sometimes, however, one channel is favored over the others. In its direct-color mode, the XGA system, for example, uses two 5-bit color channels and one 6-bit channel. The 16 bits total up nicely to two bytes of storage and allow a 65,536-color range. The extra bit is given to the green color channel because the human eye is most sensitive to brightness subtleties in the green area of the spectrum.

Beyond the standard 18-bit DAC used in the VGA system, a couple of chip makers have developed what they believe to be better ideas in

DACs. The Color-Edge Graphic system developed by Edsun Laboratories (now part of Analog Devices) found a way to increase the number of colors available from a VGA-like system without altering storage requirements. The HiColor RAMDACs from Sierra Semiconductor push the color capabilities of display adapters from 256 simultaneous on-screen colors to 32,768 or 65,536.

The CEG chip works by tinkering with the VGA color codes, reserving the uppermost 32 color codes to indicate not colors but blends of the colors of adjacent pixels. The result is smooth transitions between colors at their borders or edges. Colors blend gradually together, with a minimum loss of sharpness. More than a million blends are possible. The drawback of the Edsun CEG system is that it requires that your programs know the chip's special codes for color mixing, and few applications take advantage of it.

The HiColor chip uses the simple expedient of allocating more bits for image storage. Instead of the 8-bit maximum of VGA, the HiColor chip allows up to 16 bits to store codes. The first HiColor chips and their more recent updates (SC11481, SC11486, and SC11488) follow the standard set by TruVision's TARGA board with five bits assigned to each primary color. Other HiColor chips (SC11485, SC11487, and SC11489) also allow the use of the 16-bit system of IBM's XGA.

Note that these products don't automatically generate more colors from your programs or files. They must be specifically supported by the applications that you use in order to deliver their benefits.

Bus Links

The video system in your PC must somehow link up with the rest of its circuitry. In most display systems, the connection is intimate. Your PC's microprocessor must be able to directly intervene, injecting data right into screen memory. That means the screen memory must be within the addressing range of the microprocessor. Although some high-performance video systems (typically those with their own video processors) put their memories outside the reach of your PC's regular microprocessor, these systems cannot display the signals of standard display systems, MDA to VGA to XGA.

Either of two electrical connections can provide the logical link between screen memory and your PC's microprocessor. The link can be made at the I/O bus (which essentially equates to your PC's expansion bus) or directly to the microprocessor at its local bus. The functional difference between these two connections is speed. In most modern PCs, the microprocessor's local bus operates several times faster than the I/O bus. On the face of it, that singular advantage should give the local bus connection a big edge in performance. On actual applications, a local bus is somewhat faster but nowhere near its theoretical potential.

I/O Bus

The I/O bus connection is almost traditional. The first PCs put their video circuits on expansion boards installed in ordinary expansion slots. The choice of location was pragmatic. The required circuitry would not fit on the motherboard, so it had to go into the slots. Slot-mounted memory also gave video designers and PC owners versatility. One video adapter design would fit all PCs, opening a wide market to vendors. PC owners, in turn, got access to a huge selection of products. Moreover, upgrading the quality of display systems is easy, simply slide out one board and slip in a new one.

With the advent of the AT with its 16-bit ISA expansion bus, the advantage of using a wider bus connection became obvious. Display adapter boards with 16-bit interfaces proved themselves substantially faster than boards with 8-bit connectors. With twice the bus width, a 16-bit adapter could acquire display data quicker, delivering almost the expected doubling of performance.

Around 1987, some PC manufacturers (including industry leaders Compaq and IBM) rethought the reason for plugging video into expansion slots. The increased scale of integration left room on the motherboard that might be used by display circuitry. Moreover, where once several standards vied for acceptance as the one true video standard, VGA had assumed the role. Video was no longer a luxury, and the VGA standard made one video system the choice for nearly all PCs. As a result, these companies moved their display adapter circuitry onto the motherboard.

Although this redesign changed the physical location of display adapter circuitry, it changed nothing about its logical connection. The video circuits still linked into the PC as if it were on the expansion bus, giving the microprocessor access to video memory through the old standard addresses. Electrically, the motherboard-based video circuits remained connected to the I/O bus, notwithstanding the proximity of the high-speed microprocessor.

The I/O bus connection gives the system designer important advantages even when video circuits are installed on the motherboard. Generally, available video control circuitry is limited in its speed potential. Many of the chips simply cannot operate at the high speeds of today's microprocessors. The I/O bus is geared down to a rate tolerated by most video controllers by the bus control circuits on the motherboard. The video circuits also need access to system memory addresses, which requires tapping into address signals. The I/O bus provides the necessary address signals, so nothing more needs to be added to the PC to graft video onto the motherboard.

The I/O bus connection means that ordinary motherboard video circuitry operates exactly as if it were installed in an expansion slot. Some motherboard video systems (such as those in early IBM PS/2s) use 8-bit I/O bus connections on the motherboard, holding back performance behind that which was available from expansion bus video boards. In fact, the only advantages of motherboard video connected through the I/O bus is lower cost and the saving of one expansion slot because you need no separate display adapter.

The I/O bus connection proved satisfactory for video for such a long time, from 1981 to 1991, because the video needs of older applications were minimal. For example, with early PCs it was not a problem because most applications were character mapped. A full screen of information was simply an 80 x 25 array of characters stored in memory as two bytes per character (one byte in modified ASCII code, the other an attribute byte that specified color or emphasis). In that an entire screen of text data comprised only 4K, it took an insignificant time to transfer, even across the original PC bus (the actual transfer time would be less than 1/500th second on a 4.77 Mhz bus that is 1 byte wide).

With the increasing emphasis on graphics applications in recent years, video transfer needs have increased dramatically. A screen of standard VGA 16-color graphics, today's least common denominator, consists of 163,200 bytes of data. Move up to a True Color (24-bit) image at 1,024 x 768 resolution, and one screen of data increases to about 2.3 megabytes. If a system had no other overhead, that one screen would take a full second to transfer across the PC bus. In reality, such a transfer takes much, much longer when mediated by the system microprocessor, which must also allocate its time for memory refreshing, subtle background processes (servicing the timer interrupt, for example), and calculating the image data bound for the screen. Clearly, the several seconds per screen update required by I/O bus connections in this instance is unacceptable performance.

Local Bus

Local bus video systems take advantage of a more direct connection to the microprocessor, using the address circuits available nearer the microprocessor that operate at microprocessor speed. These signals are available thanks to new chip sets specifically designed to give access to the signals. The video circuits themselves have to respond faster to keep up with the higher speeds, or they have to inject wait states to prevent operation outside their ratings. The local bus connection to the video circuitry can be made on the motherboard itself or it can be extended to another expansion bus, such as VL Bus. As with the conventional I/O bus video connection, the physical location of the local bus video circuitry does not affect its operation or speed.

Because local bus video requires a special connection to the microprocessor in a PC, it cannot be added to existing machines the way you make other display system upgrades. Taking advantage of local bus requires a big investment, you need to either buy a new PC equipped with local bus or upgrade your existing computer with a motherboard that offers it.

The term "local bus" itself describes a technology and not an implementation. The initial flurry of PCs with local bus display systems followed no common standard. PC designers constructed their local bus connections however they saw fit. To achieve compatibility with today's applications, they mimicked ordinary VGA connections by using the same addresses for memory and the registers of their video controllers. As long as the PC designers maintained the same degree of compatibility achieved by VGA expansion boards, the details of the motherboard local bus connection were irrelevant to you as a mere PC user. The board would act exactly like an ordinary VGA system, only it would react faster.

In June, 1992, Intel Corporation released its local bus standard, which the company called the Peripheral Component Interconnect. It sets the ground rules for exactly how local bus video systems should connect with Intel's microprocessors. Although long-awaited, the PCI standard isn't particularly meaningful for you as a prospective PC purchaser. The local bus standard used on a motherboard is about as important to you as the kind of cardboard from which a milk carton is made. As long as it works and doesn't spawn anything dangerous, it serves its purpose without worry. As long as a motherboard-based local bus system works, emulating an ordinary VGA system, it doesn't matter whether it follows the PCI standard. PC manufacturers, how-ever, benefit from the PCI standard because following it assures them their creations will work properly and that they can readily transfer their local bus technology between different system designs.

Motherboard-based local bus systems impose a penalty. They restrict your upgrade options. If you ever decide to upgrade from the resolu-tion or color capabilities of the motherboard-based display system, you'll have to slide an expansion board into a slot, losing the benefit of the local bus connection. Although you won't be in any worse shape than you would be without the local bus connection, you lose what you gained from having it.

The one sure way to eliminate this local bus shortcoming is to move the local bus video system from the motherboard to some kind of plug-in adapter. You then can update your local bus video system as easily as an I/O bus system, by exchanging expansion cards. Of course, you cannot use standard ISA, EISA, or Micro Channel bus slots. By design, these bus slots provide only I/O bus connections.

In the absence of recognized standards, a special local bus slot leaves you only a little better off than a motherboard-based system. Although the slot provides upgradability, a proprietary slot can limit your upgrade choices. You can only plug in products that fit, and those are likely to come only from the original manufacturer of the PC.

Standardization is key to the success of local bus video, both success for manufacturers and for making your own long-term investment in a PC a success. Slots and video boards that follow industry-recognized standards will give you the widest selection of local bus products and upgrade potentials. An initial stab at setting a local bus connector standard was the OPTi local bus. The video industry, however, has quickly migrated to the VESA Local Bus standard and connector specification. The details of these local bus implementations are discussed in Chapter 6.

Graphics Accelerators and Coprocessors

The chief strength of any local bus implementation is the capability to quickly move data to display memory from other places in your PC. However, the recent trends in display circuitry designs have focused on minimizing the need of moving large blocks of video data from one place to another. By constructing and manipulating the on-screen image with processor power that's directly connected to display memory (rather than using a microprocessor that has to reach through a bus into display memory), massive transfers of video data can be minimized. Because less data moves across the bus, there's less of a handicap from bus overhead, no matter whether the I/O bus or a local bus is used as the transfer channel.

Two technologies are built around the concept of moving the processing power closer to display memory. Graphic accelerators use VLSI chips specially designed for carrying out important commonly used graphic operations, such as drawing lines, filling areas, or creating Windows dialog boxes. Graphic coprocessors are full-fledged microprocessors that are designed primarily for carrying out graphic operations. As with a true microprocessor, a graphic coprocessor can be fully programmed, for example, to carry out the operations of a graphic accelerator. But a graphic coprocessor can do more, almost anything within the imagination of its programmer. Although the functions and operations of a graphic accelerator are set by its hardware design (consequently, graphic accelerators are sometimes called *fixed-function chips*), the graphic coprocessor can change its personality with a change of its software.

In contrast, a traditional display system has no processing power of its own, instead relying on the intelligence of the host computer's microprocessor. Because this older design has no inherent intelligence to control the display memory that buffers each frame of the image, it is often termed a *dumb frame buffer design*.

Both graphic accelerators and graphic coprocessors add intelligence to your PC's display system to help break the bus bottleneck while lightening the load on your PC's microprocessor. Instead of the microprocessor needing to execute the instructions to create on-screen images, the graphics chips take over the chore. Where the microprocessor must move all screen-bound data into display memory through either the I/O bus or local bus, the graphics chips are directly connected to screen memory and don't require bus transfers. Instead of shipping data across the I/O bus, your PC's microprocessor sends only the software drawing commands to the graphics chips, pushing a few bytes instead of thousands across the bus. The load on the bus is so light that it makes little difference whether the graphics chips connect to your system through the I/O bus or local bus.

Only one kind of image data doesn't benefit from this graphics speed-up: stored bit images. If you have a bit image saved on hard disk that you want to put on the screen, for example, a photograph that you scanned in, the disk-based data must be transferred without modification directly to display memory.

The graphics chips bring another performance advantage. Just as numeric coprocessors can help your PC crunch through transcendental functions faster, these special-purpose graphics chips can accelerate the performance of your system in drawing images on your monitor. The instruction set of a general-purpose microprocessor is designed for versatility. The creators of the chip have no idea what some designer will do with their product, so they add the capability to do nearly anything, sacrificing overall efficiency at any particular task. The makers of the graphic processor know exactly what their creation will be used for—graphics—so they can optimize the chip's command set for graphics functions.

Graphic accelerators and coprocessors often go hand-in-hand with higher resolution display systems. Although dumb frame buffers will work for any resolution level (as long as your PC's microprocessor can access the addresses used by display memory), the prodigious amounts of data at high resolutions require the extra speed of the graphic chips for adequate performance. Graphic chips can deal with huge amounts of graphics information, hundreds of thousands of pixels, in a fraction of the time it would take your computer's native microprocessor to ponder them.

A graphics accelerator or coprocessor will often make a greater difference in the video performance of a PC than would moving to the next most powerful microprocessor. For example, adding a graphic accelerator to a 33 Mhz 486 PC will boost the speed at which it paints the screen beyond the level achievable by a 50 Mhz machine using a dumb frame buffer. The actual performance improvement varies with the application software you use, programs that merely transfer bit-images won't benefit from an accelerator or coprocessor; those that draw on the screen (such as CAD) will race ahead several times faster.

High-Level Commands

The secret weapon of the graphic chip is the high-level graphic command. Ordinary programs tell the system microprocessor how to build or manipulate an image using its normal command set. The microprocessor can only do the functions for which it was designed using the system facilities at its disposal. Even with the addition of a graphic chip, the microprocessor will continue to execute all these ordinary instructions, never asking the auxiliary chip to take over part of the action.

To bring the graphic chip into play, the microprocessor must send it instructions about what to do—those high-level graphic commands. The commands don't appear out of thin air. They must be part of the software you run on your system. Your PC's microprocessor detects the instructions and relays them to the graphic chip, which then carries them out.

The range of commands is large. Some of the more important among them include the following:

➤ *Bit block transfers* are instructions that tell the graphic chip to move data from one place to another in display memory. Instead of moving each byte of screen data through memory, the microprocessor only needs to tell the graphic chip what block to move (the source of the data) and where to put it (the destination). The graphic chip then carries out the entire data transfer operation on its own.

Often shortened to BitBlt, bit block transfers are most commonly used for scrolling the image up the screen. You can easily see the effect the command makes in video performance. When you scroll a bit image up the screen using a graphic chip, often the top part of the image snaps into its new position leaving a black band at the bottom of the screen that slowly fills with the remainder of the image. The initial quick move of the top of the image is made entirely in display memory using BitBlts. The rest of the image must be brought into display memory through the I/O bus or local bus, resulting in delays.

➤ *Drawing commands* tell the graphic chip how to construct part of an image on the screen, drawing a line, rectangle, or arc, or filling a closed figure with a solid color or pattern. Often called *graphic primitives*, these commands break the image into its constituent parts that can be coded digitally to build a shape on the screen. When your PC's microprocessor puts a line on the screen, it typically must first compute where each bit of the line will appear on the screen. The microprocessor must compute the coordinates of each pixel to appear on the screen, and then transfer the change into display memory across the bus. With a graphic chip, the microprocessor only needs to indicate the starting and ending points of a line to the chip. The graphic chip then computes the pixels and puts the appropriate values in display memory.

➤ *Sprites* are small images that move around the screen as a unit, much like an on-screen mouse pointer. General-purpose microprocessors have no provisions for handling sprites, so they must compute each bit of the sprite image anew every time the sprite moves across the screen. Many graphic chips have built-in capabilities to handle sprites. They store the bit pattern of the sprite in memory and only need instructions telling where to locate the sprite on the screen. Instead of redrawing the sprite, the graphic chip need only change the coordinates assigned its on-screen image, essentially only remapping its location.

➤ *Windowing* is one of the most common features of today's multitasking systems. Each task is given an area of the screen dedicated to its own operations and images. Keeping straight all the windows used by every task is a challenge for a general-purpose microprocessor. Graphic chips, however, are usually designed to manage windows using simple commands. Once an on-screen window is defined, it can be manipulated as a single block rather than moving individual bytes around. The windowing operations can be strictly software manipulations or the graphic chip may include special hardware provisions for streamlining the control of the windows.

In a conventional windowing system, software controls the display of each window. The layout of the screen is calculated, and the proper values for each pixel are plugged into the appropriate locations in the memory map. The image is generated by reading each memory location in sequence and using the information it contains to control the intensity of the electron beam in the display as it sweeps down the screen. Every memory location is scanned sequentially in a rigid order.

➤ *Hardware windowing* works by slicing up the memory map. Although each dot on the screen has one or more bits of memory assigned to it, the map no longer needs to be an exact representation of the screen. The video chip no longer scans each memory location in exact sequential order as the video beam traces down the screen. Instead, the memory scanned to control the beam is indicated by pointers, which guide the scan between different memory areas. Each memory area pointed to represents an on-screen window.

Each window can be individually manipulated. The memory used by a window can even be mapped into the address range of the system microprocessor while the rest of the screen is handled separately. As a consequence, most of the calculating normally required to change a window is eliminated. Screen updates speed up substantially.

> ➤ *Hardware panning* takes advantage of the display memory that's not needed as a frame buffer (for example, the extra 100K of the 256K on a VGA board that needs only about 160K for a full image). The extra memory can hold an image that's bigger than that displayed on the monitor screen. The monitor image essentially becomes a window into display memory. Instead of stretching out for 640 x 480 pixels, for example, the extra display memory might allow the filling of an 800 x 600 matrix of which only the center 640 x 480 matrix is displayed. To pan the on-screen image one way or another on the screen, the display circuits only need to change the address of the area routed through the output of the board. Changing addresses is much faster than moving blocks of bytes with BitBlt instructions, so hardware panning takes place very quickly, as long as the entire image to be displayed is held in memory.

Graphic Operating Environments

If there is any weakness in improving display performance with graphic accelerators and graphic processors, it is the need for special high-level commands. Unless a program includes the requisite instructions, the graphic chips will never swing into action. Any investment in this extra-cost hardware would be wasted.

Consequently, programs must be specially written to take advantage of your system's graphic hardware. That in itself might not seem troublesome, until you consider that more than a dozen graphic chips are in use and each has its own individual command set. To recognize and use all the available chips, a program would have to pack itself with instructions for each of the chips with which it might potentially be used. With the proliferation of different chips, the necessary code would grow inside programs like a digital cancer, swelling programs with tumors of code that will eventually doom performance.

Software drivers help programmers sidestep the need for overloading their programs with graphic code. The program itself is written to the most common subset of high-level graphic commands available from most graphic chips. The programmer uses his own, proprietary command for each of those functions. He then creates a separate program called a *software driver* that translates the commands into those used by a specific graphic chip or board build from a specific chip. When the microprocessor in the PC encounters one of the program's graphic instructions, the software driver tells the microprocessor the proper instruction to send to the graphic chip, which then carries out the operation.

Although this design makes your life easier, it fosters nightmares for most programmers, if they can even get enough sleep to have a nightmare. This strategy requires the programmer of even the simplest graphic program to be familiar with all available graphic hardware. He needs to be both a software and hardware wizard in a world where expertise in one or the other field is rare enough already.

The computer industry has circumvented this problem in two ways: leaving the writing of software drivers to the makers of display adapters (which simply shifts the requirement of double expertise from the software company to the hardware company) and the graphic operating environment.

This latter approach is simply another step like that which brought you the software driver, adding yet one more layer of software. The graphic operating environment serves as software bridges between your applications and advanced video systems that allow a single driver to be used for all applications that run under the environment. The graphic operating environment can be either an operating system in its own right (such as OS/2) or a program such as Windows that runs under another operating system (DOS).

The environment works by giving the programmer a set of software routines called *hooks* that the programmer can use to elicit certain images on the video display. The operating environment translates the hook commands into its own common language, which is translated by the graphic environments driver software into a form understood by the graphic accelerator, coprocessor, or other video innovation. Application writers need only concern themselves with the operating environment hooks. The operating environment designers, on the other hand, match their products to as many of the competing non-standard video systems as they can, or let the hardware companies do the work.

Application Interfaces

The entire set of program hooks is called the *application interface*, the intermediate translation step that allows software and hardware to come together amiably. The application interface is the official means of controlling the display system (or linking with display software) that's documented by the maker of the device. The connection can take work through any of a variety of links, from direct control of hardware registers to a top layer of software that interacts with specific drivers.

For example, the application interface IBM created for its now-discontinued 8514/A display adapter comprised a set of commands to make the display board execute bit-block transfers, draw lines, fill areas, generate patterns, and mix colors. The application interface also included text commands for proportionally spaced fonts and alphanumeric operations based on those of the IBM 3270 terminal. Commands to the 8514/A application interface took the form of BIOS function calls, except that they were entered through CALL instructions rather than software interrupts.

For the programmer, the application interface is an instruction manual that tells him how to work with the various features built into a display system. You, as a PC user, never need to deal with the application interface. Your only concern is that a specific display system you choose is compatible with the application interface of your software. If you have a program that requires an XGA display system, you want to be sure that your hardware supports the XGA application interface, which means you want true XGA compatibility.

Sometimes programmers sidestep the official application interface to take control of a display device at a lower, more intimate level. For example, many applications skirted around IBM's 8514/A application interface and sent commands directly to the display board's hardware registers to improve the performance of the system. When IBM introduced the XGA display system, the need for abiding by the application interface quickly became apparent. Although XGA completely supported the 8514/A application interface, it used entirely different hardware. Programs that took direct hardware control of the 8514/A system would not work properly with XGA display boards. You could almost hear IBM's engineers chanting, "We told you so," in the XGA documentation.

Graphic Development Systems

If you strip the graphic operating environment of its user interface, you'll end up with a set of software hooks that help applications match to hardware. Several such products, termed *graphic development systems*, are available to application developers to help them write the programs that use the operating environments. These are wonderful products because you don't have to worry about them. The programmer uses the software tools supplied by the development system to make the job of writing flashy code easier and to broaden the market for his product across a wide range of hardware. You, as the user of the application, don't have to fret about complications other than loading the appropriate driver when you start your system.

Graphic Accelerators

The number of different graphic accelerators available to display board builders appears limited only by the number of different chip makers. As of mid-1992, six products were available, all different, all incompatible. The list includes the ATI Mach 8 chip, Chips and Technology's 82C453, Integrated Information Technology's UV6000, Silicon SubSystems's (also known as S3) 86C911, and Weitek's W5086. The IBM 8514/A display board also fits the definition of a fixed-function graphic accelerator (as do the products claiming true hardware compatibility with the 8514/A standard). Each requires its own specific driver software to work with willing applications.

The most recent products are uniformly aimed at one goal, improving the rate at which Microsoft's Windows environment updates images on your monitor screen. All have similar repertories of high-level commands. For example, the S3 86C911 is designed to give a subset of the command repertory of the IBM's XGA system, eliminating the high-level commands irrelevant to the needs of Windows.

A graphic accelerator does not automatically guarantee a performance improvement on all applications. Software not designed to work with the application interface of the graphic accelerator won't gain any of the benefits of the acceleration. Often, the opposite is the case. A standard DOS program may operate more slowly through a graphic system designed to accelerate Windows performance. As with other PC hardware, your choice of a graphic accelerator depends on the applications that you want to run.

Graphic Coprocessors

A number of graphic coprocessors have been developed for various applications and adapted to PC display systems. Some of these (such as the Hitachi HD63484 and Intel 82786) never made it into the product mainstream. Intel's i860 and i960 chips also appear in some high-end graphics products, but, strictly speaking, these chips are RISC microprocessors that work well on many display tasks but are not specifically designed as graphic coprocessors. The most significant survivor is the Texas Instruments TMS34010 and its improved update TMS34020.

At heart, both chips are essentially microprocessors optimized for handling graphics. For example, even when compared to the best of today's microprocessors, the old TMS34010 is a formidable chip with awesome potential. It has the equivalent of 31 registers 32 bits wide— that's twice as many 32-bit registers as the 68000 microprocessor used in the Macintosh and nearly four times as many as used in Intel's 80386 microprocessor. The architecture of the TMS34020 is much the same, but its implementation is improved so that the chip can yield double the performance of its predecessor.

In graphics, the large number of registers is particularly valuable because they permit the many parameters often used in graphics manipulation to stay inside the processor instead of being shifted continually between the chip and memory. The pointless swapping of information out of the processor and into memory and back again is called *thrashing* and is deadly to performance.

Because of their microprocessor base and many registers, the TMS34010 and TMS34020 can handle pixel calculation tasks better than any other single chip currently in existence. They combine the best features of the general-purpose microprocessor (programmability, mathematical, and logical functions) with specialized graphics functions, such as the capability to move blocks of pixels.

Because the TI chips are fully programmable, they can mimic the function of other graphic systems. All that's required is writing the right program. However, the TI chips are at their best using an application interface designed by their creator, the Texas Instruments Graphic Architecture (TIGA). Many applications are now written to support TIGA. Although each graphic board based on the TI chips is different, TI supplies tools to make it easy for the manufacturers to mate their products to the TIGA interface. All programs that use TIGA can use all boards that support the standard with the sole requirement that different boards require that you install different software drivers (supplied with each board).

Because the TI chips are true microprocessors, they require memory to carry out their functions. Consequently, TIGA boards have two kinds of memory: display memory for the frame buffer and instruction memory for the chip's operations. As with other graphic systems, the amount of display memory will partly determine the maximum resolution of the board and the number of color planes that can be stored.

In the TIGA system, the frame buffer is usually not addressable by the microprocessor in your PC. Consequently, most of these boards require a separate display system when running without benefit of the TIGA environment (for example, for normal DOS applications). TIGA boards must then co-reside with another display adapter or have standard display adapter circuitry built-in in addition to the TIGA circuitry. (Such "built-in" circuits are often optional, such as a daughtercard that attaches to the main display board to add DOS capabilities.)

The natural mode of operation of these boards is through a monitor separate from that used for DOS applications. In such two-monitor systems, one monitor shows a DOS display (such as the commands you give a CAD program), and the other display shows what the TIGA board is doing (such as the wire frame being created by the CAD program). Although the DOS display runs in a standard mode, such as VGA, the TIGA display presents a high-resolution image. Many people either can't afford a second monitor or don't want one cluttering their desks. Consequently, most TIGA adapters allow one-monitor operation, either with on-board VGA circuitry or by allowing the output of a standard video board to loop through the TIGA board (the two boards are connected, and the output of the standard board appears at the connector on the TIGA board).

More instruction memory can be used to improve the performance of the overall display system. For example, the memory can be used to temporarily store the results of graphics commands to draw images so that images can be quickly regenerated without the need for carrying out all the math over again. Some computer-aided design applications call this feature *display-list memory*.

As with other microprocessors, the TMS-series chips can operate at different speeds. All else being equal, the higher the clock speed of the graphic coprocessor, the faster the results it will deliver.

13

Display
Adapters

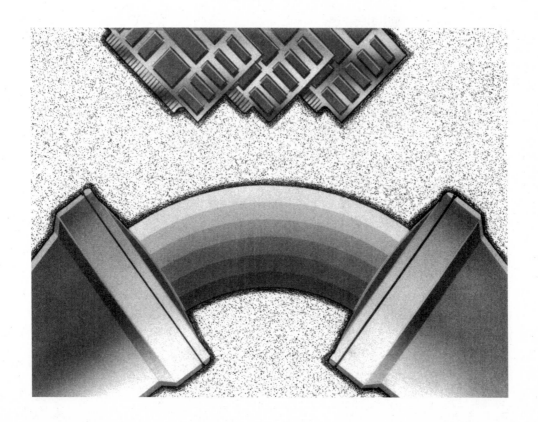

T he hardware that changes your pulsing digital PC's thoughts into the signals that can be displayed by a monitor is called the display adapter. Over the years, the display adapter has itself adapted to the demands of PC users, gaining color and graphics abilities as well as increasing its resolution and range of hues. A number of standards—and standard setters—have evolved, each improving the quality of what you see on your monitor screen. Although display adapters themselves may disappear from PCs, they will leave a legacy in the standards they set.

In the beginning, there was one—one model of IBM Personal Computer and one kind of monitor you could plug into it. As with Model T's, you had exactly one choice of color. At least monitors gave you green on black instead of straight black, but you still had no options or alternatives. Worse was what was displayed on that green screen—text that lingered ghostily or crude block graphics, the kinds of stuff you thought you outgrew when you graduated from crayons to pencils.

About the most positive thing that can be said for the original display situation was that you never had any trouble making up your mind about what you wanted. Nor did you have to worry about such trivialities as art, aesthetics, or creativity—or even the improved flow of communication and understanding that color can bring.

As soon as the PC moved from the hands of hobbyists, who were happy to have anything as long as it was a computer, into the grasp of real people trying to solve real problems, the deficiencies of the original display system became apparent. There had to be a better idea. In fact, there was more than just one. The need for better display systems has brought a profusion of ever-improving display standards, and the trend shows no sign of stopping. Where once an ordinary television set made the output of a computer look bad, today's PCs hold the potential for outdoing Cinerama.

The only difficulty you face with today's display systems is the headache of decision-making. You've got dozens of video standards and display adapters to choose from. Among these are half a dozen "official" display standards, a new standard-setting organization, and new ideas appearing almost as fast as PC models are introduced. Standards and display adapters go hand-in-hand, although their relationship is changing (along with the organizations that set the standards). The first video standards were set simply from the existence of trend-setting display adapters. That means that IBM would introduce a product, and it would immediately become the industry standard. Other companies would design their display adapters around the specifications and capabilities of the IBM product. Somewhere along the way, IBM fell victim to corporate hubris and lost its standard-setting capability. The entire computer industry wallowed for years until enough major players came together (finally with IBM's involvement as well) to create a cooperative committee to work out new standards for PCs and their display systems. Today the Video Electronics Standards Association puts an official imprimateur on the major display standards for PC products.

Today, the traditional display adapter is disappearing, becoming but another function of a PC's motherboard. Innovations like local bus video systems and PCI buses on the motherboard yield higher speeds by sacrificing the conventional display adapter design. Even if the traditional display adapter entirely disappears as a separate entity, however, the standards they use will remain an intrinsic part of every PC on the market.

Along the path of display system development, there have been a few sidetrips. For instance, before the wide acceptance of the VGA standard, the monochrome graphics system developed by Hercules Computer Technology was the primary choice for bit-image graphics on monitor screens. (Some low-cost PCs are still sold with Hercules-compatible display adapters.) Some software still holds its allegiance to the older IBM video standards set by now-obsolete display adapters. Table 13.1 shows the IBM video standards. Nearly all of these not-quite-abandoned standards are still displayable on the latest equipment (thanks to the blessing of backward compatibility deliberately engineered into IBM's display products). Even the first, rudimentary display system still hangs around as the lowest cost way to see on screen what your PC is doing.

TABLE 13.1.
IBM Video
Standards

Resolution	Colors	Mode	Character Box
MDA Monochrome Display Adapter (1981)			
720x350	1	Text	9x14
CGA Color Graphics Adapter (1981)			
640x200	16	Text	8x8
320x200	16	Text	8x8
160x200	16	Graphics	None
320x200	4	Graphics	None
640x200	2	Graphics	None
HGC Hercules Graphics Card (1982)			
720x350	1	Text	9x14
720x348	1	Graphics	None
EGA Enhanced Graphics Adapter (1984)			
640x350	16	Text	8x14
720x350	4	Text	9x14
640x350	16	Graphics	None
320x200	16	Graphics	None
640x200	16	Graphics	None
640x350	16	Graphics	None
PGA Professional Graphics Adapter (1984)			
640x480	256	Graphics	None
VGA Video Graphics Array (1987)			
720x400	16	Text	9x16
360x400	16	Text	9x16
640x480	16	Graphics	None
640x480	2	Graphics	None
320x200	256	Graphics	None
MCGA Memory Controller Gate Array (1987)			
320x400	4	Text	8x16
640x400	2	Text	8x16
640x480	2	Graphics	None
320x200	256	Graphics	None

Resolution	Colors	Mode	Character Box
Super VGA (VESA specification) (1989)			
800x600	16	Graphics	None
8514/A (1987)			
1024x768	16	Graphics	None
640x480	256	Graphics	None
1024x768	256	Graphics	None
XGA Extended Graphics Array (1990)			
640x480	256	Graphics	None
1024x768	256	Graphics	None
640x480	65,536	Graphics	None
1056x400	16	Text	8x16

Resolution (Hz) MDA	Vertical Frequency (Hz)	Horizontal Frequency Modes	Hardware Compatibility
720x350	50	18.43	None
CGA			
640x200	60	15.75	None
320x200	60	15.75	None
160x200	60	15.75	None
320x200	60	15.75	None
640x200	60	15.75	None
HGC			
720x350	50	18.10	MDA
720x348	50	18.10	MDA
EGA			
640x350	60	21.85	CGA, MDA
720x350	60	21.85	CGA, MDA
640x350	60	21.85	CGA, MDA
320x200	60	21.85	CGA, MDA
640x200	60	21.85	CGA, MDA
640x350	60	21.85	CGA, MDA

continues

TABLE 13.1.
continued

Resolution (Hz) PGA	Vertical Frequency (Hz)	Horizontal Frequency Modes	Hardware Compatibility
640x480	60	30.50	CGA
VGA			
720x400	70	31.50	CGA, EGA
360x400	70	31.50	CGA, EGA
640x480	60	31.50	CGA, EGA
640x480	60	31.50	CGA, EGA
320x200	70	31.50	CGA, EGA
MCGA			
320x400	70	31.50	CGA, EGA
640x400	70	31.50	CGA, EGA
640x480	60	31.50	CGA, EGA
320x200	70	31.50	CGA, EGA
Super VGA			
800x600	56, 60 or 72	35.00, 37.60, 48.00	VGA, CGA, EGA
8514/A			
1024x768	43.48	35.52	VGA passthrough*
640x480	43.48	35.52	VGA passthrough
1024x768	43.48	35.52	VGA passthrough
XGA			
640x480	43.48	35.52	VGA
1024x768	43.48	35.52	VGA
640x480	43.48	35.52	VGA
1056x400	43.48	35.52	VGA

NOTE: *VGA passthrough is a feature that allows the board to accept the input of a VGA signal from another board or from a VGA adapter built into the motherboard and pass it through to a monitor connected to the high-resolution board. This permits the use of a single monitor for both VGA and high-end applications.*

Consequently, that's where any discussion of the display adapters used by PCs must begin, with the first board IBM plugged into its first PCs—IBM's Monochrome Display Adapter. A technological fossil perhaps, but as enduring as its mineral-based analog. Although technology may have passed it by, the Monochrome Display Adapter remains part of many PCs, including a bewildering number of new machines.

The Monochrome Display Adapter

Introduced in 1981 along with the first PC, the *Monochrome Display Adapter* is best known by its initials, *MDA*. It's official name is even longer—the Monochrome Display and Parallel Printer Adapter—and the lengthy epithet is entirely descriptive. The "monochrome" in its name reveals the most important characteristic of the MDA. It is designed to work with single-color displays, in particular the virulent green screen that sits atop a huge number of all-IBM systems. The "display adapter" part of the name is a functional description. This board adapts the signal on the PC bus into a form that can be digested by a video system. The parallel printer adapter is a bonus, providing a connection for a printer without sacrificing another expansion slot.

Technically, the MDA is a character-mapped system with no provision for graphics other than the IBM extended character set. It uses digital signals that conform to the Transistor-Transistor Logic standard—nominally five volts to indicate a logical high, zero for a low. For a few months the only PC display system, until 1987 it produced the best-quality text available yielding the sharpest on-screen characters before the VGA system was introduced along wih the PS/2 computer line.

The excellent text quality was hardly accidental. Text was the design purpose of the system. In fact, MDA hints that IBM might never have imagined anyone wanting to draw pictures using a PC—after all, graphics were not one of the capabilities of the typical small business computer when the PC was introduced. Nor did most of the terminals of mainframe computer handle graphics.

MDA Dot Box

For legibility on par with terminals used with its larger computer systems, IBM set the character box for the MDA at 9 x 14 pixels with a typical character using a 7 x 9 matrix in the box. The extra dots space individual lines apart for greater readability, something that's most appreciated when it's not available. To put this character box on the screen in the default arrangement used by most VDTs, 80 columns and 25 rows, requires 720 pixels horizontally and 350 vertically, a total of 252,000 dots on every screen.

MDA Frame Rate

IBM compromised in how to display all those dots. At a high frame rate, displaying that amount of information would require a wider bandwidth monitor than was available (at least inexpensively) when the PC was introduced. IBM instead slowed down the frame rate to 50 Hz. and compensated for whatever flicker might develop by using long persistence phosphors in its standard monochrome display.

The lower frame rate gave the horizontal sweep of the scanning electron beam extra time to cover each line of the image. However, even with the lower frame rate, the dot density of the IBM monochrome standard demanded a higher horizontal frequency than was used by popular video monitors (and television sets), 18.1 Khz versus 15,525 Khz.

6845 Video Controller

The essence of the MDA is the *6845 video controller* and four kilobytes of dual-ported static RAM used for holding character-mapping video information. That memory is sufficient only for a single video page. The 6845 is a completely programmable device that's controlled through a series of registers. Programs can load values into the various registers of the 6845 and change the characteristics of the video signal it (and the display adapter built around it) produces. Table 13.2 lists the registers of the 6845 chip.

TABLE 13.2.
6845 Video
Controller
Registers

Register	Description	Prog. Unit	Read/Write
R0	Horizontal total	Character	Write Only
R1	Horizontal displayed	Character	Write Only
R2	Horizontal sync position	Character	Write Only
R3	Horizontal sync width	Character	Write Only
R4	Vertical total	Row	Write Only
R5	Vertical total adjust	Scan line	Write Only
R6	Vertical displayed	Row	Write Only
R7	Vertical sync position	Row	Write Only
R8	Interlace mode	None	Write Only
R9	Maximum scan line address	Scan line	Write Only
R10	Cursor start	Scan line	Write Only
R11	Cursor end	Scan line	Write Only
R12	Start address (High)	None	Write Only
R13	Start address (Low)	None	Write Only
R14	Cursor (High)	None	Read/Write
R15	Cursor (Low)	None	Read/Write
R16	Light pen (High)	None	Read Only
R17	Light pen (Low)	None	Read Only

The Cursor

The flashing cursor on the screen is created by the 6845 video controller. It's called a *hardware cursor* because the rate at which it flashes is set by system hardware and cannot be changed. However, flashing can be switched off and the size of the cursor can be altered by loading values into the appropriate registers of the 6845 video chip.

Interfacing

Not only does the MDA use different frequencies than most garden-variety monitors, it also uses a connection scheme that was odd for monitors but, because of the IBM influence and ubiquity of the PC, has become commonplace. Sometimes called *direct drive*, the TTL signals from the MDA are fourfold, a drive signal for the electron gun, an intensity bit (which causes highlighted dots and characters to glow more brightly), horizontal, and vertical synchronizing signals. All are directly connected to the part of the display circuit that handles them without the need for decoding, hence the name.

Monitors compatible with the MDA are sometimes termed direct-drive. Alternately they may be called TTL because of their adherence to the voltage levels set by the TTL circuit family. Such displays are also occasionally simply called "digital" monitors because of their use of the digital MDA signals.

These signals are assigned pins on a female nine-pin D-shell connector on the retaining bracket of the MDA. The pin-out of this connector is shown in figure 13.1.

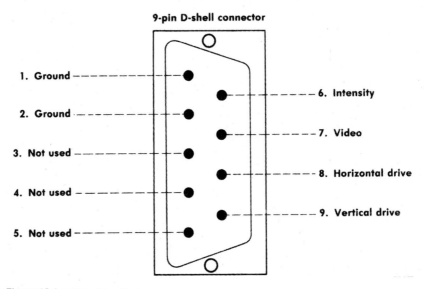

9-pin D-shell connector

1. Ground
2. Ground
3. Not used
4. Not used
5. Not used
6. Intensity
7. Video
8. Horizontal drive
9. Vertical drive

Figure 13.1. MDA Pin-Out.

The distinction of monochrome monitor types is important because only TTL or MDA monitors will work with the MDA board. Composite monochrome monitors are incompatible, as are monochrome VGA monitors. Because these other types of monitors use different connector styles, you won't even be able to plug them into an MDA display.

The Color Graphics Adapter

The first bit-mapped display adapter that IBM developed for the PC was the *Color Graphics Adapter* or *CGA*. Introduced as an alternative to the MDA in 1982, its first images dazzled a world accustomed to plain green computer screens. Compared to today's display systems, however, its spectrum was rather stark—CGA boasted the ability to show but 16 bright, pure colors (a total which misleadingly includes black, dark grey, light grey, and white). To put those colors to work other than making multi-hued text, the CGA board also featured a host of graphics modes with several different levels of resolution ranging from marginal to awful. As the name implies, the CGA system was designed to put graphics on a color screen. However, it also featured text modes and could work with monochrome displays as well—but not the IBM Personal Computer Display that was designed for the MDA board. The CGA display adapter could work with both monochrome and color composite monitors, and it even featured an output for a modulator for use with a television set. (You cannot plug a television directly into the CGA board unless, of course, the television features a monitor-style composite video input.) In addition, the CGA board also made provisions for connecting a light pen.

The CGA was designed to be a multi-mode display adapter. It could use both the character-mapped and bit-mapped display techniques, and allowed several options under each. To store its images, the CGA board was equipped with a whopping 16 kilobytes of memory which functioned as a dumb frame buffer, directly accessible by your system's microprocessor.

CGA is effectively obsolete. Display adapters matching the standard are available only as close-outs and bargain-basement imported clone board that cost as little as $10. Matching monitors are almost impossible to find except used or as close-outs. However CGA lives on in every other display system created by IBM. The color text modes of the latest display adapters mimic the CGA addressing scheme. Nearly all modern display adpaters also offer graphics modes that are backwardly compatible with software written to use CGA displays. Likely the CGA standard will live on for generations of products to come if only as a software artifact.

CGA Character Modes

The eduring text mode of the CGA system is designed much like that of the MDA system. Text mode is the boot-up default and is character-mapped in the CGA system. The chief differences between the CGA text mode and that of the MDA system are the base addresses used for memory and the character attributes that are supported.

CGA hardware also distinguished the two early IBM standards. While MDA was designed to work with a proprietary monitor with nonstandard horizontal and vertical frequencies to produce a sharper image, the CGA system opted for more standard frequencies. It was designed around the horizontal and vertical scan rates of composite video displays, which endowed the CGA system with compatibility with the greatest range of monitors available at the time—but with a sacrifice in on-screen quality.

To fit its operation under the confines of the composite video standard (which uses a 15,525 Hz horizontal rate and 60 Hz vertical rate), the CGA system divides the display into a pixel array numbering 640 horizontally and 200 vertically. To put the same 2,000 text characters on the screen in the same 80 x 25 arrangement used by the MDA allows only a dot box measuring 8 x 8 pixels. Visually and arithemetically, that means worse quality than the output of a nine-wire dot-matrix printer running in its lowest-quality draft mode.

The 16 kilobytes of memory on the CGA is sufficient to handle four pages of text. Normally, only a single page, the first one, is used in text mode. The others are, however, accessible by programs and you through both the BIOS and directly through the mode register on the CGA.

CGA Character Quality

In the CGA system, each character is allocated a 7 x 7 matrix with one dot reserved for descenders and one for letter spacing. Obviously, a descending character will occupy the full height of the dot box and thus bump into an ascending character on the line below with no separation. The fewer dots means that on-screen text will otherwise look more crude and less pleasing than that made by the MDA.

Forty-Column Text

Even those rudimentary characters are more than can be imaged sharply on a standard color television set. On most televisions, lines of text 80 characters wide appear blurry if not indecipherable because of the resolution limits of both the signals inside the set and the picture tube. To allow adequate text renderings on color televisions, IBM added a special low-resolution text mode that cuts the number of columns of text from 80 to 40. The number of rows, 25, is left the same as for other displays because it is not a problem for televisions.

Characters in 40-column text mode are made within the same 8 x 8 dot box used in 80-column mode, and they suffer the same quality limitations. They look rough but they may be more legible than 80-column characters because they are wider.

Although 40-column mode was rarely used in serious computing even in the dark ages of PCs, many programs (including many DOS utilities) make allowance for it by generating lines of text no wider than 40 characters each. That's why some of their displays look so odd most of the time. The 40-column mode is the least common denominator of all IBM text display systems. To assure that utilities would work even on the cheapest PCs, programmers wrote their utilities in this 40 column mode.

Text Colors

In any text mode, the CGA system of attributes allows up to the full 16 color palette to be displayed on the screen at once. Any character of text can be any one of the 16 colors allowed. This same attribute system is maintained today by the VGA system in its text mode.

Under the CGA attribute system, the background of the character—the dots in the 8 x 8 box that are not part of the character shape—can be separately set to one of those same 16 colors with one limitation. In the default operating mode of the system, only eight background colors are possible because the bit in the attribute byte which controls the brightness or intensity of the background color is assigned a different task. It controls the blinking of the character.

A register on the CGA board alters the definition of this attribute bit. By loading values into this register, you or a program can toggle its function between blinking and high-intensity background colors. Note, however, that this register affects all text on the screen. You cannot have both blinking characters and a high-intensity background on the screen at the same time.

The CGA forces programmers to directly manipulate this register. More advanced IBM display adapters add an extra BIOS routine that handles this function.

Border Color

Another register on the CGA controls the *border color*. The screen border is the screen area outside of the active data area in which text appears. The default colors of the CGA display—white text on a black background—hide the matching black border circling the screen. Change the background color of the text, and the border will appear, with an obnoxious sharp demarcation between it and the edge of the perimeter characters in the text display.

The Setting the CGA register for a border color, which can be any of the 16 colors displayable by the CGA system, makes for a more pleasant on-screen image. This register is called the *color select register* and is available at the I/O port 03D9(Hex). The lower four bits of this register control the border color.

Flicker and Snow

One of the most notable—and, to many people, the most obnoxious—characteristics of the CGA and many other display systems is its tendency to flash the text display off and on when the display scrolls in high-resolution text mode. Called *flicker*, it is a direct result not of the display adapter but of the sorry, slow processing speed of some the PCs in which the graphics adapters are installed interacting with impatient programs.

Scrolling an image up the screen requires that every byte used by the display must be moved because every character on the screen (and its associated attribute) must change position. The IBM display system is designed so that information is written to the screen only during the brief period called *vertical retrace*, when the scanning electron beam travels back from the bottom of the screen at the end of one frame to the top for the beginning of the next. During vertical retrace, the electron beam is *blanked*, switched off, so no matter what is sent to it, nothing gets on the screen.

If the CGA or other display memory is changed at some other time—that is, when the beam is not blanked—the display system may scan through video memory while it is being changed with the result that all sorts of odd pulses may be picked up and sent to the screen. On the screen, you see this effect as a flurry of bright dots that look like a flash of animated cartoon unconsciousness. The formal name of the quick flashes of odd images is *video noise* that's more popularly called *snow* because the randomly placed dots look somewhat like a snowstorm (if you have enough imagination).

The CGA card provides a status bit that indicates when vertical retrace is occurring. This is a "Coast is clear" signal that programs or the BIOS can query to see when it is okay to write to the screen. The vertical retrace period only provides enough time for a few lines to be updated, however. So to avoid snow, the scrolling must take place slowly, in chunks, during several retrace periods or snow may occur. IBM side-stepped this issue by turning off the electron beam for the whole time that the screen is being updated during a scroll. Instead of momentarily going black during the invisible vertical retrace, the screen turns black for a substantial—and readily visible—fraction of a second. That whole-screen blanking causes the flicker.

With a CGA adapter, the trade-off is flicker for snow. Other video adapters use faster memory that can be entirely updated within a single retrace period or different types of memory which can be updated while being read to eliminate both problems. However, even with these faster boards, waiting for video retrace can slow down screen response. Some application software gives you the choice of abiding by the rules and updating the screen using IBM's snow-elimination procedure or blasting bytes to video memory without guarantee they will slip in place without snow. With fast PCs and display adapters, this latter mode will yield higher speed without visible on-screen effects.

Graphics Modes

The CGA standard allows for graphics at three different levels of resolution named low, medium, and high—labels apropriate when the system was introduced. Today, even the CGA's highest resolution is low compared with most display systems.

With each CGA graphics resolution level, the number of on-screen dots is traded off against the number of displayable colors. The 16K of available memory creates serious limitations.

Low Resolution

The lowest resolution graphics mode of the CGA—which is not supported by IBM—breaks the screen into a display of 160 lines, each 200 dots wide. Because this display requires 32,000 pixels, only half a byte is available for the storing attributes, allowing four color planes, enough for 16 colors. All of the 16 colors possible with the CGA system can be put on a single screen in low resolution mode, but displays are so chunky that this mode is little-used.

Medium Resolution

As a compromise between color and sharpness, IBM created medium resolution mode. Based on displays of 320 lines, each 200 dots wide, the medium resolution standard allows for two color planes that permit up to four simultaneous colors to be displayed.

The four colors cannot be chosen at random, however. IBM allows four possible palettes: red, green, brown, and black; white, magenta, cyan, and black (or a selected background color); and the previous two but in high intensity colors. The palette to be used is selected using a special Bit five selects between the red/green palette (set a 0) and magenta/cyan palette (set at 1). Bit 4 selects the intensity—0 for dim, 1 for intensified. Bits 0 through 3 select the background color. The default values, set by the BIOS, are for the intensified magenta/cyan palette with a black background.

High Resolution

The highest resolution mode of the CGA assigns one bit to each pixel on the screen, allowing for individual control of an array of pixels 640 horizontally by 200 vertically. Because no additional memory is available on the CGA for storing attribute information, all pixels must be the same color and intensity. You can, however, choose what color you want them to be with the color select register.

CGA Memory Arrangement

In graphics mode, the CGA uses an unusual storage arrangement. It stores even-numbered scan lines, starting with zero, one after the other starting at absolute memory location 0B8000(Hex). The odd-numbered scan lines are stored in sequence starting at an address 2000(Hex) higher. The unusual arrangement was chosen for entirely practical hardware-design reasons.

When multiple bits are assigned to an individual pixel, they are stored as sequential bits in a given byte of storage, four pixels per byte in medium resolution mode (see fig. 13.2). The strange arrangement should not bother you because all graphic software and language automatically takes it into account.

Outputs

You can connect your video display to the CGA through one of three different connectors. The one that you choose depends on the kind of display you want to connect.

The preferred display is an IBM 5151 Personal Computer Color Display that uses TTL digital inputs through a nine-pin D-shell connector. Separate on-and-off digital signals are provided for each of three color guns (red, green, and blue), an intensity bit (which brightens all three guns simultaneously), horizontal sync, vertical sync, and ground. The pin-out is shown in figure 13.3.

In medium resolution graphics mode, each byte encodes four on-screen pixels; the two-bit pattern encodes four colors, one background or one of three foreground colors:

Bit 1	Bit 2	Bit 3	Bit 4	Bit 5	Bit 6	Bit 7	Bit 8
Fourth Pixel		Third Pixel		Second Pixel		First Pixel	

These bytes are arranged sequentially across a scan line. Scan lines then alternate across two storage areas, even lines getting stored in the lower 8K bank, odd lines in the higher 8K bank, as shown below:

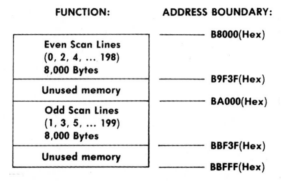

FUNCTION:

ADDRESS BOUNDARY:

- B8000(Hex)

Even Scan Lines
(0, 2, 4, ... 198)
8,000 Bytes

- B9F3F(Hex)

Unused memory

- BA000(Hex)

Odd Scan Lines
(1, 3, 5, ... 199)
8,000 Bytes

- BBF3F(Hex)

Unused memory

- BBFFF(Hex)

Figure 13.2. CGA medium resolution graphics data storage arrangement.

All of these signals are positive-going—that is, a digital high turns on the appropriate gun or indicates a synchronizing pulse—with the exception of vertical sync. When this style of connection was first becoming popular, this arrangement cause untold problems for developers because horizontal sync is normally negative-going. IBM's signal thus appears upside down.

The composite output of the CGA is provided both on an RCA-style pin jack on the retaining bracket of the card and as part of a header on the surface of the board. The signal provided at the RCA jack are compatible with both color and monochrome displays that follow the NTSC standard.

The composite output provided on the card itself is meant to operate a modulator. Other pins of this single-row header supply the voltage needed to operate the modulator (see fig. 13.4).

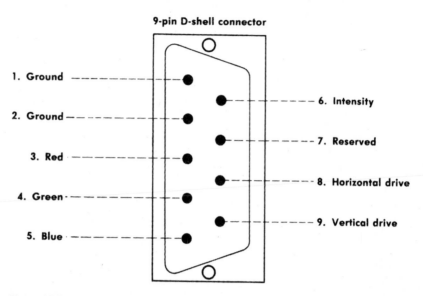

9-pin D-shell connector

1. Ground

2. Ground

3. Red

4. Green

5. Blue

6. Intensity

7. Reserved

8. Horizontal drive

9. Vertical drive

Figure 13.3. CGA RGB interface pin-out.

Black-and-White Mode

When a monochrome composite monitor is connected to the CGA, the screen will sometimes shift to a eye-straining jumble of vertical lines and shadings instead of solid color. Text can be almost impossible to read. This odd display is caused by the color subcarrier that's part of the composite video signal. It limits the bandwidth of the video signal and interferes with monochrome information, creating the odd patterns on the screen.

You can clear up the problem by switching to *black-and-white mode*, which turns off the color subcarrier. Although you can control this by loading values into a CGA register, the MODE command supplied with DOS does the job more easily. Just type the following to switch off the color subcarrier:

MODE BW

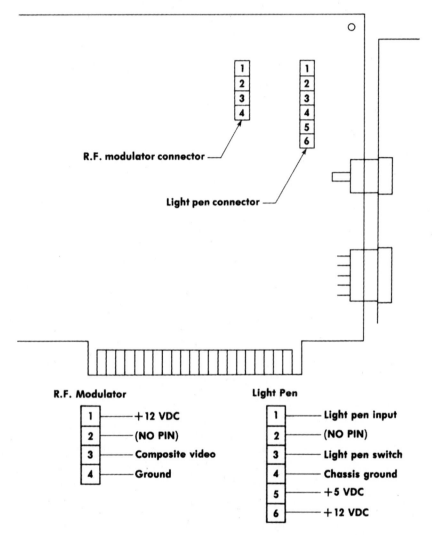

R.F. modulator connector

Light pen connector

R.F. Modulator

1	+12 VDC
2	(NO PIN)
3	Composite video
4	Ground

Light Pen

1	Light pen input
2	(NO PIN)
3	Light pen switch
4	Chassis ground
5	+5 VDC
6	+12 VDC

Figure 13.4. CGA modulator output pin-out.

Double-Scanned CGA

In these days of VGA resolution, which promises more than twice the on-screen sharpness of CGA, you might think that the PC's first graphic display standard would have been left far behind by new hardware. In fact, new PCs capable only of CGA graphic response continue to be introduced. Nearly all of these systems are mono-chrome, and most deliever higher resolution than the nominal 640 x 200 pixels of ordinary CGA. Universally, these graphic systems are found in laptop and notebook computers using Liquid Crystal Displays (LCDs).

These display systems achieve higher resolution than CGA graphics by using *double-scanning* of the CGA image. That is, instead of display-ing 640 x 200 pixels on the screen, the show 640 x 400 pixels. This double-scanning technique allows for sharper images without sacrific-ing the ability to use the CGA standard. Most importantly, double-scanned CGA allows the use of a less expansive LCD panel than a higher-quality VGA system would—few lines on the screen means fewer pixels in the panel which means lower manufacturing costs.

If double-scanned CGA were simply double-scanned, it would look as bad as any CGA screen. However in text mode, double-scanned systems use a different character generator than ordinary CGA sys-tems. Instead of duplicating pixels to stretch the character matrix, the double-scanned systems actually generate individual characters from an 8 x 16 matrix. In order words, the double-scanned text characters are double-sharp, almost as high in quality as those produced by today's standard top-quality display adapters.

Where double-scanned CGA comes up short is graphics. These systems maintain ordinary CGA addressing, so their double-scanning produces no increase in graphic sharpenss. Each pixel in an on-screen image is simply doubled in the vertical dimension. The result is bigger pixels than would be produced by a 640 x 400 pixel display system, corre-sponding to bigger grains in a photographic image. The bottom line is that ordinary double-scanned CGA graphics are not any sharper than plain old ordinary CGA graphics. In other words, the advantage of double-scanning is thus limited to sharper text and graphic compat-ibility but not higher-quality in graphics.

Sometimes, however, you can improve the quality of double-scanned CGA graphics. Some non-standard display systems—for instance, that used by the AT&T model 6300 PC-compatible computer—make 640 x 400 images in their native mode. Some software drivers for these

AT&T display systems will drive double-scanned CGA systems, yielding full 400-line quality in graphics mode. If you have a double-scanned display system, it's always worth a try to setup your graphics applications for AT&T display systems to see the effects. If the AT&T drivers work, your reward will be graphics that are twice as sharp. If the drivers don't work, your only loss will be the few minutes spent on experimentation.

Hercules Graphics

Although a step in the right direction, CGA display systems had two major drawbacks. It wasn't particularly sharp, and it required the purchase of both a video adapter and a new monitor if you wanted to add graphics to an original PC. The latter need was particularly galling if you had just invested in a monochrome system or had no need for color. Adding a second display for graphics when a system already had a perfectly good—and sharp—text-based imaging system appeared counter-productive (at least to those not in the business of selling CGAs and color displays).

Hercules Computer Technology, Inc., headed by Kevin Jenkins, developed a seemingly perfect solution, one that worked so well that it became the first universal video standard not initially promulgated by IBM.

The *Hercules Graphics Card* or *HGC* was the obvious solution, adding bit-mapped graphics to the character-mapped MDA. But Hercules had the forethought to obtain support from Lotus Development Corporation in *1-2-3*, at the time (and long afterward) the most popular program for the PC. *1-2-3* graphics were in themselves justification for the purchase of the HGC.

HGC Compatibility

The foundation for the HGC was complete emulation of the MDA. From a functional standpoint, the two boards worked exactly alike in text mode, operated at the same frequencies with exactly the same cabling and displays. Characters were formed in the same 9 x 14 pixel dot-box on a screen with a full-screen resolution of 720 x 350 pixels, a horizontal sync frequency of 18.1 Khz and a 50 Hz frame rate. All attributes of the IBM MDA—underline, blink, high-intensity, and inverse video—are supported by the HGC. The HGC even included a parallel printer port with a based address of 03BC(Hex), same as the MDA.

Although the HGC is compatible with MDA hardware and its text-mode software, it is not compatible with any IBM graphic standard. Applications must be specially written with support for the HGC. Programs written for the CGA and other IBM graphic standards will not properly execute on the HGC unless they also that HGC support.

HGC Memory

The point of departure for the HGC was its memory. Instead of the mere four kilobytes of the MDA, the HGC was equipped with a full 64K, functionally arranged in two contiguous 32K banks with base addresses of 0B0000(Hex) and 0B8000(Hex)—that is, occupying the ranges assigned to both the MDA and CGA boards.

The various video modes supported by the HGC allowed the use of this memory for several purposes. In text mode, it could be devoted to numerous text pages—up to 16. In graphics mode, it even was suffi-cient for two full-screen pages of high-resolution monochrome images.

Memory Overlap

One problem with the Hercules monochrome system was that its 64K was too large to fit into the 32K space reserved for monochrome memory. It overlapped into the color area, potentially conflicting with CGA boards plugged into the same system.

The Hercules solution was to offer degrees of compatibility controlled by a software switch. In default, boot-up mode, the HGC would activate only half of its memory, 32K starting at the 0B0000(Hex) base, eliminating the conflict. By poking a value into the software configu-ration switch register located at I/O port 03BF(Hex), the HGC would convert to use of both banks of its memory. Poking zero into the second bit (Bit 1) of the register at this port disables the second bank of memory. Poking a one enables the second bank.

A special program was supplied with the board, appropriately termed *HGC.COM*. Running this program with its FULL option put the full memory of the HGC into use. The HALF option switched off the upper bank. Later software incorporated this switching procedure in drivers designed for use with Hercules graphics.

Hercules Graphics Standards

In its graphic modes, the HGC slightly alters its on-screen resolution to 720 x 348. One bit is assigned to each pixel, allowing no attributes (other than the pixel being off or on). Eight contiguous on-screen bits are assigned each byte, 90 bytes to each 720 pixel line. The most significant bit of each byte corresponds to the leftmost on-screen pixel stored in the byte.

Lines are not stored in memory in the same order that they are displayed on the screen, however. Contiguous lines in memory display four lines apart on the screen. In effect, the screen is divided into four fields, and one line from each field in sequence is fitted into memory, then the second line from each field, and so on.

Switching to graphics mode is accomplished by poking a bit into the software configuration switch register. The first bit at this register, located at I/O port 03BF(Hex), controls the mode. Poking a zero here yields disables graphics mode; a one enables graphics mode.

The Enhanced Graphics Adapter

By 1984, the shortcomings of the CGA system had become obvious—if just from the skyrocketing white cane sales to the people who were using it regularly. The hard-to-read text displays and coarse graphics probably generated more eyestrain than anything since the insurance industry invented two-point type.

IBM's answer was a system based on a new video adapter called the *Enhanced Graphics Adapter* or *EGA*. The enhancements wrought by the new system were severalfold. It increased on-screen resolution. It brought the possibility of graphics to monochrome screens such as the venerable green IBM Personal Computer Display. And it added new

BIOS routines that augmented and extended the existing ROM-based video support built into the PC and XT.

EGA was designed to be backwardly compatible with CGA, so programs written for the older display system would work with the new board. However, EGA's sharper images required higher-frequency signals—and that meant an entirely new style of monitor.

In the long run, EGA proved to be an interim step—better but not quite good enough. After a three-year heyday, it was relegated to the background and backward compatibility. It survives as a few display modes in the VGA system. Support for EGA products—and the products themselves—is disappearing because today higher resolution technologies are simply cheaper.

EGA Resolution

The important improvement that EGA brought to the PC world was the sharper images it put on IBM's matching monitor, its Enhanced Graphics Display. EGA pushed resolution up to 640 x 350 pixels, forming characters in dot boxes measuring 8 x 14. Although the EGA dot box was a dot narrower than that used by the MDA, each characters was made from the same 7 x 9 matrix. More importantly, EGA provided enough extra space between lines on the screen so that descenders and ascending characters on adjacent rows did not touch. Color text was finally as readable as monochrome.

The EGA system also extended its 640 x 350 resolution to graphics. All previous IBM-supported graphics modes were also included in the capabilities of the VGA so that it was entirely downwardly compatible with CGA graphics.

EGA Frequencies

To fit EGA's extra dots into a video signal, IBM had to extend the horizontal scanning frequency used by the system. Instead of the television-compatible 15.575 Khz horizontal scan rate of CGA, EGA substituted 23.1 Khz. To minimize image flicker, however, the EGA design maintains the 60 Hz frame rate of CGA.

EGA Colors

Even more notable was the increase in color capability brought by the EGA standard. By altering the adapter-to-display interface, the possible palette in the EGA system was increased to 64 different hues (again, counting black and various shades of grey as separate colors). In addition, the greater memory capabilities of the EGA standard meant that the wider rainbow was possible at higher resolution levels. At its maximum resolution and maximum memory endowment, the EGA could spread 16 different shades from its 64 color palette on a 640 x 350 screen at one time.

EGA Monochrome Graphics

The EGA was also designed to eliminate the two-standard system that reigned in the IBM universe. The EGA adapter was equally adept at handling color and monochrome displays. By setting DIP switches that were cleverly arranged to be accessible through a cut-out in the card retaining bracket without popping the top off your PC, the EGA could be adapted to any standard IBM display. (Note, however, that this clearly does not include composite monitors—the EGA has not composite output. Then again, IBM never made a composite display for its personal computers.)

More importantly, the support of monochrome displays extended to graphics. The EGA provided IBM's first monochrome graphics standard. Note, however, that IBM went its own direction and did not accommodate the graphics standard used by the Hercules Graphics Card. Instead, it substituted its own standard, one compatible with EGA color graphics so that no extra effort was required to write programs compatible with both EGA monochrome and color graphics. Adopting the Hercules standard would have required programmers to develop separate code for color and monochrome graphics on the EGA.

EGA Memory

By the time the EGA was introduced, many applications had been written that moved bytes directly to video memory rather than endure the sluggishness of using IBM's primitive BIOS routines. Changing the memory arrangement used by the EGA would have made the adapter incompatible with those existing applications.

The EGA designers faced another problem. More colors and resolution automatically requires more memory. That would not be a problem except that only a finite range of addresses were reserved out of the 8088 microprocessor's range for holding video information.

The IBM solution was to make the EGA a bank-switched memory card. Its video memory was divided into four planes that could alternately be switched into the address range of the 8088.

In standard (minimal) configuration, the EGA was equipped with 64 kilobytes of RAM, split into four 16K banks. To the host system, the adapter looked like a CGA board as long as the advanced EGA modes and their bank-switching was not brought into play.

That 64K was not sufficient for the wide-palette, high-resolution modes of the EGA, so IBM provided expansion up to 256K through a memory expansion daughter card. Expansion EGA memory was allotted equally among the banks on the card, so the maximum configuration gave four banks of 64K each.

The memory of the EGA board can be switched to either the base address of the CGA or MDA to achieve compatibility with programs that write directly to video memory. In EGA modes, however, the base address of the board's memory is shifted downward to 0A0000(Hex). As a result, the entire 64K to 256K of video memory is no longer constantly addressable by the host PC's microprocessor, and writing directly to screen memory takes somewhat more ingenuity on the part of programmers. The alternative, however, was untenable—devoting a full 256K of address range to the frame buffer, which would leave almost no High DOS memory for other purposes (such as EMS— coincidentally another bank-switching system). This address-stretching solution set the pattern for all other display systems until the introduction of XGA.

EGA Interface

The EGA retained the digital signal format used by the MDA and CGA before it. To accommodate its additional color capabilities, the CGA wiring scheme was altered slightly by redefining one connection and adding two new ones. Each color gun was given two signals, essentially the individual drive signals as used on the CGA and individual intensity signals. Instead of all three guns being controlled by a single intensity signal, each gun could be brightened by itself. The two-bit digital code given to each gun allowed it four intensities—off, bright, and two intermediary levels. The combination of four levels per gun times three guns allows up to 64 hues to be displayed from the various combinations.

For compatibility with all IBM monitors, the EGA used the same connector as previous video boards, a nine-pin, female D-shell connector. The definitions of its signal pins were controlled by the setup DIP switches depending on the type of monitor that was to be connected to the board. Both the monochrome and CGA-compatible color schemes corresponded exactly with the MDA and CGA standards to allow complete compatibility. For EGA displays, the CGA intensity pin was used for the intensity signal for the green gun. Additional intensity signals were added for the red and blue guns. See figure 13.5 for the pinout.

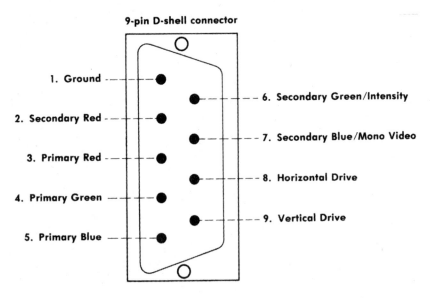

Figure 13.5. EGA pin-out.

EGA Monitor Compatibility

Because the EGA adapter cannot determine which variety of display it is connected to, you must be certain to properly match its setup to your display or risk damage to your monitor. Supplying the wrong synchronizing signals to a monochrome IBM Personal Computer Display for more than a short period can permanently damage the monitor. The symptom of an improper mating of display adapter and monitor is a blank or unreadable screen, typically crossed by a number of thin horizontal lines, and a high-pitched squeal from inside the monitor. Should you encounter these symptoms when connecting a display system, turn off your PC immediately and double-check the compatibility of your monitor and the display adapter.

At the other end of the EGA connection, matters are just as critical with IBM color and monochrome displays introduced before the EGA. Fortunately, the IBM Enhanced Color Display can determine whether it is connected to an EGA or CGA display and adjust itself to accommodate the correct synchronizing frequency. Rather than determine the frequency of the signal, however, the EGA display examines the polarity of the horizontal synchronizing signal. If the horizontal sync is positive, the monitor operates with a 15,575 Hz sync frequency. If the horizontal sync is negative-going, the display switches to a 23.1 Khz sync frequency.

EGA Compatibility with Other Display Adapters

In the IBM scheme of things, you are allowed to connect one monochrome, one color, or one of each sort of display to a system, but you can never connect more than one of each. You could, for instance, add both a CGA and MDA to your computer, but you could never use two CGAs at once. That's because both CGAs would try to locate their memories at the same addresses. Monochrome and color systems use different memory addresses, however.

The EGA follows this philosophy. If you setup an EGA to operate a color display, then it will happily co-reside with a MDA board. If you setup your EGA as a monochrome adapter, then you can also add a CGA to your system. You cannot, however, add two EGAs—even if one is setup as monochrome and one as color—because their BIOS codes and memory assignments would conflict. While a jumper on the EGA board allows you to alter its base address, the alternate address is not supported by the IBM EGA BIOS code.

Addressing the EGA

In its compatibility modes, the EGA looks to your system as though it were an MDA or CGA, depending on how you have it set up. It even sets the equipment flags appropriately to match the location assigned to its memory so that your programs might never know that they are working with an EGA. You can write simple assembly (or higher level) language procedures that directly address video memory, and they will work properly with the EGA *provided you operate within its compatibility modes.*

In the EGA's advanced graphics modes, however, you're in for surprises because you can address only one of its four pages unless you toggle the page register. Fortunately, the EGA BIOS and most application software takes care of that automatically.

The Video Graphics Array

The original IBM policy of making a display an option to its personal computers had both logical and illogical bases. It made sense because some video systems are suited better to particular applications than are others. Detached display adapters let you adopt a mix-and-match approach. It also opened up a huge market for add-on video products from third party vendors and fosters an upgrade market. Separate display adapters could be pulled out and replaced as new standards evolve and budgets allow.

But built-in video can be a logical choice in a number of applications, too. Portable computers, like the PC Portable (which does not actually have its display system built into its system board) and laptop Convertible (which essentially does) demand complete integration of the display and computer system if just for the convenience of moving one box around. The ready-made approach also offers the advantage of no-thought convenience. The system comes as a unit in one big box (may be two, one for the monitor, but at least all in one shipment) that would require no decision-making or technical expertise.

Moreover, the included-video approach is also likely to be cheaper—no need for expansion boards, interface circuitry, added development costs. IBM's first attempt at building a low-end computer, the PCjr, included its own video as part of its system board. IBM discovered that even in the age of separate display adapters, most personal computers were sold complete with their display systems already installed. With an eye to cutting costs and giving purchasers what they wanted, IBM moved the basic display adapter function to the motherboard of its second-generation of personal computer, the PS/2 line.

To minimize the downside of built-in video, IBM designed its new motherboard display circuitry to be extensible. That is, it includes built-in provisions for connecting to improved display systems are part of its design. More importantly, the on-board circuitry can work co-operatively with add-ons, potentially reducing the cost of the support needed for displays that are better than the out-of-the-box systems.

In addition, IBM designed the new display system so as not to limit your monitor options. It would accommodate either monochrome monitors so you could start to work on a budget or color displays for those who wanted flashier images. The system was designed so there was no longer a need to worry about color and monochrome incompatibilities when buying hardware or even when writing software.

The centerpiece of IBM's improved display strategy was the *Video Graphics Array* or *VGA* that's built into all Micro Channel PS/2s and included (one way or another) with nearly all compatibile computers today. In a few low-cost non-Micro Channel PS/2s, IBM stingily built in a cost-cutting offshoot of VGA technology called the *Memory Controller Gate Array* or *MCGA*. (This same abbreviation is interpreted as *Multi-Color Graphics Array*.) As the cost of full VGA support plummeted with its acceptance as a standard, this sub-standard has fallen by the wayside.

The VGA name is derived from a VLSI chip used in the implementation of the PS/2 line. Most of the circuitry of the EGA board (including emulation of Motorola's 6845 video chip) was engineered into this one logical gate-array chip, which IBM dubbed with the "video graphics array" name. The chip name quickly became the label for the entire system, probably because of its resemblance of its abbreviation to those of its predecessors, CGA, and EGA. The new name seemed like an logical outgrowth.

In fact, VGA itself is a logical outgrowth of IBM's previous video standards. It incorporates all previous video modes and extends them into new, more colorful, higher resolution territory. Yet VGA is neither the best possible video system nor does it rank as anything revolutionary. Third party video systems available even before the VGA was introduced displayed sharper or more colorful images or both. Nearly all compatible computers now include *SuperVGA* display systems that only start with VGA capabilities then add one or more higher resolutions. Even IBM has started equipping its higher-end hardware with better display systems. Even these, however, have the original VGA design at their cores. In other words, today the minimum display system you should expect in a new PC is VGA. And nearly all PCs have the capability of using software written to the VGA standard.

VGA Graphics Resolution

As with previous IBM products, the VGA standard incorporates several resolution levels in a variety of modes. But the VGA offers more modes than every before, a total of 17. Unlike previous IBM video systems, however, the top resolution offered for text and graphic modes are different.

Of the graphics modes, the sharpest bit-mapped color images made by the system achieve a resolution of 640 x 480 pixels while displaying 16 simultaneous colors selectable from a palette of 256K. This same level of resolution is also available in a two-color (white on black) mode.

While 640 x 480 pixel resolution appears to be a trifling improvement over the 640 x 350 pixels offered by the EGA adapter, the new standard has its strong points. The obvious strength is sharpness. The VGA standard allows for sharper, more colorful images than ever before.

For graphics programmers, the four-to-three relation of horizontal to vertical pixels is a blessing because it mirrors the four-to-three aspect ratio of most video monitors. The net result is square pixels—every dot is a square mosaic tile in the on-screen image—which relieves the programmer of needing to include extra steps to allow for oblong pixels and the otherwise resultant oddly-shaped figures.

VGA Text Resolution

Text resolution under the VGA standard is even sharper than that available in graphics modes. The spec calls for 720 x 400 pixels in either 16 colors or shades of grey in monochrome. Characters in this mode are more detailed than ever before, each constructed from a 9 x 16 matrix of on-screen dots, two dots taller than MDA and a dot wider than EGA.

Strangely, a forty-column mode survives, even though the VGA standard precludes the use of a television set as a display. The reason underlying this throwback mode is compatibility with older software. Programs written for 40-column displays will work on VGA systems as well as all previous display standards. In addition, a brand-new 40-column mode is available with 360 x 400 16-color text mode.

Two other new text modes allow for 30 rows of text on the screen, instead of the more common 25, by maintaining the maximal resolution and making minor alterations to the operating frequencies of the system.

VGA Colors

While more pixels mean more detail, other VGA modes also improve over previous standards by giving greater color capabilities. These wider spectrum available on the VGA system allows for greater realism to computerized image-making.

At its most colorful, the VGA standard supports up to 256 hues on the screen at one time, with the colors selectable from a total palette of 262,144. The displayable colors are selected from the palette of possibilities thanks to mapping through color look-up tables. In this mode, resolution is limited to 320 x 200 pixels, the same as medium resolution color mode on the original Color Graphics Adapter which only allowed for four simultaneous hues from a palette of 16. The number of displayable colors represent the limits of VGA memory—the limit on the number of discrete values that could be stored in pixel location in video memory. Boards with more memory often extend the 256-color mode to higher resolutions.

VGA Signals

Achieving this wide color palette required a major change in IBM display technology. Where previous IBM systems had used digital signals, the VGA system is built around analog. Only IBM's Professional Graphics Controller, which was never intended as a mainstream PC product, used analog signals in the PC environment.

One reason for switching to analog was simple logistics. The more colors that a digital system has to display, the more control signals are required (unless, of course, the system uses serial data, which would complicate both display and adapter to an extraordinary degree). The necessary number of signals increases geometrically. For instance, the 16 color palette of the CGA (that is, 2^4 colors) required four separate signals (red, green, blue, and intensity). The 64 color palette of the EGA (2^6 colors) was built around six signals. To support the 262,144 colors of the VGA system—that's 2^{18} (two to the eighteenth power) colors—would require 18 signals in a purely digital system, six signals per color. Instead of such a multiplicity of signals and wires to carry them, the VGA standard substitutes a diversity of voltage levels on three conductors. One signal on one wire is assigned to each primary color. Each signal corresponds to one of each electron gun in the cathode ray tube of the monitor. The strength of the signal controls the intensity of the beam.

The analog approach does more than just save on cabling. It makes the circuitry of the monitor quite a lot simpler. Even in a digital system, the power going to the electron beam would have to be converted from digital to analog form to be displayed, anyway. The VGA standard just puts the converter on the video card instead of in the monitor.

To convert the digital values stored in memory into analog signals to operate monitors, IBM chose to use a one-chip DAC known as the *Inmos 6171S*. Like the 6845 of the CGA and MDA, this chip has become ubiquitous in VGA-compatible display adapters as card makers seek to obtain the greatest possible compatibility with IBM's designs. The Inmos DAC is actually three DACs in one—one for each primary color. In addition, the DAC also contains the *color look-up table* for the color mapping process. The look-up table values are stored in 256 registers inside the DAC chip itself.

VGA Frequencies

As with previous new IBM video standards, taking full advantage of VGA requires an entirely new kind of monitor that operates at substantially higher synchronizing frequencies than those used by previous IBM systems.

Because each of its higher resolution images is made from a greater number of scan lines, each of those lines must be drawn more quickly. The VGA standard requires a horizontal frequency of 31.5 Khz, almost exactly double the roughly 15 Khz rate of the CGA standard and about 50% higher than the 23.1 Khz of the EGA standard.

For more stable images, the vertical refresh or frame rate of the VGA system was also increased over previous IBM standards. The VGA frame rate is 70 Hz in most display modes, although the high resolution VGA graphics modes operate at 60 Hz to squeeze more data on the screen. As a result of the faster frame rate, flicker should be less apparent in text modes. Faster phosphors can be used, which can mean less image lag and less chance of encountering the lingering ghosts endemic to most IBM monochrome screens.

VGA Memory

Storing 640 x 480 graphics in 16 colors (which take six dot-planes) requires a great deal of memory, roughly 230K. The VGA system built into PS/2 system boards is equipped with the next even memory multiple up, 256K. VGA-compatible products may stretch video memory even further—some as far as a megabyte. As with EGA, the VGA circuitry permits mapping this memory in several ways—at a base address of 0B0000(Hex) or 0B8000(Hex) to achieve compatibility with the MDA and CGA adapters or at a base address of 0A0000(Hex) for EGA and VGA graphics.

The full 256K is divided into four 64K banks, controlled by the Map Mask Register, located at 03C5(Hex) when the index at the sequencer register port 03C4(Hex) is set at 02. This register controls whether the system microprocessor can write to one or more of the banks at a given time.

Addressing within each bank is linear in VGA modes. That is, the memory arrangement puts on-screen pixels and lines into memory in the same order that they appear on the screen.

VGA Compatibility

The VGA system boasts extremely good software compatibility with previous standards and negligible hardware compatibility. The higher synchronizing frequencies and analog signals used by the VGA system require an entirely new kind of monitor. Old displays cannot be adapted to the VGA standard with but one exception. Many—but not all—multiscan-style displays (discussed in the next chapter) have a wide enough tolerance for synchronizing frequencies and analog inputs so that they can accept the signals made by previous video standards, VGA, and even higher resolution standards. Unless you have a multisync-style display with analog inputs, however, you'll need a new monitor to take advantage of VGA. Software is another matter entirely. Even with the new standard, IBM has endowed the VGA system with nearly complete compatibility with software written for previous video standards. The VGA system supports all past IBM video modes down to the lowest resolution levels, albeit occasionally in a form and format that's slightly different from the original. For instance, in the old-fashioned 200-line video modes (320 x 200 and 640 x 200 graphics), the displays are double-scanned at a 400-line rate, making on-screen image look sharper but just as chunky as on a 200-line display.

BIOS versus Register Compatibility

The software compatibility of video adapters comes in two flavors. *BIOS compatibility* indicates that a particular board reacts identically to the original that it is copied from when it receives a software command to its on-board firmware. The video BIOS then does the dirty work, poking the appropriate values into the registers on the display adapter. The video BIOS thus isolates software from the video hardware. All video boards since and including the EGA add their own BIOS code to the host system when they are installed, and the BIOS takes responsibility for matching software commands to the hardware.

This degree of compatibility ensures that the code of one video adapter will work the same as another—at least at the level of commands sent to the BIOS.

Although IBM's intention was that the BIOS level of compatibility should be sufficient, programmers often don't heed rules that IBM laid down. Sometimes to gain extra performance, programmers write software that takes direct control of video hardware. Such programs write directly to video memory and may even poke values into registers that control the functions of the video system. For programs written at this level to function properly, all the registers of a video board must work exactly like those of the prototype that they are copying. When perfect, this *register-level compatibility* assures that all programs written for one video board will work on the so-called compatible board.

IBM's VGA system maintains register-level compatibility with EGA boards and BIOS-level compatibility with CGA and MDA. That's all the compatibility that need be expected from the products of a third-party vendor. If such a product lacks register-level compatibility with either EGA or VGA, you face the prospect of programs crashing or not running at all. While the first VGA-compatible display adapter produced by third-party manufacturers often faltered in their hardware compatibility with the VGA standard, up-to-date boards have no problem making the grade. All modern VGA-compatible display adapters work well with any VGA software.

VGA Auxiliary Video Connector

For third-party manufacturers making VGA boards for PC-bus computers, true hardware compatibility with the VGA standard goes beyond the register level. It also requires one additional item, duplication of the extension to IBM Micro Channel expansion bus that's called the *VGA auxiliary video connector*. On many VGA-compatible boards, this connector is termed the *VGA Feature Connector*. This special connection permits add-on accessories to share signals and control with VGA circuitry. Add-ons can even overpower the VGA and switch it off, claiming the video output as their own.

This edge connector is usually included on most VGA-compatible display adapters. If you plan on adding an auxiliary high-resolution display systems (such as an 8514/A-compatible board) to your PC, you'll need this connector. In fact, display adapters lacking this connector cannot truly be called VGA hardware compatible.

A derivative of this design is called the *VESA Feature Connector*. The VESA connector includes the same signals as the VGA Feature Connector but uses a pin connector instead of the VGA's edge connector. Consequently, products expecting a VGA Feature Connector cannot plug into a VESA Feature Connector (and vice versa). Each of the two standards requires its own particular connecting cable. If you need to plug an auxiliary video board into your PC's VGA board, you'll want to check which type of expansion connector it uses.

VGA Color and Monochrome Integration

Although previous IBM video standards have drawn a hard line between monochrome and color, the VGA is designed to accommodate both. This is the culmination of gradual IBM progress to unite the two in one product. The MDA and CGA were completely incompatible with stand-alone systems. The EGA was capable of performing duties (and then some) of either but require that its DIP switches be properly setup—else you risk display damage. The VGA standard allows one output to be interchangeably plugged into monochrome or color VGA displays without fear of damage and with a guaranty of proper operation.

The secret is a special extra signal added to the VGA interface. This extra signal is simply feedback from the display that tells the VGA circuitry whether it's plugged into a color or monochrome display. VGA monitors are designed to send out the proper signal.

VGA Monochrome Operation

When the VGA circuitry detects a monochrome display, instead of sending out three separate signals for each color gun in the display (which, being monochrome, only has one gun), it sends out only the green signal, which the display uses to control the intensity. Of course, the color repertory of the VGA system is compromised by this operation, but the VGA compensates by translating the colors into up to 64 shades of gray, a result of the green signal being capable of handling 2^6 discrete intensities, limited by the 6-bit green channel of the DAC.

VGA Vertical Gain

The VGA system creates displays that may have one of three possible line counts—350 (for MDA- and EGA-compatible modes), 400 (for double-scanned CGA modes), and 480 (for new VGA modes). All else being equal, a display made out of fewer lines will be shorter in that the lines stay a constant width (or high, depending on your perspective). The result would be that EGA-style displays would look more than 25 percent too short on the screen—in other words, all scrunched up.

IBM displays compensate for this height difference by changing their vertical gain depending on the mode of the signal being received from the VGA. To relieve the display from the responsibility for figuring out the video mode from its signals alone, the VGA sends the display a code to indicate what number of vertical lines it is sending in each frame. The code is contained in the polarities of the vertical and horizontal synchronizing signals.

The code specifies that 480-line operation in both sync signals are negative-going. For 400-line mode, vertical sync is negative-going and horizontal is positive-going (as it in in CGA displays, which 400-line mode mimics). For 350-line mode, the code is vertical sync positive-going and horizontal sync negative-going. The remaining combination, both sync signals positive-going, is reserved.

IBM provides two methods for dealing differing times spent on each horizontal line when the number of lines change. Two dot-clocks (oscillators) are available, one each for 350- and 400-line modes. The 480-line graphics mode slightly lower the normal VGA 70 Hz frame rate to 60 Hz, allowing extra time for more lines.

VGA Connectors

Because the signals generated by the VGA are so different from those of previous IBM display systems, IBM finally elected to use a different, incompatible connector so that the wrong monitor wouldn't be plugged in with deleterious results. Although only nine connections are actually needed by the VGA system (eleven if you give each of the three video signals its own ground return as IBM specifies), the new connector is equipped with 15 pins. It's roughly the same size and shape as a nine-pin D-shell connector but before IBM's adoption of it, this so-called *high-density, 15-pin connector* was not generally available.

Figure 13.6 shows the signal assignments to this connector.

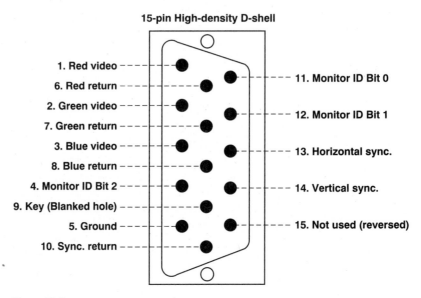

Figure 13.6. VGA pin-out.

In that the same connector is now used by all of IBM's PS/2 display systems as well as by a large number of compatible manufacturers, it is becoming more available:

Male, in-line (cable) connector,
crimp-type installation
AMP part no. 748364-1

Female, in-line (cable) connector,
crimp-type installation
AMP part no 748565-1

AMP Inc.
Harrisburg, PA
800-624-2177

71325 series connectors:

Molex Incorporated
2222 Wellington Court
Lisle, IL 60532
312-969-4550

Although many multisync-style displays will work with VGA signals, many such displays use nine-pin connectors compatible with the EGA standard. To plug one of these displays into an IBM-standard VGA connection, you'll need an adapter cable. The wiring of such a cable is shown in figure 13.7.

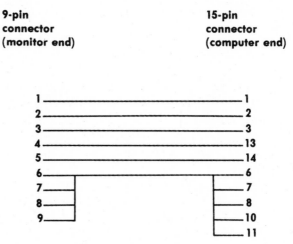

9-pin
connector
(monitor end)

15-pin
connector
(computer end)

Figure 13.7. 9-to-15 pin adapter cable for VGA.

The Memory Controller Gate Array

The lesser PS/2s like the Models 25 and 30 presented IBM with a number of problems, one of them being video. This equipment was designed to be low cost even to the extent that IBM skimped on the

Model 25 memory quota by giving it 512K instead of the DOS maximum 640K. But including VGA graphics, with its demand for 256K of RAM, would be antithetical to the cost-driven goal. But another monitor standard—or a backstep to a previous standard—would undercut the promotion of VGA as the next standard.

The compromise was to compromise, to offer some VGA hardware compatibility while slicing away three-quarters of the memory and much of the functionality. The result was a video half-breed, better than before but not as good as VGA. Its heritage is a mixture of previous IBM standards—registers arranged like those of the EGA, video modes carried over from the MDA and CGA, and hardware and two modes like that of the VGA. For lack of a better name, this system has earned the label *Memory Controller Gate Array* or *MCGA*.

MCGA Text Modes

As with the CGA, two text modes are provided by the MCGA system: one with 40-column character and one with 80-column characters. Text resolution is superior to that of the CGA because resolution was driven up to 640 x 400 pixels to match with the VGA hardware standard. Characters are formed in a 8 x 16 dot box in which every on-screen dot is addressed. A total of 16 different on-screen colors can be displayed simultaneously, draw from the full VGA palette of 256K because MCGA circuitry uses the DAC chip as VGA.

To your software, however, MCGA text looks like that of the CGA. The video buffer is assigned a base address of 0B8000(Hex), just as is the CGA.

MCGA Graphic Modes

The MCGA system offers four distinct text modes: two roughly compatible with the CGA standard and two with the VGA standard.

The CGA-compatible modes allow medium- or high-resolution CGA graphics. Both the 320 x 200 and 640 x 200 modes are double-scanned to produce 400 on-screen lines for compatibility with VGA equipment. As with other systems, however, double-scanning does not increase the sharpness of the image.

In medium resolution, CGA-compatible mode, four simultaneous colors are available, but they can be draw from the full 256K color VGA palette. Just as with the CGA, an alternate palette can be selected (through the same register), but this alternate palette can be filled with colors of your choice drawn from the full VGA repertory. In high-resolution CGA mode, foreground and background colors (the only two allowed) can be drawn from the full 256K VGA palette.

The VGA-compatible high-resolution graphics mode suffers most from the reduced memory of the MCGA system. With only 64K bytes available, the color choice at the 640 x 480 resolution level necessarily had to be sacrificed, resulting in the support of a single color plane. The color mapping capabilities of the system allow a choice from the full 256K palette for both the foreground and background color, but that's it.

The MCGA system does fully support the VGA's 320 x 200, 256 color mode, including full color mapping from the 256K VGA palette.

MCGA Software Compatibility

BIOS support provided by the MCGA system is negligible, the same level supplied by the CGA system. About the most the BIOS can do is to put strings of characters on-screen in teletype mode. MCGA does support both standard IBM CGA graphics modes, and is thus compatible with all software that sticks to IBM's rules.

The register structure of the MCGA system is quite similar to the VGA system to support its two VGA graphics modes. The differences arise because of the fewer modes and possibilities allowed by the MCGA circuitry.

MCGA Hardware Compatibility

From the hardware side, the MCGA system uses VGA-style displays and VGA connectors. The system can detect color or monochrome displays and reset its output accordingly. It also uses the same synchronizing signal polarity code to indicate whether it is operating in a 400- or 480-line mode. An MCGA system can thus use the same monitors as a VGA system, including IBM's PS/2 display line, VGA-compatible displays, and even VGA-compatible multisync-style displays.

Upgrading MCGA to VGA

The design of the Models 25 and 30 allows you to upgrade either system to full VGA graphics by adding an expansion board. When a VGA adapter is installed in either computer, the system board video circuitry is automatically switched off, and the expansion board becomes the sole video output of the computer. Because the system board video connector is inactivated, you must plug in your display to the connector on the VGA adapter board. Either the IBM Personal System/2 Display Adapter or its third-party equivalent is a suitable upgrade for either the Model 25 or 30.

Super VGA

For IBM, VGA appeared like the end of the line for standard PC display systems. The company has made no basic improvements or changes to the VGA design. To this day, it remains the standard display system in the vast majority of the IBM's personal computers. Only after four years did the company deign to add something better as standard equipment—and only then to the machines at the very top of the IBM line.

Actually, there's little to criticize in VGA as standard equipment. Although higher resolutions always look better, a dramatic step up from VGA would be invisible on the small monitors that are attached to most PCs. The detail would simply be too fine to see at normal working distances. VGA resolution is about all that's necessary for normal screen sizes, normal eyes, and normal viewing distances—and yesterday's software.

Graphic operating environments—and particularly those with multitasking capabilities (as in OS/2) or multitasking pretensions (as in Windows)—have placed greater demands on display systems. When you put several windows on the screen, you need more than a tidbit each to know what's going on, so you naturally want to squeeze as much on one screen as possible. Higher resolution lets you put more information in front of your eyes. Moreover, larger screens are becoming both available and popular, so more on-screen detail becomes both visibile and desirable.

Even when VGA was first getting off the ground and into everyone's heart and eyes, many companies tried to push beyond its 640 x 480 graphic resolution. The motiviation was to offer something more in their products. After all, adding higher resolution modes required no extra memory—designers could skimp colors at high resolution (four colors instead of sixteen) without sacrificing big numbers in advertising copy. Chipset makers added extra high resolution modes to their products, and display adapter makers followed suit.

Table 13.3 shows the bits of video memory required by the various resolutions available.

TABLE 13.3.
Bits of Video
Memory Required

Resolution	Pixels	16 colors (4-bit) memory required	256 colors (8-bit) memory required	16.7 million colors (24-bit) memory required
VGA (640x480)	307,200	153,600	307,200	921,600
Super VGA (800x600)	480,000	240,000	480,000	1,440,000
(1,024x768)	786,432	393,216	786,432	2,359,296
(1,280x1,024)	1,310,720	655,360	1,310,720	3,932,160

EGA Plus

The most popular increment up from VGA was 800 x 600 pixel resolution. At first termed *EGA Plus* because early products were not entirely VGA compatible (often using digital outputs), this level of resolution soon became known as *Super VGA* with the advent of true VGA compatibility. Super VGA simply did VGA one—or at least 50 percent—better, putting more pixels on the screen. Where Super VGA fell short was standardization. Every display adapter manufacturer had a different idea about how to put higher resolution on the screen.

Multiscanning monitors made 800 x 600 pixel and higher resolutions viewable but not entirely trouble-free. The differing standards were apt to pop images at odd places on the screen—too far left or right, too high or too low—because the timing of their signals was different. There wasn't even a standard for scan rate or refresh rate, so a given multiscanning monitor had no assurance of working with a specific Super VGA board.

The situation made several facts evident: The lack of standards made monitors look bad. The visible problem—misplaced images—appeared on monitor screens, so monitor makers were the likely candidates for blame. No one company had the marketplace power to set a new standard—except maybe IBM, but IBM abdicated responsibility by single-mindedly advocating its own high-resolution standard (8514/A) that was promoted only slightly worse than the bubonic plague. Sorting out Super VGA required a standard.

VESA

Monitor-makers were first to see a solution to the Super VGA problem. In 1987, an engineer at NEC Technologies, the company that offered the best-selling multi-scanning monitor (the MultiSync), was inspired by an idea while washing dishes in his kitchen. He conceived the idea of an industry consortium representing all the manufacturers involved in PC display systems sitting down together and coming up with their own standard. In 1988, NEC brought together many of the more prominent monitor manufacturers to try to hammer out timing standards and eliminate the off-center image problem. The result was the formation of the *Video Electronics Standards Association* or VESA. In subsequent years, nearly every display adapter manufacturer, monitor maker, and more prominent computer manufacturer had joined the organization.

VESA went beyond the initial idea of setting a hardware standard for Super VGA signals by also creating a software standard as well. But like all committees of competitors, VESA waffled. Instead of developing an iron-clad specification as IBM had done for previous display standards, VESA develop a combination of standards and guidelines that left no manufacturer in the cold nor any single set of numbers carved in stone.

800 x 600 Resolution

The committee emphasized the need for a high 72 Hz refresh rate to minimize screen flicker and there set a standard for Super VGA. But it also created a pair of "manufacturers' guidelines" to accommodate the products of member organizations that could not operate at such a high rate. After all, these committee members had stocks of old products on their shelves that were developed before the VESA standards were first promulgated. The guidelines allowed for Super VGA systems operating at 56 and 60 Hz to earn the VESA imprimateur.

Certainly, there are other justifications for the guidelines. The 56 Hz guideline is compatible with older monitors than have a bandwidth aimed only as high as handling the 35.5 Khz horizontal frequency IBM set for its 8514/A system. The 60 Hz guideline is a compromise that allows less expensive electronics with a reasonable refresh rate. On the down side, the flexible guidelines mean that you have no assurance that a given monitor will work with high refresh rate Super VGA display adapters. If a monitor will accommodate the VESA refresh rate of your Super VGA display adapter, however, the guidelines assure that the resulting image will occur in the middle of the screen.

Signal timing wasn't the only difference between the various makes of SuperVGA display adapter. Each one also had its own method for controlling its high resolution operations, essentially its own display modes. This variance was a software problem. Drivers to link boards to software had to be individually written for each display adapter because few software publishers were willing to write separate drivers for a dozen different boards.

VESA's solution was a "phantom" display mode, number 6A, that all display adapters could share. When software calls upon a Super VGA adapter to operate in that mode, it triggers the display adapter to switch into and operate compatibly in its own native 800 x 600 pixel mode. Although SuperVGA drivers are not yet universal for VESA display adapters, eventually they may be thanks to this aspect of the standard.

1024 x 768 Resolution

The next significant resolution about Super VGA's 800 x 600 pixels is 1024 x 768 pixels. VESA has worked on and developed a number of standards at this resolution level.

Along with the guidelines and standard at 800 x 600 pixels, VESA published timing recommendations for the 1024 x 768 resolution level for use in dumb frame buffer systems. This standard anticipated using the same horizontal frequency as Super VGA at its highest (72 Hz) refresh rate Beyond Super VGA, VESA has moved to developing specifications for higher resolution levels, working to develop independent standards based on IBM's 8514/A (an effort, like the IBM product itself, which it has since abandoned) and XGA systems. Beyond that, VESA provides a forum for the exchange of ideas between the engineers of various video vendors.

8514/A

In 1987, IBM's view of higher than VGA resolutions was that they were required only by special applications. The vast majority of PC users didn't require anything better than graphics made from an array of 640 x 480 pixels. For those who aspired higher, the company offered an expensive (initially about $1000) special-purpose display adapter with fixed-function acceleration circuitry, the *8514/A*, so named because it was the Adapter to match the company's model 8514 monitor.

Besides price, the 8514/A had three other strikes against it—IBM made the product available only for Micro Channel computers. Worse, the outputs of the adapter provided an interlaced video signal, which was viewed as substandard by most of the PC industry—particularly monitor makers whose products lacked the long- persistence phosphors needed to eliminate the image flicker interlacing inevitably caused. Unlike other display systems, IBM did not disclose the circuitry that made the 8514/A work, resulting in a system that was extremely difficult to clone.

Nevertheless, the 8514/A standard survived for about three years as IBM's high-resolution PC display system. Just as clone-makers were developing their own compatible products, IBM summarily abandoned 8514/A in favor of its new XGA system. However, 8514/A lives on as part of the XGA system.

The most important characteristic of the 8514/A standard was its resolution, 1024 x 768 pixels, which put about 2.5 times as much data on the screen as VGA. It uses the same DAC as the VGA system, allowing it the same potential range of 262,144 hues, although memory limits the number which can be simultaneously displayed to a substantially lower value.

8514/A Memory

One-half megabyte of memory was made the standard equipment of the 8514/A, more than enough for a 1024 x 768 pixel image four bits deep. This memory is arranged into four bit-planes, each comprising a megabit of storage, allowing 16 simultaneous on-screen colors.

That arrangement leaves 128K of memory to spare, 256 kilobits in each of the bit-planes. The memory used for the on-screen display takes up the lowest portion of that storage. The rest is put to work as auxiliary memory for the data needed to carry out such functions as area-filling and holding loadable character sets. Although this additional memory can be addressed directly by the host microprocessor just like the rest of the memory of the 8514/A, this ability is not supported by IBM. That means writing to it may destroy information that the 8514/A has stored there for another purpose.

In its VGA-compatible mode, the 8514/A divides up its half-megabyte into eight 1024 x 512 bit planes arranged in two independent banks four bit-planes deep. The hardware design of the 8514/A does not allow combining these planes into one eight-bit plane.

8514/A Memory Expansion

IBM offered a half-megabyte expansion option for the 8514/A as a daughter card. This additional memory was designed to increase the color capability of the display adapter, moving its spectrum to eight bit-planes and 256 simultaneous on-screen colors. In addition, with the additional memory both VGA-mode maps of the 8514/A also gain eight-bit depth and a full range of 256 simultaneous colors.

Dual-Screen Operation

The 8514/A system operates independently of the VGA circuitry built into its computer host. Operations that change the memory of one will not necessarily change that of the other. When the 8514/A is in its VGA mode, the two VGA systems duplicate one another. However, some operations (such as loading a palette or changing modes) may affect the 8514/A screen differently, revealing incorrect colors or a skewed greyscale. When the 8514/A is in its native mode, the two screens can be used independently. Typically, you will put text displays on the VGA screen while the 8514/A makes drawings.

8514/A Connections

The 8514/A display adapter shares the same high-density 15-pin D-shell connector with the VGA standard. Pin assignments are somewhat different. In addition to the separate signal leads provided for each color and its return, and horizontal and vertical sync, three additional leads replace the one devoted to identifying the display attached to the adapter.

The monitor identification signals provide feedback to the 8514/A board so that it knows what kind of display with which it is working. These signals prevent the 8514/A from sending a high resolution/ interlaced image to a fixed-frequency VGA display that might be plugged into its connector. This feedback scheme ensures that the display and adapter function properly together and avoids the problems that might be encountered plugging a monochrome display into a CGA adapter. Table 13.4 shows how the polarities of the synchronizing signals code different display types.

TABLE 13.4.
VGA and 8514/A
Sync Code

Mode #	Mode Function	Lines on-screen	Horiz. sync polarity	Vert. sync polarity
1	EGA	350	Positive	Negative
2	VGA text or CGA compatibility	400	Negative	Positive
3	VGA graphics	480	Negative	Negative
4	8514/A	768	Positive	Positive

Display Code Signals:				
Display Type:	8503 (Mono)	8513	8512	8514
ID Bit 0	N/C	0V.	0V.	0V.
1	0V.	N/C	N/C	N/C
2	N/C	N/C	N/C	0V.

Compatibles

After nearly three years of development, independent chip makers
finally cloned the hardware aspects of the 8514/A display adapter.
Western Digital was first to produce a truly register-compatible 8514/A
controller chip, which several manufacturers used to build boards
which could be plugged into the ISA bus. (Several board-makers had
earlier released products compatible with the 8514/A adapter interface
but not fully register compatible.) Most of these hardware-compatible
boards improved on the basic standard by recognizing that the need
for hardware compatibility extended only back to the system from the
display adapter itself. The most maligned aspect of the standard—its
interlaced monitor signals—could be avoided because software never
touched this side of the adapter.

Most non-IBM 8514/A adapters include provisions for selecting
monitor frequencies while maintaining the 1024 x 768 resolution of
the standard. Besides the IBM interlaced frequencys, most provides
for 60 Hz and 70 Hz (or higher) non-interleaved operation. The
interleaved mode allows the use of dual-frequency monitors such as
IBM's original 8514 and its successor 8515. The non-interlaced modes
require multi- scanning monitors with the capability of operating at
high refresh rates— 48 Khz with 60 Hz refresh, 56 Khz with 70 Hz
refresh.

Extended Graphics Array

Other manufacturers were slow to adopt the 8514/A standards, and
their hesitation was amply rewarded in 1990 with IBM's introduction
of its *Extended Graphics Array* video system, commonly termed *XGA*.
Just as a few manufacturers had released display adapters that match

both the 8514/A adapter interface and its hardware registers, IBM made that standard obsolete. Its XGA was backwardly compatible with only the 8514/A adapter interface. The 8514/A registers that had proved so troublesome to clone were ignored by the new standard.

From another perspective, XGA is IBM's replacement for its 8514/A display adapter. In some ways, you won't even see a difference—the current incarnation of XGA is designed to use the same monitor (IBM's 8515, a 15-inch color display that replaced the original 8514), operating at the same frequencies (35.5 KHz horizontal, 44 Hz interlaced vertical). XGA also incorporates the 8514/A Adapter Interface to allow backward compatibility with 8514/A software. Both XGA and 8514/A are made only to fit Micro Channel computers.

But XGA makes several improvements on the 8514/A. For one, it does not mandate monitor interlacing, which finally puts IBM in league with the makers of 8514/A-compatible display adapters. Aftermarket vendors have supported both interlaced and non-interlaced displays at frame rates up to 70 Hz when following the 8514/A standard. XGA permits IBM to follow the same strategy.

Unlike those compatible boards, however, XGA is not hardware-compatible with 8514/A and won't run software that takes direct register control of the 8514/A board. IBM sees XGA as a standard in its own right, one that only tips its hat at 8514/A and then continues further on into the world of graphics coprocessing.

Open Standard

Wanting to prevent the recurrence of the yawn that greeted 8514/A, IBM made XGA an open standard by fully disclosing its features and operation. Anyone with a few electronic parts and idle millions (to cover development costs) can clone it in relatively short order—say a year or so.

The world greeted XGA with a yawn anyway because the first XGA system that IBM produced matched 8514/A in its greatest perceived flaw, its use of an interlaced monitor. However, the XGA system did have its strong points—enough that most Windows accelerators incorporate most of its functions. Nor was interlacing required by the system; as with third-party 8514/A adapters, the XGA system was designed to work with either interlaced or non-interlaced monitors. To free XGA from status as a propriety standard, VESA setup a committee (of which IBM is a member) to develop XGA into an independent industry standard, a status it had not yet reached in mid-1992.

Coprocessor

The XGA board itself incorporates its own coprocessor, an IBM proprietary design, which is optimized for Windows and OS/2 Presentation Manager displays. Some of the functions it carries out include BitBlts, (Bit-block transfers), similar pixel-block transfers, line drawing, area filling, logical and arithmetic mixing, map masking, scissoring, and x-y axis addressing. (In contrast, the fixed-function 8514/A was primarily aimed for operation with Computer-Aided Design software.)

Of course, the IBM XGA coprocessor is not a mandatory part of the design of XGA boards. Manufacturers who work with the TMS34010-series of coprocessors believe that the chip can be adapted to XGA operation with appropriate software or firmware.

Hardware Sprite

XGA also adds a wealth of new features and modes to PC displays. One of these is a hardware-controlled sprite, a 64 x 64 pixel graphic image that overlays the main on-screen image without disturbing the contents of the main video memory. The sprite is moved around the screen using simple positioning commands without requiring the entire screen to be rewritten. That makes it particularly suited for moving screen elements such as fast mouse cursor.

XGA Modes

XGA has two operating modes: one in which it emulates a VGA board, the other its own Extended Graphics Mode. In VGA mode, it is hardware compatible with a conventional VGA adapter and includes all VGA features. When operating in the latter mode, it generates either 640 x 480 or 1024 x 768 pixel resolution, selected by your software. XGA also supports its own 132-column text modes with 200, 350, or 400 scan lines using characters that each measure eight pixels wide.

The VGA circuitry of the XGA adapter cannot coexist with another VGA adapter in the same PC. IBM allows for the VGA portion of its XGA adapter to be switched off for such installations. Up to eight XGA systems can be installed in a single PC.

The XGA system requires a contiguous eight-kilobyte block of memory addresses for its BIOS extension, and this block must be somewhere within the address range C0000(Hex) to DFFFF(Hex) in the High DOS memory area. The upper one kilobyte of this block is reserved for the XGA's control registers, which are used to send commands to the XGA coprocessor.

Memory

XGA also incorporates an innovative means for software to address screen memory. Actually, three different addressing schemes are supported, called *apertures*, and their accessibility and use depend on the type of microprocessor in your system and the bus width of the slot into which the XGA adapter is plugged.

The most basic of these is the 64K aperture, which can correspond to standard VGA addressing at the first 64K segment in the base of High DOS memory (addresses starting at A0000(Hex)). Alternately, this aperature can be relocated to the B0000(Hex) range. Its value is set by an on-board register. Unlike VGA, however, this aperature provides addressing to all of the memory of the XGA system (up to four mega-bytes) by paging. This aperature allows 8088 and 8086 microprocessors to use XGA memory in their limited real-mode addressing range.

A one-megabyte aperture allows XGA memory to be controlled through a one-megabyte window that can be located on any one-megabyte boundary within the first 16M of extended memory. Again, this aperature is paged to allow access to all four megabytes of XGA memory. This aperature is design to allow the 286 and 386SX micro-processors convenient access to XGA memory. It is also the widest aperature available when the XGA board is plugged into a 16-bit expansion slot.

Finally, the XGA's memory can be addressed through a four-megabyte aperature located in extended memory above the first 16M, giving a 386DX or 486 microprocessor direct (rather than paged) access to the maximum RAM of the XGA board.

Color

To achieve full-backward compatibility, XGA allows use of the color storage scheme of the VGA system. As with VGA, XGA incorporates modes that allow up to 256 simultaneous on-screen colors selected from a palette of 262,144.

Memory determines the maximum number of colors that can be displayed on the screen at a time: the low-end board with 512K of video memory allows 256 colors at the lower resolution, 16 at the higher resolution. With its current maximum of one-megabyte of VRAM, XGA allows 65,536 colors at lower resolution, 256 at high.

Because XGA uses the same DAC as VGA and 8514/A boards, it is limited to the same 262,144-color palette as the older boards are. However, XGA also incorporates a direct addressing mode which sidesteps the palette register and gives direct access to 256 on-screen colors.

In addition, XGA adds its own 16-bit *direct-color* storage format. The 16-bits are allocated between primary colors with five for red and blue and six for green. This allows 65,536 simultaneous on-screen colors. Although that range may seem limited compared to the real world spectrum, it doubles the capability of the TruVision TARGA system of 15-bit color, five bits each for red, green, and blue. In that the TARGA system has been found adequate for most video displays, XGA should be even better.

The XGA coprocessor is limited to the palette-mapped colors and cannot manipulate 16-bit direct color values. Consequently, direct color mode requires that the XGA board be used as a dumb frame buffer. However, the coprocessor can work on XGA memory at the same time as your PC's microprocessor use the memory for direct color effects.

Bus Mastering

The XGA board is designed for bus mastering operations, allowing its coprocessor to take direct memory control, not just of its own on-board VRAM, but also entirely of the system RAM in your PC. The XGA coprocessor is designed to carry out graphics calculations on data held in your PC's main memory, then speedily transfer the resulting image into the VRAM screen memory as a bus master.

Control of the XGA board is achieved through a number of memory-mapped registers that fit along with 7K of BIOS extension code into the High DOS area of your PC (memory addressed above the old DOS 640K limit). To send a command to the XGA, your software needs only to write specific bytes to certain of these memory addresses.

14

Computer Displays

A display is the keyhole you peer through to spy on what your PC is doing. You can't do your work without a display, and you can't work well without a good one. The final quality of what you see—the detail, sharpness, and color—all depend on the display that you use. No longer a function only of TV-like monitors, today's computer displays increasingly rely on new technologies to achieve flat screens and high resolutions.

You cannot see data. The information that your computer processes is nothing but ideas, and ideas are intangible no matter whether in your mind or your computer's. Although you may be able to visualize your own ideas, you cannot peer directly into the pulsing digital thought patterns of your computer. You probably have no right to think that you could—if you can't read another person's thoughts, you should hardly expect to read the distinctly non-human circuit surges of your PC.

Although most people—at least those not trained in stage magic—cannot read thoughts per se, they can get a good idea of what's going on in another person's mind by carefully observing his external appearances. Eye movements, facial expressions, gestures, and sometimes even speech can give you a general idea about what that other person is thinking, although you'll never be privy to his true thoughts. So it is with computers. You'll never be able to see electrons tripping through logical gates, but you can get a general idea of what's going on behind the screens by looking into the countenance of your computer, its *display*. What the display shows you is a manifestation of the results of the computer's thinking.

The display is your computer's line of communication to you, much as the keyboard enables you to communicate with it. Like even the best of friends, the display doesn't tell you everything, but it does give you a clear picture, one from which you can draw your own conclusions about what the computer is doing.

Because the display has no direct connection to the computer's thoughts, the same thoughts—the same programs—can generate entirely different on-screen images while working exactly the same way inside your computer. Just as you can't tell a book's contents from its cover, you cannot judge the quality of a computer from its display.

What you can see is important, however, because it influences how well you can work with your computer. A poor display can lead to eyestrain and headaches, making your computer a pain to work with. A top-quality display means clearly defined characters, sharp graphics, and a system that's a pleasure to work with.

Monitors versus Displays

Although the terms often are used interchangeably, a display and a monitor are distinctly different. A *display* is the image-producing device itself, the screen that you see. The *monitor* is a complete box that adds support circuitry to the display. This circuitry converts the signals sent by the computer (or some other device, such as a videocassette recorder) into the proper form for the display to use. Although most monitors operate under principles like those of the television set, displays can be made from a variety of technology, including liquid crystals and the photon glow of some noble gasses.

Because of their similar technological foundations, monitors, to a great extent, resemble the humble old television sets. Just as a monitor is a display enhanced with extra circuitry, the television is a monitor with even more signal conversion electronics. The television has incorporated into its design a *tuner* or *demodulator* that converts signals broadcast by television stations or a cable television company into about the same form as those signals used by monitors. Beyond the tuner, the television and monitor work in much the same way. Indeed, some old-fashioned computer monitors will work as televisions as long as they are supplied with the proper signals.

New monitors have developed far beyond their television roots, however. These monitors have greater sharpness and purity of color. To achieve these ends, they operate at higher frequencies than television stations can broadcast.

Computer displays and monitors use a variety of technologies to create visible images. A basic bifurcation divides the displays of desktop computers and those of laptop machines. Most desktop computers use systems based on cathode ray tube technology akin to that used in the typical television set. Laptop and notebook computers chiefly use liquid crystal displays. Occasionally, a desktop or portable system may be equipped with a gas-plasma display, but the displays are unusual and costly.

529

Cathode Ray Tubes

The oldest electronic image-generating system still in use is the *cathode ray tube*. The name is purely descriptive. The device is based on a special form of vacuum tube, a glass bottle that's been partially evacuated and filled with an inert gas at very low pressure. The *cathode*—another name for a negative electrode—of the tube shoots a beam or ray of electrons toward a positively charged electrode, the *anode*. (Electrons, having a negative charge, are naturally attracted to positive potentials.) Because it works like a howitzer for electrons, the cathode of a CRT is often called an *electron gun*.

Phosphors

From the gun in the neck of the tube, the electrons flow to the tube's wide, flat face where a layer of phosphorous compound lies. This phosphorus layer has a wonderful property—it glows when struck by an electron beam. To move the beam across the breadth of the tube face (so that the beam doesn't light just a tiny dot in the center of the screen), a group of powerful electromagnets arranged around the tube (the arrangement is called the *yoke*) bend the electron beam in the course of its flight.

The magnetic field set up by the yoke is carefully controlled and causes the beam to sweep each individual display line down the face of the tube.

The image you see in a CRT is the glow of the electrically stimulated phosphorous compounds, simply termed *phosphors* in the industry. Not all the phosphorous compounds used in CRTs are the same. Different compounds and mixtures glow various colors and for various lengths of time after being struck by the electron beam.

A number of different phosphors are used by PC-compatible monitors. Table 14.1 lists some of these phosphors and their characteristics.

TABLE 14.1.
Phosphors and
Characteristics

Type	Steady-state Color	Decay Color	Decay Time(ms)*	Uses or Comments
P1	Yellow-Green	Yellow-Green	15	Oscilloscopes, radar
P4	White	White	.1	Display, television
P7	White	Yellow-Green	unavail.	Oscilloscopes, radar
P11	Blue	Blue	.1	Photography
P12	Orange	Orange	unavail.	Radar
P16	Violet	Violet	unavail.	Ultraviolet
P19	Orange	Orange	500	Radar
P22R	Red	Red	.7	Projection
P22G	Yellow-Green	Yellow-Green	.06	Projection
P22B	Blue	Blue	.06	Projection
P26	Orange	Orange	.2	Radar, medical
P28	Yellow-Green	Yellow-Green	.05	Radar, medical
P31	Yellow-Green	Yellow-Green	.07	Oscilloscope, display
P38	Orange	Orange	1000	Radar
P39	Yellow-Green	Yellow-Green	.07	Radar, display
P40	White	Yellow-Green	.045	Med. persist. display
P42	Yellow-Green	Yellow-Green	.1	Display
P43	Yellow-Green	Yellow-Green	1.5	Display
P45	White	White	1.5	Photography
P46	Yellow-Green	Yellow-Green	.16	Flying spot scanners
P55	Blue	Blue	.05	Projection
P56	Red	Red	2.25	Projection
P101	Yellow-Green	Yellow-Green	.125	Display
P103	White	White	.084	P4 w/bluish background
P104	White	White	.085	High efficiency P4
P105	White	Yellow-Green	100+	Long persistence P7
P106	Orange	Orange	.3	Display
P108	Yellow-Green	Yellow-Green	125	P39 w/bluish background

continues

531

TABLE 14.1.
continued

Type	Steady-state Color	Decay Color	Decay Time(ms)*	Uses or Comments
P109	Yellow-Green	Yellow-Green	.08	High efficiency P31
P110	Yellow-Green	Yellow-Green	.08	P31 w/ bluish background
P111	Red/green	Red/Green	unavail.	Voltage penetration
P112	Yellow-Green	Yellow-Green	unavail.	Ir light pen doped P39
P115	White	White	.08	More yellow P4
P118	White	White	.09	Display
P120	Yellow-Green	Yellow-Green	.075	P42 w/ bluish background
P122	Yellow-Green	Yellow-Green	.075	Display
P123	Infrared	N/A	unavail.	Infrared
P124	Yellow-Green	Yellow-Green	.130	Yellow part of P4
P127	Green	Yellow-Green	unavail.	P11+P39 for light pens
P128	Yellow-Green	Yellow-Green	.06	Ir light pen doped P31
P131	Yellow-Green	Yellow-Green	unavail.	Ir light pen doped P39
P133	Red to Green	Red to Green	varies	current-sensitive
P134	Orange	Orange	50	European phosphor
P136	White	White	.085	Enhanced contrast P4
P137	Yellow-Green	Yellow-Green	.125	High efficiency P101
P138	Yellow-Green	Yellow-Green	.07	Enhanced contrast P31
P139	Yellow-Green	Yellow-Green	70	Enhanced contrast P39
P141	Yellow-Green	Yellow-Green	.1	Enhanced contrast P42
P143	White	Yellow-Green	.05	Enhanced contrast P40
P144	Orange	Orange	.05	Enhanced contrast P134
P146	Yellow-Green	Yellow-Green	.08	Enhanced contrast P109

Type	Steady-state Color	Decay Color	Decay Time(ms)*	Uses or Comments
P148	Yellow-Green	Yellow-Green	unavail.	Light pen applications
P150	Yellow-Green	Yellow-Green	.075	Data displays
P154	Yellow-Green	Yellow-Green	.075	Displays
P155	Yellow-Green	Yellow-Green	unavail.	Light pen applications
P156	Yellow-Green	Yellow-Green	.07	Light pen applications
P158	Yellow	Yellow	140	Medium persistence
P159	Yellow-Green	Yellow-Green	unavail.	Enhanced contrast P148
P160	Yellow-Green	Yellow-Green	.07	Data displays
P161	Yellow-Green	Yellow-Green	.07	Data displays
P162	Yellow-Green	Yellow-Green	.1	Data displays
P163	White	White	2	Photography
P164	White	Yellow-Green	.1	Displays
P166	Orange	Orange	unavail.	Ir light pens
P167	White	White	.075	Display
P168	Yellow-Green	Yellow-Green	.075	Projection
P169	Yellowish	Yellowish	1.5	Display
P170	Orange	Orange	unavail.	Enhanced contrast P108
P171	White	Yellow-Green	.2	Display
P172	Green	Green	unavail.	Light pen displays
P173	Infrared	N/A	unavail.	Light pen
P175	Red	Red	.6	Display
P176	Yellow-Green	Yellow-Green	.2	Photography
P177	Green	Green	.1	Data displays
P178	Yellow-Green	Yellow-Green	.1	Displays
P179	White	White	1	Displays
P180	Yellow-Orange	Yellow-Orange	.075	Displays
P181	Yellow-Green	Yellow-Green	unavail.	Color shutter displays
P182	Orange	Orange	50	Displays

continues

TABLE 14.1. continued	Type	Steady-state Color	Decay Color	Decay Time(ms)*	Uses or Comments
	P183	Orange	Orange	unavail.	Light pen displays
	P184	White	White	.075	Displays
	P185	Orange	Orange	30	Enhanced contrast P134
	P186	Yellow-Green	Yellow-Green	25	Displays
	P187	Yellow-Green	Yellow-Green	unavail.	Light pen P39
	P188	White	White	.05	White displays
	P189	White	White	unavail.	White displays
	P190	Orange	Orange	.1	Displays
	P191	White	White	.12	White displays
	P192	White	White	.2	White displays
	P193	White	White	.08	White displays
	P194	Orange	Orange	17	Displays
	P195	White	White	.125	Inverse displays

Approximate time in milliseconds for display to decay to 10 percent of its emission level.

The type of phosphor determines the color of the image on the screen. Several varieties of amber, green, and whitish phosphors are commonly used in monochrome displays. Color CRT displays use three different phosphors painted in fine patterns across the inner surface of the tube. The patterns are made from dots or stripes of the three additive primary colors—red, green, and blue—arrayed next to one another. A group of three dots is called a color *triad* or color triplet.

One triad of dots makes up a *picture element*, often abbreviated as *pixel* (although IBM prefers to shorten picture element to *pel*).

The makers of color monitors can individually choose each of the three colors used in forming the color triads on the screen. Most monitor makers have adopted the same phosphor family (P22), so the basic color capabilities of most multi-hued monitors are the same.

The color monitor screen can be illuminated in any of its three primary colors by individually hitting the phosphor dots associated with that color with the electron beam. Other colors can be made by illuminating combinations of the primary colors. By varying the intensity of each primary color, an infinite spectrum can be generated.

Monochrome displays have their CRTs evenly coated with a single, homogenous phosphor so that wherever the electron beam strikes, the tube glows in the same color. The color of the phosphors determines the overall color that the screen glows.

Three colors remain popular for monochrome computer displays—amber, green, and white. Which is best is a matter of both preference and prejudice. Various studies have supported the superiority of each of these colors.

> ➤ **Green**—Green screens got a head start as IBM's choice for most of its terminals and the first PC display. Green is a good selection for use where ambient light levels are low, part of its heritage from the days of oscilloscopes and radar screens (most of which remain stubbornly green). Over the last few years, however, green has fallen from favor as the screen of choice.

> ➤ **Amber**—In the 1980s amber-colored screens rose in popularity because they are, according to some studies, easier on the eyes and more readable when the surrounding environmental light level is bright. Yellow against black yields one of the best perceived contrast combinations, making the displays somewhat easier on your eyes. Amber also got a push as a de facto European monitor standard.

> ➤ **White**—Once white screens were something to be avoided, if just from their association with black-and-white televisions. A chief reason was that most early monochrome displays used a composite interface and gave low on-screen quality.

Apple's Macintosh and desktop publishing forced the world to re-evaluate white. White is the color of paper that executives have been shuffling through offices over the ages. White and black also happens to be among the most readable of all color combinations. IBM added impetus to the conversion of the entire world to white with the introduction of the VGA and its white-screen monochrome display.

If you look closely, you might see fine specs of colors, such as a bright yellow dappled into so-called "white" phosphors. Manufacturers mix together several different phosphors to fine tune the color of the monochrome display—to make it a cool, blue television white or a warm, yellowish paper white.

There's no good dividing-line between ordinary white and paper-white displays. In theory, *paper-white* means the color of the typical bond paper you type on, a slightly warmer white than the blue-tinged glow of most white monitors. But paper-whiteness varies with who is giving the name.

Often ignored, yet just as important to screen readability as the phosphor colors, is the background color of the display tube. Monochrome screen backgrounds run the full range from light grey to nearly black. Darker screens give more contrast between the foreground text and the tube background, making the display more readable, particularly in high ambient light conditions.

The background area on a color screen—the space between the phosphor dots—is called the *matrix*, and it is not illuminated by the electron beam. The color of the matrix determines what the screen looks like when the power is off—pale gray, dark green-gray, or nearly black. Darker and black matrices give an impression of higher contrast to the displayed images. Lighter gray matrices make for purer white. The distinctions are subtle, however, and unless you put two tubes side-by-side, you're unlikely to be able to judge the difference.

Color Temperature

If your work involves critical color matching, the color temperature of your monitor can be an important issue. White light is not white, of course, but a mixture of all colors. Alas, all whites are not the same. Some are richer in blue, some in yellow. The different colors of white are described by their color temperature, the number of kelvins (degrees Celsius above absolute zero) that a perfect luminescent body would need to be to emit that color.

Like the incandescence of a hot iron horseshoe in the blacksmith's forge, as its temperature gets higher, the hue of a glowing object shifts from red to orange, then to yellow, and on to blue-white. Color temperature simply assigns an absolute temperature rating to these colors.

For example, ordinary lightbulbs range from 2,700 to 3,400 kelvins. Most fluorescent lights have non-continuous color spectra rich in certain hues (notably green) but lacking other hues that makes assigning a true color temperature impossible. Other fluorescent lamps are designed to approximate daylight with color temperatures of about 5,000 kelvins.

The problem with color matching arises because pigments and paper only reflect light, so their actual color depends on the temperature of the light illuminating them. Your monitor screen emits light, so its color is independent of illumination—it has its own color temperature that may be (and is likely) different from the light on the rest of your work. Monitors are designed to glow with the approximate color temperature of daylight rather than incandescent or fluorescent light.

Alas, not everyone has the same definition of daylight. Noonday sun, for instance, ranges from 5,500 to 6,000 kelvins. Overcast days may achieve a color temperature of 10,000 kelvins because the scattered blue glow of the sky (higher color temperature) dominates the yellowish radiation from the sun. The colors and blend of the phosphors used to make the picture tube screen and the relative strengths of the electron beams illuminating those phosphors determine the color temperature of a monitor. Some engineers believe the perfect day is a soggy, overcast afternoon suited only to ducks and Englishmen, and they opt to run their monitors with a color temperature as high as 10,000 kelvins. Others, however, live in a Kodachrome world where the color temperature is the same, 5,300 kelvins, as a spring day with tulips in the park.

Persistence

CRT phosphors also differ in *persistence*, the term that describes how long the phosphor glows after being struck by the electron beam. Most monitors use medium persistence phosphors.

Persistence becomes obvious when it is long. Images take on a ghostly appearance, lingering for a few seconds and slowly fading away. Although the effect may be bothersome, particularly in a darkened room, it's meant to offset the effect of another headache-producer, flicker.

Exactly what it sounds like, *flicker* is the quick flashing of the screen image caused by the image decaying before it is re-scanned by the electron beam. The persistence of vision (a quality of the human visual system) makes rapidly flashing light sources appear continuously lit. Fluorescent lights, for example, seem to glow uninterruptedly even though they switch on and off 120 times a second (twice the nominal frequency of utility-supplied electricity).

When the periods between the electron beam passages stretch out too long for your eyes to blend them together, the lingering glow of long-persistence phosphors bridges over the gaps. Long-persistence phosphors are thus often used in display systems that are scanned more slowly than usual, such as interlaced monitors (explained later in the chapter). The IBM Monochrome display, perhaps the most notorious user of long-persistence green phosphors, is scanned 50 times a second instead of the more normal (and eye-pleasing) 60 or higher.

Long-persistence phosphors need not be green, however. Long-persistence color systems also are available for use in applications where flicker is bothersome. Most often, long-persistence color phosphors are used in interlaced systems that are scanned more slowly than non-interlaced displays.

Long-persistence phosphors also frustrate *light pens*, which depend on detecting the exact instant a dot of phosphor lights up. Because of the lingering glow, several dots will appear to most light pens to be lit simultaneously. The pen cannot zero in on a particular dot position on the screen.

Electron Guns

Monochrome CRTs have a single electron gun that continuously sweeps across the screen. Most color tubes have three guns, although some color televisions and monitors boast "one-gun" tubes. The gun count depends on what you call a gun. Like all color CRTs, the one-gun tubes have three distinct electron-emitting cathodes that can be individually controlled. The three cathodes are fabricated into a single assembly that allows them to be controlled as if they were generating only a single beam.

In a three-gun tube, the trio of guns are arranged in a triangle. One-gun tubes arrange their cathodes in a straight line, often earning the epithet *in-line guns*. In theory, in-line guns should be easier to set up, but as a practical matter, excellent performance can be derived from either arrangement.

The three guns in a color CRT emit their electrons simultaneously, and the three resulting beams are steered together by the yoke. Individual adjustments are provided for each of the three beams, however, to ensure that each beam falls on exactly the same triplet of color dots on the screen as the others. Because these controls help the three beams converge on the same triad, they are called *convergence* controls. The process of adjusting them is usually termed *alignment*.

Convergence

The three electron beams inside any color monitor must converge on exactly the right point on the screen to illuminate a single triad of phosphor dots. If a monitor is not adjusted properly—or if it is not designed or made properly—the three beams will not converge properly to one point. Poor convergence will result in images with rainbow-like shadows and a loss of sharpness and detail. Individual text characters no longer appear sharply defined but become two- or three-color blurs. Monochrome monitors are inherently free from such convergence problems because they have but one electron beam.

Convergence problems are a symptom rather than a cause of monitor deficiencies. Convergence problems arise not only from the design of the display but also from the construction and setup of each individual monitor. These problems can vary widely from one display to the next and may be aggravated by damage during shipping.

The result of convergence problems is most noticeable at the screen periphery because that's where the electron beams are the most difficult to control. When bad, convergence problems can be the primary limit on the sharpness of a given display, having a greater negative effect than wide dot-pitch or low band width (discussed later in the chapter).

Many monitor makers claim that their convergence is a given fraction of a millimeter at a particular place on the screen. If a figure is given for more than one screen location, the center of the screen will invariably have a lower figure—tighter, better convergence—than a corner of the screen.

The number given is how far one color may spread from another at that location. Lower numbers are better. A typical monitor may claim convergence of about 0.5 (one-half) millimeter at one of the corners of the screen. That figure often rises to 50 percent higher than the dot-pitch of the tube, making the convergence the limit on sharpness for that particular monitor.

Convergence problems often can be corrected by adjustment of the monitor. Many monitors have internal convergence controls. A few high-resolution (and high-cost) monitors even have external convergence adjustments. But adjusting monitor convergence is a job for the specialist—and that means getting a monitor converged can be expensive, as is any computer service call.

IBM and many other display makers now claim that their products are converged for life. Although this strategy should eliminate the need to adjust the monitors (which should be done only by a skilled technician with the correct test equipment), it also makes it mandatory to test your display before you buy it. You don't want a display that's been badly converged for life.

Shadow Masks

Just pointing the electron beams at the right dots is not enough, because part of the beam can spill over and hit the other dots in the triplet. The result of this spillover is a loss of color purity—bright hues become muddied. To prevent this effect and make images as sharp and colorful as possible, all color CRTs used in computer displays and televisions alike have a *shadow mask*, a metal sheet with fine perforations in it, located inside the display tube and a small distance behind the phosphor coating of the screen.

The shadow mask and the phosphor dot coating on the CRT screen are critically arranged so that the electron beam can hit phosphor dots of only one color. The other two colors of dots are in the "shadow" of the mask and cannot be seen by the electron beam.

The spacing of the holes in the shadow mask to a great degree determines the quality of the displayed image. For the geometry of the system to work, the phosphor dots on the CRT screen must be spaced at the same distance as the holes in the mask. Because the hole spacing determines the dot spacing, it is often termed the *dot-pitch* of the CRT.

The dot-pitch of a CRT is simply a measurement of the distance between dots of the same color. Dot-pitch is an absolute measurement, independent of the size of the tube or the size of the displayed image.

The shadow mask affects the brightness of a monitor's image in two ways. The size of the holes in the mask limits the size of the electron beam getting through to the phosphors. Off-axis from the guns—that is, toward the corners of the screen—the round holes appear oval to the gun and less of the beam can get through. As a result, the corners of a shadow mask screen are often dimmer than the center, although the brightness difference may not be distinguishable.

The mask also limits how high the electron beam intensity can be in a given CRT. A stronger beam—which makes a brighter image—holds more energy. When the beam strikes the mask, part of that energy is absorbed as heat by the mask, raising the mask temperature. In turn, this temperature rise makes the mask expand unpredictably, distorting it minutely and blurring the image. To minimize this heat-induced blur, monitor makers are moving to shadow masks made from Invar, an alloy that expands minimally as it warms.

Aperture Grilles

With all the problems associated with shadow masks, you would expect someone to come up with a better idea. Sony Corporation did exactly that, inventing the *Trinitron* picture tube.

The Trinitron uses an aperture grille—slots between a vertical array of wires—instead of a mask. The phosphors are painted on the inner face of the tube as interleaved stripes of the three additive primary colors.

The grille blocks the electron beam from the wrong stripes just as a shadow mask blocks it from the wrong dots. The distance between two sequential stripes of the same color is governed by the spacing between the slots between the wires, the *slot-pitch* of the tube. Because the electron beam fans out as it travels away from the electron gun and the stripes are farther from the gun than is the mask, the stripes are spaced a bit further apart than the slot-pitch. Their spacing is termed *screen-pitch*. For example, a 0.25 millimeter slot-pitch Trinitron might have a screen-pitch of 0.26 millimeters.

The wires of the aperture grille are quite thick, about two-thirds the width of the slot-pitch. In a Trinitron with a 0.25 slot-pitch, for example, the grille wires measure about 0.18 millimeters in diameter. The grille wires are held taut, but they can vibrate. Consequently, Trinitron monitors have one or two thin *tensioning wires* running horizontally across the screen. Although quite fine, these wires cast a shadow on the screen that's most apparent on light-colored screen backgrounds. Some people find the tensioning wire shadow objectionable, so you should look closely at a Trinitron before buying.

Trinitrons hold a theoretical brightness advantage over shadow-mask tubes. Because the slots allow more electrons to pass through to the screen than do the tiny holes of a shadow mask, a Trinitron can (in theory) create a brighter image. This added brightness is not borne out in practice. However, Trinitrons do excel in keeping their screens uniformly bright. The aperture grille wires of a Trinitron block the beam only in one dimension and, therefore, don't impinge as much on the electron beam at the screen edges.

Thanks to basic patents, Sony had exclusive rights to the Trinitron design. However, those patents began expiring in 1991, and other manufacturers were quick to begin working with the technology. Consequently, you can expect a growing number of aperture grille color monitors to come to the market.

Required Dot-Pitch

No matter whether a monitor uses a shadow-mask with a dot-pitch or an aperture grille with a slot-pitch, the spacing of image triads on the screen is an important constituent in monitor quality. A monitor simply can't put dots any closer together than the holes in the mask or grille allow. It's easy to compute the pitch necessary for a resolution level in a computer system. Just divide the screen size by the number of dots required to be displayed.

For example, a VGA text display comprises 80 columns of characters that are each nine dots wide, for a total of 720 dots across the screen. The typical 12-inch (diagonal) monitor screen is roughly 9.5 inches or 240 millimeters across. Hence, to properly display a VGA text image, the dot pitch must be smaller than .333 (or 240/720) millimeters, assuming that the full width of the screen is used for display. Often a monitor's image is somewhat smaller than full-screen width, and such displays require even finer dot pitch. The larger the display, the coarser the dot-pitch can be for a given level of resolution.

Screen Curvature

Most CRTs have a distinctive shape. At one end, a CRT has a narrow neck, which contains the electron gun or guns. Around the neck fits the deflection yoke, an external assembly that generates the magnetic fields that bend the electron beams to sweep across the inner surface of the wide face of the tube. The tube emerges from the yoke as a funnel-like flaring, which enlarges to the rectangular face of the screen itself. This face often (but now less commonly) is a spherically curving surface.

The spherical curve of the face makes sense for a couple of reasons. The curve makes the distance traveled by the electron beam more consistent at various points on the screen, edge to center to edge. A truly flat screen would require the beam to travel farther at the edges than at the center and would require the beam to strike the face of the screen obliquely, resulting in image distortion. Although this distortion can be compensated for electrically, the curving screen helps things along.

In addition, the CRT is partly evacuated, so normal atmospheric pressure is constantly trying to crush the tube. The spherical surface helps distribute this potentially destructive force more evenly, making the tube stronger.

Screen curvature has a negative side effect. Straight lines on the screen appear straight only from one observation point. Move your head closer, farther away, or to one side, and the supposedly straight lines of your graphic images will bow this way and that. The effect is most noticeable in photographs (because your eyes accommodate the curves and interpret things back into the expected straight lines).

The geometry of in-line guns simplifies tube construction and alignment sufficiently so that cylindrically curved screens are feasible. They have fewer curvilinear problems because they warp only one axis of the image. Trinitrons characteristically have faces with cylindrical curves. Most shadow-mask tubes have spherical faces.

Technology has made the reasons underlying spherical curved screens less than compelling. In the last few years, the technical obstacles to making genuinely flat screens have been surmounted. A number of manufacturers now offer flat-screen monochrome displays, which are relatively simple because compensation for the odd geometry is required by only one electron beam.

The first color flat screen was Zenith's *flat tension-mask* system. The tension-mask solves the construction problems inherent in a flat screen color system by essentially stretching the shadow mask. Its flat face and black matrix make for very impressive images. Only the case of the monitor itself is bulky and ugly to look at, and an internal fan made the first model as much a pain for the ears as the screen was a pleasure for the eyes. Since then, such monitors have become less power hungry, but they remain more costly than more conventional designs.

Resolution versus Addressability

The *resolution* of a video system refers to the fineness of detail that it can display. Resolution is a direct result of the number of individual dots that make up the screen image and, thus, is a function of both the screen size and the dot-pitch.

Because the size and number of dots limit the image quality, the apparent sharpness of screen images can be described by the number of dots that can be displayed horizontally and vertically across the screen. For instance, the resolution required by IBM's Video Graphics Array in its standard graphics mode is 640 dots horizontally by 480 vertically. The XGA display system produces an image of 1024 x 768 dots in its highest resolution mode.

Sometimes, however, the resolution available on the screen and that made by a computer's display adapter are not the same. For instance, a video mode designed for the resolution capabilities of a color television set hardly taps the quality available from a computer monitor. On the other hand, the computer-generated graphics may be designed for a display system that's sharper than the one being used. You might, for instance, try to use a television in lieu of a more expensive monitor. The sharpness you see will then be less than what the resolution of the video system would have you believe.

Actual resolution is a physical quality of the video display system—the monitor—that's being used. The video display system sets the upper limit on the display quality. In color systems, the chief limit on resolution is purely physical—the convergence of the system and the dot-pitch of the tube. In monochrome systems—which have no quality-limiting shadow masks—the resolution is limited by the *bandwidth* of the monitor, the highest frequency signal that it can handle. (Finer details pack more information into the signals sent from computer system to monitor. The more information in a given time, the higher the frequency of the signal.)

A few manufacturers persist in using the misleading term *addressability* to describe the quality of their monitors. Addressability is essentially a bandwidth measurement for color monitors. Addressability tells the monitor to point its electron guns at a specific number of dots on-screen. This definition ignores, however, the physical limit imposed by the shadow mask. In other words, addressability describes the highest quality signals the monitor can handle, but the full quality of those signals won't necessarily be visible to you on the screen.

Anti-Glare Treatment

Most mirrors are made from glass, and glass often mimics a mirror. Because of the difference between the index of refraction of air and that of glass, glass is naturally reflective. If you make mirrors, that's great. If you make monitors—or worse yet, use them—the reflectivity of glass can be a big headache. A reflection of a room light or window from the glass face of the CRT can easily be brighter than the glow of phosphors inside. As a result, the text or graphics on the display tends to "wash out" or be obscured by the brightness.

The greater the curvature of a monitor screen, the more apt it is to have a problem with reflections, because more of the environment is reflected by the screen. A spherical monitor face acts like a huge convex mirror strategically hung to give a panoramic view of shoplifters or cars sneaking around an obscured hairpin turn. The flatter the face of the monitor, the less of a worry reflection is. With an absolutely flat face, a slight turn of the monitor's face can eliminate all glare and reflections.

You can't change the curve of your monitor's face. However, there is help. Anti-glare treatments can reduce or eliminate reflections from the face of most CRTs. Several glare-reduction technologies are available, and each varies somewhat in its effectiveness.

Mesh

The lowest tech and least expensive anti-glare treatment is simply a fabric mesh, usually nylon. The mesh can either be placed directly atop the face of the screen or in a removable frame that fits about half an inch in front of the screen. Each hole in the mesh acts like a short tube, allowing you to see straight in the tube but cutting off light from the sides of the tube. Your straight-on vision gets through unimpeded, but glare that angles in doesn't make it to the screen.

As simple as this technique is, it works amazingly well. The least expensive after-market anti-glare systems use mesh suspiciously similar to pantyhose stretched across a frame.

Mechanical Glare Reduction

Glare can be reduced by mechanical means—not a machine that automatically intercepts glare before it reaches the screen, but mechanical preparation of the screen surface. By lightly grinding the glass on the front of the CRT, the face of the screen can be made to scatter rather than reflect light. Each rough spot on the screen that results from the mechanical grinding process reflects light randomly, sending it every which direction. A smooth screen reflects a patch of light, like a mirror, reflecting any bright light source into your eyes. Because the light scattered by the ground glass is dispersed, less of it reaches your eyes, and the glare is not as bright.

Coating

Glare can be reduced by applying coatings to the face of the CRT. Two different kinds of coatings can be used. One coating forms a rough film on the face of the CRT. This rough surface acts the same way as a ground-glass screen does, scattering light.

The screen also can be coated with a special compound, such as magnesium fluoride. By precisely controlling the thickness of this coating, the reflectivity of the surface of the screen can be reduced. The fluoride coating is a quarter of the wavelength of light (usually of light at the middle of the spectrum). Light going through the fluoride and reflecting from the screen thus emerges from the coating out of phase with the light striking the fluoride surface, visually canceling out the glare. Camera lenses are coated to achieve exactly the same purpose, the elimination of reflections.

Polarization

Light can be *polarized*; its photons can be restricted to a single plane of oscillation. A polarizing filter enables light of only one polarization to pass. Two polarizing filters in a row can be arranged to allow light of only one plane of polarization to pass—by making the planes of polarization of the filters parallel. The two filters will stop light entirely when their planes of polarization are perpendicular. The first filter lets only one kind of light pass, and the second filter lets only another kind of light pass. Because none of the second kind of light reaches the second filter, no light gets by.

When light is reflected from a surface, its polarization is shifted by 90 degrees. This physical principle makes polarizing filters excellent reducers of glare.

A sheet of polarizing material is placed a short distance in front of a display screen. Light from a potential source of glare goes through the screen and is polarized. When it strikes the display and is reflected, its polarization is shifted 90 degrees. When it again reaches the filter, it is out of phase with the filter and cannot get through. Light from the display, however, needs to go through the filter only once. Although this screen glow is polarized, there's no second screen to impede its flow to your eyes.

Every anti-glare treatment has its disadvantage. Mesh makes an otherwise sharp screen look fuzzy because smooth characters are broken up by the cell structure of the mesh. Mechanical treatments are expensive and tend to make the screen appear to be slightly fuzzy or out of focus. The same is true of coatings that rely on the dispersion principle. Optical coatings, Polaroid filters, and even mesh suffer from their own reflections. The anti-glare material itself may add its own bit of glare. In addition, all anti-glare treatments, and polarizing filters in particular, tend to make displays dimmer. The polarizing filter actually reduces the brightness of a display to one-quarter of its untreated value.

Even with their shortcomings, however, anti-glare treatments are amazingly effective. They can ease eyestrain and eliminate the headaches that come with extended computer use.

Overscan and Underscan

Most computer displays are rated as to their screen size. As with television sets, the measurement of the cathode ray tube (CRT or picture tube) in a computer monitor is made diagonally across its face. The active display area of a 12-inch monitor thus may measure somewhat less than nine by seven inches.

Two monitors with the same size screens may have entirely different on-screen image sizes. Composite monitors are often afflicted by *overscan*; they attempt to generate images that are larger than their screen size, and the edges and corners of the active display area may be cut off. (The overscan is often designed so that, as the components inside the monitor age and become weaker, the picture shrinks to normal size—likely over a period of years.) *Underscan* is the opposite condition in which the image is smaller than nominal screen size.

Overscan may be perfectly normal—designed into a particular display—and does not necessarily indicate any underlying problems. Image geometry is easier to control nearer the center of the screen than it is at the edges. Pulling in the reins on the image can ensure that straight lines actually are displayed straight. Excessive overscan can be intimidating and counterproductive. If overscan is excessive, you're actually getting a smaller display than you're paying for. The actual image size displayed, rather than screen size, should be taken into account when comparing monitors.

Aspect Ratio

The relationship between the width and height of a monitor screen is termed its *aspect ratio*. Today, the shape of the screen of nearly every monitor is standardized, as is that of the underlying CRT that makes the image. The screen is 1.33 times wider than it is high, resulting in the same 4:3 aspect ratio used in television and motion pictures before the wide-screen phenomenon took over.

The image on the screen need not have the same aspect ratio of the tube, however. The electronics of monitors separate the circuitry that generates the horizontal and vertical scanning signals and results in their independent control. As a result, the relationship between the two can be adjusted, and that adjustment results in an alteration of the aspect ratio of the actual displayed image. For example, by increasing the amplification of the horizontal signal, the width of the image will be stretched, raising the aspect ratio.

Normally, you should expect that the relative gains of the horizontal and vertical signals will be adjusted so that your display shows the correct aspect ratio on-screen. A problem develops when a display tries to accommodate signals based on different standards. This mismatch is particularly troublesome with VGA displays because the VGA standard allows images made with three distinct line counts—350, 400, and 480.

All else being equal, an image made from 350 lines will be less than three-quarters the height of a 480-line image. A graphic generated in an EGA-compatible mode shown on a VGA display would look quite squashed. A circle drawn on the screen would look like an ellipse; an orange would more resemble a watermelon.

Image Sizing

IBM monitors compensate for such obtuse images with the sync-polarity detection scheme. The relative polarities of the horizontal and vertical sync signals instruct the monitor in which mode and line count the image is being set. The monitor then compensates by adjusting its vertical gain to obtain the correct aspect ratio no matter the number of lines in the image.

Not all monitors take advantage of the IBM sync signaling system. Shifting display modes with such a monitor can lead to graphics displays that look crushed. Others use a technique called *autosizing* that allows the monitor to maintain a consistent image size no matter what video signal your display adapter is sending it—without regard to VGA sync coding. Monitor makers can achieve autosizing in several ways. True autosizing works regardless of the signal going to the monitor and scales the image to match the number of display lines. Mode-sensitive autosizing works by determining the display mode used for an image from the frequency of the signal. It then switches the size to a preset standard to match the number of lines in the signal. Monitors often combine VGA sync-sensing with mode-sensitive autosizing.

Image Controls

A few (far from a majority) monitors make coping with underscan, overscan, and odd aspect ratios simply a matter of twisting controls. These displays feature horizontal and vertical size (or gain) controls that allow you to adjust the size and shape of the image to suit your own tastes. With these controls—providing they have adequate range—you can make the active image touch the top, bottom, and sides of the screen bezel, or you can shrink the bright area of your display to a tiny (but geometrically perfect) patch in the center of your screen.

Size and position controls give you command of how much screen the image on your monitor fills. With full-range controls, you can expand the image to fill the screen from corner to corner or reduce it to a smaller size that minimizes the inevitable geometric distortion that occurs near the edges of the tube. A full complement of controls includes one of each of the following: horizontal position (sometimes termed phase), vertical position, horizontal size (sometimes called width), and vertical size (or height).

A wide control range is better than a narrow one. Some monitors skimp on one or more controls and limit you in how large you can make the on-screen image. Worse, sometimes a monitor maker won't include a control at all. For example, some monitors have no horizontal-size controls. As a result, you cannot adjust both the size and aspect ratio of the image.

The optimum position for these controls is on the front panel where you can adjust them and view the image at the same time. Controls on the rear panel require you to have gorilla-like arms to reach around the monitor to make adjustments while checking their effect.

Image controls come in two types: analog and digital. *Analog controls* are the familiar old knobs like you find on vintage television sets. Twist one way, and the image gets bigger; twist the other, and it shrinks. Analog controls have one virtue—just by looking at the knob you know where they are set, whether at one or the other extreme of their travel. The control itself is a simple memory system. It stays put until you move it again. Analog controls, however, also become dirty and wear out with age, and they usually allow you to set only one value per knob—one value that must cover all of the monitor's operating modes.

Digital controls give you pushbutton control over image parameters. Press one button, and the image gets larger or moves to the left. Another compensates in the opposite direction. Usually, digital controls are linked with a microprocessor, memory, and mode-sensing circuitry so that you can preset different image heights and widths for every video standard your monitor can display.

Digital controls don't get noisy with age and are more reliable and repeatable, but you never know when you're approaching the limit of their travel. Most have two-speed operation—hold them in momentarily, and they make minute changes; keep pressing the button, and they shift gears to make gross changes. Of course, if you don't anticipate the shift, you'll overshoot the setting you want, and you'll spend a few extra moments zeroing in on the exact setting you want.

Size and position controls are irrelevant to LCD and similar alternate display technologies. LCD panels are connected more directly to display memory so that memory locations correspond nearly exactly to every screen position. There's no need to move the image around or to change its shape, because it's forever fixed where it belongs.

Most CRT-based displays also carry over several controls from their television progenitors. Nearly every computer monitor has a *brightness* control, which adjusts the level of the scanning electron beam, which in turn makes the on-screen image glow brighter or dimmer. The *contrast* control adjusts the linearity of the relationship between the incoming signal and the on-screen image brightness. In other words, it controls the brightness relationship that results from different signal levels—how much brighter high-intensity is. In a few displays, both the brightness and contrast function are combined into a single "picture" control. Although a godsend to those who might get confused by having to twiddle two knobs, the combined control also limits your flexibility in adjusting the image to best suit your liking.

Other controls ubiquitous to televisions are usually absent from better computer monitors because they are irrelevant. Vertical hold, color (saturation), and hue controls only have relevance to composite video signals, so they are likely to be found only on composite-interfaced displays. The vertical hold control tunes the monitor to best decipher the vertical synchronizing signal from the ambiguous composite video signal. The separate sync signals used by other display standards automatically remove any ambiguity. Color and hue only adjust the relationship of the color subcarrier to the rest of the composite video signal and have no relevance to non-composite systems.

Flat Panel Display Systems

CRTs are impractical for portable computers, as anyone who has toted a 40-pound first-generation portable computer knows. The glass in the tube itself weighs more than most of today's portable machines, and running a CRT steals more power than most laptop or notebook machines budget for all of their circuitry and peripherals.

In lieu of the tube, laptop designers have tried just about every available alternate display technology. These include the panels packed with light-emitting diodes—the power-on indicators of the '80s—that glow at you as red as the devil's eyes. But LEDs consume extraordinary amounts of power. Consider that a normal, full-size LED can draw 10 to 100 milliwatts at full brilliance and that you need 100,000 or so individual elements in a display screen, and you get an idea of the magnitude of the problem. Certainly, the individual display elements of an LED screen would be smaller than a power-on indicator and consume less power, but the small LED displays created in the early days of portable PCs consumed many times the power required by today's technologies. LEDs also suffer the problem that they tend to wash out in bright light and are relatively expensive to fabricate in large arrays.

One alternative is the *gas-plasma screen* that uses a high voltage to ionize a gas and cause it to emit light. Most gas-plasma screens have the characteristic orange-red glow of neon because that's the gas they use inside. Gas-plasma displays are relatively easy to make in the moderately large sizes that are perfect for laptop computer screens and yield sharpness unrivaled by competing technologies. However, gas-plasma screens also need a lot of power, several times the requirements of LCD technology, at high voltages, which must be synthesized from low-voltage battery power. Consequently, gas-plasma displays are used primarily in AC-power portables. When used in laptops, the battery life of a gas-plasma-equipped machine is quite brief, on the order of an hour.

The winner in the display technology competition was the *Liquid Crystal Display*, the infamous LCD. Unlike LED and gas-plasma displays which glow on their own, emitting photons of visible light, LCDs don't waste energy by shining. Instead, they merely block light that is otherwise available. To make patterns visible, they selectively block either reflected light (*reflective LCDs*) or the light generated by a secondary source, either behind the LCD panel (*backlit LCDs*) or adjacent to it (*edgelit LCDs*). The backlight source is typical of an electroluminescent (EL) panel, although some laptops use Cold-Cathode Fluorescent (CCF) for brighter, whiter displays with the penalty of higher cost, greater thickness, and increased complexity.

A number of different terms describe the technologies used in the LCD panels themselves, terms like "supertwist," "double-supertwist," and "triple-supertwist." In effect, the twist of the crystals controls the contrast of the screen, so triple-supertwist screens have more contrast than ordinary supertwist.

The history of laptop and notebook computer displays has been one lead by innovations in Liquid Crystal Display or LCD technology. Invented by RCA in the 1960s (General Electric still makes money on royalties on RCA's basic patents), LCDs came into their own with laptop computers because of their low power requirements, light weight, and ruggedness.

An LCD display is actually a sandwich made from two plastic sheets with a very special liquid made from rod-shaped or "nematic" molecules. One important property of the nematic molecules of liquid crystals is that they can be aligned by grooves in the plastic to bend the polarity of light that passes through them. More importantly, the amount of bend the molecules of the liquid crystal give to the light can be altered by applying an electrical current through them.

Ordinary light has no particular orientation, so liquid crystals don't visibly alter it. But polarized light aligns all the oscillations of its photons in a single direction. A polarizing filter creates polarized light by allowing light of a particular polarity (or axis of oscillation) to pass through. Polarization is key to the function of LCDs.

To make an LCD, light is first passed through one polarizing filter to polarize it. A second polarizing filter, set to pass light at right angles to the polarity of the first, is put on the other side of the liquid crystal. Normally, this second polarizing filter will stop all light from passing. However, the liquid crystal bends the polarity of light emerging from the first filter so that it lines up with the second filter. Pass a current through the liquid crystal, and the amount of bending changes, which alters in turn the amount of light passing through the second polarizer.

To make an LCD display, you only need to be able to selectively apply current to small areas of the liquid crystal. The areas to which you apply current will be dark; those that you don't will be light. A light behind the LCD will make the changes more visible.

Over the past few years, engineers have made several improvements to this basic LCD design to improve its contrast and color. The basic LCD design outlined previously is technically termed *twisted nematic* technology or TN. The liquid molecules of the TN display, in their resting state, always bend light by 90 degrees, exactly counteracting the relationship between the two polarizing panels that make up the display.

By increasing the bending of light by the nematic molecules, the contrast between light and dark can be increased. An LCD design that bends light by 180 to 270 degrees is termed a "Super-twist nematic" or simply *supertwist* display. One side effect of the added twist is the appearance of color artifacts, which results in the yellowish green and bright blue hues of many familiar LCD displays.

This tinge of color can be canceled by mounting two super-twist liquid crystals back to back so that one bends the light in the opposite direction of the other. This design is logically termed a "double super-twist nematic" or simply *double supertwist* display. This LCD design is currently popular among laptop PCs with black-and-white VGA-quality displays. It does have its own drawback, however. Because there are two layers of LCD between you and the light source, double super-twist panels appear darker or require brighter backlights for adequate visibility.

Triple super-twist nematic displays instead compensate for colorshifts in the super-twist design by layering both sides of the liquid crystal with thin polymer films. Because the films absorb less light than the twin panels of double super-twist screens, less backlight—and less backlight power—is required for the same screen brightness.

LCDs also come in two styles based on how the current that aligns their nematic molecules is applied. Most LCD panels have a grid of horizontal and vertical conductors, and each pixel is located at the intersection of these conductors. The pixel is darkened simply by sending current through the conductors to the liquid crystal. This kind of display is called a *passive matrix*.

The alternate design, the *active matrix*, is more commonly referred to as *Thin Film Transistor* (or TFT) technology. This style of LCD places a transistor at every pixel. The transistor acts as a relay. A small current is sent to it through the horizontal and vertical grid, and in response, the transistor switches on a much higher current to activate the LCD pixel.

The advantage of the active matrix design is that a smaller current needs to traverse the grid so that the pixel can be switched on and off faster. Although passive LCD screens may update only about half a dozen times per second, TFT designs can operate at ordinary monitor speeds, 10 times faster. That speed increase equates to faster response—for example, your mouse won't disappear as you move it across the screen.

The disadvantage of the TFT design is that it requires the fabrication of one transistor for each screen pixel. Putting those transistors there requires combining the LCD and semiconductor manufacturing processes. That's sort of like getting bricklayers and carpenters to work together.

Color adds other complications to LCD design and manufacture—and considerable expense, on the order of an extra $2500 for a laptop equipped with color LCD. A number of technologies have been tried for color LCD screens, both *additive* (which put red, green, and blue-colored pixels side-by-side so that their output can visually combine) screens to produce colors). The most striking results have been achieved by coupling TFT technology with color to achieve bright, fast, and expensive displays. Although the best units look wonderful—often better than color CRTs—today, their prices put them in the interesting-but-impractical class.

Resolution is an important issue with LCD screens. It determines how sharp text characters and graphics will appear. Today, three resolution standards are dominant, CGA (640 x 200), double-scanned CGA (640 x 400), and VGA (640 x 480).

Most people prefer the last because it's exactly equivalent to today's most popular desktop displays, so it can use the same software and drivers.

CGA resolution is visibly inferior, producing blocky, hard-to-read characters, and is used only in the least expensive laptops.

Double-scanned CGA offers a good compromise between cost and resolution. It's actually as sharp as text-mode CGA. Graphics pose a problem as double-scanned CGA mode is not supported by a wide base of software. Under Windows, however, many double-scanned CGA systems are compatible with Toshiba and AT&T 640 x 400 pixel drivers.

VGA poses particular problems for LCD displays because it's really three more standards under a single name, operating with modes that put 350, 400, or 480 lines on the screen. Most VGA display panels have 480 rows of dots to accommodate these lines.

A problem develops with VGA images made with lower line counts. Many laptop LCD screens display only the active lines and leave the rest of the screen blank. For example, 80 lines will be left blank when 400-line mode is displayed on a 480-line LCD. The result is a black band at both the top and bottom of the screen.

This banding is particularly obnoxious in that VGA text normally displays in 400-line mode. A number of manufacturers have improved on this situation by shifting VGA text into 640 x 480 mode using larger, more legible characters to fill the screen. If you have your choice, you'll probably want your next laptop to operate in this manner.

Monitor Electronics

The image you see on screen is only part of the story of a complete display system. The video signals from your PC must be amplified and processed by the electronics inside the monitor to achieve the right strength and timing relationships to put the proper image in view.

The basic electronic components inside a monitor are its *video amplifiers*. As the name implies, these circuits simply increase the strength of (amplify) the approximately one volt signals they receive from your PC to the thousands of volts needed to drive the electron beam from cathode to phosphor. Monochrome monitors have a single video amplifier; color monitors, three (one for each primary color).

In an analog color monitor, these three amplifiers must be exactly matched and absolutely linear. That is, the input and output of each amplifier must be precisely proportional, and it must be the same as the other two amplifiers. The relationship between these amplifiers is called *color tracking*. If it varies, the color of the image on the screen won't be what your software had in mind.

The effects of such poor color tracking are all bad. You lose precision in your color control. This is especially important for desktop publishing and presentation applications. With poor color tracking, the screen can no longer hope to be an exact preview of what will eventually appear on paper or film. You may even lose a good fraction of the colors displayable by your video system.

What happens is that differences between the amplifiers will cause one of the three primary colors to be emphasized at times and de-emphasized at others, casting a subtle shade on the on-screen image. This shading effect is most pronounced in gray displays—the dominate color(s) tinge the gray.

Although you don't have to worry about color tracking in a monochrome display, the quality of the amplifier nevertheless determines the range of grays that can be displayed. Aberrations in the amplifier can cause the monitor to lose some of its gray-scale range.

The relationship between the input and output signals of video amplifiers is usually not linear. That is, a small change in the input signal may make a greater than corresponding change in the output. In other words, the monitor may exaggerate the color or gray-scale range of the input signal—contrast increases. The relationship between input and output is referred to as the *gamma* of the amplifier. A gamma of one would result in an exact correspondence of the input and output signals. However, monitors with unity gammas tend to have washed out, pastel images. Most people prefer higher gammas, in the range 1.5 to 1.8, because of their higher contrast images.

If you want a monitor that will work both with today's VGA, Super-VGA, and sharper display systems as well as old graphics adapters like CGA and EGA, you'll need a monitor with *TTL capability*. Most modern computer monitors have only analog inputs, which cannot properly display the digital (TTL) signals used by these older standards. You'll also have to check the *color support* of such monitors. To be compatible with the CGA standard, a monitor must be able to handle a 16-color digital input, sometimes called RGBI for the four (red, green, blue, and intensity) signals from which it is made. EGA compatibility requires 64-color capability.

Today's variety of signal standards makes it almost mandatory that your monitor be able to synchronize to a wide range of synchronizing frequencies. You have two frequencies to worry about—vertical frequency, which is sometimes called the refresh rate or frame rate, determines how often the complete screen is updated. The horizontal synchronizing frequency (or horizontal scan rate) indicates the rate at which the individual scan lines that make up the image are drawn.

These frequency ranges are important to you because they determine which video standards the monitor can work with. IBM's CGA requires a horizontal frequency of 15.75 Khz; MDA, 18 Khz; EGA, 22 Khz; and VGA, 31.5 Khz. At SuperVGA resolution, horizontal frequencies depend on the refresh rate used. At a 56 Hz refresh rate, 35 Khz is adequate, but at the VESA 72 Hz spec, 48 Khz is required.

The lowest frame rate normally required is the 50 Hz used by MDA signals. VGA and most other video standards use refresh rates between 60 and 70 Hz.

Interlaced systems like IBM's 8514/A and the first implementations of XGA used a trick developed for television to help put more information on a screen using a limited bandwidth signal. Instead of scanning the image from top to bottom, one line after another, each *frame* of the image is broken in half into two *fields*. One field consists of the odd-numbered lines of the image, the other the even-numbered lines. The electron beam sweeps across and down, illuminating every other line, and then starts from the top again and finishes with the ones it missed on the first pass.

What this technique achieves is an apparent doubling of the frame rate. Instead of sweeping down the screen 30 times a second (the case of a normal television picture), the top-to-bottom sweep occurs 60 times a second. While a 30-frame-per-second rate would noticeably flicker, the ersatz 60-frame-per-second rate does not. Some folks' eyes are not fooled, however, so interlaced images have earned a reputation of being flickery.

Interlacing is used on computer display signals to keep the necessary bandwidth down. A lower frame rate lowers the required bandwidth of the transmission channel. Of all the prevailing standards, only the original high-resolution operating mode of IBM's 8514/A display adapter and the first generation of XGA use interlacing. Their frame rate, 44 Hz, would cause distinct flicker. Interlacing drives the field rate up to 88 Hz. Note that you'll need a monitor that can lock to the vertical frequency of the higher field rate rather than the frame rate of an interlaced monitor.

Perhaps the most common specification that is usually listed for any sort of monitor is *bandwidth*, which is usually rated in megahertz. Common monitor bandwidth stretches across a wide range—figures from 12 to 100 Mhz are sometimes encountered.

In theory, the higher the bandwidth, the higher the resolution and sharper the image that can be displayed. In the case of color displays, the dot-pitch of the display tube is the biggest limit on performance.

In monochrome systems, however, bandwidth is a determinant of overall sharpness. The IBM display standards do not demand extremely wide bandwidths. Extremely large bandwidths are often superfluous.

The bandwidth necessary in a monitor is easy to compute. A system ordinarily requires a bandwidth wide enough to address each individual screen dot plus an extra margin to allow for retrace times. (Retrace times are those periods in which the electron beam moves but does not display—for instance, at the end of each frame when the beam must move from the bottom of the screen at the end of the last line of one frame back up to the top of the screen for the first line of the next frame.) A TTL monochrome display operating under the MDA standard shows 252,000 (or 720 x 350) pixels 50 times per second—12.6 million pixels per second. A composite display shows 128,000 (or 640 x 200) pixels 60 times per second—7.68 million pixels per second. A VGA display shows 288,000 (or 720 x 400 in text mode) pixels 70 times per second—20.16 million pixels per second.

Allowing a wide margin of about 25 percent for retrace times, it can thus be seen that for most PC applications, a bandwidth of 16 Mhz is acceptable for TTL monitors, and 10 Mhz of bandwidth is sufficient for sharp composite video displays, figures well within the claims of most commercial products. For VGA, 25 Mhz is the necessary minimum.

Table 14.2 summarizes the bandwidth required by the various IBM display standards.

TABLE 14.2.
Dot-Clocks
(Bandwidths) of
IBM Video
Standards

Video Standard	Dot-Clock
MDA	16.3 Mhz
CGA	14.3 Mhz
EGA	16.3 Mhz
PGC	25 Mhz
VGA (350- or 480-line mode)	25 Mhz
VGA (400-line mode)	28 Mhz
8514/A	44.9 Mhz

Because in real-world applications the worst-case display puts an illuminated pixel next to a dark one, the actual (as opposed to theoretical) bandwidth required by a display system is half the dot-clock plus system overhead.

Monitor Types

The world of IBM-standard monitors is marked by a profusion of confusion. In order to be certain that you are talking about the right type of display, you must describe it with specificity. Saying color or monochrome is not enough. You must also indicate the signal standard to which the monitor must abide. The standard is dictated by the video adapter that's used by the monitor, but some monitors work with different adapters, and many adapters are flexible in regard to your monitor choice. However, certain terms are in general used to describe and distinguish particular monitor types.

Monochrome

Monochrome means exactly what its root words say—"mono" means one, and "chrome" indicates color. Monochrome monitors show their images in one color, be it green, amber, white, puce, or alizarin crimson. Monochrome does not describe what sort of display adapter the monitor plugs into. Among the monitors available, you have three choices that give you long odds at finding the right combination by chance. A fourth, the multiscanning monochrome display, accepts almost any monochrome signal.

TTL Monochrome

The original display type offered by IBM—the one that plugs into the Monochrome Display Adapter—is distinctly different from any monitor standard made for any other purpose. It uses *digital* input signals and uses separate lines for both its horizontal and vertical synchronizing signals.

Its digital signals match the level used by integrated circuits of the *Transistor-Transistor Logic* family or *TTL* family. These chips operate with tightly defined voltage ranges indicating a logical one or zero. (Five volts is nominally considered a digital one, although that's the input voltage level of TTL chips. The maximum level TTL signals ever reach is about 4.3 volts.) Because of their use of TTL signals, such monitors are often called *TTL monochrome* displays. They can only be plugged into MDA or compatible display adapters (including the Hercules Graphics Board).

TTL monochrome are the least expensive monitors (and the oldest monitor technology) still sold with computer systems today. When a manufacturer wants to skimp somewhere, he may substitute a TTL monochrome display system for a monochrome VGA system. Avoid such systems if you can because fewer applications support Hercules graphics than support VGA. Consequently, you should consider such a monitor if you only want text displays and a few dollars are very important to you.

Composite Monochrome

A monitor bearing no other description other than merely "monochrome" is most likely a composite monochrome monitor. This type of monitor offers the lowest resolution of any monochrome system available for PCs, the same level as a CGA color display but without the redeeming virtue of color. Because the composite monochrome monitor uses the same signal as home and professional video systems, it is as ubiquitous as it is hard on the eyes. Designed for the mass market, the composite monochrome monitor is likely to be the least expensive available. It can be plugged into only a CGA or compatible display adapter. The built-in display of the unlamented IBM Portable Personal Computer is actually a composite monochrome monitor. About the only real use of a monochrome composite display today is in multimedia systems to preview video images.

VGA Monochrome

As with TTL monochrome monitors, VGA monochrome monitors follow a proprietary IBM standard. Unlike IBM's Personal Computer Display, the Monochrome VGA display quickly won acceptance and spawned a number of compatibles. These are all incompatible with other video standards but plug into any VGA-style output.

A VGA monochrome monitor will work with any VGA display adapter without change. It will display VGA graphics without a hitch—but also without color, of course.

Multiscanning Monochrome

Unlike the other three monochrome display types, which are designed to operate at certain fixed frequencies, the multiscanning monochrome display adapts to the signals sent to it within a wide range of frequencies. Usually, this kind of monitor can handle any standard monochrome signal, from composite to VGA. It offers no advantage over the fixed-frequency displays except an impunity from errors. You can shift it between monochrome-equipped computer systems no matter what standards they follow.

Multiscanning monochrome monitors are rare today. They appear on the market occasionally and typically disappear when demand turns out to be as great as for CP/M-based computers.

Color Monitors

Five types of color display are generally available for connecting to PCs and PS/2s. Among these are composite color, RGB (or CGA), Enhanced RGB (or EGA), VGA, and mulitscanning monitors.

Composite Color

Generic video monitors—the kind you're likely to connect to your VCR or video camera—use the standard NTSC composite video signal. This signal standard has long been used with PCs—starting with the CGA adapter and PCjr's built-in display system. Composite signals have never really gone away. They're still used where computer-generated graphics are destined for television and video productions. They also link into some multimedia systems. The 3.58 Mhz color subcarrier specified by the NTSC standard limits their color sharpness, however, so the best you can expect, should you want to use a composite color display for general use, is readable 40-column text. In other words, composite color is a special purpose product, nothing you'll want to connect for average, everyday computing.

RGB

The original color display for the IBM PC—the Personal Computer Color Display, IBM model 5151—used three discrete digital signals for each of the three primary colors. From these signals, the display type earned the acronym RGB from the list of additive primary colors: Red, Green, and Blue. To be completely accurate, of course, this style of monitor should be termed RGBI, with the final "I" standing for intensity, per the CGA standard.

Except for the interface signal, the RGB monitor works like a composite color monitor, using the same frequencies, but substituting digital signals for analog. Because there's no need for the NTSC color subcarrier, bandwidth is not limited by the interface, and RGB monitors appear much sharper than composite monitors, even though they display the same number of lines. RGB monitors work with the CGA, EGA (in its degraded CGA mode), and compatible display adapters as well as the PCjr. Because of the low resolution of CGA systems, CGA monitors are about as dead and forgotten as the PCjr.

Enhanced RGB

Moving up to EGA quality requires a better display, one able to handle the 22.1 Khz horizontal synchronizing frequency of the EGA standard. In addition, its interface is somewhat different. While still digital, it must accommodate intensity signals for each of the three primary colors. The EGA signals require a matching EGA connection on the display.

As with CGA, EGA is essentially obsolete. No new systems are sold with it anymore. Rather than getting a new monitor to work with your existing EGA card when your old monitor fails, you'll probably save time and headaches by upgrading to VGA.

VGA Displays

VGA displays were introduced by necessity with the PS/2s. They use analog inputs and a 31 Khz horizontal synchronizing frequency to match with the VGA standard. VGA is now the minimum you should demand in a computer monitor.

Multiscanning Color Displays

Color multiscanning displays were introduced even before the monochrome models. At the time, at least two competing IBM color standards were in use while only one monochrome standard was popular. Among the first color multiscanning systems was NEC's *Multisync*, a monitor so successful that any monitor in this entire class is often erroneously referred to as being a "multisync."

Multiscanning displays don't lock their horizontal and vertical synchronizing frequencies to any particular standard. Instead, they try to match the sync pulses sent to them by your computer system. By automatically adjusting themselves to the available signal, color multiscanning displays can work with just about any video standard.

The range of frequencies that they can latch on to is limited, however. For instance, a manufacturer might specify that a display can handle horizontal sync frequencies from 48 to 60 Hz. Such a display would not be able to cope with the 70 Hz signals used under the VGA standard.

Most multiscanning displays are designed to be able to handle signals even beyond the VGA standard. EGA Plus cards were initially created to capitalize on this potential. After IBM introduced its 8514/A display adapter, many manufacturers extended the range of their system to make them compatible with that standard. Now most multiscanning monitors accommodate signals affording resolutions of 1024 x 768 pixels and higher.

Inputs and Connectors

Monitors can be grouped by the display standard that they support, mostly based upon the display adapter card that they are designed to plug into. One basic guide that will help you narrow down the compatibility of a display just by inspecting its rear panel is the input connector used by the monitor. After all, if you cannot plug a monitor into your computer, odds are it won't be much good to you.

Three styles of connectors are shared by the video standards promulgated by IBM. By name, these three connectors are the RCA-style pin jack, the nine-pin D-shell, and the 15-pin "high-density" D-shell. In addition, some high-resolution monitors use three or more BNC connectors for their input signals.

Three connectors is just one fewer than the number of major IBM video standards (four). You can get into serious trouble—plugging the wrong kind of monitor into a display adapter connector into which it seemingly fits can result in fatal damage to your monitor. Obviously, you'll want to get to know which is which and what is fatal.

Pin Jacks

The bull's eye jack used on stereo and video equipment is used by IBM for the composite video connections available from the Color Graphics Adapter. Although a wealth of monitors and television sets made by innumerable manufacturers also use this connector, no display made by IBM does. However, this concession connector does give you a wealth of choices for alternate displays—that is, if you don't mind marginal quality.

Composite monitors (those dealing with the composite video and NTSC color only) rank among the most widely available and least expensive in both color and monochrome. Even better quality television sets have such jacks available.

Although you can use any composite video display with a CGA or compatible color card, the signal itself limits the possible image quality to okay for monochrome, acceptable for 40-column color, and unintelligible for 80-column color. Nevertheless, a composite video display—already a multipurpose device—becomes even more versatile with a computer input.

Daisy-Chaining

A side benefit of pin plug/composite video displays is that most have both input and output jacks. These paired jacks allow you to *daisy-chain* multiple monitors to a single video output. For instance, you can attach six composite video monitors to the output of your computer for presentations in a classroom or boardroom.

In many cases, the jacks just loop through the display (that is, they connect together). The display merely bridges the input video signal and alters it in no other manner. You can connect a nearly unlimited number of monitors to these loop-through connections with no image degradation. Some monitors, however, buffer their outputs with a built-in video amplifier. Depending on the quality of the amplifier, daisy-chaining several of these monitors can result in noticeable image degradation.

One way to tell the difference is by plugging the output of the display into the output of your computer. Most amplifiers don't work backwards, so if the display has a buffering amplifier, nothing will appear on the screen. If you do get an image comparable to the one you get when plugging into the input jack, the signal just loops through the display.

Analog Voltage Level

The specifications of composite monitors sometimes include a number describing the voltage level of the input signal. This voltage level can be important when selecting a composite display because all such monitors are essentially analog devices.

In analog monitors, the voltage level corresponds to the brightness that the electron beam displays on the screen. A nominal one-volt peak-to-peak input signal is the standard in both the video and computer industries and should be expected from any composite monitor. IBM's VGA requires a slightly different level—0.7 volts.

Termination

For proper performance, a composite video signal line must be terminated by an impedance of 75 ohms. This termination ensures that the signal will be at the proper level and that aberrations will not creep in because of an improperly matched line. Most composite input monitors (particularly those with separate inputs and outputs) feature a *termination switch* that connects a 75-ohm resistor across the video line when turned on. Only one termination resistor should be switched on in any daisy-chain, and it should always be the last monitor in the chain.

If you watch a monitor when you switch the termination resistor on, you'll notice the screen get dimmer. That's because the resistor absorbs about half the video signal. Because composite video signals are analog, they are sensitive to voltage level. The termination cuts the voltage in half and consequently dims the screen by the same amount. Note that the *dim* image is the proper one. Although bright might seem better, it's not. It may overload the circuits of the monitor or otherwise cause erratic operation.

Composite monitors with a single video input jack and no video output usually have a termination resistor permanently installed. While you might try to connect two or more such monitors to a single CGA composite output (with a wye cable or adapter), doing so is unwise. With each additional monitor, the image will get dimmer (the signal must be split among the various monitors), and the CGA adapter will be required to send out increasing current. The latter could cause the CGA to fail.

Nine-Pin D-Shell Connectors

Three different IBM video standards share the nine-pin D-shell connector: monochrome, standard RGB, and enhanced RGB. To confuse things further, many monitor makers also use the same connector for VGA and proprietary display systems.

Because of the huge potential for confusion, you must follow one important rule—know what kind of display adapter you're about to plug into. Making the wrong choice can be fatal to your display, particularly should you try to plug an IBM Monochrome Display into a CGA adapter. The mismatch of synchronizing frequencies will lead to the internal components of the display overheating and failing.

A mismatch is easy to spot—you simply can't make sense out of the image on the screen. You may see a Venetian-blind pattern of lines; the screen may flash; or it may look like the vertical hold failed in a dramatic way. Should you observe any of these patterns or hear a high-pitched squeal from your display and see nothing on the screen, immediately turn off your display. Hunt for the problem while the life of your monitor is not ticking away.

Fifteen-Pin High-Density D-Shell Connectors

The only monitors you're likely to find with 15-pin high-density D-shell connectors are those that are VGA-compatible, whether dedicated to that purpose or multiscanning.

So far, IBM has done a good job of ensuring that problems like the nine-pin mismatch won't occur with these connectors. While both monochrome and color displays use the same connectors, the VGA circuit can sense which is connected and handle either one properly.

IBM's 8514 and 8515 displays, as well as 8514/A and XGA display adapters, also use the same connector even though they at times use different signals. Again, however, IBM has incorporated coding in the signals to ensure that problems won't arise. The 8514/A and XGA adapters can sense the type of display that is connected to it and won't send out conflicting signals. The 8514 and 8515 monitors will operate happily with VGA signals, so problems won't occur if it's plugged into an ordinary VGA output.

BNC Connectors

True high-resolution systems use a separate coaxial cable for every signal they receive. Typically they use BNC connectors to attach these to the monitor. They have one very good reason. Connectors differ in their frequency-handling capabilities, and capacitance in the standard 15-pin high-density D-shell connector can limit bandwidth, particularly as signal frequencies climb into the range above 30 MHz. BNC connectors are designed for frequencies into the gigahertz range, so they impose few limits on ordinary video signals.

Monitors may use either three, four, or five BNC connectors for their inputs. A three-connector system integrates both horizontal and vertical synchronizing signals with the green signal. The resulting mix is called *sync-on-green*. Others use three connectors for red, green, and blue signals and a fourth for horizontal and vertical sync combined together. This scheme is called *composite sync*. Five connector systems use three color signals, one signal for horizontal sync, and one signal for vertical sync. These are called *separate sync* systems.

Audio Inputs

A steadily declining number of monitors, particularly those with composite inputs, have audio as well as video capabilities. This facility can be useful in at least two cases—to take advantage of the new voice synthesis and voice digitization options now becoming available for PC systems and to amplify the three-voice audio output of the PCjr. Most monitor audio amplifiers, even those with modest specifications (limited audio frequency bandwidth and output powers less than a watt), can handle either job adequately.

None of the IBM line-up of personal computers has been designed as music makers. Although you can add accessories to transform the musical mission of your PC, you'll also want to add better quality audio circuitry than you'll get with any PC. A patch cord to connect the add-on accessories to your stereo system will do just fine.

Monitor Safety

Using a PC can be hazardous, but not in the same way as other dangerous endeavors. PCs pose no chemical threats (in contrast to making PCs, which do involve environmentally sensitive chemicals and technologies) but something more insidious and invisible—electromagnetic radiation. Invisible, this potential nemesis boasts the characteristics of the perfect poison in an Agatha Christie novel: colorless, odorless, and tasteless; and after it does its deadly work, it vanishes without a trace.

All electromagnetic radiation is not bad. In fact, EMR is the source of life. Sunlight is one form of EMR. EMR also plays a major and helpful role in everyday life. The infrared rays that warm your toast, microwaves that warm your lunch, the radio signals you tune in each morning, the ultraviolet light that causes your suntan, the x-rays that help diagnose diseases—all are electromagnetic radiation.

Taken in the extreme, however, any form of EMR is dangerous. X-rays are known to cause cancer. Ultraviolet radiation causes cancers of different sorts and cataracts. Infrared radiation burns and can sear off flesh. Microwaves can cook living creatures from the inside out and have been implicated in causing cataracts. Lower frequency radio waves also hold the potential for roasting you alive and have recently been found to cause more subtle biological changes, possibly even cancer. At some point, at some overdose measure, the beneficial EMR crosses the line to become a health hazard. When it comes to computer safety, the question is where PCs and VDTs fit in the continuum from good to bad. Any equipment that generates EMR has the potential for causing health problems. Does personal computer equipment pose such hazards?

Opinions on the issue are easy to find. Anyone who gets a headache after a long day at the office is likely to implicate his PC as the culprit, and perhaps rightly so. Others point out that millions of PCs now inhabit desktops and no suspiciously large number of their regular users have mysteriously passed away on the job. The rationale is simple: I work on a computer, and I am alive; ergo my computer hasn't killed me.

Real answers, as opposed to anecdotes and opinions, are more difficult to find. One reason for lack of resolution in these questions is the world's brief experience with personal computers, hardly a decade. So direct evidence of occupational hazards of PCs is understandably absent. Moreover, all the potential hazards of PC use still may not be known or understood. Supposedly benign technologies and products often prove to have unexpected and dire side-effects long after they have become accepted in commerce and everyday life. Asbestos became widely popular as a building material in the 1930s, and more than four decades elapsed before its often-fatal consequences were definitively linked to it. Regulations were even slower in coming; for example, New York passed its first asbestos regulations in 1985. Civilizations have risen and ebbed, all the while being ravaged by deadly toxins of their own making because they did not understand the mechanism through which the problem was caused, like the lead pipes that carried much of the Roman water supply. Indeed, the health effects of extremely low frequency radiation—a part of the electromagnetic spectrum that is emitted by PCs—remain today as unknown and mysterious to the public as were the toxicologic properties of lead plumbing two millennia ago.

If any part of a PC is hazardous, it is the monitor. Monitors deal with frequencies that may be dangerous as well as forms of radiation that have been proven harmful. Monitors share many common characteristics with Video Data Terminals (or VDTs) that have been in use for nearly 40 years and about which a substantial body of health-related data has been generated. Both monitor and VDT technologies use signals of approximately the same frequencies. Both generate many of the same EMR components.

Even with VDTs, however, the issue of health effects remains unresolved after decades of study. No true consensus on the safety of VDTs—and thus, personal computer monitors—has emerged. The conflicting results of studies have lined up two opposing parties who are unlikely to be swayed by the arguments of the other. On one side are the makers of electronic equipment and the organizations that employ the people that use it. They believe that the equipment is safe. The other side, the people who actually must work at VDTs and personal computers all day long, have their doubts. It's the classic employer-employee struggle with a technological twist.

The employee viewpoint is buttressed by a variety of studies that show biological effects of electromagnetic radiation and an association between VDT use and health problems. The most infamous of these problems is the increased risk of miscarriage. For example, a famous study conducted for Kaiser Permanente in California (published in 1988) showed that among 1583 pregnant women, those who used VDTs for more than 20 hours per week had a significantly elevated rate of miscarriage.

On the other hand, VDT makers and employers rally a whole range of other studies (many of which they have funded) which have failed to find any such risk to VDT users. For example, a 1989 University of Toronto study of 800 pregnant mice subjected to electromagnetic fields of the kind given off by VDTs suggested there is no relationship between spontaneous abortion and VDT electromagnetic fields.

Although that may be good news if you're a pregnant mouse, pregnant workers may not be reassured. As in any scientific discipline, the VDT studies are subject to interpretation. Moreover, the human VDT studies are correlational rather than causal—they associate a problem with VDT use but cannot prove a true cause-and-effect relationship. The EMR from the computer terminals could be causing miscarriages, or something else about the terminals, or the way in which the particular study was conducted could have influenced the results. For example, the Kaiser study itself admits that its results may have been confounded by unmeasured workplace factors such as poor ergonomics and job-related stress. Stress rather than radiation is, in fact, a prime contender for the cause of health effects associated with VDT use.

On the other hand, a growing number of studies have found cause-and-effect relationships between EMR and biological changes in tissues grown under laboratory conditions. Some of these effects occurred when the tissues were subjected to electromagnetic fields of the same nature as those created by personal computers and VDTs.

The radiation emitted by monitors and VDTs falls into several distinct bands, some with known health effects, some in which health effects are less defined. Among the most important of these frequency ranges are x-radiation, ultraviolet radiation, microwave radiation, very low frequency radiation, and extremely low frequency radiation.

X-Radiation

Perhaps the most publicized danger involved with equipment based on cathode-ray technology—things like television picture tubes, oscilloscopes, radar screens, and computer monitors—is x-radiation.

X-rays are known to cause cancer, and the mechanism is well-understood. X-rays are *ionizing radiation*. The photons making up the X-ray signal contain sufficient energy to break up the chemical bonds in molecules, including the DNA in chromosomes. After the DNA in a cell has been changed, the genetic code of the cell is altered. The cell mutates, perhaps dying immediately or just subtly changing its activity. Once the DNA of a cell is changed, and the cell replicates, the changes are passed on to its progeny. One potential is for the growth control mechanism of the cell to change. As a result, the cell and its offspring may multiply as rapidly and uncontrollably as cancer.

The chances that any one cell would react with X-rays in such a way to cause cancer are minuscule. However, given enough rays reacting with a sufficient number of cells, the cancer potential becomes real and worrisome.

X-radiation is associated with color television screens—and thus with color computer monitors. This association is based on the scare stories of the early 1960s when early color television sets did, indeed, produce prodigious amounts of X-radiation.

One of the many ways that X-rays can be produced is through the rapid deceleration of electrons. As the electrons slow down, they have to give up energy. Depending on the momentum of the electron, some of this energy is given off as X-rays.

X-rays are classified as two types: low-energy or soft x-rays with wavelengths from one-tenth to one nanometer and high energy or hard x-rays with wavelengths shorter than one-tenth of a nanometer. Because of their low energy, soft x-rays have little penetrating power. Hard x-rays can pass through and interact with the human body. Medical x-rays are hard and they can cause cell damage. Consequently, the government has placed strict limits on exposure to them.

Early television sets used a vacuum-tube high-voltage rectifier, a small tube that generated the current to drive the electron beam in the display tube. These rectifiers were essentially miniature X-ray tubes. They functioned by passing a huge electron flux through the tube, from cathode to anode; the electrons being rapidly decelerated at the anode. X-rays were emitted in the process.

The x-ray excitement that ultimately caused the federal government to issue strict regulations on the x-radiation emitted by television sets (as well as computer terminals) was real. Certain television sets emitted x-rays of such strength you might make a radiograph of the bones in your hand using the television as an x-ray source.

Not all televisions were so dangerous, however. In fact, the culprit was proved to be defectively manufactured shunt regulator tubes that did not properly shield their anodes. The result was the emission of a concentrated, pencil-like beam of electrons through the bottom of the television set. Unless you had the television resting on your stomach—unlikely in those days of hundred-pound monster TVs—you would have been safe from its effects.

Moreover, vacuum-tube high-voltage rectifiers and shunt regulators are obsolete. They have been replaced by solid-state silicon diodes

which emit no X-radiation—electrons go through no rapid deceleration in silicon diodes. No known PC monitor uses vacuum-tube
rectifiers, so the x-radiation problem in PCs from that source should be
non-existent.

However, all CRT-based devices have another potential source of x-ray
emissions. Every CRT creates its image by shooting a ray of electrons at
the phosphors that coat the inner face of the screen. When they strike
the phosphors, these electrons also rapidly decelerate. Most of the
energy from the electron beam goes to excite the phosphors, which in
turn emit the visible light of the image. Some of it, however, can
generate x-rays. The higher the voltage inside the tube, the larger the
x-ray flux. Color tubes, which operate at potentials as high as 30
kilovolts, produce thousands of times more x-radiation than do
monochrome tubes, which operate below 20 kilovolts. (X-ray emissions increase by about a factor of ten for every one kilovolt increase.)

But it's unlikely that much x-radiation leaks out of any computer
monitor. The electron beams inside the CRTs have little energy and
produce only soft x-rays. This radiation is effectively absorbed by the
special face glass of the CRT.

Although the CRT itself looks like a simple thing—hardly more than
an oddly shaped glass bottle with some metal pins sticking out its
narrow end—it's a complex creation, believed to be the most complicated consumer product made before the advent of the microprocessor. Rather than one uniform kind of glass, the tube is crafted from
several varieties, each tailored to a specific purpose. The wide face of
the tube is thick, sometimes as much as one-half inch. It's made from
glasses rich in strontium and lead, which block the x-ray emissions
from the beam within the tube.

Regulations promulgated by the Food and Drug Administration set a
maximum limit of x-ray emissions from televisions and terminals alike
at 0.5 milliroentgens per hour at a distance of five centimeters from
the screen—that's about two inches, close-watching indeed. Devices
with greater emissions are not permitted to be sold in this country.
Moreover, the measurement of x-radiation under this standard must
be made under worst-case conditions. Not only must all controls on a
set being measured be advanced to the position maximizing x-radiation (settings at which the set is unlikely to be operated) but also

failure conditions that would result in the worst possible x-ray emissions must be simulated. (For instance, the failure of a voltage regulator who would increase the potential of the CRT electron beam.) These simulations often result in the catastrophic failure of the equipment during the test.

Compliance testing by the FDA has turned up x-ray emissions from computer terminals. For example, a 1981 study found roughly one out of 12 VDTs evaluated emitted x-radiation above the 0.5 milliroentgen per hour limit. The problems were confined to eight units (out of 91) which represented three different models. The out-of-compliance models were either recalled to be modified to comply with emissions requirements or were not permitted to be sold on the U.S. market.

The vast majority of computer monitors emit virtually no x-rays. In fact, their thick lead-enriched glass screens can actually shield you from background x-radiation.

Ultraviolet Radiation

Ultraviolet radiation is part of sunlight, a growing part owing to the diminishing ozone layer in the stratosphere. Its name describes it—ultraviolet is the invisible component of sunlight beyond the violet end of the spectrum. It has shorter waves (180 to 400 nanometers) and higher frequencies than visible light. Physically, that means that ultraviolet photons are more energetic than those of visible light. In fact, the ultraviolet spectrum spans the transitionary range between ionizing and non-ionizing radiation. UV photons can be so energetic as to cause chromosomal damage and have been implicated in causing cancer. They also can burn the skin. UV also triggers the skin's protective tanning reaction.

Unlike x-rays, however, ultraviolet is not penetrating. The thick atmospheric blanket of ozone stops them quite well; a thick blanket of cotton, or even a thin shirt, does quite a good job. Consequently, the effects of ultraviolet on the human body are limited to the places that sunlight can reach—the skin and the eyes. Today, it is generally agreed that exposure to ultraviolet radiation can cause both skin cancers, cataracts, conjunctivitis (irritation of the lining of the eye), keratitis (inflammation of the cornea), pain, and light intolerance.

Current evidence indicates that UV exposure is cumulative. That is, the longer you bathe in its rays over your lifetime and the stronger the rays, the greater the chances of unfavorable consequences. It is also believed that exposure early in life has a greater effect than later exposure.

All computer monitors emit some UV along with the visible light of their images. However, the most energetic and thus the most dangerous wavelengths cannot escape the CRT. Ordinary glass strongly absorbs ultraviolet radiation with wavelengths shorter than about 350 nanometers. The only part of the UV spectrum that may be present in CRT emissions is, therefore, the range from 350 to 400 nanometers. (Some sources list the beginning of UV radiation at 380 nanometers.)

Ultraviolet emissions are present to some extent from monitors, but the emission level declines with decreasing wavelengths and they are virtually absent in most cases at wavelengths higher than about 350 nanometers. Because most color monitors use phosphors of the same family (P22), all have similar UV emission characteristics. Invariably, however, monitor ultraviolet emissions are less than visible radiation—typically no more than 5 percent of the level of the maximum emission in the visible spectrum. In contrast, a "deluxe cool white" fluorescent tube, the kind often used in office lighting, puts out UV at a level of about 20 percent of its maximum visible emissions. Based on typical monitor brightness levels and office lighting levels mandated by OSHA, CRT emissions of UV would be a fraction (in the range of one-quarter) of the level reflected from a white sheet of paper on a desktop when the monitor is operated under the test conditions (brightness and contrast advanced fully, screen fully lit). In normal operation, UV emissions from a monitor would be substantially less. In other words, although monitors do emit a measurable amount of UV radiation, fluorescent lighting poses many times the danger of the typical computer monitor. Sunlight is substantially more dangerous.

Microwave Radiation

Microwave energy—the stuff that cooks in microwave ovens and blasts radar beams over the horizon—has well-documented effects on living cells. Like a potato or poodle in the microwave oven, they cook. The mechanism is well-understood. The energy of the microwave signal excites water and fat molecules, transferring to them as thermal energy (heat). Food is cooked by microwaves because the heat induced in them accumulates faster than it radiates away, raising the temperature. Cell proteins break down as temperature increases. Cells die. The food is cooked.

Microwaves penetrate moderate distances through living tissue. Consequently, organs inside a body can be heated (potentially killed) by microwave beams. The thermal energy of microwaves is also known to cause cataracts.

Wavelengths longer than microwaves (those typical of VHF television, FM, and standard broadcast radio signals) also cause thermal effects by transferring energy to materials, however they are not so reactive with biological tissue. They tend to penetrate without being absorbed.

Outside of the thermal effects, microwave and other radiation in the radio spectrum (that is, higher in frequency than about 30 Khz) is thought not to pose other health hazards. Some studies have implicated microwaves in causing cataracts, although most of these have been at intensities that cause thermal effects. Cataracts caused by non-thermal microwaves have reported, although the preponderance of studies have found to the contrary.

Microwave and other radio frequency heating requires very strong signals. Microwave ovens operate at levels of hundreds of watts. Computer monitors don't even draw hundreds of watts from wall outlets. Although they may emit some microwaves, the amounts are small. In fact, the government assures that such emissions will be well below the levels associated with heating effects. All computer equipment must already be certified to abide by subpart B (formerly subpart J) of part 15 of the Federal Communications Commission rules and regulations which sets interference standards that are well below (by orders of magnitude) the radiation levels necessary for thermal effects. Whereas health standards deal in volts per meter; the FCC interference standard limits emissions to microvolts per meter (the exact value depends on frequency).

Moreover, the PCs do not directly create microwave energy. Although microwaves are theoretically created as harmonics of the signals generated inside the computer, the levels of the microwave signals are essentially unmeasurable.

A possibility exists that there are nonthermal microwave effects that may be active at lower signal levels. If these effects are real, they are believed to be a result of low-frequency modulation of the microwaves. These modulation effects would be similar to the effects of direct radiation at much lower frequencies.

ELF and VLF Radiation

At the very bottom of the electromagnetic spectrum is extremely low frequency radiation. Strictly defined, ELF comprises the frequency range from 3 to 30 Hz, but in common usage, the term has been extended to any frequency below 30,000 Hz. As with all frequencies below 450 Khz, ELF is ignored in the FCC certification process. ELF has long been thought innocuous, but a number of newspaper and magazine articles have raised doubts about its safety.

Strictly speaking, the ELF of concern is not radiation but captive electric and magnetic fields that are generated by strong electric currents in power systems, appliances, and other electrical equipment (which includes computers and their peripherals). The two types of fields—electrical and magnetic—are related and arise from the same phenomena, but have individual distinguishing characteristics. *Electric fields* generate a potential (a voltage), are measured in millivolts or volts per meter, and are relatively easily shielded against using a conductive material. *Magnetic fields* generate a current (amperage), are measured in milliamps per meter or sometimes in related units of gauss, and are difficult to shield against.

A number of recent studies have correlated the strong ELF fields associated with power lines and electrical distribution systems with increased cancer risk. Electric blankets and water bed heaters have also been implicated. ELF fields similar to those generated by some computer equipment have demonstrated biological effects in the laboratory. These effects include changes in cell membrane permeability, altered prenatal development, and the promotion of the growth of cancerous cells.

ELF research has been of two types: laboratory studies on cell cultures and animal tissues and epidemiological studies—research that starts with sick people and attempts to find a common link between their backgrounds.

The epidemiological studies of power distribution systems have mostly taken the form of correlating illnesses with the exposure to ELF fields. To date, the results of these studies have been mixed. The most recent, however, have been aimed at answering the criticisms of previous studies that found a positive correlation of the conditions in which large ELF fields would be present (the fields themselves were not measured) with childhood cancers. In the United States and Sweden, correlations between cancer and strong ELF fields associated with electrical distribution systems have been found, although other, contradictory studies have also been published.

In the laboratory, the potential biological effects of ELF at levels below those which would cause the heating of tissue have been extensively investigated for about the last decade. The results of that research are beginning to show that far from being innocuous and non-interactive with biological tissue, ELF electrical and magnetic fields can be subtly active with both beneficial and harmful effects. On the positive side, ELF fields are used in treating bone fractures. The fields apparently promote bone growth and hasten healing. On the downside, ELF fields have demonstrated effects on calcium channel permeability of cell membranes which can affect a variety of cell functions, including the transmission of electrical signals in nerve tissue. The fields also have been shown to affect protein synthesis and alter circadian rhythms. ELF fields also appear to promote the growth of cancerous cells. Research has also demonstrated that developing nervous systems may be particularly susceptible to ELF fields, and that these effects may be latent, showing up only in specific situations or at later times.

Of course, not all of these dire studies stand up to scrutiny. The results of some have failed attempts at replication. And, of course, since these lab studies were carried out in vitro, there is no guarantee that the effects on human beings will be identical. However, a consensus is emerging that ELF fields can be biologically active at levels lower than were thought possible at one time.

Among the discoveries about ELF fields are that they do not behave like ionizing radiation. For instance, the fields are not energetic enough at the molecular level to change or destroy the chemical bonds in cells. They don't damage chromosomes. Instead, the ELF fields seem to mimic the electrical changes that normally occur in living cells in the body. For instance, by changing the calcium permeability of cells, they can change the response of a nerve cell to stimulation. This mimicking of normal cellular processes may be the root of the cancer-promoting potential of ELF. The membrane sites at which some ELF reactions occur appear to act as receptors for cancer promoting chemicals. In addition, ELF fields also appear to increase the chemical activity of a compound, ornithine decarboxylase. This effect has been associated with cancer promotion. In addition, ELF fields also disrupt the functions of cell gap-junctions, another effect associated with cancer growth.

Some studies have found ELF fields to have an odd aspect that complicates research. Chemical carcinogens and ionizing radiation are believed to behave in a linear fashion. That is, the dangers of each increase as the exposure level increases. While some ELF effects show a similar relationship to intensity, some studies have found "window" effects—biological effects occur only with certain field strengths (or certain frequencies) of ELF and not at higher or lower values. In addition, the window effects of ELF also appear to depend on the presence and orientation of static fields, like the earth's magnetic field. For example, one study on chick brain tissue showed changes in calcium ion flux with 60 Hz ELF fields with strengths of 35, 40, and 42.5 volts per meter, although fields of 25, 30, and 45 volts per meter showed no effect.

For health scientists, just the possibility of window effects is worrisome. If these effects are real (doubts persist that they are), they would preclude the development of exposure standards. The effects of ELF fields would vary with the individual experiencing them because the size and shape of one's body affects the strength of voltages and currents induced inside it by the ELF fields.

To complicate matters further, the waveform associated with ELF fields appears to affect their biological activity. Least active appear to be the sinusoidal waves that are characteristic of utility-supplied electricity. The most active appear to be pulsed fields like those generated by radar and fields with sawtooth waveforms, which are characteristically generated by the sweep circuitry in televisions and monitors.

Although older monitors emitted copious magnetic and electric fields—mostly above and from the left side of the sets—most manufacturers are designing new products to meet a stringent radiation standard adopted in Sweden by the Swedish Board for Measurement and Testing, internationally known by its Swedish initials, MPR.

MPR Standards

The Swedish safety standard pertains to a number of aspects of monitor emissions, including x-radiation, static electrical fields, low-frequency electrical fields and low-frequency magnetic fields. Actually, two Swedish standards exist, an old one (now termed MPR I) and a new one (MPR II), published in December, 1990. Although MPR I focused solely on alternating magnetic fields with frequencies between 1 Khz and 400 Khz, MPR II extended the standard to both electrical and magnetic fields and lowered the reach of the standard to 5 Hz. This revision has important implications for you and monitor makers. Some manufacturers claim their products meet the Swedish standard even when they only comply with MPR I. But MPR I covers only one aspect of monitor emissions—basically horizontal scanning frequencies. MPR II extends to the vertical frequency range as well as covering power line frequencies.

The MPR II standard requires particular measurements of electrical and magnetic fields to be made at various points around the monitor under carefully controlled conditions. Both types of fields are measured in two bands (5 Hz to 2 Khz and 2 Khz to 400 Khz) at distances approximating normal working distance at dozens of positions around the monitor. Electrical fields must be less than than 25 volts per meter in the lower band, 2.5 volts per meter in the upper band; magnetic fields, below 250 nanoteslas (2.5 milligauss) in the lower band and below 25 nanoteslas in the upper band.

The Swedish standards are the toughest in the world, so compliance with them is the best assurance that a monitor is as safe as possible. However, MPR compliance is not a complete assurance of safety. Safe and unsafe levels of these low-frequency fields have yet to be confidently determined. Some research actually suggests biological activity at field strengths permitted under the Swedish standards.

Radiation Protection

If, based on the current state of research, you believe ELF fields are dangerous, you can take steps to minimize your exposure to them. For instance, sit in front of your computer and display, where the ELF fields are the weakest. Avoid sitting near the sides of nearby computer monitors, particularly the left side. Because both the magnetic and electric ELF fields generated by computer equipment fall off quickly with increased distance, you can minimize your exposure by working as far from your computer and its display as is consistent with good ergonomics. In other words, don't back off so far you have to squint or strain to reach what you need to get at.

Monitors emit more ELF than do computer systems, and this radiation appears to be related to the scanning signals used by their CRTs. You can avoid the field associated with scanning signals (which may be more dangerous than the more pervasive sinusoidal waveforms) by using a display based on an alternative technology, such as an LCD display.

It's unlikely that your computer monitor will kill you. Even if the worst of the effects attributed to ELF prove true, you likely face greater risks to your health from other forms of pollution, such as the cigarette smoke you inhale (either your own or that of co-workers), the cholesterol in your bloodstream, and the peanut butter you spread on your noontime sandwich.

Buying a Monitor

The best way to judge the quality of a monitor is to look at it. Go to your dealer and scrutinize every display you're considering. If you plan to buy direct, however, you won't be able to get a good preview over the phone or through the mail. Worse, monitors are bulky, and the costs of shipping can easily overwhelm the savings you earn through negotiating a sharp deal. Nevertheless, if you know what to look for and the right questions to ask, you can assure yourself of getting the best monitor for your money. Here are some shopping hints:

Check Compatibility

The most important issue with any monitor is that it works with the display adapter you have or plan to use. If you want a low-cost monitor, you'll save by sticking to a single-standard (fixed-frequency) monitor. For the most flexibility, however, you'll want a multiscanning monitor that can accommodate both standard and non-standard signals.

With multiscanning monitors, you must match the range of horizontal and vertical frequencies that a monitor accepts with the frequencies of the signals generated by your display adapter. If you have your doubts, get your vendor's assurance that the monitor you choose will work with your specific display adapter.

Check CRT Quality

One of the biggest differences between color monitor quality levels is the picture tube used. Some manufacturers offer the same or very similar models that differ only by tube. When ordering, it is critical that you get the quality of picture tube that you need. Read the ads carefully and check the phosphor-pitch (dot-pitch or slot-pitch) of the tubes used by the monitors you're interested in. Smaller (lower numbers) is better.

Check What Is Included and Excluded

You should expect to be able to open the box, take out the monitor, and plug it into your PC. Unfortunately, some manufacturers and vendors leave out the most important link—the PC-to-monitor cable. Before you buy, be sure that you get the cable you need with your monitor. And verify that the monitor will plug into your display adapter. A few monitors, particularly the discontinued models available at steep discounts, use non-standard input connectors (for instance, a nine-pin D-shell instead of the VGA-standard 15-pin high-density D-shell). If the monitor requires an adapter to match your display adapter, make sure that the adapter is included. The necessary adapter might otherwise be hard to find—and will undoubtedly be expensive.

Make sure that a tilt-swivel stand is included with the monitor, too. Today, a stand should be considered standard equipment, although some manufacturers slight you on it. Don't forget to figure in the cost of adding a stand to a monitor that lacks one (at least if you really *want* a stand).

Figure in Shipping Costs

If you buy direct, don't forget the freight. Monitors are notoriously expensive to ship. While moderate-size displays—those 14 inches and under—can typically be sent through low-cost standard United Parcel Service, bigger monitors may incur oversize charges—if UPS will handle them at all. A big-screen, high-resolution monitor may out-weigh the UPS limit, forcing you to some alternate—and very expen-sive—freight company.

When shopping direct for a monitor, carefully check each vendor's shipping policy. The extra charges some tack on (particularly for those big screens) can easily outweigh the price differences between vendors. A monitor that's available postpaid for a few dollars more will often be the better bargain than one for a lower price that also demands you pay all the freight charges and a handling fee to boot.

Look for Shipping Damage

Not only are monitors expensive to ship, they are sensitive to shipping damage, perhaps the most damage-prone of all computer peripherals. If a monitor is dropped, its convergence might change—and always for the worse.

When you receive your monitor, be sure to check for hidden damage. Even if you see no outward signs of shipping abuse on the box (no squashed corners, no torn cardboard, no tire tracks across the top) check out the monitor thoroughly. Specifically, ensure that it turns on and its convergence is acceptable, particularly in the corners of the screen.

Weigh the Warranty

If your monitor does arrive with loose pieces rattling around in the box or a picture that requires 3-D glasses to see clearly, you won't want to ship the ailing set to the manufacturer's service depot that's an ocean away. You'll either want an immediate replacement or on-site service.

You may sacrifice both for a low price. But you'll still want to know your vendor's service policy when you order. Ask how long it will take to get a replacement—or whether you'll have to wait until the defective monitor can be returned, repaired, and finally shipped back to you. If the vendor has no service department, check the manufacturer's service policy and where the nearest repair facility is. Make a call and find out how long it takes to turn around a monitor repair.

Monitors are as reliable as any peripheral you connect to your PC, but when a problem occurs, it's likely to be expensive to repair. Consequently, the duration and coverage of the warranty of a monitor is an important consideration.

Some manufacturers warrant their picture tubes separately, often for longer than the monitor itself. This is significant additional coverage. Remember, the picture tube may make up more than half the cost of the monitor.

Again, don't forget to check how and where warranty service will be performed. If the worst happens, you'll at least want a convenient way of curing your monitor's ills.

15

Parallel Ports

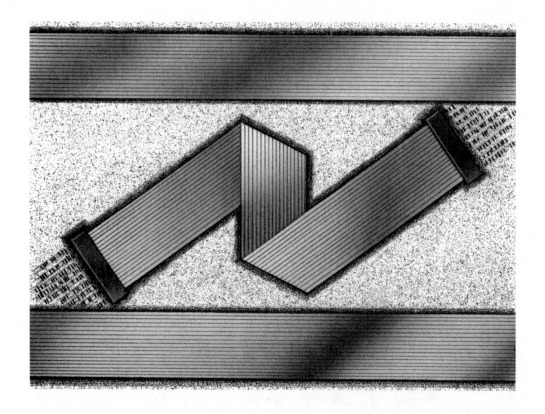

P arallel ports are well-defined, convenient, and fast—probably the most trouble-free connection you can make with your PC. Once the exclusive province of printers, an increasing number of peripherals are taking advantage of the fast, sure parallel connection. But all parallel ports are not the same nor are all parallel connections. A port that works for a printer may fail dismally when you attempt to transfer files across it. It's all a matter of design.

The term *parallel port* is almost synonymous with *printer port*. *Parallel* refers to the fact that it conducts the signals through eight separate wires—one for each bit of a byte of data—that are enclosed together in a single cable. The signal wires run in parallel from your PC to their destination. IBM made the parallel port the connection of choice for attaching printers to PCs.

In theory, eight wires means that you can move data eight times as fast through a parallel connection than through a single wire. Parallel ports are intrinsically simple because they deal with data the way your PC does—in bytes rather than bits. That's probably why IBM chose the parallel design for printer output.

Today, the parallel port remains the easiest, most foolproof way of connecting a printer to your PC. Just plug it in, and odds are that your printer will work flawlessly—or whatever flaws in its operation do appear won't have anything to do with the interconnection. The parallel port is one of the few truly plug-and-play connections in PC-dom.

Some printers (thankfully a minuscule and dwindling number) react negatively to the IBM parallel port convention, negatively enough that they may forever cease to function. Moreover, an increasing number of other peripherals try to take advantage of the speed and versatility of the parallel port, and they make demands that some ports cannot fill. If you think all parallel ports are the same, you could be surprised when you try to use an inexpensive add-in port for high-speed communications.

The differences between parallel ports are invisible. The differences might not even show up when you work with a printer. As with nearly any other product, the differences between parallel ports appear only when you push them to their limits. As applications and peripherals increase in their power demands, however, parallel ports increasingly are showing their true colors and limitations.

Parallel Information Transfer

The parallel port reflects a hardware engineer's concept of how communication should work. A signal that is in one place is connected to the distant location where it is wanted by running a wire from point to point. For every signal, another wire is added. Eight data signals take eight wires. All the signaling back and forth—for example, indications that the distant device is ready to accept data—get their own separate wires.

Such a design saves on the complex circuitry needed to bundle signals together to travel down one or two conductors. In fact, the whole connection works like a marionette—the PC operates the printer or remote device by electrically tugging on the appropriate strings. It's hard to imagine a simpler, more straightforward system.

No conversion circuitry impedes the flow of information. Moreover, the eight conductors serve as an expressway for information, moving bytes at the same speed a single bit can traverse the connection.

What the design engineer saves in time and port circuitry is made up for in the cost of cables. Instead of the two wires used by telephones and serial computer circuits, a parallel port requires at least eight wires (one for each data bit) plus more for a ground and control signals. The IBM design demands a full 25 separate connections. The result is a big, fat cable that's hard to bend—for example, when you want to back your PC against a wall to give yourself more desk space. Connectors, too, need to grow larger to accommodate all the wires and signals. And more wires means more time needs to be spent soldering or crimping the cable and connector together.

You'll note that one trade-off with the parallel interface is that the expense of extra port circuitry is balanced by the cost of a fatter cable. From the perspective of a company that manufactures computers and leaves the acquisition of printer cables to the purchaser, you can see why the parallel design makes sense.

Cable cost isn't the only downside of a parallel link. The parallel nature of the parallel port is also its undoing from an electrical standpoint. Data and control signals must travel together in a tight group down that big, thick cable. By itself, that's no problem. Parallel ports do, in fact, work well. However, the multiple signal paths tend to react with one another as they travel down the parallel cable that connects the port on your computer to the one on your printer. Signals from one lead tend to leak into others, a problem called *crosstalk*. (In telephone systems, the same tendency causes the talk in conversations in one circuit to cross over into others.)

The longer the cable, the greater the leakage. Consequently, most manufacturers recommend that PC-style parallel connections be kept under 10 feet to prevent problems. Computers and printers vary in their sensitivity to parallel port crosstalk. Some systems will work with long parallel connections, up to 50 feet long; others will balk with anything over 10 feet. The only way to tell how long a cable your system can handle is to try and see.

If you have a long printer cable—or use an extension cable—to put your printer more than 10 feet from your computer, and you can't get your system to work properly, try connecting the printer with a shorter cable. Keeping parallel cable lengths short will prevent problems. If you need a greater length than parallel cabling affords, your alternative is to use a serial connection.

The IBM Parallel Port Standard

In designing the now-standard parallel port that appeared first inside its original PC, IBM elected to follow the pattern of control signals set by one once-prominent printer manufacturer, Centronics. The connection was not formalized at the time IBM borrowed the design— Centronics had just developed a set of control signals that served well the control of computer printers. Other printer companies were adopting the Centronics design when IBM appropriated it, too.

Connectors

IBM, however, chose to go in its own direction for parallel port connectors. Where as a true Centronics printer port uses a 36-conductor Amphenol connector, IBM selected a 25-pin D-shell connector. Since then, printer makers have stuck with the 36-pin design, and IBM and nearly every other computer maker have maintained the 25-pin standard. Consequently, you'll need a special adapter cable to plug your printer into your PC in almost every case. Fortunately, the ubiquity of PCs has made the odd adapter cable a standard accessory. If you dare to make your own, table 15.1 shows a diagram of the proper connections to make.

TABLE 15.1.
IBM Parallel
Printer Cable

Connect these: 25-pin connector	To these: 36-pin connector	Connect these: 25-pin connector	To these: 36-pin connector
1	1	16	31
2	2	17	36
3	3	18	19–30,33
4	4	19	19–30,33
5	5	20	19–30,33
6	6	21	19–30,33
7	7	22	19–30,33
8	8	23	19–30,33
9	9	24	19–30,33
10	10	25	19–30,33
11	11		
12	12		
13	13		
14	14		
15	32		

Unidirectional versus Bidirectional

Since parallel ports were originally conceived to serve solely as printer outputs, the flow of data was designed to be in one direction only—from PC to printer. Only a few of the parallel port control signals needed to go the other way. Consequently, all early PCs were equipped with unidirectional parallel ports. That is, they could send but not receive data.

This one-way nature was a result of the intrinsic electrical design of the port. The parallel port was not designed to be able to supply a significant level of current. Grounding one of the data lines of the port, as might happen when sending data to it, could be destructive to the circuitry of the port. By disallowing any equipment from altering the port outputs (in effect, discouraging sending information to the port), IBM effectively precludes using the parallel port for data acquisition or reception.

IBM evidently rethought this design after the first PCs were produced, and they began to make parallel ports that were capable of bidirectional operation. However, IBM did not officially support bidirectional operation until it introduced the PS/2 line.

The parallel port support built into the very early models of IBM personal computers does, in fact, permit reading of the various data lines. As long as care is taken to keep from grounding the data lines (for instance, controlling them through resistors to keep currents low), it is possible to use even the earliest PC parallel ports bidirectionally. Because the IBM design allows the system to source 2.6 milliamps, resistors of 2.2 kilohms are sufficient. PC parallel ports can sink (absorb) up to 24 milliamps.

The whole issue of unidirectional and bidirectional ports would be academic were it not for the former being easier and cheaper to build. Although all reputable computer makers install bidirectional ports in their products, the makers of inexpensive parallel adapters or multi-function boards are apt to skimp on the circuitry. They may equip their parallel ports with unidirectional buffers.

If all you want to do is print, there is no worry whether a port is unidirectional or bidirectional. However, today you can plug a variety of devices into a parallel port. Some of these include SCSI adapters, network adapters, and data interchange systems. All of these products are designed to take advantage of the high speed of a parallel connection, but none will work with one of these unidirectional ports on a cheap parallel adapter.

Port Assignments

Each parallel port in a PC logically connects with the rest of the system through three input/output ports. One of the ports is used for transferring data to the parallel connection. Typically, your PC's microprocessor will retrieve the information to be printed from memory and transfer it to the I/O port used by the parallel adapter. This data is simply buffered and sent to the parallel connector. The other two I/O ports are used for manipulating control signals and monitoring the signals sent back by the printer, indicating its operating status.

The basic PC design allows for up to three parallel ports to be installed, each with its own triad of input/output ports. Three ranges of three I/O port addresses are reserved for parallel ports, at base addresses of 03BC(Hex), 0378(Hex), and 0278(Hex). In any system, each of these I/O address triplets must be uniquely assigned to a single parallel port. Two parallel ports cannot share the same base address.

The first of these, 03BC(Hex), was originally reserved for the parallel port that was installed on the IBM Monochrome Display Adapter card. Because the MDA card cannot be used with PS/2s, which have their own built-in display adapters, this same set of addresses was assigned to the standard equipment parallel port in each PS/2. Most compatible computers with system board video systems also use this address for their on-board parallel ports. The other two starting addresses are typically available for additional parallel ports.

Compatible systems lacking motherboard-mounted video often avoid using the 03BC(Hex) ports because there's still a small chance you might want to install an MDA video adapter in such a machine. Instead, these systems usually provide for a base address of 0378(Hex) and make some provision for reassigning the address used by the port, typically jumpers or DIP switches.

Device Names

You never need to use the I/O base addresses in the daily operation of your PC. If you need to reference a parallel port, you can instead use its DOS designation. The names LPT1, LPT2, and LPT3 are reserved for the three parallel ports the systems support. (Think of LPT as an abbreviation for Line PrinTer.) The device name PRN is equivalent to LPT1.

These logical names do not necessarily match a given set of I/O port addresses, however. At boot-up, the BIOS code of your PC searches for parallel ports at each of the three supported base addresses. The search is always performed in the order 03BC(Hex), 0378(Hex), and then 0278(Hex). The first parallel port that is found in the system is assigned the name LPT1; the second, LPT2; and the third, LPT3. If you have a monochrome display adapter or a PS/2 with a built-in parallel port, that port will always be LPT1. The values of the port available in your PC are stored in the BIOS data area starting at absolute memory location 0000:0408 with one 16-bit word reserved for storing each based address value.

As a consequence of this allocation scheme, you are assured of having an LPT1 (and PRN) device in your system no matter the I/O ports assigned to your parallel ports—providing you have at least one parallel port! If, however, you have two ports assigned to the same base I/O address, your system will assign both ports the same name, and neither is likely to work.

Port Limit

Because parallel ports come embedded in many products, it's common to find the number of parallel ports in your PC mysteriously higher than you think it should be. You can easily run into port conflicts even when you have not intentionally added extra ports. In fact, you might even exceed the official IBM parallel port maximum of three without knowing it. Or try to make two ports think they are the same one, with confusing and crashing consequences. Before you add a parallel port to your system, it's a good idea to check the number and base addresses of the ports already installed. You can check either through DEBUG or using a commercial feature reporting program.

Parallel Port Signals and Connections

Of the 25 contacts on a parallel port connector, a full 19 are used for the seemingly trivial function of transferring data. Table 15.2 shows where each connection is assigned on the standard IBM parallel port connector. The function of each of these connections is described in the following sections.

TABLE 15.2.	25-pin connector	Function	25-pin connector	Function
	1	Strobe	16	Initialize printer
IBM Parallel	2	Data bit 0	17	Select input
Cable Pin	3	Data bit 1	18	Ground
Assignments	4	Data bit 2	19	Ground
	5	Data bit 3	20	Ground
	6	Data bit 4	21	Ground
	7	Data bit 5	22	Ground
	8	Data bit 6	23	Ground
	9	Data bit 7	24	Ground
	10	Acknowledge	25	Ground
	11	Busy		
	12	Paper end (Out of paper)		
	13	Select		
	14	Auto Feed		
	15	Error		

Data Lines

The information that's to be sent to the printer to become hard copy is first loaded onto eight data lines, one for each bit of a byte of ASCII code. The signals are at standard TTL voltage, nominally a high of five volts, indicating a digital one, and a low of zero volts, indicating a logical zero.

Strobe Line

Just loading bits onto the data lines is not sufficient to indicate to the printer that it should print a character. The data bits are constantly changing, and there's no assurance in the system that all eight will simultaneously pop to the right value—and even if they did, the printer would have no way of knowing that it should (or should not) print the same character twice or more. Some way is required to signal that the computer is finished loading bits onto the data lines and that a character can be printed. The strobe line serves exactly that purpose.

The strobe signal in the IBM parallel scheme is negative. When data bits are *not* read, it is high. When a byte of data is to be transmitted, it goes low.

The timing of the data signals and the strobe signal is critical. All data lines must be at their proper value *before* the strobe signal is triggered so that the printer circuits have adequate time to assume the proper values. About one-half of a microsecond is required. The strobe signal should last for a full microsecond (long enough for the printer to realize that it's there!), and the data signals should persist slightly (another half microsecond) after the completion of the strobe. The overlap helps ensure against errors.

Busy Line

This data-strobe-and-data process allocates a minimum of two micro-seconds per character. At that rate, the parallel interface could dump 500,000 characters per second into some poor, defenseless printer. The printer needs a way to fight back, to tell the computer that it's busy blasting a character onto the paper. The *busy* signal, sent from printer to computer, accomplishes this task. It's a hold-your-horses signal. As soon as the printer receives the strobe and starts the process of print-ing a character (be it only to shove the data into an internal buffer), it trips the busy signal, sending it high.

The busy signal stays high as long as it takes the printer to prepare to receive the next byte of data. This busy condition can persist momen-tarily as the byte is loaded into a buffer or for an extended period during which the printer would be unable to accept another character for printing. For instance, the buffer may fill up, the ribbon could jam, or the printer might not have been fully initialized after being turned on.

Acknowledge Line

While the busy line is a negative signal (it commands Don't send data), another parallel port line is used for positive flow control. The *acknowledge* line carries a signal from the printer to your computer that indicates the preceding character has been properly received and dashed to paper and that the printer is ready for the next character. As with the strobe signal, acknowledge is normally a logical high that shifts low to indicate that the printer is ready for the next character. Typically, this negative-going pulse lasts about eight microseconds.

Printer Feedback

The parallel interface does more than just move data. Dedicated lines in the parallel circuit are used by the printer to signal various aspects of its condition to the host computer. The signals tell the computer that the printer is ready, willing, and able to do its job. In effect, they endow the computer with a modicum of remote-sensing capabilities.

Select

The *select* line indicates that the printer is "selected." That means that it is in its on-line condition, ready to receive information. The select line acts exactly like the on-line light on the front panel of the printer. But instead of being visible to your eyes, it's registered through the parallel port.

The select line goes high when the printer is on-line. If the select line is not high, the parallel port will not transmit data.

Paper Empty

The most common problem encountered during a print job is running out of paper. When that happens, your printer could just run the busy signal high—which would effectively stop your computer from pouring data into it. In fact, most printers do exactly that. But they do more, too, to give you some idea of what's going on (in case you can't see the printer or don't realize your paper pile has been depleted).

To indicate to your computer the exact nature of its problem, your printer pulls the *paper empty* line high. Again, it operates just like the paper out light on the printer but supplies its signal in a form your computer can understand.

Fault

One further signal, *fault*, is used as a catchall for other printer problems. This signal indicates to your computer that something is wrong without indicating exactly what. There aren't enough wires in a cable to indicate all possible printer problems. For instance, fault could indicate that the lid to the printhead chamber is open, the printhead has jammed, the printhead won't index (for instance, the drive belt is broken), or whatever other error conditions your printer can detect on its own.

The fault signal is negative-going. It's normally held high. When an error occurs, it goes low.

Many printers don't use a single-barreled defense. When something goes wrong, all the flags are raised. Busy, select, and fault all go to their warning states.

Computer Control

In the IBM parallel port scheme, three additional signals are used to control various aspects of the printer through hard-wired port connections. These initialize the printer, switch it to an on-line condition (when the printer allows such a remote-controlled change), and control line feeding.

The computer and printer are two separate organisms that can grow and change independently. That is, you can send commands to the printer to change its operation, to set new fonts, change character pitch, and so on. On its own, your computer does nothing to keep track of the commands it sends to your printer—the printer could turn into a monster that would dump the next 47 pages of your monthly report as an amorphous blob in graphics mode, and your computer wouldn't know the difference.

The printer always starts at the same point, however, with fonts, pitches, and modes all sent in a predetermined way. You can reset the printer to this condition by turning it off and then on, initializing all of its important operating parameters. The *initialize printer* or *input prime* is an alternate means of accomplishing the same end. It's like a reset button for the printer. Drive this line low from its normal high condition, and the printer initializes itself, running through its own boot-up operation.

Select Input

Some printers are designed to be switched on- and off-line by their computer hosts. The signal used for commanding the switch is called *select input* by IBM. When this signal is low, printers will accept data; when high, they will not. Many printers allow you to defeat this control by operating a DIP switch that causes the machine to always hold this line low.

Auto Feed XT

The lowly carriage return can be a confusing thing. Some printers assume that a carriage return should automatically advance paper to the beginning of the next line; others think a carriage return merely swerves the printhead back to the beginning of the line currently being printed. Most printers give you a choice—a DIP switch determines how the printer will react to carriage returns.

The *auto feed XT* signal gives your computer the choice. By holding this signal low, the printer is commanded to automatically feed one line when it detects a carriage return. Make it high, and a line feed character is required to roll the paper up to the next line.

Parallel Port Performance

The maximum operating speed of a parallel port is determined by a number of factors. The cable itself sets the ultimate limit on the frequencies of the signals that can be used. As long as it is less than about 10 feet long, however, the effects of the cable on the data throughput of a parallel port are minimal. Instead, the performance of a parallel port is mostly controlled by the values arbitrarily chosen for pulsing of the strobe and acknowledge lines used for normal parallel port flow control. When system timing is set to yield the minimal lengths of these signals, a complete character-transmission cycle requires about 10 microseconds—a speed sufficient to move 100,000 bytes in a second—that's 800,000 bits per second. Compare that to the 9,600 bps of better modems.

That high rate is the ultimate speed limit for a parallel port following the IBM standard—and one it's also unlikely to ever achieve. The characters being sent have to come from someplace, and they have to go somewhere. Processing overhead at both ends of the connection slows the orderly parallel flow substantially. The computer, for instance, must receive the acknowledge signal, then run through a BIOS routine to understand it, then load the next character into the parallel port, and finally send the strobe signal out the port. Even if the printer is equipped with its own buffer, it must go through an equivalent electronic ritual each time a character is received.

Parallel port speed thus varies with the microprocessor power in your computer. The faster the microprocessor, the quicker all of this overhead can be handled. With a vintage PC or XT pumping characters directly into a buffer, you can expect data rates about the same as those you would get with a serial port running at its top 9,600-bits-per-second speed. Modern 486-based computers often push the throughput of their parallel ports to 300,000 bps and sometimes higher.

Even with today's highest performance PCs, this microprocessor overhead remains the barrier to getting nearer to the theoretical performance limit of parallel ports. A few PCs get closer to the maximum transfer rate through the use of bus-mastering technology. Using bus-mastering parallel ports, data transfers to the parallel port can be made by the DMA controller without microprocessor intervention. With a quick DMA system, data throughput can approach the limit. The first systems with built-in bus-mastering parallel ports were the IBM PS/2 Models 90 and 95.

More important than the data throughput to the parallel port, however, is the release of the microprocessor from the drudgery of parallel control. By shifting responsibilities to the DMA system, the microprocessor gains back much of its bandwidth. As a result, overall system performance improves, particularly in a multi-user or multi-tasking environment.

16

Printers and Plotters

O f all the external peripherals people attach to their PCs, the most popular is undoubtedly the printer. Little wonder, considering that the printer is the primary means of converting your computer's intangible thoughts into the hard copy of the material world. Printers use a variety of technologies to put your PC's thoughts on paper, and each has its own advantages and disadvantages.

The term *printer* is perhaps the broadest in the language of data processing, uniting technologies as diverse as hammers, squirt guns, and flashlights. Moreover, the range of performance is wider than with any other peripheral. Various printers operate at speeds from lethargic to lightning-like, from slower than an arthritic typist with one hand tied behind his back to faster than Speedy Gonzales having just munched tacos laced with amphetamines. They're packaged as every-thing from one-pound totables to truss-stressing monsters and look like anything from Neolithic bricks to Batman's nightmares. Some dot paper with text quality that rivals that of a professional publisher and chart out graphics with speed and sharpness that puts a plotter to shame. Some make a two-year-old's handiwork look controlled.

Classifying printers runs a similar wide range. You can distinguish machines by their quality, speed, technology, purpose, weight, color, or any other of their innumerable (and properly pragmatic) design elements.

A definitive discourse on all aspects of printer technology would be a never-ending tale because the field is constantly changing. New technologies often arise, and old ones are revived and refined. New innovations are incorporated into old machines. And seemingly obsolete ideas recur again and again.

Printer Mechanics

The term *computer printer* is a general one that refers not to one kind of machine but to several. Even looking at the mechanical aspects of the typical printer's job of smudging paper with ink, you'll find that there is more than one way to put a computer's output on paper, just as there are multiple methods of getting your house cat to part with its pelt.

Impact Printers

One of the most evident demarcations between printer technologies is whether anything mechanical actually makes impact with the paper on which you want to print. Impact printers beat your paper to death. Non-impact printers cuddle and squeeze it—perhaps even electrocute it—but never slam it hard. They can use any of a diverse array of technologies from laser beams to miniature toaster heating elements that fry pigment to paper to bubbles of ink blown into place. The sole characteristic that can be assumed for a non-impact printer is that nothing forcibly smashes into the paper during the image-making process.

Typewriter Origins

At the low-priced end of the spectrum, the most popular printers rely on impact technology. All impact printers are the direct descendants of the original office typewriter, and they are perhaps best understood by examining their aged forefather.

Although an old-fashioned typewriter is a mechanical complexity (as anyone knows who has tried putting one back together after taking it apart), its operating principle is quite simple. Strip away all the cams, levers, and keys, and you'll see that the essence of the typewriter is its hammers.

Each hammer strikes against an inked ribbon, which, in turn, is pressed against a sheet of paper. The *impact* of the hammer against the ribbon shakes and squeezes ink onto the paper. Absorbed into the paper fibers, the ink leaves a visible mark or image in the shape of the part of the hammer that struck at the ribbon, typically a letter of the alphabet.

One way or another, all impact printers rely on this basic typewriter principle. Like Christopher Sholes' first platen-pecker, all impact printers smash a hammer of some kind against a ribbon to squeeze ink from the ribbon onto paper, making their mark by force. In fact, if there is any difference between an impact printer and a typewriter at all, it's the directness of the linking of the typists fingers and the on-paper output. The typewriter directly lines your fingers to the mechanism that does the printing. A printer, on the other hand, inserts your personal computer between your mind and the printed word.

In the earliest days of personal computers—before typewriter makers were sure that PCs would catch on and create a personal printer market—a number of companies adapted typewriters to computer output chores. The Bytewriter was typical of the result—a slow, plodding computer printer with full typewriter keyboard. It could do double-duty fast as your fingers could fly, but, alas, was no match for the computer's output.

One device, short-lived on the marketplace, even claimed to let you turn your typewriter into a printer merely by sitting a box on the keyboard. The box was filled with dozens of solenoids and enough other mechanical parts to make the Space Shuttle look simple. The solenoids worked as electronically controlled "fingers," pressing down each key on command from the host computer. Interesting as it sounds, this machine treaded the thin line between the absurd and surreal. More than a little doubt exists as to whether these machines, widely advertised in 1981, were ever actually sold.

Today, the most popular low-cost printers are *impact dot-matrix* printers, most often clipped to simply the name *dot-matrix*. Although they use a different character-forming method than the classic typewriter, they rely on the same hammer-and-ribbon impact-printing principle.

Impact Advantages

As with typewriters, all impact printers have a number of desirable qualities. Owing to their heritage of a century and a quarter of engineering refinement, they represent a mature technology. Their designs and functions are relatively straightforward, easy-to-understand, and reassuringly familiar.

Most impact printers can spread their output across any medium that ink has an affinity for, including any paper you might have lying around your home, from onion skin to thin cardstock. Although both impact and non-impact technologies have been developed to the point that either can produce high-quality or high-speed output, impact technology takes the lead when you perform one of the most common business needs, making multipart forms. Impact printers can hammer an impression not just through a ribbon but through several sheets of paper as well. Slide a carbon between the sheets or (better yet) treat the paper for noncarbon duplicates, and you get multiple, guaranteed-identical copies with a single pass through the mechanism. For a number of business applications—for example, the generation of charge receipts—exact carbon copies are a necessity, and impact printing an absolute requirement.

Impact Disadvantages

Impact printers reveal their typewriter heritage in another way. The hammer bashing against the ribbon and paper makes noise, a sharp staccato rattle that's high in amplitude and rich in high-frequency components, penetrating and bothersome as a dental drive or angry horde of giant, hungry mosquitoes. Typically, the impact printer rattles and prattles louder than most normal conversational tones, and it's more obnoxious than an argument. The higher speed of the impact printer, the higher the pitch of the noise, and the more penetrating it becomes.

Some printer makers have done admirable work toning down their boisterous scribes—some printers as fast as 780 characters per second are as quiet as 55 dB, about the level of a quiet PC fan. But you'll still want to leave the room when an inexpensive impact printer (the best-selling of all printers) grinds through its assignment.

Non-Impact Designs

The obvious opposite to impact technology is nonimpact printing. A number of other ways of putting images on paper without the typewriter-like hammer impact have been developed through the application of new technologies and a good deal of imagination. The leading nonimpact technologies are the inkjet, thermal, laser, wax-transfer, and dye-diffusion.

Image-Forming Methods

The terms *impact* and *nonimpact* describe the sort of devilry involved in getting any marks at all to appear on paper. But the method of making those marks is independent of what they are and how they are shaped.

Although different printing technologies have some affect on the quality of the image and what the printer is used for, other considerations are just as important in regard to image quality. Among the most important is the character-forming method used by the printer.

Fully Formed Character Printers

The original typewriter and all such machines made through the 1970s were based on the same character-forming principle as Gutenberg's original printing press. Every letter was printed fully formed from a complete, although reversed, image of itself. The character was fully formed in advance of printing. Every part of it, from the boldest stroke to the tiniest serif, was printed in one swipe of the press or clash of the typewriter hammer. The hammer (or piece of type for the printing press) acts like a mold for the letter to be produced.

In the early days of personal computing, a number of machines used this typewriter-technology and were grouped together under the term *fully formed character* printers. Other names for this basic technology were *letter-quality printers*, *daisy-wheel printers*, and a variation called the *thimble printer*.

Nearly all of the fully formed character printers that you are apt to connect to a personal computer use the impact principle to get their ink on paper. Rather than having a separate hammer for each letter, however, the characters are arranged on a single separate element that is inserted between a single hammer and the ribbon. The hammer, powered by a solenoid that's controlled by the electronics of the printer and your computer, impacts against the element. The element then squeezes the ink off the ribbon and onto the paper. To allow the full range of alphanumeric characters to be printed using this single-hammer technique, the printing element swerves, shakes, or rotates each individual character that is to be formed in front of the hammer as it is needed.

Most often, the characters are arranged near the tips of the spokes of a wheel. These machines earn the term *daisy wheel* because the hubs resemble flower petals. Hold the daisy horizontally and bend those petals upward, and the printing element becomes the thimble (or what you might call a *tulipwheel*).

Fully formed character technology produces good-quality output, on a par with better typewriters. In fact, the chief limitation is not the printing technology but the ribbon that's used. Some daisy-wheel printers when equipped with a Mylar film ribbon can give results almost as good as the work of a phototypesetter.

Although daisy-wheel printers are still available, they are outdated from the PC perspective. Their design limits them solely to text printing and crude graphics. Moreover, fully formed character printers also limit you to a few typefaces. You can only print the typefaces—and font sizes—that are available on the image-forming daisy wheels or thimbles. These machines are also slow—budget-priced machines hammer out text at a lazy 12 to 20 characters per second, and even the most expensive machines struggle to reach 90 characters per second. Other technologies (in particular, laser printers) now equal or exceed the quality of fully formed character printers, run far ahead in speed, and impose little or no price penalty.

Bit-Image Printers

The alternative to fully forming each character is making each one on the fly. The raw material for characters on paper is much the same as it is on the video screen—dots. A number of dots can be arranged to resemble any character that you want to print. To make things easier for the printer (and its designer), printers that form their characters from dots usually arrange those dots in a rectilinear matrix like a crossword puzzle grid. Because characters are formed from dots placed within a matrix, it's only natural to call such machines *dot-matrix printers*. Because most people restrict the use of the dot-matrix term to impact dot-matrix printers, these machines can be better distinguished by terming them *bit-image* printers.

Bit-Image Technologies

All popular non-impact printers and the surviving impact technology use bit-image technology. The reason is versatility. A bit-image printer can generate both text and graphics at virtually any level of quality. The dot patterns that make up individual characters are computer-controlled and can be changed and varied by your computer (or the computer-like control electronics built into the printer) without your needing to make any mechanical adjustments to the machine.

A daisy-wheel, fully formed character printer may allow you to shift from Roman to Italic typeface or from Pica to Elite type size by merely swapping printing elements (the daisy wheels themselves), but matrix printers make the switch even easier and the repertory wider. Just send a computerized instruction to the printer, and you can change the typeface in midline, double the height of each character, squeeze type to half its width, or shift to proportionally spaced script. The same dots can be formed into a chart, graph, drawing, or simulation of a half-tone photograph. Using bit-image techniques, one printer can put virtually any image on paper.

The quality and speed of the output of bit-image printers varies widely with the technology used. At the low end, dot-matrix printing can look simply awful. At the high end, better laser printers can generate book-quality output. Speeds vary from less than a page a minute to dozens of pages in the same period. The following sections describe how each of the most important bit-image printer technologies works.

Impact Dot-Matrix Printers

The prototypical bit-image printer is the impact dot-matrix machine. It uses a *printhead* that shuttles back and forth across the width of the paper. A number of thin *printwires* act as the hammers that squeeze ink from ribbon to paper.

In most dot-matrix printers, a seemingly complex but efficient mechanism controls each of the printwires. The printwire is normally held away from the ribbon and paper, and against the force of a spring, by a strong permanent magnet. The magnet is wrapped with a coil of wire that forms an electromagnet, wound so that its polarity is the opposite of that of the permanent magnet. To fire the print wire against the ribbon and paper, this electromagnet is energized (under computer control, of course), and its field neutralizes that of the permanent magnet. Without the force of the permanent magnet holding the print wire back, the spring forcefully jabs the print wire out against ribbon, squeezing ink onto the paper. After the printwire makes its dot, the electromagnet is de-energized, and the permanent magnet pulls the printwire back to its idle position, ready to fire again.

The two-magnets-and-spring approach is designed with one primary purpose—to hold the printwire away from the paper (and out of harm's way) when no power is supplied to the printer and the printhead. The complexity is justified by the protection it affords the delicate printwires.

The printhead of a dot-matrix printer is made from a number of these printwire mechanisms. Most first-generation personal computer printers and many current machines use nine wires arrayed in a vertical column. To produce high quality, an increasing number of newer impact dot-matrix printers use even more wires, typically 18 or 24. These are often arranged in parallel rows with the printwires vertically staggered, although some machines use different arrangements.

To print a line of characters, the printhead moves horizontally across the paper, and each wire fires as necessary to form the individual characters, its impact precisely timed so that it falls on exactly the right position in the matrix. The wires fire on the fly—the printhead never pauses until it reaches the other side of the paper.

A major factor in determining the printing speed of a dot-matrix machine is the time required between successive strikes of each print wire. Physical laws of motion limit the acceleration each print wire can achieve in ramming toward the paper and back. Thus, the time needed to retract and re-actuate each printwire puts a physical limit on how rapidly the printhead can travel across the paper. It cannot sweep past the next dot position before each of the print wires inside it is ready to fire. If the printhead travels too fast, dot positioning (and character shapes) would become rather haphazard.

To speed up operation, some impact dot-matrix machines print *bidirectionally*, rattling out one row from left to right, and then the next row right to left. This mode of operation saves the time that would ordinarily be wasted when the carriage returns to the left side of the page to start the next line. Of course, the printer must have sufficient memory to store a full line of text so that it can be read backwards.

Inkjets

If the term *inkjet* conjures up images of the Nautilus and giant squid or a B-52 spraying out blue fluid instead of a fluffy white contrail, your mind is on the right track. Inkjet printers are electronic squids that squirt out ink like miniature jet engines fueled in full color. Although this technology sounds unlikely—a printer that sprays droplets of ink onto paper—it works well enough to deliver image sharpness on a par with most other output technologies.

In essence, the inkjet printer is a dot-matrix printer with the hammer impact removed. Instead of a hammer pounding ink onto paper, the inkjet flings it into place from tiny nozzles, each one corresponding to a print wire of the impact dot-matrix printer. The motive force can be an electromagnet or, as is more likely today, a piezo-electric crystal (a thin crystal that bends when electricity is applies across it). A sharp, digital pulse of electricity causes the crystal to twitch and force ink through the nozzle into its flight to paper.

One secret to the success of the inkjet is that it has no ribbon to blur the image. On-paper quality can equal that of more expensive laser printers. Moreover, the "laserless" technology of the inkjet machines equates to lower costs—and lower prices. Budget inkjets rival low-end dot-matrix printers in affordable price.

But inkjets are slower at producing high quality than laser printers because they rely on a printhead that mechanically scans across each sheet instead of lightning-fast optics. Inkjets also require periodic maintenance because they use liquid ink. If not properly cared for, the ink can dry in the nozzles and clog them.

To avoid such problems, better inkjets have built-in routines that clean the nozzles with each use. Most nozzles now are self-sealing so that when they are not used, air can't get to the ink. Some manufacturers even combine the inkjet and ink supply into one easily changeable module. Nevertheless, pack an inkjet away without properly cleaning it first, and it probably won't work when you resurrect it months later.

Because inkjets are non-impact printers, they are much quieter than ordinary dot-matrix engines. About the only sound you hear from them is the carriage coursing back and forth. On the other hand, inkjets require special paper with controlled absorbency for best results, and that means that you're likely to pay more per page. If you try to get by with cheap paper that is too porous, the ink will wick away into a blur. If the paper is too glossy, the wet ink can smudge.

The liquid ink of inkjet printers can be a virtue when it comes to color. The inks remain fluid enough even after they have been sprayed on paper to blend together. This gives color inkjet printers the capability to mix their primary colors together to create intermediary tones. Although inkjets can't yet control the ink flow precisely enough to give a true-color palette, they do produce on-paper results just shy of thermal wax output. For quality color, nothing is more cost effective than an inkjet.

A new development in inkjet technology is the *solid-inkjet* or *phase-change* printer. Where classic inkjets spray volatile inks based on solvents at paper where they are fixed by the evaporation or absorption, phase-change printers melt wax that's dyed the appropriate color, flings it at paper, and lets it harden there. As with other inkjets, phase-change printers spray tiny dots of ink. When the hot dots hit the paper, they quickly cool, changing phase from liquid to solid (hence the name of the technology). The original phase-change printer, Howtek Pixelmaster, stopped there, leaving little lumps of plastic-based inks on the paper or clogging the printhead. Tektronix improved on this original by adding a *cold fuser*, a steel roller that then squashes the ink dots flat, or nearly so, as the printing medium rolls out of the printer. To make the fuser work, they also reformulated the inks from plastic compounds to a fatty wax base, something akin a crayon. Because they don't get absorbed into the paper, phase-change inks have greater saturation than traditional inkjet inks. Moreover, heat alone can remove clogs from a phase-change printhead.

Thermal

A printer that works on the same principle as a wood-burning set might seem best for a Boy Scout rather than executive on the go, but today's easy-to-tote printers do exactly that—the equivalent of charring an image on paper. Thermal printers use the same electrical heating of the word-burner, a resistance that heats up with the flow of current. In the case of the thermal printer, however, the resistance element is tiny and heats and cools quickly, in a fraction of a second. As with inkjets, the thermal printhead is the equivalent of that of a dot-matrix printer, only it heats rather than hits.

Thermal printers do not, however, actually char the paper they print on. Getting paper that hot would be dangerous, precariously close to combustion (although it might let the printer do double-duty as a cigarette lighter). Instead, thermal printers use special, thermally sensitive paper that turns from white to near-black at a moderate temperature.

Thermal technology is ideal for portable printers because there are few moving parts—only the printhead moves, nothing inside it. There are no springs and wires to jam. Moreover, the tiny resistive elements require little power to heat, actually less than is needed to fire a wire in an impact printer. Thermal printers can be lightweight, quiet, and reliable. They can even run on batteries.

The special paper is one drawback. Not only is it costly (because it is, after all, special paper) but it feels funny and is prone to discolor if it is inadvertently heated to too high a temperature. The paper can't tell the difference between a hot printhead and a cozy corner in the sun.

Gradually, thermal printers are becoming special-application machines. In that inkjets have many of the same virtues and more reasonable paper, low-cost inkjets are invading the territory of the thermal machines.

Laser Printers

The one revolution that has changed the faces of both offices and forests around the world was the photocopier. Trees plummet by the millions to provide fodder for the duplicate, triplicate, and megaplicate copies. Today's nonimpact, bit-image laser printer owes its life to this technology.

At heart, the principle is simple. Some materials react to light in strange ways. Selenium and some complex organic compounds modify their electrical conductivity. Copiers and laser printers capitalize on this by focusing an optical image on a photoconductive drum that's been given a static electrical charge. The charge drains away from the conductive areas that have been struck by light, but the charge persists in the dark areas. Pigment called a toner is then spread across the drum, and it sticks to the charged areas. A roller squeezes paper against the drum to transfer the pigment, which is fixed in place by heating or "fusing" it.

The trick to the laser printer is that the laser beam is made, as if by magic, to scan across the drum (magic because most printers use rotating mirrors to make the scan). By turning, the drum automatically advances to the next line as the scanning is done. The laser beam is modulated, rapidly switched on for light areas, off for dark areas, one minuscule dot at a time to form a bit-image. Similar optical printers use *LCD-shutter* technology which puts an electronic shutter (or an array of them) between a constant light source (which need not be a laser) and the drum to modulate the beam. *LED printers* modulate ordinary Light-Emitting Diodes as their optical source. As exotic as these different technologies sound, these imaging parts of the laser printer are of small concern in buying such a machine. Nearly all laser and laser-like printers produce similar results—you'll need an eye loupe to tell the difference—with today's incarnation of the technology producing a resolution of 300 dots per inch. You'll find that the biggest differences between lasers and related LCD shutter printers are found in their paper-handling and data-handling.

As far as color is concerned, today's affordable laser printer gives you the Model T choice—any color you want as long as it's black. The printers themselves are designed for monochrome operation and can yield other colors with toners of different hues (few of which are available).

Thermal-Wax Transfer

Today's leading technology for printing rich, pure, even, saturated colors is called *thermal-wax transfer*. Current thermal-wax engines achieve resolutions as high as today's laser standard, 300 dpi, and colors rivaling Bugs Bunny's on-screen best.

Ink makes the difference. Thermal-wax printers use wide ink transfer sheets, pure colors supported in a wax-based medium clinging to a plastic film base—sort of like a mylar typewriter ribbon with a gland condition. The ink is transferred from ribbon to paper in all its intensity by a thermal printhead as wide as the paper. A series of thermal elements, a full 300 of them per inch, heat the ribbon, melting the ink and allowing it to resolidify firmly fixed to the paper. Your choice of transfer sheet allows for monochrome or color printing from the same machine.

Compared to other technologies, thermal-wax engines are slow and wasteful. They are slow because the thermal printing elements must have a chance to cool off before advancing the 1/300th of an inch to the next line on the paper. And they are wasteful because a swath of inked transfer sheet as large as a sheet of paper is used for each of the primary colors printed on each page—that's nearly four feet of transfer sheet for one page. Consequently printing a full-color page can be expensive, typically measured in dollars rather than cents per page.

Because thermal-wax printers are not a mass-market item and each manufacturer uses its own designs for both mechanism and supplies, you're usually restricted to one source for inksheets—the printer manufacturer. Although that helps ensure quality (printer makers pride themselves on the color and saturation of their inks), it also keeps prices higher than they might be in a more directly competitive environment.

For color work, some thermal-wax printers give you the choice of three- or four-pass transfer sheets and printing. A three-pass transfer sheet holds the three primary colors of ink—red, yellow, and blue— while a four-color sheet adds black. Although black can be made by overlaying the three primary colors, a separate black ink gives richer, deeper tones. It also imposes a higher cost and extends printing time by one-third.

From these three primary colors, thermal-wax printers claim to be able to make anywhere from seven to nearly seventeen million colors. That prestidigitation requires a mixture of transparent inks, dithering, and ingenuity. Because the inks used by thermal wax printers are transparent, they can be laid one atop another to create simple secondary colors. They do not, however, actually mix.

Expanding the thermal-wax palette further requires pointillistic mixing, laying different color dots next to each other and relying on them to visually blend together in a distant blur. Instead of each dot of ink constituting a picture element, a group of several dots effectively forms a super pixel of an intermediate color.

The penalty for this wider palette is a loss of resolution. For example, a super pixel measuring 5 x 5 dots would trim the resolution of a thermal-wax printer to 60 dots per inch. Image quality looks like a color halftone—a magazine reproduction—rather than a real photograph. Although the quality is shy of perfection, it is certainly good enough for proofs of what's going to a film recorder or the service bureau to be made into color separations.

Dye-Diffusion

For true photo-quality output from a printer, today's stellar technology is the thermal *dye-diffusion* process. Using a mechanism similar to that of the thermal-wax process, dye-diffusion printers are designed to use penetrating dyes rather than inks. Instead of a dot merely being present or absent as in the case of a thermal-wax printer, diffusion allows the depth of the color of each dot to vary. The diffusion of the dyes can be carefully controlled by the printhead. In that each of the three primary colors can have a huge number of intensities (most makers claim 256), the palette of the dye-diffusion printer is essentially unlimited.

What is limited is the size of the printed area in some printers. The output of most dye-diffusion printers looks like photographs in size as well as color. Another limit is cost. The newer, more exotic technology pushes dye-diffusion machines into the pricing stratosphere. Dye-diffusions are only now knocking on the $10,000 pricing barrier.

Bit-Image Quality

The quality of the characters printed by the bit-image printer is determined by three chief factors: the number of dots in the matrix, the addressability of the printer, and the size of the dots. The denser the matrix (the more dots in a given area), the better the characters look. Higher addressability allows the printer to place dots on paper with greater precision. Smaller dots allow finer details to be rendered.

Often, even bidirectional printers slow down to single-direction operation when quality counts. To increase dot density, they retrace each line two or more times, shifting the paper half the width of a dot vertically, between passes, filling in the space between dots. Unidirectional operation helps ensure accurate placement of each dot in each pass.

A matrix measuring 5 x 7 (horizontal by vertical) dots is just sufficient to render all the upper- and lowercase letters of the alphabet unambiguously—and rather unaesthetically. The dots are big and they look disjointed. Worse, the minimal matrix is too small to let descending characters (g, j, p, q, and y) drop below the general line of type and thus makes them look cramped and scrunched up. The minimum matrix used by most commercial dot-matrix printers measures 9 x 9 dots, a readable arrangement but still somewhat inelegant. Newer 18-and 24-pin impact dot-matrix printers can form characters with 12 x 24 to 24 x 24 matrices.

Other bit-image technologies go even further. Laser printers pack tiny dots very densely, 300 per inch. A single character may be formed in a 30 x 50 matrix. The latest generation of inkjet and impact dot-matrix printers also approach that quality level.

As with computer displays, the resolution and *addressability* of dot-matrix printers are often confused. When resolution is mentioned, addressability is meant. A printer may be able to address any position on the paper with an accuracy of, say, 1/120th inch. However, if a printwire is larger than 1/120th inch in diameter, the machine will never be able to render detail as small as 1/120th inch.

The big dots made by the wide printwires will blur out the detail. Better-quality impact dot-matrix printers have smaller as well as more printwires. In addition, the ribbon that's inserted between the wires and paper serves to blur each dot hammered out by an impact dot-matrix printer. Nonimpact bit-image printers generally use dots the same size as their resolution, typically about 1/300th inch.

Laser Resolution Issues

The best resolution available in moderate cost PC printers comes from laser machines. Although the standard among most lasers is 300 dots per inch, newer printers are pushing the limits higher. Several factors control the resolution that slides out of a laser printer.

In most lasers, the resolution level is fixed primarily by the electronics inside the printer. The most important part of the control circuitry is the *Raster Image Processor*, also known as the *RIP*. The job of the RIP is to translate the string of characters or other printing commands into the bit-image that the printer will transfer to paper. In effect, the RIP works like a video board, interpreting drawing commands (a single letter in a print stream is actually a drawing command to print that letter), computing the position of each dot on the page, and pushing the appropriate value into the printer's memory. The memory of the printer is arranged in a raster just like the raster of a video screen, and one memory cell (a single bit in the typical black-and-white laser printer) corresponds to each dot position on paper.

Most dot-matrix printers accept dot-addressable graphics on the fly. That is, data bytes are sent to them and, either as soon as the bytes are received or after a full line has been accepted, the printer obediently rattles them to paper.

Laser printers can't work so quickly. They work a page at a time, (earning them the epithet *page printers*) digesting an entire sheet of graphics before committing a dot to paper. The laser mechanism is tuned to run at exactly one speed, and it must receive data at the proper rate to properly form its image. In addition, many laser printers recognize higher level graphics commands to draw lines and figures across the entire on-paper image area. To properly form these images, the laser printer needs to get the big picture of its work.

For these and other reasons, laser printers require a prodigious amount of memory to buffer full-page, bit-mapped images in their highest resolution modes. Consequently, the size of the memory in the laser printer limits the resolution of graphics that can be printed. Enough memory must be present to store a whole page at the resolution level to be printed. If not enough memory is available, only a portion of a page can be imaged, or the full page must be imaged at a lower resolution. An 8 x 10.5-inch image (about a full page on an 8.5 x 11-inch sheet) at 300 dpi requires 945,000 bytes—essentially one megabyte of printer memory. The 512K packed in some printers as standard equipment will allow only 150 dpi across a full 8.5 x 11-inch sheet. Even more memory is needed if you want to use the printer's memory for functions beside storing a raster, such as holding downloadable fonts, for example.

Most lasers operate in a *character-mapped mode* when rendering alphanumerics, so memory usage is not as great. The printer can store a full-page image in ASCII or a similar code, one byte per letter, and generate the dots of each character as the page is scanned through the printer.

The RIP itself may, by design, limit a laser printer to a given resolution. However, in many lasers, the RIP can be replaced by an add-in processor using the *video input* of the printer. The video input earns its name because its signal is applied directly to the light source in the laser in raster-scanned form (like a television image), bypassing most of the printer's electronics. The add-in processor can modulate the laser at higher rates to create higher resolutions.

Hewlett-Packard's LaserJet III series of printers introduced another sharpness-improving technology that the company called *resolution enhancement.* This technique works by altering the size of toner dots at the edges of characters and diagonal lines to reduce the jagged steps inherent in any matrix bit-image printing technique. With resolution enhancement, the actual on-paper resolution remains at 300 dpi, but the optimized dot size makes the printing appear sharper.

Some laser printers now are leaping beyond 300 dpi to 600 dpi or higher with improved RIPs. The higher resolutions also demand improved toner formulations because, at high resolutions, the size of toner particles limits sharpness much as the size of printwires limits impact dot-matrix resolution. With higher resolution laser printers, it becomes increasingly important to get the right toner, particularly should you have toner cartridges refilled. The wrong toner will limit resolution.

Graphics Printing Techniques

Bit-image printers compatible with the IBM character set give you two methods for printing graphics: *block graphics* and *all-points-addressable graphics*. The principal differences between the two are quality and compatibility. Block graphics are ugly, but any software that can generate them will operate any printer than can print them. Bit-image graphics are sharper, but require that your software know exactly how to control your printer.

Block Graphics

Think of block graphics as an extra set of characters built into a printer that permit you to draw pictures out of building blocks of simple shapes, such as squares, rectangle, triangles, horizontal and vertical lines, and so on. Each of these shapes is electronically coded and recognized by the printer as if it were a letter of the alphabet, and the printer merely lays down line after line of these block characters to make a picture, like filling in each square on a piece of graph paper with different shapes. The pictures look a little chunky because the building blocks are big, just a little under 1/8th inch across in most printer's default text modes.

All Points Addressable Graphics

The native mode of most bit-image printers allows you to decide where to place individual dots on the printed sheet using a technique called *all points addressable graphics* or *APA graphics*. With a knowledge of the appropriate printer instructions, you or your software can draw graphs in great detail or even make pictures resembling the halftone photographs printed in newspapers. The software built into the printer allows every printable dot position to be controlled—specified as printed (black) or not (white). An entire image can be built up like a television picture, scanning lines several dots wide (as wide as the number of wires in the printhead) down the paper.

This graphics printing technique takes other names, too. Because each individual printed dot can be assigned a particular location or "address" on the paper, this feature is often called *dot-addressable graphics*. Sometimes that title is simplified into *dot graphics*. Occasionally, it appears as *bit-image graphics* because each dot is effectively the image of one bit of data.

The problem with all-points-addressable graphics is that your software must know the codes for telling your printer where to put each dot. Although a number of standards have arisen in the printer industry, some manufacturers have elected to go in their own directions and use their own codes. Most, however, follow the codes set by the industry leaders. For example, most 9-pin and 24-pin impact dot-matrix printers use the same codes as Epson or IBM printers. Most laser printers use the same codes as Hewlett-Packard LaserJet printers.

Printer Control

To make what you see on paper resemble what you preview on your monitor screen, your printer requires guidance from your computer and your software to tell it exactly how to make a printout look. The computer must send the printer a series of instructions, either to control the most intimate operation of the dumb printer or to coax special features from the brainy machine.

The instructions from the computer must be embedded in the character stream because that is the only data connection between the printer and its host. These embedded instructions can take on any of several forms.

Control Characters

Some of the most necessary instructions are the most common, for instance to backspace, tab, or even underline characters. In fact, these instructions are so commonplace that they were incorporated into the ASCII character set and assigned specific values. To backspace, for instance, your computer just sends your printer a byte with the ASCII value 08, the backspace character. Upon receiving this character, the printer will backspace instead of making a mark on the paper. The entire group of these special ASCII values are termed *control characters*.

Escape Sequences

The number of ASCII characters available for printer commands are few, and the number of functions that the printer can carry out are many. To sneak additional instructions through the data channel, most printers use special strings of characters called *escape sequences*.

An escape sequence is simply a series of ASCII characters that begins with a special code symbol assigned the ASCII value of 27. This special character is often called *escape* by programmers, and is abbreviated ESC.

In most commands, the escape character by itself does nothing. It serves only as an attention getter. It warns the printer that the ASCII character or characters that follow should be interpreted as commands rather than printed.

ANSI Escape Sequences

The American National Standards Institute has defined a standard set of escape sequences for controlling printers. A partial listing of these ANSI escape sequences is given in table 16.1.

TABLE 16.1.
ANSI Control
Characters

ASCII value	Control value	Mnemonic	Function
0	^@	NUL	Used as a fill character
1	^A	SOH	Start of heading (indicator)
2	^B	STX	Start of text (indicator)
3	^C	ETX	End of text (indicator)
4	^D	EOT	End of transmission; disconnect character
5	^E	ENQ	Inquiry; request answerback message
6	^F	ACK	Acknowledge
7	^G	BEL	Sounds audible bell tone
8	^H	BS	Backspace
9	^I	HT	Horizontal tab
10	^J	LF	Line feed
11	^K	VT	Vertical tab
12	^L	FF	Form feed
13	^M	CR	Carriage return
14	^N	SO	Shift out; changes character set
15	^O	SI	Shift in; changes character set
16	^P	DLE	Data link escape
17	^Q	DC1	Data control 1, also known as XON
18	^R	DC2	Data control 2
19	^S	DC3	Data control 3, also known as XOFF
20	^T	DC4	Data control 4
21	^U	NAK	Negative acknowledge
22	^V	SYN	Synchronous idle
23	^W	ETB	End of transmission block (indicator)
24	^X	CAN	Cancel; immediately ends any control or escape sequence
25	^Y	EM	End of medium (indicator)
26	^Z	SUB	Substitute (also, end-of-file marker)

continues

TABLE 16.1.
continued

ASCII value	Control value	Mnemonic	Function
27	^[	ESC	Escape; introduces escape sequence
28	^\	FS	File separator (indicator)
29	^]	GS	Group separator (indicator)
30	^^	RS	Record separator (indicator)
31	^_	US	Unit separator (indicator)
32		SP	Space character
127		DEL	No operation
128		Reserved	Reset parser with no action (Esc)
129		Reserved	Reset parser with no action (Esc A)
130		Reserved	Reset parser with no action (Esc B)
131		Reserved	Reset parser with no action (Esc C)
132		IND	Index; increment active line (move paper up)
133		NEL	Next line; advance to first character of next line
134		SSA	Start of selected area (indicator)
135		ESA	End of selected area (indicator)
136		HTS	Set horizontal tab (at active column)
137		HTJ	Horizontal tab with justification
138		VTS	Set vertical tab stop (at current line)
139		PLD	Partial line down
140		PLU	Partial line up
141		RI	Reverse index (move paper down, backwards, one line)
142		SS2	Single shift 2
143		SS3	Single shift 3
144		DCS	Device control string
145		PU1	Private use 1
146		PU2	Private use 2
147		STS	Set terminal state
148		CCH	Cancel character
149		MW	Message writing
150		SPA	Start of protected area (indicator)
151		EPA	End of protected area (indicator)
152		Reserved	Function same as Esc X

ASCII value	Control value	Mnemonic	Function
153		Reserved	Function same as Esc Y
154		Reserved	Function same as Esc Z
155		CSI	Control sequence introducer
156		ST	String terminator
157		OSC	Operating system command (indicator)
158		PM	Privacy message
159		APC	Application program command

Some of the preceding also are implemented as standard *escape sequences* for use in seven-bit environments:

ASCII value	Control value	Mnemonic	Function
Esc D		Index	
Esc E		Vertical line	
Esc H		Set horizontal tab	
Esc Z		Set vertical tab	
Esc K		Partial line down	
Esc L		Partial line up	
Esc M		Reverse index	
Esc N		Single shift 2	
Esc O		Single shift 3	
Esc P		Device control string	
Esc [		Control sequence introducer	
Esc \		String terminator	
Esc]		Operating system command	
Esc ^		Private message	
Esc _		Application program command	

Characters shown as implemented by Digital Equipment Corporation.

De Facto Command Standards

As is so often the case with personal computer products, the standard escape sequences aren't that standard. The ANSI list is chiefly designed to handle the printing of text using fully formed character printers. Many printers have advanced graphics and other functions that transcend the ANSI design. Consequently, nearly every printer manufacturer has broadened, adapted, or ignored the standard to suit the special needs of its own printer.

Whatever standards that do exist among printers are *de facto* (after the fact), earning their status as standards simply because lots of people follow them. Usually the codes and commands used by a large manufacturer with a top-selling product will be followed by smaller companies making compatible products.

Daisy-Wheel Commands

Initially, the market for fully formed character printers was dominated by two companies: the Diablo division of Xerox and Qume, owned by the ITT conglomerate at the time the PC was introduced. (The company has changed hands several times since then.) The commands used by the printers manufactured by those two companies have emerged as compatibility standards among letter-quality printers. Even some laser printer boast either Diablo-or Qume-compatibility so that they can take over for old technology machines and work with aged word processors.

The two command sets are very similar, differing only in a few instructions. A condensed listing of the two command sets is shown in table 16.2.

TABLE 16.2.
Diablo and Qume
Control Codes
and Escape
Sequences

Control Codes			
ASCII value	Control value	Mnemonic	Function
1	^A	SOH	Perform user test continuously
2	^B	STX	Perform user test once
5	^E	ENQ	Halt continuous user test
7	^G	BEL	Sounds audible bell tone
8	^H	BS	*Backspace
9	^I	HT	*Horizontal tab
10	^J	LF	*Line feed
11	^K	VT	*Vertical tab

Control Codes			
ASCII value	Control value	Mnemonic	Function
12	^L	FF	*Form feed
13	^M	CR	*Carriage return
27		Esc	Return to normal mode
31		US	Program mode carriage motion
127		DEL	*No operation

Escape Sequences	
Escape Sequence	Function
Esc BS	*Backspace 1/120 inch
Esc LF	*Negative (backwards) line feed
Esc SO	Shift to primary mode
Esc SI	Return to normal mode
Esc RS n	*Define vertical spacing increment as n-1
Esc US n	*Set horizontal space increment to n-1
Esc VT n	*Absolute vertical tab to line n-1
Esc HT	*Absolute horizontal tab to column n-1
Esc SP	Print special character position 004
Esc SUB I	Initialize printer
Esc SUB SO	Terminal self-test
Esc CR P	Initialize printer
Esc 0	*Set right margin
Esc 1	*Set horizontal tab stop
Esc 2	*Clear all horizontal tab stops
Esc 3	*Graphic on 1/60 inch
Esc 4	*Graphics off
Esc 5	*Forward print
Esc 6	*Backward print
Esc 8	*Clear horizontal tab stop
Esc 9	*Set left margin
Esc .	Auto line feed on
Esc ,	Auto line feed off
Esc <	Auto bidirectional printing on
Esc >	Auto bidirectional printing off

continues

TABLE 16.2.
continued

Escape Sequences	
Escape Sequence	Function
Esc +	Set top margin
Esc –	Set bottom margin
Esc @T	Enter user test mode
Esc #	Enter secondary mode
Esc $	*WPS (proportional spaced printwheel) on
Esc %	*WPS (proportional spaced printwheel) off
Esc (n	Set tabs at n (n can be a list)
Esc)n	Clear tabs at n (n can be a list)
Esc /	Print special character position 002
Esc C n m	Absolute horizontal tab to column n
Esc D	*Negative half-line feed
Esc E n m	Define horizontal space increments
Esc F n m	Set form length
Esc G	*Graphics on 1/120 inch
Esc H n m 1	Relative horizontal motion
Esc I	Underline on
Esc J	Underline off
Esc K n	Bold overprint on
Esc L n n	Define vertical spacing increment
Esc M n	Bold overprint off
Esc N	No carriage movement on next character
Esc O	Right margin control on
Esc P n	Absolute vertical tab to line n
Esc Q	Shadow print on
Esc R	Shadow print off
Esc S	No print on
Esc T	No print off
Esc U	*Half-line feed
Esc W	Auto carriage return/line feed on
Esc V n m 1	Relative vertical paper motion
Esc X	Force execution
Esc Y	Right margin control off
Esc Z	Auto carriage return/line feed off

Escape Sequences	
Escape Sequence	Function
Esc e	Sheet feeder page eject
Esc i	Sheet feeder insert page from tray one
Esc x	Force execution

*Qume Sprint 11 commands shown; *indicates commands shared by Diablo 630.*

Epson and IBM Nine-Wire Commands

The closest to de facto standards for dot-matrix printers are the code and commands used by IBM and Epson. These are closely related if simply because the first IBM Graphics Printer was based on the Epson MX-80. The chief differences between the two were their character sets. IBM used the upper half of the 256 ASCII values for a variety of special symbols, the *IBM extended character set*, although Epson used those values for italics. The commands used by these two printers have become a *de facto* standard for nine-wire dot-matrix printers. A condensed table of these commands is shown in table 16.3.

TABLE 16.3.
Epson Control
Characters and
Escape Sequences

Control Codes			
ASCII value	Control value	Mnemonic	Function
7	^G	BEL	Sounds audible bell tone
8	^H	BS	Backspace
9	^I	HT	Horizontal tab
10	^J	LF	Line feed
11	^K	VT	Vertical tab
12	^L	FF	Form feed
13	^M	CR	Carriage return
14	^N	SO	[2]Turns enlarged print mode on
15	^O	SI	[2]Turns condensed print mode on
17	^P	DC1	[2]Select printer
18	^R	DC2	Turns condensed print mode off
19	^S	DC3	[2]Deselect printer

continues

TABLE 16.3.
continued

Control Codes			
ASCII value	Control value	Mnemonic	Function
20	^T	DC4	Turns enlarged print mode off
24	^X	CAN	Cancel line
127		DEL	No operation

Escape Sequences	
Escape Sequence	Function
Esc SO	[2]Turns enlarged print mode on
Esc SI	[2]Turns condensed print mode on
Esc EM	[2]Cut-sheet feeder control
Esc SP	[2]Selects character space
Esc !	[2]Selects mode combinations
Esc #	[2]MSB mode cancel
Esc $	[2]Set absolute horizontal tab
Esc %	[2]Selects active character set
Esc :	[2]Copies ROM to user RAM
Esc &	[2]Defines user characters
Esc /	[2]Set vertical tab
Esc \	[2]Move printhead
Esc <	Turn unidirectional (left-to-right only) printing on
Esc >	[2]MSB set (MSB=0)
Esc =	[2]MSB reset (MSB=1)
Esc @	[2]Initialize printer
Esc -n	Underline mode
	n=1 or 49, turns underline mode on
	n=0 or 48, turns underline mode off
Esc *n	[2]Select bit-image mode (data follows n)
	n=0, normal density
	n=1, dual density
	n=2, double-speed dual density
	n=3, quadruple density
	n=4, CRT graphics
	n=6, CRT graphics II
Esc ^	Nine-pin graphics mode
Esc 0	Set line spacing at 1/8 inch

Escape Sequences	
Escape Sequence	**Function**
Esc 1	Set line spacing at 7/72 inch
Esc 2	Set line spacing at 1/6 inch
Esc 3 n	Set line spacing at n/216 inch (n between 0 and 255)
Esc 4	[2]Turns alternate character (italics) set on
Esc 5	[2]Turns alternate character (italics) set off
Esc 6	[1]Select character set 1
	[2]Deactivate high-order control codes
Esc 7	[1]Select character set 2
	[2]Restores high-order control codes
Esc 8	Turns paper-end detector off
Esc 9	Turns paper-end detector on
Esc A n	Set line spacing at n/72 inch (n between 0 and 85
Esc B	[2]Set vertical tab stop
Esc C n	Sets form length to n lines (n between 1 and 127)
Esc C 0 n	Sets form length to n inches (n between 1 and 22)
Esc D	Set horizontal tab stop
Esc E	Turns emphasized mode on
Esc F	Turns emphasized mode off
Esc G	Turns double-strike mode on
Esc H	Turns double-strike mode off
Esc I	[2]Control code select
Esc J n	Tentative n/216-inch line spacing
Esc K	Normal-density bit-image data follows
Esc L	Dual-density bit-image data follows
Esc M	Elite-sized characters on
Esc N n	Set number of lines to skip-over perforation
	n=number of lines to skip between 1 and 127
Esc O	Turn skip-over perforation off
Esc P	[2]Elite mode off/Pica-sized characters on
Esc Q n	[2]Sets the right margin at column n
Esc R	[1]Returns to default tabs
Esc R n	[2]Selects international character set
	n=0, USA
	n=1, France
	n=2, Germany

continues

TABLE 16.3.
continued

Escape Sequence	Escape Sequences
	Function
	n=3, England
	n=4, Denmark I
	n=5, Sweden
	n=6, Italy
	n=7, Spain
	n=8, Japan
	n=9, Norway
	n=10, Denmark II
Esc S n	Superscript/subscript on mode
	n=0 or 48, superscript mode on
	n=1 or 49, subscript mode on
Esc T	Turns superscript/subscript off
Esc U n	Unidirectional/bidirectional printing
	n=0 or 48, turn bidirectional printing on
	n=1 or 49, turn unidirectional printing on
Esc W n	Enlarged (double-width) print mode
	n=1 or 49, enlarged print mode on
	n=0 or 48, enlarged print mode off
Esc X	[1]Sets margins
Esc Y	Double-speed, dual-density bit image data follows
Esc Z	Quadruple-density bit-image data follows
Esc a	[2]Justification
Esc b	[2]Set vertical tab
Esc e n	Set tab unit
	n=0 or 48, sets horizontal tab unit
	n=1 or 49, sets vertical tab unit
Esc f n	Set skip position setting
	n=0 or 48, sets horizontal skip position
	n=0 or 49, sets vertical skip position
Esc g	[2]Select 15 width
Esc i	[2]Immediate print (typewriter mode)
Esc j	[2]Immediate temporary reverse paper feed
Esc k	[2]Select family of type styles
Esc l n	Sets the left margin at column n
Esc m n	Special character generator selection

Escape Sequences	
Escape Sequence	**Function**
	n=0, control codes accepted
	n=4, graphics characters accepted
Esc p n	Proportional printing
	n=0 or 48, turn proportional printing off
	n=1 or 49, turn proportional printing on
Esc s	Half-speed printing
	n=0 or 48, turn half-speed printing off
	n=1 or 49, turn half-speed printing on
Esc z	Select letter quality or draft

Includes codes used by many printers.
[1]IBM command only
[2]Epson command only

Epson 24-Wire Commands

When dot-matrix technology advanced from 9-wire printers to 24-wire designs, graphics commands needed to be augmented to take additional print modes into account. Again, the commands for Epson's 24-wire series of printers have become as close to a standard as exists in the personal computer industry. The 24-wire extensions to the Epson command set is listed in table 16.4.

The generalized command form is as follows:

Esc*m cl c2 [graphics data]

Where m is the code number from table 16.4 and c1 and c2 specify the number of columns to use for graphics.

TABLE 16.4.
Epson 24-Pin
Graphics
Commands

Mode	Pins	Code	Density Dots/inch
Single-density	8	0	60
Double-density	8	1	120
High-double density	8	2	120
Quadruple density	8	3	240

continues

TABLE 16.4.
continued

Mode	Pins	Code	Density Dots/inch
CRT I	8	4	80
CRT II	8	6	90
Single-density	24	32	60
Double-density	24	33	120
CRT III	24	38	90
Triple-density	24	39	180
Hex-density	24	40	360

The values of c_1 and c_2 specify the number of column dots to use for the graphics display. Because one byte can code only 256 values, a second byte is used to encompass the total number of dot-columns possible. The c_1 value is least significant. To determine the proper values, divide the desired number of graphic columns by 256. The quotient is the value of c_2; the remainder is c_1.

Each 24-pin column of data in a line is encoded with three separate bytes: the first byte codes the top eight wires; the second codes the middle eight; the last codes the bottom eight. The least significant bit in each byte codes the bottom dot of the octet associated with that byte; the most significant bit codes the top dot of the octet. A value of one indicates that a dot will appear on paper.

PostScript

Laser printers are more than mere printers. Most have the brains of a complete computer. Many are smarter than the computers that they are plugged into. The instructions that they understand reflect this intelligence. Rather than mere commands, the software controls for laser printers are more like programming languages.

Among people working extensively with graphics, the most popular printer control method is Adobe Systems *PostScript* page description language. Originally developed in 1985, PostScript comprises a group of commands and codes that describe graphic elements and indicate where they are to appear on the printed page. Your computer sends high-level PostScript commands to your laser printer, and the printer executes the commands to draw the image itself. In effect, the data processing load is shifted to the printer, which, in theory, has been optimized for implementing such graphics commands. Nevertheless, it can take several minutes for the printer to compute a full-page image after all the PostScript commands have been transferred to it. (Older PostScript printers might take half an hour or more to work out a full page of graphics.)

The advantage of PostScript is its versatility. It uses outline fonts, which can be scaled to any practical size. Moreover, PostScript is device and resolution independent, which means that the same code that controls your 300 dpi printer will run a 2,500 dpi typesetter and will produce the highest possible quality image at the available resolution level. You can thus print a rough draft on your LaserJet from a PostScript file and, after you have checked it over, send the same file to a typesetter to have a photo-ready page made.

In June, 1990, Adobe Systems announced a new version of PostScript, *Level 2*, which incorporated several enhancements. The most obvious are speed and color. PostScript Level 2 can dash through documents four to five times quicker thanks to getting the font-rendering technology used in Adobe Type Manager. In addition, PostScript incorporates a new generalized class of objects called "resources" that can be precompiled, named, cached, and downloaded to the memory (or disk) inside a PostScript device. Nearly anything that's printed can be classed as a resource—artwork, patterns, and forms—and handled in this streamlined manner. PostScript Level 2 also manages its memory use much better, no longer requiring that programs preallocate memory for downloaded fonts and bit-mapped graphics. It also incorporates new file-management capabilities to handle disk-based storage inside PostScript devices. In addition, PostScript Level 2 has built-in compression and decompression capabilities so that bit-mapped images (and other massive objects) can be transmitted more quickly in compressed form and then expanded inside the printer or other device.

Color was first grafted onto PostScript in 1988, but PostScript Level 2 takes color to heart. Where each PostScript device had its own proprietary color-handling methods, with PostScript Level 2, color is device-independent. To improve color quality, the new version also allows color halftone screening at any angle, which helps eliminate moire patterns and makes sharper renderings. Level 2 also enhances font handling. Old PostScript limited fonts to 256 characters each. Level 2 allows for composite fonts, which allow an essentially unlimited number of characters. Larger fonts are particularly useful for languages that don't use the Roman alphabet (such as Japanese) or those that have a wealth of diacritical marks.

Level 2 also incorporates Display PostScript, an extension that is designed to translate PostScript code into screen images. Device-independent support for many of the more generalized printer features is also available so that paper trays, paper sizes, paper feeding, and even stapling, can be controlled through PostScript.

Of course, ordinary PostScript printers can't take advantage of these new features; Level 2 machines will be generally (though not completely) backward compatible with older code. In most cases, a PostScript Level 2 printer will handle ordinary PostScript commands without a problem, but realizing the full features of Level 2 will require new PostScript 2 software drivers.

PCL

Hewlett-Packard's *Printer Control Language*, most often abbreviated with its initials, *PCL*, was first developed as a means to control a rudimentary (by current standards) inkjet printer. As HP has introduced increasingly sophisticated laser printers, the language has been expanded and adapted. It's now on its fifth major revision, called *PCL5*.

PCL functions like an elaborate printer command set, with long strings of characters initiating the various LaserJet functions. It is not a true page-description language.

Versions of PCL before the current one have amounted to little more than a system of control codes for eliciting various printer functions, including font selection. PCL5 goes further by including more line-drawing commands and the capability to handle scalable (outline) fonts.

PCL5 was formally introduced with the announcement of the LaserJet III on February 26, 1990. It followed four earlier versions of the PCL language. Although PCL is normally associated with LaserJet printers, the initial two versions of PCL predated the introduction of the first laser printer by any manufacturer. The first printer to use the original version of PCL was the HP ThinkJet, an inkjet engine. PCL3, the third version, was the language that controlled HP's first laser printer, the original LaserJet.

Printers compatible with the PCL3 standard can use only cartridge fonts in their text modes. Full-page graphics must be generated by their computer hosts and transferred bit-by-bit to the printer.

The next major revision to PCL was a response to the needs of early desktop publishing and similar applications that demanded more than just a few cartridge-based fonts. This revision was PCL4, which added the capability to have multiple fonts on the same page and to use downloaded fonts. These were bit-mapped fonts, however, and you could print only one orientation on a given page. You could also do some rudimentary box drawing and filling of boxes.

Besides scalable fonts, PCL5 adds vector graphics, sophisticated page-formatting capability, the capability to handle portrait and landscape orientations on the same page, print white on black, and turn fonts into some pattern or shade. In addition, PCL5 incorporates a pared down version of the *HP-GL*, Hewlett-Packard's Graphics Language that has become an industry-standard means of commanding plotters.

PCL5 can yield on-paper images that are effectively identical to those made on PostScript printers, but there are substantial differences between PCL 5 and PostScript. PostScript is essentially device independent. The PostScript code sent out of a PC is the same no matter whether it is meant to control a relatively inexpensive desktop laser or an expensive typesetting machine.

As a printer language, PCL5 is device dependent. It currently works only with 300 dpi laser printers, so its code cannot be used to drive typesetters. But PCL5 is less expensive than PostScript because it requires no license to use.

PCL5 would be a curiosity were it only to be used in Hewlett-Packard printers, as it has been for the first year of its existence. But that situation is changing and making PCL5 into the latest de facto standard for controlling laser printers. A number of companies have developed controllers for laser printers that understand PCL5. These controllers are bought by printer manufacturers to build their products. Now that printer makers have easy access to these high-performance controllers, it's likely the market will soon be flooded with PCL5-compatible printers. That means that you can get PostScript quality at a lower price, which is more than enough reason to look for PCL5 compatibility in your next laser printer.

Fonts

All laser printers (and their kin, LED and LCD shutter printers) are simply glorified dot-matrix printers. Individual characters are formed from dots just like a castle can be built from a child's building blocks. Every character position is divided into a matrix like a giant tic-tac-toe playing field, and the shape of individual characters is determined by which positions in the field are light and dark.

Fonts differ in how the information for coding these light and dark patterns is stored. Generally, fonts are stored using one of two technologies, termed bit-mapped and outline.

Bit-mapped fonts encode each character as the pattern of dots that form the matrix, recording the position and color of each individual dot. Because larger character sizes require more dots, they require different pattern codes than smaller characters. In fact, every size of character, weight of character (bold, condensed, light, and so on), even each character slant (Roman versus Italic) requires its own code. In other words, a single type family may require dozens of different bit-mapped fonts.

Outline fonts encode individual characters as mathematical descriptions, essentially the stroke you would have to make to draw the character. These stokes define the outline of the character—hence the name for the technology. Your computer or printer then serves as a raster image processor (often termed a *RIP*) that executes the mathematical instructions to draw each character in memory to make the necessary bit pattern for printing. With most typefaces, one mathematical description will make any size of character—the size of each individual stroke in the character is merely scaled to reflect the size of the final character (consequently outline fonts are often termed *scalable fonts*). Consequently, one code serves any character size, although different weights and slants require somewhat different codes. A single type family can be coded with relatively few font descriptions—normal, bold, Roman, and italic combinations.

Simply scaling fonts produces generally acceptable results. However, to make the clearest, most readable text, small characters are typically shaped somewhat differently than large characters. For example, the serifs on each letter may need to be proportionally larger for smaller characters, or else they would disappear. Bit-mapped fonts automatically compensate for these effects because each size font can be separately designed. In outline fonts, the equations describing each stroke can include hints on what needs to be changed for best legibility at particular sizes. Outline fonts that include this supplementary information are termed *hinted* and produce clearer characters, particularly at large, headline, and tiny sizes.

PostScript Level 2 takes outline fonts a level further. With its *Multiple Master* fonts, some typefaces of the same family can be encoded as a single font. That is, one font definition can cover italic, Roman, and bold characters (as well as all sizes) of a given typeface.

The equations required for storing an outline font typically require more storage (more bytes on disk or in memory) than a bit-mapped fonts, but storing an entire family of outline fonts requires substantially less space than a family of bit-mapped fonts (because one outline font serves all sizes). For normal business printing, which generally involves fewer than a dozen fonts (including size variations), this difference is not significant. However, for graphic artists, publishers, and anyone who likes to experiment with type and printing, outline fonts bring greater versatility.

On the other hand, bit-mapped fonts print faster. Outline fonts have to go through an additional step (raster image processing) computations which add to printing time. Bit-mapped fonts are directly retrieved from memory without any additional footwork.

Storage and Retrieval

The information describing font characters has to be stored somewhere. Considering that many megabytes may be involved, the location of font storage can have important implications on how you use your PC and printer.

Like every dot-matrix printer, the laser printer has a few fonts built in. Ubiquitous among lasers is familiar old 10-pitch Courier, the default typeface held over from typewriter days. Probably the most endearing characteristic of Courier (at least to software and printer designers) is that it is monospaced—every character is exactly the same width, making page layout easy to control. Consequently, the bit patterns for this typeface are forever encoded into the ROMs of nearly every machine. Courier can, and usually is, pulled up at an instant's notice simply by giving a command to print a character.

A few other faces may be resident in the ROM of printers. The number depends on many factors. Generally, if the manufacturer is large, as few faces as possible will be packed in ROM; smaller manufacturers include more to give their products a competitive edge.

Font Cartridges

Additional fonts can be added in several ways. The easiest to manage is the *font cartridge*. The dot patterns for forming alternate character fonts are stored in ROM chips that are held inside each cartridge. The cartridge itself merely provides a housing for the chip and a connector that fits a mate in the printer. By sliding in a cartridge, you add the extra ROM in the cartridge to that in the printer. Many impact and laser bit-image printers have been designed to use font cartridges.

Note that each manufacturer's cartridges are different and incompatible (sometimes the cartridges of two models of printers made by the same manufacturer are incompatible), although several laser printer makers are making their machines compatible with Hewlett-Packard laser printer cartridges.

The disadvantage of the font cartridge technique, besides the cost of the fonts themselves, is the limited number of cartridge slots available. A single cartridge may hold 6 to 12 fonts. With bit-image fonts in particular, such a small capacity can be confining. To sidestep this issue, several enterprising developers have packed dozens of fonts into a single cartridge.

Downloadable Character Sets

Most laser printers also allow you to download fonts. That is, you can transfer character descriptions from your PC's memory to the RAM inside your laser printer, where the individual characters can be called up as needed just as if they were in ROM. These are called *downloadable character sets* or *soft fonts* because they are transferred as software. Typically, you buy soft fonts just like software, on floppy disks, that you copy to your PC's hard disk. You can store as many soft fonts as your hard disk can hold for use in your laser printer.

The disadvantages of soft fonts are several. Somehow, you have to transfer them from your PC to your printer, generally every time you want to use them, if you have switched off your printer in the meantime, erasing its memory of soft-font additions. Moreover, each soft font you load into your printer steals a chunk of your printer's RAM. The memory limits of your laser printer will thus constrain the number of soft fonts you can load at any given time, typically about eight if you want to leave room for printing graphics.

Some software can generate the bit patterns of fonts it needs by itself, the equivalent of having soft fonts built into the program. The software then transmits the resulting bit patterns to your printer (instead of sending a stream of characters that the printer renders into bit patterns). This technique imposes a hefty penalty—bit patterns take more memory than characters, requiring more memory inside your laser printer, more than a megabyte to print a full page at highest resolution. Worse, the greater amount of data requires longer to transmit to the printer, increasing print time.

With older printers following the Hewlett-Packard LaserJet printing standard, all but the simplest graphics required this kind of bit-image transmission, as did printing anything but cartridge fonts and soft fonts. Page description languages allow the transmission of an entire page—text and graphics—in fast, coded form. Consequently, the trend in better laser printers is to use page-description languages.

The best-known of these are PostScript and PostScript Level 2. PostScript is a proprietary product of Adobe Systems, which licenses printer makers to use it, making true PostScript printers substantially more expensive than machines without it. To avoid this cost, many manufacturers have turned to PostScript-compatible languages, which mimic PostScript but cost the printer maker less. Currently, these clones match PostScript well but have not kept up with the transition to PostScript Level 2. PostScript takes advantage of outline fonts. In fact, 35 outline fonts are built into most PostScript printers (some budget machines have as few as 17 as standard equipment).

Hewlett-Packard printers use a more modest control language, PCL (which stands for Printer Control Language). The latest LaserJet III series use PCL5, which can take advantage of outline fonts. Earlier LaserJet printers (LaserJet, LaserJet Plus, and LaserJet II series) use earlier PCL versions that don't accept outline fonts.

The bottom line is that you need a PostScript, PostScript-compatible, or PCL5-compatible printer to take advantage of most downloadable fonts.

Font Formats

All outline fonts are not the same, however. Several standards have arisen, and you must match the fonts you add to the standard used by your hardware and software. Your principal choices are Intellifont, Type 1 (PostScript), Speedo, and TrueType.

The native font format of the LaserJet III series of printers (and PCL5) is called Intellifont. Developed jointly by Agfa Compugraphic and Hewlett-Packard, it is notable as fast in rasterizing and may have the most widespread use, considering the popularity of LaserJet printers. Although you don't have to worry about font formats with cartridge fonts—if the cartridge fits, it should work—the cartridges you plug into your LaserJet or compatible printer will use Intellifont characters. Downloadable outline fonts for LaserJet III and compatible printers will use Intellifont format.

PostScript printers use Type 1 fonts, the format that probably offers more font variety than any other. You can use Type 1 fonts with Windows using Adobe Type Manager. Support for Type 1 fonts is built into OS/2 Versions 1.3 and later.

Many programs use Bitstream fonts, which have their own format called Speedo. In general, this software works by generating the characters in your PC and transferring them in bit-image form to your printer. Speedo fonts are used by Lotus 1-2-3 and Freelance (in their DOS versions). You also can use Bitstream's Speedo fonts with Windows using Bitstream's FaceLift for Windows.

Microsoft Windows 3.1 has its own format, called TrueType, that's also used by Apple's System 7 operating system for the Macintosh. Thirteen TrueType fonts come with Windows 3.1, and you can easily install more using the Windows Control Panel. TrueType is compatible with printers that use other font formats. For example, with LaserJets, for each font you want to use, TrueType generates a bit-map LaserJet font from one of its outline fonts and then downloads the font to your printer. That way, it only needs to send characters rather than bit-maps to your printer. For PostScript printers, TrueType similarly converts its fonts to PostScript outlines or bit-maps (depending on the font) and sends those to your printer.

Windows gives you font flexibility. All outline fonts packages are equipped with programs that allow them to be installed in Windows. Moreover, font managers are available for other major font formats (Adobe Type Manager, FaceLift for Windows, Intellifont for Windows).

Color Printing

A growing number of applications demand color output, and the printer industry has responded with a number of different technologies to suit individual color applications, from low cost to photo-like quality.

A number of impact dot-matrix printers allow you to add color to both the alphabets and graphics they put on paper. A few have two-color ribbons (like old-fashioned typewriters) and special software instructions to control shifting between them.

Most color printers now use ribbons soaked with three or four colors of ink and can achieve seven colors on paper by combining color pairs. For example, putting a layer of blue over a layer of yellow results in an approximation of green. To switch colors, the printers merely shift the ribbon up or down. The extra mechanism required is simple and inexpensive, costing as little as $50 extra. (Of course, the color ribbon will cost more and last shorter than its monochrome equivalent.) A few machines use multiple ribbons, each one a different color, to achieve the same effect.

Non-impact matrix printers excel at color. Inkjets are well suited to the task because their liquid inks can actually blend together on the paper before they dry. However, color inkjet printers are substantially more complex and expensive than their monochrome equivalents because each primary color requires its own separate ink reservoir and nozzle. Most thermal-wax matrix printers are particularly designed for color output. They achieve on-paper color mixing by using transparent inks that allow one color to show through another. The two hues blend together optically.

The only problem with color printers is that they need special software to bring their rainbows to life. Without the right software, you have to understand computer programming to take advantage of multicolor capabilities. Today, most impact color printers follow the standard set by the Epson JX-80, which adds one escape code to its normal command set for changing ribbon color. Thermal-wax and phase-change printers normally use PostScript, and PostScript 2 will give them a common color language.

Paper Handling

The printer must advance the paper line by line just as a typewriter does when you slam the carriage back. The various schemes developed to help printer and operator deal with this chore—the way the print-out paper is handled and the kind of paper that can be handled—must be carefully considered to match a printer to your needs.

Friction Feed

The old-fashioned typewriter moved paper through its mechanism by squeezing it between the large rubber called a *platen* and smaller rollers. The paper is additionally held around the platen above the area where the hammers strike it by a *bail arm*, which usually pivots out of the way when you load paper. The friction between the platen, smaller rollers, and bail arm keeps the paper from slipping as it is rolled past the printhead. This paper-feeding system is often called *friction feed*.

In most cases, friction feed implies that loading paper is a manual operation—you have to pull out the bail arm, insert each individual sheet, line it up to be certain that it is square (so that the printhead doesn't type diagonally across the paper), lock it and the bail arm down, and finally signal to the machine that all is well. Easier said than done, of course, and more tedious, too, should you decide to print a computerized version of the *Encyclopedia Britannica*. Worse yet, you have to stand by and give the machine your undivided attention, constantly shuffling in a fresh new sheet of paper every time the printer finishes one.

On the positive side, however, most friction-feed mechanisms will handle any kind of paper you can fit through the mechanism, from your own engraved stationery to preprinted forms, from W-2s to 1040s, envelopes, and index cards.

Automatic Sheet Feeder

Anything you can do, someone can design a machine to do, too. Whether the machine can be made affordable is another matter. Feeding paper through a friction-fed printer is no exception. A device, quite logically termed the *automatic sheet feeder* (although occasionally called *bin-feed*) can relieve your tedium and tantrums by loading most standard-size forms and plain papers into your printer without your intervention or attention. Unfortunately, sheet feeders are among the most complex accessories you can add to your computer system, many of them being much akin to the inventions of Rube Goldberg. Price rises with complexity, and sheet feeders tend also to be expensive, quite capable of ripping a multiple hundred-dollar hole in your pocket. Most sheet feeders are designed for single-layer paper; for copies, you must make two separate printings of separate sheets—no carbons. Your printing project can run into double- and triple-time when you need more than one copy.

Roll Feed

One way to reduce the number of times you have to slide a sheet of paper into the friction-feed mechanism is to make the paper longer. In fact, you could use one, long continuous sheet. Some systems do exactly that, wrapping the long sheet around a roll (like toilet paper).

The printer just pulls the paper through as it needs it. By rigidly mounting a roll-holder at the back of the printer, the paper can be kept in reasonable alignment and skew can be eliminated.

The shortcoming of this system is, of course, that you end up with one long sheet. You have to tear it to pieces or carefully cut it up when you want traditional 8.5 x 11-inch output.

Pin-Feed and Tractor-Feed

Although roll-fed paper could be perforated at 11-inch intervals so that you could easily and neatly tear it apart, another problem arises. Most friction mechanisms are not perfect. The paper can slip so that, gradually, the page breaks in the image and the page breaks at the perforations no longer correspond. In effect, the paper and the image can get out of sync.

By locking perforations in the edge of the paper inside sprockets that prevent slipping, the image and paper breaks can be kept in sync. Two different paper-feeding systems use sprocketed paper to avoid slippage. *Pin-feed* uses drive sprockets which are permanently affixed to the edges of the platen roller. Consequently, the pin-feed mechanism can handle only one width of paper, the width corresponding to the sprocket at the edges of the platen. *Tractor-feed* uses adjustable sprockets that can be moved closer together or farther apart to handle nearly any width paper that will fit through the printer.

As the names imply, a *unidirectional tractor* only pulls (or pushes) the paper through in a single direction (hopefully forward). The *bidirectional tractor* allows both forward and backward paper motion, which is often helpful for graphics, special text functions (printing exponents, for instance), and lining up the top of the paper with the top of the printhead.

Push and Pull Tractors

The original tractor mechanism for printers was a two-step affair. One set of sprockets fed paper into the printer, and another set pulled it out. For the intended purpose of tractor feeding; however, the two sets of sprockets is one more than necessary. All it takes is one set to lock the printer's image in sync with the paper.

A single set of sprockets can be located in one of two positions, either before or after paper wraps around the platen in front of the print-head. Some printers allow you to use its single set of tractors in either position. In others, the tractors are fixed in one location or the other.

Push tractors are placed in the path of the paper before it enters the printer. In effect, they push the paper through the machine. The platen roller helps to ease paper through the printer while the push tractor provides the principal force and keeps the paper tracking properly. This form of feeding has a couple of advantages. You can rip the last sheet of a printout off without having to feed an extra sheet through the printer or re-thread it. The tractor also acts bidirectionally with relative ease, pulling the paper backwards as well as pushing it forward.

Pull tractors are located in the path of the paper after it emerges from the print-making mechanism. The pull tractor pulls paper across the platen, and the paper is held flat against the platen by its friction and the resistance of pulling it up through the mechanism. The pull tractor is simpler and offers less to go wrong than push designs.

Although most pull tractors operate only unidirectionally, they work well in high-speed use on printers with flat metal (instead of round rubber) platens. Because of their high-speed operation, typically several pages per minute, the machines naturally tend to be used for large print jobs during which the waste of a single sheet is not a major drawback.

Sheet Feeders

By necessity, every laser printer has to have the complex mechanism that's so often an expensive option with other printer designs—the cut-sheet feeder. The laser printer must be able to slip a single sheet from a stack, waft it through the complex image-forming mechanism, and deliver it back to you. That today's laser printers work as well as they do is a tribute to the mechanical ingenuity of their engineers. But there are significant differences in the philosophy and convenience of the paper handling of different laser printers.

One difference is capacity. Some laser printers are made only for light, personal use and have modestly sized paper bins that hold about 50 sheets. That means every 10 to 15 minutes you have to attend to the needs to the printer, loading and removing the wads of paper that course through it. If you have a big print job, that means baby-sitting the printer—not an exciting way to spend the day.

When lasers disgorge their output, it can fall into the output tray one of two ways—face up or face down. Although it might be nice to see what horrors you have spread on paper immediately rather than saving up for a heart attack, face down is the better choice. When sheets pile on top of one another, face down means you won't have to sort through the stack to put everything in proper order.

Duplex printers take the final step—printing on both sides of each sheet of paper. If you print a lot of reports, the cost savings in cutting your paper consumption in half may pay for a more expensive duplex printer.

Paper Control

Printers differ to a great degree in how precisely they can move paper through their mechanisms. Some are designed to allow exacting tolerances and move each sheet in increments of the tiniest fractions of an inch (as small as 1/216th inch). A few still cling to their type-writer heritage and restrict you to shifting paper to one line (or half-line) at a time.

The trend has been to more precise control because it allows more format versatility in printing text—for instance, you can change line spacings from 6 lines per inch for manuscripts to 8 per inch for business letters or add a few extra inch-fractions to each line to stretch 10 pages into 12 pages when you have a tough essay assignment—and more accuracy in printing graphics.

Printers also vary in the control they afford in the other direction, the horizontal movement of the printhead across the paper. A few primitive machines still stick with the mechanical cog of the typewriter. Most modern machines, however, let you vary the character pitch in text mode and the spacing of dots and speed of printing in graphics modes. This versatility is necessary for the rendering of proportionally spaced text and for printing multiple graphic densities.

Smart and Dumb Printers

A printer is not just a brute-force paper pounder. It's got to have brains, too. Even the cheapest impact dot-matrix printer has to be smart enough to know the one exact instant it must trigger each of its printwires to ram one dot of the image on exactly the right spot on the paper. Laser printers must match each character in their font cartridges with the proper on-paper position and possibly flick their light beams seven million or more times for each sheet that rolls through. Daisy-wheel machines time their hammer blows to the exact instance the right character on its spinning wheel is lined up properly. Behind the scenes, all printers must sort embedded commands from printed characters to carry out advanced operations, such as printing bold characters or changing fonts.

Printers vary substantially in their native intelligence. Although many printers operate as little more than slaves, taking orders and carrying them out, many printers have much greater capabilities. Some can go so far as to format the data as they print it.

The old-line printer, typified by the classic all-mechanical teletype, was so dumb that it doesn't even know when it comes to the edge of the paper. It would gladly perforate its platen with the text of an entire novel if the data it was sent wasn't broken into short lines with the appropriate carriage return and line feed characters mixed in with the text. Many of today's printers have brains almost equally as primitive and rely on the computer and its software to tell them exactly what to do. Some computer programs, such as word processors designed to be used with specific printers, may include special printer driver software that adds in all sorts of extra ASCII code symbols to the data stream. Every fractional-inch movement of the printhead between proportionally spaced characters, every character to be pecked, every roll of the platen, is specifically indicated by the computer program and sent to the printer.

On the other hand, smart printers can take over these same text processing functions on their own. They can accept a nearly completely unformatted string of text, break it into proportionally spaced lines, and leave the proper margins at the top and bottom of the page. To handle these and other chores, even inexpensive printers nowadays have their own built-in microprocessors. The internal microbrain helps the printer position the proper petal of the daisy-wheel in front of the print hammer or calculate when to fire the wire of a dot-matrix printhead.

Horizontal and Vertical Tabbing

One place the intelligence of a printer can be put to use is optimizing printhead motion, making every movement of the printhead the most efficient possible. The internal microprocessor in a printer can look ahead in the memory and see what's coming up next and optimize the positioning of the printhead or print wheel by finding the shortest difference between consecutive lines. The goal is to move between printhead positions as quickly as possible. Often called *logic-seeking* printers, these machines use a number of techniques to optimize printhead movement. Using *horizontal tabbing*, they can breeze over oceans of blank space in each line without dwelling on each individual space and deciding what not to print. With *vertical tabbing,* they can be equally adept at skipping blank lines on the page. Both techniques, combined with bidirectional printing, will allow a printer so blessed to type normal documents faster than machines with the same characters-per-second speed rating that lack these features.

Consumables

Consumables are those things that your printer uses up, wears out, or burns through as it does its work. Paper is the primary consumable, and the need for it is obvious with any printer. Other consumables are less obvious, sometimes even devious, in the way they can eat into your budget.

You probably think you're familiar with the cost of these consumables. A couple months after the old dot-matrix ribbon starts printing too faintly to read, you finally get around to ordering a new $5 ribbon to hold you through for the rest of the decade. But if you buy one of today's top-quality printers (laser, thermal-wax, or dye-diffusion), you may be in for a surprise. When the toner or transfer sheet runs out, the replacement may cost as much as your old dot-matrix printer.

The reason that laser printer consumables cost so much is that a bit of the machine is used up with every page that rolls out. The organic photoconductor drum on which images are made gradually wears out. (A new drum material, silicon, is supposed to last for the life of the printer, but few printer models currently use silicon drums.) Toner is spread across each page. The charging corona or other parts may also need to be periodically replaced. Although thermal-wax printers don't waste their mechanisms, they do slurp up ink—up to four pages full of ink for every page of paper that spools through.

These consumables costs can add up. With laser printers, consumables (not including paper) cost between two and five cents a page. With thermal-wax printers, costs can range as high as five dollars a page.

Over the life of a printer, the cost of consumables can quickly exceed what you paid for the printer. More importantly, consumables costs differ with various printer models. Over the life of the typical printer, the difference in consumables cost can far overwhelm a difference in purchase price.

Because thermal-wax printers cost substantially more than laser printers, the difference in consumables costs between them don't reflect so dramatically against the purchase prices. But you can still save a dollar or more per page by opting for a machine with inexpensive consumables.

Some printers appear wasteful in their need for consumables. For example, Hewlett-Packard's LaserJets are designed with one-piece cartridges that contain both the drum and toner. The whole assembly is replaced as a single unit when the toner runs out. Other laser printers are designed so that the toner, drum, and sometimes the fuser, can be replaced individually.

The makers of the latter style of printer contend that the drum lasts for many more copies than a single shot of toner, so dumping the drum before its time is wasteful. On the other hand, the all-in-one cartridge folks contend that they design their drums to last only as long as the toner.

Surprisingly, from a cost standpoint the choice of technology doesn't appear to make a difference. (From an ecology standpoint, however, the individual replacement scheme still makes more sense.)

Cartridge Refilling

One way to tiptoe around the high cost of laser printer consumables is to have toner cartridges refilled. Most manufacturers don't recommend this. Because they have no control over the quality of the toner, they can't guarantee that someone else's replacement will work right in their machines. Besides, they miss the profits in selling toner.

Quality can really be an issue, however. For example, the resolution-enhancement technology of the HP's LaserJet III series requires toner with a particle size much smaller than that of toner used by other printers. You can't tell the difference in toner just by looking at it, but you can when blotchy gray pages pour out of the printer. When having cartridges refilled, you must be sure to get the proper toner quality.

Another consideration: with all-in-one cartridges, just refilling the cartridge with toner won't affect the drum or charger in the cartridge. Although these are engineered with extra life, the extra might not stretch two-fold. Order a refilled cartridge and you could get fresh toner packed with a worn-out drum.

On the other hand, some people report excellent results with refilled toner cartridges. Whether you'll be happy with refills depends on your personal standards as well as the quality of the refill work.

Paper

When comparing the costs of using different printer technologies, don't forget to make allowances for machines that require special paper. In most cases, approved media for such printers will be available only from the machine's manufacturer. You'll have to pay the price the manufacturer asks, which, because of the controlled distribution and special formulation, will be substantially higher than buying bond paper at the office supply warehouse.

Certainly, you can load any kind of paper that will fit into a printer. With some printers, particularly thermal machines, you won't get any image output at all if you use the wrong medium. With most printers, however, the penalty will be a substandard image. For instance, inkjet images will be blurrier with less saturated colors because of the ink absorption by the paper. Other effects may be more subtle. With laser printers, feeding may be erratic, leading to more jams, and blacks may become spotty or gray with the wrong paper. Some laser printers make particular requirements for the humidity content of the paper for proper printer operation.

If you want to use a nonapproved paper with your printer, the best bet is to try and evaluate the results you get.

Printer Sharing

Two printers aren't necessarily better than one; they're just more expensive. In a number of business situations, you can save the cost of a second printer by sharing the one among two or more PCs and their users. This strategy works because no one prints all the time; if he did, he would have no time left to create anything worth printing. Because normal office work will leave your printer with idle time, you can put it to work for someone else.

You have your choice of several printer-sharing strategies, including those that use nothing but software and those that are hardware-based.

The least expensive, in terms of out-of-pocket cost, is a simple *A/B switch box*. As the name implies, this device consists of a box of some kind that protects a multipole switch. The switch allows you to reroute all 25 connections of a printer cable from one PC to another. For example, in position A, your computer might be connected to the printer; in position B, a coworkers PC would be connected. It's the equivalent of moving the printer cable with the convenience of a switch.

True sharing systems give you the greater convenience of automatic operation. Of the various techniques, *software printer sharing* is generally the least costly. Most *zero-slot local area networks* have provisions for sharing printers. A zero-slot LAN allows you to connect several PCs as a network using their serial ports. The only expenses involved in sharing printers this way are the software itself and some (relatively cheap) cable to connect the systems together.

But there is a nonmonetary cost, too—the performance of the printer server suffers. The PC connected to the printer is forced to spend some of its time spooling the print job and controlling the printer, which can steal a good deal of performance. No worker in your office will likely want to use that PC for his daily work, unless his work mostly involves checking the output quality of the office coffee maker.

Hardware printer sharing eliminates that problem by substituting a dedicated box for spooling operations. Each PC is connected to the sharing box, which, in turn, connects directly to the printer. The disadvantage of this system is simply the expense of the added hardware.

All printer-sharing boxes are not alike. They differ in the amount of memory they make available and their arbitration systems. The memory is used to buffer print jobs so that when one PC is printing, others can continue to send printing instructions as if they are running the printer, too. No time is lost by programs waiting for printer access. More memory is generally better, although you might not need a lot should you standardize your office on Windows or Unix or some other software environment with a built-in software print spooler. With today's graphic printing job, you'll want at least a megabyte in any hardware printer sharing device.

Arbitration systems determine which PC has priority when two or more try to print at once. The best sharing systems allow you to assign a priority to every PC based on its need and the corporate pecking order. You should expect to get control software to let you manage the entire printing system to accompany the more versatile sharing devices.

Sharing devices also differ as to the number and kind of ports that they make available. You'll need a port for every PC you want to connect. You'll want parallel ports for easy connections but serial ports if PCs are located some distance (generally over 10 to 25 feet) from the sharing device.

Some printer-sharing devices plug into the I/O slots of printers. Although these devices limit the number of available ports because of size constraints, they also minimize costs because no additional case or power supply is required. A few printers are designed to be shared, having multiple or network inputs built in.

When printers are expensive, such as laser printers and thermal-wax printers, sharing the asset is much more economical than buying a separate printer for everyone and is smarter than making someone suffer with a cheap printer while the quality machine lies idle most of the day.

Buying a Printer

Any kid in a candy store will tell you exactly what he wants—everything. When forced to choose among the hundreds of available printers, you may feel the same way. Every printer has its attractions—speed, color, on-paper quality, price. In narrowing the selection down to the one right printer, you may be tempted to close your eyes and point.

Actually, making the right choice isn't hard if you methodically consider your needs and the capabilities of the printers available to you. This shopping list will help you get organized and find the right questions to ask to locate the right printer and the right printer vendor.

Compatibility

First, make a list of printers compatible with your software. Although an inexpensive printer may be tempting, it's worthless if it won't work with your software. Before you start shopping, make a list of the printers that you might at least consider using.

Check the instruction manual accompanying the software you use most for a list of printers it specifically supports. If you can't find your documentation, run through the installation process of your program and copy down the list of printers you have to choose from. When you shop, ensure that any printer you consider is on your list or will emulate one of the printers on your list.

Speed

Make sure that the speed is adequate for your needs. All else being equal, a faster printer is more desirable simply because it will get your work done quicker. Although printer speed ratings range from painfully slow to tolerable (no printer is ever fast enough), you'll find that within a given technology and price range, competing models are more equal. Still, speed can be a deciding factor.

Remember that manufacturer's speed ratings are determined theoretically rather than through testing. Although the text speeds (in pages per minute) quoted for laser printers and other page printers will be reasonably accurate, graphic speeds will be substantially slower. Character and line printers, such as dot-matrix machines, will likely turn in performances 25 to 50 percent slower than the manufacturer's figures on actual print jobs with normal page formatting.

Paper Handling

Most printers (except for those that specialize in a niche, such as label-making) will handle the standard 8.5 x 11-inch paper, or 9.5 x 11 inches for those printers using sprocket-fed media. If you need to print documents of another size, whether larger or smaller, you'll have to verify that the printer you're considering can do the job. All printers have a maximum paper size. Many tractor-fed printers have a minimum paper-width. Likewise, laser printers have particular size requirements for their media. If you need 11 x 14-inch printouts, you'll want a wide-carriage printer.

For some applications, you may need to use media other than paper—multipart forms, envelopes for correspondence, acetate for overhead transparencies. Ensure the printer you choose will work with what you want to use.

The amount of paper a printer can handle is also important. You don't want to baby-sit a printer, if just to save your hearing sitting next to an impact machine.

Tractor-feed printers will usually handle any amount of paper you can thread through them. Just be sure that a printer that can use tractors actually comes equipped with a tractor. Some older models make tractors optional.

Bin-feed (cut-sheet feeders), laser, thermal-wax, and dye-diffusion printers are all apt to use individual sheets. Consider the capacity of both the input and output bins of these printers as well as their speed of operation to determine how long you can stray from the print job before you have to feed or remove media from the printer.

Supplies

Ensure that your printer comes with the supplies you need. Most printers come with a limited supply of consumables—ribbons and special paper, if required—to get you going. You'll at least be able to test your printer. In most cases with printers that use ordinary paper, you'll be set for hundreds or thousand of pages before you need to consider buying additional consumables.

With laser printer sales, the situation may be different. Some vendors pare the prices they ask for laser printers by making the needed toner cartridge optional. Just to get the machine running, you'll have to spring for a $100 cartridge.

Make sure that you get a cartridge and other consumables you need when you order a new printer. If a laser printer is offered without a cartridge, don't forget to add the cartridge cost when you comparison shop.

Cable

Don't forget to get a cable. Connecting any printer to your PC requires a cable. A few printers—mostly older and discontinued models—have specific cabling requirements that don't precisely match the IBM standard. You'll want to ask to be sure that a standard IBM printer cable will work with the printer you buy. If not, you'll want the vendor to supply you with the correct cable for your printer.

Even if your printer uses a standard IBM connection—a cable with a 25-pin male D-shell on one end and a male 36-pin Centronics connector on the other, you won't want to forget to have one sent with your printer. There's nothing more frustrating than having a new printer and no way of connecting it to your PC.

Support

Find out who will support your prospective printer purchase. Sometime or another you'll have a need to do double-underlined, boldface, italics with your new printer, and you won't be able to figure out how to make your word processor do the trick. You'll want a support number you can call for help. Odds are your vendor won't have any more experience than you with the more exotic aspects of a printer, so a manufacturer's support line is most desirable. As with all telephone support, toll-free is best (from your perspective—you don't want to pay for a $20 call to get a $50 printer working). Some printer vendors also offer bulletin boards that will take your questions via modem.

You'll also want to check the vendor's service policy. Printers are electro-mechanical devices. That means they have both electronics and mechanical parts to fail. Consequently, service is more important for printers than just about any PC peripheral. Before you buy, check where and how you can get your printer serviced, both in and out of warranty. Many vendors are ill-equipped to handle mechanical printer repairs.

You'll find that some manufacturers have local service depots (sometimes typewriter shops) that can take care of mechanical problems without imposing the vagaries of shipping the printer back. With more expensive printers, on-site service should be available.

Warranty

Although nearly every printer is covered by a warranty, not all warranties cover everything, so check the warranty terms of the printer you're considering. Some warranties may exclude user-replaceable parts. Although that may seem logical—no one wants to warrant a ribbon—it may also cover the printhead. Unlike other peripherals, printers have parts that wear out, such as drive belts and printheads.

Both the vendor and manufacturer may offer warranties, although you might not get the latter with a close-out printer. Be sure that whoever sells you a printer will stand behind it.

Plotters

In a world in which technologies change as quickly as a chameleon climbing paisley wallpaper, plotters remain as resolute and steadfast as the Great Stoneface or your brother-in-law's bad habits. In less than a decade, microprocessors have raced ahead 20 times faster; printers have gone from hammers to lasers; hard disks have grown from five to five hundred megabytes; and plotters...well, let's say you step into a time warp, slip back 10 years, and the only proof of your travels you carry is one of today's state-of-the-art desktop plotters. One look at it, and not a soul from a decade ago would believe you a time traveler. Plotters today look the same as yesterday; they work the same; and they deliver nearly the same results.

But there's more to the story of plotter than that. Subtle changes have been made electronically and philosophically. More importantly, however, today's desktop plotters are just as useful as they ever were, notwithstanding a broadside of new competition from every quarter.

Today's desktop plotters offer the highest resolution of almost any hard copy device you can plug into your PC, typically addressable to 1/1000th of an inch. With such high accuracy, they can sketch smooth curves and skew lines without a trace of jagginess. Plotters are quick enough to serve as your only graphic output device or, in major installations, they're cheap enough to attach to workstations to take the load off a larger plotter when drafts are all that's required.

The subtle changes that have been made to desktop plotters over the last few years have made them more accessible, more usable, and generally more compatible with you and your software. Although plotters work the same way they always have—they simply control the movement of an inkpen across one or another drafting medium—they have become smarter and so have their makers.

Most plotters today are microprocessor based. The smartest plotters process the instructions they receive to move their pens as economically as possible, optimizing pen travel and pen selection to waste the least time. Manufacturers have wised up and adopted one standard language for controlling their products.

Most available plotters are designed to recognize the commands of Hewlett-Packard's HP-GL plotter language. Moreover, manufacturers now document all the details of setting up their equipment to operate with PCs and the most popular software. No longer need you stay up nights experimenting to find the right cable connections and setup parameters.

Plotter Designs

Plotter technology itself is unchanged, divided into two families: the flatbeds or X-Y plotters and roller-beds or drum plotters. The difference is simply a matter of what moves. The flatbed plotter is the magic moving hand in action. The plotting medium is held fast against the flat plotting surface (the "bed" of "flatbed"), and the mechanism moves the pen across the paper in two dimensions (the "X" and "Y") just as you would draw a picture by hand.

The roller-bed plotter restricts its pen to travel in one dimension—laterally across the width of the drafting medium—and lends new impetus to the paper. That is, to draw lines perpendicular to the movement of the pen, the paper slides underneath the pen. The "roller" in the bed is a cylinder or drum underneath the paper which provides the motive force.

Neither technology is an all-around winner. When accuracy counts, the flatbed design is the low-cost winner. Building an accurate flatbed is inherently less expensive because control over only one mechanism—that which moves the pen—is required. Roller-beds require two discrete and fundamentally different systems, one for the pen, one for the paper, to be precisely coordinated. This added complexity can translate into higher costs. But when price overrules resolution, flatbed plotters can sacrifice milli-inches of precision for affordability.

On the other hand, roller-bed plotters have an inherent speed advantage. Paper is simply less massive than overreaching mechanical arms and pen carriages, and Newton's Second Law (for those needing a refresher in freshman physics: F=ma, force equals mass times acceleration) says that it's less work to speed up a lighter object. Little wonder the fastest plotters tend to be roller-bed machines.

Flatbed plotters have one advantage: they let you use virtually any size of drafting medium up to their physical limits. Most drum or roller-bed plotters constrain your choice of widths of drafting medium because they grip it only at its edges and, for design reasons, the paper-grippers are a fixed distance apart. Narrower widths of drafting media just can't be properly gripped. However, one manufacturer, Hitachi, offers a roller-bed plotter that uses a full-width drum that can grasp any width paper down to postcard size.

With a flatbed plotter, however, you don't face minimum size limits. After all, flatbeds are just drafting tables with automated arms attached. Anything that the table will hold can be drawn on, with the proper software instructions, of course.

Plotters range in size from those that will fit atop your desk to machines that will ink sheets bigger than wallpaper. The most common machines handle drafting media up to the ANSI (American National Standards Institute) B-size, that is, with metes and bounds measuring 11 x 17 inches.

As with drafting tables, flatbed plotters require some means of securing paper to the drawing surface. Ordinary drafting tape will suffice but is hardly an elegant solution. Plotter makers have adopted several strategies to eliminate the pesky stickiness of tape. Some plotters use the magic of static electricity to hold the drafting medium down, a sticking strategy that works for all but a few media. Alternately, one manufacturer uses magnets instead of electricity to hold down drafting copy, a tactic which should work with any medium except thin sheets of iron.

Quality Issues

The most important difference between cheap and expensive plotters is precision. A better plotter has a smaller resolution or step size.

Step size is limited by a number of factors. The ultimate limit is the plotter's mechanical resolution, the finest movements the hardware can ever make owing to the inevitable coarseness of the stepper motors that move their pens. In most, but not all cases, step size is further constrained by addressability. The smallest increments in which HP-GL can move a plotter pen is 0.001 (one-thousandths) inch. The least expensive plotters often have mechanical resolutions more coarse than the addressing limits of HP-GL. In these cases, the mechanism itself limits quality. The smaller the step size, the smoother the curves a plotter can draw. Each step shows as a right-angle bump in a diagonal or curved line. At the 0.001-inch limit of HP-GL, steps are less than a third the size of a laser-printer dot—very fine indeed, essentially invisible. With less expensive plotters, however, each step may be plainly visible, resulting in a self-describing condition called the *jaggies*.

Color Issues

Desktop plotters also differ in the number of pens that they can select among automatically. Although there's a rough correspondence between color capabilities and the number of pens that a plotter can handle, you can make multicolored plots even with a one-pen engine. Most plotters allow you to pause their work and exchange pens, giving you manual control over the hues of their output. In other words, a four-pen plotter is not necessarily limited to four colors; it can ink drawings in as many tints as are available in compatible pens. More pens is a matter of convenience only.

However, a larger number of pens will let you run your plotter on auto-pilot. Start the plot and you can empty the coffee pot and socialize the morning away. You don't have to stand over the machine and anticipate when to make the change.

Besides sheer numbers, plotters offer you a choice of pen types that you can load. Which to use depends on the type of output you want to create—paper and film plots require different kinds of ink, perhaps different pen types. Some manufacturers offer refillable pens. These offer you the higher quality (thinner, more consistent lines) of a drafting pen without the hefty expense of making you buy a new one when the ink runs out.

If you have a choice of pens, you'll want to choose the most popular to have the widest possible selection. The closest to a standard among plotter pens is the design used by Hewlett-Packard machines and followed by several manufacturers. As with anything else, proprietary pen designs will limit your options and may require you to pay a higher price.

Interfacing

With plotters, compatibility is a major issue. Traditionally, plotter-makers have viewed their products as professional tools, which means that they were designed to give smug engineers their comeuppance. At minimum, you needed to have a special cable manufactured for your particular installation.

Most of that frustration lies in the past, however. The typical plotter today includes a Centronics-style parallel port that makes it as easy to connect as a dot-matrix printer.

Several machines still depend on RS-232 serial connections. Others make it an option. (All plotters reviewed here were tested using 9,600 bit per second serial transmissions so that their actual performance could be isolated from communications concerns.) If you choose to use a serial link, you'll probably want to buy the plotter maker's own serial cable that's been designed to match the needs of the particular plotter. The $50 or so you spend will stave off the Thorazine and straitjackets that sorting out a serial link usually leads to.

Unless you already have other peripherals that use it, you probably won't want to tangle with the cost, intricacies, and special software drivers required to use the IEEE-488 connection (also known as GPIB, the General Purpose Interface Bus, or HP-IB, the Hewlett-Packard Interface Bus) that some plotters make available.

Control Languages

When you say your prayers tonight, you'll want to thank your Provider for the miracle of HP-GL. Most plotter manufacturers have now adopted Hewlett-Packard Graphic Language (HP-GL) to control their machines, making that language the standard in this country. (Although HP-GL is used internationally, GP-GL is more prevalent in some markets.) Another alternative is Digital Microprocessor Plotter Language (DMPL), developed by Houston Instrument, which has several built-in functions that are not present in HP-GL, such as built-in fonts, the capability to do closed area fill with a single command, and built-in smoothing algorithms. Other plotters have their own native languages, which often work faster than HP-GL with programs that support them. But plotters that understand HP-GL will work with just about any program with a plotter output.

Performance

As with printers, most plotters have built-in RAM to buffer plotting instructions. The buffer memory helps free up your computer when you plot. A large buffer allows the plotter to absorb most or all of the instructions sent out of your PC and process them while your computer does something else. Some plotters take further advantage of their buffers by looking ahead at plotting instructions and calculating how to minimize pen movement or pen changes, drawing all black lines before switching to the red pen, for example. Such optimization can substantially trim the time required for making plots. The buffer can also allow you to make multiple copies of a plot without typing up your PC. Speed differences between plotters can be dramatic: some machines plot in half the time of others.

The output quality among plotters tends toward uniformity except in the lowest cost machines. Text renderings, however, will depend on a plotter's interpretation of HP-GL and the characteristics of any internal character sets.

Plotter Alternatives

Putting pen to paper in these days when words, music, and money flash electronically through wires at the speed of light seems about as anachronistic as stoking the furnace or paying cash. Other technologies are quicker, more colorful, and cheaper. Yet plotters persist for several reasons.

When it comes to fast graphic output, the laser printer is without peer. A typical full graphic page might pour out in less than a minute; a plotter might struggle 5 or 10 minutes on the same chore. But most laser printers (and all affordable machines) are limited to a single color and media no larger than ANSI A size (8.5 x 11 inches). Plotters deftly draw in any color that you can find in a pen and will combine color in nearly unlimited combination (as long as you're willing to manually change pens at the appropriate times). On the other hand, even the most compact of these desktop plotters handle sheets up to B size. And they are almost indifferent to the medium you give them to plot on— just match the proper pens, and they'll happily ink paper, vellum, mylar, or whatever you lay on their beds.

The comparison to color inkjet printers is nearly the same. Inexpensive inkjets won't handle large sheets. Those that will accept B-size paper likely cost more than a comparable plotter. But inkjets can stretch their color spectra through dithering and mixing inks on paper. They can even add a more natural look by shading from one hue to another, although not under direct manual control.

Plotters beat nearly all printers when it comes to accuracy: most move in steps of about 1/1000th of an inch, more than three times finer than the 300 dots per inch delivered by the typical laser engines. This extreme resolution is put to good use drawing curves from which every trace of jagginess has been expunged.

But laser printers lead when it comes to fine detail. Although the plotter can draw almost absolutely smooth diagonals thanks to their high resolution, the finest details they can create are limited to the widths of the lines drawn by their pens. Typically, the finest pen available for plotting inks a line .3 millimeters wide, about 12 times the width of the plotter's resolution or step size, about 4 times wider than the thinnest laser line.

On the other hand, plotters can draw in solid colors rather than the spotty digital dots fused to paper by the lasers or sprayed by the inkjets (not to mention the pointillism of impact dot-matrix engines). Plotter colors are pure and consistently toned.

Direct speed comparisons between printers and plotters are impossible, because they use different imaging techniques. Printers are raster-based devices; plotters draw vectors. As a result, which is faster will depend on what you want to draw.

Plotters might possibly finish simple drawings first but will lag when images become more complex than a few lines. Dot-addressed printers (as opposed to those that use a language like PostScript), on the other hand, will devote about as much time to the simplest or most complex drawings. They have to scan an entire sheet no matter how many lines are to be drawn. (PostScript printers will take somewhat longer for more complex drawings because of transfer and processing times must be added in.)

The bottom line: plotters are moderately priced, colorful, accurate, and slow. Affordable laser printers are faster but lack color capabilities and the 1/1000th inch resolution of plotters. Color lasers are quick, costly, and not quite as sharp. Color inkjets provide multiple hues, moderate speed, and costs comparable to plotters, but they lack the capability to create smooth, detailed drawings. For many applications, plotters still deliver the right combination.

17

Serial Ports

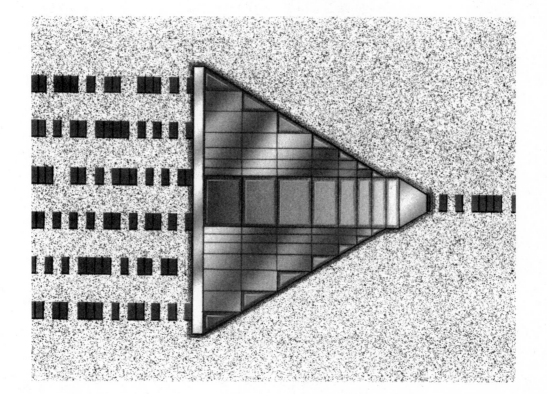

The serial port is the least common denominator of computer communications. Even the most primitive PCs and peripherals sport a serial connection. But serial communications is a many-splendored (and many-terrored) thing. Although most products follow a single industry standard, the variations lead to vexations and long nights without sleep seeking to make a recalcitrant serial port speak. The key to cutting through the confusion is understanding how serial ports work and what their signals are meant to do.

The typical PC has the personality of the local mile-a-minute gossip—the neighbor with so much to say and so little time to say it that you expect the chatterbox's head to explode from overfilling with the backlog of words. The backlog can build quickly. A typical PC can process data at a rate of *millions* of bytes per second, yet the only truly universal two-way access it has to the outside world is the serial port that hobbles along trying to exchange a few *thousands* of bytes per second. For years, from the initial PC to the first release of the PS/2 series, the standard serial port was the only bidirectional communication channel officially sanctioned by IBM for its personal computers. Even now, the serial port is the one universal communication channel.

The official term promulgated by IBM for the serial port is *asynchronous data communications port*, although that's often clipped to *async port* or *comm port*. In addition, because the variety of serial links accepted by the PC industry operates under a standard called RS-232C (one that was hammered out by an industry trade group, the Electronics Industry Association, or EIA), the common serial port is often described by its specification as an *RS-232* port.

No matter what the name, all IBM serial ports are the same, at least functionally. Each takes the 8, 16, or 32 parallel bits a computer exchanges across its databus and turns them sideways—from a broadside of digital blips into a pulse chain that can walk the plank, single-file. This form of communication earns its name *serial* because the individual bits of information are transferred in a long series.

In a perfect world, a single circuit—nothing more than two wires, a signal line, and a ground—would be all that was necessary to move this serial signal from the one place to another without further ado. Of course, a perfect world would also have fairies and other benevolent spirits to help usher the data along and protect it from all the evil imps and energies lurking about trying to debase and disgrace the singular purity of serial transfer.

The world is, alas, not perfect, and the world of computers even less so. Many misfortunes can befall the vulnerable serial data bit as it crawls through its connection. One of the bits of a full byte of data may go astray, leaving a piece of data with a smaller value on arrival as it had at departure—a problem akin to shipping alcohol by a courier service operated by dipsomaniacs. With the vacancy in the data stream, all the other bits will slip up a place and assume new values. Or the opposite case—in the spirit of electronic camaraderie, an otherwise well-meaning signal might adopt a stray bit like a child takes on a kitten, only to later discover the miracle of pregnancy and a progeny of errors that ripple through the communications stream, pushing all the bits backward. In either case, the prognosis is not good. With this elementary form of serial communications, one mistaken bit either way, and every byte that follows will be in error.

Establishing reliable serial communications means overcoming these bit-error problems and many others as well. Thanks to some digital ingenuity, however, serial communications work and work well—well enough that you and your PC can depend on them.

Synchronous and Asynchronous Communication

Two chief serial transmission methods are used to avoid the disaster of serial bit errors. In one of these, the sending and receiving systems are synchronized using some kind of auxiliary signal so that both ends of a connection are always in step. A clock, synchronized between the sending and receiving unit, precisely times the period separating each data bit. A missing bit or extra bit can be quickly detected because it (or its absence) will appear at an unexpected position in the stream of bits. It's like having all the shuttle aircraft at an airport scheduled to arrive exactly on the hour. Any airplane that hits the tarmac at another time can reasonably be expected not to be a shuttle (assuming that the shuttle service has a good reputation for on-time arrivals—possible only in the perfect world of examples, of course). Just by

checking the clock, you can distinguish shuttles from other aircraft—
or, in computer communications, a real data bit from interloping
noise. This time-synchronized form of serial transfer is called *synchronous communication* and is a technique used primarily in mainframe
systems.

This synchronized system fails whenever the sending and receiving
systems lose their mutual signal lock. The data stream then becomes
little more than noise.

The alternative is to add place-markers to the bit stream to help track
each data bit. One marker could, for example, indicate the position
assigned to a bit. A bit occurring without its marker could be assumed
errant. Of course, such a simple scheme would be grievously wasteful,
requiring two digital signals (the marker and the data bit) for every bit
of information transferred.

More workable is a compromise system. Instead of indicating each bit,
the marker could indicate the beginning of a short stream of bits. The
position of each bit in the stream could be defined by timing them at
regular intervals. Although this method is similar to synchronous
transfer, the sending and receiving systems don't have to be locked
together except for the brief interval between markers. The arrival of a
marker indicates to the receiving system to start looking for bits and
running a short-term timer. The problem of the sending and receiving
timers getting out of sync is eliminated by restarting the clock with
each marker. By keeping the period between markers short, there's not
enough time for either timer to wander too far astray.

This timed short-term system is commonly termed *asynchronous
communication* because the sending and receiving systems need not be
precisely synchronized to one another. The marker bits provide the
temporary lock needed to distinguish a short stream of data bits that
follow. Most PC serial communications use this scheme. In most
asynchronous systems, the data is broken up into small pieces, each
roughly, though not exactly, corresponding to one byte. Each of these
chunks is called a *word*, and may consist of five to eight data bits. The
most widely used word lengths are seven and eight bits, the former
because it accommodates all upper- and lowercase text characters in
ASCII code; the latter because each word corresponds exactly to one
data byte.

As serial data, the bits of a word are sent one at a time down the communication channel. As a matter of convention, the least significant bit of the word is sent out first. The rest of the bits follow in order of their increasing significance.

Added to these data bits is a very special double-length pulse called a *start* bit; it indicates the beginning of a data word. One or more *stop* bits indicate the end of the word. Between the last bit of the word and the first stop bit, a *parity* bit is often inserted as a data integrity check. Together the data bits, the start bit, the parity bit, and the stop bits make up one data *frame*.

Parity Bits

Five kinds of parity bits can be used in serial communication, two of which actually offer a means of detecting bit-level transmission errors. This error detection works by counting the number of bits in the data word and determining whether the result is even or odd. In *odd parity*, the parity bit is set on (made a logical one) when the number of bits in the word is odd. *Even parity* switches on the parity bit when the bit total of the word is even.

In *mark parity,* the parity bit is always on, regardless of the bit total of the word. *Space parity* always leaves the parity bit off. *No parity* means that the frame doesn't even provide space for a parity bit. Although foregoing a bit of data integrity (which can be provided by other means), it allows more efficient communications by squeezing more information in a given number of transmitted bits.

Signal Polarity

All of the bits of an RS-232 standard serial signal are sent down the communication line as *negative-going* pulses superimposed on a normal positive voltage that's maintained on the data line. That is, the presence of a bit in a serial word will interrupt a continuous positive voltage with a brief negative pulse.

Compared to normal logical systems, RS-232 standard data looks upside down. There's no particularly good reason for the inversion except that it's the way things have always been done, and, when it comes to communications, things work best when everybody sticks to the same standard.

Bit Rates

Another important characteristic of every serial signal is the rate at which the bits in the serial data train are nominally sent. The standard form of this measurement is amazingly simple: the number of bits per second that are sent, with the standard unit being one bit per second, or bps.

For somewhat arbitrary reasons, bit rates are enumerated in a rather odd increment. The usual minimum speed is 300 bps, although slower submultiples of 50, 100, and 150 bps are available. Faster standard speeds merely double the preceding rate, so the sequence runs 600, 1,200, 2,400, 4,800, 9,600, and 19,200, the fastest speed IBM officially supports with ordinary, microprocessor-controlled serial ports found in PS/2 Models 50 to 80.

These slow, official rates are mandatory because software control of the serial port imposes such a load on the system microprocessor that slower chips cannot deal with the fastest transmission rates. Because the highest rates cannot be supported by all software, IBM chose not to sanction higher rates in its older computers.

With the introduction of the PS/2 Models 90 and 95, IBM added a new method of serial port control that increases the serial speed potential by eliminating microprocessor overhead. In these (and newer) machines, serial ports can take advantage of bus-mastering DMA control. This expedient increases the officially sanctioned speed of these serial systems to 38,400 bps.

Even the fastest of these official speeds falls far short of the limit of serial hardware in most PCs. In fact, many software products today take advantage of the peculiar hardware design of all IBM-standard serial ports to push out data at much higher speeds, as high as 115,200 bits per second. Although serial communication can take place at much higher rates (millions or billions of bits per second in some systems), the design of the classic IBM serial port caps most personal computer hardware at the 115,200 bps rate.

Serial Hardware

The circuit at the heart of the serial ports of most IBM-compatible computers is a special chip with the express purpose of transforming parallel bus signals into a train of serial pulses. Called a *Universal Asynchronous Receiver/Transmitter,* or *UART*, this chip accepts eight data lines as a parallel input and provides a fully structured serial output. From the name, you can tell that the UART is designed to work both ways—sending and receiving. One chip can convert serial signals on a communication line into the parallel kind that your PC wants, as well as making serial from parallel. Every serial port has a UART at its heart, as do products with embedded serial ports, such as internal modems.

8250

The term *UART* describes both the function and family of integrated circuit. The exact chip goes under a numerical designation assigned by its manufacturer. Three different types of UART are used in the various computers that follow the PC standard. The oldest, slowest, and most minimal chip was used by the original PC and XT, installed on IBM's Asynchronous Communications Adapter card. Designated the 8250, this chip was adapted by most aftermarket vendors to their communications and multifunction boards so that they could precisely mimic the IBM product. The same chip was (and sometimes is) used as part of many lower-speed internal modems.

Besides providing the basic parallel-to-serial-and-back conversion, the 8250 UART also controls the flow of information and speed at which the exchange takes place. It sets the data rate of the serial signal by dividing down a 1.8432 Mhz oscillator clock supplied by your PC. The data rate is set by a divisor loaded into one of the chip's registers. Similarly, the word length, parity, and number of stop bits are set. Other registers allow your PC to monitor the chip and the progress of the communications it manages.

Wonderful as it sounds, the 8250 represents old technology. Even back in the dark ages when the original IBM PC was introduced, the chip was not highly regarded. The problem of the 8250 is that it is slow and cannot keep up with even the modest speed of AT-class computers. On the other hand, its basic design became a mandatory part of every PC because programmers had taken direct control of the registers in the chip (rather than writing their software to access it through the IBM BIOS, which was the prime culprit in limiting serial port speed). As a result, to maintain software compatibility, all later serial ports have had to duplicate the register function of the 8250 in order to remain backwardly compatible.

16450

In quest of better performance, hardware designers in 1984 turned to the 16-bit register-compatible successor of the 8250, the 16450 UART. This chip, since that time, has continued as the mainstay of most serial ports. And because expansion bus speeds have not changed substantially in the last eight years, the 16450 rates as generally fast enough for most uses.

16550A

In 1987, however, the chip of choice shifted to the higher performance 16550 or more recent 16550A. Despite performance differences, all of these more modern chips look the same to your computer, and they all will work in the same manner when called upon to do so by your software. In some cases, differences will show up between the chips. In particular, the 16550A can, however, perform more reliably in lower performance and multitasking systems.

A development other than speed, multitasking, has challenged the 16450. When one of the older UARTs (the 8250 or 16450) receives a word of data across the communication line, it has to do something with the information before it can accept another word. In most communications systems, the UART signals its microprocessor host with an interrupt, and then delivers the data word and goes back to telecommunicating. In sending data, the chip similarly accepts only one word at a time.

This process has severe drawbacks, particularly because the microprocessor may be busy with another task at the moment the UART is attempting an interrupt. Once signaled in this fashion, the processor must drop whatever it is doing to service the UART. But because the UART and communication line may first have to wait, performance suffers on both ends of the UART. Aggravating the situation are the data needs of high-speed modems like the V.32bis models.

The 16550 UART offers a neat solution to this problem: a 16-byte FIFO (first-in, first-out) on-board buffer. This modest chunk of memory allows the 16550 to keep communicating even when a multitasking computer turns its attention to other projects. When properly programmed (and using the right software because programs must be specially written to take advantage of the 16550's buffer), the 16550 can carry out its 16 bytes of communications on its own, sending or receiving data on its own while the host microprocessor engages in another task. Note that the in-chip buffer of the 16550 must be specifically enabled by your software. If the buffer is not enabled, the 16550 functions exactly the same way as the 16450 and brings no added benefit to your PC.

Chipsets

The UART chip itself is disappearing, however. Its functions are being taken over by ASICs (Application-Specific Integrated Circuits). The chipsets that most PCs are built from today typically include the circuitry of one or two UARTs. In modern one-and three-chip PCs, the UART function is hidden on the same slab of silicon along with the rest of the logic functions of the PC. In addition, some manufacturers have begun packaging several communications functions in a single package for use in multifunction boards. The Western Digital 16C552, for example, combines the electrical equivalent of two 16550 UARTs and a parallel port into one chip. Even with these more advanced chips, the internal designs of embedded UARTs will continue to mimic the stand-alone versions to ensure complete system compatibility.

UART Upgrading

Because the 16550 is completely socket-compatible with the 16450, you can replace the older chip with the newest one in a few minutes; the sole requisite is that the UART in your PC or serial card be socketed rather than soldered. The upgrade is not costly, and UARTs are available at retail from companies that sell individual electronic components. Be sure to get the latest 16550A version when you order.

I/O Addressing

In IBM and compatible computers, serial ports are simple extensions to the circuitry of the machine. Data from memory or a microprocessor register is simply moved into the UART, which makes the necessary conversion from parallel to serial data. The output of the UART is then channeled through a *serial line driver* integrated circuit, which converts the five-volt logic used by the computer to the bipolar, higher voltage system specified by the RS-232 standard.

To access the registers of the UART, your PC's microprocessor must send commands through system input/output ports. The data sent and received by the modem is also transferred to your PC through another I/O port. In fact, standard PC architecture assigns a block of eight I/O ports to each UART [and thus each asynchronous communication adapter (serial port) in your PC], although only seven are actually used.

Under DOS, IBM specifies four ranges of ports that can be used by each asynchronous communication adapter. Each range encompasses eight contiguous ports, with the ranges starting at I/O port addresses 3F8(Hex), 2F8(Hex), 3E8(Hex), and 2E8(Hex). OS/2 also communicates with asynchronous adapters through ranges of eight I/O ports but, except for the first two, uses different port ranges than does DOS. The OS/2 ports I/O addresses start at 03F8(Hex), 02F8(Hex), 3220(Hex), 3228(Hex), 4220(Hex), 4228(Hex), 5220(Hex), and 5228(Hex).

These addresses are hidden from most software and from you at the DOS prompt by the BIOS and your operating system, which, together, assign other names to each asynchronous communication adapter. When your PC boots up, the BIOS hunts through the addresses available for serial ports and transfers the base addresses of the serial ports it finds to the BIOS data area at absolute memory address 0000:0400(Hex). It searches for ports in a specific order—the order in which the I/O port base addresses are listed. DOS assigns the names COM1 through COM4 in that order to the ports it finds listed in the BIOS data area. OS/2 calls its serial ports SERIAL 1 through SERIAL 8 and has the appropriate addresses built in.

Register Function

The register at the base address assigned to each serial port is used for data communications. Bytes are moved to and from the UART using the microprocessor's OUT and IN instructions. The next six addresses are used by other serial port registers, which, in order, are as follows: the Interrupt Identification Register, the Line Control Register, the Modem Control Register, the Line Status Register, and the Modem Status Register. Another register, called the Divisor Latch, shares the base address used by the Transmit and Receive registers and the next higher register used by the interrupt enable register. It is accessed by toggling a setting in the line control register.

This latch stores the divisor that determines the operating speed of the serial port. Whatever value is loaded into the latch is multiplied by 16. The resulting product is used to divide the clock signal supplied to the UART chip to determine the bit rate. Because of the factor of 16 multiplication, the highest speed the serial port can operate at is limited to 1/16 the supplied clock signal (which is 1.8432 Mhz). Setting the latch value to its minimum, 1, results in a bit rate of 115,200.

Registers not only store the values used by the UART chip, but also are used to report back to your system how the serial conversation is progressing. For example, the line status register indicates whether a character that has been loaded to be transmitted has actually been sent. It also indicates when a new character has been received.

Although you can change the values stored in these registers manually using Debug or your own programs, for the most part you'll never tangle with these registers. They do, however, provide flexibility to the programmer.

Instead of being set with DIP switches or jumpers, the direct addressability of these registers allows all the vital operating parameters to be set through software. For instance, by loading the proper values into the line control register, you alter the word length, parity, and number of stop bits used in each serial word.

Flow Control

Besides data transmissions, the UART also creates and reacts to other signals that control its operation and how the serial conversation it engages in is managed. Control is afforded through several registers that are accessed by your computer through I/O ports. For instance, to change the speed at which the serial port communicates, you merely need to load a register with the proper number. The conversation control is handled by voltages that appear or are received on the serial port connectors on the rear panel of your personal computer.

One of these other UART functions is to arrange for the control of the flow of data across the serial line. Every serial interchange is a true conversation with two sides. When one side speaks, the other has to listen. Just as with polite conversation, if the listener isn't paying attention, nothing will be communicated. And, if the speaker rambles along too fast, the listener can be overwhelmed and miss most of what's said. Serial communications among computers is fraught with the same problems. Without properly gauging their delivery, computers may shovel out data and have it disappear into the ether unused. Even when the connection is good, the receiving equipment may be otherwise engaged and not able to give its attention to the serial information being delivered to it. Or the serial data may arrive at such a high speed that it exceeds the capacity of the receiving system to do anything with it on the fly—even saving the information for later inspection. Consequently, some means is needed for the receiving system to signal the sending system to hold on and wait until it is ready to acquire data. Several techniques for controlling the flow of serial data have evolved, all generally classed as methods of *handshaking*, which is agreeing to the terms of the transmission method.

The easiest solution is to use a special wire as a signal line that the receiving system can use to indicate that it is actually ready to receive. Because this method uses extra hardware (the flow control wire), it is termed *hardware* handshaking. This is the default flow control method used by the serial ports of today's IBM-compatible personal computers. Some communications channels do not allow the use of an extra signal wire. For example, the telephone connection used by modems (the prototypical serial communications device) only provides the two wires necessary for carrying data. With no hardware signaling mean available, some alternate method of flow control is needed. The logical way of managing such communications is to give the listener special characters that are used as semaphores to signal the speaker to slow down or stop. Another character can then be used to indicate when it's all right to speed up again. This form of flow control is termed *software handshaking* because it's not hardware. Moreover, the flow control indicators have the same tentative existence as the ideas embodied in software code.

With most software handshaking methods, the receiving system uses two distinct characters to tell the sending system when it is ready to receive a data transmission and when it can temporarily no longer accept more data. Two character pairs are commonly used in software handshaking. One, called *ETX/ACK*, uses the control code represented by the ASCII hexadecimal character 03(hex) (also called ETX—End TeXt—or Control-C) to indicate that it requires a pause in data transmission, and the ASCII character 06(hex) (ACK—ACKnowledge—or Control-F) to indicate that it's okay to resume. More common among PC products today is XON/XOFF handshaking, which uses the ASCII characters 13(hex) (also called DC1, XOFF, or Control-S) and 11(hex) (or DC3, XON, or Control-Q) to ask for pauses or resumptions of data flow.

Although most PC peripherals that used a serial connection offer the option of software handshaking, without special driver software, they will not work properly with an IBM-compatible PC. The computer doesn't even listen for the flow control characters, so it will never act upon them. The result is data overflow and characters lost from the transmission. For example, if you use a serial printer and the handshaking does not work, characters, words, or whole paragraphs may mysteriously disappear from your printouts.

Software flow control is, however, built into many application programs, for controlling peripherals, such as printers, or for relaying through modems (which cannot pass along hardware handshaking signals) to remote data sources. Many multiuser or multitasking operating systems (for example, OS/2) also come with special drivers that allow you to use the software handshaking through your system's serial ports without special applications.

Interrupts

The UART interacts with the microprocessor in your PC. It has to in order to transfer information so that the microprocessor can process the data to display or store it. To achieve the highest speed, the UART must be able to pass along data as quickly as it is received. Every time it uses flow control to stop the in-rush of information, transmission speed slows. Consequently, the UART has to pass along the data it gets as soon as possible—immediately if not sooner. It needs to get the microprocessor's attention immediately. The UART can get the attention it demands by sending a hardware interrupt to the microprocessor.

Most serial ports require that you assign them an interrupt for them to work properly. (Serial communications will work without interrupt control, but it will be severely speed constrained.) Ideally, each serial port should be assigned its own interrupt to avoid conflicts. However, the PC has few hardware interrupts available, and IBM attempted to limit the number assignable to serial ports. Two interrupts are commonly used: IRQ3 and IRQ4. The COM1 serial port normally should be given hardware Interrupt Request (IRQ) 4. Serial port COM2 normally uses IRQ3. COM3 shares IRQ3 with COM2, and COM4 shares IRQ4 with COM1.

This primitive interrupt sharing system has its drawbacks. Two or more serial devices can operate at the same time and send interrupts to your microprocessor. If two devices using the same interrupt vie for the microprocessor's attention, the chip may lose track of which port needs immediate service. As a result, commands can get confused and data lost. When assigning serial ports, it's important to avoid assigning the same interrupt to two serial devices that operate at the same time.

Mice are constantly active, always ready to issue commands to your PC. Consequently, a mouse should never share an interrupt with another device if you can avoid such an assignment. For example, if you attach a serial mouse to COM1 (which uses IRQ4), do not attach a modem to COM4 (which also uses IRQ4).

Connectors

The external manifestation of a serial port is the connector it provides for you to plug in serial devices. You can identify serial ports on an IBM-compatible computer by the type of connectors you find. Two different kinds of connectors are typically used. IBM PCs, XTs, and PS/2s all use male 25-pin D-shell connectors for their serial ports. ATs use male 9-pin D-shell connectors. The smaller connectors of the AT were mandated by the tight confines of the card-retaining bracket of the combined serial/parallel port board used in those systems. Not all 25 pins in a serial connector are actively used in the IBM scheme, allowing the use of the shorter connectors; the parallel port uses all of its pin allotment. Obviously, the serial port was the likely candidate for this size reduction.

Parallel ports, which also use 25-pin D-shell connectors, can be distinguished because they are female (that is, the connectors have holes instead of pins). Old-style MDA/CGA/EGA video connectors, which use 9-pin D-shell connectors like those of AT serial ports, also use female connectors.

In that most serial cables are equipped with 25-pin connectors at either end, an adapter is usually required to convert the AT's 9-pin connection to 25. Commercial adapters are generally available, or you can make your own. Figure 17.1 shows the proper wiring of an IBM 9-to-25 pin serial converter.

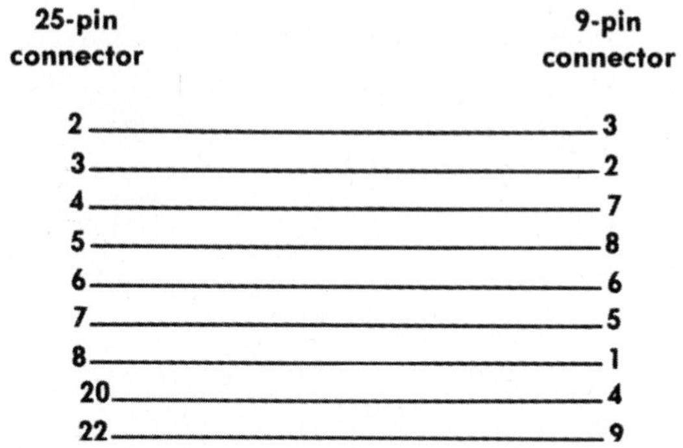

25-pin connector	9-pin connector
2	3
3	2
4	7
5	8
6	6
7	5
8	1
20	4
22	9

Figure 17.1. Wiring for a 9-to-25-pin serial adapter.

Serial Device Types

To understand how serial ports are supposed to work requires taking a giant step backward to the dark ages when huge lizards roamed the earth and personal computers were not to be found anywhere. Originally, RS-232 ports were designed to connect data terminals with modems to connect the terminals to a giant mainframe computer in some far-off city. The connection scheme was based on a typical division of labor that was near-ubiquitous in a world that had only semi-miniaturized electronics. The terminal reduced keystrokes to digital pulses and converted other pulses to characters on the screen. The modem transformed the digital signals from the terminal into analog signals that could be transmitted over telephone lines. The serial port linked them together.

In the RS-232 system, certain tightly defined names were assigned to the devices at either end of the connection. The terminal earned the epithet *Data Terminal Equipment,* or *DTE*. The modem was called *Data Communication Equipment,* or *DCE*. The difference between the two is more than just the names. Communication between the two is mediated by a very elaborate hierarchy of query signals and responses. The two behave differently and are wired differently.

No matter whether it's a DTE or DCE, the serial port on a device must function as a two-way street. Information is allowed to flow in both directions, so both ends of the connection must be able to operate as both sending and receiving devices. Every connection has two ends. One end may be the terminal and modem. At the other end, those devices may talk to a computer, another terminal, or a printer, always using another modem. No matter which end of the connection it is attached to, as long as the modem is DCE and the terminal/computer/printer is DTE, everything will work fine.

Because of the complication of both ends both sending and receiving data, often simultaneously, a single communication circuit is not sufficient to implement a true RS-232 connection. Thus, to prevent serial devices from becoming confused by hearing, and reacting to, their own transmissions, the standard serial connection uses separate wires for sending and receiving. (Modems avoid the need for separate wires by using two different signals on the same wire link.)

This use of separate wires for sending and receiving signals leads to problems. The wire one system uses for sending must be the wire the other system uses for receiving, and vice versa. If both devices sent down the same wire, no one would be listening, and no communication would take place.

By convention, the connector pins numbered 2 and 3 are used for the two communication signals. Ordinarily, DTE devices use pin 2 to send and pin 3 to receive, and DCEs use pin 3 to send and pin 2 to receive. The 9-pin equipped AT is an exception, however. Although considered DTE, it uses pin 3 on its DB-9 connector to send and pin 2 to receive. The normal 9-to-25 pin adapter supplied by IBM converts the AT to a standard 25-pin DTE-style connection.

The one important point about sending and receiving pins of serial ports is that when a normal *straight-through* cable is used, one in which the pins at one end are directly connected to the pins with the same number at the other end, DTE devices must always be connected to DCE devices, and DCE devices will only work when connected to DTE devices.

How Serial Ports Work

The RS-232 assigns particular functions to the wires in a serial cable. Besides the two conductors used for data, several others are required for hardware handshaking and to make everything work properly. The various connections and their names on standard 25-pin (DTE) and 9-pin IBM serial connectors are shown in table 17.1.

TABLE 17.1.
IBM Serial Port
Pin-Outs

25-Pin Connector		
Pin	Function	Mnemonic
2	Transmit data	TXD
3	Receive data	RXD
4	Request to send	RTS
5	Clear to send	CTS
6	Data set ready	RTS
7	Signal ground	GND
8	Carrier detect	CD
20	Data terminal ready	DTR
22	Ring indicator	RI

continues

TABLE 17.1.
continued

Current loop connections (only on IBM Async Adapter, now obsolete)	
Pin	Function
9	Transmit current loop return
11	Transmit current loop data
18	Receive current loop data
25	Receive current loop return

9-Pin (AT-Style) Connector		
Pin	Function	Mnemonic
1	Carrier detect	CD
2	Receive data	RXD
3	Transmit data	TXD
4	Data terminal ready	DTR
5	Signal Ground	GND
6	Data set ready	DSR
7	Request to send	RTS
8	Clear to send	CTS
9	Ring indicator	RI

The most important of all these assignments is number seven, the *Signal Ground*. This wire provides the necessary return path for both the data signals and the handshaking signals. This wire must be present in all serial cables.

Signal ground is separate and completely different from pin one, the *Chassis Ground*. The pin in the serial connector corresponding to this wire is connected directly to the metal chassis or case of the equipment, much as the third prong of a three-wire AC cable is. In fact, this connection provides the same safety function as the electrical ground. It ensures that the outside metal parts of the two serial devices are at the same electrical potential. It prevents you from getting a shock by touching the two devices at the same time. It carries whatever electricity might flow between the two units instead of letting your body do it (and potentially electrocuting you).

Proper Grounding

This connection is not always necessary, however, and not always desirable. It's not necessary when both devices in a serial link-up are already grounded together through their AC cables. It may not be desirable when the two serial devices are separated by a great distance and derive their power from different sources. Electrical ground potentials vary (because of differing resistances that are present in every ground return path), and it is entirely possible that grounded AC cables could put the two devices at widely different potentials. The chassis ground circuit might then carry substantial current as a *ground loop*. If the current in the loop is great enough, it can cause electrical interference. A small chance exists that it might be large enough to melt the chassis ground conductor and start a fire.

The best strategy is to follow these rules:

➤ If both serial devices in a connection are grounded through their AC cords, you do not need the chassis ground wire.

➤ If only one is grounded through its AC wire, the best bet is to ground the other device through its AC wire, too. Otherwise, you should use the chassis ground connection in your serial port.

Signal Functions

Trying to engage in serial communication would be fruitless if one or the other device at an end of the connection were turned off. Without a second device to listen, information from one would pour down the serial line and vanish into the ether, wasted. Consequently, the RS-232 specification includes two wires dedicated to revealing whether a device is attached to each end of the connection and turned on.

The signal on pin 20 is called *Data Terminal Ready* or, simply, *DTR*. It is a positive voltage sent from the DTE device to indicate that the device is plugged in, powered up, and ready to begin communication.

The complementary signal appears on pin 6. Called *Data Set Ready*, or *DSR*, a positive voltage on this line indicates that the DCE is turned on and ready to do its job.

In a normal RS-232 serial connection, both of these signals must be present before anything else happens. The DTE sends the DTR signal to the DCE, and the DCE sends the DSR signal to the DTE. Both devices then know that the other device is ready.

Normal modem hardware handshaking is implemented on two entirely different conductors. The DCE puts a positive voltage on the connection on pin 5, which is called *Clear To Send*, or *CTS*, to indicate whether it is all right to send data to the DCE. In effect, it signals to the DTE that the coast is clear. At the other end of the connection, the DTE puts a positive voltage on pin 4, called *Request To Send*, or *RTS* to indicate to the DCE that wants to receive information, too.

The important rule to remember is that unless both CTS and RTS have positive voltages on them, no data will flow in either direction. If no positive voltage is on the CTS wire, the DTE will not send data to the DCE. If no positive voltage is on RTS, then the DCE will not send data to the DTE.

The DCE issues one further signal that can affect the flow of data. Called *Carrier Detect*, or sometimes *Data Carrier Detect*, (abbreviated *CD* or *DCD*), a positive voltage on this conductor indicates that the DCE modem has a carrier signal from the modem at the other end of the connection. If no carrier is detected, then the serial signal may likely be nothing but the garbage of line noise. The CD signals help the DTE know when to be on its guard. In some cases, when CD is not positive, the DTE will refuse to accept data.

The signal on pin 22 is called *Ring Indicator*, or *RI*, and is used by a DCE modem to signal to the DTE terminal to which it is attached that it has detected ringing voltage on the telephone line. In other words, a positive voltage on RI alerts the terminal that someone is calling the modem. In most serial communications systems, this can be regarded as an optional signal because its absence usually will not prevent the flow of serial data.

A normal serial communication session follows a very particular protocol. Before anything else can happen, the hardware at both ends of the connection must be turned on and ready to go. The DTE, your computer, will assert its DTR signal and the DCE, your modem, will assert its DSR. When a telephone call awakens the modem from its lethargy, it will send an RI to the computer, which may trigger a message on the screen. Once the modem negotiates the connection with the other modem at the distant end of the call, the local modem will send a CD signal to your computer. If they were not already on during the wait before the call, your computer will assert its RTS and the modem will assert its CTS.

Type something at the computer keyboard to send to the modem or send some data from a file, and if the modem can send the bytes out fast enough to keep up, it will drop its CTS signal to tell your PC to hold off for a while. When it again makes CTS positive, your computer will resume sending data to it.

If data rolls in from the modem and your computer needs to take care of something more important, such as saving part of the transmission to disk, it will drop its RTS signal, and the modem will stop dumping data to it. When your computer finishes with its disk chores, it will assert RTS again, and data will again flow from the modem.

DTE-to-DTE Communications

As long as you want to connect a computer serial port that functions as DTE to a modem that functions as DCE, this serial connection scheme will likely work flawlessly the first time you try it. Simply sling a cable with enough conductors to handle all the vital signals between the computer and modem and, voila, serial communications without a hitch. Try it, and you're likely to wonder why so many people complain about the capricious nature of serial connections.

The problem is that you may want to connect something besides a modem to a serial port. Other common serial devices include printers, plotters, mice, digitizing pads, even video display terminals. Many of these devices are not set up to be DCE but are themselves DTE, patterned after the first computer printers that did double-duty as terminals.

Connect two DTE devices with an ordinary serial cable and the result will be that you have two serial devices tied together with a cable. You will not have a communications system at all. The two DTE units won't even listen to one another because each one will listen on the line that the other is listening on and talk on the line that the other talks on, if they even get that far. Lacking proper voltages on their DSR pins, they won't even try to talk.

All IBM-compatible computers (except the very special case of ATs with 9-pin serial connectors) are DTE. Modems and most mice are DCE and can be directly connected to IBM-style 25-pin serial ports. Serial printers operate as DTE, however, and present problems, as do many plotters and other peripherals.

The simple solution to the problem of connecting a serial printer to a PC is to use only parallel printers with PCs. But that's not always feasible—the serial connection gives a printer greater reach. Moreover, the serial connection may be the only one available to you.

Cross-Over Cables

If you need to connect another DTE device, such as a printer to your PC's serial port, you'll have to reverse pins 2 and 3 somewhere between the two ports. Special cables called *cross-over cables* do exactly that. In addition, most cross-over cables also swap the DTR and DSR leads as well as the RTS and CTS leads. In this way, the two DTE devices talk and listen to each other. The DTR signals from each device tell the other that it is ready, and the RTS signals act as flow control. A typical cross-over cable is shown in figure 17.2.

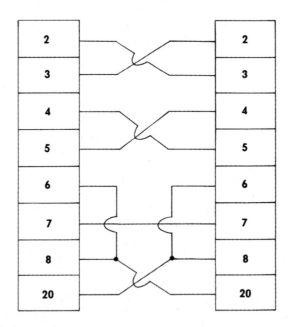

Figure 17.2. Generalized cross-over cable.

In the best of all possible worlds, such a cross-over cable between two DTE devices would work just as well as an ordinary straight-through cable between DTE and DCE. The real world is different.

The first problem is that the CD line has no corresponding match. The DTE device sends out nothing similar to a CD signal. Without the CD signal, the DTE device may be inhibited from ever sending out data.

The simple thing to do is to create a CD from something that's already at hand. Both CD and CTS have to be present for the DTE to send data out. They could be tied together, and the DTE would never know the difference. When CTS is asserted, the DTE would see CD at the same time and would know it was safe to transmit.

A variation on this theme makes the system easier to wire and more reliable. A DTE device must be turned on if it's going to produce any signal, let alone the DTR and RTS, which are flipped into DSR and CTS to let the other DTE that's party to the connection know it can send; the RTS can serve both functions. Thus one signal, RTS, through a cross-over cable can control three at the other end: DSR, CTS, and CD. These wires can actually be bridged together within the connector attached to a serial cable. In a great many cases, this cable will allow two DTE devices to communicate with one another.

This specialized cross-over cable does not work in all circumstances because not all DTE devices are wired the same. Some printers, for instance, are designed with the intention of connecting them to the serial outputs of computers that function as DTE. They consequently use a special flow-control pin on their serial connectors that differs from DTR but works in the same way. Perhaps the most common of these, used by Digital Equipment Corporation and NEC on some of their printers, devote pin 19 to flow control. Although DTR from the computer is used to control other devices, pulling its DSR, CTS, and CD high, pin 19 on these printers does the same thing. A cross-over cable that works with many such serial printers is shown in figure 17.3.

A few serial ports allow you to avoid the confusion of crossed wires and rerouted signals by making the port identity—DTE or DCE—selectable. By flipping switches or moving jumpers, you can reassign the pin definitions of these products and make them work with many serial devices using nothing more than a straight-through cable.

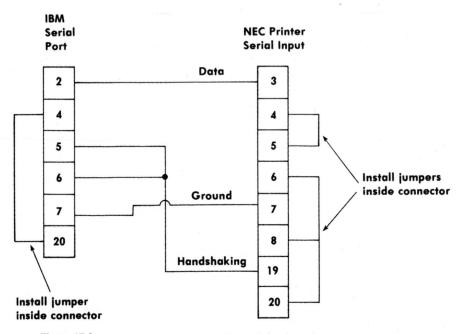

Figure 17.3. Cross-over cable for NEC and similar printers.

These indecisive ports are not a panacea, however. The serial printers that pose problems for cross-over cables by defining themselves as DTE and using pin 19 for flow control thwart the elegance of this strategy. A properly configured DCE will not provide working flow control when connected to such a DTE port through a straight-through serial cable.

One way to avoid the hassle of finding the right combination of hardware handshaking connections would appear to be letting software do it—avoiding hardware handshaking and instead using the XON-XOFF software flow control available with most serial devices. Although a good idea, even this expedient can cause hours of head scratching when nothing works as it should, or nothing works at all.

When trying to use software handshaking, it is common to have nothing happening. Without the proper software driver, your PC or PS/2 has no idea that you want to use software handshaking. It just waits for a DSR and a CTS to come rolling in from the connected serial device.

Moreover, switching to software flow control does nothing to change the sending and receiving connections of DTE and DCE. If you plan on connecting a DTE computer to a DTE printer (or whatever), you'll still need a cross-over cable even if you use software handshaking.

Null Modems

Software handshaking does free you from many of the other concerns about serial connections, however. By using local voltages, you can fool a serial port into believing that it's getting what it wants from the distant end of the cable. For instance, you can substitute the positive voltage that the PC itself provides as the DTR signal to make it believe that it has received the full complement of DSR, CTS, and CD signals by wiring the four pins together inside your serial connector.

A cable or adapter that provides this tomfoolery (usually in both directions—that is, to both ports that it is connected to) is sometimes called a *null modem*. This term has, however, lost much of its specificity. Ask for a null modem cable and you're just as likely to receive a simple cross-over cable, a cable with all of the handshaking circuits wired together, or a combination of the two that flips the data pair (pins 2 and 3) and connects the handshaking lines together. Figure 17.4 shows the wiring of a true null modem.

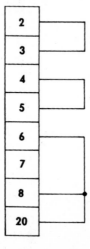

Figure 17.4. Wiring of a true null modem (a loopback connector).

The only way to be sure that such a cable is wired properly is to make it yourself. If even that's not a guarantee that it will work (or if, indeed, your skills are such that it may be a guarantee that it won't work), thoroughly scrutinize a cable wiring diagram or cable description before making your purchase.

Three-Wire Serial Connection

If the DTE device that you want to connect to your PC is a plotter or printer, you don't always have to worry about all the serial port signals. With hardware handshaking, the only thing the printer has to say to your PC is when to stop and start. A single wire can handle that. One wire also suffices for one-way data flow. A single ground will serve for both the handshaking and data signals, allowing you to hook up your serial device with as few as three wires—for data on TXD, a Signal Ground, and a handshaking line.

The reasons for making such a slimmed-down cable are several. Because there are fewer connections to make, there are fewer things to go wrong. And, when you're trying to get a system to work and you must resort to the brute force method of trial-and-error, the three-wires technique can greatly simplify your experimentation. Figure 17.5 shows two possible three-wire cables for such connections: straight-through and cross-over.

Diagnosing Serial Communication Problems

Because of all the variations in serial port connection and operation, you're apt to run into a configuration that doesn't work properly. The results of a serial mismatch range from slow or no data flow to strange characters appearing in text to serial data simply disappearing into the ether.

Sorting out such difficulties causes serial port experts to turn to their best friend, the *break-out box*. This glorified double serial connector plugs into your PC's serial port, and your serial cable plugs into it. The lights on the break-out box indicate which signals are active on the serial port. Jumpers in the break-out box let you play the equivalent of musical chairs with the serial wiring until you get a combination that lights the right lights and gets the connection working properly.

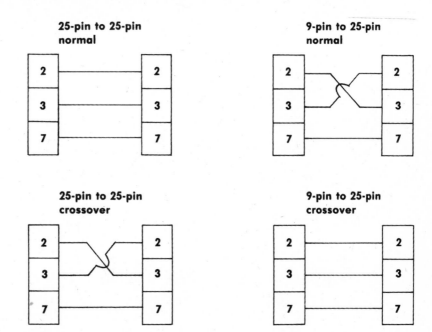

Figure 17.5. Three-wire serial cables.

But you don't need a break-out box to do basic troubleshooting. If you carefully observe the symptoms and think a bit about how serial ports work—and what can go wrong—you can often get a recalcitrant serial connection talking. The following sections are a troubleshooting guide set up as the questions you should ask yourself as you work your way through your serial problems.

Does the Port Hardware Work?

All too often we blame problems on the wrong party. What may seem to be a serial port problem could be a device disaster or cabling catastrophe. The first step in diagnosing any serial communication problem is to zero in on the area of trouble.

The chore is made easier if you already have one serial circuit that works properly. You can switch ports and see whether the problem stays with the device you are trying to use or moves with the port assignment. Check for this by moving the connection of a working serial device over to the reluctant port by moving the cable connector that's directly plugged into the port (*not* the one plugged into the serial device). If, after you alter the software to address the port being used, the serial device that you've moved works with the otherwise unwilling port, odds are that your serial port is working just fine, but you have a problem with the cabling or device attached to it.

Another preliminary check to make is whether the serial device you want to use is designed to operate as a DCE or DTE device. The cable you use will depend on the device type. When connected to an IBM-compatible computer, a DCE device should work with a straight-through cable. A DTE device connected to a PC or PS/2 will require a special cable of some kind. If the cable and device type don't match, no data will flow.

Can You Get Anything To Work?

When you don't have the luxury of having a serial port and accessory that's been proven to work, you'll have to resort to more exhaustive and exhausting testing. You can check the port by trying a known-to-be-functional serial device with it.

The best piece of test equipment is probably a Hayes-compatible modem and a known-good straight-through connecting cable. Plug the modem into the port and see if it works. If it does, you've narrowed down the problem areas to the other serial device and its cabling. If the modem doesn't work, perhaps because it was the device you were originally trying to connect to the recalcitrant circuitry, you have to dig deeper.

If you don't have a known-to-be-good serial device or the one that you have fails to work, the next step is to examine in what manner the port has failed. Actually, you've already done this in discovering that the port doesn't work. But instead of throwing up your hands in disgust, note how the failure occurred and the condition the failure left your system in.

The most common problem encountered with serial ports is that they don't work. Trying to send data to a serial port results in no response and perhaps the loss of the control of your computer, with rebooting the only medicine that will bring it back to life.

The most basic problem is that you may not have a serial port even though you think you do. You've plugged in what you think is a serial card and it isn't. Or it is a serial card but it doesn't work.

The first step is to make certain that your system recognizes the serial port. You can do so by checking the port assignments in memory using the DOS diagnostic Debug. The DUMP command (simply the letter D) in Debug will display on-screen data that is stored in memory. The particular locations of interest are those beginning at absolute address 400(hex). In PCs, XTs, and ATs, the first four bytes at 400(hex) store the port assignments of the two serial ports that the computer supports. PS/2 uses the first eight bytes to store the four port assignments that they support. As with most PC-based data, these port assignments are stored least significant byte first.

To display the serial port assignments of your system, run Debug, and then at the hyphen prompt, enter the command:

-d 40:0

This command means to dump to the display the 128 bytes starting at absolute memory location 400(hex).

For instance, if your system has one serial port, you should get a display such as this:

```
.OR80
-d          40:               0
0040:0000   F8 03 00 00 00 00 00 00-78 03 00 00 00 00 00 00   ........x.......
0040:0010   63 42 F0 C0 02 00 00 80-00 00 2A 00 2A 00 20 39   cB........*.*. 9
0040:0020   34 05 30 0B 3A 27 30 0B-0D 1C 09 0F 0B 25 66 21   4.0.:'0......%f!
0040:0030   64 20 65 12 62 30 75 16-67 22 0D 1C 64 20 01 80   d e.b0u.g"..d ..
0040:0040   4E 00 00 00 00 00 00 09-02 03 50 00 00 10 00 00   N.........P.....
0040:0050   00 18 00 00 00 00 00 00-00 00 00 00 00 00 00 00   ................
0040:0060   07 06 00 D4 03 29 30 98-00 B3 09 04 F3 5F 0B 00   .....)0......._..
0040:0070   00 00 00 00 00 01 00 00-14 14 14 14 01 01 01 01   ................
.OR60
```

The first two bytes indicate that this system has a single serial port assigned at port number 03F8(hex), exactly where it belongs.

Is There a Port Resource Conflict?

If you do have the luxury of more than one port but you also have the pain that none of them work or that they don't work in pairs, the problem could be a conflict in their port assignments. You may have two ports that are both trying to be COM1, for instance. With two different pieces of hardware responding to each of your computer's commands, neither you nor your software will have any idea which of the pair is responding when. Your system may behave intermittently or not at all.

You can easily walk into the dual port trap when your system comes equipped with a standard equipment serial output built into its system board, and you add an internal modem, multifunction board, or some mouse adapters. Because neither the computer nor the add-in product has made you specifically tangle with a serial port, you can easily forget about one of them. If it happens, as it usually does, that serial systems have chosen the same port assignment, confusion will reign until you sort it out.

The first step in analyzing any serial problem is, then, counting the number of ports in your system. Add-in serial boards, multifunction products with built-in ports, internal modems, standard-equipment system board serial ports, and mouse adapter boards that use a serial connection all count.

If you count more than two ports and have a PC, XT, or AT, you'll have to do some thinking. If one of them is an internal modem, odds are you'll be able to assign it as COM3, which is the proper thing to do. Many communication packages—presumably including the one that may have been included with the internal modem—will recognize this COM3 as a legitimate port assignment. DOS and your PC will not recognize this port, so you won't be able to use the DOS MODE command to make it accessible as a printer port. Because you're unlikely to use the DOS MODE command to manipulate your modem directly through DOS, you probably won't miss it.

Similarly, the driver software that accompanies the mouse-and-adapter board combination should allow you to assign the mouse interface to a series of ports that won't collide with your regular serial communications.

If you still end up with more than two ports, you'll have to disable the excess.

Are Interrupts Properly Assigned?

Some serial boards force you to assign serial ports and the interrupts that service them separately, perhaps through moving separate jumpers. If you receive the board with the port assignments for COM1 but its interrupt is set for COM2 or you accidentally set it up that way, the serial port may work intermittently or not at all.

Other peripherals might also attempt to use one of the interrupts that should be assigned to your serial port. For instance, a tape backup system or a bus mouse that purports not to use a serial port may try to steal interrupt 3 from your COM2 serial port.

One prime symptom of this condition is sporadic operation of the port. Sometimes it works and sometimes it doesn't, depending on what other accessories you're using. Of course, another device may totally preempt the serial port and prevent its operating at all.

The obvious solution to this sort of problem is to ensure that every port has its own interrupt, and reassign those that are in conflict—if you can. The PC and XT are notoriously short of hardware interrupts to assign to peripherals.

Do You Have Handshaking?

If your serial port suffers no interrupt or address port conflicts and otherwise seems operable but fails to work with a specific serial device, the likely cause is a lack of handshaking. This problem is most likely when your serial port failure does not totally lock up your system but, instead, allows you to abort whatever you were trying to do with the serial port, perhaps by pressing Ctrl-Break or Ctrl-C. The likely cause is that the handshake wiring of this serial circuit is not arranged properly.

Remember, unless you have software that specifically nullifies the need, a PC, XT, AT, or PS/2 requires that its handshaking demands be met before a byte leaves any serial port. In addition, mismatching DCE and DTE devices and their cables will invariably guarantee a failure of handshaking.

You can verify handshaking in two ways: testing and the empirical approach.

Testing requires a volt-ohm meter (or VOM) or a digital logic probe. Simply dig into the connector attached to the serial port in question and measure the voltages or logic states at the DSR, CTS, and CD pins. If handshaking signals are present, you should measure a positive voltage, usually in excess of five volts, when you touch each of the three pins. The indicator of the logic probe should glow when touched to these pins.

Empirically, you can connect the DSR, CTS, and CD pins directly to DTR to ensure that handshaking is present at least at the PC-end of the circuit. You can either solder the necessary wires in place (a messy solution, but one that works) or invest in a break-out box that will allow you to experiment. If, after making this adjustment, your PC acts differently, as if it has sent at least some characters to the serial device, you had a handshaking problem. (If your PC acts like it has sent out data and the serial device—such as a printer—acts as if it has received nothing, odds are your TXD and RXD lines need to be crossed, and what you thought was a DCE was a DTE device.)

Are Characters Disappearing?

If your serial device seems to work okay but loses characters from whatever is sent to it, the likely cause is a flow control problem. Typically, a serial printer will rattle out characters that appear just fine until you try to read them. Characters, words, sentences, and whole paragraphs may disappear. Lines may ignore margin settings because carriage return and line feed characters get lost on their way from computer to printer, too.

The problem is caused by handshaking working too well. Instead of the handshake signal being interrupted when the receiving device has no room to work with incoming characters, the handshake signals are locked on. To your computer, your printer always looks as if it wants more, more, more, even though it is choking on what it has already received.

Check the connection used for flow control—it may be CTS or something totally unrelated (such as DEC and NEC's pin 19)—and ensure that it is connected to DSR or CTS on your PC. In addition, verify that both devices in your serial system are using the same flow control protocol. If your computer is dumping characters under hardware control, your printer may be futilely sending XOFF after XOFF trying to stave the flow. If protocols don't match, you'll likely lose characters.

Are Print Jobs Truncated?

If your serial print jobs finish before you think they should, for instance, before the last page is printed, or if your serial print jobs suddenly stop with an error message like Device Timeout Error, the cause is simply that you forgot to add the P parameter to the end of the MODE command you used to set up your computer's serial port parameters. The printer does not respond fast enough to satisfy your computer, so it thinks something is wrong.

Do You Get Gibberish?

If your serial system gives every indication of working except all that it produces is gibberish, you probably have not properly matched serial port parameters at the two ends of the connection. Your computer is sending characters at one bit rate, and the serial device is expecting to receive them at another. Similarly, you may have your computer set for odd parity when the other end of the connection is expecting even. The two devices are not speaking the same language, so it's natural that they would get confused. The solution to the problem is simply to match the communications parameters at both ends of the connection.

18

Modems

T he greatest power and strength in using a computer comes not from sitting at a solitary keyboard but by connecting with other machines and exchanging files, programs, and information across telephone lines. Because today's telephone lines are analog and computers are digital, you need a modem to match them. But modems run a tremendous variety in speed and features.

For some reason known but to God and the infidels who figure out the most profitable hardware packages to call computers, the modem—perhaps the most desired and used computer peripheral—remains an option in all but a random sampling of portable computers. The modem is the one computer feature that lets you display the personality of your personal computer to the outside world. It puts you in touch with on-line databases, remote computer systems, far-flung friends, and even those who are still flinging around the country.

The purpose and function of the modem seem almost absurd in their simplicity. The modem merely connects your computer to the telephone line. The need for the extra device seems so absurd because both computer and telephone use ostensibly the same stuff of making and moving messages—electrical signals. Were not the giant corporations specializing in computers and telephones (we won't name names) and not such avowed rivals, you might suspect that they were in cahoots to foist such a contrived accessory on the computer marketplace.

Step back and look at what a modem does, however, and you'll gain new respect for the device. In many ways, the modern modem is a miracle worker. For instance, the best of today's modems can squeeze more than a dozen data bits through a cable where only one should fit. Even the least expensive generic modem operates like a specialized time machine that can bridge the century-wide chasm cutting between state-of-the-art computer and stone-age telephone technologies.

Far from the hatchlings of some plot by the military-industrial complex—or that even more sinister force, the telephone company—modems are a necessary bridge between digital and analog signals. The modern modem usually does much more than connect. Most are boxes chock full of convenience features that can make using them fast, simple, and automatic. The best of today's modems not only make and monitor the connection, but improve it. They dial the phone for you, even remembering the number you want and trying again and again. They listen in until they're sure of good contact, and only then let you transmit across the telephone line. Some even have built-in circuits to detect and correct the inevitable errors that creep into your electrical conversations.

Modem Operating Principles

A modem is a signal converter that mediates the communications between a computer and the telephone network. The very name "modem" indicates the role that it plays. The term is a shortening of the words *MO*dulator/*DEM*odulator. As a modulator, the modem converts the digital, direct current pulses used by the computer system into an analog signal containing the same information, a process called *modulation*.

Modulating and Demodulating

Modulation is necessary because the telephone system was designed even before electronics was invented and solid-state digital circuitry lay almost a hundred years off. The first pained words out of Dr. Bell's speaking telegraph were analog electrical signals, the same juice that flows through the receiver of your own telephone. Although strictly speaking, digital communications are older—the conventional telegraph predates the telephone by nearly three decades (Samuel F. B. Morse wondered what God had wrought in 1844)—current digital technology is only a recent phenomenon.

The telephone system was designed to handle only analog signals because that's all that speaking into a microphone creates. Over the years, the telephone system has evolved into an elaborate international network capable of handling millions of these analog signals simultaneously and switching them from one telephone set to another, anywhere in the world and possibly beyond. Although telephone companies are increasingly using digital signals to move trunk line communications between switching centers, the input and output ends of the circuit still end in conventional analog-based telephones, at least for the time being. In the future, you'll undoubtedly connect to an all-digital telephone system—ISDN is just a first step—but for today, you're still stuck with analog connections.

Modulation, and hence modems, are necessary because these analog telephone connections will not allow digital, direct current signals to pass freely or at all. The modulation process creates analog signals that code all the digital information of the computer original but can be transmitted through the voice-only channels of the telephone system.

Demodulation reverses the modulation process. At the other end of the connection, the modem as a demodulator receives that analog-coded signal and converts it back to its original digital form while preserving its information content.

The Carrier

The actual processor of modulation superimposes one signal on another. The modem as modulator starts its modulation process by generating a constant signal called the *carrier* because it carries or bears the load of the modulating information. In most systems, the carrier is a steady-state signal of constant amplitude (strength) and frequency, and coherent phase.

Modulation

The signal that's electrically mixed with the carrier to modify some aspect of it is given the same name as the process, *modulation*. Changes in the modulation result in a change in the carrier-and-modulation mix. The change in the modulation makes a corresponding change in the carrier, but not necessarily a change in the same aspect of the carrier. For instance, in FM or frequency modulation, a change in the *strength* of the modulation is reflected as a change in the *frequency* of the carrier.

Modulation brings several benefits, more than enough to justify the complication of combining signals. Because electronic circuits can be tuned to accept the frequency of one carrier wave and reject others, multiple modulated signals can be sent through a single communications medium. This principle underlies all radio communication and broadcasting. In addition, modulation allows digital, direct-current-based information to be transmitted through a medium, like the telephone system, that otherwise could not carry direct current signals.

In demodulation, the carrier is stripped away and the encoded information is returned to its original form. Although logically just the complement of modulation, demodulation usually involves entirely different circuits and operating principles, which adds to the complexity of the modem.

Short-Haul Modems

Some so-called modems aren't even modems at all. The inexpensive *short-haul modems* advertised for stretching the link between your PC and serial printer, actually involve minimal circuitry, definitely not enough to modulate and demodulate signals. So little, in fact, that often it is entirely hidden inside the shell of a simple cable connector. All that the short-haul modem does is convert the digital output of a computer to another digital form that can better withstand the rigors of a thousand feet of wire. Don't confuse short-haul modems with the real thing. A short-haul modem won't communicate over a dial-up telephone system and isn't even legal to plug into your telephone wiring.

Channel Limits

Like all great works of art, the modem is constrained to work within the limits of its medium, the telephone channel. These limits are imposed by the characteristics of analog communications and the communications medium that's used (primarily unshielded twisted-pair wire).

Signal Bandwidth

All communications channels and the signals that travel through them have a characteristic called *bandwidth*. Bandwidth merely specifies a range of frequencies from the lowest to the highest that the channel can carry or are present in the signal.

An unmodulated carrier wave has a nominal operating frequency. For example, in radio broadcasting, it's the number you dial in when you tune in your favorite station. Without modulation, the carrier wave uses only that one frequency and has essentially zero bandwidth.

The modulation that's added to the carrier contains information that varies at some rate. Traditional analog signal sources, music or voice signals, for instance, contain a near-random mix of frequencies between 20 and 20,000 Hz. Although digital signals start off as DC, which also has no bandwidth, every change in digital state adds a frequency component. The faster the states change, the more information that's squeezed down the digital channel, as measured in its bit rate (bits per second), the more bandwidth the signal occupies.

Sidebands

In the simplest modulation systems, a modulated carrier requires twice the bandwidth of the modulation signal. Although this doubling sounds anomalous, it's the direct result of the combining of the signals. Mixing the carrier and modulation results in *modulation products*. These products correspond to the frequency of the modulation *added to* the carrier plus the frequency of the modulation and *subtracted from* the carrier. The added result is often called the *upper sideband*, and the subtracted result is correspondingly called the *lower sideband*.

Because these upper and lower modulation products are essentially redundant (they contain exactly the same information), one or the other can be eliminated without loss of information to reduce the bandwidth of the modulated carrier to that of the modulation. (This form of bandwidth savings, termed *single sideband* modulation, is commonly used in broadcasting to squeeze more signals into the limited radio spectrum.)

Even with sideband squeezing, the fundamental fact remains that any modulated signal requires a finite range of frequencies to hold its information. The limits of this frequency range define the bandwidth required by the modulated signal.

Channel Bandwidth

The bandwidth of a communications channel defines the frequency limits of the signals that it can carry. This channel bandwidth may be physically limited by the medium used by the channel or artificially limited by communications standards. For instance, the bandwidths of radio transmissions are limited artificially, by law, to allow more different modulated carriers to share the air waves while preventing interference between them.

In wire-based communications channels, bandwidth is often limited by the wires themselves. Certain physical characteristics of wires causes degradations in their high-frequency transmission capabilities. The *capacitance* between conductors in a cable pair, for instance, increasingly degrades signals as their frequencies rise to the point that a high-frequency signal might not be able to traverse more than a few centimeters of wire. *Amplifiers* or *repeaters*, which boost signals so that they can travel longer distances, often cannot handle very low or very high frequencies, imposing more limits.

Most telephone channels also have an artificial bandwidth limitation imposed by the telephone company. To get the greatest financial potential from the capacity of their transmissions cables, microwave systems, and satellites, telephone carriers normally limit the bandwidth of telephone signals. One reason bandwidth is limited is so that many separate telephone conversations can be stacked atop of one another through *multiplexing* techniques, which allow a single pair of wires to carry hundreds of simultaneous conversations. Although the effects of bandwidth limitation are obvious, that's why your phone doesn't sound as good as your stereo. The telephone company multiplexing equipment works so well that you are generally unaware of all the manipulations made on the voice signals as they are squeezed through wires.

Bandwidth Limitations

One of the consequences of telephone company signal manipulations is a severe limitation in the bandwidth of an ordinary telephone channel. Instead of the full frequency range of a good-quality stereo system, from 20 to 20,000 Hz, a telephone channel will allow frequencies between only 300 and 3,000 Hz to freely pass. This very narrow bandwidth works well for telephones because frequencies below 300 Hz contain most of the power of the human voice but little of its *intelligibility*. Frequencies above 3,000 Hz increase the crispness of the sound but don't add appreciably to intelligibility.

Although intelligibility is the primary concern with voice communications (most of the time), data transfer is principally oriented to bandwidth. The comparatively narrow bandwidth of the standard telephone channel limits the bandwidth of the modulated signal it can carry, which, in turn, limits the amount of digital information that can be squeezed down the phone line by a modem.

Try some simple math and you'll see the harsh constraints faced by your modem's signals. A telephone channel typically has a useful bandwidth of about 2,700 Hz (from 300 to 3,000 Hz). At most, a carrier wave at exactly the center of the telephone channel (1,650 Hz) and burdened by both sidebands could carry data that varies at a rate of 1,650 Hz. Such a signal would fill the entire bandwidth of the telephone channel without allowing for a safety margin.

Shannon's Limit

The limit on the amount of data that can be squeezed through an analog telephone line reflects a combination of the bandwidth of the channel and the noise level in the channel. The greater the noise, the harder it is for information to compete with it. This theoretical maximum data rate is called Shannon's limit. For today's two-way dial-up telephone connections under ideal conditions, the limit reaches about 19,200 bits per second. However, practical considerations and real-world modem hardware further constrain data rates.

Safety Margin

A safety margin is necessary, however, because the quality of telephone lines varies greatly, particularly when long distance connections are involved. Because poor connections can't handle the nominal 300 to 3,000 Hz telephone bandwidth, it's ill-advised for a modem to try to take advantage of that entire frequency spread. If the connection is substandard, when the data rate reaches the fringes of the bandwidth, errors are likely to creep in.

Duplex

The usable bandwidth of a data communications channel through a modem is also limited because most modem communications are handled in *duplex* mode. The term "duplex," often redundantly called *full-duplex*, describes the capability of a communications channel to simultaneously handle two signals, usually (but not necessarily) going in opposite directions. Using these two channels, a full-duplex modem can send and receive information at the same time. Two carriers are used to simultaneously transmit and receive data. Using two carriers, of course, halves the bandwidth available to each.

Half-Duplex

The alternative to duplex communications is *half-duplex*. In half-duplex, only one signal is used, and to carry on a two-way conversation, a modem must alternately send and receive signals. Half-duplex allows more of the channel bandwidth to be put to use, but, in practice, slows data communications because, often, a modem must switch between sending and receiving modes after every block of data crawls through the channel.

Echoplex

The term "duplex" is often, and mistakenly, used to describe *echoplex* operation. In echoplex mode, a modem sends a character down the phone line, and the distant modem returns the same character, echoing it. The echoed character is then displayed on the originating terminal as confirmation the character was sent correctly. Without echoplex, the host computer usually writes the transmitted character directly to its monitor screen.

Guard Bands

Duplex does more than cut the bandwidth available to each channel in half. Separating the two channels is a *guard band*, a width of unused frequencies that isolate the active channels and prevent confusion between their separate carriers. The safety margin is, in effect, also a guard between the carriers and the varying limit of the bandwidth.

Once you add in the needs of duplex communication and the guard bands, the practical bandwidth limit for modem communications over real telephone channels that have an innate 2,700 Hz bandwidth works out to about 2,400 Hz. That leaves 1,200 Hz for each of the two duplex channels.

Modem Modulation Methods

For the job of making modulation, a modem has several methods available to it, much as AM and FM radio stations use different modulation methods. The different forms of modulation all are based on the characteristics of the carrier wave that can be changed to encode information.

Three of the primary carrier characteristics that might be used for modulation are its amplitude, its frequency, and its phase.

Amplitude Modulation

The amplitude is the strength of the signal or the loudness of a tone carried through the telephone wire. Varying the strength of the carrier in response to modulation to transmit information is called *amplitude modulation*.

One way that digital information could be coded with amplitude modulation is as two discrete strengths of the signal corresponding to the two digital states. In fact, the most rudimentary form of amplitude modulation, which has earned the special name *Carrier Wave*, or *CW*, transmission, uses the two limits of carrier strength for its code: full power and zero power. The loudness of a telephone signal is its most likely characteristic to vary, however, with both changes in the telephone line and noise that might be picked up by the line. Consequently, pure amplitude modulation is not used by modems.

Phase Modulation

Another state of the carrier that can be altered to encode information is its phase. An unmodulated carrier is a constant train of identical waves that follow one after another precisely in step. If one wave were delayed for exactly one wavelength, it would fit exactly atop the next one. The peaks and troughs of the train of waves flow by at constant intervals.

By delaying one of the waves without altering its amplitude or frequency, a detectable state change called a *phase shift* is created. The onset of one wave is shifted in time compared to those that preceded it. Information can be coded as *phase modulation* by assigning one amount of phase shift from the constant carrier to a digital one and another to a digital zero. One particular type of phase modulation called *quadrature modulation* alters the phase of the signal in increments of 90 degrees. That is, the modulated carrier will differ from the unmodulated carrier wave by a phase angle of 0, 90, 180, or 270 degrees. Although this form of modulation is useful in modem communications, it is most often used in combination with other modulation techniques.

Frequency Modulation

The other alternative modulation technique alters the frequency of the carrier in response to the modulation. For instance, a higher amplitude of modulation might be made to cause the carrier to shift upward in frequency. This technique, called *frequency modulation* is commonly used in radio broadcasting by FM stations.

Frequency Shift Keying

In the most rudimentary digital form of frequency modulation, a digital one would cause the carrier wave to change from one frequency to another. In other words, one frequency would signify a digital one, and another discrete frequency would signify a digital zero. This form of modulation is called *frequency shift keying,* or *FSK,* because information is encoded in (think of it being "keyed to") the shifting of frequency. The keying part of the name is actually left over from the days of telegraphy when this form of modulation was used for transmitting

Morse code and the frequency shift came with the banging of the telegraph key. Frequency shift keying is used in the most rudimentary of popular modems, the once-ubiquitous 300 bit-per-second modem that operated under the Bell 103 standard.

Baud Rates

With such modems one bit of data causes one corresponding change of frequency in the carrier wave. Every change of frequency or state carries exactly one bit of information. The unit of measurement used to describe the number of state changes taking place in one second is the *baud*. In the particular case of the FSK modulation, one change of state per second, one baud, conveys exactly one bit of information per second.

Depending on the number of states used in the communication system, a single transition, one baud, can convey less than or more than one bit of information. For instance, several different frequencies of tones might be used to code information. The changing from one frequency to another would take place at one baud, yet because of the different possible changes that could be made, more than one bit of information could be coded by that transition. Hence, strictly speaking, one baud is *not* the same as one bit per second, although the terms are often, and incorrectly, used interchangeably.

The number of bits that can be coded by baud varies by the inverse logarithm of the number of available states (tones, voltage, or phases). Most 1,200 bit-per-second modems operate at 600 baud with four different states available, and most 2,400 bit-per-second modems operate at 600 baud with 16 different states.

In case you're interested, the term "baud" was named after J.M.E. Baudot, a French telegraphy expert. His name is also used to describe a five-bit digital code used in Teletype systems.

FSK Modems

This 300 bit-per-second rate using the simple FSK technique requires a bandwidth of 600 Hz. The two 300 baud carriers (which require a 1,200 Hz bandwidth, two times 600 Hz) and a wide guard band fit comfortably within the 2,700 Hz limit.

Under the Bell 103 standard, which is used by most 300 bit-per-second modems, the two carrier frequencies are 1,200 and 2,200 Hz. Space modulation (logical zeros) shifts the carrier down by 150 Hz, and mark modulation pushes the carrier frequency up by an equal amount.

Because the FSK modulation technique is relatively simple, 300-baud modems are generally inexpensive. Because they don't push out to the limits of the available bandwidth, they are generally reliable even with marginal connections.

Using the same simple modulation technique and exploiting more of the 2,700 Hz bandwidth of the typical telephone line, modem speeds can be doubled to 600 baud. Beyond that rate, however, lies the immovable bandwidth roadblock.

High-Speed Modems

Modems that operate at data rates in excess of 2,400 bits per second are generally classed as *high-speed modems*. The distinction is as qualitative as it is quantitative. Above 2,400 bps, squeezing more information into the confines of the telephone line becomes increasingly difficult, requiring inventive modulation techniques quite unlike those used at lower rates.

Group Coding

A data communications rate of 300 bits per second is slow, slower than most folks can read text flowing across the screen. Even the slowest PC can absorb information at least 32 times faster, limited by the maximum serial port speed that IBM supports. Were long distance communications limited to the 300 bit-per-second rate, the only people who would be happy would be the shareholders of the various telephone companies. Information could, at best, crawl slowly across the continent.

By combining several modulation techniques, modern modems can achieve much higher data rates through ordinary dial-up telephone lines. Instead of merely manipulating the carrier one way, they may modify two (or more) aspects of the constant wave. For instance, today's most popular 1,200 and 2,400 bit-per-second modems combine frequency and phase modulation to achieve faster data flow.

These more complex forms of modulation add no extra bandwidth—remember, that's a function of the communications channel—but they take advantage of the possibility of coding digital data as changes between a variety of states of the carrier wave. For instance, the carrier wave can be phase-modulated with quadrature modulation so that it assumes one of four states.

Although you might expect these four states to quadruple modem speed, the relationship is not quite that direct. To convert states into digital information, modems use a technique called *group coding* in which one state encodes a specific pattern of bits. For example, the four different phase states are sufficient to encode the four different patterns of two digital bits. Consequently, with quadrature modulation with four states, each baud can encode any of four two-bit patterns of data—four states code two bits. Thus, a quadrature-modulated 600-baud modem can communicate at double its baud rate, 1,200 bits per second.

Group coding is the key to advanced modulation techniques. Instead of dealing with data one bit at a time, bits of digital code are processed as groups. Each group of data bits is encoded as one particular state of the carrier.

The ultimate speed of the mode is determined by the number of states that are available for coding. The relationship is not linear, however. As the number of bits in the code increases by a given figure (and thus the potential speed of the modulation technique rises by the same figure), the number of states required increases to the corresponding power of two. Twice as fast requires four states; four times faster requires 16 states; eight times as fast requires 256 states; and so on.

For example, data rates of 2,400 bps can be achieved by using a modulation method that's even more complex than quadrature modulation that yields 16 discrete states while still operating at 600 baud. Each state encodes one of the 16 different patterns of four digital bits. One baud on the telephone line carries the information of four bits going into the modem.

According to the free lunch principle, this system of seemingly getting something for nothing using complex modulation must have a drawback. With high-speed modems the problem is that the quality of the telephone line becomes increasingly critical as the data rate is increased. Moreover, as modem speeds get faster, each phone line blip carries more information, and a single error soon can have devastating effects.

Leased-Line Modems

One way to coax higher speed from a modem is to forego the one part of the connection that imposes the severe bandwidth limitation: the telephone line. Special high-grade circuits can be rented from telephone companies to whisk data from point to point at almost unbelievably high data rates (from ten thousand to millions of bits per second). The special lines are semi-permanently installed and stretch directly from one location to another, never allowed to venture through the rigors of the telephone switching system. Because these special lines are leased by the month (or other period), they are called *leased-lines* and the modems that use them are termed *leased-line* or *dedicated-line* modems. They usually lack the dialing and answering features of dial-up modems, and are meant for continuous connections.

Dial-Up Modems

In contrast, the modems with which you are likely most familiar, the ones that tie into the telephone switching system, are distinguished as *dial-up* modems. They face the constraints of the telephone system and must be capable of dealing with its special problems and shortcomings. However, they are the most useful because they can reach nearly anyone, anywhere, as long as the modems at the two ends of the call are compatible with one another.

Line Compensation

Although a long distance telephone connection may sound unchanging to your ear, its electrical characteristics vary by the moment. Everything from a wire swaying in the Wichita wind to the phone company's automatic rerouting of the call through Bangkok when the direct circuits fill up can change the amplitude, frequency, and phase response of the circuit. The modem then faces two challenges, not to interpret such changes as data and to maintain the quality of the line to a high enough standard to support its use for high-speed transmission.

Switching Modems

Perhaps the biggest limit imposed on high-speed modem communications is the use of full-duplex communications. Because a complete duplex modem circuit is essentially two complete channels, each can have (at most) only half the telephone line's bandwidth available to it. Most of the time, however, communications go only in one direction. You key in commands to a remote access system, and only after the commands are received does the remote system respond with the information that you seek. Although one end is sending, the other end is more than likely to be completely idle.

To make better use of the available bandwidth, so-called *switching modems* are designed to make use of the full bandwidth of the telephone channel, switching the direction of the signal as each end of the line needs to send data. Such modems are able to achieve a doubling of data rate without adding any complexity to their modulation. In remote mainframe access situations, where the protocol of the call fits the mold of the two ends of the connections taking turns using the phone line, switching modems can give a genuine boost to the cross-country throughput of a modem system.

Asymmetrical Modems

Switching doesn't always work, however. The change of direction of communication isn't instantaneous. The modem has no way of knowing when to switch other than listening for a pause in the data stream. Some delay to recognize such a pause must be built into the system. Further, when the direction of the call changes, the modem may be called to adjust for line differences (the characteristics of a telephone connection are not necessarily the same in both directions, the two directions of communication may take entirely different paths). In all, switching the direction of the data movement can take a full second.

Although a second pause may not be burdensome when you're simply sending characters and watching a response on the screen, it can be overwhelming when transferring a file. Most file-transfer protocols (for instance, XMODEM and Kermit) are designed to send a small block of data to the remote system, which then checks it for accuracy, and finally sends a brief return message that the data was received intact or that it was bad. A switching modem may require a full second or more for each turn-around and confirmation. In that some protocols use blocks only 256 or 512 bytes long between confirmations, sending a file amounts to the classic hurry-up-and-wait syndrome. The modems blast a block across the line, then loll around for a much longer period awaiting a confirmation.

In an attempt to get the best of both worlds, *asymmetrical modems* cut the waiting by maintaining a semblance of two-way duplex communications while optimizing speed *in one direction only* by shoehorning in a low-speed (typically 300 bps) channel in addition to the high-speed one. As with a switching modem, asymmetrical modems can flip-flop the direction of the high-speed communications. They rely on algorithms to determine which way is the best way. Typically, the high-speed channel is used for transferring blocks of data while the confirmations trickle back on the lower speed channel. FAX modems use this scheme.

Fallback

Most modems use at most two carriers for duplex communications. These carriers are usually modulated to fill the available bandwidth. Sometimes, however, the quality of the telephone line is not sufficient to allow reliable communications over the full bandwidth expected by the modem. In such cases, most high-speed modems incorporate *fallback* capabilities. When the top speed does not work, they attempt to communicate at lower speeds that are less critical of telephone line quality. The pair of modems might first try 9,600 bps and be unsuccessful. They next might try 4,800, then 2,400, and so on until reliable communications are established.

Multiple-Carrier Modems

Although most modems rely on a relatively complex form of modulation on one or two carriers to achieve high-speed, one clever idea now relegated to a historical footnote by the latest modem standards is the *multiple-carrier modem*, which uses relatively simple modulation on several simultaneous carrier signals. One of the chief advantages of this system comes into play when the quality of the telephone connection deteriorates. Instead of dropping down to the next incremental communications rate, generally cutting data speed in half, the multiple-carrier modems just stop using the carriers in the doubtful regions of the bandwidth. The communication rate may fall off only a few percent in the adjustment. (Of course, it could dip by as much as a normal fallback modem as well.)

Data Compression

Although there's no way of increasing the number of bits that can cross a telephone line beyond the capacity of the channel, the information-handling capability of the modem circuit can be increased by making each bit more meaningful. Many of the bits that are sent through the telecommunication channel are meaningless or redundant, they convey no additional information. By eliminating those worthless bits, the information content of the data stream is more intense, and each bit is more meaningful. The process of paring the bits is called *data compression.*

The effectiveness of compression varies with the type of data that's being transmitted. One of the most prevalent data compression schemes encodes repetitive data, eight recurrences of the same byte value might be coded as two bytes, one signifying the value and the second the number of repetitions. This form of compression is most effective on graphics, which often have many blocks of repeating text. Other compression methods may strip out start, stop, and parity bits. Modem manufacturers often claim that their proprietary data compression methods might reduce the number of bits that need to be transferred by 50 percent, effectively doubling communications speed.

Data compression need not take place in the modem. You can also compress files inside your PC *before* you send them out to your modem. Sending a file compressed to half its size will take half as long to transmit. *File compression* streamlines the digital coding of files, allowing them to be squeezed down to a fraction of their normal size. Sort of like dehydrating soup, the vital contents can be more easily stored and reconstituted when needed.

The same trick can help when stretching storage resources, too. Program distributors can save costs by perhaps doubling the capacity of each floppy disk they use. And anyone with a hard disk oozing data out its seams can save, by choosing compression instead of a hardware upgrade, a few dollars instead of a few thousand to increase storage capacity. Nearly all file-compression programs allow multiple files to be grouped together in a single archive file and provide utilities (or options) for checking which file is in what archive.

File compression has become standard in places where storage space is at a premium and time for transferring data must be minimized. Electronic bulletin boards almost universally deal in archives, files compressed one way or another to take best advantage of their resources. Most archival data compression products began as *shareware* products that were distributed through bulletin boards that they served. They were distributed free, but required a modest licensing fee for continuing (and commercial) use, relying on word-of-mouth to advertise their capabilities. As others beyond bulletin board operators and their users have discovered the usefulness of file-compression programs, commercial vendors have joined the list of suppliers, both tailoring compression for special applications and joining the mainstream with archiving utilities that pack data tightly as possible.

The first program to win wide acceptance for file compression and archiving among bulletin board operators was ARC from System Enhancement Associates. Since its introduction in 1985, ARC has been revised a number of times and has been distributed as shareware. ARC uses two forms of compression (repeated-character and dynamic Lempel-Ziv compression) of which the program itself picks the most effective. Files compressed using ARC are distinguished by their use of the file name extension .ARC.

Many bulletin boards have abandoned ARC file compression for a competing product, PKzip from PKware Inc. Reasons vary. Some people did not like SEA's aggressive use of the legal system against PKware. Others found PKzip to be faster, more efficient, and more versatile in file compression. As with ARC, PKzip is distributed as shareware.

These programs differ in the algorithms they use for streamlining data, whimsically identifying their particular techniques as crunching, squashing, compressing, squeezing, imploding, distilling, almost anything short of transmogrification (and that may appear at any time). Necessarily they yield different file formats. Although some are compatible with the formats used by others, you have no guarantee that one compression program can decompress a file packed by another.

One word of warning. Once a file is compressed, it usually can be compressed no further. Consequently, modems with built-in file compression, such as those that follow the MNP5 or v.42bis standards, won't be able to further compress such files. In fact, sometimes MNP5 takes longer to transmit a compressed file than sending the file would take without using MNP5 compression. Software compression programs are thus an alternative rather than supplement to hardware data compression in modems.

Error Checking and Error Correction

Because all higher speed modems operate closer to the limits of the telephone channel, they are naturally more prone to data errors. To better cope with such problems, nearly all high-speed modems have their own built-in *error-checking* methods (which detect only transmission errors) and *error correction* (which detects data errors and corrects the mistakes before they get passed along to your PC). These error-checking and error-correction systems work like communications protocols, grouping bytes into blocks and sending cyclical redundancy checking information. They differ from the protocols used by communications software in that they are implemented in the hardware instead of your computer's software. That means they don't load down your computer when it's straining at the limits of its serial ports.

It can also mean that software protocols are redundant and a waste of time. As mentioned before in the case of switching modems, using a software-based communications protocol can be counterproductive with many high-speed modems, slowing the transfer rate to a crawl. Most makers of modems using built-in error-checking will advise against using such software protocols.

All modem error-detection and error-correction systems require that both ends of the connection use the same error-handling protocol. In order that modems can talk to one another, a number of standards have been developed. Today, the most popular are MNP4 and v.42, both defined below as standards. You'll also sometimes see a couple abbreviations describing error-handling methods: LAPB and LAPM.

LAPB stands for Link Access Procedure, Balanced, an error-correction protocol designed for X.25 packet-switched services, such as Telebit and Tymnet. Some high-speed modem makers adapted this standard to their dial-up modem products before the v.42 standard was agreed on. For example, the Hayes Smartmodem 9,600 from Hayes Micro-computer Products includes LAPB error-control capabilities.

LAPM is an acronym for Link Access Procedure for Modems and is the error-correction protocol used by the CCITT v.42 standard.

Modem Standards

Neither men nor modems are islands. Above all, they must communicate and share their ideas with others. One modem would do the world no good; it would just send data out into the vast analog unknown, never to be seen (or heard) again, sort of like writing a letter to the editor of your local newspaper.

But having two modems isn't automatically enough. Like people, modems must speak the same language for the utterances of one to be understood by the other. Modulation is part of the modem language. In addition, modems must be able to understand the error-correction features and data-compression routines used by one another. Unlike most human beings who speak any of a zillion languages and dialects, each somewhat ill-defined, modems are much more precise in the languages they use. The have their own equivalent of the French Academy and standards organizations.

In the United States, the first standards were set long ago by the most powerful force in the telecommunications industry, the telephone company. More specifically, the American Telephone and Telegraph Company, the Bell System, which promoted various Bell standards, the most famous being Bell 103 and Bell 212A. After the Bell System was split into AT&T and the seven regional operating companies (Baby Bells, a situation also known as AT&T and the seven dwarfs), other long distance carriers broke into the telephone monopoly. Moreover, other nations have (not surprisingly) become interested in telecommunications.

As a result of these developments, the onus and capability to set standards moved from AT&T to an international standards organization, the *Comite Consultatif International Telegraphique et Telephoneique,* or CCITT (in English, International Telegraph and Telephone Consultative Committee). All of the high-speed standards used by modems today and the immediate future are sanctioned by the CCITT. These standards include v.22bis, v.32, v.32bis, v.42, and v.42bis.

Along the way, a modem and software maker, Microcom, developed a series of standards prefixed with the letters MNP, such as MNP4 and MNP5. The letters stand for Microcom Networking Protocol.

Standards are important when buying a modem because they are your best assurance that a given modem can successfully connect with any other modem in the world. In addition, the standards you choose will determine how fast your modem can transfer data and how reliably it will work. The kind of communications you want to carry out will determine what kind of modem you need. If you're just going to send files electronically between offices, you can buy two nonstandard modems and get more speed for your investment. But if you want to communicate with the rest of the world, you'll want to get a modem that meets the international standards. The following sections describe the most popular standards for modems that are connected to PCs.

Bell Standards

Bell 103 comes first in any list of modem standards, not just alphabetically, but because it was the first widely adopted standard, and it remains the standard of last resort, the one that will work when all else fails. It allows data transmissions at a very low speed. As noted, Bell 103 uses very simple FSK modulation; thus, it is the only standard in which the baud rate (the rate at which signal changes) is equal to the data rate.

Bell 212A is the next logical step in a standards discussion because it was the next modem standard to find wide application in the United States. It achieves a data transfer rate of 1,200 bits per second by adding quadrature modulation to a frequency modulated 600-baud signal. Consequently, a Bell 212A modem operates at 600 baud and transfers information at 1,200 bits per second. Although at one time the most widely used communication standard in America, many foreign countries prohibited the use of Bell 212A, preferring instead the similar international standard, v.22.

MNP Standards

Microcom Networking Protocol is an entire hierarchy of standards, from MNP Class 1, a no-longer-used error-correction protocol, to MNP Class 10, Adverse Channel Enhancements, which is designed to get the most data transfer performance from poor connections. MNP does not stand alone but works with modems that may conform to other standards. The MNP standards specify technologies rather than speeds. MNP Classes 2 through 4 deal with error control and are in the public domain. Classes 5 through 10 are licensed by Microcom and deal with a number of modem operating parameters.

MNP2 is designed to work with any modem that's capable of full-duplex communications. It works by confirming each byte as it is sent by having the receiving modem echo back each character. The sending modem can compare what it sent out with what came back to see if any errors occurred during transmission. Of course, this two-way street of data cuts effective transmission rates to half of what would otherwise be possible.

MNP3 improves on MNP2 by working synchronously instead of asynchronously. Consequently, no start and stop bits are required for each byte, trimming the data transfer overhead by 25 percent or more. Although MNP3 modems exchange data between themselves synchronously, they connect to PCs using asynchronous data links, which means they plug right into RS-232 serial ports.

MNP4 is basically an error-correcting protocol but also yields a bit of data compression. It incorporates two innovations. *Adaptive Packet Assembly* allows the modem to package data in blocks or packets that are sent and error-checked as a unit. The protocol is adaptive because it varies the size of each packet according to the quality of the connection. *Data Phase Optimization* eliminates repetitive control bits from the data traveling across the connection to streamline transmissions. Together these techniques can increase the throughput of a modem by 120 percent at a given bit-rate. In other words, using MNP4, a 1,200 bit-per-second modem could achieve a 1,450 bit-per-second throughput. Many modems have MNP4 capabilities.

MNP5 is purely a data-compression protocol, which squeezes some kinds of data into a form that takes less time to transmit. MNP5 can compress some data by a factor up to two, effectively doubling the speed of data transmissions. On some forms of data, such as files that have been already compressed, however, MNP5 may actually increase the time required for transmission.

MNP6 is designed to help modems get the most out of telephone connections independent of data compression. Using a technique called *Universal Link Negotiation*, modems can start communicating at a low speed, then, after evaluating the capabilities of the telephone line and each modem, switch to a higher speed. MNP6 also includes *Statistical Duplexing*, which allows a half-duplex modem to simulate full-duplex operation.

MNP7 is a more efficient data-compression algorithm (Huffman encoding) than MNP5, which permits increases in data throughput by a factor as high as three on some data.

MNP9 (there is no MNP8) is designed to reduce the transmission overhead required by certain common modem operations. The acknowledgment of each data packet is streamlined by combining the acknowledgment with the next data packet instead of sending a separate confirmation byte. In addition, MNP9 minimizes the amount of information that must be retransmitted when an error is detected by indicating where the error occurred. Although some other error-correction schemes require all information transmitted after an error to be resent, an MNP9 modem needs only the data that was in error to be sent again.

MNP10 is a set of *Adverse Channel Enhancements* that help modems work better through poor telephone connections. Modems with MNP10 will make multiple attempts to set up a transmission link, adjust the size of data packets they transmit according to what works best over the connection, and adjust the speed at which they operate to the highest rate that can be reliably maintained. One use envisioned for this standard is cellular modem communications, the car phone for data.

CCITT Standards

V.22 is the CCITT equivalent of the Bell 212A standard that delivers a transfer rate of 1,200 bits per second at 600 baud. It actually uses the same form of modulation as Bell 212A but is not compatible with the Bell standard because it uses a different protocol to set up the connection. In other words, although Bell 212A and v.22 modems speak the same language, they are unwilling to start a conversation with one another. Some modems support both standards and allow you to switch between them.

V.22bis was the first true world standard, adopted into general use in both the United States and Europe. It allows a transfer rate of 2,400 bits per second at 600 baud using a technique called trellis modulation that mixes two simple kinds of modulation, quadrature and amplitude modulation. Each baud has 16 states, enough to code any pattern of four bits. Each state is distinguished both by its phase relationship to the unaltered carrier and its amplitude (or strength) in relation to the carrier. There are four distinct phases and four distinct amplitudes under v.22bis, which, when multiplied together, yield the 16 available states.

V.32 is an international high-speed standard that permits data transfer rates of 4,800 and 9,600 bits per second. At its lower speed, it uses quadrature amplitude modulation similar to Bell 212A but at a higher baud rate, 2,400 baud. At 9,600 bits per second, it uses trellis modulation similar to v.22bis but at 2,400 baud and with a greater range of phases and amplitudes.

Note that while most Group III FAX machines and modems operate at 9,600 bits per second, a FAX modem with 9,600 bps capability is not necessarily compatible with the v.32 standard. Don't expect a FAX modem to communicate with v.32 products.

V.32bis extends the v.32 standard to 14,400 bits per second and allows fallback to intermediary speeds of 7,200 and 12,000 bits per second in addition to the 4,800 and 9,600 bit-per-second speeds of v.32. Note that all of these speeds are multiples of a basic 2,400 baud rate. The additional operating speeds that v.32bis has and v.32 does not are generated by using different ranges of phases and amplitudes in the modulation.

At 14,400 bits per second, there are 128 potentially different phase/amplitude states for each baud under v.32bis, enough to encode seven data bits in each baud. Other data rates (including v.32) use similar relationships for their data coding. Because there are so many phase and amplitude differences squeezed together, a small change in the characteristics of a telephone line might mimic such a change and cause transmission errors. Consequently, some way of detecting and eliminating such errors becomes increasingly important as transmission speed goes up.

V.fast is the informal working title for a new standard being developed by the CCITT that's expected to be adopted in the spring of 1993. Under ideal conditions, it will allow dial-up communications at data rates of 19,200 bits per second without data compression.

V.42 is a worldwide error correction standard that is designed to help make v.32, v.32bis, and other modem communications more reliable. v.42 incorporates MNP4 as an "alternative" protocol. That is, v.42 modems can communicate with MNP4 modems, but a connection between the two won't use the more sophisticated v.42 error-correction protocol. At the beginning of each call, as the connection is being negotiated between modems, a v.42 modem will determine whether MNP4 or full v.42 error correction can be used by the other modem. v.42 is preferred, MNP4 being the second choice. In other words, a v.42 will first try to set up a v.42 session; failing that, it will try MNP4; and failing that, it will set up a communications session without error correction.

V.42bis is a data-compression protocol endorsed by the CCITT. Different from and incompatible with MNP5 and MNP7, v.42bis is also more efficient. On some forms of data, it can yield compression factors up to four, potentially quadrupling the speed of modem transmissions. (With PCs, the effective maximum communication rate may be slower because of limitations on serial ports, typically 38,400 bits per second.) Note that a v.42bis-only modem cannot communicate with an MNP5-only modem. Unlike MNP5, a v.42 modem never increases the transmission time of "incompressible" data. Worst-case operation is the same speed as would be achieved without compression.

All-Digital Dial-Up Telecommunications

Eventually, today's modem standards will be replaced by the next step in PC-to-PC communications, all digital dial-up telecommunications. After all, nearly all traffic between telephone exchanges throughout the world is digital. The only archaic analog step is the stretch between the exchange and your home or office (called *POTS* by those in the know, Plain Old Telephone Service). Although the last 10 years have seen improvements in the speed of moving digital data through this ancient link—dial-up modems have moved from transfer rates of a paltry 300 bits per second to a 38,400 bps and more—it has no future.

Certainly you'll still talk on the telephone for ages to come (if your other family members give you a chance, of course), but the nature of the connection may finally change. Eventually, digital technology will take over your local telephone connection. In fact, in many parts of America and the rest of the world, you can already order a special digital line from your local telephone company and access an all-digital switched system. You get the equivalent of a telephone line, one that allows you to choose any conversation mate who's connected to the telephone network (with the capability of handling your digital data, of course) as easily as dialing a telephone. At least three such services are currently or will soon be available in many locations. All are known by their initials: SDS 56, ISDN, and SMDS. Eventually, you'll probably plug your PC into one of them, or one of their successors.

SDS 56

Already available from some telephone operating companies in some exchanges, *Switched Data Services 56* (sometimes shortened to

Switched-56) gives you a single digital channel capable of a 56 kilobit-per-second data rate. Its signals are carried through conventional copper twisted-pair wiring (the same old stuff that carries your telephone conversations). To link to your PC, you need special head-end equipment, the equivalent of a modem, for your PC. (This equipment is priced in the range of better v.32 modems.) Of course, because the signal stays digital, there's no need for modulation or demodulation. The signal stays error free through its entire trip.

In some locales, SDS 56 is no more expensive than an ordinary business telephone line. However, installation costs can be substantially higher, and some telephone companies may add extra monthly maintenance charges in addition to the normal dial-up costs.

To take advantage of SDS 56, you also need someone with whom to communicate who also has SDS 56 services. Currently SDS 56 is not an internationally agreed on standard, so your access to the service and its subscribers will be less universal than telephone-based modem links. The chief advantages of linking through SDS 56 are higher speed, greater reliability, and data integrity.

ISDN

The initials stand for *Integrated Services Digital Network*, although waggish types will tell you it means "I Still Don't Know" or "It Still Does Nothing." The latter seems most apt because ISDN has been discussed for years with little to show for all the verbiage.

The problem is one of perception rather than reality because many strides have already been made in bringing ISDN into your home and office. ISDN is an internationally supported standard, one that promises eventually to replace your standard analog telephone connection. And the onslaught of ISDN is gaining momentum. In fact, by the end of 1994 more than half the telephone connections in the country are scheduled to have access to ISDN.

As with SDS 56, ISDN takes advantage of the copper twisted-pair wiring that's already in place linking homes and offices to telephone exchanges. Instead of a single analog signal, an ISDN line carries three digital channels: two B (for Bearer) channels, which can carry any kind of data (digitally encoded voice, FAX, text, and numbers) at 64,000 bps, and a D (or Delta) channel, operating at 16,000 bps, that can carry control signals and serve as a third data channel. The three channels can be independently routed to different destinations through the ISDN system.

A single ISDN wire will allow you to transfer uncompressed data bi-directionally at the 64,000 bps rate, exactly like a duplex modem today but with higher speed and error-free transmission thanks to its all-digital nature. Even during such high-speed dual-direction connections, the D channel would still be available for other functions.

One key element of ISDN is that it makes do with today's ordinary twisted-pair telephone wiring. Neither you nor the various telephone companies need to invest the billions of dollars required to rewire the nation for digital service. Instead, only the central office switches that route calls between telephones, which today are mostly plug-in printed circuit boards, need to be upgraded.

Of course, this quick fix sounds easier than it is. The principal barriers aren't technological, however, but economic. The changeover is costly and, because telephone-switching equipment has long depreciation periods, does not always make business sense for the telephone company.

Once you have access to ISDN, you won't be able to plug your PC directly into your telephone line, however. You'll still need a device to interface your PC to the ISDN line. You'll need to match your equipment to the line and prevent one from damaging the other using a device called an ISDN Adapter. Such adapters may have analog ports that will allow you to connect your existing telephones into the ISDN network. ISDN Adapters are already becoming available for use in the limited areas that already have ISDN.

SMDS

If you need to move more data fast, the alternative is *Switched Multimegabit Data Service*. Still in its infancy, SMDS is backed by no universal standard but is instead easing itself into the market. One implementation provides some government offices with dial-up links supporting 1.45 megabit-per-second data transfers. Other systems with 1.2 to 30 Mbps rates have been proposed.

Modem Control

Besides its basic purpose of converting digital data into modulated audio signals, the modem is often called on to handle other chores of convenience. For instance, it may be called on to automatically dial or answer the phone or report the condition of the telephone line. These features of the modem must be able to be controlled by your computer, and the modem must be able to signal your computer about what it does and what it finds out.

Dual Modes

Most modems operate alternately in one of two modes. In *command mode*, the modem receives and carries out instructions sent by your computer. In *communications mode*, it operates as transparently as a modem can, merely converting data.

Changing modes is mostly a matter of sending control characters to the modem. The characters can only be received and processed in command mode. In communications mode, they would be passed along down the telephone line.

Shifting from command mode to communications mode is easy; the modem is already handling commands, so adding one more to its repertory is no big deal. Shifting back from communications mode to command mode is more problematic. In communications mode, the modem is supposed to be relaying all the data it receives down the telephone line. The most widely used method for initiating the switch from communications to command mode involves a *guard period*, a brief interval during which no data is sent, then sending a set of characters unlikely to be found in a normal communications string, followed by a final guard period. This mode-switching method is patented by Hayes Microcomputer Products, a modem manufacturer (which was, in turn, named after Dennis Hayes, its founder), and must be licensed by all modems that use it. Most modems use guard periods of one second and three plus signs as the command character sequence.

Hayes Command Set

Today, most modems use a standardized set of instructions called the *Hayes command set*, named after the Hayes company that developed it for its modems. For the most part, the Hayes command set comprises several dozen modem instructions that begin with a two-character sequence called *attention characters*. Other characters specifying the command follow the attention character. Because the AT is part of nearly every command, the Hayes command set is also termed the *AT command set*, most often by Hayes' competitors that don't want to give the competition credit. A modem that understands the Hayes command set (or the AT command set) is said to be *Hayes-compatible*.

The AT command set itself is not patented (although it is not useful without incorporating the patented mode-switching method). The basic Hayes command set is listed in table 18.1.

TABLE 18.1.
Hayes Extended
Command Set

Command	Function
AT	Attention (used to start all commands)
ATIn	Request product code and ROM checksum:
	0=modem sends its 3-digit product code
	1=request numeric checksum of firmware ROM
	2=request OK or ERROR state of ROM checksum
A/	Repeat last command (No AT or Return)
A	Answer without waiting for ring
Bn	Bell mode—set 1200 bps protocol compatibility:
	0=CCITT v.22/v.22bis
	1=Bell 212A
Cn	Carrier state:
	0=off
	1=on
Dn	Dial telephone number n

Special dialing commands:	
P	Pulse dialing
R	Reverse mode (use answer frequencies when originating a call)
S	Dial stored number
T	Tone dialing

continues

TABLE 18.1.
continued

Special dialing commands:	
W	Wait (for second dial or access tone)
@	Wait for quiet answer
,	Pause (a delay in dialing sequence)
!	Flash (on-hook for 1/2 second)
;	Return to command mode after dialing
En	Echo modem commands:
	0=no
	1=yes
Fn	Full or half duplex operation:
	0=half
	1=full
Hn	Hook:
	0=on hook (hang up)
	1=off hook
Ln	Loudness or speaker volume:
	0=low
	1=low
	2=medium
	3=high
Mn	Mode of speaker operation:
	0=off
	1=on
	2=always on
	3=disable speaker when modem receives a carrier signal while modem is dialing
On	On-line state:
	0=modem returns to the on-line state
	1=modem returns on-line and retrains equalizer (2400 bps mode only)
Qn	Quiet command for result codes:
	0=commands are sent
	1=commands are not sent
Sn=x	S-register commands:
	n=S-register number
	x=value to set register to
Sn?	Display value of S-register n
Vn	Verbose mode for result codes:
	0=use digits
	1=use words

Special dialing commands:

Xn	Enable extended result code and mode setting:
	0=basic (300 bps)
	1=extended (no dial tone or busy signal detection)
	2=extended (detects dial tone but not busy signals)
	3=extended (no dial tone detect but detects busies)
	4=extended (detects both dial tones and busy signals)
Yn	Long space disconnect:
	0=disabled
	1=enabled; disconnects after receiving 1.6 sec break
Z	Fetch configuration profile from nonvolatile memory
&Cn	Data Carrier Detect handling:
	0=modem keeps DCD (RS-232 pin 8) always on
	1=DCD tracks data carrier detected by modem
&Dn	Data Terminal Ready handling:
	0=modem ignores DTR line (RS-232 pin 20)
	1=modem assumes asynch command state when DTR goes off
	2=DTR off switches modem off hook, out of answer mode, and back to command state
	3=DTR switching off initialized modem
&F	Fetch factory configuration profile from ROM
&Gn	Guard tone selection:
	0=no guard tones
	1=550 Hz guard tones
	2=1800 guard tones
&Jn	Telephone jack selection
	0=RJ-11/RJ-41S/RJ-45S
	1=RJ-12/RJ-13
&Ln	Leased-line or dial-up line selection:
	0=dial-up operation
	1=leased-line
&Mn	Asynchronous/Synchronous mode selection:
	0=asynchronous
	1=synchronous mode 1—async dialing, then switch to synchronous operation

continues

TABLE 18.1.
continued

Special dialing commands:	
	2=synchronous mode 2—stored number dialing
	3=synchronous mode 3—manual dialing
&Pn	Pulse dial make/break pulse length selection
	0=39% make, 61% break (US and Canada standard)
&Rn	Request to send/Clear to send handling (sync mode only):
	0=CTS (RS-232 pin 5) tracks RTS (pin 4)
	1=modem ignores RTS and turns CTS on when ready to receive synchronous data
&Sn	Data Set Ready handling:
	0=modem forces DSR on whenever modem is turned on
	1=DSR (RS-232 pin 6) operates according to EIA specifications
&Tn	Test mode:
	0=terminates any test in progress when last command on a line
	1=initiates local analog loopback test
	3=initiates local digital loopback
	4=conditions modem to perform remote digital loopback when requested by another modem
	5=prohibits remote digital loopback
	6=initiates remote digital loopback with another modem
	7=initiates remote digital loopback with self-test
	8=initiates remote digital loopback with self-test
&W	Write active configuration profile to memory
&Xn	Select synchronous transmit clock source (sync mode only):
	0=modem generates timing and sends through pin 15
	1=modem's host computer generates timing and sends it to modem on pin 24, which modem routes to pin 15
	2=modem derives timing from incoming signal and supplies it to pin 15
&Zn	Store telephone number
	n=string of digits compatible with Dial command

Most AT commands follow the attention characters with one letter that specifies the family of the command and another character that indicates the nature of the command. For instance, H is standard for

Hook. H0 means put the phone "on the hook" or hang up. H1 indicates that the modem should take the phone off the hook, that is, make a connection to the line.

Several commands and their modifiers can be combined on a single line after an initial attention command. For example, to command a Hayes or Hayes-compatible modem to dial information on a tone-dialing line, the proper sequence of commands would read ATDT15511212. The AT is the attention signal, D is the Dial command, the T tells the modem to use tones for dialing, and the 15511212 is the number of the telephone company information service.

All AT commands must be followed by a carriage return. The modem waits for the carriage return as a signal that the computer has sent the complete command and that the modem should start processing it.

Extended Hayes Command Set

At the time the Hayes command set was developed, modems had relatively few special features. As modems became more sophisticated, they became more laden with capabilities and features. The original Hayes command set had to be extended to handle all the possibilities. Note that many Hayes-compatible modems recognize only the original command set. All of their features, if they have them, may not work with software that expects the extended Hayes set.

S-Registers

The extensions to the original Hayes command set include so many new functions that the command language might have become ungainly and confusing. After all, there are only 26 letters in the alphabet that might be used for one-letter commands. Hayes added the facility of a special register or memory area called the *S-Register* inside its modems that allows the setting of the modem's operating parameters. By setting the value contained by the S-register, a variety of modem functions can be controlled. S-register settings are shown in table 18.2.

TABLE 18.2.
Hayes Modem
S-Registers

Register	Range	Units	Description	Default
S0	0–255	rings	answer on ring #	0
S1	0–255	rings	count number of rings	0
S2	0–127	ASCII	escape code	43
S4	0–127	ASCII	character used as return	13
S4	0–127	ASCII	character used as line feed	10
S5	0–32, 127	ASCII	character used as backspace	8
S6	2–255	sec.	time to wait for dial tone	2
S7	1–255	sec.	time to wait for carrier	30
S8	0–255	sec.	length of comma pause	2
S9	1–255	.1"	response time, carrier detect	6
S10 S11	1–255	.1"	delay before hang up reserved	7
S12 S13	20–255	.02"	escape code dead time reserved	50
S14	bit-mapped	modem options	AA(Hex)	
	bit 0	reserved		
	bit 1	command	echo	
			0=no echo	
			1=echo	
	bit 2	result codes		
			0=enabled	
			1=disabled	
	bit 3	verbose mode		
			0=short form result codes	
			1=verbose result codes	
	bit 4	dumb mode		
			0=modem acts smart	
			1=modem acts dumb	
	bit 5	dial method		
			0=tone	
			1=pulse	
	bit 6	reserved		
	bit 7	originate/answer mode		
			0=answer	
			1=originate	

Register	Range	Units	Description	Default
S15			reserved	
S16	bit-mapped	modem test options		
bit 0	local analog loopback			
	0=disabled			
	1=enabled			
bit 1	reserved			
bit 2	local digital loopback			
	0=disabled			
	1=enabled			
bit 3	status bit			
	0=disabled			
	1=enabled			
bit 4	initiate remote digital loopback			
	0=disabled			
	1=enabled			
bit 5	initiate remote digital loopback with test message and error count			
	0=disabled			
	1=enabled			
bit 6	local analog loopback with self test			
	0=disabled			
	1=enabled			
bit 7	reserved			
S17			reserved	
S18	0–255	sec.	test timer	0
S19			reserved	
S20			reserved	
S21	bit-mapped		modem options	0
bit 0	telco jack used			
	0=RJ-11/RJ-41S/RJ-45S			
	1=RJ-12/RJ-13			
bit 1	reserved			
bit 2	RTS/CTS handling			

continues

	Register	Range	Units	Description	Default
TABLE 18.2. continued					

0=RTS follows CTS

1=CTS always on

bit 3,4　DTR handling

　　　0,0=modem ignores DTR

　　　0,1=modem to command state when DTR goes off

　　　1,0=modem hangs up when DTR goes off

　　　1,1=modem initializes when DTR goes off

bit 5　DCD handling

　　　0=DCD always on

　　　1=DCD indicates presence of carrier

bit 6　DSR handling

　　　0=DSR always on

　　　1=DSR indicates modem is off-hook and in data mode

bit 7　long space disconnect

　　　0=disabled

　　　1=enabled

Register	Range	Units	Description	Default
S22	bit-mapped		modem option register	76(Hex)

bit 0,1　speaker volume

　　　0,0=low

　　　0,1=low

　　　1,0=medium

　　　1,1=high

bit 2,3　speaker control

　　　0,0=speaker disabled

　　　0,1=speaker on until carrier detected

　　　1,0=speaker always on

　　　1,1=speaker on between dialing and carrier detect

bit 4-6　result code options

　　　0,0,0=300 baud modem result codes only

　　　1,0,0=modem does not detect dial tone or busy

　　　1,0,1=modem detects dial tone only

　　　1,1,0=modem detects busy signal only

　　　1,1,1=modem detects dial tone and busy

　　　other settings undefined

Register	Range	Units	Description	Default
bit 7	make/break pulse dial ratio			
	0=39% make, 61% break			
	1=33% make, 67% break			
S23	bit-mapped		modem option register	7
bit 0	obey request from remote modem for remote digital loopback			
	0=disabled			
	1=enabled			
bit 1,2	communication rate			
	0,0=0 to 300 bps			
	0,1=reserved			
	1,0=1200 bps			
	1,1=2400 bps			
bit 3	reserved			
bit 4,5	parity option			
	0,0=even			
	0,1=space			
	1,0=odd			
	1,1=mark/none			
bit 6,7	guard tones			
	0,0=disabled			
	0,1=550 Hz guard tone			
	1,0=1800 Hz guard tone			
	1,1=reserved			
S24			reserved	
S25	0–255	.01"	delay to DTR	5
S26	0–255	.01"	RTS to CTS delay	1
S27	bit-mapped	modem options register	40(Hex)	
bit 0,1	transmission mode			
	0,0=asynchronous			
	0,1=synchronous with async call placement			
	1,0=synchronous with stored-number dialing			
	1,1=synchronous with manual dialing			

continues

Register	Range	Units	Description	Default
TABLE 18.2. continued				
bit 2	dial-up or lease-line operation			
	0=dial-up line			
	1=leased-line			
bit 3	reserved			
bit 4,5	source of synchronous clock			
	0,0=local modem			
	0,1=host computer or data terminal			
	1,0=derived from received carrier			
	1,1=reserved			
bit 6	Bell or CCITT operation			
	0=CCITT v.22 bis/v.22			
	1=Bell 212A			
bit 7	reserved			

Response Codes

Commands sent to a Hayes-compatible modem, by their very name and nature, are one-way. Absent some means of confirmation, you would never know whether the modem actually received your command, let alone acted on it. Moreover, you also need some means for the modem to tell you what it discovers about your connection to the telephone line. For instance, the modem needs to signal you when it detects another modem at the end of the line and when that connection is broken.

Part of the Hayes command set is a series of *response codes*, which serve that feedback function. When the modem needs to tell you something, it sends back, via the same connection used to send data between your computer and modem, code numbers or words to apprise you of the situation. In the Hayes scheme of things, you can set the modem to send simple *numeric* codes, consisting solely of codes (which you can then look up in your modem manual, if you have one) or *verbose* responses, which may be one or more words long in something close to everyday English.

Typical responses include "OK" to signify that a command has been received and acted on, "CONNECT 1,200" to indicate that you've linked with a 1,200 bit-per-second modem, and "RINGING" to show that the phone at the other end of the connection is ringing. Hayes response codes are listed in table 18.3.

TABLE 18.3.
Hayes Response Codes

Numeric code	Verbose code	Definition
0	OK	Command executed without error
1	CONNECT	Connection established (at 300 bps)
2	RING	Phone is ringing
3	NO CARRIER	Carrier lost or never detected
4	ERROR	Error in command line or line too long
5	CONNECT 1,200	Connection established at 1,200 bps
6	NO DIALTONE	Dial tone not detected in waiting period
7	BUSY	Modem detected a busy signal
8	NO ANSWER	No silence detected while waiting for a quiet answer
10	CONNECT 2,400	Connection established at 2,400 bps

Note that because the response codes flow from your modem to your computer as part of the regular data stream, you may accidentally confuse them with text being received from the far end of your connection.

Modem Features

The broad term "features" describes various subtle, and some not-so-subtle, ways in which modems differ from one another. For the most part, the features of a modem taken together determine how easily and conveniently you can put it to work. A no-frills modem, for example, may require that you spin the dial of your phone with your index finger or answer incoming calls before turning them over to your computer system when you hear the carrier tone of the modem at the other end of the line. Many people are willing to put up with such petty inconveniences to save the price of a modem.

Although none of the tasks that features-deficient modems foist on you will tax your mind or constitution, a no-frills modem short-changes the capabilities of your computer. With a full-featured modem, your PC can dial the phone faster and with fewer errors and can handle the chore automatically when you're not around. Or with the latest memory-resident communication software, your PC can dial the full-featured modem and collect your messages while you're in the midst of browbeating data into shape with another program.

Actually, nearly every modem made today, including the lowest budget models made in obscure foreign lands, has all the standard features that you might normally want. Once you start integrating features into circuit chips, adding a few more features is not an arduous process. The only time you're likely to run into a modem deficient in today's convenience features is when you try to make do with one manufactured to yesterday's standards, the modem you inherit from some corporate higher-up, one that you find lying face-down in the gutter and you nurse back to life, one that you buy used from a shady looking character in a trench coat on a deserted street corner.

Of the various features of a state-of-the-art modem, the ones you should expect in any new product that you buy are discussed in the following sections.

Auto-Answer

An auto-answer modem is capable of detecting incoming ringing voltage (the low-frequency, high-voltage signal that makes the bell on a telephone ring) and seizing the telephone line as if it had been answered by a person. Upon seizing the phone line, the auto-answer modem sends a signal to its host computer to the effect that it has answered the phone. The computer then can interact with the caller.

An auto-answer modem allows you or others to call into your computer system without anyone being present to answer the telephone and make the connection to your computer.

Auto-Dial

An auto-dial modem is capable of generating pulse-dial or DTMF (dual-tone modulated frequency or Touch-tone) dialing signals independent of a telephone set.

An auto-dial modem can dial the telephone under computer command, for instance, after hours when you're asleep and phone rates are low. Without auto-dial, you would have to dial the phone yourself, listen for the screech of the far-end modem's answer, plug in your modem, and finally hang up the phone.

Automatic Speed Sensing

Before a connection is made, you may have no way of knowing at what speed a distant modem will be operating. Most of today's modems can automatically adjust for the speed of the distant modem if it is within the speed range that can be handled. High-speed modems usually negotiate the highest possible shared speed to operate at using proprietary protocols.

Many modems also attempt to adjust to the speed at which you send them data, again if it is within the range of speeds that the modem can handle. The attention code of the Hayes command set conveys enough data that a modem can lock into the data and appropriately match its operating speed to that of the information flow.

Acoustic Couplers

Really vintage modems made no electrical contact with telephone lines at all. That's because years ago hooking your modem directly to the phone line was neither practical or legal. It wasn't practical before the now-common modular telephone plug-and-jack arrangement allowed anyone to plug in telephone equipment without fear of embarrassment or electrocution. It wasn't legal because telephone company regulations dating long before the AT&T telephone monopoly was split up did not permit individuals to directly connect modems to their telephone lines.

Instead of electrical connections, vintage modems sent their signals to telephones as sound waves. A device called an *acoustic coupler* was used to convert the tone-like analog signals made by the modem into sounds which are then picked up by the microphone in the telephone handset and passed through the telephone network again as electrical signals. To make the sound connection a two-way street, the acoustic coupler also incorporated a microphone to pick up the squawks emanating from the earpiece loudspeaker of the telephone handset, convert them into electrical signals, and supply them to the modem for demodulation.

Acoustic couplers can take many forms. In early equipment, the acoustic coupler was integral to the modem, a special cradle in which you lay the telephone handset. Today you're more likely to see couplers made from two rubber cups designed to engulf the mouthpiece and earpiece of a telephone handset. This latter form of acoustic coupler persists because it allows modems to be readily connected and disconnected from non-modular telephones, those that you cannot unplug to directly attach a modem. This conductibility is especially important for roving computers that may be called on to tie their internal modems into non-modular pay station and hotel room telephones.

Although acoustic couplers were normally used only at low speeds, typically ordinary Bell 103 communications at 300 baud, high-speed acoustic couplers that operate at speeds up to 9,600 bits per second are available.

Direct-Connect Modems

Modems that directly plug into the electrical wires of the telephone system are called, quite logically, *direct-connect* modems. Almost in tribute to the acceptance of the modular telephone wiring system, nearly every modem that you can buy today is direct-connect.

Asynchronous Modems

Almost any modem that you buy for normal use with your PC will feature *asynchronous transmission*. This odd-sounding term describes a method of exchanging information between two different computer systems that operate completely independently and do not share any timing information.

Normally, the time at which a pulse occurs in relation to the ticking of a computer's system clock determines the meaning of a bit in a digital signal, and the pulses must be synchronized to the clock for proper operation. The asynchronous transmissions, however, such as the digital pulses are not locked to the system clock of either computer. Instead, the meaning of each bit of a digital word is defined by its position in reference to the clearly (and unambiguously) defined start bit. Because the timing is set within each word in isolation, each word of asynchronous signal is self-contained and essentially independent of any time relations beyond its self-defined bounds.

The signals of modems that use the telephone system are generally asynchronous because it is more expensive and difficult to synchronize signals through the telephone system through which signals may be rerouted at any time without any warning.

Synchronous Modems

Most dedicated-line modems use a special communication technique often used among mainframes called *synchronous transmission*. In this method of transmitting data across phone lines, the two ends of the channel share a common time base, and the communicating modems operate continuously at substantially the same frequency and are continually maintained in the correct phase relationship by circuits that constantly monitor the connection and adjust for the circuit conditions. Higher speed modems, 2,400 bits per second and beyond, often use synchronous transmissions.

In synchronous transmissions, the timing of each bit independently is vital, but framing bits (start and stop bits) are unnecessary, which makes this form of communication a bit (actually two or three bits) faster. One problem in using it is that before information can be exchanged, not just the two ends of the connection must be synchronized but also the link between the modem and computer must be synchronized. Auto-dialing features usually won't work in synchronous mode because, without a connection, there's nothing to synchronize to, and the connection cannot be made without dialing.

Autosynchronous Modems

Hayes solved the dialing problem for synchronous communications by adding an *autosynchronous* feature to their newest higher speed modems. This special mode allows the connection between PC and modem to operate asynchronously. The modem translates those signals into synchronous mode before sending them down the telephone line. It also works the other way and translates synchronous signals from the far end of the line into asynchronous for sharing with the host computer. The autosynchronous features can help PCs talk to mainframe and other computers that use synchronous communication as easily as they communicate with other PCs.

Modem Packaging

Perhaps the biggest choice you have in buying a new modem is whether it installs inside your PC as an *internal modem* or connects outside your PC through a cable as an *external modem*. Internal modems are like any other expansion cards that plug into a vacant slot inside your PC. External modems are additional boxes to find a place for on your desk.

In many cases when you have to choose between actual products, physical appeal may be the best guiding factor because often exactly the same circuitry is available in the different packages.

There are a few practical reasons for preferring one style of modem packaging over another. External modems offer the advantage of portability, you can move your external modem between different computer systems, even those that are not IBM-compatible, simply by pulling the plug. Moving an internal modem requires popping the lid off your PC and the recipient's PC and all the folderol that follows.

Additionally, internal modems can restrict you to certain computer systems. Some internal modems are built as full-length expansion cards, which means you can install them only in full-size PCs, XTs, ATs, and hardware compatibles. You'll need a different modem for a foreshortened computer (like the Tandy 1000). When you make the move from PC to PS/2 architecture, you'll also have to shell out the cash for a new internal modem. Most laptops and the PCjr can use only internal modems that were specifically designed for their proprietary expansion buses.

If you have a PC with its original, minimal 63.5-watt power supply, adding an internal modem—an older, full-length modem card in particular—may limit the number of other expansion boards that you can plug into your system. Such modems are notoriously power-hungry and may leave few watts for other cards, such as hard disks and EMS boards.

On the other hand, internal modems tend to be a few dollars cheaper than external models because the internal units don't need extra packaging or power supplies (although they need some extra signal circuitry). You can also forego the cost of a serial cable, which might cost you $30 or more from a local dealer. With an internal modem, you don't have to deal with a tangle of cords, plugs, or transformers vying for the few holes in your wall outlet, extra boxes on your desk, or another thing to switch off when you put your system to sleep at night.

Port Assignments

Other than matters of power supply, the impact on your system resources will be the same no matter the style of modem you choose. Although external modems require a serial port and cable, internal modems also require the use of a serial port address, which means you still lose the use of that address by a serial port, COM1 or COM2 (or COM3 or COM4 in PS/2s and the latest DOS versions). If you use versions of DOS before 3.3, you'll only be able to add one serial port in addition to the port or address used by either an external or internal modem. Although some internal modems can have their addresses set as COM3 or COM4, you must be sure that the communications software that you choose can control the ports beyond COM2.

If there is any general rule, it's that you should choose an external modem for its flexibility and its capability to move to new and different computer systems; choose an internal modem for its neatness and lower overall cost.

Connecting and Using a Modem

Unlike other common peripherals, modems often are not plug-and-play devices, external modems particularly. Perhaps that's to be expected because they plug into serial ports.

Modem Cabling

The easiest part of installing a modem is hooking up the cable. Modems connected to the serial ports used by PCs and PS/2s use "straight-through" cables. Only AT-style serial ports with nine-pin connectors require adapters to match them to most modems.

The problems begin with software. In the interactions of various communications packages with modems, a number of serial port control lines are brought into play. Some communications programs, such as PC-Talk III, make minimal use of the indications modems provide. Others monitor every connection. Consequently, the number of control lines that must be connected, and thus the number of wires that must be available in the cable that links your modem to your computer, depends on the communications software that you plan to use. In some situations, the minimal triad, pins 2, 3, and 7, will suffice. Other programs require the full complement of 10 connections. The moral to be drawn from this story is that should you not know the type of cable required by your modem, use a straight-through serial cable equipped with at least 10 conductors.

Modem Switch Settings

Modems themselves can be programmed to treat their various connections in different ways to match the needs of software. For instance, some programs require that the modem keep them abreast of the connection through the Carrier Detect signal. Other programs couldn't care less about Carrier Detect but carefully scrutinize Data Set Ready. To accommodate the range of communications applications, most modems have setup switches that determine the handling of their control lines. In one position, a switch may force Carrier Detect to stay on continually, for example. The other setting might cause the status of Carrier Detect to follow the state of the modems conversations.

These switches take two forms, mechanical and electrical. Mechanical switches are generally of the DIP variety. In the prototypical modem, the original Hayes Smartmodem 1200, these switches are hidden behind the front panel of the modem. (To get to them, carefully pry up the trailing ears of the sides of the bezel, first one side, and then the other of the black front panel of the modem. Then pull it forward and off.)

Most commercial modems that use DIP switches are patterned after the Hayes Smartmodem 1200. Its DIP switch settings are shown in table 18.4.

TABLE 18.4.
Hayes Smartmodem DIP Switch Settings

Switch	Name	Function	Equiv. Command
1	DTR Recognition On/Off	*Up*—Modem recognized DTR signal; computer can make modem hang up or not answer with DTR lead (RS323 pin 20) *Down*—Modem ignores DTR	
2	Result Code Select	*Up*—Verbose result codes (Codes sent as English words) *Down*—Numeric result codes	ATV1 ATV0
3	Result Code On/Off	*Up*—Result codes are sent to computer *Down*—Result codes are sent	ATQ1 ATQ0
4	Character Echo On/Off	*Up*—Modem echoes commands it receives in command mode *Down*—Modem does not echo characters unless in half-duplex mode and on-line	ATE1 ATE0
5	Autoanswer On/Off	*Up*—Modem automatically answers calls on first ring *Down*—Modem will not answer incoming calls	ATSO=1 ATSO=0
6	Carrier Detect On/Off	*Up*—Modem sends signal to computer to indicate character detected (RS3232 pin 8) *Down*—Modem does not change status of pin 8 to reflect detected carrier. Defaults to making carrier always appear present	
7	RJ11/ RJ12 Select	*Up*—Modem connected to single-line RJ11 telephone jack *Down*—Modem connected to multi-line service using RJ12 or RJ13 jack. This setting will make in-service indicators illuminate on multiline phones when the modem goes off-hook.	
8	Command Recognition	*Up*—Disables Smartmodem 1200 command recognition *Down*—Enables Smartmodem 1200 command recognition	

The other kind of switch is electrical, exemplified by the Smartmodem 2400. Made from EEPROM memory, these switches are set by sending commands to the modem from your computer. Because of their EEPROM nature, they retain their settings even when the modem is turned off or unplugged.

Other modems may follow this pattern exactly or may use another memory technology, for instance, battery backed-up dynamic RAM. A few don't make any effort toward removing the volatility. Such modems require you to reprogram their settings every time you turn them on. Although you can't do much to make modem memory non-volatile when it's not, you can make life easier using disk memory. Simply add the modem settings you want to enforce to the setup strings that many communications software packages send to the modem before they begin to make a connection.

The setup commands for the industry-standard Smartmodem 2400 are shown in table 18.5. These commands for the Smartmodem 2400, which has no DIP switches, duplicate the functions of the DIP switches of the Smartmodem 1200.

TABLE 18.5.
Hayes Smartmodem 2400 Setup Commands

Switch	Name	Substitute Command
1	DTR Recognition On/Off	*On*—Make bit 3 of S-register 21 equal 1; bit 4 equal 0 *Off*—Make bits 3 and 4 of S-register 21 equal to 0
2	Result Code Select	*Verbose codes*—Send command ATV1 to modem *Numeric codes*—Send command ATV0 to modem
3	Result Code On/Off	*On*—Send command ATQ1 to modem *Off*—Send command ATQ0
4	Character Echo On/Off	*On*—Send command ATE1 to modem *Off*—Send command ATE0 to modem
5	Autoanswer On/Off	*On*—Send command ATSO=1 to modem *Off*—Send command ATSO=0
6	Carrier Detect On/Off	*On*—Set bit 5 of S-register 21 to a value of 1 *Off*—Set bit 5 of S-register 21 to a value of 0

Switch	Name	Substitute Command
7	RJ11/ RJ12 Select	*RJ11*—Set bit 0 of S-register 21 to a value of 0 *RJ12*—Set bit 0 of S-register 21 to a value of 1
8	Command Recognition	*Dumb*—Set bit 4 of S-register 14 to a value of 1 *Smart*—Set bit 4 of S-register 14 to a value of 0

Buying a Modem

Buying a modem is like a treasure hunt. The best values are hidden and you have to dig them out. But if you know what to look for, and what to ask for, you'll find you can easily strike it rich.

Start by determining your communications needs. You've got to know what you're after when you start the search, what kind of communications you want to carry out and how fast. Once you've made that decision, you can check out features and additional values (like software) that modem manufacturers offer you. Although everyone inevitably has his own priorities and concerns, this shopping list will help you find the right drive and the right vendor.

The kind of communications you want to carry out will determine what kind of modem you need. If you're just going to send files electronically between offices, you can buy two non-standard modems and get more speed for your investment. But if you want to communicate with the rest of the world, you'll want to get a modem that meets the international standards.

Speed

Determine how fast you want to communicate. Speed is the major factor in setting the price of a modem. Faster modems are more complex and more exacting, consequently, they cost more. If you don't need the fastest modem in the world, you can save big. If you rarely transfer files, you probably don't need high speed. But if you're moving dozens or hundreds of kilobytes every day, a

9,600 bit-per-second or faster modem can pay for itself in lower phone bills in a matter of months.

Standards

The speed you want will, for the most part, determine what standard you'll want your modem to follow. But don't forget about error correction and data compression. Although software methods of both work reasonably well at lower speeds, at 9,600 bits per second or higher, you'll want the hardware to do the work.

Not all modems support speeds lower than the one that they are primarily designed to operate at. For instance, a 9,600 bit-per-second modem doesn't necessarily include the capability to operate at 2,400, 1,200, or even 300 bits per second. If you need these speeds, you'll have to be sure that the modem you choose includes them.

Just because a modem has lower speeds doesn't mean that it will automatically switch to slower operation when the telephone line proves bad. You'll want a modem with automatic fallback to negotiate the highest possible speed at which a connection can operate.

The Hayes AT command set is as close to a standard for modem control as there is in the industry. A modem that is Hayes-compatible will work with the widest range of software including nearly every communications program. In addition, phone dialers and similar utilities may require a Hayes-compatible modem.

Packaging

Internal modems are generally less expensive (except in the case of proprietary modems made for particular laptop and notebook PCs) than external modems but are more difficult to move between systems.

An external modem somehow needs to connect to a serial port on your PC. Although some pocket modems will plug directly into a port connector, most modems require a cable. Few modems come equipped with the necessary cable, so be sure to order a serial cable when you buy your modem. Almost universally, you will require a straight-through serial cable, although the standard seven connections (rather than the full 25 of the serial connector) are generally sufficient.

Like any expansion board, an internal modem requires a free expansion slot to plug into. Make sure that you have a slot available in your PC. In addition, an internal modem needs a free COM port address. If you have four serial ports in your system already, you generally cannot install an internal modem.

If you have a laptop computer, a pocket modem is a great way of avoiding the high price of proprietary internal modems. A pocket modem is an external modem small enough to slip into the case along with your laptop or notebook PC, yet can do everything that a full-size modem can. In addition, a pocket modem can extend the battery life of your laptop computer.

Pocket modems can be designed to run either on internal batteries or draw their power from the telephone line itself. If you've ever gotten stuck with a dead battery in an emergency, you already know the advantage of line power.

Port Usage

You want the most flexibility in an internal modem so that you can still retain two or three serial ports for other functions (such as scanners, mice, and so on). If the modem doesn't support COM3 and COM4, you may lose the capability to address one of your system's serial ports after you install the modem.

Software

Check whether any software comes with the modem. More than any other PC peripherals, modems are likely to come with software, typically a full-fledged communications program. This software can be more than just a free program; it can be a key to unlocking particular modem features (such as the capability to use higher-numbered serial ports). Be sure to ask what you get when you order, and make sure that it comes in the box when you get the modem.

Quality Issues

Modem standards indicate only what signals a modem can deal with under ideal conditions, but not every connection is ideal. Modems vary in their capability to accommodate noisy telephone lines, changing levels, and other signal problems. Check modem specification to determine how well the product can deal with noise, what its minimum signal is, and other signal-recovery features like echo-cancellation.

Don't forget hardware reliability. As with other computer peripherals, the more reliable modems are those with fewer components (because there's simply less to go wrong). Look for a modem that uses the latest electronics (VLSI and Surface-Mount Components). More compact modems by necessity use these space-saving (and reliability-increasing) technologies.

Support

Find out who supports the modems you consider, and what kind of support they offer. When you have a problem with a modem, you have two avenues of support. Most of the time, you'll first want to give a call to the vendor who sold you the modem. So check what the vendor offers for support before you buy. A toll-free support line is ideal, particularly one that's attended 24 hours a day.

Before you buy, ask the salesman about his company's support policy. Does it have a support number at all? When is support available? You'll probably test your modem in the evening or late night when telephone charges are lowest. Will support be there when you need it? Is the support line toll-free? Are there enough people to answer your questions immediately or do you have to wait, presumably forever, for someone to call you back? Technical support that depends only on the salesperson who wrote down your credit card number is usually as good as no support at all.

Modem manufacturers differ in their support policies. Although many will try to help you with your problems (sometimes only after wending your way through the corporate hierarchy), others may not even be in business any more, or they may be located in some foreign land lacking telephone connections with the United States and the 20th century. In that you may have to rely on the modem manufacturer for help when your pleas to the vendor go unanswered, you'll want the manufacturer of your modem to be at least reachable. A modem vendor with a consumer support line is a godsend, particularly if the line is toll-free. Technical support through a bulletin board service can be helpful, but remember, it will be difficult to connect to the BBS if you cannot make your modem work!

Product warranties are given both by the manufacturer and the vendor. However, the latter is usually more important because you'll get the most direct help with your modem from the vendor.

The easy-to-quantify issue is the length of the warranty. A modem warranty should extend past the first connection to at least 90 days. You'll find better products, and better vendors, will offer modem warranties measured in years.

How that warranty is honored is important. The easiest to deal with is a replacement policy under which the modem vendor will send you a replacement modem when you send yours back. If the vendor elects to repair your modem instead, you may be disconnected for weeks.

A return policy is also helpful if you cannot get your modem to work with your particular PC configuration. Subtle incompatibilities may make one modem unhappy in your system. If so, you'll want to be able to return the modem and try another model without suffering a restocking fee.

Manufacturers' warranties are trickier to get a handle on. In general, the warranty period starts when the product is sold to your vendor, not to you, so it may expire sooner than you think. Worse, a manufacturer may choose not to recognize its warranty if you don't buy from an authorized dealer. So it's important to clarify whether you get a manufacturer's warranty when you buy your modem. And of course, a manufacturer's warranty is meaningless if the modem manufacturer is out of business or beyond your reach in the depth of the Pacific Basin.

FAX

FAX, short for facsimile transmissions, gives the power of Star Trek's transporter system (but without the aliens and pyrotechnics) to anyone who needs to get a document somewhere else in the world at the speed of light. Although FAX doesn't quite dematerialize paper, it does move the images and information a document contains across continents and reconstructs it at the end of its near-instantaneous travels. The recipient gets to hold in his own hands a nearly exact duplicate of the original, the infamous reasonable facsimile.

From that angle, FAX is a telecopier, a Xerox machine with a thousand miles of wire between where you slide the original in and the duplicate falls out. In fact, the now aging telecopiers made by Xerox Corporation were the progenitors of today's FAX machines.

Functionally, however, FAX works like television for paper. Much as a television picture is broken into numerous scan lines, a FAX machine scans images as a series of lines, one at a time, and strings all the lines scanned on a document into a continuous stream of information. At the receiving end, another FAX machine converts the data stream into black-and-white dots on another sheet of paper, duplicating the pattern of the original.

In actual application, FAX plays the role of a modem for pictures. Although, in the West, data is sent across wires in digital bytes representing the alphabet of a handful of symbols, the FAX machine serves the same purpose where pictograms rule. Squeezing kanji and katakana characters down an ASCII modem may have the same pleasant effect as swallowing a porcupine whole, but FAX can digest the lot with nothing getting stuck in its throat and nary a burp. Quite understandably, about half the world's two million FAX machines are installed in Japan.

FAX is becoming increasingly important in Western business, too. It is the fastest and most cost-effective way of getting on-paper images from one place to another. Contracts complete with signatures, prescriptions, plans, charts, graphs, drawings, and page layouts all slip through the FAX connection with equal facility. FAX is cheaper than any other method of moving business information fast, a fraction of the cost of a next-day courier and even priced under telex. Only a fast ASCII blast and electronic mail compare. But, as they say everywhere from vaudeville to revival meetings, the best is yet to come. Engineers have linked FAX machines and PCs to create instant and automatic graphics communications systems. From humble beginnings as task masters ruling over FAX machines, PCs are becoming FAX stations that create, manage, send, receive, and display FAX images. FAX and the

PC can link electronic publishing systems with the world or tie the world of FAX images into your PC screen. With the latest PC-based FAX systems, you can create an investment newsletter in PageMaker or Ventura Publisher and deliver it around the world overnight without ever touching a sheet of paper.

In addition, the PC is becoming the FAX gateway for larger computer systems and networks. Although mainframe FAX links are marred by high costs (some cost as much as $12,000) and incompatibilities (early mainframe FAX products didn't work under the Group 3 standard), PC FAX systems are inexpensive and completely compatible. The PC is the logical link between the mainframe database and worldwide distribution of graphic information.

FAX Origins

The concept of facsimile transmissions is hardly new. As early as 1842, Alexander Bain patented an electro-mechanical device that could translate wire-based signals into marks on paper. Newspaper wire photos, which are based on the same principles, have been used for generations.

The widespread use of FAX in business is a more recent phenomenon, however, and its growth parallels that of the PC for much the same underlying reason. Desktop computers did not take off until the industry found a standard to follow, the IBM PC. Similarly, the explosive growth of FAX began only after the CCITT (an abbreviation for the French rendering of the International Telegraph and Telephone Consulative Committee, an organization that is part of the United Nations) adopted standards for the transmission of facsimile data.

The original system, now termed Group 1, was based on analog technology and used frequency shift keying, much as 300 baud modems do, to transmit a page of information in six minutes. Group 2 improved that analog technology and doubled the speed of transmission, up to three minutes per page.

The big break with the past and breakthrough was the CCITT's adoption in 1980 of the Group 3 FAX standard, which is entirely digitally-based. Using data compression and modems that operate at up to 9,600 bits per second, full-page documents can be transmitted in 30 to

60 seconds using the Group 3 standard. The data compression makes the speed of transmitting a page dependent on the amount of detail that it contains. In operation, the data-compression algorithm reduces the amount of data that must be transferred by a factor of 5 to 10. On the other hand, a bad phone connection can slow FAX transmissions as FAX modems automatically fall back to lower speeds to cope with poor line quality.

Under the Group 3 standard, two degrees of resolution, or on-paper sharpness, are possible (which also affects speed): standard, which allows 1,728 dots horizontally across the page (about 200 dots per inch) and 100 dots per inch vertically; and fine, which doubles the vertical resolution to achieve 200 x 200 dpi and requires about twice the transmission time.

In 1984, the CCITT approved a super-performance facsimile standard, Group 4, which allows resolutions of up to 400 x 400 dpi as well as higher speed transmissions of lower resolutions. Although not quite typeset quality (phototypesetters are capable of resolutions of about 1,200 dpi), the best of Group 4 is about equal to the resolving capability of the human eye at normal reading distance. However, today's Group 4 FAX machines require high-speed, dedicated lines and do not operate as dial-up devices. The ill-fated (now discontinued) Zap Mail services offered by Federal Express were based on Group 4 facsimile equipment.

PC-Based FAX

From a practical viewpoint, the most important application of PC-based FAX today is its capability to send and receive documents to and from the installed base of facsimile equipment. With FAX, there is no question of compatibility because the Group III standard requires that all graphic information be distilled to the same transmission format that guarantees compatibility with any FAX-compatible system.

Transmitting to FAX machines offers several advantages. FAX reception is essentially automatic. The FAX machine answers the line and starts its chore of churning out paper. When the transmission ends, it hangs up and waits for the next call. Unattended operation is not just possible but a design intent. With a FAX board in your PC, every FAX machine in the world becomes a remote printer, ready at any time to pour out its output.

The first link-ups between FAX and the PC were mere handshakes, but today the affair has become more intimate. When the two technologies first met, they kept their individual identities and joined together only through a serial port. With the latest innovations, however, the FAX machine and PC are combined into a single entity as easily as adding an expansion board to your computer.

One of the first PC-to-FAX connections was made by Xerox Corporation by tying an ordinary facsimile machine, their modem 895, to a PC. The FAX machine then functioned as a normal FAX machine, scanning, transmitting, and regenerating documents. The PC took control. It sent commands to the FAX machine to dial the phone and deliver transmissions to entire groups of recipients. The PC could also access the FAX data stream, recording it on disk, storing documents, or previewing images before they were sent or after they were received. A software utility could convert standard ASCII files into FAX-compatible data.

The new approach does away with the FAX machine entirely. Instead, it substitutes a FAX-compatible, high-speed modem that installs inside the PC. The PC itself creates the FAX images, or they can be derived from a peripheral image scanner. When a FAX transmission is received, it is displayed on the monitor screen or printed using a standard dot-matrix or laser printer. Special software can convert ASCII and even some graphic files into FAX format. Incoming and outgoing calls are managed much as they are in the linked FAX and PC systems. Images can be graphically edited either before or after transmission.

In truth, the capabilities of the two systems have converged. Once FAX data is in any PC, it can be similarly manipulated. The only important difference is that systems that link a PC to a FAX machine can also function separately while the FAX machine-in-a-PC is inseparable. On the other hand, two separate machines costs substantially more than a simple PC enhanced with a FAX modem board and adds more clutter to the office.

The primary advantage of either link-up is convenience. Without the connection, you'd have to print out a document made by your PC, and then scan it into the FAX machine. When you receive something without the PC-to-FAX connection, you would have the paper copy as the starting ground for any manipulations you'd want to make. Unless you have a scanner, that means pulling out the scissors and rubber cement if you want to make changes.

Link PC and FAX, and you can work on the screen, editing with painting programs or electronic publishing editors. With OCR software, you can even convert FAX documents into ASCII text to edit. Going the other direction, you can create FAX documents using your word processor or, with the appropriate conversion software, any other program. Instead of printing the results, you send them by FAX.

Creating FAX on the PC gives your work an added advantage, an apparent increase in resolution. By their nature, scanners have to make do with whatever they are force-fed. Unless the edge of a character or line perfectly matches the edge of a scanning cell, the question as to whether the corresponding dot should be black or white will be ambiguous. As a result, scanned characters can have fuzzy or jagged edges. When the character is made by a computer to be printed using a FAX machine, however, each dot can be optimally placed to give the sharpest apparent resolution. FAX text and graphics created on a PC thus look better than anything that's scanned in. Drivers for Windows allow you to print to FAX as easily as an ordinary printer.

Your PC can also be the base of an attack-FAX system. Instead of feeding the same sheet through your Group III machine a hundred times for a hundred different recipients, you send all the copies at once with a couple of keystrokes on your PC. Your PC-to-FAX program will churn out all the copies to everyone on an electronic mailing list with little more bother than sending one.

The chief disadvantage of PC-based FAX is that the system is substantially more complex than operating a FAX machine. Any secretary or executive can run a FAX machine. PC-to-FAX not only requires some knowledge (and confidence) in running a computer, but also it imposes the additional steps of booting up the machine, running software, prying your way through menus, and making sure that the ancillary equipment is powered-up and ready. If you want to ship document A to point B, pushing it through a dedicated FAX machine will be easier, cheaper, and less frustrating.

At its best, PC-to-FAX is a complementary technology to the FAX machine. If you want to move text that you've written on your word processor to Anchorage or Taipei, PC-to-FAX is quicker and less complicated than dragging it through your dot-matrix printer on the way to the FAX machine. The same goes for pictures you've brushed up through PC Paint or combination images you've created with PageMaker. You'll even get better quality at the distant end of the connection because PC-to-FAX programs know how to manipulate electronic images to yield the best quality output.

Commercial FAX Products

The price of adding FAX to your PC has reached new lows thanks to the availability of low-cost FAX modem chip sets. With but a handful of inexpensive parts, a boardmaker can craft a full Group III-compatible modem. Prices are now under $300. Almost universally, PC-to-FAX modems are made from the VLSI (Very Large Scale Integration) chips made by Rockwell Corporation. These chips cut costs, increase reliability, and practically guarantee that all of these FAX systems will be equally impervious (or susceptible) to line noise and completely compatible with the signal requirements of both the telephone system and Group III standard.

But all FAX boards are not the same. Some operate only at half-speed, 4,800 bps, doubling FAX send and transmission times. These are a choice only when your need for FAX is rare. (But if it is, you wouldn't be considering FAX at all, now would you?) Another difference between boards is intelligence. FAX boards can be either smart or dumb.

By today's standards, the classic FAX board is dumb. Although it can send and receive FAX transmissions, schedule transmissions, and even broadcast them to a long list of recipients, it lacks its own native intelligence. It depends on its computer host to control every step of its operation.

In contrast, the smart FAX board is built around a microprocessor. The computer host tells the board what to do. The details are left to the control of the brain on the board itself. As a result of this division of labor, more of the microprocessor power of the host computer is available for other purposes without sacrificing transmission speed. Dumb boards cannot send and receive FAX in the background because they monopolize the bandwidth of your PC's microprocessor in order to process high bit-rate data. A microprocessor on the FAX board can offload most of this FAX labor and execute it while your PC's microprocessor is working on another application. Consequently, FAX transmissions and reception can occur while the host computer is used for some other purpose.

A microprocessor on a FAX board in itself is not necessary for background FAX operation, however. Some dumb FAX systems deliver background operation with their own software or using multitasking environments, such as DoubleDos or DESQview. Although background operation with such dumb products is possible, it is not always desirable. When the computer must divide its time between multiple chores, the operation of the entire system slows down.

The various available FAX products also differ in the amount of background capability they offer. FAX is not a single operation. Most FAX boards are called on not only to manage sending files or receiving them, but also to convert ASCII files to FAX format, to schedule calls, and to manage errors (such as encountering a busy signal when calling out). Some FAX products run a number of these procedures in the foreground while nevertheless claiming background capabilities.

Whether background operation is needed for all FAX functions depends on how the system is used and by whom. Most people might not care about background operation in sending FAX but need its power during reception.

Smart FAX products are naturally costlier because, by definition, they include a microprocessor, a relatively expensive type of integrated circuit. In addition, to make a FAX board capable of background operation without host intervention, a wealth of additional components and circuitry is required. The board needs a microprocessor, at least 64K of RAM, PROM, and additional support chips. Moreover, the on-board microprocessor adds substantial length to the development period of the FAX product, pushing up the cost to create it.

The big difference between PC-to-FAX systems is software. Most systems give you menus to keep the inherently complex process manageable, but the menu hierarchies differ substantially. Some make sending the same FAX to a list of people quick and easy; others are demanding and confusing.

PC-to-FAX systems also differ in their capabilities. For example, some systems allow you to manipulate images before you send and after you receive them; others relegate image-editing to other programs. Although some PC-to-FAX systems won't flinch at 100-page transmissions, others balk long before the century mark.

In other words, selecting a PC-to-FAX system is more than a matter of buying a FAX board to slide into an expansion slot. If you want to get the most from FAX, you'll want to find a full-featured product that offers the capabilities you need.

19

Mass Storage Systems

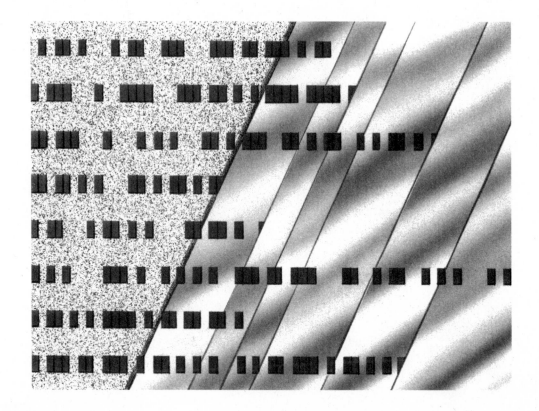

Mass storage is where you put the data you need immediately at hand but which won't fit into memory. Designed to hold megabytes and retrieve them at a moment's notice, mass storage has traditionally been the realm of magnetic disks, but other technologies and formats now serve specialized purposes and await their chances to move into the mainstream.

The difference between genius and mere intelligence is storage. The quick-witted react fast, but the true genius can call upon memories, experiences, and knowledge to find real answers. PCs are no different.

Putting a fast microprocessor in your PC would be meaningless without a means to store programs and data for current and future use. Mass storage is the key to giving your PC the long-term memory that it needs.

Essentially an electronic closet, mass storage is the place where you put information that you don't want to hold in your hands but don't want to throw away, either. As with the straw hats, squash rackets, wall-paper tailings, and all the rest of your dimly remembered possessions that pile up out of sight behind the closet door, retrieving a particular item from mass storage can take longer than when you have what you want at hand. And if you don't keep it organized, you may never find what you're looking for, or the whole horde may crash down on you.

Personal computers use several varieties of mass storage. In most PCs, the primary mass storage mediums are the hard disk drive and, to a lesser extent, the floppy disk drive, both of which are based on magnetic recording technology. For specialized storage, other technologies are also becoming prominent, primary among them laser-based optical systems. For the mass storage of data you need less readily, streaming and cassette tape drives are often the leading choice.

All of these media share the defining characteristics of mass storage. They deal with data en masse in that they store thousands and millions of bytes at a time. They also store that information on-line. To earn their huge capacities, the mass storage system moves the data out of the direct control of your PC's microprocessor. Instead of being held in your computer's memory where each byte can be directly accessed by your system's microprocessor, mass storage data requires two steps to use. First, the information must be moved from the mass storage device into your system's memory. Then it can be accessed by the microprocessor.

Mass storage can be either on-line storage, instantly accessible by your microprocessor's commands, or off-line, requiring some extra intervention (such as sliding a cartridge into a drive) for your system to get the bytes that it needs. Sometimes the term near-line storage pops up, referring to systems in which information isn't instantly available but can be put into instant reach by microprocessor command. The jukebox, an automatic mechanism that selects CD ROM cartridges (sometimes tape cartridges), is the most common example.

Moving bytes from mass storage to memory determines how quickly stored information can be accessed. In practical on-line systems, the time required for this access ranges from less than 0.01 second in the fastest hard disks to 1,000 seconds in some tape systems, spanning a range of 100,000 or five orders of magnitude.

By definition alone, the best off-line storage systems have substantially longer access times than the quickest on-line systems. Even with fast-access disk cartridges, the minimum access time for off-line data is measured in seconds because of the need to find and load a particular cartridge. On the other hand, the slowest on-line and fastest off-line storage system speeds overlap because the time to ready an off-line cartridge can be substantially shorter than the period required to locate needed information stored written on a long on-line tape.

Various mass storage systems span other ranges as well as speeds. Storage capacity reaches from as little as the 160K of the single-sided floppy disk drive to the multiple gigabytes accommodated by helical tape systems. Costs run from under $100 to more than $10,000.

The best way to put these huge ranges into perspective is to examine the technologies that underlie them. All mass storage systems are unified by a singular principle: they use some kind of mechanical motion to separate and organize each bit of information they store. To retain each bit, they make some kind of physical change to the storage medium, burning holes in it, blasting bits into oblivion, changing its color, or, most commonly, altering a magnetic field.

Magnetic Storage

Magnetic storage media have long been the favored choice for computer mass storage. The primary attraction of magnetic storage is nonvolatility. That is, unlike most electronic or solid-state storage systems, magnetic fields require no periodic addition of energy to maintain their state once it is set.

The issue is permanence. Magnetic fields have the wonderful property of being static and semi-permanent. On their own, they don't move or change. The electricity used by electronic circuits is just the opposite. It's constantly on the go and seeks to dissipate itself as quickly as possible. The difference is fundamental. Magnetic fields are set up by the spins of atoms that are physically locked in place. Electric charges are carried by mobile particles, mostly electrons, that not only refuse to stay in place but also are individually resistant to predictions of where they are or are going.

But, given the right force in the right amount, magnetic spins can be upset, twisted from one orientation to another. Because magnetic fields are amenable to change rather than being entirely permanent, magnetism is useful for data storage. After all, if a magnetic field were permanent and unchangeable, it would present no means of recording information. If it couldn't be changed, nothing about it could be altered to reflect the addition of information. It would be the equivalent of trying to carve cuneiform in a diamond using a banana as your only tool. You could never make your mark on any facet of posterity.

At the elemental particle level, magnetic spins are eternal, but taken collectively, spins can be made to come and go. A single spin can be oriented in just a single direction, but in virtually any direction. If two adjacent particles spin in opposite directions, they cancel one another out when viewed from a larger, macroscopic perspective.

Altering those spin orientations takes a force of some kind, and that's the key to making magnetic storage work. That force can make an alteration to a magnetic field, and once the field has been changed it will keep its new state until some other force acts on it.

The force that most readily changes one magnetic field is simply another magnetic field. (Some permanent magnets can be demagnetized simply through heating them sufficiently, but the demagnetization is actually an effect of the interaction of the many minute magnetic fields of the magnetic material itself.)

Despite their different behavior in electronics and storage systems, magnetism and electricity are manifestations of the same underlying elemental force. Both are electromagnetic phenomena. One result of that commonality makes magnetic storage particularly desirable to electronics designers: magnetic fields can be created by the flow of electrical energy. Consequently, evanescent electricity can be used to create and alter semi-permanent magnetic fields just as an all too mortal sculptor can hew a creation that will last for generations.

Once set up, magnetic fields are essentially self-sustaining. They require no energy to maintain because they are fundamentally a characteristic displayed by the minute particles that make up the entire universe (at least according to current physical theories). On the submicroscopic scale of elemental particles, the spins that form magnetic fields are, for the most part, unchangeable and unchanging. Nothing is normally subtracted from the spins: they don't give up energy even when they are put to work. Spins can affect other electro-magnetic phenomena, for example, used in mass to divert the flow of electricity. In such a case, however, all the energy in the system comes from the electrical flow, the magnetism is a gate, but the cattle that escape from the corral are solely electrons.

The magnetic fields that are useful in storage systems are those large enough to measure and effect changes on things that we can see. This magnetism is the macroscopic result of the sum of many microscopic magnetic fields, many elemental spins. Magnetism is a characteristic of submicroscopic particles. (Strictly speaking, in modern science magne-tism is made from particles itself, but we don't have to be quite so particular for the purpose of understanding magnetic computer storage.)

Magnetic Materials

Three chemical elements are magnetic: iron, nickel, and cobalt. The macroscopic strength as well as other properties of these magnetic materials can be improved by alloying them, both together and with nonmagnetic materials, particularly rare earths like samarium.

Many particles at the molecular level have their own intrinsic magnetic fields. At the observable (macroscopic) level, they do not behave like magnets because their constituent particles are organized (or disorganized) randomly so that, in bulk, the cumulative effects of all their magnetic fields tend to cancel out. In contrast, the majority of minute magnetic particles of a permanent magnet are oriented in the same direction. The majority prevails, and the material has a net magnetic field.

Some materials have the capability to be magnetized. That is, their constituent microscopic magnetic fields can be realigned so that they reveal a net macroscopic magnetic field. For instance, by subjecting a piece of soft iron to a strong magnetic field, the iron will become magnetized.

Magnetic Storage

If that strong magnetic field is produced by an electromagnet, all the constituents of a magnetic storage system become available. Electrical energy can be used to alter a magnetic field, which can be detected later. Suppose that you put a lump of soft iron within the confines of an unenergized electromagnet. Any time you return, you can determine whether the electromagnet has been energized in your absence merely by checking for the presence of a magnetic field in the iron. In effect, you've stored exactly one bit of information.

To store more, you need to be able to organize the information. You need to know the order of the bits. In magnetic storage systems, information is arranged physically the way data travels serially in time. Instead of being electronic blips that flicker on and off as the milliseconds tick by, magnetic pulses are stored like a row of dots on a piece of paper, a long chain with both beginning and end. This physical arrangement can be directly translated to the temporal arrangement of data used in a serial transmission system just by scanning the dots across the paper. The first dot becomes the first pulse in the serial stream, and each subsequent dot follows neatly in the data stream as the paper is scanned.

Instead of paper, magnetic storage systems use one or another form of media, generally either a disk or long ribbon of plastic tape, covered with a magnetically reactive mixture. The form of medium directly influences the speed at which information can be retrieved from the system.

Digital Magnetic Systems

Computer mass storage systems differ in principle and operation from tape systems used for audio and video recording. Whereas audio and video cassettes record analog signals on tape, computers use digital signals.

In the next few years, this situation will likely change as digital audio and video tape recorders become increasingly available. Eventually the analog audio and video tape will become historical footnotes, much as the analog vinyl phonograph record was replaced by the all-digital compact disc.

In analog systems the strength of the magnetic field written on a tape varies in proportion to the signal being recorded. The intensity of the recorded field can span a range of more than six orders of magnitude. Digital systems generally use a code that relies on patterns of pulses, and all the pulses have exactly the same intensity.

The technological shift from analog to digital is rooted in some of the characteristics of digital storage that make it the top choice where accuracy is concerned. Digital storage resists the intrusion of noise that inevitably pollutes and degrades analog storage. Every time a copy is made of an analog recording, the noise that accompanies the desired signal essentially doubles. That's because the background noise of the original source is added to the background noise of the new recording medium while the desired signal itself does not change. This addition of noise is necessary to preserve the nuances of the analog recording; every twitch in the analog signal adds information to the whole. The analog system cannot distinguish between noise and nuance. In digital recording, however, there's a sharp line between noise and signal. Noise below the digital threshold can be ignored without losing the nuances of the signal. Consequently, a digital recording system can eliminate the noise buildup in making copies. Moreover, noise can creep into analog recordings as the storage medium deteriorates, whereas the digital system can ignore most of the added noise of age. In fact, properly designed digital systems can even correct minor errors that get added to their signals.

Saturation

Digital recordings avoid noise because they ignore all strength variations of magnetic field except the most dramatic. Digital recordings just look for the unambiguous "it's either there or not" style of digital pulses of information. Analog systems achieve their varying strengths of field by aligning the tiny molecular magnets in the medium. A stronger electromagnetic field causes a greater percentage of the fields of these molecules to line up with the field, almost in direct proportion to the filed strength, to produce an analog recording. Because digital systems need not worry about intermediate levels of signal, they can simply lay down the strongest possible field that the tape can hold. This level of signal is called *saturation* because much as a saturated sponge can suck up no more water, the particles on the tape cannot ever produce a stronger magnetic field.

Although going from no magnetic field to a saturated field would seem to be the widest discrepancy possible in magnetic recording, and therefore the least ambiguous and most suitable for digital information, this contrast is not the greatest possible. Nor is it easy to achieve. Magnetic systems attempt to store information as densely as possible, trying to cram it in so every magnetic particle holds one data bit. Magnetic particles are extremely difficult to demagnetize, but the polarity of their magnetic orientation is relatively easy to change. Digital magnetic systems exploit this capability to change polarity, and they record data as shifts between the orientations of the magnetic fields of the particles on the tape. The difference between the tape being saturated with a field in one direction and the tape saturated with a field in the opposite direction is the greatest contrast possible in a magnetic system, and is exploited by nearly all of today's digital magnetic storage systems.

Coercivity

One word that you may encounter in the description of a magnetic medium is *coercivity*, a term that describes how strongly a magnetic field resists change, which translates into how strong a magnetic field a particular medium can store. Stronger stored fields are better because the more intense field stands out better against the random background noise that is present in any storage medium. Because a higher coercivity medium resists change better than a low coercivity material, it's also less likely to change or degrade because of the effects of external influences. Of course, a higher coercivity and its greater resistance to change mean that a recording system requires a more powerful magnetic field to maximally magnetize the medium. Equipment must be particularly designed to take advantage of high coercivity materials.

With hard disks, which characteristically mate the medium with the mechanisms for life, matching the coercivity of a medium with the recording equipment is permanently handled by the manufacturer. The two are matched for once and for all when a drive is made. Removable media devices (floppy disks, tape cartridges, cassettes, and other removable media devices) pose more of a problem. If media are interchangeable and have different coercivities, you face the possibility of using the wrong media in a particular drive. Such problems often occur with floppy disks, particularly when you want to skimp and use cheaper double-density media in high-density or extra-density drives.

Moreover, the need for matching drive and medium makes upgrading a less-than-simple matter. Obtaining optimum performance requires that changes in media be matched by hardware upgrades. Even when better media are developed, they may not deliver better results with existing equipment.

As storage media have been miniaturized, the coercivity of the magnetic materials used has generally increased. The greater intrinsic field strength makes up for the smaller area on which data is recorded. With higher coercivities, more information can be squeezed into the tighter confines of the newer storage formats. For example, the coercivity of the magnetic coatings of 3.5-inch floppy disks is much higher than that of 5.25-inch disks. The coercivity of DC2000 tape cartridges is much higher than that of older DC6000 designs. Although invisible to you, the coercivities of tiny, modern hard disk drives are much higher than big, old drives.

Coercivity is a temperature-dependent property. As the temperature of a medium increases, its resistance to magnetic change declines. That's one reason you can demagnetize an otherwise "permanent" magnet by heating it red hot. Magnetic media dramatically shift from being unchangeable to changeable (meaning a drop in coercivity) at a material-dependent temperature called the *Curie temperature*. Magneto-optical recording systems take advantage of this coercivity shift by using a laser beam to heat a small area of magnetic medium that's under the influence of a magnetic field otherwise not strong enough to affect the medium. Only the area heated by the laser above its Curie temperature (rather than the whole area under the magnetic influence) is changed by the external magnetic field. Because a laser can be tightly focused to a much smaller spot than is possible with traditional disk read/write heads, using such a laser-boosted system allows data to be defined by tinier areas of recording medium. A disk of a given size can store more data when its magnetic storage is optically assisted. Moreover, such media are resistant to the effects of stray magnetic fields (which may change low coercivity fields) as long as they are kept at room temperature.

The unit of measurement of coercivity is the *Oersted*. The coercivities of floppy disks range from 300 to 750 Oersteds. The coercivity of the medium used in magneto-optical drives is often higher than 6,000 Oersteds.

Retentivity

Another term that appears in the descriptions of magnetic media is *retentivity*, which measures how well a particular medium retains or remembers the field that it is subjected to. Although magnetic media are sometimes depended on to last forever, the stored magnetic fields begin to degrade as soon as they have been recorded. A higher retentivity assures a longer life for the signals recorded on the medium.

No practical magnetic material has perfect retentivity, however. The random element of modern physical theories assures that. Even the best hard disks slowly deteriorate with age, showing an increasing number of errors as time passes after data has been written. To avoid such deterioration of so-called permanent records, magnetically stored recordings should be periodically refreshed. Tapes stored in mainframe computer libraries, for example, are refreshed periodically (in intervals from several months to several years depending on the personal philosophy and paranoia of the person managing the storage). Although noticeable degradation may require several years, perhaps a decade or more, the tape caretakers do not want to depend on media written long ago.

If you're worried about the impermanence of magnetic recording, you can do the same thing the professionals do, refresh your storage. As a practical matter, that means backing up, and then restoring your hard disk, copying floppy disks, or simply making new backup tapes. Hard disks, the storage medium that most people depend on and worry about, take an extra step to completely refresh. After you back up your hard disk, you should reformat and repartition it before restoring the data to it again. Low-level reformatting rather than simple DOS formatting is required because the address marks put on the disk during the low-level format process also deteriorate with age, and these magnetic markings are only written (or rewritten) during the low-level formatting process. An inadvertent change in these sector markings can lead to Sector Not Found or similar errors that make data impossible to recover with DOS. Rewriting them with a low-level format can rejuvenate a cantankerous old disk.

Several hard disk utility packages, such as the Norton Utilities from Symantec Corporation and PC Tools from Central Point Software, have special "non-destructive" low-level formatting procedures directly aimed at hard disk rejuvenation. These work by copying all the data stored on a disk track to another location on the disk, low-level reformatting the original sector to refresh it (including its sector identification markings), and then rewriting the original data back to the track. The advantage of these systems is convenience. Although these utilities still recommend that you make a full disk backup before running the disk rejuvenation routine, they relieve you of the need to make a full restoration of the backup (unless in the rare case that something goes wrong with the rejuvenation process).

Flux Transitions

The 1s and 0s of digital information are not normally represented by the absolute direction in which the magnetic field is oriented, but by a change from one orientation to another so that they can take advantage of the most easily detected maximal magnetic change, from saturation in one direction to saturation in the other. These dramatic changes are termed *flux transitions* because the magnetic field or flux makes a transition between each of its two allowed states. In the very simplest magnetic recording systems, the occurrence of a flux transition would be the equivalent of a digital 1; no transition, a digital 0.

Of course, the system must know when to expect a flux transition, or else it would never know that it had missed one. Somehow the magnetic medium and the recording system must be synchronized with one another so that the system knows the point at which a flux transition should occur. In other words, the needs of digital recording are more complex than they at first seem. Instead of simple bit-for-bit recording, digital magnetic storage requires an elaborate coding system to keep the data straight.

Data Coding

Certainly assigning a single flux transition the job of storing a digital bit could be made to work, but this obvious solution is hardly the optimal one. For instance, to prevent errors, a direct one-to-one correspondence of flux-to-data would require that the pulse train on the recording medium be exactly synchronized with the expectations of the circuitry reading the data, perhaps by carefully adjusting the speed of the medium to match the expected data rate. A mismatch would make all the data being read or written incorrect. It might take several spins of the disk, each spin lasting more than a dozen milliseconds, to get back in sync.

By including extra flux transitions on the disk to help define the meaning of each flux change on a magnetic medium, it is possible to eliminate the need for exact speed control or other physical means of synchronizing the stored data. All popular magnetic recording systems use this expedient to store data asynchronously. However, all of these asynchronous recording schemes also impose a need for control information to help make sense from the unsynchronized flux transition pulse train.

Single-Density Recording

In one of the earliest magnetic digital recording schemes called *frequency modulation*, or *FM* recording, the place where a flux transition containing a digital bit was going to occur was marked by an extra transition called a *clock bit*. The clock bits form a periodic train of pulses that enables the system to be synchronized. The existence of a flux change between those corresponding to two clock bits indicated a digital 1, and no flux change between clocks indicated a digital 0.

The FM system requires a reasonably loose frequency tolerance. That is, the system could reliably detect the presence or absence of pulse bits between clock bits even if the clock frequency was not precise. In addition, the bandwidth of the system is quite narrow, so circuit tolerances are not critical. The disadvantage of the system is that two flux changes were needed to record each bit of data, the least dense practical packing of data on disk.

Initial digital magnetic storage devices used the FM technique, and for years it was the prevailing standard. After improvements in data packing were achieved, FM became the point of reference, often termed *single-density recording*.

Double-Density Recording

Single-density implies that there's something better, and that something is called *modified frequency modulation* recording (*MFM*) or *double-density recording*. Once the most widely used coding system in hard disks in PCs and still used by all PC floppy disk drives, double-density recording eliminates the hard clock bits of single-density to pack information on the magnetic medium twice as densely.

Instead of clock bits, digital 1s are stored as a flux transition and 0s as the lack of a transition within a given period. To prevent flux reversals from occurring too far apart, an extra flux reversal is always added between consecutive 0s.

Group Coded Recording

Even though double-density recording essentially packs every flux transition with a bit of data, it's not the most dense way of packing information on the disk. Other data coding techniques can as much as double the information stored in a given system as compared to double-density recording.

Both FM and MFM share a common characteristic, a one-to-one correspondence between bits of data and the change recorded on the disk. Although such a correspondence is the obvious way to encode information, it is not the only way. Moreover, the strict correspondence does not always make the most efficient use of the storage medium.

The primary alternative way of encoding data is to map groups of bits to magnetic patterns on the magnetic storage medium. Encoding information in this way is called *group coded recording* or *GCR*.

On the surface, group coding appears like a binary cipher. Just as in the secret codes used by simplistic spies in which each letter of the alphabet corresponds to another, group coding reduced to an absurdity would record a pattern of flux transitions, such as TTNT, where T is a transition and N is no transition.

Just as simple translations buy the spy little secrecy (such transpositional codes can be broken in minutes by anyone with a rudimentary knowledge of ciphering), they do little for the storage system. Where these translations become valuable is in using special easy-to-record patterns of flux transitions for each data group, typically with more transitions than there are bits in the data group. This technique succeeds in achieving higher area densities because the real limit on data storage capacity is the spacing of flux transitions in the magnetic medium. The characteristics of the magnetic medium, the speed at which the disk spins, and the design of the disk read/write head determine the minimum and maximum spacing of the flux changes in the medium. If the flux changes are too close together, the read/write head might not be able to distinguish between them; too far apart and they cannot be reliably detected.

By tinkering with the artificial restraints on data storage, more information can be packed within the limits of flux transition spacing in the medium.

Run Length Limited

Run length limited, or *RLL,* is one special case of group coded recording that is designed to use a complex form of data manipulation to fit more information in the storage medium without exceeding the range limits of its capability to handle flux transitions. In the most common form of RLL, termed *2,7,* each byte of data is translated into a pattern of 16 flux transitions.

Although this manipulation requires double the number of flux transition bits to store a given amount of information, it has the virtue that only a tiny fraction of the total number of 16-bit codes is needed to unambiguously store all the possible 8-bit data codes. There are 256 8-bit codes and 65,536 16-bit codes. Consequently, the engineer designing the system has a great range of 16-bit codes to choose from for each byte of data. If particularly astute, the designer can find patterns of flux translations that are particularly easy to record on the disk. In the 2,7 RLL system, the 16-bit patterns are chosen so that each digital 1 between two and seven digital 0s in the resulting 16-bit data stream of flux transitions. The 16-bit code patterns that do not enforce the 2,7 rule are made illegal and never appear in the data stream that goes to the magnetic storage device.

Although the coding scheme requires twice as many bits to encode its data, the pulses in the data stream better fit within the flux transition limits of the recording medium. In fact, the 2,7 RLL code ensures that flux transitions will be three times farther apart than in double-density recording because only the digital 1s cause flux changes, and they are always spaced at least three binary places apart. Although there are twice as many code bits in the data stream because of the 8-to-16 bit translation, the code bits corresponding flux transitions will be three times closer together on the magnetic medium while still maintaining the same spacing as would be produced by MFM. The overall gain in storage density achieved by 2,7 RLL over MFM is thus 50 percent.

The penalty of the greater recording density RLL is that much more complex control electronics and wider bandwidth electronics in the storage device are required to handle the higher data throughput.

Advanced RLL

A more advanced RLL coding system (*3,9 RLL* or *advanced RLL*) improves not only on the storage density that can be achieved on a disk, but is also more tolerant of old-fashioned disks. 3,9 RLL differs from 2,7 RLL in that it uses a different code that changes the bit pattern so that the number of sequential 0s is between three and nine. 3,9 RLL still uses an 8-to-16 bit code translation, but it ensures that digital 1s will never be closer than every four bits. As a result, 3,9 RLL allows data to be packed into flux transitions four times denser. The net gain, allowing for the loss in data translation, amounts to 100 percent. Information can be stored about twice as densely with 3,9 RLL as ordinary double-density recording techniques.

This seemingly extraordinary data-packing capability is a result of the various artificial limits enforced in most data storage systems. Until recently, most storage devices were designed for double-density recording, and they followed tightly defined interface standards for the connections between themselves and their control electronics. However, new interfacing schemes for hard disks isolate the data coding from the stream of data sent to the computer host. Drive manufacturers are thus free to use whatever form of data coding they like, and neither you nor your PC ever knows the difference. Consequently, with modern hard disk drives, the form of data coding that's used is rarely revealed (unless you take a critical look at the manufacturer's specification sheet). The information is simply irrelevant to you when you use an advanced disk interface.

Data Compression

In group coding, the correspondence between each bit pattern in the input data and the flux transitions represented by it is independent of all the other bit patterns in the data stream. Each pattern directly corresponds to its own pattern of flux transitions. The group coding system can mindlessly match bit pattern for flux pattern to achieve the optimal storage density of each byte of data.

But group coding does not represent the most efficient way of squeezing information into a storage medium. Many of the bytes in a stream of data are redundant. Their information content could be represented in some other manner using many fewer bytes. Group coding seeks to represent the stream of individual bytes without regard to content, simply ensuring that each pattern can be faithfully reproduced. Group coding does nothing to guarantee that the actual information is encoded in the data stream as efficiently as possible.

In contrast to the local view taken by the group coding mechanism, data compression systems take a global view. By examining the patterns of bytes rather than the bit patterns inside each byte, the compression system seeks to find patterns that can be more efficiently represented. The goal of the data-compression system is to eliminate redundancy, separating the bulk from the content. In effect, the compression system squeezes the air out of the data stream. The result is like deflating a blimp. The resulting limp bag will fit in confines too tight for a 300 foot-long dirigible but can readily be reinflated with helium to its original size and purpose. Similarly, data compression can reduce fat files into their slimmest possible representation, which can later, through a decompression process, be reconstituted into their original form.

Most compression systems work by reducing recurrent patterns in the data stream into short tokens. For example, the two-byte pattern "at" could be coded as the single byte "@," cutting the storage requirement in half. Most compression systems don't permanently assign tokens to bit patterns but, instead, make the assignments on the fly. They work on individual blocks of data one at a time, starting afresh with each block. Consequently, the patterns stored by the tokens of one block may be entirely different from those used in the next block. The key to decoding the patterns from the tokens is included as part of the data stream.

The compression ratio compares the resulting storage requirements to the uncompressed data storage requirements. For example, a compression ratio of 90 percent would reduce storage requirements by 90 percent. The compressed data could be stored in 10 percent of the space required by its original form.

Lossless versus Lossy Compression

Most compression systems assume that you want to get back every byte and bit that you store. When you pump the helium back into your deflated blimp, you expect to get an airship, not a gray golf ball. Similarly, you don't want numbers disappearing from your spreadsheets or commands from your programs. You assume that decompressing the compressed data will yield everything you started with, without losing a bit. The processes that deliver that result are called *lossless compression systems*.

Sometimes, however, your data may contain more detail than you need. For example, you might scan a photo with a true-color 24-bit scanner and display it on an ordinary VGA system with a color range of only 256 hues. All the precise color information in your scan is wasted on your display, and the substantial disk space you use for storing it could be put to a better use.

Analog images converted to digital form and analog audio recordings that are digitized often contain subtle nuances beyond the perception of most people. Some data reduction schemes called *lossy compression systems* ignore these fine nuances. The reconstituted data does not exactly replicate the original. For viewing or listening, the restored data is often good enough. Because lossy compression systems work faster than lossless schemes and because their resulting compression ratios are higher, they are often used in time- and space-sensitive applications, digital image, and sound storage.

Compression Implementations

Compression is simply a data transformation much like all the other manipulations made by a microprocessor. Consequently, an ordinary software program can convert your PC's microprocessor into an excellent data compressor.

Such software-only compression systems can be used to increase disk or tape capacity. Some software compression systems work as software drivers. They intercept the data stream headed for your hard disk, reroute it through a compression algorithm run by your PC's microprocessor, and pass the result to your disk instead of the original data. Many tape backup systems incorporate their own compression systems that transform that data as it is being passed from hard disk to tape (or floppy disk) drive. In either case, when the compressed data is later read, the compressed data stream is captured, its bytes processed by a complementary decompression algorithm, and the results passed to your application software.

The advantage of software-only compression is that it involves only software. You pay for nothing other than the program and almost miraculously get two times more storage space. The downside is the time required for processing. Software compression can slow disk response because of the time required by your PC's microprocessor to carry out the data transformations. Moreover, the systems that work as software drivers can encounter problems with hard disks that don't precisely conform to the DOS standard. Moreover, the driver software may not work with operating systems other than DOS.

Stand-alone software compression programs are also available to shrink files so that they require less time to transmit or a smaller disk space to store. Because these need not work in real time by trying to hide invisibly inside normal disk operations, they can more extensively evaluate files to determine the optimum compression method, even resorting to different schemes for various parts of a file or piling several compression schemes atop one another. (Because they are time insensitive, these programs can try more complex compression methods and thus avoid the rule that a compressed file can be compressed no further.)

These compression programs typically include a means for packing a number of files into a single unit. They are popular among users of electronic bulletin board systems because the smaller compressed files minimize expensive telephone line connection time. The leading commercial programs are ARC from System Enhancement Associates and PKzip from PKware.

You can take a load off your microprocessor with a compression coprocessor board. The coprocessor substitutes its power for that of your microprocessor in compression operations, eliminating the performance handicap of software compression. However, the coprocessor requires a driver to intercept disk (or tape) read and write operations and thus may be incompatible with non-DOS operating systems.

A number of hard disks now incorporate device-level compression, which moves the compression coprocessor from an expansion board to the disk drive itself. Such disks can store more information than their resources would otherwise allow. Because the compression circuitry is part of the drive itself and automatically fits in the middle of the data stream, there's no need for software drivers to make this form of compression work. Moreover, because device-level compression uses a coprocessor chip, there's no performance penalty.

Note that the same compression methods typically are used by software, coprocessor, and device-level compression. As a result, using more than one of these methods is counterproductive. The compressed output of one cannot be further compressed. Moreover, files compressed by compression utilities, such as ARC or PKzip, cannot be further compressed by any of these means. You'll get optimum speed and storage usage by using only one compression system.

Sequential and Random Access Media

The original electronic mass storage system was magnetic tape, actually a thin strip of paper on which a thin layer of refined rust had been glued. Later, the paper gave way to plastic, and the iron oxide coating give way to a number of improved magnetic particles based on iron, chrome dioxide, and various mixtures of similar compounds.

Tape Recording

The machine that recorded on these ribbons was the Magnetophone, the first practical tape recorder, made by the German company Telefunken. From this World War II-vintage device, able to capture only analog sounds, tape recording gradually gained the capability to record both video and digital data. Today both data cassettes and streaming tape systems are based on the direct offspring of the first tape recorder.

These tape media have a very straightforward design. The tape simply moves from left to right past a stationary read/write head. When a current is passed through an electromagnetic coil in this head, it creates the magnetic field needed to write data onto the tape.

When the tape is later passed in front of this head, the moving magnetic field generated by the magnetized particles on the tape induces a minuscule current in the head. This current is then amplified and converted into digital data. The write current used in putting data on the tape overpowers whatever fields already exist on the tape, both erasing them and also imposing a new magnetic orientation to the particles representing the information to be recorded.

Sequential Media

A fundamental characteristic of tape recording is that information is stored on tape one-dimensionally, in a straight line across the length of the tape. This form of storage is called sequential because all of the bits of data are organized one after another in a strict sequence, like those paper-based dots. In digital systems, one bit follows after the other for the full length of the tape. Although the width of the tape may be put to use in multi-track and the helical recording used by video systems, conceptually these, too, store information in one dimension only.

In the Newtonian universe (the only one that appears to make sense to the normal human mind), the shortest distance between two points is always a straight line. Alas, in magnetic tape systems, the shortest distance between two bits of data on a tape may also be a long time. To read two widely separated bits on a tape, all the tape between them must be passed over. Although all the bits in between are not to be used, they must be scanned in the journey from the first to second bits. If you want to retrieve information that's not stored in order on a tape, the tape must shuttle back and forth to find the data in the order that you want it. All that tape movement to find data means wasted time.

In theory, there's nothing wrong with sequential storage schemes; depending on the storage medium that's used, they can be very fast. For instance, one form of solid-state computer memory, the all-electronic "shift register," moves data sequentially at nearly the speed of light.

The sequential mass storage systems of today's computers are not so blessed with speed, however. Because of their mechanical foundations, most of tape systems operate somewhat slower than the speed of light. For instance, while light can zip across the vacuum of the universe at 186,000 miles per second (or so), cassette tape crawls along at 1 7/8 inches per second. Although light can get from here to the moon and back in a few seconds, moving a cassette tape that distance would take about 10 billion times longer, several thousand years.

Although no tape stretches as long as the 238,000 mile distance to the moon, sequential data access can be irritatingly slow. Instead of delivering the near-instant response most of today's impatient power users demand, picking a file from a tape can take as long as 10 minutes. If you had to load all your programs and data files from tape, you might as well take up crocheting to tide you through the times you're forced to wait.

Random Access Media

On both floppy and most hard computer disks, the recorded data is organized differently to take advantage of the two-dimensional aspect of the flat, wide disk surface. Instead of being arranged in a single straight line, disk-based data is spread across several concentric circles like lanes in a circular race track or the pattern of waves rolling away from a splash. Some optical drives follow this system, but many other optical systems modify this arrangement, changing the concentric circles into one tightly packed spiral that continuously winds from the edge to the center of the disk. But even these continuous-data systems behave much as if they had concentric circles of information.

Tracks

The mechanism for making this arrangement is quite elementary. The disk itself moves in one dimension under the read/write head, which scans the tape in a circle as it spins and defines a *track*, which runs across the surface of the disk much like one of the lanes of a racetrack. In most disk systems the head, too, can move, or else the read/write head would be stuck forever hovering over the same track and the same stored data, making it a sequential storage system that wastes most of the usable storage surface of the disk.

In most of today's disk systems, the read/write moves across a radius of the disk, perpendicular to a tangent of the tracks. The read/write head can thus quickly move between the different tracks on the disk. Although the shortest distance between two points (or two bytes) remains a straight line, to get from one byte to another, the read/write head can take shortcuts across the lanes of the racetrack. Once the head reaches the correct track, it still must wait for the desired bit of information to cycle around under it. However, disks spin relatively quickly (300 revolutions per minute for most floppy disks and 3,600 rpm for most hard disks), so you only need to wait a fraction of a second for the right byte to reach your system.

Because the head can jump from byte to byte at widely separated locations on the disk surface and because data can be read and re-trieved in any order or at random in the two-dimensional disk system, disk storage systems are often called *random access devices*, even though they fall a bit short of the mark with their need to wait while hovering over a track.

The random access capability of magnetic disk systems makes the combination much, much faster than sequential tape media for the mass storage of data. In fact, disks are so superior and so much more convenient than tapes that tape is almost never used as a primary mass storage system. Usually tape plays only a secondary role as a backup system. Disks are used to store programs and files that need to be loaded on a moment's notice.

In optical systems with a single continuous track spiral, the read/write head still must move radially across the disk if just to follow the long spiral. But because it still can leap from one part of the continuous track to another, the moving head also endows these systems with fast random access speeds. Moreover, because the head can follow the track inward without jogging and briefly skipping over an unreadable disk area, these continuous track systems can smoothly read long blocks of data at high speeds. Consequently, they offer both excellent random access speeds and high continuous data transfer rates.

In modern hard disks, the actual physical track arrangement has become irrelevant. Using special electronics, disk designers are able to mask the physical characteristics of the drive and make it respond as if it has some other geometry. Using such a masking process, engineers can make otherwise incompatible drives function in PCs. For example, neither DOS nor most BIOSs allow the use of more the 1,024 tracks (or cylinders) on a hard disk. Using this masking technique, the logical disk geometry your PC sees can be kept within this limit even if the drive itself actually has 2,048 tracks.

Sectors

Tracks are usually broken down into smaller segments called *sectors*. The number of sectors on each track varies from 8 on some floppy disks to 51 or more on some modern, high-capacity drives. On disks that use device-level interfaces, the number of sectors is the same on all tracks, even though information has to be squeezed in more tightly on the tracks nearer the center of the disk because the track diameter is smaller. Normally, the sector size is 512 bytes in the IBM scheme of things.

Each sector is unambiguously identified with special magnetic markings on the disk. These sector identifications are part of the format of the disk. Figure 19.1 shows the contents of a typical sector identification.

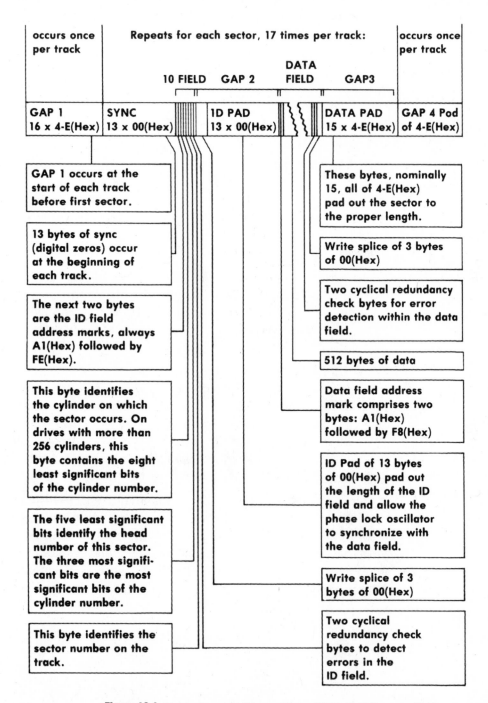

Figure 19.1. Typical sector ID markings (ST5061412 controller).

Zone-Bit Recording

An increasing number of drives use a number of tricks to pack more sectors on the longer tracks nearer the outer edge of disk platters. Special electronics hide these odd sector arrangements from your computer, disguising the sector arrangement so that it looks as if all tracks are equally endowed with sectors.

The technology behind squeezing in more sectors is complex. Nominally, hard disks spin at a constant rate. If they alter their speed so that they spin faster when the read/write head is over the longer outer tracks so as to pack in more data, access time would suffer. Although the head could dash about quickly, the system would have to wait while the disk spun up or down to the appropriate speed for reading or writing.

Using a technique called *zone-bit recording* solves this problem. Instead of changing disk speed, zone-bit drives alter the frequency at which their electronics operate depending on the zones (a continuous group of tracks) that the head hovers over. The different frequencies result in different data densities.

Conventional disks that use constant frequencies end up recording at lesser densities on the outer tracks of disk platters because more of the medium spins under the head in a given period. Zone-bit recording allows maintaining a nearly constant data density across the disk. Using higher frequencies at the outer tracks of a disk increases their data density to that of the inner tracks. This, in turn, can substantially increase overall disk capacity without compromising reliability.

The drive must somehow mask its actual physical characteristics so that it looks to your PC as if it has a standard geometry, such as tracks of 17 sectors, each sector storing 512 data bytes. DOS can't deal with disks that magically change from having 17 sectors per track one minute to 23 sectors, then to 31. This masking process is simplified using a system-level interface.

Translation Mode

The number of heads, tracks, and sectors are important when configuring your PC. These values determine the signals the drive controller must send to your drive to find a given byte of data. Normally, you indicate these values when you run your PC's setup procedure. The masking techniques used to hide the actual number of tracks and sectors mean that you configure your system to the logical track and sector arrangement created by the drive electronics rather than the actual physical configuration of the drive.

Some state-of-the-art drives go further. They not only mask their physical characteristics but also have enough intelligence so that the drive can sense what parameters (the number of heads, cylinders, and sectors) your PC expects. The drive then automatically matches those parameters. This feature is called *translation mode*.

A drive that supports translation mode will accept any drive parameters you choose with your PC's setup procedure, providing you don't specify more capacity than the drive is capable of supplying. For example, you could buy an 80-megabyte drive that supports translation mode, and it will automatically adapt to emulate whatever number of heads and cylinders you've entered into your setup program.

Translation mode has one drawback, however. Once you format a drive with translation mode, its logical configuration is set and cannot be changed without reformatting the drive. Although the drive can still automatically adapt, your data cannot.

A problem arises should the CMOS configuration memory of your PC be corrupted. For example, if you replace the battery in your PC and have to reconfigure your system, you'll have to remember the old drive parameters you had set to recover the data you stored. Or if you want to transfer a drive and its data between different systems, you'll have to be sure to use the same setup parameters in each system.

Unfortunately, a translation-mode drive offers no help as to what parameters to use other than telling you its capacity. Consequently, as a future reference you should label your hard disk with the parameters (or drive type) you had set when you formatted it.

Clusters

DOS doesn't deal with tracks or sectors. Instead, it allocates disk storage into handy groups of sectors called *clusters*, sometimes called *allocation units*. Each cluster is an interchangeable unit of a standard size that can vary from 512 to 8,096 bytes depending on disk type, its format, and the DOS version that you use.

To store a file on disk, DOS breaks it down into a group of clusters, perhaps hundreds of them. Each cluster can be drawn from anywhere on the disk. Sequential pieces of a file do not necessarily have to be stored in clusters that are physically adjacent.

The earliest, and now obsolete, versions of DOS follow a simple rule in picking which clusters are assigned to each file. The first available cluster, the one nearest the beginning of the disk, is always the next one used. Thus, on a new disk, clusters are picked one after another, and all the clusters in a file are contiguous.

When a file is erased, its clusters are freed for reuse. These newly freed clusters, being closer to the beginning of the disk, will be the first ones chosen when the next file is written to disk. In effect, DOS first fills in the holes left by the erased file. As a result, the clusters of new files may be scattered all over the disk.

The earliest versions of DOS use this strange strategy because they were written at a time when capacity was more important than speed. The goal was to pack files on the disk as stingily as possible.

Starting with Version 3.0, DOS doesn't immediately try to use the first available cluster closest to the beginning of the disk. Instead, it attempts to write on never-before-used clusters before filling in any erased clusters. This helps assure that the clusters of a file will be closer to one another, a technique that improves the speed of reading a file from the disk.

File Allocation Table

To keep track of which cluster belongs in which file, DOS uses a file allocation table, or FAT, essentially a map of the clusters on the disk. When you read to a file, DOS automatically and invisibly checks the

FAT to find all the clusters of the file; when you write to the disk, DOS checks the FAT for available clusters. No matter how scattered over your disk the individual clusters of a file may be, you, and your software, only see a single file no matter how the clusters are scattered.

It's important to keep cluster size small because clusters are the smallest possible storage unit on a disk. Consequently, the smallest batch file you create will steal at least one cluster of disk space. It is possible that a 10-byte batch file could occupy 8,192 bytes on the disk. On the average, every file larger than one cluster will also waste half a cluster worth of disk space. Moreover, every directory, even those not containing files, will also steal at least one cluster from a disk. Consequently, the smaller the cluster size, the less disk space will be wasted on unused storage. DOS versions through 3.3 used FATs with 12-bit cluster numbers, allowing a total of 4,096 uniquely named clusters. With 8,192 byte clusters, the maximum possible disk (or partition size) was 33,554,432, the infamous old DOS 32M limit. DOS 4.0 and later allow 16-bit FAT entries, which allow a total of 65,536 uniquely named clusters. With cluster size kept at a space-saving 2,048 bytes, the maximum permissible disk size is 134,217,728 (or 128M). Larger disks or partitions, up to 512M, are accommodated by increasing cluster size, stepwise, through 4,096 to 8,192 bytes. DOS 5.0 can handle even larger disks by dividing them into multiple partitions, each kept within the limits imposed by the combination of cluster and FAT entry size.

Control Electronics

Mass storage systems usually consist of three parts, which are sometimes combined. The actual drive or transport (complete with its own internal electronics) handles the medium itself, spooling the tape or spinning the disk. The controller electronics generate the signals that control the transport from commands given by the host computer system. And the host adapter converts the signals generated by the host computer, for our purposes, the signals that travel on the ISA, EISA, Micro Channel, or local bus, into those that are compatible with the controller.

Primeval Controllers

Before the appearance of the IBM XT, most controllers for mass storage devices were often free-standing circuit boards that were installed in the same housing as the hard disk drive itself. A separate host adapter card would convert the signals of the host computer to those of the standard favored by the controller. The host adapter and controller were linked by a kind of glorified parallel port. Control functions were distributed in three places: the host adapter inside the computer, the controller itself which was typically mated in the cabinet with the mass storage device, and the transport electronics that were part of the mass storage device itself.

Many early add-ons for PCs, such as hard disks and tape backup systems, used this separate controller-adapter-disk drive system. The manufacturers of these products had good reason to do this. This design allowed mass storage equipment to mate with virtually any computer system simply by substituting a different host adapter. Off-the-shelf controllers could be designed so that they could be matched to any computer system, giving them the widest possible market. After all, before the PC there was no such thing as a truly universal bus standard. When incompatible computers of unlike designs were sold in quantities of dozens and hundreds (unlike the millions of standardized IBM-style machines sold today), this technique opened large enough markets to make the manufacture of mass storage systems economically feasible.

Moreover, there was a good, practical reason for separating the host adapter and controller. The combination of controller and host adapter circuitry would likely consume more board space than would fit into an ordinary PC expansion slot.

Combined Host Adapter and Controller

Although neither the PC bus nor the Micro Channel qualify as universal standards, their huge user bases easily justify the manufacture of products designed exclusively for them. As the success of the first IBM personal computer began to prove such acceptance was coming, controller manufacturers began to integrate the host adapter and storage system controller electronics onto a single expansion board. Today, most mass storage systems use this approach, mating with the storage device on one end and the PC's expansion bus (whatever standard it might follow) on the other. This single board is also called a *controller* because that's its primary function, and its combination nature is taken for granted.

The IBM XT hard disk subsystem heralded the change from the host adapter-controller system. The XT controller unified the host adapter and controller functions on a single, dense circuit board. This pioneering controller, initially made for IBM by Xebec Corporation, set the pattern for the next generation of devices. The great majority of hard disk controllers follow this two-in-one pattern. The AT followed this scheme, using a control developed by Western Digital Corporation— specifically, model WD1002. Because software was written to take advantage of the features of this specific controller, it set the trend for all designs that followed. Nearly all hard disk controllers used in PCs to this day emulate the features of the WD1002.

Embedded Controllers

The next logical step in controller design is to move the circuitry out of the expansion slot and put it on the drive. This change is called *integrating* or *embedding* the controller function in their storage devices. This technology is technically termed integrated drive electronics, although in general use the abbreviation IDE often refers to a specific kind of disk interface, one that uses the AT expansion bus for its connections, which is formally (and correctly) termed the AT Attachment or ATA interface, or simply the AT interface.

The small computer system interface, or SCSI, represents one of the fullest implementations of an embedded disk controller. SCSI, discussed in detail later in this chapter, operates as a fully arbitrated expansion bus and allows device-independent interchanges of data at high speeds.

Integrated Hard Disk Cards

The alternate strategy to putting the expansion board-based electronics on the hard disk is to put the hard disk on the expansion board. This also integrates the drive electronics, and, in fact, the first true embedded interfaces were used on hard disk cards, which put all three essential functions (host adapter, controller, and storage device) together on a single board-like assembly that would slide into a standard expansion slot. Of course, this strategy is only effective when you don't require access to the medium used by the mass storage device, characteristic only of hard disks. Miniaturization and standardization have made embedded control electronics on conventionally mounted drives the preferred interface choice.

Device-Level Interfaces

The whole purpose of the controller is to link a disk or tape drive with its computer host. So that the widest variety of devices can be connected to a controller, the signals in this connection have been standardized.

The interface can appear at one of two levels. A device-level interface is designed to link a particular kind of device to its host. The interface is particular to the signals developed by that device and will generally work with no other. A system-level interface connects at a higher level, after all the signals from the device have been converted to the kind used by the host computer system. The signals used by a system-level interface are not specific to any single kind of device. For example, tape drives, hard disks, floppy disks, even scanners and printers all can use the same system-level interface. Each would require its own specific device-level interface. Three device-level interfaces are regularly used in PC-based mass storage systems. These include the floppy disk interface and two hard disk interfaces, ST506 and the Enhanced Small Device Interface or ESDI.

Floppy Disk Interface

Floppy disks follow a standard that's simply referred to as the *floppy disk interface*. This connection scheme is also used by a number of inexpensive tape backup systems. In operation, it's much like a glorified serial port that's had a few new command lines added to it to handle the particular functions associated with the floppy disk drive. Only a few signals are required to control the two floppy disk drives normally attached by a single cable to the controller.

Two drive-select signals are used to individually select either the first or second drive, A or B. (In four-drive systems, the signals for A in the second cable control drive C, and those of B control D.) If the signal assigned to a particular drive is not present, all the other input and output circuits of the drive are deactivated, except for those that control the drive motor. In this way, two drives can share the bulk of the wires in the controller cable without interference. However, this control scheme also means that only one drive in a pair can be active at a time. You can write to drive B at the same time as you read from drive A. That's why you must transfer the data held on a disk (or file) from one drive into memory before you can copy it to another drive.

One wire is used for each drive to switch its spindle motor on and off. These are called *Drive Select A* and *Drive Select B*. Although it is possible to make both motors spin simultaneously, rules laid down by IBM admonish against activating these two lines to make both floppy disk drive motors run at the same time (this saves power in the severely constrained PC system and is a moot issue in the single-drive XT system). Of course, the two drives in your PC may run simultaneously for brief periods due to a delay built into most drives that keeps their motors running for a few seconds after the motor-enable signal stops.

Two signals in the floppy disk interface control the head position of each of the attached drives. One, step pulse, merely tells the stepper motor on the drive with its drive select active to move one step (exactly one track) toward or away from the center of the disk. The direction signal controls which way the pulses move the head. If this signal is active, the head moves toward the center.

To determine which of the two sides of a double-sided disk to read, one signal, called *write select*, is used. When this signal is active, it tells the disk drive to use the upper head. When no signal is present, the disk drive automatically uses the default (lower) head.

Writing to disk requires two signals on the interface. The write data signal comprises the information that's actually to be written magnetically onto the disk. It consists of nothing but a series of pulses corresponding exactly to the flux transitions that are to be made on the disk. The read/write head merely echoes these signals magnetically. As a fail-safe to preclude the possibility of accidentally writing over valuable data, a second signal called *write enable* is used. No write current is sent to the read/write head unless this signal is active.

Four signals are passed back from the floppy disk drive to the controller through the interface. Two of these help the controller determine where the head is located. Track 0 indicates to the controller when the head is above the outermost track on the disk so that the controller knows from where to start counting head-moving pulses. Index helps the drive determine the location of each bit on a disk track. One pulse is generated on the Index line for each revolution of the disk. The controller can time the distance between ensuing data pulses based on the reference provided by the index signal.

In addition, the write-protect signal is derived from the sensor that detects the existence or absence of a write-protect tab on a disk. If a tab is present, this signal is active. The read-data signal comprises a series of electrical pulses that exactly matches the train of flux transition on the floppy disk.

Controllers

The basic purpose of the floppy disk controller is to convert the requests from the BIOS or direct hardware commands that are couched in terms of track and sector numbers into the pulses that move the head to the proper location on the disk. For the most efficient operation, the controller must also remember where the head is located, index the head as necessary, and report errors when they occur.

In its translation function, the floppy disk controller must make sense from the stream of unformatted pulses delivered from the drive. The controller first must find the beginning of each track from the Index pulse, and then mark out each sector from the information embedded in the data stream. Once it identifies a requested sector, the controller must then read the information it contains and convert it from serial to parallel form so that it can be sent through the PC bus. In writing, the controller must first identify the proper sector to write to, which is a read operation, and then switch on the write current to put data into that sector before the next sector on the disk begins.

Most of the hard work of the controller is handled by a single integrated circuit, the 765 controller chip. The 765 works much like a microprocessor, carrying out certain operations in response to commands that it receives through registers connected to your computer's I/O ports. This programmability makes the 765 and the floppy disk controllers made from it extremely versatile, able to adapt to changes in media and storage format as the PC industry has evolved. None of the essential floppy disk drive parameters are cast in stone or the silicon on the controller. The number of heads, tracks, and sectors on a disk are set by loading numbers into the registers of the 765. The values that the controller will use are normally loaded into the controller when you boot up your computer. You ordinarily don't have to worry about them after that. With the right on-board support circuitry and BIOS code, the same controller can often handle floppy disks ranging from ancient 8-inch monsters to the latest extra-density (2.88M) 3.5-inch pocket-liners. Because older designs could not foresee the potential of future floppy disk formats, however, not all controllers are compatible with all floppy disk formats. And to get full use of more recent floppy configurations, you'll need a version of DOS or other operating system designed to accommodate them (see Chapter 20).

Special software can reprogram your controller to make it read, write, and format floppy disks that differ from the IBM standard. Two types of software perform this reprogramming. Copy-protection schemes may alter vital drive parameters by misnumbering sectors, adding extra sectors, or a similar operation that cannot be duplicated using normal IBM parameters. Disk compatibility software alters the controller programming to make the floppy disk drives in your system act like those used by other computers, such as those that use the CP/M operating system. Note, however, that although the IBM system is flexible, it cannot handle all possibilities, such as Commodore or Apple disks. Those computers used entirely different drive control hardware, which the 765 cannot mimic.

Over the last decade, the floppy disk controller has evolved from an entity of its own to a few circuits on the system board. The original design that IBM plugged into its first PC was also adopted by the XT and Portable PC. With the AT, the floppy disk circuitry was packaged alongside the hard disk control circuitry on the system's hard disk controller, saving an expansion slot. With the advent of the PS/2 series, the floppy disk controller was put onto the system board.

Modern PC-compatible computers can use any of these three designs. All work equally well. The main design considerations are slot usage and cost. Some clone-makers find it less expensive to slide in an expansion board rather than building floppy disk circuitry on the system board. Although these designs may waste an expansion slot, that's rarely a consideration for a company trying to package a PC as cheaply as possible. For you, as a PC purchaser, the chief floppy controller issue arises when you upgrade: if you install a new hard disk controller, replacing one that incorporated floppy disk circuitry, you'll need to replicate your old floppy disk circuitry in your upgrade.

Connectors

The floppy disk interface has changed subtly over the years. The original PC and XT floppy disk controller used an edge connector to attach to the floppy disk cable. AT and more recent controllers generally use pin connectors. In either case, the same signals appear at the same pins. The connectors on floppy disks are changing as well. Nearly all 5.25-inch drives use edge connectors; most 3.5-inch drives use pin connectors.

In addition to the edge connector on the card, PC and XT controllers provide a second, 37-pin connector on the card option retaining bracket. All the signals necessary for running a third and a fourth floppy disk are available there. Most newer floppy disk controllers only provide for two drives, although a few four-drive controllers are available from third-party manufacturers.

ST506/412

The original hard disk interface used in the IBM XT, AT, and some models of PS/2 computers followed an industry standard device-level interface called *ST506/412*. Unlike the names of other interfaces that are acronyms, the ST506 name has little significance. The initials stand for Shugart Technology, the company that originated the interface, and the numbers just distinguish this design from others, much like the model number of automobiles or cameras.

As with the floppy disk interface, ST506 transfers data to and from the disk drive in serial form. Bits are read as flux transitions from the disk and delivered in original form to the controller through a single data wire. The data separator in the controller then figures out which bits are meaningful data and which are formatting or sector identification information.

The stream of actual data bits then goes to a deserializer circuit, which converts the serial train of bits into parallel data compatible with the bus of the host computer. At the same time, the data is checked for errors, and most of the errors are corrected.

The ST506 standard does not specify the data coding method of the signal recorded on disk or passed through the interface. It only provides a serial channel between drive and controller. Consequently, ST506 accommodates MFM, RLL, and advanced RLL coding methods. However, drives must be able to deal with the higher frequencies of advanced modulation methods. The disk controllers themselves determine the modulation method and data coding, so the choice of controller determines what's recorded on disk. Unlike the floppy disk interface, the ST506 interface uses two cables, a wide control cable with 34 connections and a smaller data cable with 20. Table 19.1 shows the functions assigned to each of these connections.

TABLE 19.1.
ST506/412
Cable Pin-Out

Control cable:			
Pin	Function	Pin	Function
1	Head select 8	2	Ground
3	Head select 4	4	Ground
5	Write gate	6	Ground
7	Seek complete	8	Ground
9	Track 0	10	Ground
11	Write fault	12	Ground
13	Head select 1	14	Ground
15	Reserved	16	Ground
17	Head select 2	18	Ground
19	Index	20	Ground
21	Ready	22	Ground
23	Step	24	Ground
25	Drive select 1	26	Ground
27	Drive select 2	28	Ground
29	Drive select 3	30	Ground
31	Drive select 4	32	Ground
33	Direction in	34	Ground

Data cable:			
Pin	Function	Pin	Function
1	Drive selected	2	Ground
3	Reserved	4	Ground
5	Reserved	6	Ground
7	Reserved	8	Ground
9	Reserved	10	Reserved
11	Ground	12	Ground
13	MFM write data +	14	MFM write data –
15	Ground	16	Ground
17	MGM read data +	18	MFM read data –
19	Ground	20	Ground

In new PCs, the ST506 interface is essentially obsolete. Hard disk makers long ago stopped designing new drives using the interface, and few new drives using it are available. Its primary defect was speed. ST506 was designed in the days when PC performance was 50 or more times slower than today's best machines. Back then, it moved data faster than any PC could possibly absorb it. Today, PCs far outclass ST506 drives.

The ST506 interface itself was not suitable for upgrading. Because it is a device-level interface, the timing of its signals is directly matched to physical attributes of the drives using it. That is, its operating frequencies are forever tied to a transfer rate governed by the spin of the disk. None of these values can be changed without altering the others. Faster disks thus require a new, faster interface.

ESDI

A faster version of ST506 is essentially what ESDI was designed to be— the same control and data signals upgraded to higher speeds. In fact, many of the first ESDI products simply boosted the speed at which data was transferred between transport and controller from ST506's 5 Mhz to 10 Mhz.

ESDI uses similar connections to those of the ST506 interface, including the same two-cable system. The two interfaces are not compatible, however. You cannot plug an ESDI drive into an ST506 interface and expect the system to work. Nor will an ST506 drive work through an ESDI connection. The pin-out of the ESDI connection scheme is shown in table 19.2.

TABLE 19.2.
ESDI Cable
Pin-Out

Control cable:			
Pin	Function	Pin	Function
1	Head select 3	2	Ground
3	Head select 2	4	Ground
5	Write gate	6	Ground
7	Config/Status data	8	Ground
9	Transfer acknowledge	10	Ground

continues

TABLE 19.2.
continued

Control cable:			
Pin	Function	Pin	Function
11	Attention	12	Ground
13	Head select 0	14	Ground
15	Sector/Addr mark found	16	Ground
17	Head select 1	18	Ground
19	Index	20	Ground
21	Ready	22	Ground
23	Transfer request	24	Ground
25	Drive select 1	26	Ground
27	Drive select 2	28	Ground
29	Drive select 3	30	Ground
31	Read gate	32	Ground
33	Command data	34	Ground

Data cable:			
Pin	Function	Pin	Function
1	Drive selected	2	Sector/Address mark found
3	Seek complete	4	Address mark enable
5	Reserved for step mode	6	Ground
7	Write clock +	8	Write clock –
9	Cartridge changed	10	Read reference clock +
11	Read reference clock –	12	Ground
13	NRZ write data +	14	NRZ write data –
15	Ground	16	Ground
17	NRZ read data +	18	NRZ read data –
19	Ground	20	Index

However, ESDI isn't quite so simple. The interface specification allows for slower and faster speeds (some drives now send signals at 25 Mhz) and pins down more aspects of drive and system design. ESDI was also designed with the idea of adapting the interface to tape systems, although it has not won wide acceptance for that application.

Of all the improvements made by ESDI, its higher speed has the most important implications. To make information move faster while maintaining the same spin rate as ST506 drives (3,600 revolutions per minute), the typical ESDI hard disk drives must pack twice as much data onto each track to be read during each revolution. Most ESDI drives thus lay 34 or more sectors on each track, doubling data density as well as transfer rate.

As with the ST506 standard, the ESDI is a device-level interface. Its connections are fundamentally made directly to the device that's to be connected to the system. In the case of hard disks, ESDI goes beyond ST506 by allowing configuration and bad track information to be stored on the drive itself. Instead of requiring the host computer to know what kind of disk drive is connected through the interface (either through an XT-style BIOS extension or through CMOS configuration memory, each ESDI drive tells the controller how many tracks, cylinders, and such it has. Instead of requiring that you test for and type in all the bad tracks on the drive, it lets the manufacturer test the disk, flag the bad tracks, and store that information on the disk in a standardized form that the controller can directly access. Unfortunately, few PCs take advantage of this information; most still require that you configure their CMOS memory for vital drive parameters as you would with ST506 drives.

The biggest virtue of ESDI has proven to be its similarity to ST506, coupled with higher speed. Installing an ESDI drive system hardly differs from installing an ST506 drive, yet you get higher performance. After a brief moment in the sun, however, ESDI has fallen from favor. Its split drive/controller design no longer makes sense for PC or drive designers, and it is running into a performance roadblock. Its serial data channel is reaching its upper speed limit. Disk interfaces allowing parallel transfers are taking its place. By late 1991, most hard disk manufacturers had spurned ESDI for new drive development, instead turning exclusively to system-level interfaces.

System-Level Interfaces

In contrast to device-level interfaces, system-level interfaces allow the mass storage designer a great deal of freedom. The inner workings of the storage device are hidden from the interface, all that comes out is formatted data compatible with the host computer. Although conventional device-level designs push the raw data stream from the disk or other device through the interface—along with the data goes device formatting information, such as sector identifications and the like—system level interfaces transfer only active data. The system level passes along only an executive summary of the device's information; device-level interfaces must include the footnotes, page numbers, and irrelevant digressions. Without all the chaff, the system-level interface can move more data even when operating at exactly the same clock rate as a device-level interface.

Moreover, today's system-level interfaces are not constrained by the serial limitations of the popular device-level interfaces. For example, the AT Attachment interface passes data 8 or 16 bits at a time; the latest SCSI connections allow transfers up to 32 bits wide. Although the system-level interfaces aren't clocked as fast as the quickest device-level interfaces, they deliver greater throughput. In fact, the lower clock speed of the system-level interfaces is an advantage that reduces design and radiation problems.

In addition, because the actual device is hidden from the interface signals, the system-level design allows technical innovation without altering compatibility. New technologies for higher capacities, greater security, or even faster throughput can be accommodated without violating the standard. Because all the essential circuitry of each device's controller is built into any system-level interface device, you don't need to carefully match an AT interface hard disk to a controller, for example, to get a working system. You don't have to worry whether a particular drive can handle RLL data coding or what its ESDI transfer rate may be. The manufacturer has already done that for you. These advantages, and many more, have made system-level interfaces the designs of choice for today's PC peripherals.

AT Attachment

The dominant hard disk interface for PCs has become the AT Attachment design, a natural outcome considering that the interface is based on the ISA expansion bus, which is (of course) the most widely used computer bus of all. In performance, this system-level interface outclasses every device-level interface by a wide margin and comes up second only to the latest incarnations of the SCSI design.

Although the AT interface began as a design chosen for its low cost for small capacity drives, it has grown up. The trend to the AT interface has dramatically accelerated over the last couple of years for three very good reasons. The interface holds distinct advantages for disk drive makers, computer makers, and computer buyers.

First, the most important. You, as a computer buyer and user, gain a great deal of convenience from AT interface drives. Connecting them is easy; they require only two cables, a signal cable and a power cable. Most of the worries in connecting a traditional hard disk are absent. You have no need to fret about proper terminations or where which drive gets plugged into the daisy-chain cable.

In the AT interface scheme, the drives and not the cable determine what drive letter is assigned to each. Moreover, you don't have to worry about such things as RLL data coding or modulation technique. In fact, most of the latest ATA drives make the system setup procedure easier than ever, tolerating a wide range of setup parameters.

AT interface connections also offer some of the highest data transfer rates of any hard disk interfacing scheme for personal computers. AT interface data transfer speeds can be as much as two to three times higher than the old performance leader, ESDI. Moreover, the AT interface promises to put more megabytes in your PC for a lower price than the more conventional hard disk interfaces.

Computer makers benefit from AT interface technology because they don't need to put separate hard disk controllers in their products. That is an immediate cost benefit; the manufacturer doesn't have to pay for the unneeded controller and can pass along the lower price to you. In addition, AT interface drives can also lower assembly cost because there's one less cable and one less expansion board to install in the system.

Of course, building a special AT interface connector to a system board adds to the manufacturer's cost of making a system. But today's latest chip sets that form the basis for system board designs have internal AT interface support, giving the system manufacturers a hard disk interface at essentially no charge. The added system board connector may be the only cost added by including an AT interface for hard disks and other peripherals.

Integrating control electronics on the drive to make an AT interface might not at first seem to benefit the hard disk maker. After all, the integration makes a more complex product that should be more expensive to manufacture. But other benefits won by IDE and improvements in other areas of disk design have made the integration of control electronics a big plus for hard disk and other device manufacturers.

As with all electronics, the trend for the control circuitry on hard disk drives has been toward large scale integration, combining all the needed functions into one large chip (or a small set of larger chips). Although engineering functions onto a VLSI chip is expensive, manufacturing is less so, and assembly can be cheaper. VLSI means fewer components, so there's less to install. There's also less to fail, so AT interface drives can cost less to warrant and maintain.

But for disk manufacturers, the best part of any AT interface is the freedom it affords hard disk designers in getting the most capacity possible from a given mechanism. All the vital details of disk design and operation are effectively hidden from the host computer by the AT interface connection. AT interface drives can break traditional rules and limits with impunity. Your system never knows the difference. You get the gain without conventional hard disk pains.

History

The idea for using an ordinary AT interface for linking hard disks to PCs goes back to the primeval days when Compaq Computer Corporation was developing its long-discontinued Portable II computer. Work on designing the new interface started in 1985 as a means to minimize the number of slots required to integrate a hard drive into the computer. The Portable II would be short of slots, and eliminating a slot-mounted hard disk controller would free one more slot. In this first design, the controller was still a separate board built by Western Digital Corporation to Compaq specifications but coupled directly to the drive.

The term *Integrated Drive Electronics* first appeared in early 1986, when Compaq worked with Western Digital and the Magnetic Peripherals division of Control Data Corporation (the division is now part of Seagate) to integrate the WD controller chip onto a CDC half-height, 5.25-inch, 40-megabyte hard disk drive. In this implementation, the controller was grafted onto the hard disk assembly, but its circuitry was identifiable as a controller separate from the rest of the drive's electronics. This drive was first used in the Deskpro 386, in which it connected to a multifunction board in one of the machine's expansion slots. At this time, the specification was first expanded to handle two drives through one connection.

In the middle of 1986, in parallel with the CDC effort, Compaq and Conner Peripherals started a joint development effort to emulate what was then called the IDE interface with a gate array that was integrated with the rest of the control electronics of the hard disk. At this point, the controller had truly become integrated in an effort to reduce the cost and complexity of the hard disk system while improving its reliability. The AT interface connector was first moved to the system board with Compaq's Portable III.

Once the benefits of the AT-bus connection were proved, other disk makers adopted the standard. But because no official standard or even unofficial guidelines had been promulgated, each drive maker added its own nuances and variations to the interface. Consequently, early drives based on the AT interface from different manufacturers may suffer compatibility problems, principally when you attempt to connect two drives of a different make to a single AT interface connector.

An industry group called the CAM (Common Access Method) Committee was formed in October, 1988, from companies that make and use hard disk drives to develop an AT interface standard. The group formalized the specifications for the AT Attachment interface in March, 1989, and in November, 1990, submitted the specifications as a proposed standard to the American National Standards Institute. In 1991, a standard was finally and formally approved.

Implementation

In purest form, an AT interface drive would be one you could slide directly into an expansion slot inside your PC—a hard disk card. The drive would use exactly the same signals as any other expansion board and exactly the same connector. After all, the expansion bus is the real AT interface.

True AT interface drives are different. Contrary to what you would expect from the interface name, drives that use the AT interface specification do not use a direct connection to the standard ISA expansion bus. Instead, they attach to a special connector with signals somewhat different from those floating around on the ISA bus.

One reason for this difference is that the expansion buses inside computers are not designed to have cables plugged into them. Their circuitry is not optimized for transmitting signals beyond the back plane of the system board. Moreover, you wouldn't want to plug a full-height 5.25-inch hard disk directly into an expansion slot, at least if you wanted any hope of further expanding your system. The drive would be just too big and clumsy. Instead, the AT drive interface uses a special connector on the system board of PCs compatible with the standard. Alternatively, a small host adapter board (which should never be called a controller card because the control electronics are on the drive) can be used to adapt a PC using the ISA or EISA expansion bus to accept an AT interface drive. Micro Channel and local bus signals differ substantially from those used by the AT interface, so those buses are not directly compatible with AT interface drives. However, because of the popularity of drives using the AT interface, some board makers have made conversion products that allow you to connect AT interface drives to Micro Channel systems or local bus slots.

The AT interface for hard disks doesn't aim for full plug compatibility with the ISA bus. Instead, it modifies the bus signals somewhat to give it more reach and less complexity. You simply don't need all 98 connections of the ISA expansion bus to run a hard disk drive. For example, hard disk drives are not normally memory-mapped devices, so there's no need to give a hard disk control of all 24 addressing lines of the AT bus.

Instead of direct access to bus addressing, in the AT interface design the cable going to the hard disk is connected to address-decoding logic circuitry. Thanks to this circuitry, only the signals sent to the addresses used in controlling the hard disk are sent to the drive. The address lines themselves become superfluous. The actual addresses used by the AT interface connection are not part of the specification but are determined by the circuitry and BIOS of the host computer.

In addition to address-decoding logic, the AT interface design adds buffering circuits to allow the connection to safely transverse the length of cable running to the disk drive. Because of the relatively high speed of these signals, corresponding to the 8 Mhz bus clock of the ISA expansion bus, the length of this connecting cable is severely constrained. Under the AT interface specifications, signal cables are limited to 18 inches total length.

The AT interface specification reduces the 98 pins used by the two ISA bus connectors to a single 40-pin connector. Besides the 16 bits of data (some AT interface drives and host adapter implementation may use just 8 bits, exactly as some expansion boards have only 8-bit connectors), a variety of control signals are provided for. These signals manage the functions of the AT interface drive through input/output registers in the control circuitry on the drive. Among these control signals are those to request reading or writing data, make DMA transfers, check the results of running diagnostics, and indicate which of the two drives that can be connected to an AT interface port is to perform a given function. The interface also provides a "spindle sync" signal to allow two drives to spin synchronously as is required for some implementations of drive array.

The 40 connections of the AT interface are made using a pin connector rather than the edge connector used for expansion boards. A pin connector (often called a *header*) comprises two rows of square, gold-plated pins spaced 0.1 inch apart in both directions.

To prevent you from hooking up the ATA signal cable improperly, these AT interface connectors are keyed. That is, of the 40 pins in two rows that make up the host connector, pin 20 is not present (for example, it may be clipped off). The corresponding hole on the cable connector is plugged. If you try to plug in the connector upside down (or backward, depending on your point of view about these things), the plug will hit a pin rather than the pin 20 space it expects, thus preventing you from plugging in the connector.

Seven of the connections of the AT Attachment interface (numbers 2, 19, 22, 24, 26, 30, and 40) are grounds, scattered among the signals to provide them some degree of isolation from one another. Sixteen pins (3 through 18) are devoted to data, although the specification allows for 8-bit connections using only the odd-numbered 8 pins in the sequence. The remaining 16 pins are assigned various signal control functions, such as those to manage reading or writing data, make DMA transfers, and coordinate the operation of two drives.

The AT Attachment signals primarily concerned with controlling the transfer of data across the interface are given their own dedicated connections. Commands to the drives and the responses from the drives (including error indications) are passed through 17 8-bit registers.

The two drives permitted under the AT Attachment standard share all the connection and receive all signals across the interface indiscriminately. To signal which drive should act on a given command, the AT Attachment uses a special control register. The same register also determines the head, track, and sector that is to be used at any given time.

Seven signals are used to select among the registers. The registers are divided into two groups: control block registers and command registers, which are indicated by two interface signals. Activating the Drive Chip Select 0 signal (pin 37) selects the control block registers. Activating the Drive Chip Select 1 signal (pin 38) selects the command block registers. When the drive I/O write signal (pin 23) is active, the registers that accept commands from the host are accessible through the interface data lines. When the drive I/O read signal (pin 25) is active, the registers indicate drive status through the data lines.

Drive Address Bus 0 through 2 and located on pins 35, 33, and 36 (in conjunction with the other signals) control which register is currently selected and accessible through the data lines. The AT Attachment standard defines two read- and one write-control block registers as well as seven read- and seven write-command block registers. Of these, one write-command block register selects the active drive and head (up to 16 heads are allowed). Two registers select the drive track (allowing up to 65,536 tracks on a single drive), the sector to start reading from or writing to, and the number of the track to be read or written. The read registers indicate which drive and head are active as well as which track and head are being scanned. Other registers provide status information and define errors that occur during drive operation.

The number of register bits available sets the logical limits on device size: up to 16 heads, 65,536 tracks, and 256 sectors per track. In that many PCs are incapable of handling more than 1,024 tracks, the maximum practical capacity of an AT Attachment drive is 2,147,483,648 bytes (two gigabytes).

During active data transfers, separate signals are used as strobes to indicate that the data going to or coming from the drive or values in the control registers is valid and can be used. The falling edge of the drive I/O read signal (pin 25) indicates to the host that valid data read from the disk is on the bus. The falling edge of the drive I/O write signal (pin 23) indicates that data on the bus to be written on disk is valid.

The drive 16-bit I/O signal (pin 32) indicates whether the read or write transfer comprises 8 or 16 bits. The signal is active to indicate 16-bit transfers. Normally, AT Attachment transfers are accomplished through programmed I/O, the standard mode of operation using the standard AT hard disk BIOS. However, the AT Attachment standard optionally allows direct memory access (DMA) transfers. Two signals control handshaking during DMA data moves. The drive signals that it is ready to read data and transfer it in DMA mode by asserting the DMA request signal (pin 21). The computer host acknowledges it is ready to accept that data with the DMA acknowledge signal (pin 29). If the host cannot accept all the data at once, it removes the DMA acknowledge signal until it is ready to receive more.

In DMA write operations, the host PC uses DMA acknowledgments to indicate that it has data available, and the active drive uses DMA request for handshaking to control the flow of data. The drive I/O read and write signals indicate in which direction the data should flow (as a disk read or write).

An AT Attachment disk drive can interrupt the host computer to gain immediate attention by activating the drive interrupt signal (pin 31). On programmed I/O transfers, the drive generates an interrupt at the beginning of each block of data (typically a sector) to be transferred. On DMA transfers, the interrupt is used only to indicate the command has been completed. (The interrupt used is determined by the host's circuitry.)

A drive can signal to the host computer that it is not ready to process a read or write request using the I/O channel ready signal (pin 27). Normally, this signal is activated; the drive switches it off when it cannot immediately respond to a request to transfer data.

The drive reset signal (pin 1) causes the drive to return to its normal power-on state, ignoring transfers in progress and losing the contents of its registers (returning them to their default values). Normally, this signal is activated briefly (for at least 25 microseconds) when the host computer is turned on so that the drive will initialize itself. Activating this signal thereafter will cancel the command in progress and reinitialize the drive.

The passed diagnostics signal (pin 34) is used by the slave drive to indicate to its host that it is running its diagnostics. The "passed" in the name does not refer to the diagnostics being completed successfully, but that the results are ready to be passed along to the host system. Actual results (and the command to actually execute diagnostics) are given through the AT Attachment registers.

The spindle sync/cable select signal (pin 28) can be used at the drive manufacturer's option either to make the drives spin synchronously (as is required by some drive array technologies) or to set drive identification as master or slave by the cable rather than using a jumper or switch on the drive. When used as a spindle synchronizing signal, the master drive generates a periodic pulse (typically once each revolution of the disk although the actual timing is left to the drive manufacturer), and the slave uses this signal to lock its spin to the master. When this connection is used as a cable select signal, supplying a ground on pin 28 causes a drive to function as the master (drive 0); leaving the connection open causes the connected drive to act as the slave (drive 1).

A single signal, termed drive active/drive 1 present, located on pin 39, indicates that one of the drives is active (for instance, to illuminate the drive activity indicator on the system front panel). The same pin is used by the host signal to determine whether one or two AT Attachment drives are installed when the power is switched on. The drive assigned as the slave is given a 400 millisecond period during system startup to put a signal on this pin to indicate its availability; after waiting 450 milliseconds to give the slave drive time to signal, the master drive puts its signal on the pin to indicate its presence to the host computer. The drive switches its signal off and converts the function of the signal to drive activity when the drive accepts its first command from the host computer or after waiting 31 seconds, whichever comes first.

As comprehensive as the AT Attachment standard is, it doesn't define everything. Most importantly, it governs only the connection between the PC and drive. Everything upstream (inside the computer) is left to the designer of the host PC. AT Attachment does not indicate the logical location of its control registers. The decoding logic that determines those values is part of the host adapter circuitry of the PC. The system BIOS (or add-in BIOS) provides the needed information for establishing the link.

The system BIOS is thus critical to getting AT Attachment drives to operate properly. Some older BIOSs may not be able to properly control AT Attachment drives. In particular, AMI BIOSs dated before 9 April 1990 were not completely compatible. To use an AT Attachment drive in a system with one of these older BIOSs, you'll have to replace the BIOS.

Without a doubt, AT Attachment will continue to grow and flourish because it brings two worlds together, not just the disk and PC but you and drive makers. AT Attachment gives you the easiest and most worry-free of all interfaces to install. Drive manufacturers get the potential for more speed and capacity. And both you and the manufacturers win with lower prices.

Performance

Speed is the most promising aspect of the AT interface, but early drives didn't deliver on that promise. Through the end of 1991, most AT interface drives were merely modifications of older products and designs with the necessary control electronics grafted on. Consequently, these drives were held back by issues related to the performance constraints of old interfaces, such as drive rotation rate and data density. New drive designs aimed specifically at system-level interfaces are pushing the AT interface ahead. The potential of the AT interface is great because it's based on the AT bus, and it should be able to deliver throughput that exactly matches the host computer's bus. No additional limits need be imposed by other standard interfaces that the signal must traverse through. The ST506 and ESDI interfaces, on the other hand, force information going to and from the disk to slow to a single-file serial rate from 1/3 to 1/12 the potential of the ISA bus.

The potential throughput of the AT interface connection is exactly the same as the ISA bus. At a nominal 8 Mhz clock rate, an 8-bit AT interface connection can move data as quickly as 4 megabytes per second (each transfer requires two bus cycles, so the interface moves each byte at half the bus's clock rate). In 16-bit form, potential throughput doubles to 8 megabytes per second.

These speeds represent theoretical maximums. Your actual performance will differ because real-world throughput is limited by the mechanical speed of the drive. However, AT interface devices can approach the speed limit of the interface if they use large on-board buffers and those buffers are full of the data requested from the computer hosts. This design isolates the data request from the mechanical delays of operating the drive.

SCSI

Pronounced "scuzzy" by much of the computer industry (but sometimes "sexy" by its staunchest advocates), SCSI is a system-level interface that provides what is essentially a complete expansion bus into which to plug peripherals. SCSI isn't simply a connection that links a device or two to your PC. Rather, it functions like a sub-bus.

SCSI devices can exchange data among themselves without the intervention of the host computer's microprocessor. In fact, these devices can act across the SCSI bus even while other transfers are shifting across the host computer's normal expansion bus.

As with any expansion bus, any of a variety of device types can be connected to the SCSI bus almost indiscriminately, all communicating to your PC through a single port connection. Up to seven SCSI devices can be daisy-chained to one SCSI port. All the devices function independently, under the control of the host system through the SCSI port.

As with the AT interface, SCSI provides a parallel connection between its devices and the SCSI adapter. In most SCSI systems only a single cable, albeit one with a wealth of conductors, is needed for a SCSI linkup. The basic pin-out is shown in table 19.3.

TABLE 19.3.
SCSI Cable
Pin-Out

Pin	Function	Pin	Function
1	Ground	2	Data line 0
3	Ground	4	Data line 1
5	Ground	6	Data line 2
7	Ground	8	Data line 3
9	Ground	10	Data line 4
11	Ground	12	Data line 5
13	Ground	14	Data line 6
15	Ground	16	Data line 7
17	Ground	18	Parity line (data)
19	Ground	20	Ground
21	Ground	22	Ground
23	Ground	24	Ground
25	No connection	26	Terminator Power
27	Ground	28	Ground
29	Ground	30	Ground
31	Ground	32	Attention
33	Ground	34	Ground
35	Ground	36	Busy
37	Ground	38	Acknowledge
39	Ground	40	Reset
41	Ground	42	Message

continues

TABLE 19.3.
continued

Pin	Function	Pin	Function
43	Ground	44	Select
45	Ground	46	C/D
47	Ground	48	Request
49	Ground	50	I/O

In 1991, a new revision of SCSI was introduced to help fix some of the problems in mating SCSI devices together, as well as increase the speed of SCSI transfers. Referred to as *SCSI 2*, the revision broadened the original 8-bit bus to wide SCSI, which can use either 16 or 32 data lines. In addition, the speed of SCSI transfers was doubled in a derivation called *fast SCSI*. Originally, the extra signal lines of the revised standard were added on a supplemental connector, but a new one-connector version was also adopted.

Operation and Arbitration

All devices connected to a single SCSI bus function independently, under the control of the host system through the SCSI adapter. Rather than just using signals on dedicated conductors on the bus that can be understood by devices as dumb as a light bulb, SCSI presupposes a high degree of intelligence in the devices it connects, and provides its own command set, essentially its own computer language, for controlling the devices.

Not only is SCSI more like an expansion bus of a computer than a traditional hard disk interface, it resembles today's more advanced Micro Channel and NuBus designs. Like the latest computer buses, SCSI provides an arbitration scheme. Arbitration allows the devices connected to the bus to determine which of them can send data across the bus at a given time. Instead of being controlled by the host computer and suffering delays while its microprocessor does other things, the arbitration of the SCSI bus is distributed among all the devices on the bus.

Arbitration on the SCSI bus is handled by hardware. Each of the up to seven SCSI devices is assigned a unique identifying number, usually by setting jumpers or DIP switches on the drive in a manner similar to the drive-select jumpers on an ST506 device.

When a device, called the initiator, wants to access the SCSI bus, it waits until the bus is free, and then identifies itself by sending a signal down one of the SCSI data lines. At the same time, it transmits a signal down another SCSI data line corresponding to the other SCSI device, called the target, that the initiator wants to interact with. The eight data lines in the SCSI connection allow the unique identification of seven SCSI devices and one host.

Note that SCSI devices can initiate arbitration on their own, independent of the host. Two SCSI devices can also transfer information between one another without host intervention. For instance, a SCSI hard disk might back itself up to a SCSI tape drive without requiring the attention of (and robbing performance from) its host computer. Better than background operation, this form of backup represents true parallel processing in the computer system.

In addition, SCSI provides for reselecting. That is, a device that temporarily does not need bus access can release the bus, carry out another operation, and then resume control. For instance, you could command a disk drive to format, and it could carry out that operation without tying up the bus. The net result is, again, true parallel processing.

Because SCSI is a high-level interface, it also isolates the computer from the inner workings of the peripherals connected to it. For instance, the SCSI standard allows hard disks to monitor their own bad tracks independently from the computer host. The disk drive itself reassigns bad tracks and reports back to its computer host as if it were a perfect disk. In addition, a hard disk drive could be designed to automatically detect sectors that are going bad and reassign the data they contain elsewhere, all without the host computer or the user ever being aware of any problems.

Compatibility

SCSI hard disks entirely isolate the host computer from concerns about disk sectors and tracks. The SCSI system deals with data at a higher level, as blocks, so any block-oriented device can take advantage of the connection scheme. This arrangement works well in the Macintosh environment because the Mac operating system has built-in provisions for dealing with SCSI. PC DOS and MS-DOS lack such provisions, however, so SCSI host adapters for IBM-standard systems must convert sector and track requests into their SCSI equivalent. As a result, the system gets, at best, an indirect look at the disk drive. At worst, the overhead required for the address conversions can considerably slow the performance of an IBM-based SCSI system. This symptom was particularly noticeable in the first generation of SCSI devices and host adapters. Drive and host adapter manufacturers have learned to use more of SCSI's speed but you'll still find a wide variance in the throughputs of the SCSI host adapters on the market. The quickest adapters approach the performance potential of the interface; the worst adapters drag speed down to the level of the ancient interfaces.

The Apple Macintosh implementation of SCSI has been criticized for being at variance from the otherwise accepted industry standard, but the only place it varies is with the connector choice. The standard SCSI hookup uses a single, special 50-pin connector. In the existing asynchronous implementation of SCSI, more than half of the wires in the connectors are used as grounds (redundant signal return lines). The Macintosh uses a 25-pin miniature D-shell connector much like that used by serial ports and does away with many of the redundant ground connections. The more compact size of this connector was probably one reason for its choice. It also makes cabling easier and more convenient.

A bigger compatibility issue arises when trying to take advantage of SCSI's capability to link multiple devices to one host adapter. Some devices just won't work with others. The incompatibilities arise out of the flexibility of the SCSI standard itself. Although the specification strictly defines all hardware parameters, it is much looser when it comes to software features. Much of the SCSI command set is optional, devices only have to implement the features that they will use. Moreover, the SCSI specification provides no standard means of the host computer controlling SCSI devices through the interface. That's left up to the system designer.

Although this approach works well in the environment that SCSI was originally designed for—minicomputers, in which the device maker also configures the host adapter to match a particular computer system—it fails in the multi-splendored DOS world. Today two competing standards, called CAM and ASPI, are primarily used for SCSI control by DOS computer systems. Unfortunately, the two standards go in different software directions.

The Common Access Method, or CAM, Committee, the same group that helped develop the AT Attachment standard, has developed its own implementation of the SCSI standard that allows access to SCSI devices directly through your PC's operating system. Although a CAM standard has not been formally adopted by any standard-setting organization, the specification has been around long enough that many manufacturers use it for their products. Such CAM-compliant SCSI host adapters have on-board BIOSs that will link with your operating system. Programs written to take advantage of CAM can then make requests to your operating system and have them carried out by the appropriate SCSI device. Unfortunately, DOS is not currently CAM-compliant, although OS/2 Version 2.0 is.

The Advanced SCSI Programming Interface (ASPI) is an alternate SCSI control system that was originally developed by host adapter maker Adaptec (the "A" in ASPI originally meant Adaptec, but the company yielded to change to broaden the appeal of the standard) and is now widely used in the PC industry. Adaptec calls it a "de facto standard." ASPI uses a layered approach to the software interface using driver software. Programs communicate and send commands to SCSI devices through an individual software driver for each device. An overall ASPI driver links the individual device drivers to the SCSI system hardware.

The BIOS on an ASPI-compliant host adapter merely provides fundamental services that establish the link with the ASPI driver.

In general, the ASPI BIOS provides WD1002 emulation. That is, it will allow you to connect one or two SCSI hard disks to the host adapter and have them mimic a Western Digital WD1002 ST506-style hard disk controller and its associated disks. Without further ado or drivers, the first SCSI disk will be able to boot your system as drive C:, and the second serves as drive D:. That's as far as the BIOS support goes, however. Without loading software drivers, your ASPI-based system cannot recognize further hard disks or other SCSI devices.

To completely set up an ASPI system, you must install all the required device drivers in your PC's CONFIG.SYS file. You'll have to install the ASPI driver when you install your host adapter and install a driver for each SCSI device you connect (except the first two hard disks). Because the device-specific software drivers need the ASPI driver to link to the SCSI system, you should ensure that the ASPI driver entry precedes that of other SCSI device drivers in your PC's CONFIG.SYS file.

One problem you may encounter getting your ASPI system to work may have its roots in impatience. If you originally bought your SCSI host adapter along with a hard disk and were anxious to get things running, you may have simply connected everything as if it were an IDE AT interface or ESDI hard disk. The hard disk probably would have worked just fine (thanks to the WD1002 emulation of the BIOS), but when you later try to install a CD-ROM player, its driver won't be able to find the ASPI driver you failed to install. You'll get an obscure error message about the lack of an ASPI driver that will likely make you scratch your head for hours. The solution to this problem is to fetch the disk that came with your SCSI host adapter and install the ASPI driver.

Most software drivers search for their target devices when they are booted into your system. Consequently, all of your external SCSI devices should be running when you switch on your PC. Either turn on your SCSI devices before you switch on your PC or use a power director (outlet box) to ensure that your entire computer system, PC and SCSI peripherals, switch on simultaneously.

Caching

All mass storage devices, be they magnetic hard disks, floppies or optical, face two primary performance constraints: access speed and transfer rate. Access speed is the inevitable delay between the instant your computer requests a particular byte or block of information from the disk drive and when that information is located on the disk. In specifications, it is represented by a number termed *average access time*, which describes the mean time (in milliseconds) required for the read/write head of a drive to move between disk tracks. Transfer rate describes the speed at which the information stored on the disk can be moved into the working memory of your PC. It is usually measured in megabytes per second.

Both access speed and transfer rate are issues of design, but their ultimate limits arise from mechanical issues. Access speed is principally determined by the speed at which the disk mechanism can fling its head about. Smaller heads, having less inertia, can generally be snapped into place more quickly, although a more robust mechanism can bestow a measure of snap to heavier head assemblies. Transfer rate limitations arise mostly from the combination of the rotational rate of the disk and the density at which information is stored on each track. The faster the disk spins and the closer data bits are fitted together on the disk, the more bits will spin by the head in a given period, producing a quicker flow of information.

Because of the mechanical nature of these speed limits, any miraculous improvement in their performance is impossible. Because laws of motion involving inertia and other principles that scientists hold dear preclude instantaneous acceleration, access delays can never be eliminated from mechanical systems. More to the point, practical mechanisms can never lower the delays past the point that some people, likely including yourself, won't be bothered by them. Similarly, the rotation rates of disks are limited by such issues as mechanical integrity (spin a disk too fast and centrifugal force will tear it apart), and the packing of data is constrained by the capability of the read/write technology to resolve individual bits on the disk surface.

The big problem with these mechanical limits is that they are orders of magnitude lower than the electronic and logic limits of computers. A computer thinks in nanoseconds and microseconds but has to wait milliseconds when it needs data from disk. It may need to wait further when it needs to transfer a large block of information from a mass storage device.

The best way to hurdle these mechanical barriers is with caching. A suitable device cache allows required information to be retrieved at near electronic speeds.

The cache can bring a second, additional benefit to DOS-based systems. DOS is essentially a single-threaded operating system. That is, DOS steps through each of its functions one at a time, waiting for the last function to be completed before it advances to the next. In writing to a disk, for example, DOS waits until the write operation is completed before it returns control to you.

DOS doesn't have to work that way. Caches can add a degree of concurrency to the operating system by returning control of your system to you while the disk write operations are completed. This simple expedient can be sufficient to cut the time required to write to your disk system by half.

Hardware versus Software Caches

Caching is generally classified into two types, hardware and software, depending on the type of memory used to build the cache. But caching is better distinguished by where in the system it takes place. The hardware/software line is drawn in implementation. The hardware-based cache requires that you add some kind of additional memory to your system to use for caching. Software-based caches use part of the RAM in your PC to build the cache. As with data compression, there are three potential logical locations for a mass storage cache: on the device itself, in its controller or host adapter, or in your PC's RAM.

Although much has been written about the advantage of hardware versus software caching, the issues all boil down to cost. To add hardware caching to a PC means installing additional memory. Although during the DRAM shortage of a couple of years ago, the cost of memory imposed a severe penalty; today the RAM for a reasonable cache (1 megabyte) is almost trivial. However, the difference in cost between a cached disk controller or host adapter and one without is much more substantial. A cached controller may cost three to five times more.

A software cache requires generally no additional memory in your system, instead taking advantage of whatever leftover RAM you want to assign to disk acceleration. If you have no spare RAM, you can add extra megabytes for no more than the cost of SIMMs (single in-line memory modules).

The logical location of the cache determines the ultimate performance advantage it can add to your system. Although every kind of cache helps minimize the slowdowns imposed by the mechanical nature of disk storage, some help sidestep system bottlenecks better than others. At the same time, some caches are easier to deal with and offer fewer compatibility problems than others.

Device-Mounted Caches

The straightforward place to put a hardware cache is on the disk drive itself. That way, the cache can be added to the system invisibly, and at no cost for extra memory or software. The drive itself would simply appear faster to you and your software.

The disk-based cache has three primary shortcomings. It's not entirely adaptable to all kinds of hard disks. It works best with disks that use system-level interfaces, such as SCSI (the Small Computer System Interface) and AT interface, which separate the actual data stored on the disk from housekeeping information (sector identifications) in the disk's electronics. Moreover, the on-disk cache does nothing to improve the performance of other parts of the disk system that hinder performance, such as the interface and the expansion bus. Finally, disk-based caching cannot do anything to improve the performance of an existing disk system. To gain its benefits, you must slide in a new disk drive.

Controller-Based Caches

The next logical place to put a cache is on the disk controller or host adapter. This location adds the flexibility of endowing any disk, old or new, with a cache. It also can overcome some of the limits imposed by the disk interface. When the data you need is in the cache, it can be sent to your system as fast as the expansion bus can carry it without concern for the transfer rate through the disk interface. But that still leaves a bottleneck in many systems, the bus itself. Expansion buses operate at a fraction of the speed than quicker microprocessors can handle data, so the bus connection can lead to a substantial slowdown in even cached disk performance. And because controller-based caches require extra hardware, they add to the cost of your mass storage system.

Software Caches

The final place to put a cache is in your system's own memory using a software-mediated product. Because such a location is downstream from the expansion bus, it can not only accelerate the mechanical aspects of disk performance but also break through the bus bottleneck. The memory used in the software cache is the fastest RAM in your system, directly connected to your PC's microprocessor.

The drawbacks of the downstream software cache are several. The cache steals away RAM that could be otherwise used by programs. Because most caches operate as software drivers, they may be invisible to programs that direct control of disk hardware, resulting in conflicts that could corrupt disk data. And because the software cache must be controlled and maintained by your PC's main microprocessor, they can slow down your system somewhat.

The first and last of these problems should be no cause for worry. Any cache will need additional memory, and the downstream software cache uses the least expensive RAM available, simple memory expansion for your system board without the necessity for outboard hardware controllers. Moreover, better software caches minimize their memory impact, a characteristic discussed later in this chapter.

The microprocessor overhead extracted by a software cache should, for the most part, be invisible to you. Few, if any, software caches run continually in the background, sapping clock cycles from your system's microprocessor. Most instead swing into action only when your PC is accessing its disk subsystem. With reasonable sizes of cache, the acceleration gained overwhelms the microprocessor overhead. For example, cache overhead may shave off 2 percent of your microprocessor's power during disk activity while improving disk performance by 50 percent or more. The net gain, 48 percent, or more, more than makes up for the overhead.

Compatibility problems are more difficult to eliminate because they result from fundamental mismatches between utility software and the cache driver software. Fortunately, these days only one very specific variety of software is likely to crash into a cache: hard disk utilities and specialty disk drivers, such as Disk Manager (from On-Track Computer Systems) and SpeedStor (from Storage Dimensions), that are used to match non-standard hard disks to PCs. With the latest releases of cache software and these utilities, most of the problems have been worked out. Earlier program versions may have problems. However, any software that chooses to directly access the registers of a hard disk controller (for whatever purpose) may subvert the cache and cause data to disappear.

If you run into such difficulties, you have an easy solution, simply switch off the cache while you take advantage of the disk utility. Because most such programs are used only occasionally (for example, file recovery or disk optimization), the time and trouble required to switch off the cache won't amount to much.

Cache Operation

Commercial disk caching programs differ in three principal ways: how they handle read operations, how (and whether) they cache disk write operations, and their usage and management of system memory. Getting the right cache for your PC and the way you work requires investigating all three.

Read Buffering

The fundamental function of a disk cache is buffering read operations. The cache software fills its memory with the data it anticipates your system and software will need and supplies that information from its buffers on request at RAM speed when there is a cache hit. If there is a miss, the cache directs the software to retrieve data from disk at disk speed.

The design issues control how efficient that read cache operates, and, thus, how often it speeds up disk operations. These issues include how the memory of the cache is filled with data, how the contents of memory are updated, and how the cache recognizes whether needed information is contained in its memory.

The first appears simple. After all, before you can expect to read anything in a cache, there must be something there. But filling a cache is a task akin to augury; the cache control software must make a stab at predicting your system's future needs. Most caches take a straightforward approach, reading somewhat more than your application software requests of a given disk track or (less commonly) file. The underlying assumption is that you'll need more of what you're already looking at.

After a few read requests, the cache memory will fill up, and the control software is faced with the problem of what to save and what to discard to make room for new data. Several different algorithms are used by the writers of software caches. Most are variations of least frequently used (LFU) and least recently used (LRU) designs, in that order of popularity. The former discards the data in the cache that your system has asked least often. The latter throws away the data that was requested the longest time previously. The LFU technique is more complex and demands more from system resources, so LRU often performs better. Even so, in typical systems the gain performance in using the two techniques falls within about 8 percent of one another, close enough to be a draw.

Keeping track of the data in the cache is a matter of minimizing the time required to determine whether needed data is held within the cache. In general, cache programs assign tags to associate data in memory with that on the disk. The exact handling of this information, like the other details of caching algorithms used by specific products, is a matter of great secrecy among most commercial cache publishers. For the most part, publishers treat their technology as if it were black magic, but even more mysterious.

Despite such proprietary thaumaturgy, even cache publishers admit that read performance differs little among commercial software disk caches. You probably won't see a difference whether you use a costly third-party cache or one that comes free with your PC or operating system when all you do is read from your hard disk.

Accelerating write operations is another matter entirely. Some caches (generally the free ones) ignore write operations entirely, forcing direct disk access (and the resultant delays) when your software wants to store or change data in mass storage. The underlying philosophy is to be safe although slow.

Write Buffering

The reason for this conservative approach is that caching write operations is fraught with dangers. Overcoming them takes a lot of development time, making a cache with write buffering more expensive to create.

The biggest worry comes with delayed writing. That is, when the cache accumulates data to be written to disk for a preset period or until a time when your system is no longer busy. The system can then write the data to disk without slowing anything down. In addition, it can reorganize the data to optimize the head movement of the drive and eliminate multiple, sequential changes to a disk sector by only writing the last of them to disk.

All the while the cache is collecting and holding information, your system reacts as if the disk has been written to at RAM speed. Press the Save button, and you immediately regain control of your system so that you can go on to something else.

To gain this responsiveness, however, you put your data at risk. Between the time your software thinks it has written to disk and the data actually is stored, it is vulnerable to accidental or intentional power failure. You may think that an important file has been written and switch off your PC, and whatever data was still held in the write cache would evaporate with the flow of electricity through your machine. Moreover, the damage can be worse than just losing a file. Some operating systems and operating environments are designed to automatically recover when a power failure terminates their operation midstream. But this software may expect to have its disk changes written in a particular order that the write cache might violate for sake of speed. The operating system might thus be thwarted in its efforts to recover and rebuild itself. Even worse, it may rebuild itself incorrectly and become a disaster.

To avoid such problems, many disk caches avoid caching writes entirely or do not employ delayed writing techniques. Caches that do allow delayed writings typically make it an optional feature that can be defeated by those who are especially concerned about data integrity. They may also allow you to set the maximum allowable writing delay. The shorter the delay, the less data will be at risk (but the less performance improvement you can expect). Write-caching programs may also intercept warm boot commands (the Ctrl-Alt-Del keystroke sequence) and force the flushing of the cache, writing all of its contents to disk, immediately before allowing the reboot to occur. Of course, this strategy does no good with a cold (power off) boot.

An alternative write-caching technology eliminates delayed writing and, instead, relies on operating your disk drive concurrently with other operations to give an apparent performance increase. The technique is simple in concept. The cache accepts data from your application and immediately begins writing it to disk. However, instead of holding back your system while the data is doled out through the drive interface and drive mechanism, it yields control to your software as soon as the information has been written into the cache memory. The actual writing to disk continues for some time afterward, concurrent with the continuation of normal operation of your PC.

Such concurrent writing technology is not risk free. Switching off your PC immediately after control returns to a program after a disk write can result in lost data because everything may not have been spooled off to disk. However, there will be no unpredictable period of vulnerability as would be the case with delayed writing systems. As soon as the drive activity indicator goes out, you're safe to switch off or reboot your PC.

The time saved by concurrent writing approaches that of delayed writing with a properly designed caching program. Both techniques require the same time to transfer information into the cache, and both return control of your system immediately thereafter. Although delayed writing may minimize the time actually spent in writing to disk, these savings will likely be invisible to you.

Memory Usage

Memory marks another major difference between software caching programs. Certainly all respectable commercial caching products are now able to make use of all principal PC memory types—conventional (DOS), expanded (EMS), and extended (XMS) memory—but they differ substantially in how efficiently the memory needs of the cache can be shared with other system resources.

Nearly every software-based speed-up technology that can be applied to a PC requires some memory usage, but caches and print spoolers are notorious for their needs for huge blocks of RAM. The more memory devoted to such speed-up technologies, the greater the performance gain. But the memory used for these functions must be drawn from somewhere, and that increasingly means away from the resources that could be used for executing programs. Every megabyte devoted to your disk cache is one less megabyte usable by Windows or the applications running under Windows, for example.

Most of the time you are left to allocate the memory between the various functions of your PC. After all, every computer setup is unique—you may want a huge cache while others may want the greatest possible program space. Allocating memory yourself requires carefully examining the needs of your software. With print spoolers, for example, you must devote enough memory to handle the largest print job or else your gain may be for naught, you'll still be stuck waiting for your printer when the spooler fills up. The memory that you allocate to the spooler for this worst-case scenario is then forever drawn away from the reach of your software.

A trend among caching programs is to make memory allocation dynamic. That is, they take memory away from your system only when you need it or they share memory with other functions.

Caches differ substantially in their capability to share. Many simply don't. After all, at $30 to $50 per megabyte, adding more RAM to accommodate the cache is not an overwhelming expenditure. Some caches, however, dynamically allocate memory among themselves and other functions, such as RAM disks and print spoolers. With these caches you need to devote less RAM to gain the same level of performance improvement from all memory-hogging functions.

Using a Cache

Once you elect to install a software cache in your system, you have a number of decisions to make. Among the first is whether to take advantage of write caching or rely solely on speeding up read operations. The decision hinges on two factors: how you work and your willingness to take a risk.

If you use your PC only casually, if you don't want to bother thinking about managing your system, if you don't think you can remember to pause a few seconds to flush the cache before rebooting or switching your system off, you may want to avoid write caching. One instance of brain fade, pushing your power switch before the cache has finished writing to your disk, and you'll ever afterward curse caching.

Even if you're careful, write caching imposes a risk, an extended risk of power failure and software crashes. Realistically, the risk is very small. You're no more likely to lose data in your write cache from such causes as you would any other information. But you are adding slightly to a period of great vulnerability. If you want to eke out the most possible acceleration from a disk cache, you'll want a product that handles write caching in some manner. The decision between delayed writing or concurrent writing again depends on your personal assessment of the risk involved.

After you choose a product, you'll need to install it. In doing so, you'll be faced with the toughest decision of all, how much of your system's RAM to devote to the cache. The basic rule is that the more memory you devote to caching, the more you will enhance the performance of your disk drive. Software caches smaller than 64K may not be large enough to overcome the handicaps of their own operating overhead. Most cache publishers recommend a minimum of 256K to 384K be devoted to a software cache with 512K to 1M being preferred. At that level, you can expect a hit ratio approaching 90 percent with normal disk usage.

What kind of memory to use is another issue. Among the basic choices, DOS, extended, or expanded, the worst is DOS. Every byte you steal from DOS memory is one that cannot be used by your software. Moreover, you simply can't make a large cache from DOS memory because, by definition, there's not a lot of DOS memory.

In 8088-based computers (XT-class), your best choice is expanded memory. Of course, getting expanded memory for a cache will involve adding an expanded memory board. You may find that the cost of a memory board and that of a hardware disk caching controller will be quite similar. In this case, there's little reason to prefer one over the other because XT systems face no bus bottleneck; the entire system is equally slow.

With 286-based AT-class systems operating at 10 Mhz or less, you have your choice of extended or expanded memory, most of which will have to be installed in expansion slots. Your choice between the two memory types does not matter; they'll deliver approximately equal performance. Moreover, a hardware cache may have a speed advantage because of its lack of software overhead. The bus bottleneck will be the same for memory boards or hardware caches.

As the system clock speeds rise above 10 Mhz and race ahead of the bus clock, performance issues begin to favor software over hardware caching, providing the memory used for the software cache is system board memory. A memory board installed in an expansion slot will suffer the bus bottleneck and be unable to deliver performance better than a hardware cache.

In these faster systems, extended memory should be preferred for your software cache. Even when expanded memory is emulated by fast system board RAM, it cannot quite keep up with plain extended memory. Expanded memory requires additional system management overhead, which is not required by extended memory.

20

Floppy Disks

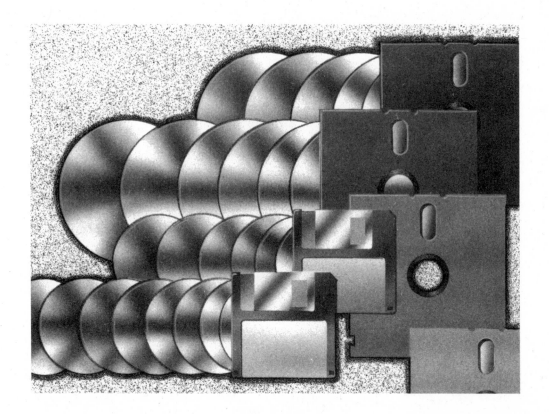

T he floppy disk is the premiere data exchange medium for PCs and the most popular backup system. Except for a few notebook computers, all PCs come with at least one floppy disk drive as standard equipment. Although floppy disk drives come in a variety of sizes and capacities—disks measure from 2.5 to 8 inches in diameter and store from 160K to 2.88M each—all work in essentially the same way.

Since the first PC booted up, the floppy disk has been a blessing and a curse, subject of the same old saw usually reserved for kids, spouses, and governments—"You can't live with them, and you can't live without them."

You can't live without floppy disks because they provide the one universal means of information interchange, data storage, and file archiving used by PCs. They are convenient—you can stuff half a dozen 3.5-inch floppy disks into a shirt pocket—and easy to use. Slide a disk into a slot, press a button, or close a door, and you have another megabyte or so on-line.

But most people have a hard time living with floppy disks because of their frustration factor. Floppy disks are slow and small. No matter how much a floppy disk holds, it will be a few kilobytes shy of what you need. Moreover, floppy disks are plagued by problems. Subtle magnetic differences between disks often have no apparent effect until months after you have trusted your important data to a disk that can no longer be read. A profusion of standards means that you need to carefully match disks to drives, drives to controllers, and the whole caboodle to DOS. You never seem to have the right drive to match the disk that came in the box of software—or enough space for all the drives you need to match the proliferating floppy disk standards. Indeed, floppies are like taxes—something that everyone lives with and no one likes.

The floppy disk itself is only part of a system. Just as a nail is worthless in the abstract—without the hammer to drive it in place and the arm to swing the hammer—so is a floppy disk, unless you have all the other parts of the system. These parts include the floppy disks, called the *media*; the floppy disk drive mechanism; the floppy disk drive controller; and the disk operating system software. All four elements are essential for the proper (and useful) operation of the system.

Media

The floppy disk provides a recording medium that has several positive qualities. The flat disk surface allows an approximation of random access. As with hard disks, data are arranged in tracks and sectors. The disk rotates the sectors under a read/write head, which travels radially across the disk to mark off tracks. More important, the floppy disk is a removable medium. You can shuffle dozens of floppies in and out of drives to extend your storage capacity. The floppy disk in the drive provides on-line storage. Off-line, you can keep as many floppy disks as you want.

The term *floppy disk* is one of those amazingly descriptive terms that abound in this age of genericisms. Inside its protective shell, the floppy disk medium is floppy—flexible—and looks like a wide, flat disk. The disks are stamped out from wide rolls of the magnetic medium like cutting cookies from dough.

The wide rolls look like hyperpituitary audio or video tape, and that's no coincidence. Its composition is the same as for recording tape—a polyester substrate on which a magnetic oxide is bound. Unlike tape, however, all floppy disks are coated with magnetic material on both sides. The substrate is thicker than tape, too—about three mils.

Single-Sided Disks

Even though all floppy disks have an oxide coating on both sides, many disks are sold as *single-sided*. Rather than restricting the coating to one side, the manufacturer of single-sided floppy disks restricts its testing to one side. Only one side of a single-sided disk is *certified* for recording. The manufacturer of the disk only guarantees that one side will work properly. By convention, the bottom surface of the disk is used in single-sided floppy disk drives.

The actual testing of the floppy disk is one of the most costly parts of the manufacturing process. Testing two sides takes more time and inevitably results in more rejected disks. Two sides provide more space in which problems can occur. Both single-sided and double- sided floppy disks may be made from exactly the same batch of magnetic medium.

Many people cut the price they pay for floppy disks by substituting their own testing (during the floppy disk format process) for that ordinarily performed by the manufacturer. They buy single-sided disks and format them double-sided. This process shifts the cost of the rejected disks, which should be usable as single-sided media if you want to hand a copy of one of your data files to a friend, from manufacturer to user.

Disk makers will tell you that their testing is more thorough and critical than what you can accomplish with your disk drives, and they are right. But your application may not be crucial enough to require the absolute (or nearly so) certainty of factory testing.

High-Density Disks

Not all magnetic media are the same. Different manufacturers have their own secret formula for the right magnetic coating to spread on the disk. One of the differences is in the size of magnetic particles that actually remember the data. So called *high-density* disks use a magnetic medium with a notably finer grain, allowing the disk to pack more information into a smaller space. These floppy disks have higher coercivities than normal density floppies.

All floppy disk drives use MFM recording that produces *double-density* recording. Hence, normal and high-density disks are double-density even though many manufacturers reserve the double-density term for lower capacity 5.25-inch floppy disks. Some computers used floppies termed *quad-density* with capacities in between those of normal and high-density floppies (720K on a 5.25-inch disk), but this format was never adopted as an IBM or DOS standard.

You can often format a normal density disk as though it were a high-density floppy, particularly with 5.25-inch disks, because most floppy disk drives of that size cannot tell the difference between the media. Although you sometimes will get a large number of errors, many normal-density floppy disks format just fine at high density. Only with the passing of time does the difference in coercivities take its toll. As these wrongly formatted disks age, they develop read errors much more quickly than properly formatted disks. Consequently, your seemingly secure storage becomes unreliable. Lose enough files (and one should be enough), and you won't want to experiment in such short-sighted penny-savings.

Extra-High Density Disks

The latest incarnation of the floppy disk pushes the storage capacity of a single disk to a new high, four megabytes each, about 2.88 megabytes with standard DOS formatting. Although the same size and shape as their predecessor normal and high-density floppy disks, these *extra-high density* floppy disks use an entirely different magnetic material (barium-ferrite) with a substantially higher coercivity than even high-density disks. Moreover, the magnetic particles of the medium are aligned vertically—perpendicular to the disk surface—rather than laterally as with other floppy disks. Consequently, extra-high density floppy disks are so different that they require a new kind of drive mechanism. Normal and high-density floppy disks cannot be used for extra-high density recording (although the extra-high density drives are backwardly compatible with older media used at the rate capacity of each medium).

Disk Sizes

Floppy disks have been made in sizes from 12 inches to 2 inches with untold variety in between. Only three of these sizes have acquired any degree of acceptance in the PC community: 8-inch, 5.25-inch, and 3.5-inch diameters. Disks with a 2.5-inch diameter were used for a brief period by one notebook computer. The numbers describe the diameter of the disk coated with magnetic medium. All disks are covered with a plastic sheath or shell that extends their dimensions.

The biggest floppies came first. Introduced in 1971, the 8-inch floppy disk had become a standard among small-computer systems before the first IBM PC was introduced. These large floppies had a number of features going for them. They were compact—at least compared to the ream of paper that could hold the same amount of information—convenient, and standardized. Above all, they were inexpensive to produce and reliable enough to depend on. From the computer hobbyists' standpoint, the random-access capability of these disks made them a godsend for good performance, at least when compared to the only affordable alternative, the cassette tape.

By the time IBM introduced its first PC, other computer makers had moved to the 5.25-inch floppy, a size introduced in 1976. IBM followed the trend and adopted the size. Because these disks were smaller than the older 8-inch variety, these 5.25-inch floppies were called *diskettes* by some. The name later spread to even smaller sizes.

When the PC rolled out, each computer manufacturer had its own data storage format (and capacity) for the small disks. More than 50 different data formats were used by various manufacturers at one time or another. The prestige of the IBM name and the success of PC sales made the IBM format the first true standard for 5.25-inch floppy disks.

The primary advantage of the 5.25-inch floppy was its compact size, which made desktop computers possible. On the down side, the smaller size meant smaller capacities. The first IBM-standard 5.25-inch floppy disks stored only 160K, compared to the megabyte capacity of the 8-inch disk.

Portable laptop computers forced the issue of still smaller disks on the world even before the introduction of the PS/2 series made them standard across the IBM product line. Besides being compact, the 3.5-inch floppy medium also boasts more storage capacity (owing to oxide advances and a precision design) and greater ruggedness (because of the tough plastic shell).

5.25-Inch Floppies

The 5.25-inch disk is a sandwich in which the bologna is the disk. Appropriately named, the disk is 5.25 inches across; the shell it fits in extends to a full 5.5 inches square. The layout of a 5.25-inch floppy disk is shown in figure 20.1.

The shell is folded from a tough, flexible plastic and sonically welded together. Inside the shell is a layer of non-woven cloth, the liner that serves to reduce the friction of the disk spinning against the shell and sweep contaminants off the disk.

The large hole in the center of the shell enables the drive hub of the disk drive to fit through. The hole cut out in the outer shell of the disk allows the drive mechanism to clamp onto the disk and spin it without slippage. The liberal lateral and longitudinal play of the disk in its shell allows it to be precisely centered on the hub.

The hub clamp is shaped like a truncated cone. The narrower portion slips into the hub hole of the disk, and as it is forced down against the drive hub itself to clamp the disk, its increasing diameter forces the disk into the proper position. The clamp holds the disk against the hub by pressing down against a narrow (about 1/16th inch) circle of disk around the hub hole.

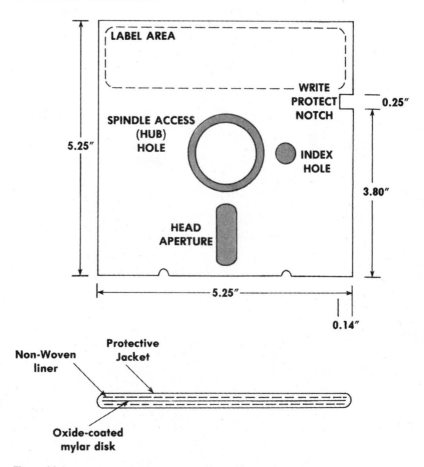

Figure 20.1. Layout of 5.25-inch floppy disk.

This area of the disk is the most prone to wear and damage. Centering can warp and tear it; the disk spinning before clamping can wear at it. To forestall damage, many disks are equipped with protective *hub rings*, which reinforce this vital center area of the disk. Some disks have rings on both sides; others only one (which should be on the bottom, where the most wear would take place). Some disks (primarily high-density floppies) don't have any. The hub rings are one more thing to get out of alignment on the disk. The tighter tolerances of high-density recording make alignments more critical, hence to omission.

Index Hole

A smaller hole in the floppy shell not far from the hub hole is designed to allow mechanical indexing of the disk. If you rotate a 5.25-inch disk inside its shell (spread your fingers inside the hub hole to rotate it without touching the magnetic surface), eventually you can make a small hole in the disk line up with the one in the disk shell. This is the *index hole*.

The original concept behind the index hole was that a light shining against the disk could detect the hole and precisely determine the radial position of the disk. Detection of the hole provided an absolute marker of where the disk was in its rotation.

Some disks had multiple holes. Some floppy disk drives used these holes to mark the beginning of each sector of storage. Because of the absolute marking method that was fixed by the disk hardware itself, these floppy disks were called *hard-sectored*.

The floppy disk drives used in ordinary PCs don't use the hole in the floppy for any purpose whatsoever. It's just an artifact from previous designs. PC floppy disk drives mark off their sectors magnetically. Because the position of each sector can be changed by software—the operating system that controls the drive—such floppy disks are said to be *soft-sectored*.

Ignoring holes is easier than making do without them, so disk drives based on soft-sectoring can use disks designed for hard- or soft-sectoring. Systems designed for hard-sectoring cannot use soft-sectored disks, however. If you have such a machine left over from the dark ages of desktop computing, you might want to think about hoarding floppies—if you can find a source of supply.

Sector Count

The actual format of data on soft-sectored floppy disks varies under the control of the software that you use. IBM's original DOS 1.0 knew only one floppy disk format that put 40 tracks on one side of a 5.25-inch floppy disk, each track divided into eight sectors. The total capacity of such a disk was 160 kilobytes. When double-sided disk drives and a new version of DOS became available, the capacity of each disk doubled.

DOS 2.0 brought additional formats. The operating system was adjusted to put nine sectors on each of forty tracks. This version of DOS was backwardly compatible with the earlier versions and would let any double-sided drive read, write, or format disks with one or two sides and eight or nine sectors per track.

The high-density disks introduced with the AT and DOS 3.0 gained their extra storage space by increasing the density of data in both directions. Under the new DOS with high-density floppy disks and matching drives, 80 tracks were laid on each side of the disk with 15 sectors per track.

The extra-high density magnetic medium has not been used for 5.25-inch floppies.

High-Density Incompatibility

To achieve that greater number of tracks, the read/write head of high-density floppy disk drives was made narrower. The result of this change is a backward incompatibility in writing and formatting double-density disks. Although a high-density drive can read, write, and format any IBM 5.25-inch floppy disk format, the disks it makes may not be readable on a double-density drive. The narrow head doesn't fill the entire track with magnetic data, and whatever magnetic fields are left outside the range of the narrow head may confuse the wider head of a double-density drive (see fig. 20.2).

Generally, if you format a double-density disk in a double-density drive, the data that a high-density drive puts on that disk also will be readable by the double-density drive. However, if you write anything on a disk with a double-density drive and write over it using a high-density drive, that disk will likely be unreadable by a double-density drive (although the high-density drive may have no trouble reading back what it has written).

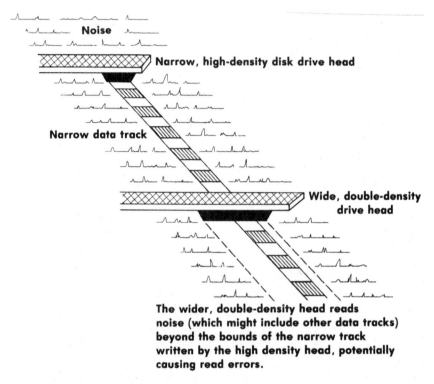

Noise

Narrow, high-density disk drive head

Narrow data track

Wide, double-density drive head

The wider, double-density head reads noise (which might include other data tracks) beyond the bounds of the narrow track written by the high density head, potentially causing read errors.

Figure 20.2. Double- versus high-density floppy disk heads.

Head Access Aperture

The large oval hole or slot—it's shaped sort of like an elongated racetrack—in both sides of the disk shell allow the read/write head(s) of the floppy disk drive to contact the disk surface. Two rules govern this slot, termed the *head access aperture*: the end of the disk closest to this hole goes into the disk drive first; never touch the disk surface itself, which can be seen through this hole. Those two rules are about all you need to know to operate a floppy disk drive successfully.

Write-Protect Notch

The shell surrounding the disk is generally square except for a notch near one corner. Called the write-protect notch, this cutout is sensed by a switch inside the disk drive. If the slot is found, you have write access to the disk, enabling you to read, write, or format the disk. If the notch is covered with a write-protect tab or a piece of tape, the disk drive sensor won't find it. The drive then will report to your computer that the disk is write-protected, and you will not be able to write to or format the disk.

Eight-inch disks also have write-protect notches, but they work just the opposite. The absence of a notch indicates to the drive that you can write on the disk. Uncovering the notch write protects the disk.

The scheme used by 5.25-inch disks has several advantages. If you insert a disk upside down, the write-protect notch will be in the wrong place, and the drive won't be able to find it. You are prevented from trying to write to an upside down disk, possibly destroying valuable data. Special disks without notches can be made that can never be written to (disk duplicating machinery does not have to obey the notch rule). With these special notchless disks, distribution copies of software can be protected from accidental erasures or alterations.

You cannot override the physical write-protection afforded by the notch through software. Even though you may get the message Abort, Retry, Ignore? (or, with newer versions of DOS, Abort, Retry, Fail?) after a write-protect error, telling the system to Ignore won't override the protection. You can, however, remove the write-protect tab or carefully cut the disk shell so as to make your own notch.

If you like to live dangerously, you also could cut the wire from the switch that senses the write-protect notch in the disk drive. After you make your first mistake and destroy your only copy of a program or data file, you'll discover how valuable hardware write-protection can be.

Flippy Disks

Another unlamented aberration in floppy disks was the so-called *flippy disk* that could be flipped over in a single-sided disk drive so that you could use the other side of the disk. Because the write-protect notch was the only thing that prevented the disk from being flipped, innovative entrepreneurs cut an extra notch in the other side of the disk shell. With that expedient, you could slide the flippy into your floppy either side up.

The usefulness of the flippy is limited in the PC market—not since the first generation of the original PC have single-sided disks been installed in PCs. Moreover, the design has a fatal flaw. When a disk is flipped over, it turns in the opposite direction. In so doing, it bends the nap of the liner in the disk shell in the opposite direction, tends to dislodge the dirt it has collected, and scatters that dirt all over the disk again, severely shortening the life of the magnetic coating on the disk.

At one time, some software was distributed on flippies—one side holding IBM PC information, the other the same data in Apple II format. Because IBM machines didn't recognize the Apple disks (and vice versa), your PC would think such a flippy is just a single-sided disk. Unless you have two computer systems, one matching each standard, you won't be tempted to flip that flippy over. If you do, you should guarantee the life of the programs it contains by making yourself a duplicate copy and putting the flippy safely away.

3.5-Inch Floppies

Portable computers and down-sized machines like Apple's Macintosh drove the need for still smaller floppy disks. A variety of abortive attempts, including a miniaturized 5.25-inch system that had two inches of diameter loped off, finally led to the near-universal acceptance of the demonstrably superior 3.5-inch system originally promulgated by Sony. In their favor, 3.5-inch disks are convenient critters, exactly shirt-pocket size, and they are tough and reliable enough to be tossed around with impunity. The layout of a 3.5-inch floppy disk is shown in figure 20.3.

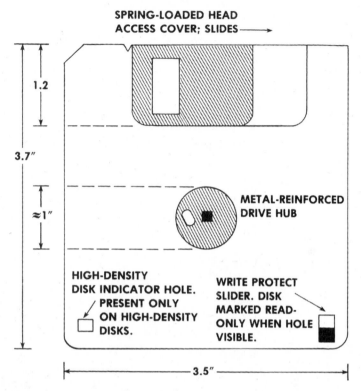

Figure 20.3. Layout of 3.5-inch floppy disk.

Tough Shell

The 3.5-inch system embodies several improvements over the veteran 5.25-inch design. Most notable is its hard shell, tough and only slightly flexible. The hard shell protects the fragile disk while enabling you the freedom of carrying out such crimes, forbidden with 5.25-inch disks, of writing on an already applied disk label with a ballpoint pen. Unlike the bigger disks that leave a large head-access swath of the disk vulnerable to dirt, dust, and fingerprints, the 3.5-inch design covers the vulnerable access area with a spring-loaded sliding metal shield or shutter, which opens automatically only when you insert a disk into a drive. This protection means that 3.5-inch disks don't need the protection of a sleeve or shuck.

Insertion Key

Unlike 5.25-inch disks, the 3.5 is designed to prevent improper insertion. One corner is truncated so that a disk will only fully engage in a disk drive when correctly oriented.

Write-Protection

Instead of a write-protect notch and tap, the 3.5-inch design uses a hole and a plastic slider. When the slider blocks the hole, you can read, write, and format the disk. When the slider is moved back to reveal the hole (or is entirely absent, as it is on many software distribution disks) the disk is write-protected.

More Tracks

The storage capacity of the 3.5-inch disk proves that less can be more. Although less than half the surface area is available for recording on a 3.5-inch disk compared to a 5.25-inch disk, the standard format of the little disk actually can pack in more data, up to 720K at normal density, 1.44M at high-density. The larger capacities result from the use of a more finely grained medium with better magnetic properties and greater precision. The old problem of disk centering is reduced by a the 3.5-inch disk's metal hub, which allows easier, more positive mechanical action with less chance of damage or wear. Instead of 48 or 96 tracks per inch, the 3.5-inch design squeezes in 135 per inch. Because of the cramped quarters, however, only 80 of these narrow tracks fit on a disk.

Sector Count

The lower capacity IBM 3.5-inch drives, used by the IBM Convertible and some compatible computers, use the same physical and logical layout as ordinary double-sided, double-density disks—512 byte sectors arranged nine per track—and increase capacity solely by doubling the number of tracks per disk side (up to 80 tracks) to attain 720K per disk. The high-density disks used by the PS/2 line and nearly all more recent compatibles double the density of the data in each track (to fit 18 sectors per track) to achieve their 1.44M limit. Single-sided 3.5-inch disks are not supported in the IBM universe.

Your disk drive can tell whether you have put a normal density or high-density floppy disk into it. An extra *high-density notch* marks the disks with greater capacity.

Extra-high density disks maintain the same number of tracks as their predecessors (80) at the same 135-tracks-per-inch spacing as high-density floppies but double the number of sectors per track, from 18 to 36. The track width is maintained at the same value as older floppy disk styles. This arrangement enables extra-high density floppy disk drives to read and write 720K and 1.44MB floppies without compatibility problems.

2.5-Inch Floppies

In 1989, Zenith Data System introduced a novel and short-lived 2.5-inch floppy disk system patterned after the double-density 3.5-inch drive system. The arrangement of tracks and sectors on the drive was the same for the two media, giving both a capacity of 720K, but the 2.5-inch drives obviously packed information more tightly. The reason for the smaller size was to make floppy disk drives fit into the tiniest possible package—Zenith believing that no one would want a notebook computer that could not use removable media. Unfortunately for Zenith, no one wanted to use a nonstandard floppy disk drive that lacked the primary capacity for which people insisted in having floppies in their PCs—moving data to the desktop computers by exchanging disks. Although you could back up your files to one of the tiny floppies, you had to connect the Zenith notebook computer to your desktop machine as though it had no floppy disk drive when you wanted to transfer data. After the Zenith experience, no other manufacturer opted for 2.5-inch drives.

Floppy Disk Drives

As computer equipment goes, floppy disk drives are simple devices. The essential components are a *spindle motor*, which spins the disk, and a stepper motor that drives a metal band in and out to position the read/write heads, an assembly collectively called the *head actuator*. A manual mechanism is provided for lowering a hub clamp to center and lock the disk in place and to press the heads against the surface of the disk. In all except the single-sided drives of the original PC, two heads, which pinch together around the disk to read and write from either side of the medium, are used. The tracks on either side of the disk are interleaved so that one head is not directly over the other but is instead slightly offset.

Speed Control

All of the electronics packed onto the one or more circuit boards attached to the drive unit merely control those simple operations. A servo system keeps the disk spinning at the correct speed. Usually an optical sensor looks at a stroboscopic pattern of black dots on a white disk on the spindle assembly. The electronics count the dots that pass the sensor in a given period to determine the speed at which it turns, adjusting it as necessary. Some drives use similar sensors based on magnetism rather than optics, but they work in essentially the same way—counting the number of passing magnetic pulses in a given period to determine the speed of the drive.

Head Control

Other electronics control the radial position of the head assembly to the disk. The stepper motor that moves the head reacts to voltage pulses by moving in one or more discrete steps of a few degrees (hence the descriptive name of this type of motor). Signals from the floppy disk controller card in the host computer tell the disk drive to which track of the disk to move its head. The electronics on the drive then send the appropriate number of pulses to the stepper motor to move the head to the designated track.

The basic floppy disk mechanism receives no feedback on where the head is on the disk. It merely assumes that it gets to the right place because of the number of steps the actuator makes. Because the drive does its best to remember the position of the head, hard reality can leave the head other than in its expected place. For example, you can reach in and manually jostle the head mechanism. Or, you may switch off your computer with the head halfway across the disk. When the power is off, all the circuitry forgets, and the location of the head becomes an unknown.

Note that the stepper motors in most double-density floppy disk drives sold today can trace all 40 tracks used by the IBM floppy disk format. Some earlier computers did not require all 40 tracks. Consequently, some drives made for these computers—usually those drives closed out at prices that seem too good to be true—may not have a full 40-track range. Caveat emptor!

Head Indexing

So that the head can be put in the right place with assurance, the drive resorts to a process called *indexing*. The drive moves the head as far as it will go toward the edge of the disk. When the head reaches this index position, it can travel no farther, no matter how hard the actuator tries to move it. The drive electronics make sure that the actuator moves the head a sufficient number of steps (a number greater than the width of the disk) to ensure that the head will stop at the index position. After the head has reached the index position, the control electronics can move it a given number of actuator steps and know exactly where on the radius of the disk the head is located.

Extra-High Density Drives

To cope with the extra-high density recording medium, extra-high density floppy disk drives required a radical innovation—an extra head for each surface. The extra-high density medium is so difficult to work with that it requires a separate erase head. The extra head is fixed to the same actuator as the read/write head and moves with it track-to-track. When writing data, the erase head prepares the area for the read/write head by aligning the disk flux transitions in the same direction. The read/write head then can change their orientation to record data.

DOS Requirements

Functionally, there's no difference between the full- and half-height 5.25-inch units. They run exactly the same with all software—except half-height drives should not be used with DOS 2.0 or earlier. Because of the slower mechanism of the smaller drives, IBM increased a few time constants in DOS 2.1, which was made available at the same time as the PCjr.

Not only do DOS 3.0 and later versions take into account the requirements of half-height drives, these later versions of DOS also support high-density (1.2 megabyte), 5.25-inch drives. You must use DOS 3.0 or later with 1.2M floppy disks.

The first DOS version to support 3.5-inch drives was DOS 3.2, which supports only the 720K drives used by the PC Convertible. The high-density 3.5-inch drives with a 1.44M capacity used by the PS/2 series require either DOS 3.3 (or later) or OS/2. Extra-high density floppy disk drives require DOS 5.0 or later.

Floppy Disk Controllers

Although operating a floppy disk drive seems simple, it's actually a complex operation with many levels of control. When you press the Save button while running an application program, your button press does not connect directly to the drive. Instead, the keystroke is detected by your computer's hardware and recognized by its BIOS. The BIOS, in turn, sends the appropriate electronic code to your application program. The program then makes one or more requests to DOS to write something to disk. DOS sends instructions to the BIOS, and the BIOS sends codes to ports on the disk control hardware. Finally, this hardware tells the drive where to move its head and what to do.

The penultimate piece of hardware in this chain is the *floppy disk controller*. It has two purposes in operating your system's floppy disks: one is to translate the logical commands from your computer system, which are usually generated by the BIOS, into the exact electrical signals that control the disk drive. The other function is to translate the stream of pulses generated by the floppy disk head into data in the form that your computer can deal with.

The best way to understand the operation of the floppy disk controller is to examine the signals that control the floppy disk drive and those that the drive sends to its computer host.

Two, *Drive Select A* and *Drive Select B* are used to individually select either the first or second drive, A or B. (In four-drive systems, the signals for A in the second cable control drive C, and those of B control D.) If the signal assigned to a particular drive is not present, all the other input and output circuits of the drive are deactivated, except for those that control the drive motor. In this way, two drives can share the bulk of the wires in the controller cable without interference. However, this control scheme also means that only one drive in a pair can be active at a time. You can write to drive B at the same time as you read from drive A. That's why you must transfer the data held on a disk (or file) from one drive into memory before you can copy it to another drive.

One wire is used for each drive to switch its spindle motor on and off. These wires are called, individually, *Drive Select A* and *Drive Select B*. Although it is possible to make both motors spin simultaneously, rules laid down by IBM admonish against activating these two lines to make floppy disk drive motors run at the same time (this saves power in the severely constrained PC system and is a moot issue in the single-drive XT system). Of course, the two drives in your PC may run simultaneously for brief periods due to a delay built in most drives that keeps their motors running for a few seconds after the Motor Enable signal stops. Two signals control the head position. One, *Step Pulse*, merely tells the stepper motor on the drive to move one step—that's exactly one track—toward or away from the center of the disk. The *Direction* signal controls which way the pulses move the head. If this signal is active, the head moves toward the center.

To determine which of the two sides of a double-sided disk to read, one signal, called *Write Select*, is used. When this signal is active, it tells the disk drive to use the upper head. When no signal is present, the disk drive automatically uses the default (lower) head.

Writing to disk requires two signals. *Write Data* comprises the information actually to be written magnetically onto the disk. It consists of nothing but a series of pulses corresponding exactly to the flux transitions to be made on the disk. The read/write head merely echoes these signals magnetically. As a fail-safe to preclude to possibility of accidentally writing over valuable data, a second signal called *Write Enable* is used. No write current is sent to the read/write head unless this signal is active.

The data rate of the data signal varies with the disk drive type. A normal density floppy accepts and sends data at a rate of 250 kilobits per second. A high-density drive operates at 500 kilobits per second. An extra-high density drive operates at one megabit per second.

The controller receives four signals back from the floppy disk drive.

Two of these signals help the controller determine where the head is located. *Track 0* indicates to the controller when the head is above the outermost track on the disk so that the controller knows from where to start counting head-moving pulses. *Index* helps the drive determine the location of each bit on a disk track. One pulse is generated on the Index line for each revolution of the disk. The controller can time the distance between ensuing data pulses based on the reference provided by the Index signal.

The *Write Protect* signal is derived from the sensor that detects the existence or absence of a write-protect tab on a disk. If a tab is present, this signal is active.

The *Read Data* signal comprises a series of electrical pulses that exactly matches the train of flux transition on the floppy disk. The data rates correspond to those used for writing to the disk. In its control function, the floppy disk controller must convert the requests from the BIOS or direct hardware commands that are couched in terms of track and sector numbers into the pulses that move the head to the proper location on the disk. For the most efficient operation, the controller must also remember where the head is located, index the head as necessary, and report errors when they occur.

In its translation function, the floppy disk controller must make sense from the stream of unformatted pulses delivered from the drive. It first must find the beginning of each track from the Index pulse and then mark out each sector from the information embedded in the data stream. After it identifies a requested sector, it then must read the information it contains and convert it from serial to parallel form so that it can be sent through the PC bus. In writing, the controller first must identify the proper sector to write to—which is a read operation—then switch on the write current to put data into that sector before the next sector on the disk begins.

Most of the hard work of the controller is handled by a single integrated circuit, the 765 controller chip. (In contemporary PCs, the function of the 765 is often integrated inside chip sets.) The 765 works much like a microprocessor. It carries out certain operations in response to commands that it receives through registers connected to your computer's I/O ports.

This programmability makes the 765 and the IBM floppy disk controller extremely versatile. None of the essential floppy disk drive parameters are cast in stone or the silicon on the controller. The number of heads, tracks, and sectors on a disk are set by loading numbers into the registers of the 765. Usually, the normal IBM operating values are loaded into the controller when you boot up your computer. You ordinarily don't have to worry about them after that.

Special software can reprogram your controller to make it read, write, and format floppy disks that differ from the IBM standard. Two types of software perform this reprogramming. Copy-protection schemes may alter vital drive parameters by misnumbering sectors, adding extra sectors, or a similar operation that cannot be duplicated using normal IBM parameters. Disk compatibility software alters the controller programming to make the floppy disk drives in your system act like those used by other computers, such as those that use the CP/M operating system. Note, however, that although the IBM system is flexible, it cannot handle all possibilities, such as Commodore or Apple disks. Those computers used entirely different drive control hardware that the 765 cannot mimic.

Controller Integration

IBM has used three distinct styles of floppy disk controller—stand-alone, combined, and integrated. The original design used in the first PC was also adopted by the XT and Portable PC and used a stand-alone floppy disk controller. The PCjr used a separate but functionally identical design. The floppy disk controller of the AT and XT Model 286 were combined with the hard disk controller. All PC/2 models have their floppy disk controllers built into their system board circuitry. The extra-density controllers of more recent PS/2s are similarly integrated. Compatible computer manufacturers have adopted all of these designs.

Format Compatibility

All computers in the IBM PC and PS/2 families (as well as completely compatible computers) could, in theory, support standard double-density, double-sided floppy disk drives. (Although PS/2s can operate normal density 5.25-inch floppy drives, finding matching drives for these machines can be difficult.) Normal-density floppies are thus the only truly universal storage system across the PC product line, making their media the one format with the widest range of compatibilities.

High-density 5.25-inch drives with 1.2M data capacity are supported by IBM hardware only in AT and later computers (including the XT Model 286). The BIOS of earlier machines—PCs, XTs, Portable PCs, and the PCjr—is unable to handle the larger number of tracks used by these drives. Similarly, 3.5-inch drives are not supported by the hardware machines earlier than the PS/2 series, with the exception of the Convertible, the initial versions of which were only capable of handling 720K drives.

The primary culprit is generally your system BIOS. The BIOS stores all the instructions your computer knows on its own for matching the 765 to different floppy disk types. If your system BIOS lacks the instructions needed to make a 3.5-inch drive work, you can't, for example, plug such a drive into your PC and expect it to play properly.

Determining whether your PC is compatible with a given type of floppy disk drive can be as easy as checking your system's owner's manual or as difficult as trial-and-error experimentation. One place to start is with the date your system was made. Computers designed before the IBM AT was announced in August, 1984, are likely to recognize only double-density (360K) 5.25-inch floppy disk drives because high-density 5.25-inch drives were not introduced until the first AT was. Systems designed before IBM introduced its ill-starred PC Convertible laptop computer are unlikely to use double-density 3.5-inch drives because IBM introduced the 720K format with that machine. IBM began using high-density 3.5-inch drives with the introduction of its PS/2 series in 1987, although a few manufacturers anticipated this format.

If you don't know when your system was designed or introduced, you're not out of luck. You can take a quick look at your PC's setup procedure—either the setup procedure you can select from the keyboard when your computer boots or the disk-based setup program that accompanied your computer when you bought it. Check the options that setup gives you for floppy-disk drives.

The setup program used by most computers since the introduction of the AT includes a set of choices from which you select which style of floppy disk drive you have installed as drive A and B. Check what your choices are. If the style of floppy disk drive that you want to install is listed in setup, you're home free—your floppy disk upgrade will work with your PC after a simple mechanical installation job.

If your PC does not have a setup program, it was likely designed by the old school—in the days before the AT. Consequently, your system most likely knows only about double-density 5.25-inch floppy disk drives.

Laptop computers are an entirely different matter. Most laptop computer manufacturers recognize the problems of media incompatibility and allow for some means of connecting an external 5.25-inch floppy disk drive to their products. Most of these add-on drives attach to dedicated proprietary floppy disk ports on the laptop computer. These manufacturers offer their own products (typically expensive) for adding floppy disk drives.

The lack of direct support for a given floppy disk drive type by your PC does not mean that you're forever precluded from adding that variety of floppy disk drive. You just need to take a few extra steps to teach your PC how to handle the renegade drive.

You must use one of three strategies: adding driver software, upgrading your floppy disk controller along with the floppy disk drive, or altering the BIOS of your computer. The first is the universal approach, the least expensive, and the one that requires the least tinkering with the solid-state secrets of your PC. It's also the most limited.

Driver software supplements the code that's contained in your system BIOS with special instructions for handling the new type of floppy disk drive. The drivers load through your system's CONFIG.SYS file just like any other device driver would.

That's the first limitation of using driver software—your system has to boot up before the driver can be read. Consequently, driver software is not an adequate solution for your boot floppy, drive A. It's the classic Catch 22—the system can't boot from the floppy because it has to read the driver first, but to read the driver it must first boot the system.

Moreover, because the driver loads after DOS takes control of your PC, driver software is operating-system specific. You'll need a different driver for DOS than you will for OS/2 or Unix. In many cases, you may not be able to find driver software for operating systems other than DOS. If you're planning on moving up to a new operating system, you probably won't want to go the driver route.

Some software, such as some disk utilities and backup programs, takes direct hardware control of floppy disk drives, ignoring software drivers. These applications may not work on a floppy disk drive that uses a software driver. Worse, the software may *try* to work and spin the floppy disk drive into chaotic operation. This, in turn, may destroy the data on floppies you put into the drive.

Software drivers also add a petty irritation. Because DOS brings them to life after all other disk drives in your system have been initialized through your system's BIOS, they take on drive letter identifications further down the line than the last BIOS-based drive. So your new driver-based floppy will likely be recognized as drive D rather than drive B. All told, software drivers are technically the least desirable way of matching a foreign floppy disk drive to a PC. Unfortunately, they also are the only universal method of doing so, sometimes the only method permitted by a given PC. Apart from the perfect hardware match, driver software is also the least expensive means of matching a floppy to your PC.

Many floppy disk kits include a software driver to help you upgrade systems that need one. Note that this driver is used in addition to the DRIVER.SYS program that comes with recent versions of DOS. The driver that comes with the floppy disk drive tells your PC how to operate the floppy disk drive; DRIVER.SYS tells your system how to recognize that new floppy disk drive.

In many PCs, you can match an odd floppy disk drive by changing your floppy disk controller. Many—but far from all—modern floppy disk controllers come equipped with an add-on BIOS that adds the necessary instructions to your system's existing BIOS to allow it to control any standard floppy disk drive type. But if you want to add a new floppy disk controller with BIOS support to your PC, you have to be careful. Older controllers and the least expensive recent controllers do not have the necessary BIOS code built in.

To ensure that you get the BIOS you need, you have to ask when you order a particular controller whether it has its own BIOS. Better yet, check when you order a new floppy controller to be sure that it will allow you to use a specific floppy disk drive type with your PC.

Computers that have their floppy disk control circuitry built into their system boards will require that you disable the system board floppy circuitry before you add a new controller card. If you cannot disable the system board floppy disk control circuitry of your PC, then you won't be able to add a new controller. Micro Channel PS/2s also foreclose on the possibility of controller-based BIOS upgrades because Micro Channel-based floppy controller cards are virtually impossible to find.

The most satisfying solution to the floppy incompatibility problem is adding a new BIOS to your PC so that all the needed floppy disk instructions will be built into your computer. This change requires that you remove two (or four) large integrated circuit chips from the system board of your PC and replace them with new ones. That part of the job takes only a few minutes (after you open and disassemble your PC).

The more difficult part of the job is finding a BIOS upgrade that will work with your computer. Although several companies manufacture BIOSs, these companies aim their sales efforts at providing chips to computer makers. They don't ordinarily deal in single-piece quantities with individual end-users like you.

Moreover, unless a BIOS upgrade is available from the original maker of your PC, you have no guarantee that the new BIOS will actually work with your computer. You generally cannot buy a BIOS off the shelf. What you can do is contact the dealer who originally sold you your computer and ask if its manufacturer offers a BIOS upgrade. If such an upgrade is available, your dealer will be the best (and likely only) source of supply.

Drive and Cabling Configuration

The IBM floppy system is the standard for all floppy disk systems. It was designed so that you can install floppy disk drives with a minimum of thought—which gives you an idea of what manufacturers think of their assembly line workers. Once you understand a few simple rules, you can do as good a job as—or better than—they can.

Drive-Select Jumpers

The cabling used in a floppy disk subsystem apparently presumes that a drive attached to it already knows whether it is supposed to be drive A or B in your system. However, for compatibility reasons, all floppy disk drives are created equal with a common design for all drive letters. In order that a given floppy disk drive can assume the identity of A or B, drive manufacturers equipped their products with DIP switches or jumpers to select the appropriate appellation. Termed drive-select jumpers, most floppy disk drives allow you to select one of four potential identities.

For reasons related to their function—they essentially switch some of the connections delivered by the cable—drive-select jumpers can usually be found on a drive near the edge connector onto which you attach the cable. Usually you'll be faced with an array of jumpers or switches, probably about either, each labeled with a not-too-meaningful combination of two or three letters and numbers. The drive-select jumpers can be identified (when they are labeled) by their two character prefix DS. From there different disk drive manufacturers go in two directions. Some start numbering the drive-select settings with one and count up to four; others start with one and venture only as far as three.

Drive-Select Settings

In the IBM scheme of things, which of these settings applied to drive A or B—or even C or D—has no relevance. All floppy disk drives in an IBM-style computer are set to be the second drive in the system. A special twist to the floppy disk connecting cable sorts out the proper disk drive identity.

To configure a floppy disk drive for installation in an IBM-style system, you should invariably set it as the second drive, paying no attention to whether it will be A or B. With drives with which the drive-select jumpers are numbered starting with zero, all floppy disk drives should be set as one. With drives with which the number of the drive-select jumpers begins with one, all drives should be set as two.

Drive Cabling

The special twist that sorts out the drive identities is exactly that—a group of five conductors in the floppy disk cable are twisted in the run to one of its connectors. This twist reverses the drive-select and motor control signals in the cable as well as rearranging some of the ground wires in the cable (which effectively makes no change).

Because all drives are set up as the second drive, this reversal makes the drive attached to the cable after the twist the first drive, drive A. In other words, drive A is attached to the connector at the end of the cable, the one where the wire twist takes place. Drive B is attached to the connector in the middle of the length of the cable. The third connector, at the end of the cable with no twist, goes to the floppy disk controller.

Single Drive and Straight-through Cables

With hard disk drives, you can use a straight-through cable—that is, one without the twist near the last connectors—to operate a single disk drive by moving the drive-select jumper of the connected hard disk to the first drive position. This tactic *will not work* with floppy disk drives. The twisted part of the cable moves not only the drive-select conductor but also the motor control conductor. Therefore, you cannot use a straight-through cable with a single floppy disk drive in your computer system.

If you make your own floppy disk cable to handle a single drive, you'll have to abide by the IBM drive select numbering scheme. You have to make a twist in the conductors, as shown in figure 20.4.

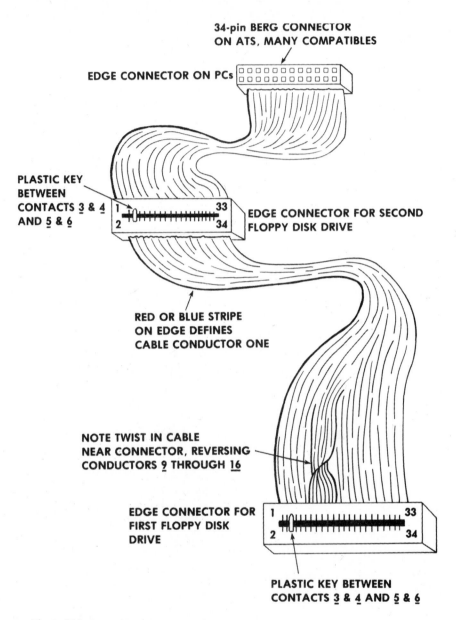

Figure 20.4. Two-drive floppy disk cable.

Terminating Resistor Networks

In the floppy disk system originally developed by IBM and used by compatible computer makers, there was but one physical difference between drives A and B. Drive A always had a *terminating resistor network* installed. Drive B always did not. In three or four floppy disk drive systems, drive C always had a terminating resistor. Drive D did not.

That simple rule proved more confusing than most people could deal with. Consequently, modern floppy disk drives are often equipped with a non-removable terminating resistor pack.

Purpose

The terminating resistor is used to absorb the excess current that flows through the connection between the floppy disk controller and the drive electronics. The circuits are designed so that a specific current is expected to flow through them. The terminating resistor network forces the proper current to flow so that no excess is left in the system. Without the terminating resistor, the signal going to the floppy disk drive would be mismatched and may bounce back and forth through the circuitry before finally decaying, possibly resulting in errors. By absorbing the excess, the terminating resistor prevents those potential errors.

Two terminating resistors—for example, having a resistor network installed on both disk drives in a system—would cause too much current to flow, which can lead to the premature failure of the circuits themselves. The terminating resistor network is always located on the last drive that is physically connected to the cable because that's where the signal reflections would occur.

Removable terminating resistors are typically rated at 2.2 kilohms (an ohm being the basic unit of electrical resistance; a kilohm being 1000 ohms). Non-removable terminating resistors are nominally rated at 1 kilohm. Consequently, two drives with non-removable terminating resistors will have approximately the same value as a properly terminated system. If only one drive with a non-removable resistor is installed in a PC—either alone or in conjunction with a drive with a

2.2K terminating resistor pack installed—the mismatch will only be half what it would be by breaking the hard-and-fast rule. That's actually close enough to eliminate most problems. If you have a drive with a removable termination, you'll still want to abide by the rules because otherwise the terminating resistance can get too high or low.

Identification

Identifying terminating resistor packs is quite easy. They usually take on one of two forms—either housed in a single in-line package or, more usually, in a dual in-line package that looks like an ordinary integrated circuit (except that it is sometimes blue or amber instead of black and may be shinier). Single in-line packages usually resemble small oblong blocks, about an inch long, an eighth inch thick, and half an inch high. Nine separate leads, at one-tenth inch spacing, project from the bottom of the network and into a socket or directly through the printed circuit board of the floppy disk drive electronics. Non-removable terminations usually take the single in-line form.

In most contemporary floppy disk drives, the termination resistor stands out because it's the only socket-mounted device on the circuit board. Figure 20.5 illustrates common terminating resistor types.

Location

The terminating resistor network in most floppy disk drives is found adjacent to the edge connector to which you plug in the drive. Because the network must be removed from a generic drive in roughly half its installations, the resistor network is generally accessible near the rear edge of the printed circuit board holding the electronics of the drive. Usually, it is near or adjacent to the drive select jumpers or switches.

Removal

For the most part, when you need to make a floppy disk drive with a removable termination either drive B or drive D, you only need pull out the resistor. SIP networks should be removable just by pulling them firmly away from their sockets. DIP networks may require the use of a chip puller, or you can pry them up with a small screwdriver.

(can be black, blue, or opaque amber)

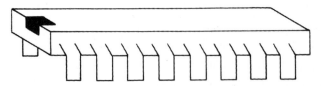

1. **Dual in-line package; usually has eight *pairs* of "legs".**

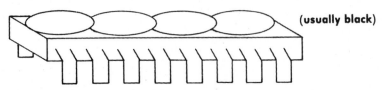

(usually black)

2. **Sometimes the dual in-line package appears "lumpy".**

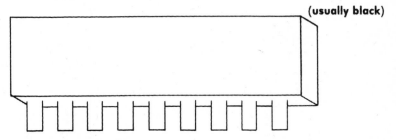

(usually black)

3. **Single in-line package generally has nine "legs".**
   Sometimes it, too, appears lumpy.

Figure 20.5. Terminating resistors.

Disk Care

The rules governing the care of floppy disks are all based on the prevention of damage. Two forces can impair the function of floppies—physical damage and magnetism.

Magnetic Enemies

The latter is the more insidious. Invisible magnetic fields can alter or erase the data you have stored on your floppy disk. For instance, if the File Allocation Table of the disk is damaged, you may never be able to recover information from your disk even though it's still written on the disk.

Sources of potentially damaging magnetism abound in the office. For instance, the ringers inside old-fashioned telephones—the Bell telephones that have actual ringing bells inside them—are operated by powerful electromagnets. Whenever the phone rings, it sets up a magnetic field that can erase disks that are near or underneath the telephone. The field is not too strong, however, and keeping your disks a few inches from the phone should be sufficient.

Other common disk-damaging devices include magnetized scissors, those clever little paper-clip holders with ring magnets at the top to hold the clips in readiness, and even the motorized playthings found on some executives' desks. Even some monitors may exude magnetic fields from their power supplies or degaussing coils.

Physical Dangers

Physical damage includes anything that may alter the surface or substrate of the floppy disk. Any alteration—be it a coating of dust, oily fingerprints, or a physical tear or crease—is enough to interfere with the proper operation of the disk.

Writing on a disk label with a ballpoint pen, a commonly cited problem, creases the disk. When the head scrapes over the disk, the crease causes a slight, temporary loss of contact with the disk. The data that might be read during that period are lost, resulting in a disk error. Folding or creasing the disk, even within its protective shuck, causes the same problem.

Dirt and fingerprints are cumulative and work slowly, wearing out the disk and your disk drive mechanism. They can combine together to literally gum up the works. Loose labels and write-protect tabs can come free and also damage your disk or drive mechanism.

Disk Care Recommendations

The best way to prevent disk problems is to take good care of your disks. Always keep them in their protective sleeves when they are not being actively used. Before you switch off your computer, remove the disk from the drive and put it away. Although IBM computers offer little risk of damaging a disk when they are powered down, even inside the machine a disk can collect potentially destructive dust on its surface. It's much less likely to inside its sleeve.

Keep your disks organized in a disk file cabinet. Although most are made from plastic and thus offer no magnetic shielding, they automatically put your disks far enough away from most magnetic sources that magnetic damage is minimized. Just don't put your magnetized scissors inside with the disks. The file cabinet also protects the disks from physical damage besides keeping you organized.

Radical Recovery of 5.25-Inch Floppies

The protective (generally black) plastic shell of the 5.25-inch floppy disk deflects most woes that might afflict your data. Sometimes, however, it becomes the problem rather than the solution. When one of your floppy disks suffers some tremendous indignity—say from being trod upon by the local high school cross-country team wearing their cleats—the damage done to the shell may be all that stands between you and reading your data from the disk. The shell might get so bent it won't fit into the drive slot or so corrugated that the disk won't turn inside it. If you've got data on such a disk, all is not lost— at least not yet.

Radical surgery can give you a chance to see what's left on the disk. Using the radical recovery technique, you may be able to save your data, though your disk has met its demise. (The harder shell of 3.5-inch floppies normally prevents the problems afflicting 5.25-inch floppies that are amenable to radical repair.)

Radical recovery merely means separating the disk from its shell for one last spin in your disk drive. To get the disk out of its shell, you can either break the sonic welds holding the shell closed (more difficult than it sounds) or slice off one edge of the shell with a scissors or paper cutter.

After you have opened the shell, carefully slide the disk out, touching its surface as little as possible. With most disk drives, you can gently insert this naked disk right into the slot, watching carefully as you operate the lever to lower the head that the centering hub actually engages the center hole of the vulnerable disk.

Some floppy disk drives have an anti-head crash lock that prevents you from lowering the head without a disk *in its shell* being present in the drive. If that's the case for yours, you'll have to sacrifice a second, good-quality disk. Slice the new disk open, pull out the disk itself, and reinsert the disk from the corrupted shell.

After you have your bad floppy in a disk drive, copy its contents to a new disk to substitute for the old. You should be able to get more than a few spins from your reconstituted disk. You stand a good, though hardly perfect, chance of recovering the information stored on it.

Note that some companies—notably Polaroid—offer a free data recovery service for their warranteed disks. If the disks that you use are covered by such a warrant, do not try the radical recover because it will likely void the aforesaid warranty. Instead, let the disk manufacturer dig out your data. The disk maker stands a better chance of getting back your data, and you'll suffer fewer heartaches and headaches.

21

Hard Disks

I n most PCs, the hard disk is the principal mass storage system. It holds all of your programs and data files and must deliver them to your system at an instant's notice. Hard disks differ by technology, interface, speed, and capacity, all of which are interrelated.

A PC without a hard disk demonstrates solid-state senility. All that's left of long-term memory are the brief flashbacks that can be loaded (with great effort and glacial speed) from floppy disks. What's left is a curiosity to be nursed along until death overtakes it, probably your own demise because a PC without a hard disk will make you wish you were dead.

The hard disk is the premiere mass storage device for today's PCs. No other peripheral can approach the usefulness of the hard disk's combination of speed, capacity, and straightforward user installation. In fact, without today's big, fast disks you probably wouldn't even consider a quick 32- or 64-bit microprocessor. You couldn't keep enough data in your system to make the fast chip useful.

The hard disk puts the bulk of your programs and data at your fingertips, ready for instant access. It can speed up everyday work by loading programs in a fraction of the time required by floppy disks. By storing and sorting through data very quickly, it will make many of your programs seem to run faster. The hard disk will even make the rest of your computer system seem more responsive.

The hard disk deals in megabytes, hundreds of them. In one second, the disk has to be able to remember or disgorge the information equivalent of the entire contents of a physics textbook or a novel. And it must be equally capable of casting aside its memories and replacing them with revised versions to keep your system up to date. That's a big challenge, particularly for a device that may be no larger than a deck of playing cards and uses less power than a night light.

In the first decade of PCs, hard disks evolved from high-priced luxuries to simple necessities. In fact, the evolution of the PC echoes and emphasizes the changed perception of the hard disk. The first PC made no provision for a hard disk. The XT brought hard disk capabilities. The AT put the emphasis on hard disk performance. Micro Channel PS/2s made the hard disk standard equipment (though by then, no self-respecting PC lacked a hard disk drive). Windows and OS/2 make a 100-megabyte hard disk mandatory.

Depending on your needs and demands, hard disks can be expensive or cheap. They come in various sizes and speed ratings. You can scrounge through ads and find decade-old drives that will still plug into your PC at prices that will make Scrooge smile, and you weep while you wait and wait for its ancient technology to catch up with the demands of a modern microprocessor. Today's drives have little in common with their forebears of as little as five years ago. They're smaller, more responsive, have several times the capacity, and several times the life and reliability. They don't even plug into your PC the same way as early hard disks. Finding the right hard disk requires understanding what's inside a drive, what the different mechanisms and technology are, and what best mates with a modern machine.

Naming Conventions

The place to begin any discussion is getting a handle on what you're talking about. The name *hard disk* seems straightforward enough, distinguishing such products from the other familiar mass storage device, the floppy disk. While the floppy disk is based on a flexible carrier for its magnetic medium, the hard disk uses a rigid, or hard, substrate called a *platter* (which, of course, has a disk shape). The name is merely descriptive but hardly exhaustive or universal. Hard disk drives wear several other monikers, some apt and accurate, others not.

IBM, for example, favors the term *fixed disk* to hard disk. The reasoning is that the platter in a hard disk is fixed inside the drive, rather than being removable as is a floppy disk. Of course, some hard disk drives use removable media, destroying the "fixed" distinction.

Winchester Disk Drives

Perhaps the most familiar synonym for hard disk drive is Winchester disk drive, often clipped simply to Winchester by those in the know. In truth, few of today's hard disks have the right to wear the label "Winchester." And that's good.

Winchester refers to the underlying technology used by the read/write head in the disk drive. The head in a Winchester drive is attached to a slight airfoil, like an airplane wing, and operates as a flying read/write head, floating a few microinches (millionths of an inch) above the surface of the disk. Unlike the airplane wing that moves through the air to gain the lift that levitates it, the air moves and the read/write head stands still (at least in the direction of the airflow). The spinning of the disk in the drive itself stirs up the air to raise the head. The advantage of this design is that the head does not touch the disk, at least when the disk is spinning, so there's no rubbing or wear of the disk surface. At the same time, the read/write head is close enough (6 to 12 microinches in a modern drive) that the magnetic fields of the medium and head don't spread too far.

How the name "Winchester" got associated with this technology has become part of computer folklore. The first drive to use this technology was developed by IBM Corporation at its Hursley Laboratory, which happens to be located near Winchester in England. But that felicitous location has nothing to do with the drives epithet. Rather, the name resulted from a bit of word association. The original IBM disk drive that used this technology was code-named "3030" because it had two sides, each of which could store 30 megabytes. To some people, this designation recalled the famous Winchester 3030 repeating rifle that, according to legend, won the West. The name Winchester carried over to the like-numbered disk drive. The moniker not only stuck but was generalized to the flying head technology on which the drive was based.

A new head technology, called Whitney, results in much smaller, faster, and sturdier assemblies that have replaced the original Winchester head design in many, if not most, products. Future hard disk drives may abandon the flying head for one that swims in a thick liquid. Likely, however, the Winchester name will persist in general use for all hard disk drives.

Bernoulli Technology

Iomega Corporation's Bernoulli Box removable media drives turn Winchester technology upside down. Instead of using the airflow generated by the spinning disk to lift the head above a rigid disk, these drives use a flexible disk that bends around the head under the force of the air pressure. The advantages of this system are that the spinning disk has much lower mass and is more resistant to head crashes. The disadvantage is that the medium is constantly flexed and eventually wears out.

The name is drawn from the Bernoulli theorem or principle, first propounded by the 18th century Swiss mathematician and physicist Daniel Bernoulli. His principle states that the total energy at any point in a fluid system is constant; thus, faster moving fluids exert less pressure. The faster air flows over a surface, the lower the pressure. Airplane wings are designed as airfoils that force air to travel a greater distance over the top of the wing compared to the bottom, resulting in a lower pressure atop the wing. The higher pressure underneath the wing lifts the wing and airplane. Winchester hard disk heads use airfoils, and they also work because of the Bernoulli principle. In other words, Iomega's Bernoulli name is accurate but not restrictive to their product.

No matter the terminology, hard disk, Winchester, or fixed disk, the underlying principles are the same in high-speed magnetic mass storage systems, as are your concerns in installing, using, and taking advantage of these systems.

873

Understanding Hard Disks

Not all hard disks are created equal. Different hard disk models are made from different materials using different technologies and under different standards. As a result, the performance, capacities, and prices of hard disks cover a wide range from a few hundred dollars to tens of thousands. Understanding these differences will help you be better able to judge the quality and value available in any disk product. You'll also better understand what you need to do to get one running and keep it that way.

The hard disk is actually a combination device, a chimera that's part electronic and part mechanical. Electrically, the hard disk performs the noble function of turning evanescent pulses of electronic digital data into more permanent magnetic fields. As with other magnetic recording devices, from cassette recorders to floppy disks, the hard disk accomplishes its end using an electromagnet (its read/write head) to align the polarities of magnetic particles on the hard disks themselves. Other electronics in the hard disk system control the mechanical half of the drive and help it properly arrange the magnetic storage and locate the information that is stored on the disk.

Drive Mechanism

The mechanism of the typical hard disk is actually rather simple, comprising fewer moving parts than such exotic devices as electric razors and pencil sharpeners. The basic elements of the system include a stack of one or more platters, the actual hard disks themselves. Each of these platters serves as a substrate upon which is laid a magnetic medium in which data can be recorded. Together, the platters rotate as a unit on a shaft, called the *spindle*. Typically the shaft connects directly to a spindle motor that spins the entire assembly (see fig. 21.1).

The first disk drives (back in the era of the original IBM Winchester) used synchronous motors. That is, the motor was designed to lock its rotation rate to the frequency of the AC power line supplying the disk drive. As a result, most motors spun the disk at the same rate as the power line frequency (3,600 resolutions per minute), which equals the 60 cycles per second of commercial power in the United States.

Synchronous motors are typically big, heavy, and expensive. They also run on normal line voltage, 117 volts AC, which is not desirable to have floating around inside computer equipment where a couple of errant volts can cause a system crash. As hard disks were miniaturized, disk makers adopted a new technology, the servo-controlled DC motor, that eliminated these problems. A servo-controlled motor uses feedback to maintain a constant and accurate rotation rate. That is, a sensor in the disk drive constantly monitors how fast the drive spins and adjusts the spin rate should the disk vary from its design specifications.

Constant Spin

Unlike floppy disk drives, most hard disk platters are kept constantly spinning (at least while the disk drive is powered up) because achieving a stable spin of the massive stack of platters at their relatively high speeds may require 10 to 30 seconds for a 5.25-inch disk drive; half that time or less for 3.5-inch and smaller drives because there's less inertia to overcome. The constant spin earns the hard disk one of its two biggest benefits, the data recorded on it is nearly instantly accessible. Floppies, on the other hand, require that you wait a half-second or so until they get spinning up to speed.

In some applications, particularly notebook computers, the constantly spinning hard disk takes a toll. Keeping the disk rotating means constant consumption of power by the spindle motor, which means shorter battery life. Consequently, some hard disks aimed at portable computers are designed to be able to cease spinning when they are not needed. Typically, the support electronics in the host computer determine when the disk should stop spinning. In most machines that means if you don't access the hard disk for a while, the computer assumes you've fallen asleep, died, or had your body occupied by aliens and won't be needing to use the disk again. When you do send out a command to read or write the disk, you then will have to wait while it spins back up to speed, possibly as long as several seconds. Subsequent accesses then occur at high hard disk speeds until the drive thinks you've died again and shuts itself down.

Latency

Despite the quick and constant rotation rate of a hard disk, it cannot deliver information instantly on request. There's always a slight delay that's called *latency*. This term describes the period after a command to read to or write from a hard disk and before the disk rotates to the proper angular position to locate the specific data needed. For example, if a program requests a byte from a hard disk and that byte has just passed under the read/write head, the disk must spin one full turn before that byte can be read from the disk and sent to the program. If read and write requests occur at essentially random times in regard to the spin of the disk (as they do), on the average the disk will have to make half a spin before the read/write head is properly positioned to read or write the required data. Normal latency at 3,600 rpm means that the quickest you can expect your hard disk, on the average, to find the information you want is 8.33 milliseconds. For a computer that operates with nanosecond timing, that's a long wait, indeed.

Because hard disk electronics expect drives to spin at 3,600 rpm and early disk interfaces (the means by which the disk drive was connected to its computer host) expected the disk to operate at that speed, most servo-controlled hard disks spun at 3,600 rpm. Nothing dictates that a disk must spin at this speed, however, and using today's embedded interfaces (AT Attachment and SCSI), engineers are free to select any disk rotation rate they like. Many disks now spin faster than 3,600 rpm because a faster spinning disk can deliver better performance, all else being equal. Some hard disks now spin as fast as 5,400 rpm. These faster spinning disks trim latency to deliver data more quickly. A 5,400 rpm disk reduces latency from the 8.3 milliseconds of a 3,600 rpm drive to 5.5 ms.

Note that disk rotation speed cannot be increased indefinitely. Centrifugal force tends to tear apart anything that spins at high rates, and hard disks are no exception. Disk designers must balance achieving lower latencies with the self-destructive tendencies of rapidly spinning mechanisms.

Data Transfer Rate

The speed of the spin of a hard disk also influences how quickly data can be continuously read from a drive. At a given storage density (which disk designers try to make as high as possible to pack as much information in as small a package as possible), the quicker a disk spins, the faster information can be read from it. As spin rates increase, more bits on the surface of the disk pass beneath the read/write head in a given period. This increase directly translates into a faster flow of data, more bits per second.

The speed at which information is moved from the disk to its control electronics (or its PC host) is termed the *data transfer rate* of the drive. Data transfer rate is measured in megabits per second, megahertz (typically these two take the same numeric value), or megabytes per second (one-eighth the megabit per second rate). While older device-level hard disk interfaces constrained hard disk data rates, system-level interfaces allow designers freedom in selecting the data transfer rate. Higher rotation rates help designers achieve higher transfer rates. The trend is, of course, to higher transfer rates. The limiting factor is usually the highest frequencies that the control electronics and cable connection between drive and electronics can safely handle.

The Disk Within

The disk spinning inside the hard disk drive is central to the drive in more ways than one. The diameter of this platter determines how physically large a drive mechanism must be. In fact, most hard disk drives are measured by the size of their platters. When the PC first burst upon the world, hard disk makers were making valiant attempts at hard disk platter miniaturization, moving from those 8 inches in diameter to 5.25-inch platters. Today the trend is to ever-smaller platters. Most large-capacity drives bound for desktop computer systems now use 3.5-inch platters. Those meant for PCs in which weight and size must be minimized (which means, of course, notebook and smaller PCs) have platters measuring 2.5, 1.8, or 1.3 inches (currently the smallest) in diameter.

To increase storage capacity, both sides of a platter are used for storing information, each surface with its own read/write head. (One head is on the bottom where it must fly below the platter.) In addition, manufacturers often put several platters on a single spindle, making a taller package with the same diameter as a single platter. The number of platters inside a hard disk also influences the speed at which data stored on the hard disk can be found. The more platters a given disk drive uses, the greater the probability that one of the heads associated with one of those platters will be above the byte that's being searched for. Consequently, the time necessary to find information is reduced.

Adding platters has drawbacks besides increasing the height of a drive. More platters means greater mass, so their greater inertia will require longer to spin up to speed. This is not a problem for desktop machines; power-on memory checks typically take longer than it does for even the most laggardly hard disk to spin up. But an additional wait will be annoying in laptop and notebook computers that slow down and stop their hard disks to save battery energy. Additionally, since each surface of each platter in a hard disk has its own head, the head actuator mechanism inevitably gets larger and more complex as the number of platters increases. Inertia again takes its toll, slowing down the movement of the heads and increasing the access time of the drive. Of course, drive makers can compensate for the increased head actuator mass with more powerful actuators, but that adds to the size and cost of the drive.

Platter Composition

The platters of a hard disk are precisely machined to an extremely fine tolerance measured in microinches. They have to be; remember, the read/write head flies just a few microinches above each platter. If the disk juts up, the result is akin to a DC-10 encountering Pike's Peak, a crash that's good for neither airplane nor hard disk. Consequently, disk makers try to ensure that platters are as flat and smooth as possible.

The most common substrate material is aluminum, which has several virtues. It's easy to machine to a relatively smooth surface. It's generally inert, so it won't react with the material covering it. It's non-magnetic so it won't affect the recording process. It's been used for a long while (since the first disk drives) and is a familiar material. And above all, it's cheap.

A newer alternative is the glass platter, although the actual material used can range from ordinary window glass to advanced ceramic compounds akin to space shuttle skin. Glass platters excel at exactly the same qualities as do aluminum platters. On the positive side, they hold the advantage of being able to be made smoother. But because glass is newer, it's less familiar to work with. Consequently, larger hard disk manufacturers are waiting to see how the glass-plattered products of smaller makers work out before shifting their production to the new substrate material.

Areal Density

The smoothness of the substrate affects how tightly information can be packed on the surface of a platter. The term used to describe this characteristic is *areal density*, that is, the amount of data that can be packed onto a given area of the platter surface. The higher the areal density, the more information can be stored on a single platter. Smaller hard disks require greater areal densities to achieve the same capacities as larger units.

Areal density is generally measured in megabytes per square inch of disk surface. Current products achieve values on the order of 100 to 200M per square inch.

A number of factors influence the areal density that can be achieved by a given hard disk drive. The key factor is the size of the magnetic domain that encodes each bit of data. Manufacturers make read/write heads smaller to generate smaller fields and fly them as closely to the platter as possible without risking the head running into the jagged peaks of surface roughness. The medium itself affects the possible areal density.

Oxide Media

The first magnetic medium used in hard disks was made from the same materials as used in conventional audio recording tapes—ferric or ferrous oxide compounds, essentially fine grains of rather exotic rust. As with recording tape, the oxide particles are milled in a mixture of other compounds including a glue-like binder and often a lubricant. The binder also serves to isolate individual oxide particles from one another. This mud-like mixture is then coated onto the platters.

The technology of oxide coatings is old and well developed. The process has been evolving for more than 50 years, and now rates as a well-understood, familiar, and obsolete technology. New hard disk designs have abandoned oxide media, and with several good reasons. Oxide particles are not the best storers of magnetic information. Oxides tend to have lower coercivities, and their grains tend to be large when compared to other, newer media technologies. Both of these factors tend to limit the areal density available with oxide media. The slight surface roughness of the oxide medium compounds that of the platter surface, requiring the hard disk read/write head to fly farther away from it than other media, which also reduces maximum storage density. In addition, oxide coatings are generally soft and are more prone to getting damaged when the head skids to a stop, when the disk ceases its spin, or when a shock to the drive causes the head to skitter across the platter surface, potentially strafing your data as effectively as an attack by the Red Baron.

Thin-Film Media

In nearly all current hard disk drives, oxide coatings have been re-placed by thin-film magnetic media. As the name implies, a thin-film disk has a microscopically skinny layer of a pure metal, or mixture of metals, mechanically bound to its surface. These thin films can be applied either by plating the platter much the way chrome is applied to automobile bumpers or by sputtering, a form of vapor plating in which metal is ejected off a hot electrode in a vacuum and electrically attracted to the disk platter.

Thin-film media hold several special advantages over oxide technol-ogy. The very thinness of thin-film media allows higher areal densities because the magnetic field has less thickness in which to spread out. Because the thin-film surface is smoother, it allows heads to fly closer. Thin-film media also have higher coercivities, which allow smaller areas to produce the strong magnetic pulses needed for error-free reading of the data on the disk.

One reason that thin film can be so thin and support high areal densities is that, as with chrome-plated automobile bumpers and faucets, plated and sputtered media require no binders to hold their magnetic layers in place. Moreover, as with chrome plating, the thin films on hard disk platters are genuinely hard, many times tougher than oxide coatings. That makes them less susceptible to most forms of head crashing, the head merely bounces off the thin-film platter just as it would your car's bumpers.

Contamination

Besides shock, head crashes can also result from contaminants such as dust or air pollution particles on the media surface, which can strike the head and upset its flight. The head touching the disk surface may result in a nick to the media, which not only destroys the storage capability of the media in the area struck by the head but also can loosen particles of media that can, in turn, cause further contamination and crashing.

Fortunately, the almost universal use of thin-film media and more robust drive mechanisms has made head crashes things of the past. Although you should still be careful with your hard disk (no sense tempting fate or your service contract), in normal use you need not worry about crashes. Most of today's hard disk drives are designed for the rigors of portable computers—computers designed to be moved during operation, say when an airplane hits a pocket of turbulence—so a nudge now and again won't destroy the disk.

To be on the safe side and guard against contamination of the platter surface with dust, hair, and other floating gunk, most hard disks keep all their vulnerable parts in a protective chamber. In fact, this need to avoid contamination is why nearly all PC hard disks use non-removable media, sealed out of harm's way.

The disk chamber is not completely airtight. Usually a small vent is designed into the system to allow the air pressure inside the disk drive to adjust to changes in environmental air pressure. Although this air exchange is minimal, a filter in this vent system traps particles before they can enter the drive. Microscopic pollutants, such as corrosive molecules in the air, can seep through the filter, however, potentially damaging the disk surface. Although the influx of such pollutants is small (the hard disk vent does not foster airflow, only pressure equalization), it is best not to operate a hard disk in a polluted environment. You wouldn't want to be there to use it, anyhow.

Removable Media Drives

Removable hard disks put the hard disk platter (or platters) in a plastic cartridge that can be withdrawn from the disk drive mechanism and separately stored. Other platters can be inserted in the drive and interchanged, much like floppy disks.

Sealing these removable platters from the atmosphere is practically impossible. As a consequence, removable media drive manufacturers often use very tough plated media in their products to make them more resistant to head crash damage. Usually, they suck the air and, they hope, the contaminants, out of the cartridge before they allow the platters to begin to spin.

In addition, the head actuator of the removable media drive must be toughened up and some means must be found to move the head from a great distance from the platters (so that the platters can be safely removed or inserted into the drive) to a tiny distance (so that they can fly the proper distance from the platter). These robust mechanisms are inherently slower than the fastest hard disks, imposing a penalty on the average access times of such products.

To circumvent such difficulties, a new product puts the entire drive mechanism in a removable cartridge form. Motor, platter, head, actuator, and protective chamber are fashioned into one removable unit. Such removable drives have all the security advantages of other removable media devices. In addition, they can be built more like hard disks, with fewer contamination and crash worries and greater speed. Currently, their sole drawback is a higher price.

A new alternative is the hard disk carrier that turns any 3.5-inch drive into a removable unit. The carrier has two parts: a mounting assembly that installs permanently inside a drive bay in your PC and the carrier itself into which you bolt a disk drive. The carrier then slides in and out of the mounting assembly. You plug in the drive before you boot up, and you pull it out at the end of the day to lock it in your safe or put it under your pillow.

Read/Write Heads

Besides the platters, the only other moving part in most hard disk drives is the head system. In nearly all drives, one read/write head is associated with each side of each platter and flies just above or below its surface. Each of these read/write heads is flexibly connected to a more rigid arm which supports the flying assembly. Usually several of these arms are linked to form a single moving (usually pivoting) unit.

Altitude Effects

The height at which the read/write head of a hard disk flies is one factor in determining the ultimate storage capacity of the drive. Magnetic fields spread out with distance, so the farther the head is from the disk, the larger the apparent size of the field generated by a flux transition on the disk. Moving the head closer shrinks the apparent size of the flux transitions, allowing them to be packed closer together on the disk surface and increasing the capacity of the disk. The typical 1980s vintage hard disk head flew about 10 to 12 microinches above the surface of the platter. Newer heads fly closer, on the order of 5 microinches. These lower heights are possible thanks to smoother platters and smooth thin-film media.

Contact Media

Magnetic fields spread out with distance, so the closer the read/write head flies to the platter surface, the more focused its fields and the smaller the area it can write to and read from. Lowering the flying height of a hard disk head thus increases the hard disk's potential storage capacity.

The limiting case is flying at zero altitude. Just as with barnstorming pilots, flying at such a low height is fraught with danger. Just as trees, barns, and other obstacles loom in the way of low-flying aircraft, surface imperfections of hard disks can have similar deleterious consequences on a low-flying head. When the head has no ground clearance, it runs into a further problem, friction. The head constantly rubbing against the disk surface will soon wear something out. It doesn't matter whether the platter or the head succumbs; the result is the same, a disfunctional disk.

Nevertheless, the optimum flying height for a hard disk head is zero. Drive makers have found a way around the problem of friction: constant lubrication for the head in the form of a viscous liquid. In effect, the head swims instead of flies, and the liquid prevents both from wearing out. In coming years, expect to see these contact disks as an alternative to flying head designs.

Head Actuators

Each read/write head scans the hard disk for information. If the head was fixed in position as is the head of a tape recorder, it would only be able to read a narrow section of the disk. The head and the entire assembly to which it is attached must be able to move to take advantage of all the recordable area on the hard disk. The mechanism that moves the head assembly is called the *head actuator*. Usually the head assembly is pivoted and is swung across the disk by a special head actuator solenoid or motor.

Modern head actuator designs also help increase hard disk capacity. This increase is achieved by precision. One of the most important limits on the density of data storage in a disk system is the capability of the mechanism to exactly and repeatedly locate a specific location on the disk surface that will store a bit of information. The more precise the mechanism, the tighter it can pack data. The better actuators (along with the dimensional stability of the rigid platters themselves) are used in the hard disk for a more stable, more precise storage environment that can reliably pack information at a greater density.

Head Actuator Types

The head actuator is part of an electro-mechanical system that also includes the electronics that control the movement of the head. Two distinct types of electronic systems are commonly used in hard disk designs: open-loop actuators and closed-loop actuators. Open-loop systems are essentially obsolete in modern hard disk drives. They played an important role, however, in the development of the hard disk drive. The disks used in the XT and AT were based on open-loop systems.

Specific types of hard disk mechanisms are associated with these open-loop and closed-loop design techniques. Most open-loop systems used band-stepper technology. Today's closed-loop hard disks almost universally use servo-voice coil actuators. Whether the loop is open or closed merely indicates whether direct feedback about the head position is used in controlling the actuator. An open-loop system gets no direct feedback; it moves the head and hopes that it gets to the right place. Closed-loop systems give the drive feedback about the location of the read/write head over the platters. Consequently, closed-loop drives can have higher storage densities because the head can be more precisely placed when it knows its exact location above the disk platters.

Band-Stepper Actuators

The band-stepper actuator is, in principle, the same mechanism used to move floppy disk heads. Typically, the band-stepper actuator uses a stepping motor to generate the force to move the head. A stepping motor is a special direct current motor that, instead of spinning, turns in discrete increments in response to electrical pulses from the control electronics. The electronics of the band-stepper system send out a given number of pulses and assume that the stepper motor rotates that number of steps. The band of the band-stepper is simply a thin strip of metal that couples the rotating shaft of the motor to the linear travel of the head. Each pulse from the control electronics moves the head across one track of the hard disk. The speed at which this form of actuator can operate is limited by the rate at which pulses can reliably be sent to the motor.

The advantages of the band-stepper design are its electrical simplicity and the capability to use all platter surfaces for storing data. On the downside, practical stepper motor designs limit the number of tracks (one track per step, remember) and the speed at which the head can move (and data be found) because each pulse must be individually recognizable by the actuator with some error margin allowed for. Modern microelectronics have eliminated electrical simplicity as an issue, and higher areal densities achievable by other designs permit larger storage even if one of the platter surfaces in the drive cannot be used for storage. As a result, band-stepper hard disks are obsolete, and no current products from the major disk vendors use this technology.

Servo-Voice Coil Actuators

The closed-loop system gets a constant stream of information regarding the head position from the disk, so it always knows exactly where the head is. The system determines the location of the head by constantly reading from a special, dedicated side of one platter, the servo surface, which stores a special magnetic pattern that allows the drive mechanism to identify each storage location on the disk.

The most common of the closed-loop actuator systems uses a voice coil mechanism that operates like the voice coil in a loudspeaker, hence the name servo-voice coil actuator. In this design, a magnetic field is generated in a coil of wire (a solenoid) by the controlling electronics, and this field pulls the head mechanism against the force of a spring. By varying the current in the coil, the head mechanism is drawn farther from its anchoring spring and the head moves across the disk. In this design, the voice coil mechanism connects directly to a pivoting arm, which also supports the read/write head above the platter. The varying force of the voice coil swings the head radially in an arc across the platter surface.

Because of its closed-loop nature, the servo-voice coil system need not count out each step to the disk location it needs to travel to. It can quickly move to approximately the correct place, and in milliseconds, fine-tune its location based on the servo information. This speed and the tight track spacing afforded by closed-loop positioning have made servo-voice coil hard disks the current choice of all major hard disk manufacturers.

Dual-Actuator Drives

Even the servo-voice coil mechanism has to obey the laws of physics. It cannot move the head instantly from one track to another, so there is always a slight delay when the head has to search out a particular byte. One of the principal goals in improving hard disk performance is minimizing this delay. Drive makers have squeezed about all they can get out of traditional mechanisms by reducing the mass (and thus inertia) of the head assembly. Dramatic speed improvements require a radical change.

One such departure from traditional design first developed by Conner Peripherals is the dual-actuator hard disk. Instead of a single head per platter, the Conner design uses two, each attached to its own independent actuator. Either head can scan across the entire surface of the platter. With properly designed electronics, this mechanism can cut latency in half on isolated disk operations and can eliminate the delays imposed by head movement on back-to-back read or write requests.

Latency can be trimmed by installing the two head actuators at diametrically opposed positions across the disk. The drive electronics can determine which head is nearest the desired data and use it for the read or write operation. Because one of the heads will have to be within half a revolution of the desired data, the rotational latency is one-half the time it takes the platter to make a complete spin.

When read and write requests are stacked, this two-head system can effectively eliminate track access delays. One head can seek while the other is reading or writing and thus be ready for the next drive operation. This technique does not work with current versions of DOS, however, because DOS requires one disk operation to be completed before requesting another one. More advanced operating systems, such as Novell NetWare, can take full advantage of this design.

Landing Zone

Hard disks are most vulnerable to head crash damage when they are turned off. As soon as you flick the off switch on your computer, the platters of its hard disk must stop spinning, and the airflow that keeps the heads flying stops. Generally, the airflow decreases gradually, and the head slowly progresses downward, eventually landing like an airplane on the disk media.

In truth, however, any head landing is more of a controlled crash and holds the potential for disk damage. Consequently, most hard disks, even those with thin-film media, have a dedicated landing zone reserved in their media in which no data can be recorded. This landing zone is usually at one edge or the other of the actual data storage area.

Park and Lock

Usually a software command is necessary to bring the head to the landing zone and hold it there while the disk spins down. This process is called *head parking*. Some drives are designed so that whenever their power is switched off, the head automatically retracts to the landing zone before the disk spins down. Such drives are termed automatic head parking.

Even when the read/write head touches down in the proper landing zone when the power to the disk drive is turned off, potential problems can still arise. An impact or other shock to the system can jar the head out of the landing zone, bouncing it across the vulnerable medium. To guard against such disasters, a growing number of hard disks lock their read/write heads in place at the landing zone when power is removed. This feature is generally termed automatic park and lock. Nearly all modern hard disk drives have park and lock.

Disk Geometry

A combination of the hard disk mechanism, its controller, and the software operating it all dictates the manner in which data is arranged on the platter. Unlike floppy disks, which are often interchanged, hard disks need not fit any particular standard because their media are never at large, always sealed inside the drive mechanism. Because platters cannot be removed from drives (providing you don't take matters into your own hands with a can opener and crowbar), they have no need of interchangeability. The physical layout of the data on disk is thus left to the imagination of the disk's designer.

The disk designer is not given free rein, however, because of one overriding necessity: compatibility with DOS and the IBM hardware standard. Certain disk parameters must arbitrarily be set at values that true compatibility requires. Of course, where there's a roadblock, there's an engineer with a pocket calculator figuring out exactly how much effort sidestepping it will take. Today's advanced drive electronics allow the designers the widest possible latitude in selecting hard disk parameters. Whatever doesn't match the PC standard, the electronics fake so that your PC doesn't know about the rules violations. Consequently, what your PC sees follows the IBM standard to the letter, but what goes on inside the drive is the engineer's business.

To understand this parameter monkey business, you first need to know a bit of hard disk geography, where the drive puts your bytes. The storage arrangement is called the drive's geometry and it determines the setup parameters of the drive used in its installation.

Tracks

No matter the type magnetic media or style of head actuator used by a disk, the read/write head must stop its lateral motion across the disk whenever it reads or writes data. While the head is stationary, the platter spins underneath it. Each time the platter completes one spin, the head traces a full circle across its surface. This circle is called a *track*.

Cylinders

Each head traces out a separate track across its associated platter. Because the combination of all the tracks traced out at a given head actuator position forms the outline of a solid cylinder, such a vertical stack of tracks is often called a *cylinder*.

Typical PC hard disks have between 312 and 2,048 cylinders (or tracks per platter), although most PCs are limited to using fewer. The number of cylinders is permanently determined when the drive is manufactured by the magnetic pattern written on the servo surface (which you cannot alter) of the drive.

Sectors

Most hard disks systems further divide each track into short arcs, termed *sectors*. The sector is the basic storage unit of the drive. (DOS gathers together several sectors to make its basic unit of storage for disk files, the cluster.) Sectors can be soft, marked magnetically with bit patterns embedded in the data on the track itself, or hard, set by the drive mechanism itself.

Soft sectors are demarcated using a low-level format program, and their number can vary almost arbitrarily, depending on the formatting software and the interface used for connecting the disk. In the standard hard disk configuration of any DOS or OS/2 version, each hard disk sector holds 512 bytes of data. Drives using the ST506 interface and MFM data coding almost invariably have 17 on each track. Shifting to RLL increases the sector count to 25 or 26. ESDI drives usually have about 34 sectors per track. AT Attachment and SCSI hard disks might have almost any number of sectors per track. They may even put differing numbers of sectors on inner and outer tracks.

The sector count on any given track of a traditional hard disk is the same as every other track because hard disks once almost invariably used constant angular velocity recording. This technology sets the speed of the disk's spin at a constant rate so that in any given period over any given track, the drive's read/write head hangs over the same length arc (measured in degrees) of the disk. The actual length of the arc, measured linearly (in inches or centimeters) varies depending on the radial position of the head. Sectors on tracks farther from the center of the disk are longer. Despite their greater length, however, the outer-track sectors hold the same data as the shorter inner sectors. Constant angular velocity equipment is easy to build because the disk spins at a constant number of rpm. Old vinyl phonograph records are the best example of constant angular velocity recording, the black platters spun at an invariant 33, 45, or 78 rpm.

A more efficient technology, called *constant linear velocity recording*, alters the spin speed of the disk depending on how near the center tracks the read/write head lies so that, in any given period, the same length of track passes below the head. When the head is above the outer tracks of the disk, where the circumference is greater, the slower spin allows more data to be packed into each track. Using this technology, more sectors could be packed onto the longer outer tracks. Constant linear velocity recording thus permits more information to be packed on a disk. For this reason, constant linear velocity recording is used for high-capacity media such as audio compact discs.

But constant linear velocity recording is ill-suited to hard disks. For the disk platter to be properly read or written, it must be spinning at the proper rate. Hard disk heads regularly bounce from the outer tracks to the inner tracks as your software requests them to read or write data. Slowing or speeding up the platter to the proper speed would require a long wait, perhaps seconds because of inertia, which would shoot the average access time of the drive through the roof.

Zone-bit recording offers a compromise solution. Disk spin is kept constant but the drive alters its electronics to pack more sectors on the outer tracks. Ordinarily, this would cause havoc with familiar software (such as DOS and formatting programs), which expect the same number of sectors in every track. But because the disk interface is integrated into the drive, the physical format of the drive can be completely hidden from the software. The disk electronics translate the drive's odd format into one more like conventional disk drives.

Currently zone-bit recording is used by relatively few companies because the technology is protected by patents. Moreover, it only works with intelligent interfaces, so it is less likely to be used in small drives that would most benefit from its greater-storage-from-nothing capabilities.

Write Precompensation

Constant angular velocity recording has another drawback. The shorter sectors closer to the spindle require data to be packed into them more tightly, which squeezes the magnetic flux reversals in the recording medium ever closer together. The capability of many magnetic media to hold flux transitions falls off as the transitions are packed more tightly. Pinched together, they produce a feebler field and induce a lower current in the read/write head.

One way of dealing with this problem is to write on the disk with a stronger magnetic field as the sectors get closer to the spindle. By increasing the current in the read/write head when it writes nearer the center of the disk, the on-disk flux transitions can be made stronger. They can then induce stronger currents in the read/write head when that area of the disk is read.

This process is called write precompensation because the increased writing current compensates for the fall-off in disk responses nearer its center at a place logically before the information is stored on the disk.

The 1,024 Cylinder Limit

Disk designers are not free to use any geometry for these products. The design of the PC constrains them, principally because of decisions made when IBM originally engineered its systems (which the rest of the PC industry dutifully copied, limits and all, for compatibility's sake). For example, IBM's engineers severely constrained the size and number of file allocation table entries and limited the number of cylinders that its hardware and software could reach.

For personal computer models up to the first generation of ATs and their compatibles, the maximum possible cylinder count for a hard disk totaled 1,024. This limit was enforced throughout the hardware and software of the system. Both DOS and the hard disk controller refused to peek above track 1,024. Although you could put a hard disk with a larger cylinder count into such systems, only the first 1,024 cylinders were accessible because neither DOS nor the controller could count higher.

This low cylinder count can be a severe limitation because the current trend in hard disk design is toward lower drives, 3.5-inch drives that stand one-inch tall. The low head room means that fewer platters can be stacked in the drive. The only way to fill the smaller housing with more data is to pack it more densely on each platter, which means adding more cylinders.

Although software drivers can compensate for the inability of early versions of DOS (before 3.3) to handle greater cylinder counts, the controllers of all PCs and XTs limit the addressability of cylinders beyond 1,024. This hardware limit also applies to ATs and compatibles that use the Western Digital WD1002 series of controllers or those designed to be exactly compatible with them. Starting with the WD1003 series, however, this limit was removed. To take advantage of larger disks with such controllers, you'll still need a driver or more recent version of DOS.

Translation Mode

Drive makers have found a better way around the problem: sector translation or translation mode. Essentially, the hard disk translates its own geometry from one arrangement to another. For example, while a drive might have 2,048 cylinders and three heads, the drive electronics are designed to respond as if the drive was actually built with only 1,024 cylinders and six heads, sneaking under the limit. Because the translation occurs in the drive hardware itself, neither you nor your system has to worry what the actual physical cylinder and head arrangement might be. Sector translation works most effectively on embedded interface drives, AT Attachment and SCSI, which give the disk designer full control over all aspects of the disk controller hardware.

A few manufacturers take this translation one step further. Not only can some of their drives make the translation, the final arrangement is flexible and the drive itself can determine what's best. For example, some Seagate AT Attachment drives check your system to see what drive geometry it expects, and then the drive changes like a chameleon to that configuration.

The 32-Megabyte Addressing Limit

DOS versions before 4.0 limited the maximum size of disk addressable as a single unit to 32 megabytes. For compatibility with older software (particularly hard disk utilities), many people still stick with this limit and partition their hard disks into 32M volumes.

The limit arose from a combination of factors: the space IBM and Microsoft allowed for the file allocation table and the number of sectors that were assigned to each cluster. DOS normally divides files into clusters of four sectors. It keeps track of which clusters are part of which file using the file allocation table. The number of clusters that DOS can address is limited by the overall size of the file allocation table and the size of each entry in the table.

In versions of DOS before 3.0, each entry in the file allocation table was a byte and a half (12 bits), allowing a maximum of 4,096 clusters to be identified. In these early versions of DOS, clusters were made from eight sectors, totaling 4,096 bytes each. Under this scheme, the maximum size for a standard DOS volume would be 16 megabytes.

Starting with DOS version 3.0, each file allocation table entry was allowed to be either 12 or 16 bits, depending on disk capacity. With disks smaller than about 16 megabytes, 12-bit allocation units are used. Larger disks get the 16-bit file allocation table entries, permitting a total of 65,536 entries. With the larger number of allocation table entries, cluster size was reduced to four sectors or 2,048 bytes.

Not all of those entries are useful, however, because versions of DOS from 3.0 to 3.32 (and, for compatibility reasons, OS/2 version 1.0) limit the size of the file allocation table itself to 16,384 entries. That number of entries coupled to the cluster size of four sectors results in the 32-megabyte addressing limit of DOS. Larger disks are not possible using this scheme because no space is available for recording more than 16,384 file allocation table entries.

DOS 4.0 breaks the 32-megabyte limit by allocating up to 65,536 bytes to the file allocation table. This change alone effectively quadruples the maximum hard disk capacity to 128 megabytes. This limit is, of course, also imposed by the 16-bit size of file allocation table entries as well.

DOS versions 5.0 and later allow you take steps beyond this 128-megabyte partition limit by altering the size of each cluster. For example, doubling the size of each cluster from four to eight sectors (2,048 to 4,096 bytes each) effectively doubles the maximum disk size without changing the size of FAT entries. In fact, even before DOS 5.0, some hard disk management programs resorted to this technique to break the old 32- and 128-megabyte limits. DOS 5.0 allows a cluster to be made from up to 16 sectors (8,192 bytes).

As clever as it is, this technique has its drawbacks. It can be wasteful. Disk space is divvied up in units of a cluster. No matter how small a file (or a subdirectory, which is simply a special kind of file) may be, it occupies, at minimum, one cluster of disk space. Larger files take up entire clusters, but any fractional cluster of space that's left over requires another cluster. On average, each file on the disk will waste half a cluster of space. The more files, the more waste. The larger the clusters, the more waste. Unless you work exclusively with massive files, increasing cluster size to increase disk capacity is a technique to avoid whenever possible.

DOS 5.0 was also designed to use the smallest cluster size possible for a given disk capacity. Consequently, disks with capacities up to 134,217,728 bytes could be addressed as a single unit with 2,048-byte clusters. With 8,192-byte clusters, the maximum size of a single unit or disk partition is 536,870,912 bytes. DOS 5.0 handles larger disks, but requires partitioning them into these half-gigabyte chunks.

Disk Parameters

Taken together, the number of platters (or heads), the number of cylinders, and the point at which write precompensation begins make up the set of disk parameters. These three numbers are required by the disk drive controller to properly operate a disk drive.

In early model computers, such as the IBM XT and early add-on disk subsystems, the disk parameters were permanently encoded into the ROM firmware of the disk controller itself. Using this technique, every controller had to be matched to the disk drive model that it was to operate.

A few aftermarket suppliers had a better idea. They recorded the disk parameters on the disk itself in a place that would be reachable in the same way across may different models of disk drive. As part of the boot-up process, the disk drive would be commanded to read back its identifying information, loading it into the controller. Thereafter, the controller could properly run the drive.

With the IBM AT, a new method of getting disk parameters to the controller was developed. The parameters were stored in the CMOS setup memory of the computer. The controller read the parameters from the CMOS and could then properly run the drive. This same technique is used by the PS/2 series of computers.

ESDI and SCSI drives permit the drive parameters to be embedded in the system. For instance, ESDI drives can record their parameters on the disk itself because the location and means of accessing this information is standardized. (Nevertheless, some computers require knowing the disk parameters of ESDI drives.) Because SCSI is a system level interface, the issue doesn't even arise. The controller electronics are part of the drive and there is no chance of mismatch.

With the AT Attachment interface and automatic translation mode, you don't have to worry about any of these parameters. As long as you set your system for the proper drive capacity, the disk itself will make the right parameter match.

Table 21.1 lists the essential drive parameters of most of the commonly available hard disks that may be used in ATs and similar computers.

TABLE 21.1.

Parameters for Common Hard Disks

ALPS

Ampex

Area

Atasi

Atasi

MFM Interface: Model	Capacity	Cylinders	Heads	Sectors
DRND-10A	10	615	2	17
DRND-20A	20	615	4	17
DRPO-20D	20 (RLL)	615	2	26
RPO-20A	20 (RLL)	615	2	26

MFM Interface: Model	Capacity	Cylinders	Heads	Sectors
PYXIS-7	5	320	2	17
PYXIS-13	10	320	4	17
PYXIS-20	15	320	6	17
PYXIS-27	20	320	8	17

ATA Interface: Model	Capacity	Cylinders	Heads	Sectors
A120	124	1024	4	60
A180	181	1488	4	60
MD-2060	61	1024	2	60
MD-2080	80	1323	2	60

MFM Interface: Model	Capacity	Cylinders	Heads	Sectors
AT-3020	17	645	3	17
AT-3033	28	645	5	17
AT-3046	39	645	7	17
AT-3051	43	704	7	17
AT-3051+	44	733	7	17
AT-3053	44	733	7	17
AT-3075	67	1024	8	17
AT-3085	71 (RLL)	1024	8	26
AT-3128	109	1024	8	26

ESDI Interface:				
AT-676	765	1632	15	54
AT-6120	1051	1925	15	71

BASF

MFM Interface: Model	Capacity	Cylinders	Heads	Sectors
6185	23	440	6	17
6186	15	440	4	17
6187	8	440	2	17
6188-R1	10	612	2	17
6188-R3	21	612	4	17

Bull

MFM Interface: Model	Capacity	Cylinders	Heads	Sectors
D-530	26	987	3	17
D-550	43	987	5	17
D-570	60	987	7	17
D-585	71	1166	7	17

C. Itoh

MFM Interface: Model	Capacity	Cylinders	Heads	Sectors
YD-3042	44 (RLL)	788	4	26
YD-3082	87 (RLL)	788	8	26
YD-3530	32	731	5	17
YD-3540	45	731	7	17

Control Data

MFM Interface: Model	Capacity	Cylinders	Heads	Sectors
94155-19	18	697	3	17
94155-21	18	697	3	17
94155-25	24	697	4	17
94155-28	24	697	4	17
94155-36	30	697	5	17
94155-38	31	733	5	17
94155-48	40	925	5	17
94155-51	43	989	5	17
94155-57	48	925	6	17
94155-67	58	925	7	17
94155-77	64	925	8	17
94155-85	71	1024	8	17
94155-86	72	925	9	17
94155-96	80	1024	9	17
94155-120	102 (RLL)	960	8	26
94155-135	115	960	9	26

continues

TABLE 21.1.
continued

Control Data

MFM Interface: Model	Capacity	Cylinders	Heads	Sectors
94205-30	25	989	3	17
94205-41	38 (RLL)	989	3	26
94205-51	43 (RLL)	989	3	26
94205-77	65 (RLL)	989	5	26
94335-55	46	1072	5	17
94335-100	83	1072	9	17
94335-150	128 (RLL)	1072	9	26

Control Data

ESDI Interface: Model	Capacity	Cylinders	Heads	Sectors
94156-48	40	925	5	17
94156-67	56	925	7	17
94156-86	72	925	9	17
94166-101	84	969	5	34
94166-141	118	969	7	34
94166-182	152	969	9	34
94186-265	221	1412	9	34
94186-324	270	1412	11	34
94186-383	319	1412	13	34
94186-383H	319	1224	15	34
94186-383S	338	1412	13	36
94186-442	368	1412	15	34
94186-442H	368	1412	15	34
94196-383	338	1412	13	34
94196-766	664	1632	15	54
94211-106	89	1024	5	34
94246-182	160	1453	4	54
94246-383	338	1747	7	54
94316-111	98	1072	5	36
94316-136	120	1268	5	36
94316-155	138	1072	7	36
94316-200	177	1072	9	36
94356-111	98	1072	5	36
94356-155	138	1072	7	36
94356-200	177	1072	9	36

Control Data

ATA Interface: Model	Capacity	Cylinders	Heads	Sectors
94204-65	65	948	5	26
94204-71	71	1032	5	26
94204-74	65	948	5	26
94204-81	71	1032	5	26
94208-75	60	969	5	26
94244-219	191	1747	4	54
94244-274	241	1747	5	54
94244-383	338	1747	7	54
94246-182	160	1453	4	54
94246-383	338	1747	7	54
94314-136	120	1068	5	36
94354-90	79	1072	5	29
94354-111	98	1072	5	36
94354-126	111	1072	7	29
94354-133	117	1272	5	36
94354-135	119	1072	9	29
94354-155	138	1072	7	36
94354-160	143	1072	9	29
94354-172	157	1072	9	36
94354-186	164	1272	7	36
94354-200	177	1072	9	36
94354-230	211	1272	9	36

Control Data

SCSI Interface: Model	Capacity	Cylinders	Heads	Sectors
24221-125M	110	1024	3	36
24221-209M	183	1024	5	36
94161-101	86	969	5	26
94161-121	120	969	7	26
94161-141	140	969	7	26
94161-155	150	969	9	36
94161-182	155	969	9	36
94171-300	288	1365	9	36
94171-344	335	1549	9	36
94171-350	300	1412	9	46
94171-375	375	1549	9	35
94171-376	330	1546	9	45

continues

TABLE 21.1.
continued

Control Data

SCSI Interface: Model	Capacity	Cylinders	Heads	Sectors
94181-385D	337	791	15	36
94181-385H	330	791	15	55
94181-574	574	1549	15	36
94181-702	601	1546	15	54
94181-702M	613	1549	15	54
94191-766	676	1632	15	54
94191-766M	676	1632	15	54
94211-91	91	969	5	36
94211-106	91	1022	5	26
94211-209	142	1547	5	36
94221-125	107	1544	3	36
94221-190	190	1547	5	36
94221-209	183	1544	5	36
94241-383	338	1261	7	36
94241-502	43	1755	7	69
94351-90	79	1068	5	29
94351-111	98	1068	5	36
94351-126	111	1068	7	29
94351-128	111	1068	7	36
94351-133	116	1268	7	36
94351-133S	116 (SCSI-2)	1268	7	36
94351-134	117	1068	7	36
94351-155	138	1068	7	36
94351-155S	138 (SCSI-2)	1068	7	36
94351-160	142	1068	9	29
94351-172	150	1068	9	36
94351-186S	163 (SCSI-2)	1268	7	36
94351-200	177	1068	9	36
94351-200	177 (SCSI-2)	1068	9	36
94351-230	210	1272	9	36
94601-767H	665 (SCSI-2)	1356	15	64
94601-767M	676	1508	15	54

Century Data

ESDI Interface: Model	Capacity	Cylinders	Heads	Sectors
CAST 10203E	55	1050	3	35
CAST 10304E	75	1050	4	35
CAST 10305E	94	1050	5	35
CAST 14404E	114	1590	4	35
CAST 14405E	140	1590	5	35
CAST 14406E	170	1590	6	35
CAST 24509E	258	1599	9	35
CAST 24611E	315	1599	11	35
CAST 24713E	372	1599	13	35

Century Data

SCSI Interface: Model	Capacity	Cylinders	Heads	Sectors
CAST 10203S	55	1050	3	35
CAST 10304S	75	1050	4	35
CAST 10305S	94	1050	5	35
CAST 14404S	114	1590	4	35
CAST 14405S	140	1590	5	35
CAST 14406S	170	1590	6	35
CAST 24509S	258	1599	9	35
CAST 24611S	315	1599	11	35
CAST 24713S	372	1599	13	35

CMI

MFM Interface: Model	Capacity	Cylinders	Heads	Sectors
CM3206	10	306	4	17
CM3426	20	615	4	17
CM5205	4	256	2	17
CM5206	5	306	2	17
CM5410	8	256	4	17
CM5412	10	306	4	17
CM5616	13	256	6	17
CM5619	15	306	6	17
CM5826	21	306	8	17
CM6213	11	640	2	17
CM6426	21	615	4	17
CM6426S	22	640	4	17
CM6640	33	640	6	17

continues

TABLE 21.1.
continued

| MFM Interface: | | | | |
Model	Capacity	Cylinders	Heads	Sectors

CMI

| MFM Interface: | | | | |
Model	Capacity	Cylinders	Heads	Sectors
CM7660	50	960	6	17
CM7880	67	960	8	17

Cogito

| MFM Interface: | | | | |
Model	Capacity	Cylinders	Heads	Sectors
CG-906	5	306	2	17
CG-912	11	306	4	17
CG-925	21	612	4	17
PT-912	11	612	2	17
PT-925	21	612	4	17

Conner

| ATA Interface: | | | | |
Model	Capacity	Cylinders	Heads	Sectors
CP-342	40	805	4	26
CP-344	43	788	4	26
CP-2024	21	653	2	32
CP-2034	32	823	2	38
CP-2064	64	823	4	38
CP-2084	85	548	8	38
CP-2304	209	1348	8	39
CP-3000	43	976	5	17
CP-3022	21	622	2	33
CP-3024	22	636	2	33
CP-3044	43	1047	2	40
CP-3102	104	776	8	33
CP-3104	105	776	8	33
CP-3111	112	832	8	33
CP-3114	112	832	8	33
CP-3184	84	832	6	33
CP-3204/F	213	683	16	38
CP-3304	340	659	16	63
CP-3364	362	702	16	63
CP-3504	509	987	16	63
CP-3554	544	1054	16	63
CP-4024	22	627	2	34
CP-4044	43	1104	2	38
CP-30064	61	762	4	39
CP-30084	84	526	8	39

Conner

ATA Interface:				
Model	Capacity	Cylinders	Heads	Sectors
CP-30084E	85	905	4	46
CP-30104	120	1522	4	39
CP-30174E	170	903	8	46
CP-30204	213	683	16	38

Conner

SCSI Interface:				
Model	Capacity	Cylinders	Heads	Sectors
CP-340	42	788	4	26
CP-2020	21	642	2	32
CP-3020	21	622	2	33
CP-3040	42	1026	2	40
CP-3100	105	776	8	33
CP-3180	84	832	6	33
CP-3200/F	213	1366	8	38
CP-30060	61	1524	2	39
CP-30080	84	1053	4	39
CP-30100	120	1522	4	39
CP-30200	213	2119	4	49

Disctec

ATA Interface:				
Model	Capacity	Cylinders	Heads	Sectors
RHD-20	21	615	2	34
RHD-60	63	1024	2	60

Disctron

MFM Interface:				
Model	Capacity	Cylinders	Heads	Sectors
D-503	3	153	2	17
D-504	4	215	2	17
D-506	5	153	4	17
D-507	5	306	2	17
D-509	8	215	4	17
D-512	11	153	8	17
D-513	11	215	6	17
D-514	11	306	4	17
D-518	15	215	8	17
D-519	16	306	6	17
D-526	21	306	8	17

continues

TABLE 21.1.
continued

Epson

MFM Interface:				
Model	Capacity	Cylinders	Heads	Sectors
HD850	11	306	4	17
HD860	21	612	4	17

Fuji

MFM Interface:				
Model	Capacity	Cylinders	Heads	Sectors
FK301-13	10	306	4	17
FK302-13	10	612	2	17
FK302-26	21	612	4	17
FK302-39	32	612	6	17
FK303-52	40	615	8	17
FK305-26	21	615	4	17
FK305-39	32	615	6	17
FK305-39R	32 (RLL)	615	4	26
FK305-58R	49 (RLL)	615	6	26
FK309-26	20	615	4	17
FK309-39	32	615	6	17
FK309-39R	30 (RLL)	615	4	26

Fuji

SCSI Interface:				
Model	Capacity	Cylinders	Heads	Sectors
FK308S-39R	31	615	4	26
FK308S-58R	45	615	6	26
FK309S-50R	41	615	4	26

Fujitsu

MFM Interface:				
Model	Capacity	Cylinders	Heads	Sectors
M2225D	21	615	4	17
M2225DR	32 (RLL)	615	4	26
M2226D	30	615	6	17
M2226DR	49 (RLL)	615	6	26
M2227D	40	615	8	17
M2227DR	65	615	8	26
M2230AS	5	320	2	17
M2230AT	5	320	2	17
M2231	5	306	2	17
M2233AS	11	320	4	17
M2233AT	11	320	4	17
M2234AS	16	320	6	17

Fujitsu

MFM Interface: Model	Capacity	Cylinders	Heads	Sectors
M2235AS	22	320	8	17
M2241AS	25	754	4	17
M2242AS	43	754	7	17
M2243AS	68	754	11	17
M2243R	110 (RLL)	1186	7	26
M2243T	68	1186	7	17

Fujitsu

ATA Interface: Model	Capacity	Cylinders	Heads	Sectors
M2611T	45	1334	3	33
M2612T	90	1334	4	33
M2613T	135	1334	6	33
M2614T	180	1334	8	33
M2622T	330	1435	8	56
M2623T	425	1435	10	56
M2624T	520	1435	12	56
M2631T	45	916	2	48

Fujitsu

ESDI Interface: Model	Capacity	Cylinders	Heads	Sectors
M2246E	172	823	10	35
M2247E	143	1243	7	64
M2248E	224	1243	11	64
M2249E	305	1243	15	64
M2261E	326	1658	8	53
M2262E	448	1658	11	48
M2263E	675	1658	15	53

Fujitsu

SCSI Interface: Model	Capacity	Cylinders	Heads	Sectors
M2245SA	148	823	10	35
M2247S	138	1243	7	65
M2247SA	149	1243	7	36
M2247SB	160	1243	7	19
M2248S	221	1243	11	65
M2248SA	238	1243	11	36
M2248SB	252	1243	11	19
M2249S	303	1243	15	65

continues

TABLE 21.1. continued

	SCSI Interface: Model	Capacity	Cylinders	Heads	Sectors
	M2249SA	324	1243	15	36
Fujitsu	M2249SB	343	1243	15	19
	M2263HA	672	1658	15	53
	M2266HA	1079	1658	15	85
	M2611SA	45	1334	2	34
	M2612SA	90	1334	4	34
	M2613SA	136	1334	6	34
	M2614SA	182	1334	8	34
	M2622SA	330	1435	8	56
	M2623SA	425	1435	10	56
	M2624SA	520	1435	12	56

	ESDI Interface: Model	Capacity	Cylinders	Heads	Sectors
Hewlett-Packard	HP-97544E	340	1457	8	57
	HP-97548E	680	1457	16	57
	HP-97556E	681	1680	11	72
	HP-97558E	1084	1962	15	72
	HP-97560E	1374	1962	19	72
	HP-D1660A	333	1457	8	57
	HP-D1661A	667	1457	16	57

	SCSI Interface: Model	Capacity	Cylinders	Heads	Sectors
Hewlett-Packard	HP-97544S	331	1447	8	56
	HP-97544T	331 (SCSI-2)	1447	8	56
	HP-97548S	663	1447	16	56
	HP-97548T	663 (SCSI-2)	1447	16	56
	HP-97549T	1000 (SCSI-2)	1911	16	64
	HP-97556T	673 (SCSI-2)	1670	11	72
	HP-97558T	1075 (SCSI-2)	1952	15	72
	HP-97560T	1363 (SCSI-2)	1952	19	72
	HP-C2233S	238 (SCSI-2)	1511	5	49
	HP-C2234S	334 (SCSI-2)	1511	7	61
	HP-C2235S	429 (SCSI-2)	1511	9	73

Hitachi

MFM Interface:				
Model	Capacity	Cylinders	Heads	Sectors
DK301-1	10	306	4	17
DK301-2	15	306	6	17
DK502-2	21	615	4	17
DK511-3	30	699	5	17
DK511-5	42	699	7	17
DK511-8	67	823	10	17
DK521-5	42	823	6	17

Hitachi

ESDI Interface:				
Model	Capacity	Cylinders	Heads	Sectors
DK512-8	67	823	5	34
DK512-12	94	823	7	34
DK512-17	134	823	10	34
DK514-38	330	903	14	51
DK515-78	673	1361	14	69
DK522-10	103	823	6	36

Hitachi

SCSI Interface:				
Model	Capacity	Cylinders	Heads	Sectors
DK512C-8	67	823	5	34
DK512C-12	94	823	7	34
DK512C-17	134	819	10	34
DK514C-38	321	903	14	51
DK515C-78	661	1261	14	69
DK522C-10	88	819	6	35

IMI

MFM Interface:				
Model	Capacity	Cylinders	Heads	Sectors
5006	5	306	2	17
5007	5	312	2	17
5012	10	306	4	17
5018	15	306	6	17
7720	21	310	4	17
7740	43	315	8	17

continues

TABLE 21.1.
continued

MFM Interface: Model	Capacity	Cylinders	Heads	Sectors
Kalok				
KL320	21	615	4	17
KL330	32 (RLL)	615	4	26

ATA Interface: Model	Capacity	Cylinders	Heads	Sectors
Kalok				
KL343	42	676	4	31
KL3100	105	820	6	35
KL3120	120	820	6	40
P5-125	125	2048	2	80
P5-250	251	2048	4	80

SCSI Interface: Model	Capacity	Cylinders	Heads	Sectors
Kalok				
KL341	40	644	4	26

MFM Interface: Model	Capacity	Cylinders	Heads	Sectors
Kyocera				
KC20	21	615	4	17
KC30	32 (RLL)	615	4	26

ATA Interface: Model	Capacity	Cylinders	Heads	Sectors
Kyocera				
KC40GA	41	1075	2	26

SCSI Interface: Model	Capacity	Cylinders	Heads	Sectors
Kyocera				
KC80C	87	787	8	28

MFM Interface: Model	Capacity	Cylinders	Heads	Sectors
Lapine				
3522	10	306	4	17
LT10	10	615	2	17
LT20	20	615	4	17
LT200	20	614	4	17
LT300	32 (RLL)	614	4	26
LT2000	20	614	4	17
Titan 20	21	615	4	17
Titan 30	32 (RLL)	615	4	26
Titan 3532	32 (RLL)	615	4	26

Maxtor

MFM Interface: Model	Capacity	Cylinders	Heads	Sectors
XT1050	38	902	5	17
XT1065	52	918	7	17
XT1085	68	1024	8	17
XT1105	82	918	11	17
XT1120R	104 (RLL)	1024	8	26
XT1140	116	918	15	17
XT2085	72	1224	7	17
XT2140	113	1224	11	17
XT2190	159	1224	15	17

Maxtor

ATA Interface: Model	Capacity	Cylinders	Heads	Sectors
7040A	41	1170	2	36
7080A	81	1170	4	36
8051A	43	745	4	28
LXT-200A	207	1320	7	45
LXT-213A	213	1320	7	55
LXT-340A	340	1560	7	47

Maxtor

ESDI Interface: Model	Capacity	Cylinders	Heads	Sectors
P1-08E	969	1778	9	72
P1-12E	1051	1778	15	72
P1-13E	1160	1778	15	72
P1-16E	1331	1778	19	72
P1-17E	1470	1778	19	72
XT4170E	157	1224	7	35
XT4175E	149	1224	7	34
XT4179E	158	1224	7	36
XT4230E	203	1224	9	35
XT4280E	234	1224	11	34
XT4380E	338	1224	15	35
XT8380E	360	1632	8	54
XT8610E	541	1632	12	54
XT8800E	694	1274	15	71

continues

TABLE 21.1.
continued

SCSI Interface:				
Model	Capacity	Cylinders	Heads	Sectors
XT81000E	889	1632	15	54
7040S	40	1155	2	36
7080S	81	1155	4	36
LXT-50S	48	733	4	32
LXT-100S	96	733	8	32
LXT-200S	191	1320	7	33
LXT-213S	200	1320	7	55
LXT-340S	340	1560	7	47
P0-12S	1027	1632	15	72
P1-08S	696	1778	9	72
P1-12S	1005	1216	19	72
P1-17S	1470	1778	19	72
XT4170S	157	1224	7	36
XT4280S	241	1224	11	36
XT4380S	337	1224	15	36
XT8380S	360	1632	8	54
XT8702S	616	1490	15	54
XT8760S	675	1632	15	54

Maxtor appears beside the SCSI Interface section (rows 7040S onward).

MFM Interface:				
Model	Capacity	Cylinders	Heads	Sectors
310	2	118	2	17
321	5	320	2	17
322	10	320	4	17
323	15	320	6	17
324	20	320	8	17
450	10	612	2	17
512	25	961	3	17
513	41	961	5	17
514	58	961	7	17

Memorex

MFM Interface:				
Model	Capacity	Cylinders	Heads	Sectors
1302	20	830	3	17
1303	34	830	5	17

Micropolis

Micropolis

MFM Interface: Model	Capacity	Cylinders	Heads	Sectors
1304	41	830	6	17
1323	35	1024	4	17
1323A	44	1024	5	17
1324	53	1024	6	17
1324A	62	1024	7	17
1325	71	1024	8	17
1333	34	1024	4	17
1333A	44	1024	5	17
1334	53	1024	6	17
1334A	62	1024	7	17
1335	71	1024	8	17

Micropolis

ATA Interface: Model	Capacity	Cylinders	Heads	Sectors
1743-5	112	1140	5	28
1744-6	135	1140	6	28
1744-7	157	1140	7	28
1745-8	180	1140	8	28
1745-9	202	1140	9	28

Micropolis

ESDI Interface: Model	Capacity	Cylinders	Heads	Sectors
1352	30	1024	2	36
1352A	41	1024	3	36
1353	75	1024	4	36
1353A	94	1024	5	36
1354	113	1024	6	36
1354A	132	1024	7	36
1355	151	1024	8	36
1516-10S	678	1840	10	72
1517-13	922	1925	13	72
1518-14	993	1925	14	72
1518-15	1064	1925	15	72
1538-15	872	1925	15	71

continues

TABLE 21.1.
continued

Micropolis

ESDI Interface: Model	Capacity	Cylinders	Heads	Sectors
1551	149	1224	7	34
1554-7	158	1224	7	36
1554-11	234	1224	11	34
1555-8	180	1224	8	36
1555-9	203	1224	9	36
1555-12	255	1224	12	34
1556-10	226	1224	10	36
1556-11	248	1224	11	36
1556-13	276	1224	13	34
1557-12	270	1224	12	36
1557-13	293	1224	13	36
1557-14	315	1224	14	36
1557-15	338	1224	15	36
1566-11	496	1632	11	54
1567-12	541	1632	12	54
1567-13	586	1632	13	54
1568-14	631	1632	14	54
1568-15	676	1632	15	54
1652-4	92	1249	4	36
1653-5	115	1249	5	36
1654-6	138	1249	6	36
1654-7	161	1249	7	36
1663-4	197	1780	4	36
1663-5	246	1780	5	36
1664-6	295	1780	6	54
1664-7	345	1780	7	54

Micropolis

SCSI Interface: Model	Capacity	Cylinders	Heads	Sectors
1373	73	1024	4	36
1373A	91	1024	5	36
1374	109	1024	6	36
1374A	127	1024	7	36
1375	146	1024	8	36
1488-15	675	1628	15	54

Micropolis

SCSI Interface: Model	Capacity	Cylinders	Heads	Sectors
1528-15	1354 (SCSI-2)	2106	15	84
1576-11	243	1224	11	36
1577-12	266	1224	12	36
1577-13	287	1224	13	36
1578-14	310	1224	14	36
1578-15	332	1224	15	36
1586-11	490	1632	11	54
1587-12	535	1632	12	54
1587-13	579	1632	13	54
1588-14	624	1632	14	54
1588-15	668	1632	15	54
1596-10S	668	1834	10	72
1597-13	909	1919	13	72
1598-14	979	1919	14	72
1590-15	1049	1919	15	71
1673-4	90	1249	4	36
1673-5	112	1249	5	36
1674-6	135	1249	6	36
1674-7	158	1249	7	36
1683-4	193	1776	4	54
1683-5	242	1776	5	54
1684-6	291	1776	6	54
1684-7	340	1776	7	54
1773-5	112	1140	5	28
1774-6	135	1140	6	28
1774-7	157	1140	7	28
1775-8	180	1140	8	28
1775-9	202	1140	9	28

Microscience

MFM Interface: Model	Capacity	Cylinders	Heads	Sectors
4050	45	1024	5	17
4060	68 (RLL)	1024	5	26
4070	62	1024	7	17
4090	95 (RLL)	1024	7	26

continues

TABLE 21.1.
continued

Microscience

MFM Interface:				
Model	Capacity	Cylinders	Heads	Sectors
HH312	10	306	4	17
HH315	21	612	4	17
HH330 (RLL)	33	612	4	26
HH612	10	612	2	17
HH712A	10	612	2	17
HH725	21	612	4	17
HH738	33 (RLL)	612	4	26
HH825	21	612	4	17
HH830	33	612	4	26
HH1050	45	1024	5	17
HH1060	66 (RLL)	1024	5	26
HH1075	62	1024	7	17
HH1080	95 (RLL)	1024	7	26
HH1090	80	1314	7	17
HH1095	95 (RLL)	1024	7	26
HH1120	122	1314	7	26
HH2012	10	306	4	17

Microscience

ATA Interface:				
Model	Capacity	Cylinders	Heads	Sectors
7040	47	855	3	36
7070-20	86	960	5	35
7100	107	855	7	35
7100-20	120	960	7	35
7100-21	121	1077	5	44
7200	201	1277	7	44
7400	420	1904	8	39
8040	43	1047	2	40
8040/MLC	42	1024	2	40
8080	85	1768	2	47
8200	210	1904	4	39

Microscience

ESDI Interface:				
Model	Capacity	Cylinders	Heads	Sectors
5040	46	855	3	35
5070	77	855	5	35
5070-20	86	960	5	35
5100	107	855	7	35
5100-20	120	960	7	35

Microscience

ESDI Interface:				
Model	Capacity	Cylinders	Heads	Sectors
FH2777	688	1658	15	54
FH21200	1062	1921	15	72
FH21600	1418	2147	15	86
HH2120	128	1024	7	35
HH2160	160	1276	7	35

Microscience

SCSI Interface:				
Model	Capacity	Cylinders	Heads	Sectors
6100	110	855	7	36
FH3414	367	1658	8	54
FH3777	688	1658	15	54
FH31200	1062	1921	15	72
FH31600	1418	2147	15	86
HH3120	121	1314	5	36
HH3160	169	1314	7	36

Miniscribe

MFM Interface:				
Model	Capacity	Cylinders	Heads	Sectors
1006	5	206	2	17
1012	10	306	4	17
2006	5	306	2	17
2012	10	306	4	17
3006	5	306	2	17
3012	10	612	2	17
3053	44	1024	5	17
3085	71	1170	7	17
3212	10	612	2	17
3412	21	615	4	17
3425	21	615	4	17
3438	32 (RLL)	615	4	26
3650	42	809	6	17
3675	63 (RLL)	809	6	26
4010	8	480	2	17
4020	17	480	4	17
5330	25	480	6	17
5338	32	612	6	17
5440	32	480	8	17

continues

TABLE 21.1.
continued

MFM Interface:				
Model	**Capacity**	**Cylinders**	**Heads**	**Sectors**
5451	43	612	8	17
6032	26	1024	3	17
6053	44	1024	5	17
6074	62	1024	7	17
6079	68 (RLL)	1024	5	26
6085	71	1024	8	17
6128	110 (RLL)	1024	8	26
6212	10	612	2	17
7426	21	612	4	17
8225	20 (RLL)	771	2	26
8225C	21	798	2	26
8412	10	306	4	17
8425	21	615	4	17
8434F	32 (RLL)	615	4	26
8438	32 (RLL)	615	4	26
8450	41 (RLL)	771	4	26
8450C	40	748	4	26

Miniscribe (MFM Interface)

ATA Interface:				
Model	**Capacity**	**Cylinders**	**Heads**	**Sectors**
7040A	36	980	2	36
7080A	72	980	4	36
8051A	43	745	4	28
8225AT	21	745	2	28
8438XT	32	615	4	26
8450AT	42	745	4	28
8450XT	42	805	4	26

Miniscribe (ATA Interface)

ESDI Interface:				
Model	**Capacity**	**Cylinders**	**Heads**	**Sectors**
3085E	72	1270	3	36
3130E	112	1250	5	36
3180E	157	1250	7	36
6170E	130	1024	8	36
9000E	338	1224	15	36
9230E	203	1224	9	36
9380E	338	1224	15	36
9424E	360	1661	8	54
97803	676	1661	15	54

Miniscribe (ESDI Interface)

Miniscribe	SCSI Interface: Model	Capacity	Cylinders	Heads	Sectors
	3085S	72	1255	3	36
	3130S	115	1255	5	36
	3180S	153	1255	7	36
	7080S	81	1155	4	36
	8051S	45	793	4	28
	8225S	21	804	2	26
	9000S	347	1220	15	36
	9230S	203	1224	9	36
	9380S	347	1224	15	36
	9424S	355	1661	8	54
	9780S	668	1661	15	54

Mitsubishi	MFM Interface: Model	Capacity	Cylinders	Heads	Sectors
	MR521	10	612	2	17
	MR522	20	612	4	17
	MR533	25	971	3	17
	MR535	42	977	5	17
	MR535R	65 (RLL)	977	5	17

Mitsubishi	ESDI Interface: Model	Capacity	Cylinders	Heads	Sectors
	MR5301E	65	977	5	26

Mitsubishi	SCSI Interface: Model	Capacity	Cylinders	Heads	Sectors
	MR535S	65	977	5	26
	MR537S	65	977	5	26

MMI	MFM Interface: Model	Capacity	Cylinders	Heads	Sectors
	M106	5	306	2	17
	M112	10	306	4	17
	M125	20	306	8	17
	M212	10	306	4	17
	M225	20	306	8	17
	M306	5	306	2	17
	M312	10	306	4	17
	M325	20	306	8	17

continues

TABLE 21.1.
continued

MFM Interface:				
Model	Capacity	Cylinders	Heads	Sectors
M5012	10	306	4	17
D3126	20	615	4	17
D3142	42	642	8	17
D3146H	40	615	8	17
D5114	5	306	2	17
D5124	10	309	4	17
D5126	20	612	4	17
D5127H	32 (RLL)	612	4	26
D5146	40	615	8	17
D5147H	65 (RLL)	615	8	26
D5452	71	823	10	17

NEC (MFM Interface)

ATA Interface:				
Model	Capacity	Cylinders	Heads	Sectors
D3735	56	1084	2	41
D3755	105	1250	4	41
D3761	114	915	7	35

NEC (ATA Interface)

ESDI Interface:				
Model	Capacity	Cylinders	Heads	Sectors
D3661	118	915	7	36
D5652	143	823	10	34
D5655	153	1224	7	35
D5662	319	1224	15	34
D5681	664	1633	15	53

NEC (ESDI Interface)

SCSI Interface:				
Model	Capacity	Cylinders	Heads	Sectors
D3835	45	1084	2	41
D3855	105	1250	4	41
D3861	114	915	7	35
D5882	665	1633	15	53
D5892	1404	1678	19	86

NEC (SCSI Interface)

MFM Interface:				
Model	Capacity	Cylinders	Heads	Sectors
NDR320	21	615	4	17
NDR340	42	615	8	17
NDR360	65 (RLL)	615	8	26
NDR1065	55	918	7	17

Newbury Data (MFM Interface)

Newbury Data

MFM Interface: Model	Capacity	Cylinders	Heads	Sectors
NDR1085	71	1025	8	17
NDR1105	87	918	11	17
NDR1140	119	918	15	17
NDR2085	74	1224	7	17
NDR2140	117	1224	11	17
NDR2190	160	1224	15	17

Newbury Data

ESDI Interface: Model	Capacity	Cylinders	Heads	Sectors
NDR4170	149	1224	7	34
NDR4175	157	1224	7	36
NDR4380	338	1224	15	36

Newbury Data

SCSI Interface: Model	Capacity	Cylinders	Heads	Sectors
NDR3170S	146	1224	9	26
NDR3280S	244	1224	15	26
NDR4380S	319	1224	15	34

Okidata

MFM Interface: Model	Capacity	Cylinders	Heads	Sectors
OD526	31 (RLL)	612	4	26
OD540	47 (RLL)	612	6	26

Olivetti

MFM Interface: Model	Capacity	Cylinders	Heads	Sectors
HD662/11	10	612	2	17
HD662/12	20	612	4	17
XM5210	10	612	4	17

Otari

MFM Interface: Model	Capacity	Cylinders	Heads	Sectors
C214	10	306	4	17
C507	5	306	2	17
C514	10	306	4	17
C519	15	306	6	17
C526	10	306	8	17

continues

TABLE 21.1.
continued

Panasonic

MFM Interface: Model	Capacity	Cylinders	Heads	Sectors
JU-116	20	615	4	17
JU-128	42	733	7	17

Prairietek

ATA Interface: Model	Capacity	Cylinders	Heads	Sectors
120	21	615	2	34
240	42	615	4	34

Priam

MFM Interface: Model	Capacity	Cylinders	Heads	Sectors
502	46	755	7	17
504	46	755	7	17
514	117	1224	11	17
519	160	1224	15	17
3504	44	771	5	17
ID20	26	987	3	17
ID40	43	987	5	17
ID45	50	1166	5	17
ID45H	44	1024	5	17
ID60	59	1018	7	17
ID62	62	1166	7	17
ID75	73 (RLL)	1166	5	25
ID100	103 (RLL)	1166	7	25
ID130	132	1224	15	17
ID230	233 (RLL)	1224	15	25
V130R	39 (RLL)	987	3	26
V150	42	987	5	17
V160	50	1166	5	17
V170	60	987	7	17
V170R	91 (RLL)	987	7	26
V185	71	1166	7	17
V519	159	1224	15	17

Priam

ESDI Interface: Model	Capacity	Cylinders	Heads	Sectors
617	153	1225	7	36
623	196	752	15	34
628	241	1225	11	36
630	319	1224	15	34

Priam

ESDI Interface: Model	Capacity	Cylinders	Heads	Sectors
638	329	1225	15	36
ID120	121	1024	7	33
ID150	159	1276	7	35
ID160	158	1225	7	36
ID250	248	1225	11	36
ID330	338	1225	15	36
ID330E	336	1218	15	36

Priam

SCSI Interface: Model	Capacity	Cylinders	Heads	Sectors
717	153	1225	7	36
728	241	1225	11	36
738	329	1225	15	36
ID330S	338	1218	15	36

Quantum

MFM Interface: Model	Capacity	Cylinders	Heads	Sectors
Q510	8	512	2	17
Q520	18	512	4	17
Q530	27	512	6	17
Q540	36	512	8	17

Quantum

ATA Interface: Model	Capacity	Cylinders	Heads	Sectors
PRO 40AT	42	965	5	17
PRO 80AT	84	965	10	17
PRO 120AT	120	814	9	32
PRO 210AT	209	873	13	36
PRO LPS52AT	52	751	8	17
PRO LPS80AT	86	616	16	17
PRO LPS105AT	105	755	16	17
PRO LPS240AT	235	723	13	51

Quantum

SCSI Interface: Model	Capacity	Cylinders	Heads	Sectors
Q160	200	971	12	36
Q250	53	823	4	36
Q280	80	823	6	36

continues

TABLE 21.1.
continued

Quantum

SCSI Interface: Model	Capacity	Cylinders	Heads	Sectors
PRO 40S	42	965	5	17
PRO 80S	84	965	10	17
PRO 120S	120	814	9	32
PRO 210S	209	873	13	36
PRO LPS52S	52	751	8	17
PRO LPS80S	86	616	16	17
PRO LPS105S	105	755	16	17
PRO LPS240S	235	723	13	51

Rodime

MFM Interface: Model	Capacity	Cylinders	Heads	Sectors
RO101	3	192	2	17
RO102	6	192	4	17
R0103	9	192	6	17
RO104	12	192	8	17
RO201	5	321	2	17
RO201E	11	640	2	17
RO202	11	321	4	17
RO202E	22	640	4	17
RO203	16	321	6	17
RO203E	33	640	6	17
RO204	22	320	8	17
RO204E	44	640	8	17
RO251	5	306	2	17
RO252	10	306	4	17
RO3045	37	872	5	17
RO3055	45	872	6	17
RO3060R	49 (RLL)	750	5	26
RO3065	53	872	7	17
RO3075R	59 (RLL)	750	6	26
RO3085R	69 (RLL)	750	7	26
R05065	53	1224	5	17
RO5090	74	1224	7	17
RO5130R	114 (RLL)	1224	7	26

Rodime	ATA Interface: Model	Capacity	Cylinders	Heads	Sectors
	RO3058A	45	868	3	34
	RO3095A	80	923	5	34
	RO3099AP	80	1030	4	28
	RO3121A	122	1207	4	53
	RO3128A	105	868	7	34
	RO3135A	112	923	7	34
	RO3139A	112	523	15	28
	RO3199AP	112	1168	5	28
	RO3209A	163	759	15	28
	RO3259A	213	990	15	28
	RO3259AP	213	1235	9	28

Rodime	ESDI Interface: Model	Capacity	Cylinders	Heads	Sectors
	RO5075E	65	1224	3	35
	RO5125E	109	1224	5	35
	RO5180E	153	1224	7	35

Rodime	SCSI Interface: Model	Capacity	Cylinders	Heads	Sectors
	RO652A	20	306	4	33
	RO652B	20	306	4	33
	RO752A	20	306	4	33
	RO3055T	45	1053	3	28
	RO3057S	45	680	5	26
	RO3058T	45	868	3	34
	RO3085S	70	750	7	26
	RO3088T	76	868	5	34
	RO3090T	75	1053	5	28
	RO3128T	105	868	7	34
	RO3129TS	105	1091	5	41
	RO3130T	105	1053	7	28
	RO3139TP	112	1148	5	42
	RO3199TS	163	1216	7	41
	RO3259T	210	1216	9	41
	RO3259TP	210	1189	9	42
	RO3259TS	210	1216	9	41

continues

TABLE 21.1.
continued

SCSI Interface: Model	Capacity	Cylinders	Heads	Sectors
RO5075S	61	1219	3	33
RO5078S	61	1219	3	33
RO5125S	103	1219	5	33
RO5178S	144	1219	7	33
RO5180S	144	1219	7	33

Rodime

ATA Interface: Model	Capacity	Cylinders	Heads	Sectors
SHD-3101A	105	1282	4	40

Samsung

SCSI Interface: Model	Capacity	Cylinders	Heads	Sectors
SHD-3201S	211	1376	7	43

Samsung

MFM Interface: Model	Capacity	Cylinders	Heads	Sectors
ST124	21	615	4	17
ST125	21	615	4	17
ST138	32	615	6	17
ST138R	33 (RLL)	615	4	26
ST151	43	977	5	17
ST157R	49 (RLL)	615	6	26
ST206	5	306	2	17
ST212	10	306	4	17
ST213	10	615	2	17
ST225	21	615	4	17
ST225R	21 (RLL)	667	2	31
ST238R	32 (RLL)	615	4	26
ST250R	42 (RLL)	667	4	31
ST251	43	820	6	17
ST252	43	820	6	17
ST253	43	989	5	17
ST277R	65 (RLL)	820	6	26
ST278R	65 (RLL)	820	6	26
ST279R	65 (RLL)	989	5	26
ST406	5	306	2	17
ST412	10	306	4	17
ST419	15	306	6	17
ST506	5	153	4	17

Seagate Technology

MFM Interface:				
Model	Capacity	Cylinders	Heads	Sectors
ST1100	83	1072	9	17
ST1106R	91 (RLL)	977	7	26
ST1150R	128 (RLL)	1072	9	26
ST4026	21	615	4	17
ST4038	31	733	5	17
ST4051	42	977	5	17
ST4085	71	1024	8	17
ST4086	72	925	9	17
ST4096	80	1024	9	17
ST4097	80	1024	9	17
ST4135R	115 (RLL)	960	9	26
ST4144R	123 (RLL)	1024	9	26

Seagate Technology

ESDI Interface:				
Model	Capacity	Cylinders	Heads	Sectors
ST1111E	98	1072	5	36
ST1156E	138	1072	7	36
ST1201E	177	1072	9	36
ST2106E	92	1024	5	36
ST2182E	160	1452	4	54
ST2383E	337	1747	7	54
ST4182E	160	969	9	36
ST4383E	338	1412	12	36
ST4384E	338	1224	15	36
ST4442E	390	1412	15	36
ST4766E	676	1032	15	54
ST4767E	676	1399	15	63
ST4769E	691	1552	15	53

Seagate Technology

ATA Interface:				
Model	Capacity	Cylinders	Heads	Sectors
ST125A	21	404	4	26
ST138A	32	604	4	26
ST157A	45	560	6	26
ST274A	65	948	5	26
ST280A	71	1032	5	27
ST325A	21	615	4	17

Seagate Technology

continues

Seagate Technology

ATA Interface:				
Model	Capacity	Cylinders	Heads	Sectors
ST351A	43	820	6	17
ST1057A	53	1024	6	17
ST1090A	79	1072	5	29
ST1102A	89	1024	10	17
ST1111A	98	1072	5	36
ST1126A	111	1072	7	29
ST1133A	117	1272	5	36
ST1144A	130	1001	15	17
ST1156A	138	1072	7	36
ST1186A	164	1272	7	36
ST1201A	177	1072	9	36
ST1239A	211	1272	9	36
ST1480A	426	1474	9	62
ST2274A	241	1747	5	54
ST2383A	338	1747	7	54
ST3051A	43	820	6	17
ST3096A	89	1024	10	17
ST3120A	107	1024	12	17
ST3144A	131	1001	15	17

Seagate Technology

SCSI Interface:				
Model	Capacity	Cylinders	Heads	Sectors
ST125N	21	407	4	26
ST138N	32	615	4	26
ST157N	49	615	6	26
ST177N	61	921	5	26
ST225N	21	615	4	17
ST251N	43	820	4	26
ST251N-1	43	630	4	34
ST277N	65	820	6	26
ST277N-1	65	630	6	34
ST296N	80	820	6	34
ST1090N	79	1068	5	29
ST1096N	80	906	7	26
ST1111N	98	1068	5	36
ST1126N	111	1068	7	29
ST1133NS	116 (SCSI-2)	1268	5	36
ST1156N	138	1068	7	36

Seagate Technology

SCSI Interface: Model	Capacity	Cylinders	Heads	Sectors
ST1156NS	138 (SCSI-2)	1068	7	36
ST1162N	142	1068	9	29
ST1186NS	163 (SCSI-2)	1268	7	36
ST1201N	177	1068	9	36
ST1201NS	177 (SCSI-2)	1068	9	36
ST1239NS	210 (SCSI-2)	1268	9	36
ST1400N	331 (SCSI-2)	1476	7	62
AT1480N	426 (SCSI-2)	1476	9	62
ST2106N	91	1022	5	36
ST2125N	107	1544	3	45
ST2209N	179	1544	5	45
ST2383N	337	1261	7	74
ST2502N	435	1755	7	69
ST4182N	155	969	9	35
ST4250N	300	1412	9	46
ST4376N	330	1546	9	45
ST4385N	330	791	15	55
ST4702N	601	1546	15	50
ST4766N	676	1632	15	54
ST4767N	665 (SCSI-2)	1356	15	64
ST41200N	1037	1931	15	71
ST41520N	1352 (SCSI-2)	2102	17	ZBR
ST41600N	1352 (SCSI-2)	2101	17	75
ST41650N	1415 (SCSI-2)	2107	15	87
ST41651N	1415 (SCSI-2)	2107	15	ZBR

Seimens

ESDI Interface: Model	Capacity	Cylinders	Heads	Sectors
1200	174	1216	8	35
1300	261	1216	12	35
4410	322	1100	11	52
5710	655	1224	15	48
5810	688	1658	15	54

continues

TABLE 21.1.
continued

SCSI Interface:				
Model	Capacity	Cylinders	Heads	Sectors
2200	174	1216	8	35
2300	261	1216	12	35
4420	334	1100	11	54
5720	655	1224	15	48
5820	688	1658	15	54
6200	1062	1921	15	72

Seimens

MFM Interface:				
Model	Capacity	Cylinders	Heads	Sectors
SA604	5	160	4	17
SA606	7	160	6	17
SA607	5	306	2	17
SA612	10	306	4	17
SA706	6	320	2	17
SA712	10	320	4	17

Shugart

MFM Interface:				
Model	Capacity	Cylinders	Heads	Sectors
SQ225F	20	615	4	17
SQ306F	5	306	2	17
SQ306R	5	306	2	17
SQ306RD	5	306	2	17
SQ312	10	615	2	17
SQ312RD	10	615	2	17
SQ312F	20	612	4	17
SQ319	10	612	2	17
SQ325	20	612	4	17
SQ325F	20	615	4	17
SQ338F	30	615	6	17
SQ340AF	38	649	6	17

Syquest

MFM Interface:				
Model	Capacity	Cylinders	Heads	Sectors
TM244	41 (RLL)	782	4	26
TM246	62 (RLL)	782	6	26
TM251	5	306	2	17
TM252	10	306	4	17
TM261	10	615	2	17
TM262	21	615	4	17

Tandon

MFM Interface:

Tandon

Model	Capacity	Cylinders	Heads	Sectors
TM262R	20 (RLL)	782	2	26
TM264	41 (RLL)	782	4	26
TM344	41 (RLL)	782	4	26
TM346	62 (RLL)	782	6	26
TM361	10	615	2	17
TM362	21	615	4	17
TM362R	20 (RLL)	782	2	26
TM364	41 (RLL)	782	4	26
TM501	5	306	2	17
TM502	10	306	4	17
TM503	15	306	6	17
TM602S	5	153	4	17
TM603S	10	153	6	17
TM603SE	21	230	6	17
TM702	20 (RLL)	615	4	26
TM702AT	8	615	4	17
*TM703	10	733	5	17
TM703AT	31	733	5	17
TM705	41	962	5	17
TM755	43	981	5	17
TM3085	71	1024	8	17
TM3085R	104 (RLL)	1024	8	26

SCSI Interface:

Tandon

Model	Capacity	Cylinders	Heads	Sectors
TM2085	74	1004	9	36
TM2128	115	1004	9	36
TM2170	154	1344	9	36

MFM Interface:

Teac

Model	Capacity	Cylinders	Heads	Sectors
SD150	10	306	4	17
SD510	10	306	4	17
SD520	20	615	4	17

continues

TABLE 21.1.
continued

ATA Interface:				
Model	Capacity	Cylinders	Heads	Sectors

Teac

SD340-A	43	1050	2	40
SD380	86	1050	4	40

SCSI Interface:				
Model	Capacity	Cylinders	Heads	Sectors

Teac

SD340S	43	1050	2	40
SD380-S	86	1050	4	40

MFM Interface:				
Model	Capacity	Cylinders	Heads	Sectors

Toshiba

MK53FA/B	43	830	5	17
MK53FA/B	64 (RLL)	830	5	26
MK54FA/B	60	830	7	17
MK54FA/B	90 (RLL)	830	7	26
MK56FA/B	86	830	10	17
MK56FA/B	129 (RLL)	830	10	26
MK134FA	44	733	7	17

ATA Interface:				
Model	Capacity	Cylinders	Heads	Sectors

Toshiba

MK234FC	106	845	7	35

ESDI Interface:				
Model	Capacity	Cylinders	Heads	Sectors

Toshiba

MK153FA	74	830	5	35
MK154FA	104	830	7	35
MK156FA	148	830	10	35
MK250FA	382	1224	10	35
MK355FA	459	1632	9	53
MK358FA	765	1632	15	53
MK556FA	152	830	10	35

SCSI Interface:				
Model	Capacity	Cylinders	Heads	Sectors

Toshiba

MK153FB	74	830	5	35
MK154FB	104	830	7	35
MK156FB	148	830	10	35
MK250FB	382	1224	10	35
MK232FB	45	845	3	35

Toshiba	SCSI Interface: Model	Capacity	Cylinders	Heads	Sectors
	MK233FB	76	845	5	35
	MK234FB	106	845	7	35
	MK355FB	459	1632	9	53
	MK358FB	765	1632	15	53

Tulin	MFM Interface: Model	Capacity	Cylinders	Heads	Sectors
	TL213	10	640	2	17
	TL226	22	640	4	17
	TL238	22	640	4	17
	TL240	33	640	6	17
	TL258	33	640	6	17
	TL326	22	640	4	17
	TL340	33	640	6	17

Vertex	MFM Interface: Model	Capacity	Cylinders	Heads	Sectors
	V130	26	987	3	17
	V150	43	987	5	17
	V170	60	987	7	17

Western Digital	MFM Interface: Model	Capacity	Cylinders	Heads	Sectors
	WD262	20	615	4	17
	WD344R	40 (RLL)	782	4	26
	WD362	20	615	4	17
	WD382R	20 (RLL)	782	2	26
	WD383R	30 (RLL)	615	4	26
	WD384R	40 (RLL)	782	4	26
	WD544R	40 (RLL)	782	4	26
	WD582R	20 (RLL)	782	2	26
	WD583R	30 (RLL)	615	4	26
	WD584R	49 (RLL)	782	4	26

Western Digital	ATA Interface: Model	Capacity	Cylinders	Heads	Sectors
	WD93024	20	782	2	27
	WD93028	20	782	2	27

continues

TABLE 21.1. continued	ATA Interface: Model	Capacity	Cylinders	Heads	Sectors
	WD93034	30	782	3	27
Western Digital	WD93038	30	782	3	27
	WD93044	40	782	4	27
	WD93048	40	782	4	27
	WD95024	20	782	2	27
	WD95028	20	782	2	27
	WD95034	30	782	3	27
	WD95044	40	782	4	27
	WD95058	40	782	4	27
	WD AB130	32	733	5	17
	WD AC140	42	980	5	17
	WD AC160	62	1024	7	17
	WD AC280	85	980	10	17
	WD AH260	63	1024	7	17

This table was compiled from actual installations, manufacturers' data, and other sources and is believed to be accurate for the models listed.

Many of the drives use sector translation, and the figures listed represent values found to operate satisfactory in actual computer systems rather than the actual physical configuration of the drives.

Drive Arrays

When you need more capacity than a single hard disk can provide, you have two choices: trim your needs or plug in more disks. But changing your needs means changing your lifestyle, foregoing instant access to all of your files by deleting some from your disk, switching to data compression, or keeping a tighter watch on backup files and intermediary versions of projects under development. Of course, changing your lifestyle is about as easy a teaching an old dog to change its spots. The one application with storage needs likely to exceed that capacity of today's individual hard disks (1.5 gigabytes and climbing) is serving a network, which makes a total lifestyle change for network server about as probable as getting a platoon of toddlers to clean up a playroom littered with a near-infinite collection of toys.

Consequently, when the bytes run really low, you're left with the need for multiple disks. In most single-user PCs, each of these multiple drives will act independently and appear as a separate drive letter (or group of drive letters) under DOS. Through software, such multiple drive systems can even be made to emulate one large disk with a total storage capacity equal to that of its constituent drives. Because DOS only does one thing at a time, such a solution is satisfactory, but it's hardly the optimum arrangement where reliability and providing dozens of users instant access is concerned. Instead of operating each disk independently, you can gain higher speeds, greater resistance to errors, and improved reliability by linking the drives through hardware to make a drive array or what has come to be known as a *redundant array of inexpensive disks,* or *RAID.*

The premise of the drive array is elementary—combine a number of individual hard disks to create a massive virtual system. But a drive array is more than several hard disks connected to a single controller. In an array, the drives are coordinated, and the controller specially allocates information between them. For example, in some drive arrays, the spin of each drive is synchronized, and any single data byte may be spread among several physical hard disks.

The obvious benefit of the drive array is the same as any multiple disk installation: capacity. Two disks can hold more than one, and four more than two. But drive array technology can also accelerate mass storage performance and increase reliability.

Data Striping

The secret to both of these innovations is the way the various hard disks in the drive array are combined. They are not arranged in a serial list where the second drive takes over once the capacity of the first is completely used up. Instead, data is split between drives at the bit, byte, or block level. For example, in a four-drive system, two bits of every byte might come from the first hard disk, the next two bits from the second drive, and so on. The four drives could then pour a single byte into the data stream four times faster; moving all the information in the byte would only take as long as it would for a single drive to move two bits. Alternatively, a four-byte storage cluster could be made from a sector from each of the four drives. This technique of splitting data between several drives is called *data striping.*

At this primitive level, data striping has a severe disadvantage: the failure of any drive in the system results in the complete failure of the entire system. The reliability of the entire array can be no greater than that of the least reliable drive in the array. The speed and capacity of such a system are greater but so are the risks involved in using it.

Redundancy and Reliability

By sacrificing part of its potential capacity, an array of drives can yield a more reliable, even fault-tolerant, storage system. The key is redundancy. Instead of a straight division of the bits, bytes, and blocks each drive in the array stores, the information split between the drives can overlap.

For example, in a four-drive system instead of each drive getting two bits of each byte, each drive might store four. The first drive would take the first four bits of a given byte; the second drive would take the third, fourth, fifth, and sixth bits; the third drive would take the fifth, sixth, seventh, and eighth bits; the fourth drive would take the seventh, eighth, first, and second bits. This digital overlap allows the correct information to be pulled from another drive when one encounters an error. Better yet, if any single hard disk should fail, all of the data it stored could be reconstituted from the other drives.

This kind of system is said to be fault-tolerant. That is, a single fault, the failure of one hard disk, will be tolerated, meaning the system will operate without the loss of any vital function. Fault tolerance is extremely valuable in network applications because the crash of a single hard disk does not bring down the network. A massive equipment failure thus becomes a bother rather than a disaster.

This example array represents the most primitive of drive array implementations, one that is particularly wasteful of the available storage resources. Advanced information-coding methods allow higher efficiencies in storage so that a strict duplication of every bit is not required. Moreover, advanced drive arrays even allow a failed drive to be replaced and the data that was stored on it to be reconstructed without interrupting the normal operation of the array. A network server with such a drive array wouldn't have to be shut down even for disk repairs.

RAID Implementations

Just connecting four drives to a SCSI controller won't create a drive array. An array requires special electronics to handle the digital coding and control of the individual drives. The electronics of these systems are proprietary to their manufacturers. The array controller then connects to your PC through a proprietary or standard interface. SCSI is becoming the top choice. Currently, most drive arrays are assembled by computer manufacturers for their own systems, but a growing number are becoming available as plug-in additions to PCs.

Five levels of RAID technology are now recognized, termed RAID 1 through 5. (Sometimes engineers talk about RAID 0, which means a single ordinary disk drive—in other words, not an array at all.)

The numerical designations are actually arbitrary and are not meant to indicate that RAID 1 is better or worse than RAID 5. Which implementation is best depends on what you most want to achieve with a drive array: efficient use of drive capacity, fewest number of drives, greatest reliability, or quickest performance. For example, RAID 1 provides the greatest redundancy (thus reliability), and RAID 2 the best performance (followed closely by RAID 3). The numbers simply provide a label for each technology that can be readily understood by the cognoscenti.

RAID 1

The simplest of drive arrays, RAID 1, consists of two equal-capacity disks that mirror one another. One disk duplicates all the files of the other, essentially serving as a backup copy. Should one of the drives fail, the other can serve in its stead.

This reliability is the chief advantage of RAID 1 technology. The entire system has the same capacity as one of its drives alone. In other words, the RAID 1 system yields only 50 percent of its potential storage capacity, making it the most expensive array implementation. Performance depends on the sophistication of the array controller. Simple systems would deliver exactly the performance of one of the drives in the array. A more sophisticated controller could potentially double data throughput by simultaneously reading alternate sectors from both drives. Upon the failure of one of the drives, performance would revert to that of a single drive, but no information (and no network time) would be lost.

RAID 2

The next step up in array sophistication is RAID 2, which interleaves bits or blocks of data as explained earlier in the description of drive arrays. The individual drives in the array operate in parallel, typically with their spindles synchronized.

To improve reliability, RAID 2 systems use redundant disks to correct single-bit errors and detect double-bit errors. The number of extra disks needed depends on the error-correction algorithm used. For example, an array of eight data drives may use three error-correction drives. High-end arrays with 32 data drives may use seven error-correction drives. The data, complete with error-detection code, is delivered directly to the array controller. The controller can instantly recognize and correct for errors as they occur, without slowing the speed at which information is read and transferred to the host computer. The RAID 2 design anticipates that disk errors occur often, almost regularly. At one time, mass storage devices might have been error-prone, but no longer. Consequently, RAID 2 can be overkill except in the most critical of circumstances.

The principal benefit of RAID 2 is performance; because of their pure parallel nature, it and RAID 3 are the best-performing array technologies, at least in systems that require a single, high-speed stream of data. In other words, it yields a high data transfer rate. Depending on the number of drives in the array, an entire byte or even a 32-bit double-word could be read in the same period it would take a single drive to read one bit. Normal single-bit disk errors don't hinder this performance in any way because of RAID 2's on-the-fly error correction.

The primary defect in the RAID 2 design arises from its basic storage unit of multiple sectors. As with any hard disk, the smallest unit each drive in the array can store is one sector. File sizes must increase in units of multiple sectors, one drawn from each drive. In a 10-drive array, for example, even the tiniest two-byte file would steal 10 sectors (5,120 bytes) of disk space. (Under DOS, which uses clusters of four sectors, the two-byte file would take a total of 20,480 bytes!) In actual application this drawback is not severe because systems that need the single-stream speed and instant error-correction of RAID 2 also tend to be those using large files, for example, mainframes.

RAID 3

RAID 3 is one step down from RAID 2. Although RAID 3 still uses multiple drives operating in parallel, interleaving bits or blocks of data. Instead of full error correction, it allows only for parity checking. That is, errors can be detected but without the guarantee of recovery.

Parity checking requires fewer extra drives in the array, typically only one per array, making it a less expensive alternative. When a parity error is detected, the RAID 3 controller reads the entire array again to get it right. This rereading imposes a substantial performance penalty. The disks must spin entirely around again, yielding a 17 millisecond delay in reading the data. Of course, the delay appears only when disk errors are detected. Modern hard disks offer such high reliability that the delays are rare. In effect, RAID 3 compared to RAID 2 trades off fewer drives for a slight performance penalty that occurs only rarely.

RAID 4

RAID 4 interleaves not bits or blocks but sectors. The sectors are read serially, as if the drives in the array were functionally one large drive with more heads and platters. (Of course, for higher performance a controller with adequate buffering could read two or more sectors at the same time, storing the later sectors in fast RAM and delivering them immediately after the preceding sector has been sent to the computer host.) For reliability, one drive in the array is dedicated to parity checking. RAID 4 earns favor because it permits small arrays of as few as two drives, although larger arrays make more efficient use of the available disk storage.

The dedicated parity drive is the biggest weakness of the RAID 4 scheme. In writing, RAID 4 maintains the parity drive by reading the data drives, updating the parity information, and then writing the update to the parity drive. This read-update-write cycle adds a performance penalty to every write, although read operations are unhindered.

RAID 4 offers an extra benefit for operating systems that can process multiple data requests simultaneously. An intelligent RAID 4 controller can process multiple input/output requests, reorganize them, and read its drives in the most efficient manner, perhaps even in parallel. For example, while a sector from one file is being read from one drive, a sector from another file can read from another drive. This parallel operation can improve the effective throughput of such operating systems.

RAID 5

RAID 5 eliminates the dedicated parity drive from the RAID 4 array and allows the parity-check function to rotate through the various drives in the array. Error checking is thus distributed across all disks in the array. In properly designed implementations, enough redundancy can be built in to make the system fault-tolerant.

RAID 5 is probably the most popular drive-array technology currently in use because it will work with almost any number of drives, including arrays as small as two, yet permits redundancy and fault tolerance to be built in.

Drive Packaging

You don't have to be a hardware wizard to figure out that a hard disk has to fit where you want to install it. As drive form factors shrink, however, you would think that these concerns would go away. This issue becomes one of making a tiny drive big enough to bolt into yesterday's giant-size drive bays. But physical drive installation isn't so simple. Today you're more likely than ever to try to squeeze a second (third or whatever) drive into the confines of a fully-expanded PC. Moreover, matching drive and bay size isn't enough. You've also got to pack in a controller or host adapter and wring out enough juice to power the drive product you choose.

Internal Hard Disks

It should be obvious that your drive must fit where you want to put it. It must have a form factor that matches one of the available drive bays in your computer or, if it is smaller, you need an adapter kit to fit it in.

Mounting a hard disk is much the same as installing a floppy disk drive. Unlike floppy disk drives, however, hard disks have no controls, knobs, or removable media that require user attention. Consequently, hard disks do not require front panel access and can be buried inside your computer without sacrificing anything other than a glance at the drive activity indicator LED on the front of most hard disks. Many small footprint desktop computers do exactly that. Space for an inch-high 3.5-inch hard disk drive may be nothing but a bay bent from a slice of sheet steel appended in some opportune place inside the system. Without an instruction manual or vivid imagination, you would never find where they've tucked away a tiny hard disk drive. Drives now consume so little power that proper cooling no longer dictates mounting position.

Most systems still provide half-height 5.25-inch bays for hard disk storage. With a modern 3.5-inch hard disk drive, your only concern is that you get a mounting kit to match the drive to the larger bay, or be sure that your system provides some way of installing a small disk in a larger bay. For example, the trays that ALR tower-style computers use for both hard and floppy disk drives easily accommodate either 5.25-inch or 3.5-inch drives without adapters. In general, AT-style cases that use rails to mount drives will require adapters. Systems in which drives directly screw in generally will accept a small drive in a large bay if you're willing to forego the sturdiness of screwing in both sides of the drive. Systems designed from the start with 3.5-inch bays pose no installation problems unless you want to cram in an ancient 5.25-inch drive (in which case your best option may be to take a circular saw to the drive, shave a few inches off, and the drive will fit without a problem, although this technique will compromise the access time of the drive, stretching it from milliseconds to millennia).

If you don't have sufficient space inside your computer for disk expansion, two alternative strategies are available to you. When your add-on storage needs are huge, you can opt to move the disk drive outside the chassis, in which case your expansion opportunities are essentially unlimited. Because of their need for multiple hard disks, nearly all drive arrays are installed externally. At the other end of the storage spectrum, if you have an ISA-bus computer, you can opt for a hard disk card, a small hard disk combined with its own controller that fits into an expansion bus slot instead of a disk drive bay. Both external disks and hard disk cards are discussed in the following sections.

Hard Disk Power

Power is a problem with every hard disk, including the tiniest hard card, that's installed in factory-issue IBM PCs. The constant spin of the hard disk platters that gives near-instant response extracts one penalty: the drive must continually draw power to keep up the spin even when your PC is doing something that doesn't involve the disk.

Older hard disks, for instance, the behemoth full-height 5.25-inch drives of the AT age, have electrical requirements that could strain computers with smaller power supplies, such as the 63.5 watt original PC and 100 watt clone machines. You can work around such problems by installing a larger power supply in computers that are deficient in wattage.

On the other hand, modern 3.5-inch drives draw a fraction of the power of the dinosaurs (most are under 10 watts, many under 5), so power issues rarely arise. Moreover, any PC with a 135 watt or larger power supply should have enough reserves for at least one hard disk drive no matter the vintage of the disk. Stick with a modern desktop PC, most of which have 200 watt power supplies and a modern hard disk, and drive power will not be a problem.

The power difficulty you'll likely encounter is finding a connector to plug into the drive. Many systems provide too few drive power connectors for full expansion. Check your PC before you order a new hard disk to ensure that a power connector is available for the new drive. If not, add a wye cable to your shopping list.

A wye cable is designed to intercept the power connector meant for one drive and split it two ways. This cable has one male drive power connector (like the power jacks on the backs of most disk drives) and two female connectors (matching the one you remove from the power jack on the back of a drive). Plug the connector you remove from the drive jack into the male plug, and you're left with two female plugs that will accommodate two disk drives.

Disk Controllers

Any hard disk you install must also electronically match the computer in which it is to be used. You need a spare connection from your existing hard disk controller or host adapter or you need to install a second controller/adapter.

Some early PCs pose particular problems. For example, while the controller of an XT can handle a second disk drive, both drives must have the same hardware parameters (including use of the old ST506 interface). You cannot mix MFM and RLL drives on one controller. Even though both drive types use the ST506 interface, the RLL controller can provide only RLL signals.

Modern PCs and drive interfaces allow you more freedom. ESDI permits you to use two drives (with that interface, of course) of any capacity. AT Attachment host adapters are equally flexible. SCSI host adapters allow up to seven drives to be connected, and all seven can have different setup parameters.

If you want to install a hard disk in a system that has not had a hard disk before (for example, because you're building it from scratch) or if you want to change interfaces (for example, to replace an aged ST506 drive with a low-cost AT Attachment unit), you'll need a new controller or host adapter. Don't forget that many systems combine the hard disk and floppy disk control functions in one PC expansion board. If you replace such a controller with a new interface, don't forget to get a new host adapter with floppy disk circuitry or a separate floppy disk controller board.

External Hard Disks

External chassis units were once, and briefly, the only hard disks that you could attach to your PC. They simultaneously solved two problems of the first PC: inadequate space and inadequate power. Another advantage often cited by the manufacturers of these devices was that they added no heat inside your PC. The external chassis also allows you to use very large drives, eight-inch and larger disks, with your PC. None of these arguments make sense in an age of 500-megabyte drives only slightly larger than a deck of playing cards. But external drives still thrive for several reasons: the advent of drive arrays, the versatility of plugging in and moving between systems, and laptop computers with no other provisions for hard disk expansion. Moreover, there's nothing inherently evil about external drive installation. The only real drawback is the additional costs involved, not just the dollars required to pay for an extra box and power supply.

Most often external drives are assembled by system houses, companies that buy raw disk drives, controller electronics, and the other hardware needed to make a complete system and put everything together into one no-hassle package. While the system integrator is one level removed from the original disk drive manufacturer and adds his own profit to the price you have to pay, the bargain is not necessarily bad. The system integrator not only assembles the complete unit, saving you the trouble, but also the integrator usually tests the finished product, adding one degree of quality control and eliminating a degree of worry.

Where still available, the external chassis hard disk subsystem comprises a complete mass storage subsystem, one that includes the disk drive proper, a case with built-in power supply, and a host adapter card. Ancient external drives were packaged with the actual drive controller in the external chassis and used a simple host adapter in your PC. For a while, external drives put the controller inside your PC. Modern units have gone back to the old-fashioned design with the actual controller in the external box. Actually, the controller is an embedded interface built into the hard disk itself, and the board in your PC is simply an ordinary AT Attachment or SCSI host adapter.

In any case, the external chassis must be connected to your computer by a cable of some kind. The FCC provides a tremendous incentive for manufacturers to make these connecting cables as short as possible, shorter cables are less likely to radiate interference, so getting FCC certification for external drives with shorter cables is easier. But short cables can severely restrict your flexibility in positioning the drive where you want it. You might be forced to put the unit to the left of your computer and have to rearrange your desk around the needs of the disk drive.

No matter the length of the cable, it's also one more thing to get in the way. And it's one more thing to go wrong. Connectors are the most troublesome part of any circuit and one of the elements most likely to fail.

On the other hand, external drives can be somewhat easier to install. For the most part, you won't have to deal with nuts, bolts, and screws because the external chassis is usually supplied to you completely assembled. Instead, you only need to plug the host adapter into an expansion slot inside your computer, and then link the external chassis and the adapter with the cable supplied by the manufacturer.

Hard Disk Cards

In 1985, the hard disk makers at Quantum Corporation hit upon an idea with so much promise that they created a new company to develop and promote it. The company was Plus Development Corporation; the idea, the HardCard, essentially a hard disk on a standard-size PC expansion card. Since then, Plus Development has gone on to develop other products, and to be absorbed back into Quantum. Nevertheless, the original idea must still be regarded as inspired. The all-in-one HardCard package eliminated all the hardware worries in installing a hard disk. It required no cables, no bloody knuckles, and no worries about an errant touch on a delicate circuit causing a $100-per-hour repair job. In addition, the HardCard was a perfect fit for systems that had no drive bays available for adding another disk. The original HardCard used a proprietary disk controller and a special low-power, low-profile disk drive, all manufactured by Japanese electronics giant Matsushita Industrial Corporation. In effect, it was the first integrated drive electronics (IDE) product for PCs sold in the consumer market.

The first HardCard was a modest device. Its capacity was 10 megabytes, it performance only on par with the ordinary XT hard disk. And it was expensive, priced at about three times the level of do-it-yourself hard disk systems of equivalent performance and capacity. Since then, Plus has developed the product to capacities beyond 100 megabytes with performance on par with separate hard disk drives. Modern HardCards also use the same 16-bit bus interface as other hard disk host adapters and controllers. To date, however, no Micro Channel hard disk cards have been developed.

Even the low-capacity original HardCard was enough to prove the viability of the combined hard-disk-on-an-expansion-board idea, now generally termed the hard disk card. Several manufacturers followed suit, often simply bolting a short disk controller to a small-format hard disk. Most of these have disappeared from the market as a result of Plus aggressively protecting its patents on the card-in-a-slot concept. In that nearly all new PCs come with a hard disk as standard equipment and most people have now worked up the courage to tackle normal drive installation, the HardCard's particular product niche is becoming small indeed.

HardCards still have their value. They make an ideal supplement to standard equipment drives, one that can be installed even by folks whose manual dexterity is rivaled only by their capability to fly through the air unassisted. They also serve as a convenient way of setting up multiple PCs in a corporation. You can write all the files you want to install on several PCs onto a single HardCard, and transfer all the files (even the file structure) to the native hard disk in each machine. Just plug the master HardCard into each machine in turn and issue a single XCOPY command.

Disk Performance Issues

When shopping for hard disks, many people become preoccupied with disk performance. They believe that some drives find and transfer information faster than others. They're right. But the differences between drives are much smaller than they used to be, and, in a properly set up system, the remaining differences can be almost completely equalized.

The performance of a hard disk is directly related to design choices in making the mechanism. The head actuator has the greatest effect on the speed at which data can be retrieved from the disk with the number of platters exerting a smaller effect. Because the head actuator designs used by hard disk makers have converged, as have the number of platters per drive because of height restrictions of modern form factors, the performance of various products has also converged.

Clearly, however, all hard disks don't deliver the same performance. The differences are particularly obvious when you compare a drive that's a few years old with a current product. Understanding the issues involved in hard disk performance will help you better appreciate the strides made by the industry in the last few years and show you what improvements may still lie ahead.

Average Access Time

You've already encountered the term latency, which indicates the average delay in finding a given bit of data imposed because of the spin of the disk. Another factor also influences how much time elapses between the moment the disk drive receives a request to reveal what's stored at a given place on the disk and when the drive is actually ready to read or write at that place. This is the speed at which the read/write head can move radially from one cylinder to another. This speed is expressed in a number of ways, often as a seek time. Track-to-track seek time indicates the period required to move the head from one track to the next. More important, however, is the average access time (sometimes called average seek time), which specifies how long it takes the read/write head to move on the average to any cylinder (or radial position). Lower average access times, expressed in milliseconds, are better. The type of head actuator technology, the mass of the actuator assembly, the physical power of the actuator itself, and the width of the data area on the disk all influence average access time. Voice-coil actuators are quicker than stepper designs. Lighter actuators have less inertia and can accelerate and settle down faster. A more powerful actuator mechanism can knock around the head assembly with greater alacrity. And the narrower the band on the disk holding information, the shorter the distance the head must travel between tracks.

Real world access times vary by more than a factor of 10. Old technology drives responded with average access times as long as 150 milliseconds. The newest drives are closer to 10 milliseconds. Dual-actuator drives can virtually eliminate the access time required on consecutive read or write requests.

How low an average access time you need depends mostly on your impatience. Quicker is always better. In the past it cost more. Today, however, the differences are smaller and almost inconsequential. The only accepted guidelines are the IBM specifications for its various products. The first hard disk installed in an IBM personal computer resided in the XT and had a specified average access time of 85 milliseconds. The next generation IBM personal computer, the AT, required a drive with an average access time of 40 milliseconds.

With 386 and more recent computers, however, the IBM guidance falls by the wayside. The company has installed drives with various access times in different computer models, so no one figure can offer real guidance. The next performance level of the AT drive is about 28 milliseconds, which serves the first generation of 386-based PCs quite well. Fast 386 machines (25 Mhz and above) and 486SX machines are better served by drives operating in the vicinity of 20 milliseconds. Machines based on the 486DX and better microprocessors can benefit from drives with average access times of 15 milliseconds or better.

Elevator Seeking

Advanced disk controllers, particularly those used in disk arrays, are able to minimize the delays caused by head seeks using a technique called *elevator seeking*. When confronted with several read or write requests for different disk tracks, the controller organizes the requests in the way that moves the head the least between seeks. Like an elevator, it courses through the seek requests from the lower numbered tracks to the higher numbered tracks, and then goes back to the next requests, first taking care of the higher numbered tracks, and then working its way back to the lower numbered tracks. The data gathered for each individual request is stored in the controller and doled out at the proper time.

Elevator seeking improves performance in drive systems that receive multiple requests for data almost simultaneously. DOS, as a single-threaded operating system, cannot take advantage of this access-acceleration technique. DOS requires that each seek request be fulfilled before it sends the next request to the disk. In network systems, however, multiple seek requests can and do occur simultaneously. Elevator seeking can substantially cut the disk access time in such systems.

Data Transfer Rate

Once a byte or record is found on the disk, it must be transferred to the host computer. Another disk system specification, the data transfer rate, reflects how fast bytes are batted back and forth, which is how quickly information can shuttle between microprocessor and hard disk. The transfer rate of a disk is controlled by a number of design factors completely separate from those of the average access time.

Through the years, the factor constraining the transfer rate of particular computer systems has shifted from the host microprocessor to the disk interface to the bus and to the disk drive. For example, the limit on the transfer rate of the original IBM Personal Computer XT was the 8088 microprocessor itself, which was unable to process information as quickly as even the laggardly ST506 interface. PCs based on the 386 microprocessor finally raced ahead of disk and interface performance, so drive manufacturers have begun to concentrate on improving the throughput of these aspects of disk systems.

One limit in transfer rate that cannot be exceeded is the data transfer rate of the interface connecting a hard disk to its host computer. A drive cannot move information faster than the interface allows. The old ST506 interface is the slowest currently in use. Although both RLL and Advanced RLL help speed it up, AT Attachment, SCSI, and ESDI hold greater potential.

The transfer rate of a hard disk is expressed in megahertz (Mhz) or megabytes per second (or M/sec, which is one-eighth the megahertz rate). The old ST506 standard specified a transfer rate of 0.625 M/sec. Using RLL coding boosts the ST506 interface to 0.9375 M/sec. As originally propounded, ESDI delivered a 1.25 M/sec transfer rate, but more advanced products have pushed that value to 3.125 M/sec. With an eight-bit connection, the AT Attachment interface permits a transfer rate of 4 M/sec; with a 16-bit connection, 8 M/sec. The original SCSI connection permitted a 5 M/sec transfer rate. Fast SCSI 2 boosts that to 10 M/sec. Sixteen-bit wide SCSI 2 matches that figure; 32-bit wide SCSI 2 doubles it to 20 M/sec; and 32-bit wide SCSI 2 coupled with Fast SCSI 2 pushes it all the way to 40 M/sec. Remember, of course, that because ST506 and ESDI are device-level interfaces, actual throughput of drives using them will fall to lower values because transfer overhead must be deducted from the raw rates given here (see Chapter 20).

Another interface issue may limit transfer rates below the highest of these values: the host computer bus. The ISA bus has a maximum effective transfer rate of 8 M/sec, and will constrain faster SCSI links. EISA connections can be as high as 33 M/sec; Micro Channel as low as 10 M/sec (16-bit bus operating at 10 Mhz), although a 32-bit Micro Channel connection starts at 20 Mhz and may offer rates as high as 40 M/sec in advanced transfer modes. All local bus links exceed basic disk interface transfer rates.

Note that all of these rates are peak values that cannot be sustained for long periods, so effective transfer rates through bus connections will necessarily be lower than the values given (see Chapter 6).

Today's disk and bus interfaces are rarely the bottlenecks constricting disk transfer rates. Physical factors in the construction of the drive nearly always constrain the transfer rate to a lower value. The primary constraint results from the combination of the speed of a disk's spin and its track density, that is, the number of 512-byte sectors in each track. The faster the platter spins and the denser the data on each track, the more information will pass under the read/write head in a given period. With device-level interfaces, this raw stream of data is what is passed through the interface. The product of spin speed and the capacity of each track yields the raw data rate. Most system-level interfaced drives made through about 1991 were based on the same mechanisms used for the device-level drives, and so achieved the same actual throughputs despite the greater potential of their interfaces. The situation was the equivalent of having a 16-lane interstate highway with only three licensed cars on the road. As manufacturers have turned away from device-level interfaces and concentrated on improving system-level interfaced drives with new designs (such as faster rotation rates, zone-bit recording, and on-disk caching), actual throughputs are rising. The high transfer rates of the most advanced interfaces give engineers substantial growing room, however.

If you check the specification of many SCSI hard disk drives and host adapters, you'll likely see several figures given for transfer rate. For example, a SCSI host adapter may specify the disk-to-adapter transfer rate (5 M/sec) and an adapter-to-host transfer rate (20 M/sec or even 33 M/sec). Without some performance-enhancing feature on the host adapter, the lower figure would be the more accurate representation of the speed you could expect from such a system. However, disk caching on the host adapter will allow such a host adapter to operate near the higher adapter-to-host transfer rate.

Sector Interleave

Back in the days when microprocessors lagged behind hard disk performance, system engineers worried about adequately slowing drive performance to achieve an optimum match with the host PC. Sector interleaving was the primary method of achieving the happiest marriage. Interleave is no longer an issue with most modern hard disks.

The sector interleave of a hard disk refers to the relationship of the logical arrangement of sectors in a track to their actual physical arrangement. For example, sectors might be numbered 1 through 17 and data is stored sequentially in them. But on the disk, consecutively numbered sectors need not be laid next to each other. The actual order is not important to the disk controller because it reads the sector identification (essentially the number assigned the sector) rather than checking the sector position on the disk when it needs to find a particular sector. This mapping between the logical and physical sector locations is determined by the low-level format of the hard disk.

Sector interleaving works by forcing the disk drive to skip a given number of sectors when DOS tells it to read consecutive sectors. For instance, DOS may instruct the drive to read sectors one and two. The hard disk system reads sector one, and then the arrangement of sectors causes it to skip the next six sectors before reading the sector bearing the number two identification. The time that elapses while the six unread sectors pass by gives the host computer a chance to catch up with the disk.

The ratio of the length of a sector to the distance between the start of two logically consecutive sectors is termed the *interleave factor*. Because the length used for measuring interleave is one sector, often only the right-side factor in the ratio is used to describe the interleave. Thus, a disk in which no sectors are skipped would be said to have an interleave factor of 1:1 or simply 1. If five sectors are skipped between each one that's used, the interleave factor would be 1:6 or 6.

Although interleaving would appear to invariably slow the transfer rate of a disk system, the optimum interleave actually helps improve performance. Higher or lower interleave values impair performance, and setting an interleave too low has the most dramatic and deleterious effect. Consider, for example, what happens when a PC is not ready for the next sector being read from the disk, the disk must complete an entire spin before the sector can be read again, typically a delay of about 17 milliseconds (at 3,600 rpm). If skipping one sector is sufficient to give the PC time to catch up, the added delay is only one millisecond (assuming 17 sectors per track). In this case, the proper interleave makes the disk system 17 times faster than not interleaving, a compelling argument for achieving the optimum interleave.

Note that erring on the high side yields less of a penalty than too low of an interleave. Skipping an extra sector delays the next sector read by only 1 millisecond compared to the 17 milliseconds imposed by erring on the low side.

Because of the tremendous penalty for setting interleave factors too low, IBM was perhaps overly conservative in specifying interleave factors for the XT and AT hard disks. The XT used an interleave of 6; the AT, 3. These systems often achieve somewhat better disk performance with lower transfer rates. Specialty programs such as SpinRite (from Gibson Research) will allow you to determine the optimum interleave for the hard disk in your system. Note that while a 1:1 interleave might appear optimum, it rarely is. Most AT and better computers that use hard disks without track buffering typically work best with a interleave factor of 2. Interleave is not an issue with hard disks that have track buffers, which means essentially all modern disks with system-level interfaces (AT Attachment and SCSI) and ESDI drives.

Cylinder Skewing

Although a 1:1 interleave factor sounds like the most desirable, it is not without its problems. After the disk drive head finishes reading one track, it must be repositioned slightly to read the next. As with any mechanical movement, repositioning the head requires a slight time. Although brief, this repositioning period is long enough that should the head try to move from the end of one track to the beginning of another, it will get there too late. Consequently, you have to wait while the whole track passes below the head until it is ready to read the beginning of the second track.

This problem is easily solved by the simple expedient of not aligning the starting points of all tracks along the same radial line. By offsetting the beginning of each track slightly from the end of the preceding track, the travel time of the head can be compensated for. Because the beginning of the first sector of each track and cylinder thus do not line up but are somewhat skewed, this technique is called *track skewing* or *cylinder skewing*.

Track Buffering

With modern hard disks and controllers, interleave has become irrelevant. Control electronics (either on an expansion board or embedded in the drive) use track buffering (on-disk buffer memory that stores the contents of an entire track) to better match the information needs of the host computer. When you send a read request to a controller with a track buffer, it reads the entire disk track no matter how much information you actually need. If you need information from two consecutive sectors, they are read from the controller's buffer independently of the spin of the disk. Disks in track-buffered systems operate best with a 1:1 interleave. Nearly all except the oldest ESDI drives are designed to work with track-buffered controllers, have built-in track buffers, or use some even more advanced transfer optimizing method.

Disk Caching

The ultimate means of isolating your PC from the mechanical vagaries of a hard disk seeking is *disk caching*. Caching eliminates the delays involved in seeking when a read request (or write request in a system that supports write caching) involves data already stored in the cache; the information is retrieved at RAM speed. Similarly, the cache pushes the transfer rate of data stored in the cache up to the ceiling imposed by the slowest interface between the cache and host microprocessor. With an on-disk cache, the drive interface will likely be the primary constraint; with a hardware cache in the disk controller or host adapter, the bus interface is the limit; with a software cache, microprocessor and memory access speed are the only constraints.

Buying a Hard Disk

Because the technical differences between hard disk drives for single-user PCs are converging, you have fewer worries about choosing the right hard disk than ever before. Just about any current (as opposed to close-out) product you buy will deliver excellent performance and a long, trouble-free life. But you face a number of other issues that will help determine which disk to buy and where to buy it from.

Capacity

Undoubtedly the biggest trade-off with hard disks is capacity versus price. The issue is primarily personal: only you can judge what you can afford. The best strategy is to get more than you think you'll need because then it will take you a bit longer to use all the available storage.

Today, only tightwads and those caught in 10-year time warps buy 20- or 40-megabyte drives. These capacities are clearly inadequate for state-of-the-art software. Add in Windows 3.1 and a few of its applications, and you'll be pushing past the limits of a 40-megabyte drive. OS/2 version 2.0 will tax a 60-megabyte drive. In other words, start your thinking at 100 megabytes. You'll probably find the best combination of useful capacity and low cost-per-megabyte in products around 200 megabytes.

Performance

Forget all the nuances of performance unless you're optimizing a network server. Otherwise, invest in a few megabytes of extra RAM for your PC and use a software disk cache. SMARTDRV.SYS, which accompanies current versions of MS-DOS and Windows, will more than compensate for the differences in different hard disks.

System Compatibility

Although it usually comes low on the list of buying concerns, the most important consideration with any hard disk drive is that it work with your PC. Several issues are involved.

If you want an uncluttered life without the need for special software and still want to squeeze the most capacity from your drive, the drive's physical configuration (number of heads and cylinders) must match one of the drive parameters listed in your PC's setup procedure. You'll have to ask the vendor of your hard disk for the head and cylinder count (it's usually not advertised) and match it to the table in your PC's manual or the display you get when selecting a drive type during your PC's setup procedure. You can avoid such problems by opting for a drive with automatic sector translation mode or an advanced installation program.

If you're adding a second hard disk to your system, the best choice is to match your first drive. If you cannot make an exact match, choose the same interface so that you won't need a second drive controller. If, however, you have an ST506 drive in your PC, you'll be better off discarding it and buying a slightly larger AT Attachment drive. The extra bytes will cost you nearly nothing and you'll get better performance with fewer worries.

Remember, an older AT Attachment drive may not be compatible with another manufacturer's product. If your PC has an AT Attachment drive that was made before 1990, the only drive compatible with your existing unit may be its exact twin. More recent products should cooperate without a problem, however.

Some SCSI controllers won't work with specific PCs or disk drives, although the situation is improving. If you opt to go SCSI, you're best off getting a matched drive and controller to assure against compatibility conflicts.

Controller and Host Adapter Issues

If you want to upgrade your PC from an old drive to one that uses a high-performance interface, you'll require a new hard disk controller or host adapter. Don't forget to factor in its price when you consider your new drive. And don't forget that support of the controller is as important as support of your hard disk.

If you want a high-performance interface, resign yourself to ousting your present drive or get your vendor's absolute assurance that your new drive and controller will work while your old unit is also installed in your PC. You want to be sure that you can return the new drive without paying a restocking charge should it prove incompatible. If a vendor doesn't offer you that much assurance, he's not sure the drive will work in your system, and you should share his doubts.

Cables

Make sure that cables are included in any package deal, both as a convenience and to keep costs under control. You don't want to get a new drive on Friday afternoon and not be able to use it till Tuesday because you have to wait for the cables you didn't know you needed to arrive by Pony Express. Remember, bought separately, cables can add $10 to $20 to the cost of your system. That's easily the difference in price between two vendors of the same model hard disk. The one that includes cables with the drive will often be the better buy.

Physical Factors

You don't want to get stuck with a hard disk that has to sit on top of your PC because it doesn't fit inside. Make sure that your system has room for any drive you buy. With 5.25-inch hard disk, the issue is simple—full-height or half-height to fit the drive bay you have available. With 3.5-inch drives, you may have to consider the exact height of the drive in inches to see whether it will fit.

You'll also want to make sure that you have the mounting hardware that you require for your drive. If your system uses standard AT-size hard disk rails, make sure that the drive you order comes with rails. Some vendors will give you a choice of Compaq-size rails, ask for them if you need them.

Don't expect vendors to support more obscure drive mounting schemes; instead, check your system. You'll probably find that its manufacturer had the foresight to put the needed hardware into its vacant drive bays, just waiting for you to make an upgrade.

Drive Reliability

The Mean Time Between Failures (MTBF) of a hard disk gives a general indication of its reliability. Today, the figures are almost ridiculous. Where drives were once rated at about 25,000 hours, most are now rated in the range 100,000 to 160,000 hours; that's 11 to 18 years. Some manufacturers now list their MTBF figures as 300,000 or more hours, 34 years. Your PC (or you, for that matter) should last as long. A long MTBF is an assurance of a long-lasting drive. But you'll also want to consider how the manufacturer backs up its MTBF claim. A 500,000 hour MTBF is meaningless if the manufacturer gives you only a 90-day warranty.

Warranty

Hard disk drives may be warranted by the vendor or the manufacturer. You'll probably depend more on the vendor's warranty, so that should be your first concern.

The easy-to-quantify issue is the length of the warranty. A hard disk warranty should extend for at least 90 days. You'll find that better products, and better vendors, will offer hard disk warranties measured in years.

How that warranty is honored is important. Because you have no control over what happens to a drive that you return for repair, you should prefer a warranty that gives you a replacement drive (at least if the product dies in its first few weeks of life) rather than risking getting your old drive back as a time-bomb, waiting to go off the second the warranty expires.

Manufacturers' warranties are trickier to get a handle on. In general, the warranty period starts when the product is sold to your vendor, not to you, so it may expire sooner than you think. Worse, a manufacturer may choose not to recognize its warranty if you don't buy from an authorized dealer. So it's important to clarify whether you get a manufacturer's warranty when you buy your drive.

At least the drive manufacturer has the facilities for properly handling repairs and a reputation to uphold, so you shouldn't worry about having your drive repaired rather than replaced by the manufacturer.

Support

Depending on the manufacturer of the hard disk, you may have one or two avenues of support for the drive you buy. In most cases, the preferred first choice for support is the vendor who sold you the drive. You'll want to check out what the drive vendor offers.

Before you buy, ask the salesman about the company's support policy. Check to see whether the vendor even has a support telephone number. Because you'll probably install your drive in the evening, you'll want to be sure that the number is staffed at any conceivable hour you might call (say around the clock). Check whether the support line is toll-free and that there are enough people to answer your questions immediately. You don't want to have to wait, perhaps forever, for someone to call you back.

Some vendors depend solely on the drive manufacturer's support staff. Drive makers run a wide range in the support they offer end users. Some won't even talk to you. They deal only with vendors, not with the real users of their products. Others prefer that you start with your dealer, but will help in a pinch. Some have consumer support lines, a few are even toll-free.

Installing a Hard Disk

Once you've selected a hard disk (and are sure that it will work with your system) and have it in your hands, you must physically install it. Hard disk drives fit into bays exactly like any other device (see Chapter 19). The one unique aspect of hard disk installation is the cabling. Each drive interface has its own particular cabling requirements. You'll typically have to deal with two or three cables, each with its own particular concerns.

The Power Cable

All drives require power to run their motors and their control electronics, and most drives, regardless of size or interface, use the same kind of power connection. The primary exceptions are the 3.5-inch hard disks meant for installation in IBM's PS/2 internal drive bays, which have their power and signal connectors integrated into a single plug-in unit. With other drives, the power connection is a standard device power plug, a nylon connector that accommodates four separate wires, one of which is redundant. Note that the AT Attachment standard also recognizes a miniaturized power connector like that used by some 3.5-inch floppy disk drives.

In most PCs, the wires follow a standardized color code (for the most part, exceptions exist). A red wire carries 5 volts of direct current for operating the disk drive logic and control circuitry. An orange wire moves the 12 volts that is used to power the disk drive spindle motor. And a black wire (and often a yellow one) provides the return path, the ground, for the other two voltages.

The nylon connectors are keyed by chamfers on two corners so that you cannot plug them in backwards (or upside down, depending on your perspective) and send the wrong voltage jolting into the circuits of your disk drives.

Proper drive installation requires only that you slide a power connector into your disk drive, ensuring that it seats all the way into the jack on the back of the hard disk. Much effort sometimes is required to slide the plug all the way into the jack. Be careful and prevent undue stress on the drive. Instead of simply pushing the plug into the jack, put one finger on the plug and your thumb on the jack and squeeze the two together.

ST506 and ESDI Cabling

The two popular device-level hard disk interfaces used with PCs share a common cabling system. Originally developed for use with the ST506 interface, the identical cabling scheme was carried over to ESDI. Both involve two cables, a data cable and a control cable.

The Data Cable

In the ST506 and ESDI environment, the hard disk data cable is also quite straightforward. Usually a ribbon cable, it comprises 20 conductors. On the disk drive end, the cable terminates in a female edge connector. To provide the keying that prevents inadvertent reversal, a plastic insert is often placed between the second and third rows of pins in this edge connector, and the mating circuit board edge on the disk drive is slotted between the matching contacts.

Because ribbon cables are polarized and generally marked with a colored leader corresponding to the number one conductor, you should have no problem properly orienting a hard disk data cable even if the plastic key is absent. The colored leader on the edge of the cable that indicates the location of conductor number one always goes to the side of the hard disk contact, the edge of which is closest to the keying slot (see fig. 21.1).

The other end of the cable generally features a header connector that slips over the golden pins of a circuit board header. This end of the cable usually is not keyed, although sometimes a header pin is removed and the corresponding hole in the connector is plugged. Usually the circuit board on which the header is mounted is stenciled with a legend identifying a few pin numbers. The keying stripe on the cable is always oriented toward pin 1 or pin 2, away from pins 19 and 20.

Most hard disk controllers provide headers for plugging in two data cables, one for each disk drive that the controller is capable of operating. Usually these headers are labeled as J3 and J4, and the lower number jack is meant for the first hard disk.

Plugging the data cable into the wrong disk drive controller header is not a fatal error. Although the disk drive system will not operate properly, no damage is likely to result. Symptoms of this condition include the drive seeming to operate properly, rattling its head around and lighting its activity indicator (because the control cable in the proper position ensures the drive does what it is supposed to do), but error messages appear on-screen (because the controller is not receiving data on the pins that it expects to). Moving the cable to the correct header will bring the disk drive to life, barring other problems.

The Control Cable

The signals from the controller that specify what the hard disk drive is supposed to do are relayed through a 34-conductor cable. Much like floppy disk cables, the hard disk control cable is designed to daisy-chain two devices; one end of the cable plugs into the controller, and two connectors are provided for attaching to individual disk drives.

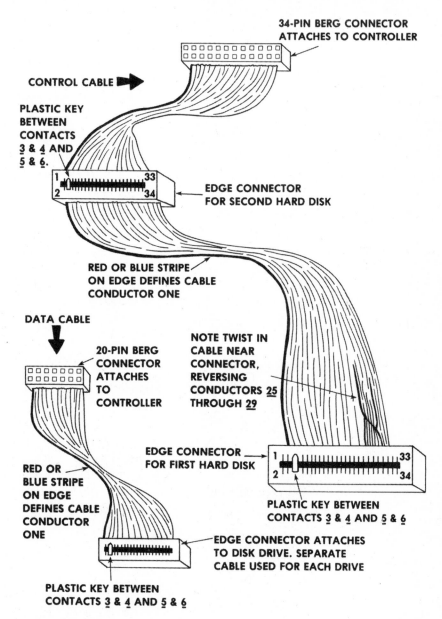

34-PIN BERG CONNECTOR ATTACHES TO CONTROLLER

CONTROL CABLE

PLASTIC KEY BETWEEN CONTACTS 3 & 4 AND 5 & 6.

EDGE CONNECTOR FOR SECOND HARD DISK

RED OR BLUE STRIPE ON EDGE DEFINES CABLE CONDUCTOR ONE

DATA CABLE

20-PIN BERG CONNECTOR ATTACHES TO CONTROLLER

NOTE TWIST IN CABLE NEAR CONNECTOR, REVERSING CONDUCTORS 25 THROUGH 29

RED OR BLUE STRIPE ON EDGE DEFINES CABLE CONDUCTOR ONE

EDGE CONNECTOR FOR FIRST HARD DISK

PLASTIC KEY BETWEEN CONTACTS 3 & 4 AND 5 & 6

EDGE CONNECTOR ATTACHES TO DISK DRIVE. SEPARATE CABLE USED FOR EACH DRIVE

PLASTIC KEY BETWEEN CONTACTS 3 & 4 AND 5 & 6

Figure 21.1. ST506 and ESDI cables.

IBM's hard disk daisy-chain scheme is reminiscent of that used by floppy disks, and the hard disk control cable is very similar to the floppy disk control-and-data cable. For instances, both cables have several conductors twisted near the first disk drive connector, that is, the connector that is plugged into what DOS recognizes as drive C:. The connector in the middle of the cable, without the twist, gets plugged into drive D:.

Despite the similarity of the cable twist, hard disk control cables and floppy disk control-and-data cables are not the same. Each of these two species of disk drive cables twists different conductors in the ribbon cable. Substituting one for the other will not be successful.

If you have a number of loose, uninstalled floppy control-and-data hard disk control cables, to avoid confusion you should plainly identify the nature of each one. One good strategy is to use an indelible ink marker to label the drive connectors with the proper identifying letters, A and B for floppy cables, C and D for hard disk cables. Or mark on the ribbon cable itself "floppy" or "hard disk."

Drive Select Jumpers

Every hard disk must be uniquely definable by the system that it is resident in. Although DOS uses drive letters, such as the familiar C:, the drive letter is only a logical identification. The hardware of your system also requires a unique physical identification for each drive. Every ST506 and ESDI hard disk is thus assigned a device number or a drive select number, much as floppy disks are. Device numbers generally are selected by jumpers or DIP switches located on the hard disk itself.

Special Cabling Concerns

No matter the drive letter that DOS assigns to a hard disk, the IBM ST506 and ESDI hard disk scheme requires that each hard disk be set up as the second hard disk drive. For hard disks that start numbering with device one, an IBM hard disk must be number two. For hard disks that start numbering with zero, an IBM hard disk must be set as number one.

Both drives in a system are thus set with the same device number. The control cable takes care of distinguishing one drive from another. The twist in the cable makes the drive plugged into the connector at the end of the cable appear to the system as the first drive. The other disk, set up as the second drive and connected by a length of cable without a twist, appears exactly as it should, as the second drive.

No hard and fast rule says you must obey the IBM scheme. As long as you know what you're doing, you can use a straight-through or twisted cable, as your heart leads you. The secret to success is knowing how to set the drive select jumpers on your hard disk for your particular configuration.

To use a straight-through control cable to connect a single hard disk to your IBM standard controller, you must set the drive select jumper on the disk drive to reflect it as being the first drive in your system. To daisy-chain two hard disks on a single control cable that does not have a twist before the last connector on the cable, set the drive you want to be recognized as C: as the lowest drive select number in your system; the drive to be recognized as D: as the second-lowest drive select.

Using More Than Two Hard Disks

Most ST506 and some ESDI hard disks support drive select values in excess of two. The IBM cabling scheme never uses these settings. Instead, the system favored by IBM and most compatible makers uses separate disk drive controllers for each pair of hard disks. With AT interface drive, you must do likewise with host adapters. SCSI host adapters will allow up to seven disks or other devices to be connected. However, you can connect fewer, connect a second host adapter for more than seven drives, or use a separate host adapter for each drive, should you want (and have incendiary currency in your pocket).

The hard disks attached to each controller or host adapter are assigned drive select numbers, SCSI IDs, or whatever in exactly the same way it would be in a two-drive system. With standard IBM cabling (a twist in the control cable near the connector for drive C), both drives connected to each controller are jumpered as the second physical hard disk in the system.

The different drive-select numbers assigned to each hard disk, either through jumpers or the cable twist, merely serve to distinguish the two units at the controller. Drive letter assignments are actually issued by DOS.

DOS follows a strict order in assigning drive letters, starting by giving the letter C: to the first hard disk (or other device) it finds in its logical search. This search begins with reading through the system BIOS, and then progresses through the device drivers in the system's CONFIG.SYS file.

The BIOS search involves not just the firmware contained in the system or planar board ROM but also the code in add-in peripheral expansion boards including any hard disk controllers. Most disk controllers assign a memory address of C8000(hex) to the start of the code they contain; most also allow you to set an alternate address of D8000(hex). Memory is searched sequentially, so the drives attached to the controller with the lower starting address —C8000(hex) in this case—will be detected first and eventually assigned the first hard disk drive letters. When the controller using memory starting at the D8000(hex) address are found, they will be assigned the next available drive letters, regardless of their drive select settings. Note that when only a single disk controller is present and it is assigned the secondary base address of D8000(hex), it will be the first to be recognized. The drive or drives connected to it will be issued DOS assignments starting with C.

The general rule is that drive select jumpers (and cable twists) distinguish the hard disks attached to a given controller, and base memory addresses distinguish controllers.

AT Attachment Cabling

The AT Attachment scheme simplifies cabling in other ways. All the signals in the cable are extended to each of the two drives that potentially can be attached to a single host connector. Both drives that can be connected to a host AT Attachment port through the cable receive exactly the same signals on the same pins. No weird twists in the ribbon cable are used to distinguish the drives from one another as is required in IBM's ST506 and ESDI connection arrangements. Instead, the signals to and from individual AT Attachment-interfaced drives are distinguished by control signals and timing.

Multiple Drives

When two drives are connected to a single AT Attachment port, they do not behave as equals, however. One drive is designated the master, the other is the slave. However, the master is master only in nomenclature. The master drive does not control the slave. Its only superior function is to perform signal decoding for both drives in the two-drive system.

All AT Attachment drives hold the potential for being master or slave. The function of each is determined by jumper settings on the drive itself. With a jumper in one position, a drive will act as the master. In another position, it will be a slave.

Only one master and one slave are permitted in a single AT Attachment connection, so each of the two drives in a single AT Attachment chain must have its master/slave jumpers properly set for the system to work. Most drives are shipped jumpered for operation as the master, so you'll only have to adjust the second AT Attachment drive you add to the short chain.

Terminations

AT Attachment drives do not normally require you to adjust terminations when you install them as you need to do with ST506 or ESDI drives. In the AT Attachment design, terminations are unnecessary. Exactly like plugging expansion cards into an expansion bus, the AT Attachment bus is designed to be properly loaded with any of its possible loads—zero, one, or two drives. Essentially, then, AT Attachment installation means that you plug in your hard disks. That's about all.

SCSI Connections

Putting together a SCSI system has its own set of concerns. You need to set SCSI identification numbers, link together all the drives, and properly terminate the entire chain of devices.

SCSI ID Numbers

SCSI allows you to connect its seven devices in any order simply by chaining them together in any order. To distinguish one device from another, SCSI requires that you assign each one a unique SCSI ID number in the range 0 to 6. (The host adapter is automatically device 7.)

Most external SCSI devices are assigned their ID number by a push button or rotary switch on the rear panel of the equipment. Internal SCSI devices, such as hard disks, typically have several jumpers or switches that set their SCSI ID. The most basic rule is simple: the SCSI ID number must be unique, so never assign to two or more devices in the same SCSI chain the same ID number.

Although the SCSI standard itself allows complete freedom in assigning SCSI ID numbers (the only difference between them is that higher numbers get higher priority during arbitration), some host adapter software developers are more rigid in their SCSI ID requirements. Most host adapters that have Western Digital WD1002 controller emulation built into their boot ROMs require that any SCSI drive meant to boot your PC uses the ID number 0. In any case, you should check the SCSI ID of all of the SCSI devices connected to your host adapter when you install a new hard disk to avoid conflicts.

SCSI Cabling

Because SCSI is a bus, you connect devices by daisy-chaining. That is, you run a straight cable (no twists like the ST506) from the host adapter to each SCSI device.

Internal SCSI devices like hard disks use a simple flat ribbon cable with multiple connectors attached to it. All connectors have identical signals, so you can use any convenient connector for any SCSI device. The devices and host adapter use SCSI ID numbers to sort out which commands and data go where.

External SCSI cabling is somewhat different. You run a cable from the host adapter to the first device in the external SCSI chain. For the next device, you plug another cable into the first device, and then plug the other end of the cable into the second device. Just continue in the same manner adding another cable for each additional device.

Most external SCSI devices have two SCSI connectors to facilitate such daisy-chaining. It doesn't matter which of the two connectors on the SCSI device to which you attach each cable. Functionally, both connectors are the same; each is equally adept at handling incoming and outgoing signals.

Under the SCSI standard, there must be at least 0.3 meters of cable between any two external SCSI devices. The total length of all cables in the SCSI chain should be no more than six meters. External SCSI cables should be shielded.

The standard SCSI connector has 50 pins and looks like an enlarged Centronics printer connector. A few host adapters and some external SCSI devices use 25-pin D-shell connectors (like the parallel ports on the back of your PC). You'll need an adapter cable to match these devices. It's best to put any 25-pin SCSI device at the end of the SCSI daisy-chain.

After you finish connecting your SCSI cables and terminating your daisy-chain, you'll want to be sure to snap in place the retaining clips or wires on each SCSI connector to be sure each connector is held securely in place. This mechanical locking is particularly important with SCSI connections because the wiring works like old-fashioned Christmas lights, if one goes out, they all go out. Not only will whatever SCSI device that has a loose connector be out of touch, all other devices after the loose connector in the chain will also lose communication. Moreover, because the chain will no longer be properly terminated, even the devices earlier in the chain may not work reliably. Locking the wire on each SCSI connector will help assure that none of the connectors accidentally gets loosened.

SCSI Terminations

Eventually, your SCSI daisy-chain will come to an end. You'll have one last device to which you have no more peripherals to connect. To prevent spurious signals bouncing back and forth across the SCSI cable chain, the SCSI standard requires that you properly terminate the entire SCSI system. The three most popular means of terminating SCSI devices are internally with resistor packs, externally with dummy termination plugs, and using switches. Resistor packs are components attached directly to circuit boards, such as with ST506 and ESDI drives. Unlike the other interfaces, SCSI devices typically use three (instead of one) resistor packs for their terminations. Most PC-based SCSI host adapters and hard disks come with termination resistors already installed on them.

You can easily identify terminating resistors as three identical components about an inch long and one-quarter to three-eights inch high and hardly an eighth of an inch thick. Most commonly, these resistor packs are red, brownish yellow, or black and shiny, and they are located adjacent the SCSI connector on the SCSI device or host adapter. When necessary, you remove these terminations simply by pulling them out of their sockets on the circuit board.

External SCSI terminators are plugs that look like short extensions to the SCSI jacks on the back of SCSI devices. One end of the terminator plugs into one of the jacks on your SCSI device, and the other end of the dummy plug yields another jack that could be attached to another SCSI cable. Some external terminators, however, lack the second jack on the back. Generally, the absence of a second connector is no problem because the dummy plug should only be attached to the last device in the SCSI chain.

Switches, the third variety of termination, may be found on both external and internal drives. Sometimes a single switch handles the entire termination, but occasionally a SCSI drive will have three banks of DIP switches that all must be flipped to the same position to select whether the termination is active. These switches are sometimes found on the SCSI device itself or on the case of an external unit.

A few external SCSI devices rely on the terminators on the drive inside their cases for their terminations. For these you'll have to take apart the device to adjust the terminators.

According to the SCSI specification, the first and last device in a SCSI chain must be terminated. The first device is almost always the SCSI host adapter in your PC. If you install a single internal hard disk to the host adapter, it will be the other end of the chain and thus require termination. Similarly, a single external hard disk will also require termination.

With multiple devices connected to a single host adapter, the termination issue becomes complex. Generally, the host adapter will be one end of the SCSI chain, except when you have both internal and external devices connected to it. Only then should you remove the terminators from your host adapter. In that case, the device nearest the end of the internal SCSI cable should be terminated, as should the external device at the end of the daisy-chain of cables, the only external device that likely has a connector without a cable plugged into it. Remove or switch off the terminators on all other devices.

Hard Disk Setup

Once a drive is physically installed and cabled in place, you must let your computer know what you've done. With PCs, XTs, and third-party systems with disk parameters encoded into firmware, you needn't do anything. The firmware sends the proper message to the system and lets it know what's going on. With ATs and later computers, however, you must take positive steps to set up your system for a new hard disk.

AT Drive Types

Starting with the AT (and the XT Model 286), IBM increased your hard disk choices by storing disk configuration information in a different way. Fifteen configurations are built into the hard disk BIOS, and half a byte of CMOS storage is used as a pointer to indicate which set of parameters are to be used. These configurations are in the same form as disk parameters, and they should match the parameters of the disk you choose to use.

When you run the AT Setup program, you're inserting the proper information for the disk drive you have into this special memory location. Each of the two drives that the standard IBM controller supports can be any of the drive types in the list. Mixing drive types is, indeed, permitted.

Later IBM and compatible computers have expanded the different configurations that are predefined in the memory of the controller and have necessarily expanded the CMOS pointer storage to a full byte. These systems, too, allow you to connect two different drive types to a single controller.

IBM is generally consistent about what numbers it assigns to each drive type. The first 15 types used by the AT retain their numbers even in the wider collections available in later machines.

Although compatible computer manufacturers usually copied IBM for the first 15 drive type choices, many makers went in their own directions for the later extrapolations. Indeed, many began to offer a wider choice of hard disk types even before IBM. The parameters are specific to each BIOS incarnation and vary among manufacturers and sometimes among system models. In general, you can check your various drive options by running the setup program provided with your PC, either on a setup disk or built into its BIOS.

Unsupported Drives

You can work around this lack of support for the drive you want to add in several ways. The easiest is to use a drive with automatic sector translation, which will make the best match possible as long as you set your system up for the correct capacity. Otherwise, matching an unsupported drive will require extra software or foregoing some of the capacity of your drive.

Special drive installation software, such as On-Track Computer System's Disk Manager and Storage Dimension's SpeedStor, set up software drivers to match unsupported disks to your system. Run the installation software and select the proper disk model from a menu, and the match is automatically made. The only shortcoming to this software setup system is that it works only with DOS.

If you can come close to matching your drive's parameters, however, you can generally get a specific hard disk to work by matching the drive type number of a unit with fewer cylinders than the drive you have. For instance, if you have a drive with 1,224 cylinders, choose a drive type with the same number of heads as your new drive but with 1,024 cylinders. The penalty for this expedient is a loss of capacity: other 200 cylinders will not be accessible on your system.

Similarly, you can specify fewer heads than your system actually has, but in such a case you're likely to give up much more capacity to make a match. Do this only as a last resort.

Drive Activity Indicator

Nearly all hard disks have a drive activity indicator, a small red or green LED that glows when the drive is being accessed by your system. If you're installing a new hard disk into some systems, however, you may notice that this LED lights as soon as you switch on the power to your system and stays on all the time. Most of the time this constant glow is not an indication of a problem. Rather, it results from the IBM AT hard disk design.

All IBM computers with internal hard disk mounting allow for a front panel drive activity indicator. In every case, the signal that controls this indicator is derived from the hard disk controller and not the disk drive itself, so it reflects what the controller tells the drive to do and not what the drive is actually doing. The controller makes the drive think that it is constantly selected and active, causing the constant glow of its light. If a red light inside your computer bothers you, you can often disconnect the LED on the drive or clip one of its leads.

Hard Disk Formatting

A new hard disk is like a newborn babe: although some capabilities are built-in, its mind and memory are essentially blank. It has to learn about the world before it can do what it was designed for. For example, many drives must construct the individual sectors that they use for storage from the undifferentiated lengths of individual tracks.

Much like floppy disk drives, the organization of a hard disk drive is called its *format*. Hard disks differ from floppies in that two levels of organization wear the same title, the low-level format and the DOS format. Both are necessary to use a disk under DOS, but each has its own role and requires its own procedure to set up.

Low-Level Formatting

All drives must have their sectors individually defined on each track. Hard disks with device-level interfaces typically came with their tracks and cylinders predefined, either by the steps of its stepper motor head actuator or by the servo tracks on the servo platter of a voice-coil actuated drive, but the sectors were nowhere to be seen or sensed. Before data can be written on such a disk, the sectors have to be marked to serve as guideposts so that the information can later be found and retrieved. The process by which sectors are defined on the hard disk is called *low-level formatting* because it occurs at a control level below the reaches of normal DOS commands.

Creating a low-level format requires running a low-level formatting program. Some versions of DOS shipped with IBM-compatible computers include such a program with names like LLFORMAT or HDPREP. Most disk diagnostic programs also include low-level formatting routines. Low-level formatters for pre-1987 IBM Personal Computers were included with the Advanced Diagnostics programs that IBM sold to accompany its PC and AT systems. The low-level formatting program for PS/2-series machines is included on the reference disk that accompanies each computer, but it is hidden. To use this low-level formatting program, boot your PS/2 from its Reference Diskette. At the first screen where you are asked to press Enter to continue, press the Enter key. You should then see the Main Menu, which offers you seven menu selections. Ignore them. Instead, press the Ctrl and A keys (Ctrl-A) simultaneously. Your machine will then load its Advanced Diagnostics. You can choose the low-level format routine from the menu.

Many of the manufacturers of aftermarket ST506 and ESDI hard disk controllers include the necessary program for low-level formatting a hard disk connected to their product in the controller's ROM firmware. These routines are normally executed through the GO command of the DOS DEBUG program. For instance, a number of these routines are accessed by typing the following instruction at the DEBUG hyphen prompt:

    G=C800:5

If you try this with your controller and it doesn't work, you'll likely lock up your system. If it works, you'll be prompted on the screen. The built-in low-level formatting routines of some vary a few bytes in position in their add-in BIOSs. You may want to try starting execution at C800:6 or C800:8 if the first example does not work. Other than locking up your computer, you won't do any damage. In particular, you won't hurt any data on a new hard disk because there's nothing there to begin with.

Most hard disk drives with system-level interfaces (which means most hard disks) now come with their low-level formats already in place. Some don't even permit low-level formatting—for example, AT Attachment drives that may use sector translation that makes the actual geometry of the drive indecipherable by your PC. The manufacturers of these drives assume that once the hard disk is formatted at the factory, it never needs to be formatted again.

Formatting for Disk Rejuvenation

As noted in Chapter 19, all magnetic media tend to deteriorate with age. That is, the flux transitions in the hard disk medium tend to get weaker as time passes. As soon as a flux transition is written, it gradually loses strength. Eventually, it can become weak enough to be ambiguous and result in an error when it is read. The flux transitions in the data areas of your hard disk get rejuvenated every time you write to them, starting their long trek to deterioration all over again. The low-level format information is written once and never gets rejuvenated, at least if you don't low-level format your disk again.

Some people believe that low-level formatting their disk periodically will increase its reliability and help forestall disk errors. In fact, with older drives that permit it, a low-level format can eliminate disk errors. Backing up such a drive and running its low-level format program once every couple of years is an excellent idea, even if it doesn't prolong the life of the disk, the backup you make may become valuable should disaster strike your system. Newer drives use higher coercivity media that are more resistant to age deterioration. Most disk makers believe that low-level format rejuvenation is no longer necessary with their current products.

Bad Tracks and Sectors

In the manufacture of hard disk platters, defects occasionally occur in the magnetic medium. These defects will not properly record data. Sectors in which these defects occur are called bad sectors; the tracks containing the sectors are called bad tracks.

Your computer can deal with bad sectors by locking them out of normal use. During the low-level formatting process, the sectors that do not work properly are recorded and your system is prevented from using them. The only ill effect of reserving these bad sectors is that the available capacity of your hard disk may diminish by a small amount.

Some low-level formatting programs require that you enter bad sector data before you begin the formatting process. Although this seems redundant (the format program will check for them anyhow), it's not. Factory checks for bad sectors are more rigorous than the format routine. This close scrutiny helps minimize future failure. Tedious as it is, you should enter the bad sector data when the low-level format program calls for it. The listing of bad sectors is usually on a sheet of paper accompanying the disk drive or on a label affixed to the drive itself.

The only time when a bad sector is an evil thing is when it occurs on the first track of the disk. The first track (Track 0) is used to hold partition and booting data. This information must be located on the first track of the disk. If it cannot be written there, the disk won't work.

Should you get a hard disk with a bad Track 0, return it to the dealer from whom you bought it. If you reformat a disk after a head crash and discover that Track 0 is bad during the format process, you need a new disk.

Partitioning

Once the low-level format is in place on a hard disk, you must partition it. Partitioning is a function of the operating system. Partitioning sets up the logical structure of the hard disk in a form that is compatible with the operating system.

The IBM program for partitioning is called FDISK. After low-level formatting your disk, you must run FDISK before you can do anything else with the disk using the DOS (or OS/2) operating system.

DOS Formatting

The final step in preparing a disk for use is formatting it with the operating system you intend to use. With DOS, that means running the FORMAT program. The current DOS FORMAT program does not overwrite the data areas of a hard disk (which means it won't rejuvenate them). It simply refreshes the file allocation table. (That's why you can unformat disks. By storing a copy of the FAT elsewhere on the disk, the unformatting program can reconstruct the FAT to find all the files hidden by the DOS formatting operation.)

Note that IBM operating systems are backward-compatible but not forward-compatible. If you format a hard disk under DOS 5.0 and you boot from a floppy with DOS 3.3 on it, you may not be able to read your hard disk. You will either get an error message or see strange things on your screen, such as file names consisting of odd combinations of numbers and smiley faces. Never write to a hard disk using a version of DOS that is earlier than the format on the disk. If you do, the disk will be irreparably damaged.

22

Optical
Storage

Optical storage technologies promise a unique mixture of permanence, removable cartridges, and high capacities. Four different systems are available—CD ROM, WORM, rewritable optical, and Floptical drives—and each has its own role. None currently can take the place of other mass storage devices, but each has its own unique virtues that promise a long run on the PC playbill.

If the best advice for a young graduate in the '60s was "plastics," the prime opportunity for a naive youth today would be optics. Controlled beams of light promise to revolutionize nearly every industry. In fact, claims for the application of light go so far as curing cancer.

Plastics was sage but safe advice in the '60s because the potential had already been proven. The same holds true for optics. Light waves have already joined electrical signals in carrying long-distance traffic. Lasers have taken over from radar the role of the speeder's arch-nemesis on superhighways. And His Master's Voice is now more regularly unwound optically from spinning CDs than from the black vinyl phonograph records of ages gone by.

In the computer field, optical threatens long-established magnetic storage not with one but four different technologies—the CD ROM, WORM, rewritable optical, and Floptical disk drives. Each is optimized for a specific role in PCs, and each has advantages that old magnetic media are hard-pressed to match.

Chief among these is storage density. Beams of laser light can simply be focused to sharper points than can magnetic fields (which typically are not focused at all). Already, optical devices achieve on the order of 10 times more storage in a given area than can magnetic drives. On the horizon are new optical techniques that promise to push storage densities 100 times higher than today without even focusing the light.

Optical storage can also be permanent. Most optical storage media are rated for ten or more years of error-free storage. Expected lifetimes stretch into the centuries—far, far longer than anyone would trust the vagaries of magnetic storage.

Optical storage media and drives are also rugged. There's no need for low-flying magnetic read/write heads, no contact between the medium and the read/write mechanism most of the time, and an inherent ability to look beyond surface damage to the data stored safely within the medium.

Surprisingly, however, in this age of comparisons with the speed of light—the ultimate highest velocity in the universe—optical storage systems suffer most from performance deficits. Even the best optical systems lag far behind their magnetic equivalents. So far, optical has not become the highest-speed storage system, but the other virtues are sufficient to earn one or more optical systems a place in your PC.

Of the four common optically based storage systems for PCs, three of them (CD ROM, WORM and rewritable optical) are best distinguished by the means, mechanism, and party which puts data onto each disk. Floptical drives achieve the same end as rewritable optical drive (in fact, they are rewritable optical drives) but are mechanically distinct. The means by which the data are recorded determines how you can use each optical storage system.

CD ROMs require that all the data they store come prerecorded on the disk. The CD ROM drives that you slide into your PC can only read what's recorded on disk. That is, after all, how the medium earned its name. It's Read-Only Memory. As such, it can be a perfect distribution mechanism, allowing a publisher to stamp out multiple copies of important files (anything from programs to databases to image or sound files) and distribute them to millions of waiting PCs.

WORM drives give you the ability to write data into optical storage. But like stone tablets carved for the ages, the WORM can never change. What you write becomes a permanent record, your mark for posterity. If you need to keep archives or make an unalterable audit trial, no medium keeps you as honest as WORM.

Rewritable optical drives are the optician's answer to the hard disk. As with magnetic hard disk drives, you can read or write at random to the rewritable optical drive, megabytes at a time. The only difference is that the rewritable optical drive augments the magnetic recording method with a focused light beam that allow it to record smaller bits on a tougher recording medium.

Floptical drives are to ordinary floppy disk drives as rewritable optical drives are to conventional magnetic hard disk drives. Again, the recording mechanism remains magnetic, but the fine-focusing of light helps squeeze ever more data onto a thin, flexible diskette.

CD ROM

As its name implies, CD ROM is fundamentally an adaptation of the Compact Disc digital audio recording system—rock and roll comes to computer storage. As with conventional audio Compact Discs, digital data is written to a CD ROM master disk using special recording equipment that blasts microscopic pits on the surface of a disk. The information encoded in the pits can be read simply by detecting changes in reflectivity (the pits are darker than background of the shiny silver disk).

Because these data pits are a mechanical feature, merely dimples in the disk, their tiny patterns of encoded information can be duplicated on millions of disk copies using pressing equipment similar to that used to squeeze out old-fashioned vinyl LP albums. Once a CD ROM disk is pressed, however, the data it holds cannot be altered. The pits are present for eternity.

Sometimes the terms rewritable CD ROM and read-only CD ROM pop up in the media. Note that these words are self-contradictions—something that's rewritable can't be read-only (as in the acronym ROM). While some systems have been proposed that allow you to write your own CDs—notably Tandy Corporation's long-promised THOR and Sony's miniaturized recordable CDs promised for 1992 release—these are not a ROM at all but rewritable systems enhanced with the capability of reading CDs. The name CD ROM indicates the origins and purpose of the system. CD stands for Compact Disc, the audio playback choice of the current generation of stereo fanciers. ROM stands for Read Only Memory. Like the ROM chips inside your PC, CD ROM disks store digital information in unalterable form. The CD ROM is a source of digital code designed for delivery and not recording.

Whereas conventional read-only memory is based on special stamp-sized slices of silicon, CD ROM uses a silvery spinning disk about five inches in diameter. That disk bears more than a superficial resemblance to the CDs that spin in your stereo system. In fact, the disks and the bits stored on them are much the same. The primary difference between audio and computer CDs is the content of the information that's stored, not the mechanism or means. Both stereo system CDs and CD ROMs record digital information. The stereo system CD player translates the digital code into the analog music (or something that passes for music among the cognoscenti) that pounds out of loudspeakers. The digital noise on the CD ROM stays digital and is processed in that form by your PC.

The audio CDs and CD ROM discs are so similar that most CD ROM systems that work with your PC will, in fact, play the music CDs in your collection—if you have the right program to control the disk player. Music playback abilities are built into most computer CD ROM players. Many even have headphone jacks on their front panels or audio outputs on the back to provide for your listening as well as data processing enjoyment. Most manufacturers include the necessary audio playback software with the CD ROM players that they provide for PCs.

The reciprocal is not true, however. Audio CD players generally will not play CD ROM medium—at least they won't reveal the contents of the CD ROM in any recognizable form (other than audio noise). Getting access to the data on a CD ROM disk requires a computer CD ROM player.

Computer CD ROM players are more expensive than stereo models because retrieving computer data is more demanding. A tiny musical flaw that might pass unnoticed even by trained ears could have disastrous consequences in a data stream. Misreading a decimal point as a number, even zero, can have disastrous consequences on calculations (except, perhaps, if you're calculating your own paycheck). To minimize, if not eliminate, such problems computer CD ROM players have error correction circuitry that's much more powerful than that built into stereo equipment. In addition, CD ROM players require a special kind of remote control—the ability to execute the commands issued by your PC. By itself, the computer CD ROM player does nothing but spin its disk. Your computer must tell the player what information to look for and read out. And your computer is needed to display—visually and aurally—the information the CD ROM player finds, be it text, a graphic image, or a musical selection. Fortunately, CD ROM disks are designed to be an interchangeable medium; you need only one CD ROM player for as many disks as you want to use. Much like the one in your stereo system, the computer CD ROM player allows you to interchange disks, so one player allows access to an entire library of CD ROM media.

The similarity between stereo and computer CDs extends to function as well. As with music CDs, the digital CDs for your computer are foremost a publishing medium. Just as newspapers, books, videos, and records provide a means through which you can carry home entertainment and information in a convenient form, so does the CD ROM.

The CD ROM medium is perfectly suited to this application. The disks themselves are easy to manufacture—they can be made on the same presses as music discs—and inexpensive compared to more traditional publishing processes. The capacity of the typical CD ROM disk is huge, however, making paper publishing look like a product of the Dark Ages. A single CD holds up to 600 megabytes—the equivalent of 300,000 pages of text, about 150 full-length books.

Media

The heart of the CD ROM system is the disk itself. The CD ROM system just doesn't make sense without the availability of disks with data already stored upon them. Because you can't write to a CD ROM, you can't do anything with the drive unless you have something to read. In other words, a CD ROM player is not something to buy in the abstract—you must have some software in mind that you want to slide into it. After all, if nothing but Hawaiian music was available on audio CD, who but the most dedicated or depraved listeners would buy a player?

CD ROM disks are available in wide variety, though not yet for everyone's tastes. There is great potential for growth because of how inexpensive and easy to duplicate the disks are.

CD ROM disks store information exactly the same way it's stored on the CDs in your stereo system, only instead of getting up to 75 minutes of music, a CD ROM disk holds hundreds of megabytes of data. That data can be anything from simple text to SuperVGA images, to programs, and the full circle back to music for multimedia systems.

The silver disk puts digital data into optical form. The digital data on audio or computer CD ROM is coded as pattern of bits represented by the presence or absence of light absorbing pits beneath the surface of the CD. The overall CD is shiny and reflects light well; the pits don't. A laser beam is focused on the disk and reflects back into a photodetector, which can tell the difference in the brightness of the reflection of a pit or unharmed disk. The pattern of bits codes digital data.

The pits in the CDs that you slide into your player—whether a music disc or a data disk—are embossed (or stamped) in place. That was one of the appeals of the original audio CD system to record manufacturers. CD disks are manufactured in basically the same way as old-fashioned vinyl albums. First, a disk master is recorded on a special machine with a high-powered laser that blasts the pits in a blank recording master. The master is made into a mold that is then used to stamp out copies of the original CD much like dies are used to stamp out coins. One a CD is stamped, its surface is aluminized to reflect light (except where the pits are), and a clear plastic cover is applied over the entire surface to protect the pits from chemical and physical abuse (oxidation and scratches). The principal differences between the CD and phonograph record manufacture are that the CD has only one recorded side, and the details are finer.

Actually, the precision of the CD manufacturing process isn't a significant part of the cost of the disk. Most of the price is attributable to the cost of the data on the disk, the royalty that's paid to the people who create, compile, or confuse the information that's to be distributed. You pay a similar price for the data that's stored in books, but for your book purchase you get something bigger and more tangible—it feels like it should be worth more.

While the costs of manufacturing a single book or CD ROM disk are on the same order of magnitude, CD ROMs appear to give you less for more because they hold so much information. Data weighs more in book form, so those who buy by the pound think books are the better value. On a fact-for-fact and pennies-per-fact basis, however, CD ROMs are substantially less expensive than books. The data is just as valuable; it's just less tangible.

CDs are long-lived for two reasons. First, the protective clear plastic layer prevents abuse (in fact, CDs are more vulnerable to scratches on their label side than the side that is scanned with the playback laser), and because the system is designed so that nothing actually touches the playback surface of the CD. The data pits are sealed within layers of the disk itself and are never touched by anything other than a light beam—they never wear out, and acquire errors only when you abuse the disks purposely or carelessly (for example, by scratching them against one another when not storing them in their plastic jewel boxes). Although error correction prevents errors from showing up in the data, a bad scratch can prevent a disk from being read at all.

For the distribution of digital information—music or data—the Compact Disc is typically the most affordable alternative for moving hundreds of megabytes to thousands of locations. This low cost makes the CD ROM the premiere digital publishing medium. Hundreds of CD ROM titles are available, each one holding an encyclopedia of data.

Players

If there is any weak link in the CD ROM system, it is the players. CD ROM players set the rate at which information encoded on the CD ROM can be found and transferred. And those rates are slow, indeed.

The basic problem underlying this laggardly performance is the audio origins of the CD ROM system. The needs of playing back music and retrieving data are entirely different. Music requires a data transfer rate that's slow by data processing measures. One goal in designing high-fidelity music systems is adequate playing time. The CD was designed to accommodate moderate-length classical music compositions—that meant playing just over an hour to accommodate Beethoven's Ninth Symphony. Spread 600 megabytes over 60 minutes, and you get a data transfer rate of 166Kb/second. Allow for overhead (such as formatting information) and the rate is even lower. Hardly coincidentally, the net data transfer rate of most CD ROM players is 150Kb/sec.

It gets worse. To cram as much music as possible on each Compact Disc, the system uses constant linear velocity recording. That is, the spin rate of the disk platter varies depending on how far the read/write head is located from the center of the disk. As the head moves from track to track, the spin rate of the disk changes. With music, which is normally played sequentially, that's no problem. The speed difference between tracks is tiny, and the drive can quickly adjust for it. Make the CD system into a random-access mechanism, and suddenly speed changes become a big issue. The drive might have to move its head from the innermost to outermost track, requiring a drastic speed change. The inertia of the disk spin guarantees a wait while the disk spins up or down. Moreover, the optical head of the CD system is substantially more massive than the flyweight mechanisms of hard disks—that means a longer wait for the head to settle into place. Add these factors together, and the average access time of a CD ROM player can be as high as 300 milliseconds.

The slow speed of CD ROMs may gradually improve. NEC has already introduced a double-speed player. By spinning disks at twice the rate of other CD ROM players, the new drives boost the data transfer rate of the CD ROM system to 300Kb/second with no change in the media. Although the data rate still may seem small, dramatic improvements can be seen in the performance of digital video and animation systems that have their data recorded on CD ROM.

There is a good side to the audio foundation of CD ROM technology. CD ROM players have inherited a lot of convenience features from their audio siblings. For instance, many machines accept disks exactly like stereos do—with drawers that slide out at the press of a button. Just lay your disk in the drawer, press the button again, and it's loaded.

Some CD ROM players make the job even easier. You load your disks into a special carrier that resembles the plastic jewel-box case that most commercial music CDs come in. When you want to load a disk into the CD ROM player, you slide the whole carrier into a waiting slot. Most people buy a carrier for each CD ROM disk they have because of this convenience and the extra protection the carrier affords the disk—no scratches and no fingerprints, guaranteed! CD ROM changes use multiple-disk cartridges exactly like those used by audio CD changers.

Software

Once a CD ROM player is properly installed in your computer system, you can access the disk you slide in as if it were just another DOS drive. The CD ROM player will have its own drive letter, and you can check what's on the disk as simply as executing a DIR command.

You might not have access to the data that's stored on the disk so easily, however. Most CD ROMs contain their own searching software that you must run to read the data stored there. But don't worry about having to learn to use another software package. Most of these programs will give you a menu-driven interface that's easy to use, completely intuitive. Sponges and several varieties of lichens are reputed to have mastered the ins and outs of these programs.

While easy on you, these programs are not easy on your system. They may require a huge amount of memory to run. Most will demand your system be filled to its full DOS 640K limit. In fact, these memory-hogging programs may even require you to eject your favorite TSR programs before you can start to use your CD ROM.

And the CD ROM programs may carve their own storage space from your hard disk, hundreds of kilobytes of it for their files. To compound the misery, each CD ROM disk you have will likely require its own data access software. If you get several CD ROM disks, you'll need quite a lot of storage just for the programs that accompany each one.

In other words, if you want to install and use a CD ROM player, you'll have to start with a PC with a full dose of DOS memory—640K—one that includes a hard disk drive. CD ROM driver and retrieval software will also require that you use DOS 3.10 or later on your system.

Standards

Unlike other peripherals that you might want to add to your PC, the CD ROM player and its media have been completely standardized. The same CD ROM disks will fit the currently available mechanisms so that you're assured your new digital library will be readable and should remain so far into the future. You don't have to worry about how a given brand may affect the compatibility of your CD ROM system.

You do have to ensure that the CD ROM disks you buy are compatible with your computer's software architecture. Many disks are sold in special versions for PCs or Macintosh computers, with different access software to match the target computer. Hence, when you order a disk, it is important to specify what kind of computer you are using.

The data on CD ROM disks is stored in a particular format—an arrangement of tracks and sectors similar to that of hard disks—and, thankfully, one format has become a standard across the industry. Nearly all CD ROM disks and CD ROM players available today conform to the High Sierra format or its more recent upgrade, the ISO 9660 specification.

The only practical difference between these two standards is that the driver software supplied with some CD ROM players, particularly older ones meant for use with High Sierra formatted disks, may not recognize ISO 9660 disks. You're likely to get an error message that says something like "Disc not High Sierra." The problem is that the old version of the Microsoft CD ROM extensions—the driver that adapts your CD ROM player to work with DOS—cannot recognize ISO 9660 disks.

To meld CD ROM technology with DOS, Microsoft Corporation created a standard bit of operating code to add onto DOS to make the players work. These are called the DOS CD ROM extensions, and several versions have been written. The CD ROM extensions before Version 2.0 exhibit the incompatibility problem between High Sierra and ISO 9660 noted above. The solution is to buy a software upgrade to the CD ROM extensions that came with your CD ROM player from the vendor who sold you the equipment. A better solution is to avoid the problem and ensure that any CD ROM player you purchase comes with Version 2.0 or later of the Microsoft CD ROM extensions.

Interface

The connection between CD ROM players and your PC also has been, for the most part, standardized. The majority of CD ROM players that you can buy today use the Small Computer Systems Interface (SCSI) to link with your computer. A few CD ROM players connect through a serial port and a few others use proprietary connections or the AT interface similar to that of AT Attachment hard disk drives.

Serial-connected CD ROMs don't make much sense when you're talking about moving 600 megabytes of data at 150Kb/second and all you have is a 9,600 bit-per-second connection. Proprietary interfaces are quick, but they leave you stuck with the classic proprietary problem—your sources of supply (not to mention repairs and spare parts) may be severely limited.

WORM

Move the recording mechanism for CD ROMs from the factory to your PC and you have the general concept for the WORM drive. WORM stands for Write-Once, Read Multiple times (or Many times), and that's exactly what the system does. A laser beam reacts with the inner media of an optical disk and blasts spots dark, forever changing the disk. The pattern of light and dark spots made by the laser corresponds to bits of data stored.

Because both CD ROM and WORM store information similarly (as those pesky dark spots), you'll find many similarities between the two technologies. As with CD-ROMs, WORM drives store data as permanent physical changes in the disk surface that alter the disk's reflectivity. But the WORM drive can't dig pits as can the CD ROM master recorder. The WORM media is already safely encapsulated in plastic when you receive it, so pit-blasting in the CD ROM sense won't work. Instead of digging, WORMs work by chemically darkening or evaporating the reflective medium inside their disks.

The already-encapsulated form of WORM disks has another ramification—WORM disks are not easily duplicated by stamping as are CD-ROMs. The surface of the WORM disk is always smooth no matter what happens inside. Consequently, every WORM disk must be written individually. Each disk is either an original or, that wonderful oxymoron, an original copy. Duplicating a disk means reading the data from one and streaming it over to another—a transfer of hundreds of megabytes at optical rates. If there ever were a million-selling prerecorded WORM disk, you wouldn't want to be responsible for pressing the buttons to make the copies.

As a result of these issues, WORM technology fits a very limited, very specialized niche—actually, three of them: data acquisition, archival backup storage, and data retrieval systems. In data acquisition, you need a permanent record of the measurement you've made or other data. A WORM drive accommodates megabytes of information and keeps you honest by not permitting you to doctor the data later. As a backup system, WORM drives offer moderate speed, large capacity, the ability to interchange cartridges, and (again) permanence. Data retrieval systems, where megabytes are put on line for reference, benefit from the capacity of WORM, its ability to create and store megabytes rather than just read them like CD ROM, and (yet again) permanence.

WORM disks are no more indestructible than any computer medium you can throw in the fireplace. Compared to other forms of computer storage, however, WORM comes off well. While common phenomena like the magnetic fields of telephone bells and the aurora borealis conspire against all forms of magnetic storage, today's optical WORM disks are safe from just about everything except acetone rains. Magnets—no matter how strong—won't alter the data. Even the current corroding atmosphere can't get through the tough plastic coating of the disks.

The claimed life for WORM optical cartridges is ten years, versus three years for magnetic media. Barring cataclysm, the data on a WORM cartridge will endure longer than the expected life of the host computer.

Standards

Because WORM is a specialized, niche technology, the range of available products is small. But a small range doesn't mean a lack of variety, particularly when it comes to standardization.

Although more than a dozen companies manufacture WORM drives, two firms dominate the industry—Literal (formerly Information Storage, Inc.) and Panasonic. Most of the available WORM products follow one of three standards, two of which are defined by standard-setting organizations, one of which is proprietary.

Both the International Standards Organization (ISO) and the American National Standards Institute (ANSI) have created specifications outlining WORM storage systems. The two systems are physically incompatible; a cartridge for a drive that follows one standard won't work in a drive design to match the other. The differences aren't little, easily resolvable things like sector size or color of the cartridges. The standards vary, but indisputable differences such as the size of the cartridge, the capacity of the cartridge, and the data storage format on the cartridge. Although most WORM cartridges use disks measuring about 5.25 inches in diameter, the protective shell wrapped around these disks varies in thickness and mechanical accouterments, rending different manufacturers' products non-interchangeable. You can't even slide a cartridge meant for one drive into a drive made under a different WORM standard.

The digital contents of the cartridges also varies. The ISO standard allows for a total cartridge capacity of about 650 megabytes. Among other manufacturers, Pioneer, Laser Magnetic Storage, and Hitachi make drives that conform to ISO specifications. The ANSI standard allows for capacities of about double that sanctioned by the ISO, 1.2 gigabytes per disk. ISO cartridges are somewhat thicker than ANSI cartridges. Literal makes drives that conform to the ANSI standard.

Literal also makes another product that's a half-breed—it is a thick shell like that of the ISO standard, but the 5.25-inch disk inside stores as much data as an ANSI disk—1.2 gigabytes.

Panasonic follows the beat of its own drummer and is able to fit about 940 megabytes into its proprietary cartridge. Contrary to what you might expect, the Panasonic proprietary standard yields the lowest cost per megabyte of WORM systems.

Besides the 5.25-inch WORM drives most often used by personal computers, larger systems are also available for applications that are even more specialized. Among the most popular of these are 12-inch disks that provide the basis for immense digital libraries and information retrieval systems. A single 12-inch cartridge can hold 6 megabytes—3.2 per side. Those prodigious amounts can be multiplied by jukeboxes, WORM cartridge changers that automatically select and load cartridges when the data stored on them are required. The leading manufacturer of 12-inch WORM systems is Sony.

Media

In general, the various cartridges used by personal computer WORM standards consist of a thin metalized film medium encapsulated in a clear polycarbonate plastic disk. The actual disk is further protected by a high-impact plastic shell with a sliding metal door that allows access for the optical read/write head of the drive.

WORM disks are sold with the optical equivalent of a low-level format already in place. Some of the first WORM drives formatted their cartridges with grooves that the laser beam tracked to write and read information. This style of formatting has been superseded in nearly all existing drives by flat disks on which servo information is blasted onto (and through) the disk with a laser during manufacture.

As with floppy disks, WORM disks can be either single-sided or double-sided. But unlike magnetic media, however, WORM cartridges must be physically flipped over to access the second side, exactly as you would with an old-fashioned vinyl phonograph record.

Drives

The one-way data flow means that WORM drives are necessarily more expensive than CD ROM players simply because CD ROM players don't need recording circuitry and WORM drives do. The lasers in WORM drives require higher power to do their recording as well. Moreover, the smaller market for WORM technology means that the drives don't benefit so handsomely from the economies of scale. In fact, WORM drives often cost ten times as much as CD ROM players.

WORM drives are not a degraded form of rewritable optical technology. The two systems use quite different technologies. Although both systems are based on laser beams, their operating principles are quite unalike. Most rewritable disks rely on a special optically bistable medium that can be shifted between two states of reflectivity (which may differ only by a few percent) under the joint influence of the laser and a magnetic field. Hence, they are magneto-optical systems. The WORM drive uses a laser to ablate a hole in a thin metal film (actually, the laser only pokes a tiny hole in the medium; surface tension enlarges it to its final form).

WORM drives themselves conform to the 5.25-inch form factor used by older hard disks (except, of course, those that use 12-inch and other sized cartridges!). Nearly all available WORM drives require a full-height drive bay, although a half-height model is available from Ricoh. While at one time all WORM drives used proprietary interfaces, the SCSI connection is now dominant in the field. Nearly any WORM drive that you buy today will have a SCSI interface.

With the development of rewritable optical disks, many people consider WORM technology to be an orphan, or worse, a retiree—still around after all these years but with no purpose left in life. Actually, orphan is closer to the truth. Unlike other products that disappear in the dust riled up by onrushing technology, WORM drives have hung on, always on the periphery of the consciousness of the computer industry, just as orphans and other social problems always lurk in the background. Like orphans, WORM drives hold great promise, at least if you take you time investigate their potentials.

WORM drives are orphans, too, because they have no close kin— cousins, maybe, but no real brothers and sisters, no parents (of course), and likely no offspring. They are related to other optical technologies as closely as people are related to jellyfish and birds of paradise. If you have an application that requires large capacities and unalterable permanence, WORM may be your only choice—now and for a long time.

Rewritable Optical Disks

For people used to the flexibility of floppy and hard disk drives, neither CD ROM nor WORM appears to be a real solution. Data come and go, changing and transforming many times a day, hour, even millisecond. Even if information were unchanging, your mind probably isn't. The lure of the PC is that the data you work with is malleable and not carved in stone.

Rewritable optical technology combines that malleability of hard disk data with the density and permanence of optical storage. Surprisingly, rewritable optical drives accomplish exactly what their name implies. Data can be written on their disks in a form that can be read optically. The written data can be—but need not be—permanent. At any later time you can change and rewrite what's on the disk. The potential of rewritable optical technology is so promising that various manufacturers have developed (or are developing) at least three technologies—dye-polymer, phase-change, and magneto-optical—to make it possible. All three yield both the high storage densities that only optical media can provide along with the potential for upgrading their storage contents as your data changes. Each, however, has its weaknesses.

Dye-Polymer Storage

The rewritable technology closest in concept to CD ROM or WORM is dye-polymer. This recording method relies on special materials that change their physical characteristics in response to the heat applied by a laser beam. In the dye-polymer system, a dye-tinted inner polymer sheet is sandwiched between a translucent protective cover. The dye-polymer media reacts to the heat of the laser beam by swelling, producing a small bump wherever the laser strikes. The bump changes the reflectivity of the disk, and this change in reflectivity can be detected by the same optical system used in a Compact Disc player. To erase the disk so that it can be rewritten, the beam of another laser forces the dye-polymer bump to relax and return to its original reflectivity.

The advantage of this system is that in playback it is compatible with ordinary CD ROM disks. In fact, dye-polymer disks can be made to be compatible with ordinary CD ROM players, in effect giving you a machine that you can use in your home to make CDs—but one at a time.

The disadvantage is that the dye-polymer is a physical reaction, one that can be reversed only a finite number of times. As with the metals that fatigue in the skins of airliners, the dye-polymer layer eventually loses its ability to bump and bump back. Great strides have been make in pushing the life of the dye-polymer materials from a few cycles to hundreds, even hundreds of thousands, but even that's not sufficient to mimic a hard disk, parts of which may change thousands of times a day.

The premiere example of the dye-polymer technology—and the one that has received the most publicity—is the Tandy High-performance Optical Recording system, developed by Tandy Corporation. Despite its first announcement years ago, THOR remains in development and is not available commercially.

Phase-Change Storage

In phase-change rewritable optical systems, the recording medium is cycled between crystalline and amorphous states to store the ones and zeros of digital code. That is, the recordable material can arrange itself into the regularly ordered lattice of a crystal or into a form in which its constituent molecules are randomly organized like a compressed powder. While the chemical make-up of the medium remains the same as it changes between states, its reflectivity is altered. The result is that the medium can be made into tiny light and dark patches that can be used to encode digital information.

In effect, these state changes are effectively the same media alteration that's used in some WORM drives. Some commercial products actually use this technology to function as dual-purpose units—a single drive can handle both rewritable and WORM cartridges. Just slide in the kind of disk you want to use—almost. Differing WORM and rewritable cartridge standards complicate matters.

Phase-change technology suffers from the same weakness as dye-polymer—the recording medium has a finite life. The physical change from crystalline to amorphous fatigues the material until it can no longer be altered.

Whether the fatigue-prone dye-polymer and phase-change technologies can be used successfully as computer storage depends on their use and the number of state changes they can safely endure. Typical phase-change media are rated for lives in excess of ten thousand cycles. While just a few thousand cycles may sound sufficient for use in computer disk storage, even a million cycles may be woefully inadequate in a conventional PC mass storage system. While you may not erase and rewrite the entire contents of your disk drive very often, DOS busily rewrites the file allocation table on the disk every time you create or add to a file. That may happen thousands a times a day. If used like an ordinary magnetic disk, state-change optical media may quickly fail, with errors occurring first in the most important storage area on the disk, the FAT.

That's not to say phase-change and dye-polymer media are entirely unworkable; they're just not amenable to normal DOS operations. By clever engineering, FAT changes can be minimized, for example by moving the FAT before it becomes overwrought. State-change disks can also be effective when buffered by traditional magnetic hard disk media—ongoing changes are made to the hard disk, and only occasionally are those changes spooled off to the optical drive. State-change disks are also suitable for specialized applications that require a limited number of write cycles. A writable digital disk storage system for home audio is an example, the purpose for which the Tandy THOR system is primarily targeted. Because most people will record only a few times (even a few thousand) on a given part of a disk, the medium would not be unduly stressed.

Magneto-Optical Storage

The third technological choice, magneto-optical, is currently the most widely used rewritable optical method. Consequently, most rewritable optical drives are today called magneto-optical or MO drives.

The magneto-optical name describes the principal used in these products. The recording medium in each disk is fundamentally a magnetic material (but one unlike you'll find on hard disks and floppies) that relies on magnetic fields to store information. The optical part is used only to assist the magnetic mechanism, to refine its perceptions. A tightly focused laser beam points out where the magnetic mechanism is to write data onto the disk, and prepares the medium to make it recordable. In reading, however, MO drives are purely optical. The laser by itself reads the magnetically stored data from the disk.

The combination of optical and magnetic technologies results from necessity. As can be seen from the other rewritable optical technologies, the principal problem is not making the medium rewritable, but maintaining rewritability over many write operations. Materials that are physically altered in recording suffer fatigue, which limits their life. The best example is the WORM system that alters the disk to such an extent—with parts of the medium blasted into oblivion and beyond—that writing is possible only once. Magnetic materials don't physically change during the recording process. Only the fields of the particles of magnetic medium are altered. The particles themselves don't change.

Changes in magnetic polarity are well understood and generally believed to be completely reversible. After all, that's how traditional magnetic media—hard disks and floppies—work. Because MO drives are based on this well-understood principle, they are generally considered to be capable of an unlimited number of write-rewrite cycles. There's no worry about stress, fatigue, failure, and data loss. But magnetics and optics don't go together especially well. Other than blasting away the magnetic medium as if it were part of a WORM disk to get rid of the fields of individual magnetic particles, a laser by itself cannot alter the magnetism of a material. Of course, writing magnetically and reading optically offers no hope in delivering on the unique promise of optical storage. If a magnetic head were used to write data, it could pack information no more densely than the information would be packed on a conventional Winchester disk. There would be no incentive to use the fine probe of a laser beam to read the disk—no reason for optical technology to be used at all.

MO drives rely on a technical twist that allows the light beam to make only the small area it illuminates recordable by a conventional magnetic field. Another trick is used to allow the laser to determine the alignment of the magnetic fields of particles on the disk.

Write Operation

The writing process for an MO system relies on the combined effects of magnetic fields and laser-beam optics. The drives use a conventional magnetic field, called the bias field, to write data onto the disk. Of course, the nature of the field is limited by the same factors in Winchester disks—the size of the magnetic domains that are written is limited by the distance between the read-write head and the medium and is, at any practical distance, much larger that the size of a spot created by a focused laser.

To get the size of a magnetic domain down to truly minuscule size, MO drives use the laser beam to assist magnetic writing. In effect, the laser illuminates a tiny area within a larger magnetic field, and only this area is affected by the field.

This optical-assist in magnetic recording works because of the particular magnetic medium chosen for use in MO disks. This medium differs from that of ordinary Winchester drives in having a higher coercivity, a resistance to changing its magnetic orientation. In fact, the coercivity of an MO disk is about an order of magnitude higher than the 600 or so Oersteds of coercivity of the typical Winchester disk.

This high coercivity alone gives MO disks one of their biggest advantages over traditional Winchesters—they are virtually immune to self-erasure. All magnetic media tend to self-erase; that is, with the passing of time their magnetic fields lose intensity because of the combined effects of all external and internal magnetic fields upon them. The fields just get weaker. The higher the coercivity, the better a medium resists self-erasure. Consequently, MO disks with their high coercivities are able to maintain data more reliably over a longer period than Winchester disks.

The quoted lifetime for MO disks is 10 to 15 years. While that's difficult to prove because MO drives have not even existed for ten years, many people in the industry view that claimed lifetime as conservative. Traditional magnetic media require refreshing every few years to guarantee the integrity of their contents. Mainframe computer data tapes are typically refreshed every two years. MO media promise to substantially extend the time between refreshes, if not eliminating the need for refreshing entirely.

The high coercivity of MO media also makes the disks resistant to the effects of stray magnetic fields. While a refrigerator magnet means death to the data stored on a floppy disk, it would likely have no effect on an MO disk (but you still wouldn't want to clamp your MO disks to your system unit with refrigerator magnets). This resistance to stray fields means that you have to worry less about where and how you store MO cartridges.

Along with such benefits, the higher coercivity of MO media brings another challenge: obtaining a high enough magnetic flux to change the magnetic orientation of the media while keeping the size of recorded domains small. Reducing this high coercivity is how the laser assists the bias magnet in an MO drive.

The coercivity of the magnetic medium used by MO disks, as with virtually all magnetic materials, decreases as its temperature increases and becomes zero at a media-dependent value called the Curie temperature. By warming the MO disk medium sufficiently close to the Curie temperature, the necessary field strength to initiate a change can be reduced to a practical level. The magnetic medium used by MO disks is specifically engineered for a low Curie temperature, about 150 degrees Celsius.

The same laser that's used for reading the MO disk can simply be increased in intensity to heat up the recording medium to its Curie temperature. This laser beam can be tightly focused to achieve a tiny spot size. While the magnetic field acting on the medium may cover a wide area, only the tiny spot heated by the laser actually changes its magnetic orientation, because only that tiny spot is heated high enough to have a sufficiently low coercivity.

Practical mechanisms based on this design have one intrinsic drawback: the bias magnetic field must remain oriented in a single direction during the process of writing a large swath of a disk, a full sector, or track. The field cannot change quickly because the high inductance of the electromagnet that forms the field prevents the rapid switching of the magnet's polarities. The field must be far larger and stronger than those of Winchester disks because the magneto-optical head is substantially further from the disk—it doesn't fly but rides on a track.

Because of this inability of the magnetic field to change rapidly, the bias magnet in today's MO drives can align magnetic fields in a given area of a disk track but one direction each time that portion of a track passes beneath the read/write head. For example, when the bias field is polarized in the upward direction, it can change downward-oriented fields on the disk to upward polarity but it cannot alter upward-oriented fields to the downward direction.

Practical MO systems today thus require a two-step rewriting process. Before an area can be rewritten on the disk, all fields in that area must be oriented in a single direction. In other words, a given disk area must be separately erased before it can be recorded. In conventional MO drive designs, this erasure process requires a separate pass under the bias magnet with the polarity of the magnet temporarily reversed. After one pass for erasing previously written material, the field of the magnetic head is reversed again to the writing orientation. The actual information is written to disk on a second pass under the head. The only areas that change magnetic polarity then are those struck with and heated by the laser beam.

The penalty for this two-step process is an apparent increase in the average access time of MO drives when writing data. The extra time for a second pass is substantial. Although speeds vary, many MO drives spin their disks at a leisurely 2,400 revolutions per minute, roughly a third slower than Winchesters disks (which typically operate at about 3,600 RPM). Each turn of such an MO disk therefore requires 25 milliseconds. Even discounting head movement, the average access time for writing to an MO drive cannot possibly be faster than at least 37.5 milliseconds. (On the average, the data to be erased will be half a spin away from the read-write head, 12.5 milliseconds, and a second spin to write the data will take an additional 25 milliseconds.) Understandably most manufacturers are working on "one-pass" MO drives and are speeding the spins of their disks. Some drives now spin faster, at the same 3,600 RPM rate as hard disks. The 3.5-inch MO drives typically operate at 3,000 RPM.

The MO drive also suffers another performance handicap. While Winchester read-write heads are typically flyweight mechanisms weighing a fraction of a gram, the read-write heads of MO drives are massive assemblies of magnetic and optical parts. Typically this MO head mounts on a sled that slides on parallel steel tubes that act as a track. Moving that massive head requires a robust mechanism and, thanks to the principal of inertia, takes substantially longer to speed up, slow down, and settle as compared to a Winchester head. In fact, when it comes to average access time, there is almost no comparison between Winchesters, which can now write data as quickly as 15 milliseconds between random bytes, and MO drives which, at their current best, are no faster than 60 ms.—not counting the twice-around write penalty.

The optical sled used by MO drives isn't without its redeeming qualities, however. Unlike the Winchester drive head, which must fly micro-inches above the media surface to pack data tightly on the disk, optical heads can work at a distance. The guide rods absolutely fix the distance between head and disk that's truly huge compared to Winchesters—and with that distance comes safety. Head crashes are impossible on MO drives because the head is restrained from moving close to the media. In fact, only the laser beam ever touches the disk surface (or should—keep your fingers out of the protective door in the MO cartridge!).

As with CDs, the optically active surface of an MO disk is sealed beneath a tough layer of transparent plastic, again minimizing damage. The laser beam focuses through the clear covering. Because the beam is out of focus at the surface of the disk and only converges to a spot underneath the clear surface layer, imperfections such as scratches or dust on the top of the disk have relatively little effect on the accuracy of disk reading or writing. Of course, MO drives also incorporate error correction to minimize the appearance of errors in the stream of stored data.

Read Operation

At the field strengths common to electronic gear, light beams are generally unreactive with magnetic fields. Fiber-optic cables, for example, are impervious to the effects of normal electromagnetic noise that would pollute ordinary wires. Consequently, getting a laser to read the miniscule magnetic fields on an MO disk is a challenge.

The trick used in MO technology is polarization. The MO disk is read by a laser beam that is reflected from the disk surface as in other technologies, but in the MO drive the laser beam is polarized. That is, the plane of orientation of its photons in the laser beam are all aligned in one direction.

When the polarized beam strikes the magnetically aligned particles of the disk, the magnetic field of the media particles causes the plane of polarization of the light beam to rotate slightly, a phenomenon called the Kerr effect. While small, as little as a 1 percent shift in early MO media but now reportedly up to 7 percent, this change in polarization can be detected as reliably as the direct magnetic reading of a Winchester disk. A polarized beam passing through a second polarizing material diminishes in intensity depending on how closely the polarity of the beam is aligned with that of the second material. In effect, the polarity change becomes a readily detected intensity change.

Standards

Even with MO drives, data exchange depends on standardization; the cartridges written on one machine must be readable by others. From diverse beginnings, MO products have gone a long way to achieve the necessary standardization to the extent that ISO has propounded a set of specifications for 5.25-inch and 3.5-inch MO cartridges. The ISO standard guarantees that any ISO-standard cartridge can be used in any drive supporting the ISO standard. Although that sounds like a straightforward statement, it has its complexities.

For 5.25-inch MO disks, the ISO standard is actually a dual standard. It allows cartridges of two types, those that store data in 1,024-byte sectors and those that store data in 512-byte sectors. Because larger sectors mean less overhead—among other things, fewer sector identification markers are required—1,024-byte-per-sector cartridges can store more data, about 650 megabytes per cartridge (about 325 per side) versus 594 (often rounded to 600) megabytes for 512-byte-per-sector cartridges (about 297 megabytes per side). The actual capacity of each cartridge varies and is inevitably smaller than these figures because, as with hard disks, magneto-optical cartridges may have bad sectors which cannot be used for data storage. The smaller, 3.5-inch cartridges store about 128M using 512 bytes per sector, 25 sectors per track, and 10,000 tracks on a cartridge.

Under the ISO standard, a 5.25-inch drive must be able to read and write both 512- and 1,024-byte-per-sector cartridges. Drives produced before the standard was adopted (or by companies not recognizing the standard) may be limited to one or the other size. Some manufacturers offer drives that support not only ISO cartridge standards but their own, proprietary storage formats. For example, the Tahiti drive produced by Maxtor augments its ISO abilities with a special format and data storage method that packs up to one gigabyte per cartridge. Using constant linear velocity recording, it fills the longer, outer tracks of each disk with more sectors full of data. In contrast, the ISO standards call for constant angular velocity recording (meaning the disk spins at a constant rate), which puts the same number of sectors—and the same amount of data—on every disk track.

The strongest point of the ISO standard is that it strictly defines the MO cartridge and the media it contains. Not only does this aspect of the standard assure physical compatibility of cartridges, it also insure that multiple sources of supply will be available, potentially making media less expensive.

As with all too many personal computer "standards," however, the ISO standard is not a panacea that guarantees cartridges written in one MO drive will be readable by another. Although the ISO standard does specify the physical format in which data is stored on the disk, it does not indicate the logical format. Different system integrators may opt for their own disk partitioning schemes, and the software drivers used by one MO system vendor may not recognize the partitioning used by another maker. Note that few MO drive integrators opt to use standard DOS partitioning, although the introduction of Version 5.0 may change their perspective on DOS.

Performance

Besides the issue of average access time and the spin speed of the disks (which determines data transfer rate), the format of an MO cartridge can determine the overall performance of the MO system. The way the capacity of an MO cartridge is carved up (as well as the disk's formatting and even the number of bytes per sector) affects the data throughput performance of a drive. A cartridge partitioned for standard 32-megabyte DOS volumes may deliver half the effective throughput of a drive using a proprietary partitioning scheme that allows the entire capacity of one cartridge side to be addressed as a single volume. This performance effect arises because larger volumes on MO cartridges result in larger DOS storage clusters, and larger clusters reduce the overhead involved in extended data transfers.

Performance of MO drives also varies more widely than conventional hard disks because the ISO standard specifies that MO drives use the Small Computer System Interface (SCSI) to connect to their hosts. While this interface choice has its advantage in flexibility (for example, up to seven SCSI devices can be connected to a single host adapter), SCSI also can be a handicap for DOS users. ISO magneto-optical drives, like all SCSI devices in DOS-based computers, can be severely constrained by performance of the SCSI host adapter used. A good SCSI host adapter will allow an MO drive to a transfer data at the speed data can be recovered from the spinning disk, a rate on par with today's best Winchester hard disks. A poor SCSI adapter may limit mass storage throughput to 10 percent its possible peak rate and make the overall system look painfully slow.

Media

Despite their common name, most 5.25-inch cartridges are filled with optical disk platters that actually measure 130 millimeters (5.12 inches) in diameter. The cartridges themselves measure .43 x 5.31 x 6.02 inches (HWD) and somewhat resemble 3.5-inch floppy disks in that the disk itself is protected by a sliding metal shutter. So-called 3.5-inch magneto-optical disks have platters that are actually 90 millimeters across in a cartridge shell about the same size and appearance as a 3.5-inch floppy disk, only the MO disks are thicker.

The magnetic medium on an MO disk is constructed from several layers. First, the plastic substrate of the disk is isolated with a dielectric coating. The actual magneto-optical compound—an alloy of terbium (a rare earth element), iron, and cobalt—comes next, protected by another dielectric coating. A layer of aluminum atop this provides a reflective surface for the tracking mechanism. This sandwich is then covered by 0.30 millimeters of transparent plastic. Disks are made single-sided, then two are glued together back-to-back to produce two-sided media.

Unlike conventional Winchester disks that store data on number of concentric tracks or cylinders, under the ISO standard MO drives use a single, continuous spiral track much like the groove on an old vinyl phonograph record. The spiral optimizes the data transfer of the drive because the read/write head does not need to be moved between tracks during extended data transfers. It instead smoothly scans across the disk.

Capacity is an oft-cited advantage of optical media generally and MO products specifically. But the capacities of MO systems are not that much larger than what purely magnetic drives offer. In fact, 3.5-inch magneto-optical drives offer less capacity than today's state-of-the art 3.5-inch magnetic hard disks. Even 5.25-inch magneto-optical drives do not outshine the capacities of magnetic drives despite their greater storage densities.

But direct comparisons between Winchester and MO capacities are misleading. The quoted capacities of both type of drive are in roughly the same ballpark, but the technologies are playing different games. Drives using 5.25-inch disks may quote roughly similar capacities for either technology, a maximum of about a gigabyte. But Winchester drives might use up to eight internal disks or platters (15 recordable surfaces) to achieve that capacity, while the higher data packing density of MO drives allow them to reach the same figure with a single platter locked inside a removable cartridge.

The capacities quoted for MO cartridges don't take into account how much storage is actually on-line. Although 5.25-inch MO drives are quoted with capacities in the range 600 to 1,000 megabytes, only half of the figure that manufacturers commonly quote is actually available at any one time. The disks in today's cartridges array their storage across two sides, and current MO drives have a single read/write head, so only one side of a cartridge can be read from or written to at a time. To access the other side, you have to physically remove the cartridge from the drive, flip it over, and slide it back in. Consequently, only half of the total capacity of the cartridge is actually on-line at a time.

On the other hand, while MO drives are usually rated with capacities per cartridge, a single drive has an effectively unlimited capacity. Run out of space, and you only need slide in a new cartridge or flip over the one that's in the drive. You can stock up on as many cartridges as you can afford (the price per cartridge currently is about $250). Of course, only about 300 megabytes of that unlimited total can be accessed at a time.

Most makers of MO drives also offer jukebox systems, sometimes termed "autochangers." These units can automatically shift between several disks to achieve astonishing near-line storage abilities, 50 to 100 gigabytes. It's called near-line storage because you have to put up with a slight wait as the autochanger finds the correct cartridge and spins it up to speed. The jukeboxes are not priced to put them in the budgets of most individual PC owners. They are products for information servers.

Applications

The spiral tracks of MO cartridges demonstrates that designers of the drives recognize that the technology is not at its best when randomly accessing data, but rather favors large sequential transfers. Consequently, current MO drive systems are not aimed at universally replacing Winchester hard disks as primary mass storage media. Their role today is seen as secondary mass storage—the uncharted territory that lies between hard disks and streaming tape.

In other words, MO drives are not for every application, but they have significant strengths that make a particularly good choice when a safe, secure means of storing hundreds of megabytes is required. Graphics and audio/visual systems are particular candidates because MO cartridges provide the capacity needed for easy exchange of extremely large files. Engineers, for example, can put huge CAD files on disks to archive them.

MO drives can also make an excellent backup medium, particularly for network applications. A single cartridge can back up all but the largest hard disks. Moreover, the capability to rewrite cartridges allows them to fit into the traditional arrangement in which backup media are routinely recycled. Compared to tape media, restoration of files from MO disks is fast and easy. However, MO cartridges are substantially more expensive than open-reel or cartridge tapes of the same capacity by a factor of at least two.

MO disks can also serve as an excellent archival medium. Cartridges are compact enough to carry several in a briefcase or lock securely in a safe. Data stored on them is safe for long term storage because MO media are virtually free from self-erasure and resist external magnetic perils, thanks to their high coercivity.

In some systems, MO drives could replace hard disks as the primary mass storage system. With suitable caching software, the apparent performance of MO disks can be hoisted nearly to the level of a conventional hard disk. The lag in access time will still become apparent during cache misses, however.

Writing an obituary for hard disks is probably premature. Rewritable magneto-optical disks probably won't displace Winchester technology soon. Like most new technologies, MO will likely achieve its greatest success in a new role, one that it will likely define itself. As it stands now, MO technology is both useful and available. And it affords possibilities that may change the way you use your PC.

Floptical

Just as magneto-optical drives interbreed two different technologies, so does the Floptical disk drive. Whereas MO drives seek to pry marketshare away from traditional hard disks, Floptical diskettes aim at the old-fashioned floppy disk.

The primary lure of the Floptical diskette is capacity. Whereas conventional floppy disks now hold up to about 2.88 megabytes, the current implementations of Floptical drives store 21 megabytes of formatted data (25M unformatted) in the same sized package.

Not only are Floptical diskette identical in size with 3.5-inch floppies, the old-technology floppies will slide into a Floptical disk drive. The drives are backwardly compatible with 1.44M and 720K (but not 2.88M) floppy disks. The new drives will both read and write conventional magnetic diskettes.

This compatibility is possible because Floptical technology is a magnetic recording process. Your data never spurts through a light beam or laser. By using special high-density recording media and special heads, the storage density is increased above that of floppy disks.

The principal problem with ordinary floppy disks is entirely different from those faced by the high-capacity magnetic storage leader, the hard disk. Hard disks are limited in the density of data they can store by the distance the read/write head flies above the media. Floppies put their heads in contact with the drive, so they could in theory (and all else being equal) exceed the storage densities of hard disks.

The problem with floppies is that they are, well, floppy. Because the medium is not dimensionally stable, it is difficult if not impossible to reliably recover narrow, closely spaced tracks. The disk expands and contracts with temperature changes and deforms as it spins around inside its shell.

Floptical drives use an optical servo track to solve the problem. A special optical servomechanism keeps the magnetic read/write head in position to properly write and read the disk. The optical servo information is embedded in the disk during its manufacture and cannot be altered by the recording process. In fact, it cannot be erased by normal means. You can run a Floptical disk under a bulk degausser and it won't lose its servo information.

23

Tape

Tape is for backup, your insurance that a disaster won't erase every last vestige of your valuable data. You can also use some of the standardized tape systems as exchange media, the floppy disk for the age of megabytes. Tape systems come in a number of formats with different capacities, speeds, and levels of convenience. The best, however, is the one that's the least trouble to use.

Faith is trusting your most valuable possessions—purportedly to protect them—to a sealed black box filled with machinery you don't understand, fragile machinery at that, honed to split-hair tolerances and vulnerable to a multitude of ills—electroshock, impact, even old age. One misstep and your treasures can be destroyed.

Such groundless, even misguided, trust should have no place in business and definitely no role in the rigorous world of personal computer, but that's exactly what you do every time you save a file to your hard disk drive. You send data to a complex, sealed black box with the hope of someday retrieving it. Technology has given us this faith—but just in case the faith is misplaced, technology has also bequeathed us with the tape to use for backup systems.

With tape, you can quickly make a copy of your most valuable data on a movable medium that you can take to preserve somewhere safe. When disaster strikes—as it inevitably will—you always have your tape copy as a backup, ready to replace the original. The concept is simple but far from perfect. You've a variety of tape systems to choose from and all share one undesirable quality—you have to pay for them.

The price is more than monetary. Making a tape backup also extracts a toll in convenience. From a miracle or wonder drug, it's more like castor oil for your computer. It's unpalatable and has little per-ceived value in the abstract, no matter what you have to pay for it. You put up with it because you've been told it's good for you in some way that you hope to never need test. But no matter how much sugar is mixed in with it, you'd still wish it (and the need for it) would go away. It won't, so you might as well swallow hard and take advantage of the protection that tape offers you and your PC.

Background

Tape was the first magnetic mass storage system, harking back to the last days of World War II. Although first used for voice and music, tape soon invaded the computer world, first as a convenient alternative to punched cards and punched paper tape, the primary storage system used by mainframe computers. Later, information transfer became an important use for tape. Data bases could be moved between systems as easily as carting around one or more spools of tape. After magnetic disks assumed the lead in primary storage, tape systems were adapted to backing them up.

Personal computers have benefited from the evolution of tape in the mainframe environment. Never considered as primary storage—except in the nightmares of the original designers of the first PC, who thoughtfully included a cassette port on the machine for its millions of users to ignore—tape started life in the PC workplace in the same role it serves today, as a backup medium. Although some software vendors have eyed the huge, cheap storage of tape cartridges as a file interchange medium, the attempts at establishing it as a standard for such purposes have been but flirtations. For years, it has beckoned, but it's never taken itself seriously enough to maintain a long-lasting relationship.

As a physical entity, tape is both straightforward and esoteric. It's straightforward in design, providing the perfect sequential medium— a long, thin ribbon that can hold orderly sequences of information. The esoteric part involves the materials used in its construction.

Tape consists of two essential layers, the *backing* and the *coating*. The backing provides the support strength needed to hold the tape to-gether while it's flung back and forth across the transport. Progress in the quality of the backing material has mirrored developments in the plastics industry. The first tape was based on paper. Shortly after the introduction of commercial tape recorders at the beginning of the '50s, cellulose acetate (the same plastic used in safety film in photography for three decades previously) was adopted. The state-of-the-art plastic is polyester, of double-knit leisure-suit fame. In tape, polyester has a timeless style of its own—flexible and long wearing with a bit of stretch. It needs all of those qualities to withstand the twists and turns of today's tortuous mechanisms, fast shuttle speeds, and abrupt changes of direction.

Coatings also have evolved over the decades, as they have for all magnetic media. Although most tapes are coated with doped magnetic oxides, coatings of pure metal particles in binders and and even vapor-plated metal films have been used for tape. Tape coatings are governed by the same principles as other magnetic media; the form is different but the composition remains the same.

In backup systems, the packaging of the tape is as important as its composition. The form that the tape package takes determines the mechanism required for writing to and reading from it.

In general, the trend has been to package tape in an ever-more convenient form. Tape started out as loose spools that required threading as elaborate as threading a vintage 16mm film projector. Clever engineers got the idea of putting both the supply and take-up reels (or spools) in a single cartridge so threading was minimized. Once the cartridges were standardized, the tape engineers concentrated on cramming more data into the cartridges.

The result of these efforts is the diversity of tape systems now available for plugging into your PC. Four major types of tape systems (as well as a few out-of-the-mainstream technologies) are sometimes used in personal computer systems, all of which were originally designed for other purposes. These include open-reel tape, cassettes, quarter-inch cartridges, and helical-scan tape.

Open-Reel Tape

The classic computer tape medium uses individual tape spools termed *open-reel tape* because the spools are not kept inside protective shells, as are other computer tape formats. All of the Big-Brother-style computer films of the '50s and early '60s used the jerky, back-and-forth movement of big open reel tape transports as a symbol of the vast computer power of the age. At the time, the big reels of tape were the primary storage systems of those computers, and the back-and-forth rocking of the tape was the machine's quest to find a given record. As you can imagine, put to such purposes, the average access time of the tapes was measured in seconds and could stretch for an eternity—particularly when the right tape was not mounted on the transport.

From a diversity of formats, one standard quickly evolved in open-reel tape. The tape, nominally one-half inch wide, is split into nine parallel tracks, each running the full length of the tape. One track is used for each bit of a byte of data, the ninth track containing parity-checking information. Every byte is recorded in parallel, a lateral slice across the tape. Because of these physical characteristics of the medium, open-reel tape is often termed *half-inch* or *nine-track* tape.

Individual reels of tape can be of almost any diameter larger than the three-inch central hole. The most common sizes are seven and ten-and-one-half inches in diameter. Tape lengths vary with reel size and with the thickness of the tape itself. A ten-inch spool holds 2500 to 3600 feet of tape.

As open-reel technology has evolved, the distance between each byte has been gradually reduced, packing an increasing amount of information on every inch of tape. Originally, open-reel tapes were recorded using FM signals, packing 800 bytes on every linear inch of the tape. Advancing to MFM doubled the capacity to 1600 bpi. This density is now the most common in open-reel tape. More exotic transports push data densities up to 3200 or even 6250 bpi.

Data are recorded on open-reel tape in distinct blocks, each separated by a stretch of blank tape called the *inter-block gap*. The length of this gap can vary from a fraction of an inch to several inches, depending on characteristics of the overall system (involving such factors as how quickly the host computer can send and receive information from the tape subsystem). Together, the tape length, data density, and inter-block gap determine the capacity of a single reel of tape. The common 1600 bpi density and a reasonable inter-block gap can put about 40 megabytes on a ten-inch reel.

Although once considered great, that 40 megabytes isn't much by today's PC storage standards. It takes awfully large reels to pack a workable amount of information. And that's the chief disadvantage of open-reel tape. Tape reels are big and clumsy, and the drives match. When a single reel is more than ten inches across, fitting a drive to handle it inside a 5.25-inch drive is more than difficult. Ten-inch reels themselves are massive, and spinning (and stopping) them requires a great deal of torque, which means large, powerful motors—again something incompatible with the compact necessities of the PC. In fact, most open-reel tape transports dwarf the typical PC. Some look more like small refrigerators.

Open-reel drives also tend to be expensive because they are essentially low-volume yet precision machinery. Even the least expensive open-reel system costs more than a good, high-speed PC—$3000 and up. Unlike other PC peripherals, the price of open-reel tape has been stable for years. There are no breakthrough technologies on the horizon that will revolutionize nine-track tape and its pricing.

On the positive side, age and mass can be virtues when it comes to system and data integrity. Because of the low density used in recording, each flux transition on an open reel tape involves a greater number of oxide particles, making it potentially more resistant to degradation (all other oxide characteristics being equal). The big, heavyweight drives are generally sturdy, designed for industrial use, and should last nearly forever when attached to a PC.

As a backup system alone, open reel tape is not much of a bargain, however. Other tape systems, particularly the various cartridge formats, are less expensive and—according to their design specifications—as reliable or even more reliable. For most people, cartridges are also easier to use.

Open-reel tape excels as a data-interchange medium, however. Almost any 1600 bpi tape is readable on almost any open-reel transport. Although block lengths and inter-block gaps may vary, these differences are relatively easy to compensate for. Consequently, open-reel remains the medium of choice for shifting information between mainframe and minicomputers. For instance, most mailing lists are delivered on open-reel tapes. An open-reel transport opens this world to the personal computer, allowing the interchange of megabytes of information with virtually any other system. Although most open-reel systems for PCs concentrate on the interchangeability of the tapes, they also include provisions for making open-reel backups. Think of the backup capability as a bonus rather than the reason for buying an open-reel system.

3480 Cartridges

Operators of mainframe computers endured the inconveniences of open-reel tape for more than 20 years before an accepted successor appeared on the scene. A new tape system that's essentially a cross between cartridges and open-reel is replacing old-fashioned, open-reel tapes in its role of backup storage. Because of its newness, however, the system has not yet proven a successor to open-reel tape as an interchange medium.

Termed *3480* after the model number of the first IBM machine that the new media addressed, the system is based on cartridges that are little more than open-reel tapes stuffed into a protective shell. The tape is still half an inch wide, and it runs through the drive much like open reel tapes. The drive mechanism pulls the tape out of the cartridge, winds it onto a tape-up spool, shuttles it back and forth to find and write data, and rewinds it back into the cartridge when it is done. In effect, the cartridge is just an oddly shaped all-enclosing reel that doesn't itself rotate. Not only can people more easily slide tape into drives, but automatic mechanisms can locate tapes and load them. Such mechanisms are often called *juke boxes* because they work like the classic '50s Wurlitzers that gave three plays for a quarter, selecting the songs to play from an internal array of disks—complete with big windows so you could stare in amazement at the mechanical wonder.

The 3480 system holds a bigger advantage over open-reel than just convenience in mounting tapes, however. The upgrade to 3480 also brings double the number of tracks, and a once or twice more doubling is promised in the future by IBM. In IBM's current implementation, these 18 tracks are written in two parallel sets of nine tracks simultaneously, which doubles the data transfer speed and throughput of the system. In addition, the recording density is higher than open-reel tapes, increasing both capacity and the data speed of the system. The result of this redesign is that a cartridge with less than a quarter the volume of an open-reel tape (3480 cartridges measure 4.75 x 4.25 x .75 inches) can hold much more data—can hold hundreds of megabytes.

The drawback of these innovations is the high price. All 3480 tape transports that are currently available are big ticket ($20,000-plus) products designed for the mainframe market.

Several companies worked at adapting the 3480-style cartridge into systems that would be practical (and affordable) for PC applications. These systems shared only the medium with the mainframe technology, using different data formats than the true IBM 3480 tape drive. From the PC perspective, these systems have faded into obscurity, probably because they lacked the big advantage of open-reel tape. They weren't capable of exchanging information with mainframes.

Cassette Tape

Introduced originally as a dictation medium, cassettes grew both up and down—into a stereophonic music recording medium that spawned a market for equipment sometimes costing thousands of dollars—and down into the realm of cheap, portable recorders costing $10–20. These low-end machines represent the cheapest way to magnetically record information ever created. Although originally conceived solely for dictation, using modem-like methods, they could record digital signals modulated onto audible tones. Low prices and ready accessibility made cassettes the choice of early computer hobbyists for recording data and pushed cassettes into the commercial market as a distribution medium for computer software, mostly for inexpensive home-style computers.

When the PC was first brought to market, the cassette was seen as a viable storage alternative, at least among the home and hobbyist computer markets, by industry watchers with eyeglasses as thick as bathyscaph portholes. Even IBM caught cassette mania and elected to build a port for attaching a cassette machine into every PC.

Little more than a year later the marketplace myopia improved, and the storage needs of the PC showed the shortcomings of audio cassette technology adapted to data: slow speed and sequential access. The modulation-audio method of recording yielded a data rate about equivalent to a 1200-bit-per-second modem, and finding data on a tape took a long time or a lot of guessing with your finger on the fast-forward button. These practical matters led to the cassette port being dropped from the XT and all subsequent IBM computers. Among PCs, the cassette as a primary data storage device is mostly of historical interest only.

In the last few years the cassette mechanism has proven a compelling platform, however. Teac developed a new, high-speed cassette transport aimed particularly at data storage. It abandoned the audio cassette standard used by earlier systems and pegged its performance on par with higher priced cartridge-based backup systems using a digital recording system. The result was called the *digital cassette* or D/CAS for short. These data-only cassettes now represent a viable secondary storage technology.

Developed—and patented—by the Dutch Philips conglomerate, the audio cassette was just one of many attempts to sidestep the biggest complaint against open-reel tape systems, that the tapes were difficult to handle and hard to thread through the recording mechanism. The idea did not originate with Philips. An earlier attempt by RCA, which used a similar but larger cassette package, failed ignobly in the marketplace. The Compact Cassette, as it was labeled by Philips, was successful because it was more convenient and did not aspire so high. It was not designed as a high-fidelity medium, but grew into that market as technology improved its modest quality. While the RCA cartridge was about the size of a thin book, the Compact Cassette fit into a shirt pocket and was quite at home when it was on the go in portable equipment. Size and convenience led to its adoption as the autosound medium of choice, then the general high-fidelity medium of choice (even before the introduction of the Compact Disc, cassettes had earned the majority of the music market).

The basic cassette mechanism simply takes the two spools of the open-reel tape transport and puts them inside a plastic shell. The shell protects the tape because the tape is always attached to both spools, eliminating the need for threading.

The sides of the cassette shell serve the purpose of the side of the tape reel—holding the tape in place so that the center of the spool doesn't pop out. This function is augmented by a pair of Teflon slip sheets, one on either side of the tape inside the shell, that help to eliminate the friction of the tape against the shell. A clear plastic window in either side of the shell lets you take a look at how much tape is on either spool, how much is left to record on or play back.

The reels inside the cassette themselves are merely hubs that the tape can wrap around. A small clip that forms part of the perimeter of the hub holds the end of the tape to the hub. At various points around the inside of the shell, guides are provided to ensure that the tape travels in the correct path.

The shell is thickened at the edge that is open to allow the record/playback head and the drive puck to be inserted against the tape.

The cassette also incorporates protection against accidental erasure of valuable music or information. On the rear edge of the cassette—away from where the head inserts—is a pair of plastic tabs protecting hole-like depressions in the shell. A finger from the cassette transport attempts to push its way into this hole. If it succeeds, it registers that the cassette is write-protected. Breaking off one of these tabs therefore protects the cassette from accidental erasure. To restore recordability, the hole only needs to be covered up. Cellophane or masking tape—even a Band-Aid or file folder label works for that purpose. There are two such tabs, one to protect each side of the tape. The tab in the upper left protects the top side of the cassette. (Turn the cassette over and the other side becomes the top—but the tab that allows recording on this side still appears in the upper left.)

More recent audio cassettes may have additional notches on the rear edge to indicate to automatic sensing cassette decks the type of tape that's inside the cassette shell. Audio tape comes in four varieties, which require different settings on the cassette recording for optimal operation.

The Teac data cassettes add one huge notch on the backbone of the cassette that works as a key to lock out audio cassettes from their digital mechanisms. Even were the notch not there, ordinary audio tapes wouldn't work in the Teac mechanism. The high-speed cassette system requires special cassettes designed to match its magnetic and mechanical requirements.

The first Teac system used two tracks on each cassette, one for recording in each direction. However, the mechanism was bi-directional and automatically used both sides. Not only did you not need to flip over a tape in the Teac system, you were prohibited from doing so. The asymmetrical placement of the identifying notch absolutely precludes the use of the wrong side of a tape.

The first Teac D/CAS system was able to put a full 60M on one tape. That was quickly increased to 160M. In 1991, Teac introduced a new mechanism (their model number MT-2ST/F50) which pushed capacity to 600M. Using a standard SCSI-2 interface, it is able to move information onto tape at a rate of up to 242K per second. Teac plans to push up capacity to 2.5G cassettes by 1993, and to 10G in 1995.

Quarter-Inch Cartridges

A few years after the cassette was introduced to take dictation, 3M Company first offered a quarter-inch tape cartridge as a data recording medium. First put on the market in 1972, these initial quarter-inch cartridges were designed for telecommunications and data acquisition applications calling for the storage of serial data such as programming private business telephone exchanges and recording events. No one could have imagined that the quarter-inch cartridge would evolve into the premiere personal computer backup medium. There were no PCs.

The initial concept behind the quarter-inch tape cartridge appears to be the same as that of the cassette—put the two spools of tape from the open-reel system into an easy-to-handle plastic box. In function, operation, and construction the two—the cassette and cartridge—are entirely different because the needs of dictation and data storage were entirely different. Compared to the cassette, the tape cartridge required greater precision and smoother operation. To achieve that end, a new mechanical design was invented by Robert von Behren of the 3M Company, who patented it in 1971.

The Quarter-Inch Cartridge Mechanism

Instead of using the capstan drive system like cassettes, the quarter-inch cartridge operates with a belt-drive system. A thin, isoelastic belt stretches throughout the cartridge mechanism, looping around (and making contact with) both the supply and take-up spools on their outer perimeters. The belt also passes around a rubber drive wheel, which contacts a capstan in the tape drive.

The capstan moves the belt but is cut away with a recess that keeps it away from touching the tape. The friction of the belt against the outside of the tape reels drives the tape. This system is gentler to the tape because the driving pressure is spread evenly over a large area of the tape instead of pinching the tape tightly between two rollers. In addition, it provides for smoother tape travel and packing of the tape on the spools. The tape is wound and the guide and other parts of the mechanism arranged so that the fragile magnetic surface of the tape touches nothing but the read/write head (see fig. 23.1).

For sturdiness, the cartridge is built around an aluminum baseplate. The rest of the cartridge is transparent plastic, allowing the condition of the tape and the mechanism to be readily viewed.

The essence of the design is that the cartridge itself acts as the tape drive. It contains the tape guides, the tape, and the tape-moving mechanism. While that means that the data cartridge is somewhat more expensive to make, drives are less expensive because they essentially need only a motor and a head. The design also ensures the best possible consistency of alignment of the tape and minimizes the need for adjustments to the drive.

Early Systems

The initial cartridge, called the DC300A by 3M Company, held 300 feet of tape in a package almost the size of a paperback book— a full 6 × 4 × 5/8 inches. The cartridge mechanism was designed to operate at a speed of 30 inches per second, using phase encoding (single-density recording) to put at a density of 1,600 bits per inch serially (one track at a time) on the tape, resulting in a data rate of 48 kilobits per second. Two or four tracks were used one at a time. Drives for this format were made by 3M Company, Kennedy, Qantax, DEI, and, briefly, IBM.

In 1979 DEI quadrupled the speed and capacity of the quarter-inch cartridge by introducing a drive that recorded four tracks in parallel, still at 30 inches per second and 1600 bits per inch. The new mechanism achieved a 192 kilobit per second data rate using standard DC300A tapes. Even though these cartridges only held 1.8 megabytes unformatted—one megabyte formatted, the same as an 8-inch floppy disk—using this recording method, the data rate was high enough to interest the computer industry.

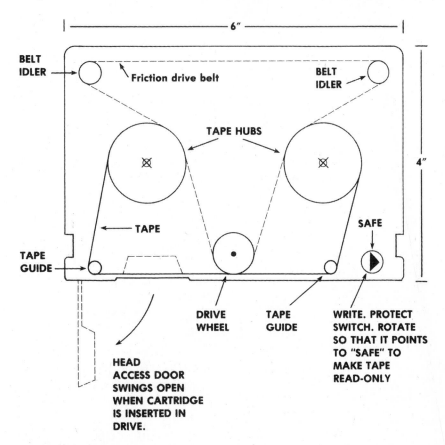

Figure 23.1. Quarter-inch cartridge mechanims (DC-600 style cartridge is shown; the DC2000 is similar but smaller).

A year later another four-track drive for the DC300A cartridge was introduced. The capacity of the system was increased to about 15M by shifting to MFM recording and pushing the data density to 6,400 bits per inch. Although the 192 kilobit per second transfer rate and 30 inch per second speed were maintained, data was transferred serially, one track at a time. As late as 1988, this ground-breaking drive was still in production, although it was not longer used in mass-market PC products, being superseded in those applications by higher capacity systems.

Since then, tape lengths have again been increased, to a now-standard 600 feet in a cartridge that was first designated DC600. Current implementations of cartridge technology use cartridges the same size and shape as the 3M originals. However, capacities have blossomed into the gigabyte range thanks to multitrack heads, high-density recording media, and error correction. Up to 100 gigabytes of storage per cartridge are envisioned.

The DC600 cartridge is now a thing of the past—but in name only. New designations have been added to take into account other media and tape length differences that affect storage capacities. The series of full-size quarter-inch cartridges is now termed DC6000. The last three (or so) digits of tape cartridge model numbers of most tape cartridges are used to designate the tape capacity.

QIC

Only the media was the same in early products based on quarter-inch cartridges. Each drive manufacturer went in his own direction, not only varying the number of tracks and density of data on the tape but even how the tape drive connected with its computer host. Every tape system was proprietary, a situation that doesn't give a computer supervisor a feeling of security when he has a lifetime of data packed onto cartridges. Proprietary standards means whatever is stored on tape is at risk to the whims of the manufacturer. A discontinued product line could render tape unreadable in the future as drives break down. Moreover, the diversity of tape systems meant that each manufacturer essentially had to start from scratch in developing each model.

To try to lessen the chaos in the tape cartridge marketplace, a number of tape drive manufacturers—including DEI, Archive, Cipher Data, and Tandberg—met at the National Computer Conference in Houston in 1982. They decided to form a committee to develop standards so that a uniform class of products could be introduced. The organization took the name Working Group for Quarter-Inch Cartridge Drive Compatibility, a name often shortened into QIC Committee. In November, 1987, the organization was officially incorporated as Quarter-Inch Cartridge Standards, Inc.

The QIC Committee was formed primarily of drive manufacturers who do not sell directly to the PC market and initially concerned itself with physical standardization. Data formats were left for system integrators to develop—and, in general, each one designed his own. With time the committee has developed into a trade association and it recognized the need for format standardization, too. Today, it promulgates standards at all levels of the application of tape.

The first standard developed by the committee to reach the market-place in a commercial product was *QIC-02*, a nine-track version of a DC300 tape drive. The first units were shipped in 1983. The QIC-24 standard put 60MB on a DC6000 cartridge using nine tracks; QIC-120, 125M; QIC-150, up to 250M across 18 tracks. Later standards incorporate the drive capacity as part of the designation.

QIC-compatible drives with 525M capacity were first put on the market in 1990 as QIC-525. In 1991, capacity was pushed to 1 gigabyte (QIC-1000) and then 1.35 gigabytes (QIC-1350). Drives with 2.1 gigabyte capacities began shipping in 1992 (QIC-2100).

As capacities have increased, so have data densities and read/write speeds. The largest capacity QIC systems sold today (QIC-1000, QIC-1350, and QIC-2100) lay 30 tracks across the quarter-inch width of the ferric-oxide tape they use. To achieve their capacities without increasing the number of tracks, QIC-1000 writes with a data density of 36 kilobits per inch, QIC-1350 at 51 kilobits per inch, QIC 2100 at 68 kilobits per inch. The higher density of QIC-2100 requires 950 Oersted tape while the other standards use 760 Oersted media.

Proposed standards for DC6000-size cartridges will push storage capacities higher by boosting the number of tracks and, later, the data density. The proposed 10 gigabyte-per-tape standard will squeeze 144 tracks across a tape; the 35 gigabyte proposal will put 216 tracks on the tape.

The simple act of locating and identifying tracks is no long so simple with that many tracks. Consequently, the high-capacity proposals rely on servo technology to follow each of the many narrow tracks, a technique similar to that used to shoehorn more tracks into specialized disk systems. Similarly, the advanced high-capacity tape systems use Advanced Run Length Limited data coding to get more useful capacity from the magnetic medium.

Minicartridges

If standard quarter-inch cartridges have any drawback, it's their size. Squeezing drives to handle a six-by-four cartridge into a standard 5.25-inch drive bay is a challenge; fitting one in a modern 3.5-inch bay is an impossibility. Seeking a more compact medium, quarter-inch cartridge makers cut their products down to size, reducing tape capacity while preserving the proven drive mechanism. The result was the *minicartridge*. The smaller size was adopted by the QIC Committee, which now promulgates standards for it.

The first minicartridge was introduced by 3M Company with the model designation *DC2000*, so minicartridges are often called DC2000-style cartridges. As with DC6000-size cartridges, the model designations of most minicartridges encode the cartridge capacity as their last digits. A DC2080 cartridge is designed for 80M capacity; a DC2120 for 120M.

The minicartridge package measures just under 3.25 x 2.5 x 0.625 inches. As originally developed, it held 205 feet of tape with the same nominal quarter-inch width used by larger cartridges. Drives easily fit into standard 3.5-inch bays. Cartridge capacities are lower than full-size cartridges—if just because there's less tape inside—but capacities are keeping up with normal hard disk sizes. The QIC Committee envisions the small cartridges eventually holding 30 gigabytes.

The number of manufacturers of minicartridge tape drives is surprisingly small. In 1992, they totaled about eight: Alloy, Ardat (one division of Archive), Braemar, Colorado Memory Systems, Irwin Magnetic (another Archive division), Mountain, 3M Company, and Wangtek. Other names are found on the market, but they are usually affiliates of one of these makers. For example, Maynard is the retail arm of Archive, and Irwin is now a division of Maynard. Summit is a spin-off production group for Mountain.

QIC-40

The first major standard used with minicartridges was *QIC-40*. The standard was originally designed primarily to be a low-cost backup medium for DOS- and OS/2-oriented systems. To keep user expenses under control, it connected to PCs using a conventional floppy disk controller. The first drives simply plugged into a vacant connector on your PC's floppy disk cable, limiting systems with a minicartridge drive to a single floppy drive. Modern drives link in various ways to allow two floppy drives to be used in the host PC.

Under the QIC-40 standard, 20 tracks were arrayed across the width of the tape, each one of which held roughly two megabytes of data. Each track was divided into 68 segments of 29 sectors. Each sector stored 1024 bytes. The standard specifies modified frequency modulation (MFM) recording, the normal output of a floppy disk controller. At standard data rates and tape speeds, information was packed at a density of 10,000 bits per inch. Tape speed depended on the kind of floppy disk controller that you used. A normal-density controller (one that worked only with 360K floppies) produced a data rate of 250 kilobits per second, resulting in a tape speed of 25 inches per second. High-density controllers, which operate at 500 kilobits per second, yielded a tape speed of 50 inches per second.

QIC-40 also specified the data format. Sectors were assigned to files in much the same way that disk space is allocated. Each tape had the equivalent of a file allocation table that listed the bad sectors contained on the tape so that no bytes are risked on bad or marginal media. Data on the tape were specifically structured under the QIC-40 format (see fig. 23.2).

One-third of the possible 60 megabyte capacity of a DC2000 tape under the QIC-40 format was devoted to identifying the format structure of the tape and to data error-correction. Two methods of error correction were used, cyclical redundancy checking and a Reed Solomon code (an efficient error-correction algorithm that's used, among other places, in interplanetary communications—really!). The resulting theoretical error rate was extremely low—one in 10^{14}—one bad bit in 100 trillion. Do the math and that should ensure that less than one tape in two hundred thousand had a single bit error. If achieved, the result would be fewer errors than you might expect with a typical disk drive.

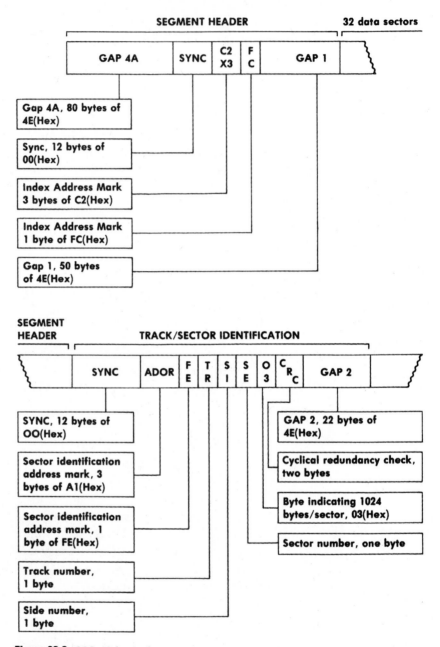

Figure 23.2. QIC-40 logical structure.

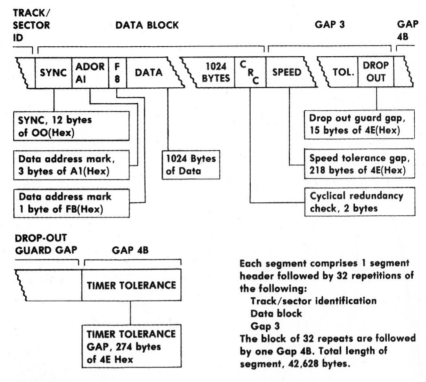

Figure 23.2. continued

The chief disadvantage of QIC-40 was time. Using QIC-40 often was an exercise in patience. Because of the use of the floppy disk interface, data transfers were limited to floppy disk speeds. Early QIC-40 drives also required as long as half a minute to index their read/write heads to find the edge of the tape before they would start a backup session. They had to properly position themselves over the very narrow tracks on the tape. Modern drives have eliminated this lengthy wait.

As with floppy disks, however, QIC-40 tapes required formatting before they could be used. Because the tapes had much greater capacity than floppy disks, the formatting process took commensurately longer—one full-speed pass across the head for each track. That added up to about an hour for 40 megabytes. To save formatting time, many manufacturers of QIC-40 systems allowed partially formatting a tape to a lower capacity, often in two megabyte increments representing a single track. The better solution that's now used by most manufacturers of more modern tape formats is the *preformatted cartridge*. Many media vendors will sell minicartridges with the formatting already done at only a slight premium over the price of unformatted tapes.

The formatting requirement of QIC-40 and subsequent minicartridge standards is not all bad. Along with the bother comes a number of benefits. For example, during the format process, bad sectors can be reserved. Because the tape is formatted with a file allocation tape, individual tape sectors can be accessed randomly. While the tape still must be shuttled to any given spot, the format allows each sector to be unambiguously identified without reference to its neighbors. That means you don't have to read through the whole tape just to find a single file. As a result, a QIC-40 tape can mimic the operation—though not the random-access speed—of a floppy disk. In addition, formatted tapes make appending files to a partially used tape easy because the system can quickly find where it left off writing to the tape.

QIC-80

The next setup from QIC-40 is the QIC-80, which essentially extrapolates on the earlier standard. QIC-80 defines not only the physical arrangement of tracks on the tape and data density but also the logical data format on the tape (which, in theory, should make cartridges made on one drive interchangeable with those made on another—a goal that is finally being achieved), error correction (which theoretically reduces tape error rate below that of the disk being backed up), and the data compression schemes that can optionally be used. Tape drives that follow the QIC-80 standard can read but not write cartridges conforming with the older QIC-40 standard.

The principal on-tape difference between the older and newer standards is that QIC-80 puts more, narrower tracks on a tape—32 instead of 20. In addition, the density of data on each track is increased from 10,000 bits per inch to 12,500. The net difference is an effective doubling of tape capacity to 80 megabytes.

Although QIC-80 drives can use floppy disk controllers, they need not. Their interface is based on the 765 floppy disk controller chip or its equivalent, which may be part of a separate host adapter board or a spare channel in your PC's existing floppy disk controller. Which form this circuitry takes determines how easy a specific minicartridge system is to install. Some drives plug directly into any spare floppy disk drive connectors in your system. Others intercept the signals from your floppy disk controller before it goes to your drives, adding a wire and a bit of confusion inside your PC. Still others use extra expansion boards with their own dedicated electronics (which are still based on floppy disk controller chips).

Although the QIC-80 interface is based on a traditional floppy disk controller, the standard also supports the higher data rate used by extra-density floppy disk drives, one megabit per second. Extended length tapes that are 50 percent longer can increase the capacity of a QIC-80 system to 120 megabytes per cartridge. Most QIC-80 systems also offer the option of data compression, which can nominally yet again double cartridge capacity. (As with any data compression system, the compression ratio varies with what's being compressed—while programs may compress by only 10 percent, graphic files often can be reduced by 90 percent.) Consequently, most makers of QIC-80 systems advertise them by their theoretical maximum capacity, 250 megabytes.

QIC-100

The next number up from QIC-80 on the standards roster is *QIC-100*, but the nomenclature is misleading. QIC-100 is an older standard than QIC-80. Moreover, where the QIC-40 and QIC-80 names hint at the nominal capacities of the systems, QIC-100 does not. Under the QIC-100 standard, only 40MB could be packed on a tape.

The purpose of the additional 40MB standard was performance. By using its own controller rather than sharing one with floppy disk drives, QIC-100 allowed for the option of higher data transfer rates. Of course, the additional cost of the controller also meant that QIC-100 systems were more expensive floppy based systems. QIC-100 proved an aberration and never achieved the mainstream acceptance of QIC-40 or QIC-80. Even the QIC Committee describes the QIC-100 standard as "aging," the only minicartridge standard with that designation.

QIC-100 allowed for serial data writing across 12 or 24 serpentine tracks at a density of 12,000 flux reversals per inch. The standard was looser than QIC-40 and did not define a block length. As with QIC-40, QIC-100 tapes required formatting prior to their use.

QIC-100 has been superseded by QIC-128, which can pack 86MB on a DC2110 cartridge or 128MB on a DC2165 cartridge using either a QIC-100 style interface or SCSI.

Future Minicartridge Standards

The QIC Committee has defined standards for minicartridges that will extend the life of the familiar medium well into the next century.

The immediate step up from QIC-80 will be QIC-500M, a format that will pack up to 500MB on a minicartridge without data compression. QIC-500M drives are designed to be backwardly compatible with QIC-40 and QIC-80 and will read tapes produced under the older standards. A new cartridge with higher coercivity tape (900 Oersted), designated QIC-143, will be required to achieve the half-gigabyte capacity. As with QIC-40 and QIC-80, QIC-500M drives can connect to PCs using a floppy disk interface. However, the standard also allows for drives to use the AT Attachment interface. Data compression— exactly the same algorithm used by QIC-80—can push per-tape capacity to one gigabyte.

A higher-speed alternative is QIC-410M, which is designed to link to PCs using a SCSI-2 connection. This standard is not backwardly compatible with existing standards and packs only 410MB per cartridge (potentially doubled with compression). However, the SCSI interface promises higher speeds.

The next step up is QIC-875M, designed to use the same 900 Oersted minicartridges as QIC-410M and QIC-500M but put 875MB on them. The standard requires a data density of 67,733 bits per inch and 38 tracks across the tape. Drives conforming to QIC-875 will read both QIC-410M and QIC-40/80 tapes. QIC-875M drives will also use a SCSI-2 connection.

Further in the future is QIC-3GB, the step up from QIC-410M, with which it will be backwardly read-compatible. QIC-3B will use another new tape type in its cartridges (which will be designated QIC-138).

As the name indicates, the standard will fit three gigabytes of uncompressed data on each cartridge, double that with compression.

The QIC Committee has also proposed a ten-gigabyte minicartridge standard and is dreaming about one for 35-gigabyte minicartridges.

Minicartridge Compatibility

Following a QIC standard does not necessarily ensure the interchange-ability of tapes between drives of different manufacturers. Although the existing standards define a format for data on a tape, not all makers of tape backup systems follow these standards.

The standards actually fall a bit short. They fall short of actually specifying the exact arrangement of the tape file structure. That's left to the individual software developers who make the backup program to run the tape system. As a result, while tapes are interchangeable between different drives and can be read without regard to the equipment used, your backup software might not be able to make sense of the results. Because there's no compatibility of file structure, you can read every byte on a tape in any system, but all you might end up with is a big pile of data—files can run into one another and even inter-mingle.

Helical-Scan Systems

The basic principle of all of the above tape systems is that the tape moves past a stationary head. The speed the tape moves and the density of data on the tape together determine how fast information can be read or written, just as the data density and rotation rate of disks controls data rate. Back in the '50s, however, data rate was already an issue when engineers tried to put television pictures on ordinary recording tape. They had the equivalent of megabytes to move every second, and most ordinary tape systems topped out in the thousands. The inspired idea that made video recording possible was to make the head move as well as the tape to increase the *relative* speed of the two.

Obviously, the head could not move parallel to the tape. The first videotape machines made the head move nearly perpendicular to the tape movement. Through decades of development, however, rotating a head at a slight angle to the tape so that the head traces out a section of a helix against the tape has proven to be the most practical system. The resulting process is called *helical scan* recording. Today two helical-scan systems are popular, eight-millimeter and DAT (which is short for *Digital Audio Tape*).

In a helical-scan recording system, the rotating heads are mounted on a drum. The tape wraps around the drum outside its protective cartridge. Two arms pull the tape out of the cartridge and wrap it about halfway around the drum. So that the heads travel at an angle across the tape, the drum is canted at a slight angle, about five degrees for eight-millimeter drives, about six degrees for DAT.

Helical-scan recording can take advantage of the entire tape surface. Conventional stationary-head recording systems must leave blank areas—*guard bands*—between the tracks containing data. Helical systems can and do overlap tracks. Although current eight-millimeter systems use guard bands, DAT writes the edges of tracks over one another.

This overlapping works because the rotating head drum actually has two (or more) heads on it, and each head writes data at a different angular relationship (called the *azimuth*) to the tracks on the tape. In reading data, the head responds strongly to the data written at the same azimuth as the head and weakly at the other azimuth. In DAT machines, one head is skewed twenty degrees forward from perpendicular to its track; the other head is skewed backward an equal amount.

Eight Millimeter

Probably the most familiar incarnation of eight-millimeter tape is in miniaturized camcorders. Sony pioneered the medium as a compact, high-quality video recording system. The same tapes were later adapted to data recording by Exabyte Corporation and first released on the PC market in 1987. Exabyte remains the sole supplier of eight-millimeter digital tape drives.

Video recorders have in the past been used as the basis of tape backup systems. However, these relied on converting digital computer signals into an analog format that could be recorded on tape as if it were a video signal. Alpha Microsystems used this approach in a product the company called *Videotrax*.

In the Videotrax backup system, a single expansion card in the host computer converts hard disk or other system data into NTSC (National Television Standards Committee) video signals, which can then be backed up and stored on a conventional videocassette recorder. Although either a VHS or a Betamax machine (or even a professional-caliber U-magic) can be used, Alpha Micro offered its commercial systems based on VHS recorders. The Videotrax system combines Alpha Micro's proprietary digital-to-video conversion board with a specially modified VHS machine that can be remotely controlled by a PC. The host computer can take command of tape travel during the backup, or you can run the system manually.

To minimize the problem of dropouts—sections on the tape that lose tiny bits of video information—Videotrax wrote multiple copies of data to tape, a procedure called *redundancy* that is successful because it is statistically unlikely that each of the copies will suffer dropout degradation. The problem with redundancy is that writing multiple copies takes time and space. Backing up 80 megabytes required a complete two-hour video tape—and the two hours it took to fill it.

The eight-millimeter helical system created by Exabyte shares only the cassette with the eight-millimeter video recording system. The cassette resembles an audio cassette in that it has two hubs within its plastic shell, but the tape is much wider (eight millimeters, of course, that's 0.315 inch compared to 0.150 inch for cassette tape) and a hinged door on the cassette protects the tape from physical damage. The cassette itself measures 3.75-inches by 2.5-inches and is about half an inch thick.

The Exabyte eight-millimeter system was designed from the ground up for digital recording. It does not use or process video signals in any way.

In the original eight-millimeter system, the head drum rotated at 1800 revolutions per minute while the tape traveled past it at 10.89 millimeters per second to achieve a track density of 819 per inch and a flux density of 54 kilobits per inch. That's enough to squeeze 2.5 megabytes on a single cartridge. Improvements have extended the capacity to five megabytes without compression and up to 10G with compression. The tape can be rapidly shuttled forward and backward to find any given location (and block of data) within about 15 seconds.

Eight-millimeter drives tend to be quite expensive. Complete systems cost thousands of dollars. A raw drive alone starts over $1,000. Its primary market is backing up file servers, machines that can benefit from its huge capacity.

Digital Audio Tape

Developed originally as a means to record music, *Digital Audio Tape* was first released as a computer storage medium in 1989. Using a tape four millimeters wide (and sometimes called *four-millimeter tape*), DAT uses tiny cartridges to stored huge amounts of data. The first DAT system was capable of packing 1.3 gigabytes into a cassette measuring only 0.4 x 2.9 x 2.1 inches (HWD). The secret is the most dense storage of any current computer tape medium, 114 megabits per square inch on special 1450 Oersted metal particle tape (the same material as used by eight-millimeter digital tape systems). A cassette holds either 60 or 90 meters of this tape; the shorter tapes storing 1.3G; the longer tapes, 2.0G.

In a DAT drive the tape creeps along requiring about three seconds to move an inch at a rate of eight millimeters per second. The head drum, however, spins rapidly at 2000 revolutions per minute, putting down 1869 tracks across a linear inch of tape with flux transitions packed 61 kilobits per inch.

DAT technology has two important strengths: access speed and capacity. In the audio realm the DAT medium was designed for rapid access to information—finding a musical selection—hence, once translated into the computer realm it could locate a file in about 15 seconds. While access speed is of little importance for backups, quick times make for easy file restorations.

Nonstandard Tape Systems

A number of tape systems have been developed by clever engineers which, while often brilliant, have failed to ignite the market. Typically these nonstandard systems excelled in one or more characteristics (such as price, performance, capacity, or convenience) but never yielded an overall package that bettered the established formats. Most have disappeared quietly into the ages—and usually with good reason. You can still encounter some of these technologies as close-outs and, increasingly, in museums (or in PCs that should be in museums). Among these forgotten and forgettable formats were DC1000 cartridges, servo-formatted tapes, and spooled tape.

DC1000 Cartridges

About the same length and width as DC2000s but thinner, DC1000 cartridges used 150 mil (thousandths of an inch) wide tape—the same width as audio cassette tape—and held 10 to 20 megabytes. In a world where 200-megabyte hard disks are becoming the norm, the fate of such a small capacity system would not be hard to predict.

Tape systems based on the DC1000 cartridge at one time proved popular mostly because of their low prices. In fact, when interfaced through a floppy disk controller, DC1000 systems were among the least expensive tape systems available for small computer systems. Irwin Magnetic dominated the industry and essentially set its own standard for such products.

The DC1000 had no inherent flaw but low capacity. The format was unable to keep up with the fast growth in hard disk capacities. Moreover, the prices of DC2000 systems fell while the QIC Committee was able to wring ever larger capacities from the tapes. The marketplace simply outgrew DC1000.

Servo-Formatted Minicartridges

For a period, DC1000 was successful, so Irwin Magnetic adapted some of its technology to the larger DC2000 cartridges. Instead of using the standard QIC-40 or QIC-80 format on DC2000 tapes, Irwin developed its own proprietary (and QIC-incompatible) embedded-servo tape format. The servo data on the tape helps positively position the read/write head in relation to the thin track on the tape, allowing the use of a less precise, lower cost tape drive.

Again, there was nothing inherently wrong with the technology. In fact, future high-capacity QIC formats will use a variation on the same scheme. The system worked so well that at one time Irwin Magnetic had about half of the market for minicartridge tape drives. However, other companies were able to push the prices of their QIC-80 products below that of the Irwin drives, and the company lost market share. Although the drives are still available, the company is disappearing, acquired by Archive Corporation and later folded into the company's other operations.

Spooled Tape

For a brief while one company, Interdyne, offered what could be viewed as a cross between quarter-inch cartridges and open reel tape—or even 3480 cartridges with narrower tape and without the cartridge. The design was called *spooled tape*. You slid a plastic-cased spool of quarter-inch tape into a drive that automatically threaded it onto an integral tape-up spool. As with many tape backup systems, the Interdyne spooled tape drive used a floppy disk controller. In theory, the cartridgeless cartridges could be cheaper than other designs, but the Interdyne design failed to catch on.

Tape Operation

Tape drives are often described by how they work as well as what kind of medium they use. Most of the different technologies span many media. All influence how quickly the tape system operates and how convenient it is to use.

Start-Stop Tape

The fundamental difference between tape drives is how they move the tape. Early drives operated in *start-stop* mode. That is, they handled data one block (which could range from 128 bytes to a few kilobytes) at a time, and wrote it to tape as it was received. Between blocks of data, the drive would stop moving the tape and await the next block. The drive had to prepare the tape for each block, identifying the block so that the data could be properly recovered. The start-stop operation was necessary with early PCs for another reason—most computers were so slow that they could not move data to the drive as fast as the drive could write it to tape.

Streaming Tape

In 1981, DEI and Archive introduced the first quarter-inch cartridge *streaming tape* drives. These products were capable of accepting data and writing it to tape continuously without needing to stop. Because the tape did not have to stop between blocks, the system could accept data faster. It also lowered the cost of the drive because it did not have to accelerate the tape quickly or brake the motion of the tape spools so a lighter weight mechanism could be used. Nearly all PC tape drives are now capable of streaming data to tape.

Parallel Recording

The nine-track tapes that set the first standard for computer tape recording spread each byte across their tracks, one bit per track with one track for parity. A tape was good for only one pass across the read/write head, after which the tape would need to be rewound for storage.

Serpentine Recording

Most PC tape systems, on the other hand, write data serially. With multiple tracks available, these use a recording method called *serpentine recording*. The data bits are written sequentially, in one direction, on one track at a time, continuing for the length of the tape. When the end of the tape is reached, the direction of its travel is reversed, and the read/write head cogs down one step to the next track. At the end of that pass, the process is repeated until all the tracks are filled.

Other Issues

When buying a tape drive or its media, you confront other issues besides the tape format. Among these are the way the drive installs in (or out) of your PC and the media that you slide into the drive.

Internal and External Drives

Internal and external units are generally much the same—the only effective difference is that you need a free drive bay to install an internal system. External systems tend to be costlier because they require a case and a connecting cable. However, they offer the advantage that you can shuttle a single backup drive between several PCs (providing you equip each with the necessary host adapter).

Better still are external drives that link to PCs through standard bi-directional parallel ports. Because nearly every PC has a parallel port built in, you can shuttle one of these machines around without the worry of adding host adapters. Such drives usually attain the speeds of other units that use floppy disk interfaces. If you have a number of PCs to regularly back up, a single external tape drive can do the job.

Internal drives are the choice when you don't want a lot of clutter or want to save the cost the drive manufacturer charges for packaging and powering an external unit. As with other peripherals you install internally, you've got to have a free bay for an internal tape drive, and the bay will require front panel access. Nearly all internal tape drives require the power as used by disk drives—positive five volts DC for their logic, 12 volts for their drive motors—and they link to your PC's power supply with a standard drive power connector.

Media Matching

As with other removable media drives, cartridges (or whatever) serve as the raw material that a tape drive works upon. Although most tape media are entirely different from tape cartridges used in audio and video products, some data tape cartridges are physically similar to their other worldly counterparts—D/CAS, eight millimeter, and DAT cassettes. Considering the premium prices charged for data-certified media, substituting audio or video cassettes can be tempting, indeed. Even within the real world of computer products, it's sometimes tempting to substitute a cheaper minicartridge for those officially sanctioned for a tape drive.

Unfortunately, data tapes are engineered with different characteristics such as coercivity and retentivity. Audio cassettes won't fit a D/CAS machine because of the coding notch in the backbone of the latter. Audio and video helical-scan cassettes will fit computer drives, however. However, computer systems put much more stringent requirements on their media. While a drop-out on an audio tape will likely be undetectable (powerful error-correction circuitry assures of that), the same tape flaw could result in an error and loss of data in a computer system. With eight-millimeter tape, matching the right medium is more critical because eight-millimeter video tapes are designed for analog recording and computer systems put digital data recorded into saturation onto their tapes.

Much as metal tape won't sound very good when used in a stereo that is not "metal ready," the wrong tape in a data system can result in unacceptably high error rate. If you value your data, do not attempt to use a tape not certified for the data density that your system uses.

Backup Software

The tape drive is only part of a true backup system. Just as important is the software that runs the system. The software determines what you can do with a tape drive and how you do it.

Almost universally today's backup software gives you (or should) menu control and some means of automating your regular backup procedure—for example, a batch mode or command-driven option. If you only make occasional backups, you probably won't want to spend the time to learn an elaborate command structure, so these menu-controlled systems are often best. However, if you want to automate the backup process and make untended backups, you'll either want software that can be run in command mode or a program that has provisions to automatically swing into action while you count sheep, without worrying whether it will actually work and whether you've left your PC switched on.

Generally, two backup techniques have evolved—image and file-by-file backups—with manufacturers each developing their own format standard for their own tapes.

Image Backups

The image backup is a bit-for-bit copy of the original disk. Bytes are merely read from the disk and copied on tape without a glance to their content or structure. Because little processing overhead is involved, these image backups can be fast.

The problem with image backups is that they typically require restoring to exactly the same drive as was backed up because they read the bad tracks with the good, unused disk areas with those that are used. Obviously, this technique is not very versatile if you want to exchange data between systems—or if your hard disk crashes and must be replaced. One solution to this problem is adding intelligence to the restoration program so that it can add the needed structure when moving files back to disk from tape.

Another image problem is that the image backup is an all-or-nothing process. While it may be the fastest way of moving all the information from a disk to tape, it fails when it comes to backing up a single file. Along with that file, the rest of the entire disk contents would have to be backed up—a big waste of time.

File-by-File Backups

File-by-file backups add structure to the information as it is backed up. Although processing overhead tends to slow down file-by-file systems, finding files within the structure (and hence, individual file restoration) is easier.

The problem with file-by-file backups is the time required to process the file structure data. In the past this processing time slowed most systems so severely they were unable to supply data to tape drives fast enough to keep the tape streaming. Once the drive reverted to start-stop recording, backup times skyrocketed.

More powerful PCs and better backup software have changed this situation. Most PCs are powerful enough to read disk data, process it, and send it to a tape drive fast enough to keep the drive streaming. Because file-by-file backups can be more efficient because they back up only the data you need to back up, they can take a performance lead over image backups. Consequently, file-by-file backing up has almost completely replaced the image backup process today.

File-by-file backup systems afford several methods of selecting which files are to be written to tape. Your choices often include specifying files by typing in their names, some identifying characteristics, or tagging files by choosing them from a menu-like display.

Several identifying characteristics help you select files. The most popular of these, which should be expected as normal file selection options, include archive bits, which indicate whether a file has been previously backed up; date stamps, which allow you to back up files that have been changed after a given date; and subdirectory searches, which include all files in the daughter directories of the one being backed up. Some software also allows you to specifically exclude files from a backup session, either by name or tagging.

Most tape systems allow you to give a name to every backup session that can be later read to identify a tape if, for instance, you neglect to put a physical label on it. Many backup systems also allow you to embed a password so the secrecy of your data won't be compromised if a tape is lost or stolen.

Cost Issues

For most people, the most important factor in guiding their backup choice is cost. In general, more buys more—speed, capacity, compatibility, and convenience.

The most expensive systems for PCs today are those that use nine-track open-reel tapes. They earn their keep by giving your data the utmost security as well as providing a portal through which you can access and exchange data with other computer systems. Next in the price spectrum are the helical-scan systems. You pay for their prodigious capacities and advanced spinning-head technology.

In quarter-inch cartridges, larger DC6000-style systems are the most expensive but are also fastest and have the larger capacity.

Tape Requirements

With any removable media system, the cost of the medium can quickly eclipse the price of the hardware. Consequently, you will be tempted to limit the number of tapes in which you invest.

For most backup scenarios, you will want sufficient media capacity to hold a minimum of three complete backups. For greater peace of mind or more elaborate backup rituals—such as keeping a separate backup for each day of the week—your media needs increase. Most people actively use between six and ten tapes in their regular backup routine.

You should also figure in the cost of periodically replacing any media that can wear out. All tape media and all disks except for cartridge hard disks will eventually wear out.

The exact amount of life to expect from a particular medium depends on your own personal paranoia. According to one major media manufacturer, DEI, DC600-style cartridges should last 5000-6000 passes across the read/write head. On the other hand, cautious mainframe managers may routinely replace open-reel tapes after they've been used as few as 50 times. A good compromise, according to DEI, would be annual replacement of your backup tapes.

When you look beyond backing up, other considerations can overrule the price differences between systems. For instance, when you absolutely need access to mainframe tapes or want to interchange information, you'll have to bite the bullet and budget for an open-reel tape drive.

A Backup Strategy

The best backup system is the one that you're most likely to use—and use routinely. No matter how good or expensive it may be, a backup system is worthless if you never bother to put it to work. The backup system that's easiest and most convenient to operate is the one least likely to be ignored—and the one most likely to help when disaster strikes.

No matter the backup hardware you choose, you still need a backup system. That system requires more than just hardware, even more than software. To make it work, you must adhere to a strict backup routine after you make one overall backup of all the files on your hard disk.

If you plan on overseeing all of your backups as they happen, the fastest backup system is always the more endurable. But if your time is valuable and you don't mind leaving your PC running overnight (and have the faith that it will, indeed, continue to run overnight), taking advantage of automatic backup programs will make the time spent backing up meaningless. If you don't have to wait, it doesn't matter how long it takes.

Even a slow backup system is better than none. And even an occasional backup beats not having any. All it takes is one disk crash, however, for you to learn how important it is to take the time—no matter how long—to keep your backups current.

The best backup system is the one that enforces the routine that you're most likely to follow, the one that assures you have protection when the worst does happen. A backup system that does not get used (or used often) is not a backup system at all.

Index

Note: Bold page numbers indicate the location of a term's definition or the first in-context usage of the term.

M

U

V

W

X

Y-Z

College Marketing Group
50 Cross Street
Winchester, MA 01890

ATT: **Cheryl Read**